World Development Report 1991
The Challenge of Development

Published for the World Bank
Oxford University Press

Oxford University Press

OXFORD NEW YORK TORONTO DELHI
BOMBAY CALCUTTA MADRAS KARACHI
PETALING JAYA SINGAPORE HONG KONG
TOKYO NAIROBI DAR ES SALAAM
CAPE TOWN MELBOURNE AUCKLAND
and associated companies in
BERLIN IBADAN

First printing June 1991

ISBN 0-19-520869-2 clothbound
ISBN 0-19-520868-4 paperback
ISSN 0163-5085

The Library of Congress has cataloged this serial publication as follows:
World development report. 1978–
[New York] Oxford University Press.
v. 27 cm. annual.
Published for The World Bank.
1. Underdeveloped areas—Periodicals. 2. Economic development—
Periodicals. I. International Bank for Reconstruction and Development.

HC59.7.W659   330.9′172′4   78-67086

Foreword

World Development Report 1991, the fourteenth in this annual series, synthesizes and interprets the lessons of more than forty years of development experience. This Report, together with last year's on poverty and next year's on the environment, seeks to provide a comprehensive overview of the development agenda.

The 1990s began with dramatic changes. Many countries in Eastern Europe and elsewhere initiated ambitious reforms of their economic and political systems. These reforms reflect both the accumulated evidence on economic policies and fundamental changes in the political environment. Not only in Eastern Europe, but also in Africa, Asia, Latin America, and the Middle East, people are seeking escape from poverty and oppression to gain control over their own destinies and find better lives for themselves and their families. Against the backdrop of these transitions, this year's Report links the historical debates that counseled policymakers in their past decisions, the lessons of experience, and the evolving thought on how best to proceed.

One of the most valuable lessons relates to the interaction between the state and the market in fostering development. Experience shows that success in promoting economic growth and poverty reduction is most likely when governments complement markets; dramatic failures result when they conflict. The Report describes a market-friendly approach in which governments allow markets to function well, and in which governments concentrate their interventions on areas in which markets prove inadequate.

The Report looks at four main aspects of the relationship between governments and markets. First, investing in people requires an efficient public role. Markets alone generally do not ensure that people, especially the poorest, receive adequate education, health care, nutrition, and access to family planning. Second, essential for enterprises to flourish is an enabling climate—one that includes competition, adequate infrastructure, and

institutions. Competition fosters innovation, the diffusion of technology, and the efficient use of resources. Third, successful economic development requires the integration of countries with the global economy. Openness to international flows of goods, services, capital, labor, technology, and ideas spurs economic growth. Fourth, a stable macroeconomic foundation is essential to sustained progress. Restoring the confidence of the private sector is now a major challenge for several countries with a long history of macroeconomic instability.

What are the prospects for rapid development in the years ahead? The Report notes that a favorable international climate is critical for future development. The effects of the policies of industrial countries on development grow, as more developing countries turn outward and the world becomes more and more interdependent. But the Report stresses that, above all, the future of developing countries is in their own hands. Domestic policies and institutions hold the key to successful development. With strong and sustained reforms at home, the Report concludes, the pace of development can be substantially increased—to lift millions of people out of poverty by the end of the decade.

Like its predecessors, *World Development Report 1991* includes the World Development Indicators, which offer selected social and economic statistics on 124 countries. The Report is a study by the staff of the World Bank, and the judgments made herein do not necessarily reflect the views of the Board of Directors or the governments they represent.

Barber B. Conable
President
The World Bank

May 31, 1991

This Report has been prepared by a team led by Vinod Thomas and comprising Surjit S. Bhalla, Rui Coutinho, Shahrokh Fardoust, Ann E. Harrison, Daniel Kaufmann, Elizabeth M. King, Kenneth K. Meyers, Peter A. Petri, and N. Roberto Zagha. T. N. Srinivasan, Mark Rosenzweig, and Francisco Sagasti collaborated closely and provided extensive advice. The team was assisted by Sushenjit Bandyopadhyay, Fernando J. Batista, Marianne Fay, Jon Isham, Kali Kondury, Stefan Krieger, and Yan Wang. Stanley Fischer played a principal role in the initial stages of the Report's preparation. The work was carried out under the general direction of Lawrence H. Summers.

Many others in and outside the Bank provided helpful comments and contributions (see the bibliographical note). The International Economics Department prepared the data and projections presented in Chapter 1 and the statistical appendix. It is also responsible for the World Development Indicators. The production staff of the Report included Kathryn Kline Dahl, Connie Eysenck, Alfred F. Imhoff, Hugh Nees, Kathy Rosen, Walton Rosenquist, and Brian J. Svikhart. Cartographic services were provided by Jeffrey N. Lecksell, Gregory George Prakas, and Eric M. Saks. Library assistance was provided by Iris Anderson and Jane Keneshea. The support staff was headed by Rhoda Blade-Charest and included Laitan Alli, Trinidad S. Angeles, and Lupita Mattheisen. Clive Crook was the principal editor.

The advice and support of Professor Bela Balassa (1928–1991) are respectfully acknowledged. His contributions to this and past *World Development Report*s were valuable in understanding development. The core team remembers fondly David A. Renelt (1964–1991), who contributed to the Report.

Contents

Boxes

Text figures

Text tables

Statistical appendix tables

Acronyms and initials

DAC Development Assistance Committee of the Organisation for Economic Co-operation and Development

EC The European Community (Belgium, Denmark, Germany, France, Greece, Ireland, Italy, Luxembourg, Netherlands, Portugal, Spain, and United Kingdom)

ERR Economic rate of return

DFI Direct foreign investment

GATT General Agreement on Tariffs and Trade

GDP Gross domestic product

GNP Gross national product

G-7 Group of Seven (Canada, France, Germany, Italy, Japan, United Kingdom, and United States)

IBRD International Bank for Reconstruction and Development

IDA International Development Association

IFC International Finance Corporation

IMF International Monetary Fund

LIBOR London interbank offered rate

NGOs Nongovernmental organizations

NIEs Newly industrializing economies

ODA Official development assistance

OECD Organisation for Economic Co-operation and Development (Australia, Austria, Belgium, Canada, Denmark, Finland, France, Germany, Greece, Iceland, Ireland, Italy, Japan, Luxembourg, Netherlands, New Zealand, Norway, Portugal, Spain, Sweden, Switzerland, Turkey, United Kingdom, and United States)

PPP Purchasing power parity

TFP Total factor productivity

UNDP United Nations Development Programme

Unesco United Nations Educational, Scientific, and Cultural Organization

UNICEF United Nations Children's Fund

WHO World Health Organization

Definitions and data notes

A note on data selection

The data used in this *World Development Report* cover a range of time periods and are from more than 100 countries (both industrial and developing). Data availability was the primary criterion for usage; other criteria varied from chapter to chapter. For details, see the technical note at the end of the main text.

Country groups

For operational and analytical purposes the World Bank's main criterion for classifying economies is according to their gross national product (GNP) per capita. Every economy is classified as low-income, middle-income (subdivided into lower-middle and upper-middle), or high-income. In addition to classification by income, other analytical groups are based on regions, exports, and levels of external debt.

In this edition of *World Development Report* and its statistical annex, the World Development Indicators (WDI), minor changes to country classification have been introduced. The changes are: (a) the "nonreporting nonmembers" group is now "other economies" and includes only Albania, Cuba, Democratic People's Republic of Korea, and the Union of Soviet Socialist Republics (USSR); (b) "total reporting economies" is replaced by "world." Note that the definition of "oil exporters" has been changed (see the definition in the analytical groups below). As in previous editions, this Report uses the latest GNP per capita estimates to classify countries. The country composition of each income group may therefore change from one edition to the next. Once the clas-

sification is fixed for any edition, all the historical data presented are based on the same country grouping. The country groups used in this Report are defined as follows.

- *Low-income economies* are those with a GNP per capita of $580 or less in 1989.
- *Middle-income economies* are those with a GNP per capita of more than $580 but less than $6,000 in 1989. A further division, at GNP per capita of $2,335 in 1989, is made between lower-middle-income and upper-middle-income economies.
- *High-income economies* are those with a GNP per capita of $6,000 or more in 1989.

Low-income and middle-income economies are sometimes referred to as developing economies. The use of the term is convenient; it is not intended to imply that all economies in the group are experiencing similar development or that other economies have reached a preferred or final stage of development. Classification by income does not necessarily reflect development status. (In the World Development Indicators, high-income economies classified by the United Nations or otherwise regarded by their authorities as developing are identified by the symbol †). The use of the term "countries" to refer to economies implies no judgment by the Bank about the legal or other status of a territory.

- *"Other economies"* are Albania, Cuba, Democratic People's Republic of Korea, and the Union of Soviet Socialist Republics (USSR). In the main tables of the World Development Indicators, only aggregates are shown for this group, but Box A.2 in the technical notes to the WDI contains key indicators reported for each of these countries.

- *"World"* comprises all economies, including economies with less than 1 million population, which are not shown separately in the main tables. See the technical notes to the WDI for aggregation methods used to retain the same country group across time.

Analytical groups

For analytical purposes, other overlapping classifications based predominantly on exports or external debt are used in addition to geographic country groups. The lists provided below are of economies in these groups that have populations of more than 1 million. Countries with less than 1 million population, although not shown separately, are included in group aggregates.

- *Oil exporters* are countries for which exports of petroleum and gas, including reexports, account for at least 50 percent of exports of goods and services. They are People's Republic of the Congo, Islamic Republic of Iran, Iraq, Libya, Nigeria, Oman, Saudi Arabia, Trinidad and Tobago, United Arab Emirates, and Venezuela. Although the USSR meets the established criterion, because of data limitations it is excluded from this group measure.
- *Severely indebted middle-income countries* (abbreviated to "severely indebted" in the World Development Indicators) are twenty countries that are deemed to have encountered severe debt-servicing difficulties. These are defined as countries in which three of the four key ratios are above critical levels: debt to GNP (50 percent), debt to exports of goods and all services (275 percent), accrued debt service to exports (30 percent), and accrued inter-

est to exports (20 percent). The twenty countries are Argentina, Bolivia, Brazil, Chile, People's Republic of the Congo, Costa Rica, Côte d'Ivoire, Ecuador, Arab Republic of Egypt, Honduras, Hungary, Mexico, Morocco, Nicaragua, Peru, Philippines, Poland, Senegal, Uruguay, and Venezuela.

- *OECD members*, a subgroup of "high-income economies," comprises the members of the Organisation for Economic Co-operation and Development except for Greece, Portugal, and Turkey, which are included among the middle-income economies.

Geographic regions (low-income and middle-income economies)

- *Sub-Saharan Africa* comprises all countries south of the Sahara except South Africa.
- *Europe, Middle East, and North Africa* comprises the middle-income European countries of Bulgaria, Czechoslovakia, Greece, Hungary, Poland, Portugal, Romania, Turkey, and Yugoslavia, and all the economies of North Africa and the Middle East, and Afghanistan. For some analyses in *World Development Report*, Eastern Europe (Hungary, Poland, Romania, and Yugoslavia) is treated separately.
- *East Asia* comprises all the low- and middle-income economies of East and Southeast Asia and the Pacific, east of and including China and Thailand.
- *South Asia* comprises Bangladesh, Bhutan, India, Myanmar, Nepal, Pakistan, and Sri Lanka.
- *Latin America and the Caribbean* comprises all American and Caribbean economies south of the United States.

Data notes

- *Billion* is 1,000 million.
- *Trillion* is 1,000 billion.
- *Tons* are metric tons equal to 1,000 kilograms, or 2,204.6 pounds.
- *Dollars* are current U.S. dollars unless otherwise specified.
- *Growth rates* are based on constant price data and, unless otherwise noted, have been computed with the use of the least-squares method. See the technical note to the World Development Indicators for details of this method.
- *The symbol* / in dates, as in "1988/89," means that the period of time may be less than two years but straddles two calendar years and refers to a crop year, a survey year, or a fiscal year.

- *The symbol* .. in tables means not available.
- *The symbol* — in tables means not applicable.
- *The number* 0 or 0.0 in tables and figures means zero or a quantity less than half the unit shown and not known more precisely.

The cutoff date for all data in the World Development Indicators is April 30, 1991.

Historical data in this Report may differ from those in previous editions because of continuous updating as better data become available, because of a change to a new base year for constant price data, and because of changes in country composition in income and analytical groups.

Economic and demographic terms are defined in the technical note to the World Development Indicators.

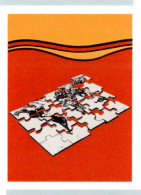

Overview

Development is the most important challenge facing the human race. Despite the vast opportunities created by the technological revolutions of the twentieth century, more than 1 billion people, one-fifth of the world's population, live on less than one dollar a day—a standard of living that Western Europe and the United States attained two hundred years ago.

The task is daunting, but by no means hopeless. During the past forty years many developing countries have achieved progress at an impressive pace. Many have achieved striking gains in health and education. Some have seen their average incomes rise more than fivefold—a rate of progress that is extraordinary by historical standards. So if nothing else were certain, we would know that rapid and sustained development is no hopeless dream, but an achievable reality.

Nonetheless, many countries have done poorly, and in some living standards have actually fallen during the past thirty years. That is why poverty remains such a formidable problem and why substantial economic progress has yet to touch millions of people. The sharp contrast between success and failure is the starting point for *World Development Report 1991*. Why have country experiences been so different? What must developing countries do if the productivity and well-being of their people are to increase rapidly during the next decade? What can the international community do to spur development and alleviate poverty? These questions are all the more pressing because nearly 95 percent of the increase in the world's labor force during the next twenty-five years will occur in the developing world.

The processes driving economic development are by no means fully understood. But much can be learned from experience. History shows, above all, that economic policies and institutions are crucial. This is encouraging, because it implies that the countries which have failed to prosper can do better. But it is also challenging, because it obliges governments everywhere (not just in developing countries) as well as the multilateral agencies to take account of the factors that have promoted development and put them to work.

A central issue in development, and the principal theme of the Report, is the interaction between governments and markets. This is not a question of intervention versus laissez-faire—a popular dichotomy, but a false one. Competitive markets are the best way yet found for efficiently organizing the production and distribution of goods and services. Domestic and external competition provides the incentives that unleash entrepreneurship and technological progress. But markets cannot operate in a vacuum—they require a legal and regulatory framework that only governments can provide. And, at many other tasks, markets sometimes prove inadequate or fail altogether. That is why governments must, for example, invest in infrastructure and provide essential services to the poor. It is not a question of state or market: each has a large and irreplaceable role.

A consensus is gradually forming in favor of a "market-friendly" approach to development. The Report describes the various elements of this strategy, and their implementation in a wide variety of country contexts. It goes further. It stresses the complementary ways markets and governments

1

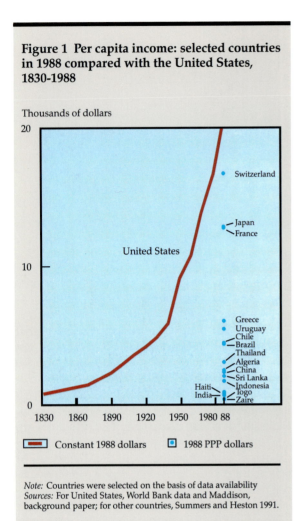
can pull together. If markets can work well, and are allowed to, there can be a substantial economic gain. If markets fail, and governments intervene cautiously and judiciously in response, there is a further gain. But if the two are brought together, the evidence suggests that the whole is greater than the sum. When markets and governments have worked in harness, the results have been spectacular, but when they have worked in opposition, the results have been disastrous.

The world economy in transition

The technological changes of this century have enabled countries to use their resources much more productively than ever before. Living conditions have improved beyond recognition, not just in industrial countries but also in most developing countries. The pace of this improvement has seemed to accelerate with time. It took the United

Kingdom sixty years to double its real income per person, starting in 1780. Many developing countries matched the achievement within twenty years, after World War II.

The real income gap between the industrial countries and some developing countries, notably those in East Asia, has narrowed dramatically since World War II. But the gap between the industrial countries and the developing countries of other regions has widened. The 1980s were a difficult decade for most countries—though per capita income in China and India, the most populous countries, and Asia as a whole, grew substantially. In the past quarter century, per capita income grew little in such countries as Argentina, Jamaica, Nigeria, and Peru; in Nicaragua, Uganda, Zaire, and Zambia, it declined. Many poor countries have per capita real incomes that are much lower than that of the United States at the beginning of the nineteenth century (Figure 1). However, the gaps between rich and poor in infant mortality and life expectancy have narrowed more quickly—thanks to the spread of medical technology, environmental sanitation, better nutrition, education, and the natural limits to achievement in such indicators (Figure 2).

The crucial question for the future is whether national and international policies will permit the potential created by technological progress to be exploited. Sustainable development requires peace. War and its aftermath in the Middle East have cast a cloud of uncertainty over that region. Ethnic strife, civil wars, and international conflicts, as well as natural disasters, continue to destroy the fragile base of development in many parts of the world. By conservative estimates, wars have been directly responsible for 20 million deaths since 1950. That includes more than 12 million deaths from civil wars in the developing world. Far and away, the most important cause of famine in developing countries in recent years has been not inadequate agricultural output or poverty, but military conflict.

Rapid development also requires that economic integration expand for all. The boundaries that separate national markets for goods, capital, and labor have continued to be eroded. Worldwide trade has expanded by more than 6 percent a year since 1950, which is more than 50 percent faster than the growth of output. Global integration in trade, investment, factor flows, technology, and communication has been tying economies together. But it remains to be seen whether this trend will continue.

Increasing exposure to external influences undoubtedly puts the developing countries at risk. High industrial-country fiscal deficits, potentially high international interest rates, weaknesses in the financial institutions in the United States, deterioration of some aspects of the financial situation in Japan, and protracted and inconclusive negotiations in the Uruguay Round of trade talks will all take their toll. But global integration in the flow of goods, services, capital, and labor also brings enormous benefits. It promotes competition and efficiency, and it gives poor countries access to basic knowledge in medicine, science, and engineering.

Sustained development depends on global conditions and especially on country policies. Recently, countries in Eastern Europe embarked on ambitious programs of economic reform. The Soviet Union grappled with difficulties of economic and political transformation. A number of developing countries initiated policy improvements similar to the earlier ones elsewhere. Democracy swept through Eastern Europe as well as parts of the developing world.

The staff of the World Bank has made projections for the world economy in the 1990s. If there are no major adverse shocks and generally good policies, average per capita real incomes in the industrial countries might grow by about 2.5 percent a year (Table 1). This could be achieved with an inflation rate of 3–4 percent and a real interest rate of about 3 percent. If world trade expands more than 5 percent a year and recent policy reforms continue and are consolidated, per capita real incomes in the developing countries might grow by roughly 3 percent a year. Better or worse external conditions could raise or lower this outcome by 0.5–1.0 percentage point. More extreme scenarios

Figure 2 Life expectancy at birth: selected countries in 1985 compared with Japan, 1900-85

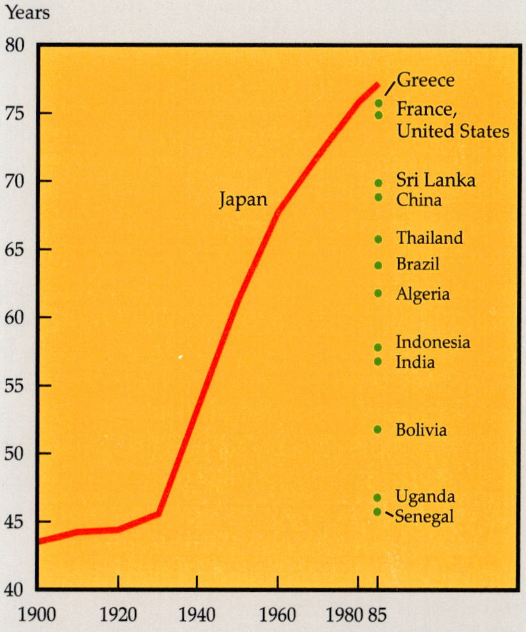

Note: Countries were selected on the basis of data availability.
Sources: World Bank data; United Nations 1991.

(for example, substantially lower growth rates in industrial countries) are plausible, but not likely, particularly during a period as long as a decade.

Country studies which support these projections suggest that, under more vigorous and comprehensive reforms, the developing countries' long-term income growth could be improved by

Table 1 Growth of real GDP per capita, 1965–2000
(average annual percentage change, unless noted)

Group	Population, 1989 (millions)	1965–73	1973–80	1980–89	Projection for 1990s[a]
Industrial countries	773	3.7	2.3	2.3	1.8–2.5
Developing countries	4,053	3.9	2.5	1.6	2.2–2.9
Sub-Saharan Africa	480	2.1	0.4	− 1.2	0.3–0.5
East Asia	1,552	5.3	4.9	6.2	4.2–5.3
South Asia	1,131	1.2	1.7	3.0	2.1–2.6
Europe, Middle East, and North Africa	433	5.8	1.9	0.4	1.4–1.8
Latin America and the Caribbean	421	3.8	2.5	− 0.4	1.3–2.0
Developing countries weighted by population[b]	4,053	3.0	2.4	2.9	2.7–3.2

a. Projected on the basis of the two main scenarios (baseline and downside) discussed in Chapter 1.
b. Using population shares as weights when aggregating GDP growth across countries.
Sources: World Bank data and World Bank 1991a.

1.5–2 percentage points—on average, about twice the improvement from better external conditions. What, in detail, those reforms might be is the subject of the body of the Report. These projections also contain a warning: if recent reforms are reversed, the outcome might easily be much worse.

Paths to development

The challenge of development, in the broadest sense, is to improve the quality of life. Especially in the world's poor countries, a better quality of life generally calls for higher incomes—but it involves much more. It encompasses, as ends in themselves, better education, higher standards of health and nutrition, less poverty, a cleaner environment, more equality of opportunity, greater individual freedom, and a richer cultural life. This Report is concerned primarily with economic development, in itself a broad idea. Any notion of strictly economic progress must, at a minimum, look beyond growth in per capita incomes to the reduction of poverty and greater equity, to progress in education, health, and nutrition, and to the protection of the environment.

Thinking on development has shifted repeatedly during the past forty years. Progress has not moved along a straight line from darkness to light. Instead there have been successes and failures, and a gradual accumulation of knowledge and insight. On some matters, a fairly clear understanding has emerged, but many questions still remain contentious and unanswered.

Climate, culture, and natural resources were once thought to be the keys to economic development. Rapid industrialization, using explicit and implicit taxes on agriculture to fund industrial investment, was for many years a much-favored strategy. After the Great Depression and through the 1960s, most policymakers favored import substitution combined with fostering infant industries. In its day this view was endorsed, and the strategy supported, by external aid and finance agencies.

These views have not stood the test of time. Now there is clearer evidence, from both developing and industrial countries, that it is better not to ask governments to manage development in detail. Discriminatory taxes on agriculture have almost always turned out to be taxes on growth. Economic isolation behind trade barriers has proved costly. Retarding competition and interfering with prices, deliberately or accidentally, have very often proved counterproductive.

As the importance of openness and competition has been realized, the conviction has grown that they are insufficient by themselves. Investing in people, if done right, provides the firmest foundation for lasting development. And the proper economic role of government is larger than merely standing in for markets if they fail to work well. In defining and protecting property rights, providing effective legal, judicial, and regulatory systems, improving the efficiency of the civil service, and protecting the environment, the state forms the very core of development. Political and civil liberties are not, contrary to a once-popular view, inconsistent with economic growth.

As a matter of arithmetic, the growth of output can be accounted for as the growth of capital and labor and changes in the productivity of those inputs. Productivity has grown much more slowly in developing countries than in industrial countries. In the nearly seventy countries examined for the Report, changes in the use of capital made a large contribution to changes in output. But the key to explaining the differences in the growth of output from country to country is the growth of productivity.

Growing productivity is the engine of development. But what drives productivity? The answer is technological progress, which is in turn influenced by history, culture, education, institutions, and policies for openness in developing and industrial countries. Technology is diffused through investment in physical and human capital and through trade. Strong evidence links productivity to investments in human capital and the quality of the economic environment—especially the extent to which markets are distorted.

The Report looks at several indexes of market distortion, such as the parallel-market premium on the exchange of foreign currency and restrictions on trade. Far more economies have had severely distorted price systems than only moderately or slightly distorted ones. Most of the countries with severely distorted prices did poorly in output growth and productivity. At the opposite extreme, the few economies that had relatively undistorted price systems did well. In the middle the results are more ambiguous: some economies were successful, but others did much less well. In general, a relatively undistorted price system, other things being equal, has a better chance of promoting growth than a heavily distorted one. A range of evidence also suggests what can be gained by reducing interventions in the market. For instance, various degrees of reforms in Chile, China, Ghana, India, Indonesia, the Republic of

Korea, Mexico, Morocco, and Turkey during the 1980s were generally followed by improvements in economic performance.

Is this view really consistent with the remarkable achievements of the East Asian economies, or with the earlier achievements of Japan? Why, in these economies, were interventions in the market such as infant-industry protection and credit subsidies associated with success, not failure? First, these governments disciplined their interventions with international and domestic competition. This meant that interventions had to be carried out competently, pragmatically, and flexibly; if one failed, it was likely to be removed. Instead of resisting market competition, governments tried to anticipate it—and when they were proved wrong, they were quick to undo the harm. Second, these governments, on the whole, were careful to ensure that intervention did not end up distorting relative prices unduly: in trade, they successfully neutralized the bias against exports that is usually a by-product of protection. Third, their intervention was more moderate than in most other developing countries. In that respect, these economies refute the case for thoroughgoing dirigisme as convincingly as they refute the case for laissez-faire.

In several respects, government intervention is essential for development. What then are the conditions under which government intervention is likely to help, rather than hinder? Economic theory and practical experience suggest that interventions are likely to help provided they are market-friendly. That means:

• *Intervene reluctantly.* Let markets work unless it is demonstrably better to step in. Certain actions involving public goods readily pass this test in principle because the private sector does not usually carry them out: spending on basic education, infrastructure, the relief of poverty, population control, and environmental protection. Certain other actions usually fail the test. For instance, it is usually a mistake for the state to carry out physical production, or to protect the domestic production of a good that can be imported more cheaply and whose local production offers few spillover benefits.

• *Apply checks and balances.* Put interventions continually to the discipline of the international and domestic markets. The Republic of Korea withdrew its support for the heavy chemicals industry when market performance showed that the policy was failing.

• *Intervene openly.* Make interventions simple, transparent, and subject to rules rather than offi-

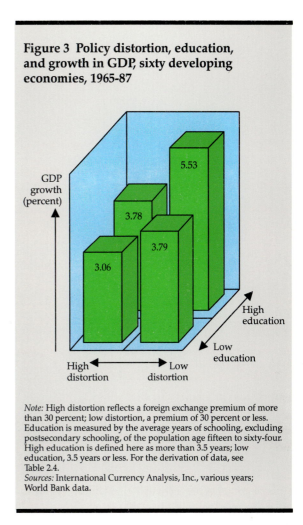

Figure 3 Policy distortion, education, and growth in GDP, sixty developing economies, 1965-87

Note: High distortion reflects a foreign exchange premium of more than 30 percent; low distortion, a premium of 30 percent or less. Education is measured by the average years of schooling, excluding postsecondary schooling, of the population age fifteen to sixty-four. High education is defined here as more than 3.5 years; low education, 3.5 years or less. For the derivation of data, see Table 2.4.
Sources: International Currency Analysis, Inc., various years; World Bank data.

cial discretion. Prefer, for example, tariffs to quantitative controls.

The complementarity of a sound policy climate and market-friendly interventions is one of the most encouraging lessons of development experience. Analysis suggests, for example, that there may be an interaction between different forms of investment (human, physical, and infrastructure) and the quality of policies (Figure 3). Among a sample of sixty developing economies during the period 1965–87, those with distorted policies and a low level of education grew, on the average, by 3.1 percent a year. The economies that had either higher levels of education or fewer policy distortions did better, growing at 3.8 percent a year. But the countries that had both—that is, a higher level of education and fewer distortions—grew at 5.5 percent a year. There also seems to be such a complementarity between increasing physical capital and economic policies. This research does not by

Figure 4 The interactions in a market-friendly strategy for development

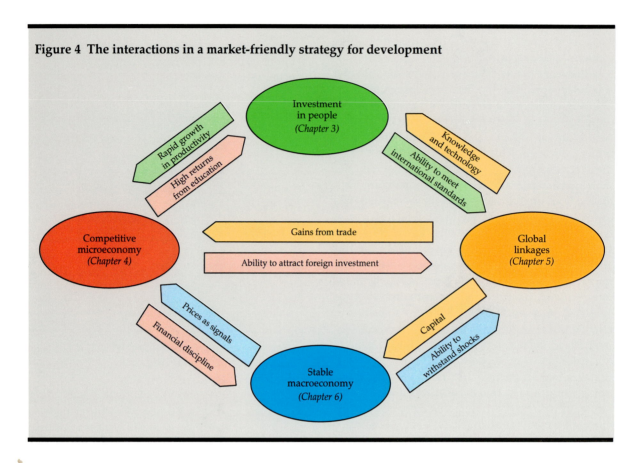

itself show causation, but it suggests that the results from moving forward on several fronts at once can be exceptionally good.

Elements of a market-friendly approach

The Report looks at the relation between governments and markets under four broad headings: human development, the domestic economy, the international economy, and macroeconomic policy. These areas of activity are interrelated. A relatively undistorted domestic economy rewards those who build up their human capital more generously than does a distorted one; at the same time, education makes the domestic economy more productive by speeding the adoption of new technology. To take another example, a stable macroeconomy helps the domestic price system because it clears away the fog of inflation. But microeconomic efficiency also makes it easier to keep inflation low: with fewer unviable enterprises, there will be less need for subsidies to swell the public sector deficit. All four sets of actions are worth doing in their own right. But because of such linkages, the results will probably be disproportionately strong if done together (see Figure 4).

Investing in people

The economic returns from public and private investments in people are often extremely high. Markets in developing countries cannot generally be relied upon to provide people—especially the poorest—with adequate education (especially primary education), health care, nutrition, and family planning services.

Rapid population growth is a crucial concern in some countries such as Bangladesh and in some parts of the world such as the Sahel. The growth of the population typically slows as people's education and incomes grow and they move to cities. Yet in many countries, investments in education, health, and family planning have been necessary, in addition to income growth, to reduce fertility and slow the pace of population growth. Effective family planning programs have informed people of the private and social costs of high fertility, encouraged couples to reduce family size, and helped to meet the demand for contraceptives. Such programs have worked best in countries that have also instituted policies to improve education for women and increase their opportunities for work in the modern sector.

Many governments are investing far too little in human development. In Brazil and Pakistan rapid growth alone was insufficient to improve the social indicators substantially. In Chile and Jamaica, however, these indicators improved even in periods of slow growth. Among low-income countries, Guinea and Sri Lanka have the same per capita income, but average life expectancy is some two-thirds longer in Sri Lanka. Among middle-income countries, Brazil and Uruguay have similar per capita incomes, but infant mortality is two-thirds lower in Uruguay. By some estimates Shanghai has a lower infant mortality rate and longer life expectancy than New York City.

In addition to increasing the quantity of human investment, governments must improve its quality. Too often, capital investments go forward with inadequate provision for the recurrent expenditures they entail, which results in wasteful under-utilization. And expenditures are frequently poorly targeted and involve a great deal of leakages. There is a need to reduce heavy subsidies for higher education and to spend much more on primary education, from which the returns are relatively higher. The case for a similar switch in spending from expensive curative health care systems to primary systems is also strong.

More care is required to ensure that public programs reach their intended beneficiaries. Examples of well-designed and well-targeted social expenditures include a program to increase primary school enrollment in Peru; the provision of rural health facilities in the state of Kerala in India; efforts to reduce infant mortality in Malaysia; and health programs to raise life expectancy in Chile, China, and Costa Rica. There are useful opportunities for partnership with the private sector. Involving the private sector permits services to be delivered more effectively, as in the cases of education in Kenya, the Philippines, and Zimbabwe; and of health care in Rwanda and Zambia.

The climate for enterprise

Domestic and external competition has very often spurred innovation, the diffusion of technology, and an efficient use of resources. Japan, the Republic of Korea, Singapore, the United States, and Europe's most successful economies have all established global competitive advantage through the rigors of competition. Conversely, systems of industrial licensing, restrictions on entry and exit, inappropriate legal codes concerning bankruptcy and employment, inadequate property rights, and price controls—all of which weaken the forces of competition—have held back technological change and the growth of productivity.

Examples of such restrictions at various times include Argentina's policy of favoring incumbent firms for new industrial investment; barriers to entry or exit in many African countries, China, India, and Eastern Europe; sheltered national markets for parts of Europe's computer industry; extensive price regulations in Brazil, the Arab Republic of Egypt, and Indonesia; capacity licensing in India and Pakistan; and state control of selected industries in almost all developing countries. When regulatory reforms to correct the obstacles have been undertaken—as in Ghana, India, Indonesia, and recently many other countries—they have paid off.

An efficient domestic economy also requires public goods of correspondingly high quality. These include, most fundamentally, a regulatory framework to ensure competition, and legal and property rights that are both clearly defined and conscientiously protected. It also requires investment in infrastructure, such as irrigation and feeder roads, which have proven to provide high returns. The returns from research and development in agriculture, for instance, can be extremely high: witness maize in Peru, rubber in Malaysia, wheat in Chile and Pakistan, and cotton in Brazil.

Domestic policy should confront entrepreneurs with the information that is embodied in prices, and it should then equip them (by means of investments in infrastructure and institutions) to respond. A detailed study of the World Bank's investment projects in developing countries confirms that market incentives work. The rate of return to public and private sector projects implemented under policies that do little to distort prices is consistently higher than under policies that result in more distortions (Figure 5). A substantial improvement in policy is associated with a 5–10 percentage point increase in the rate of return for projects, or a 50–100 percent increase on average. Also evident are the general positive effects of institution-building and investing in infrastructure on returns from projects. Again, this confirms that good policies and investments (including external financing) are complementary.

Integration with the global economy

When international flows of goods, services, capital, labor, and technology have expanded quickly, the pace of economic advance has been rapid. Openness to trade, investment, and ideas has

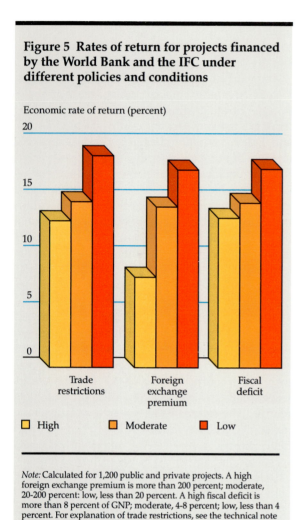

Figure 5 Rates of return for projects financed by the World Bank and the IFC under different policies and conditions

Economic rate of return (percent)

High   Moderate   Low

Trade restrictions   Foreign exchange premium   Fiscal deficit

Note: Calculated for 1,200 public and private projects. A high foreign exchange premium is more than 200 percent; moderate, 20-200 percent; low, less than 20 percent. A high fiscal deficit is more than 8 percent of GNP; moderate, 4-8 percent; low, less than 4 percent. For explanation of trade restrictions, see the technical note for Chapter 4 at the end of the main text.
Source: World Bank data.

been critical in encouraging domestic producers to cut costs by introducing new technologies and to develop new and better products. A high level of protection for domestic industry, conversely, has held development back by decades in many places. The effect of import competition on firms in, for instance, Chile and Turkey, and the effect of greater competition in export markets on firms in Brazil, Japan, and the Republic of Korea confirm the decisive contribution to efficiency that the external economy can make.

The international flow of technology has taken many forms: foreign investment; foreign education; technical assistance; the licensing of patented processes; the transmission of knowledge through labor flows and exposure to foreign goods markets; and technology embodied in imports of capital, equipment, and intermediate inputs. Policies to promote these flows include greater openness

to investment and to trade in goods and services. Nontariff barriers, which are especially distorting, need to be phased out, and tariffs reduced, often substantially.

Governments also need to play a more positive role. To get the most out of technology transfer, appropriate education and on-the-job training will be required. As in Japan and the Republic of Korea, government agencies and industry associations can collaborate to gather and disseminate information on technology, and to help develop quality control for exports.

Governments in the *industrial countries* have a responsibility—if not to the developing world, then to their own people—to grant exporters in the developing countries access to their markets. Without such access, reforms in the developing countries may go to waste. For several decades, the industrial countries had been reducing their tariffs; in the 1980s, however, nontariff barriers were steadily raised. Between 1966 and 1986, the share of imports to countries that belong to the Organisation for Economic Co-operation and Development (OECD) that were affected by nontariff measures is estimated to have doubled. In 1986, more than 20 percent of imports from the developing countries were covered by "hard-core" measures alone. Freeing trade within regions—as in the case of Europe's Project 1992, the United States-Canada Free Trade Agreement of 1989, and the proposed free trade agreement for Canada, Mexico, and the United States—is beneficial. But it remains to be seen whether regional blocs will support or hinder the goal of a more open global trading system. At any rate, a renewed commitment to the General Agreement on Tariffs and Trade (GATT), together with a greater willingness by all countries to undertake unilateral trade reform, is highly desirable.

The macroeconomic foundation

A stable macroeconomic foundation is one of the most important public goods that governments can provide. Experience shows that when government spending has expanded too far, the result has often been large deficits, excessive borrowing or monetary expansion, and problems in the financial sector, which have been quickly followed by inflation, chronic overvaluation of the currency, and loss of export competitiveness. Excessive borrowing can also lead to domestic and external debt problems, and to the crowding out of private investment. Restoring the confidence of the private sector is now a basic aspect of efforts to spur renewed growth and generate employment in several countries with a history of macroeconomic instability, including Argentina, Bolivia, Côte d'Ivoire, and Ghana.

Fiscal and financial instability have sometimes been partly inflicted on governments by external events—or by internal shocks such as civil wars or natural disasters. But governments can choose how to respond to such pressures. In such countries as Côte d'Ivoire, Mexico, Kenya, and Nigeria, the response to a temporary economic upswing was an unsustainable increase in public spending. Countries such as Botswana, Chile, Colombia, Indonesia, the Republic of Korea, Malaysia, Mauritius, and Thailand have managed to keep their macroeconomic policies on course, and their broader economic performance has benefited accordingly.

A government can maintain a prudent fiscal policy by looking carefully at the division of economic tasks between the government and the private sector. That, as the Report argues, is desirable in any case. In reappraising their spending priorities, implementing tax reform, reforming the financial sector, privatizing state-owned enterprises, and using charges to recover the cost of some state-provided services, governments can meet the goals of microeconomic efficiency and macroeconomic stability at the same time.

Developing countries are also affected by the macroeconomic policies of the *industrial countries,* especially when these policies reduce the supply of global savings relative to their demand and raise real interest rates. An adequate supply of external capital (concessional and nonconcessional) is essential—which calls for strong efforts by the World Bank and other multilateral agencies, as well as bilateral sources. The decline in voluntary private lending to developing countries needs to be reversed. The debt crisis remains an obstacle to growth. Overcoming it requires the implementation of comprehensive adjustment programs and return to regular creditworthiness; expanding the number of countries covered by commercial-debt and debt-service reduction; more concessional rescheduling for the poorest debtor countries; expansion of debt forgiveness and deepening the concessionality of other debt relief measures by official bilateral lenders; and an increase in equity and quasi-equity investment.

Rethinking the state

The approach to development that seems to have worked most reliably, and which seems to offer most promise, suggests a reappraisal of the respective roles for the market and the state. Put simply, governments need to do less in those areas where markets work, or can be made to work, reasonably well. In many countries, it would help to privatize many of the state-owned enterprises. Governments need to let domestic and international competition flourish. At the same time, governments need to do more in those areas where markets alone cannot be relied upon. Above all, this means investing in education, health, nutrition, family planning, and poverty alleviation; building social, physical, administrative, regulatory, and legal infrastructure of better quality; mobilizing the resources to finance public expenditures; and providing a stable macroeconomic foundation, without which little can be achieved.

Government intervention to protect the environment is necessary for sustainable development. Industrial countries as well as developing countries face serious problems of environmental degradation. In addition to air and water pollution, sustained development is threatened by the depletion of forests, soil, village ponds, and pastures. Appropriate policies include proper pricing of resources, clearer property rights and resource ownership, taxes and controls on pollution, and investment in production alternatives. The experience of many countries suggests that market reforms can also help to protect the environment. But specific environmental actions are needed. Finding the least costly way to confront environmental ills is a high priority.

What might prevent a realignment of the roles of state and market? Will the political and social structures permit it to be implemented? Is it more or less likely to go forward under governments that are accountable to their people and that defend political and civil liberties? It has often been argued that a democratic polity makes economic development more difficult to achieve. Reform almost always comes at the expense of certain vested interests, and macroeconomic stabilization usually means at least a temporary rise in unemployment. The claim is that only authoritarian governments can make the hard choices.

This is patently false. The evidence from large samples of countries does not go so far as to show that individual freedoms by themselves spur economic growth, but it offers no support at all for the view that they hold growth back. Neither does it endorse the notion that authoritarian governments, on average, show greater promise for achieving rapid growth. And looking beyond growth to the other elements of economic development, the lesson of experience is even less equivocal: political freedoms, and civil liberties—such as a free press and the free flow of information—seem to be associated with progress in health and education in large groups of countries.

The interactions between political systems and economic policies are complex. Clearly, economic policies are not chosen in a vacuum. All but the most repressive governments need to retain a measure of popular support for their actions. Often this support has been bought with an assortment of damaging policy interventions (such as high tariffs, currency overvaluation, and industrial licensing) as well as corruption and wasteful public spending. Military spending remains high in many industrial as well as developing countries. Among the latter, it is well in excess of the combined public expenditures on education and health in many countries such as Angola, Chad, Iraq, the Democratic People's Republic of Korea, Uganda, or Zaire. Insecure authoritarian governments have been at least as prone as democratic ones to go down this path. At the end of it, all too often, lies an economic and political crisis that sets development back years.

Many countries have suffered a vicious circle of harmful interventions that entrench special interests and lead to rent-seeking and the ''capture'' of the state. Governments sometimes intervene in the market to address political instability and other political constraints. But the result is that all too often, the combination of pervasive distortions and predatory states leads to development disasters. Reversing this process requires political will and a political commitment to development. Implementing the economic reforms considered in this Report is one way to confront the political constraints on development.

Reform must look at institutions. The establishment of a well-functioning legal system and judiciary, and of secure property rights, is an essential complement to economic reforms. Reform of the public sector is a priority in many countries. That includes civil service reform, rationalizing public expenditures, reforming state-owned enterprises, and privatization. Related economic reforms include better delivery of public goods, supervision of banks, and legislation for financial development. Strengthening these institutions will increase the quality of governance and the capacity of the state to implement development policy and enable society to establish checks and balances.

Experience also suggests that a relatively equitable distribution of income and assets broadens the base of political support for difficult changes. But caution is needed. Redistribution through distorting prices (such as subsidized credit) can be damaging, and the benefits in any case often go to the less needy. Many of the policies recommended in this Report would tilt the distribution of income in favor of the poor. Reducing trade protection generally promotes exports and raises the incomes of the poor by supporting labor-intensive activities, for instance, as does spending more on primary education and preventive health care, improving the functioning of labor markets, and enhancing labor mobility. Some countries could improve equity by reforming their highly regressive tax systems. Land reform can also be beneficial, as in China, Japan, and the Republic of Korea, although its feasibility in many other countries has been questioned. Subsidies, targeted to the poor, for the consumption of basic food, may be needed. Everywhere, well-designed safety nets are essential to protect the most vulnerable from the short-term costs of reform.

The speed and sequencing of policy reform have often been decisive. Again, it is hazardous to generalize. Swift reforms may help to neutralize the resistance of interest groups opposed to change; or more gradual reforms may allow time to address their concerns. But countries such as Ghana, Indonesia, the Republic of Korea, Mexico, and Turkey seem to show that packages of comprehensive reform, with at least some bold changes made at the start of the program, are more likely to succeed. Comprehensive reforms can make heavy demands on the administrative capacity of governments. Some argue that moving too quickly can raise unemployment, skew the distribution of income, and promote the overrapid depletion of natural resources. But the social cost of failing to reform can be very great, as Argentina, Côte d'Ivoire, Peru, and Eastern Europe all found out in the 1980s. Swift and comprehensive reforms, with measures to reduce poverty and protect the environment directly, will usually be the right way forward.

Priorities for action

The recent slowdown in many industrial countries and renewed economic uncertainty have cast a cloud over the global prospects for development. The task is formidable: for many of the world's poorest countries, decades of rapid growth will be needed to make inroads on poverty. And priorities and constraints vary widely across countries at different stages of development. Yet the opportunity for rapid development is greater today than at any time in history. International links, in the form of trade and flows of information, investment and technology, are stronger now than forty years ago. Medicine, science, and engineering have all made great strides; the benefits are available worldwide. And policymakers have a better understanding than before of the options for development.

To seize this opportunity, industrial countries, developing countries, and external aid and lending agencies need to act. The *industrial countries* need to

• Roll back restrictions on trade. The Uruguay Round of trade talks must not be allowed to fail. Nontariff barriers to trade need to be dismantled. Developing countries would benefit from being granted unrestricted access to industrial-country markets—some $55 billion in additional export earnings, or as much as they receive in aid.

• Reform macroeconomic policy. Reduced fiscal deficits, stable financial systems, stable currencies, low and stable interest rates, and steady non-inflationary growth would transform the climate for development in the rest of the world.

The *industrial countries and multilateral agencies*, including the World Bank can strengthen development prospects by enhancing the quantity and quality of external financial assistance. They need to

• Increase financial support. More external financing, both concessional and nonconcessional, would greatly strengthen the development effort. Many developing countries continue to struggle with heavy burdens of external debt. Further progress in extending debt relief to the middle- and low-income countries is needed.

• Support policy reform. Additional financing will be far more effective when it supports sound domestic policies. Experience shows that it pays lenders and borrowers alike to ensure that investments and market-friendly policies go together.

• Encourage sustainable growth. The global community has a great responsibility to take common action to protect the earth's environment, and to support the control of environmental degradation in developing countries.

But the developing countries' prospects are principally in their own hands. Domestic reforms ensure the benefits of better external conditions. The *developing countries* need to

• Invest in people. Governments must spend more, and more efficiently, on primary education, basic health care, nutrition, and family planning. That requires shifts in spending priorities; greater efficiency and better targeting of expenditures, and in some cases greater resource mobilization.

• Improve the climate for enterprise. Governments need to intervene less in industrial and agricultural pricing, to deregulate restrictions to entry and exit, and to focus instead on ensuring adequate infrastructure and institutions.

• Open economies to international trade and investment. This calls for far fewer nontariff restrictions on trade and investments, substantially lower tariffs, and a decisive move away from discretionary forms of control.

• Get macroeconomic policy right. Macroeconomic policy needs to ensure that fiscal deficits are low and inflation kept in check. Appropriate, market-based incentives for saving and investment are essential if domestic resources are to play their essential part in financing development.

In each of these areas, the challenge to policymakers is to exploit the complementarities between state and market. They can transform the outlook for economic development by having the state intervene less where it may (for example, in production), and more where it must (for example, in environmental protection), by strengthening institutions and capabilities, by finding nondistortionary ways to promote equity, and by fostering checks and balances in governments.

Succeeding in development is indeed the most pressing of all the challenges that now confront the human race. Incomplete though our understanding still is, enough has been learned in the past forty years to point the way. Strategies in which governments support rather than supplant competitive markets offer the best hope for meeting the challenge of development.

The world economy in transition

Radical change is under way in the global economy. Recently more than a dozen countries have launched major economic reforms. Democracy has swept Eastern Europe and is making inroads in the developing world. The European Community has moved closer to political and economic union. If these events are cause for optimism, others are not. War in the Middle East, increasing difficulties with the Soviet Union's economic transition, and slowing world growth have been setbacks.

This Report will show that what matters most for any country's economic development is its own approach to economic policies and institutions. But global economic conditions are important. So whereas the rest of this Report is largely about what countries themselves can do to improve their performance, this chapter looks at the global context in which those actions will be cast.

In some ways the international economy will be unfavorable to development in the coming decade. Interest rates may remain high, and growth is likely to remain slow worldwide. No early end to the debt crisis is in sight—nor is any substantial resumption in North-South capital flows. The need to protect the environment poses an additional challenge. Yet there are also favorable signs for development. Real reform is being carried out in Eastern Europe. Ghana, Indonesia, Mexico, and other countries are striving to sustain their earlier programs of reform; Peru, Tanzania, and Viet Nam, for example, have embarked on new ones. If more countries do the same—and if their actions find support in greater openness in international trade and finance—rapid progress is indeed possible.

The long view

Economic history shows that it is possible for countries to develop rapidly and indeed that for many countries the pace of change has accelerated. It shows at the same time that many countries have developed very slowly, if at all. The key to development, clearly, is to understand why the range of experience has been so wide.

The time required for substantial changes in the quality of life has shrunk steadily over the centuries (Figure 1.1). Beginning in 1780, the United

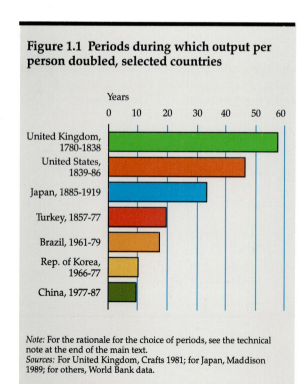

Figure 1.1 Periods during which output per person doubled, selected countries

Years

United Kingdom, 1780-1838

United States, 1839-86

Japan, 1885-1919

Turkey, 1857-77

Brazil, 1961-79

Rep. of Korea, 1966-77

China, 1977-87

Note: For the rationale for the choice of periods, see the technical note at the end of the main text.
Sources: For United Kingdom, Crafts 1981; for Japan, Maddison 1989; for others, World Bank data.

Kingdom took fifty-eight years to double its output per person. Starting in 1839, the United States took forty-seven years. Starting in the 1880s, Japan did it in only thirty-four years. After World War II, many countries doubled their per capita output even faster than Japan: for example, Brazil in eighteen years, Indonesia in seventeen, the Republic of Korea in eleven, and China in ten. This change in pace indicates that the industrial revolution gained momentum over a long period, whereas catching up has been a more and more rapid process.

The pace of progress has hastened not only for income and material consumption, but also for other aspects of welfare. Many developing countries have approached the life expectancies of the industrial world in a remarkably short time (Figure 1.2). These changes reflect better diet, housing conditions, and access to medical care. The latter, in turn, were possible thanks to increases in food production and distribution, growth in family incomes, medical advances, public investments in safe drinking water and sanitary waste disposal, and, more recently, the development of health care systems.

Technological progress, more than any other single factor, has fueled this economic advance. Innovations have produced great strides in agriculture, industry, and services. Famines disappeared from Western Europe in the mid-1800s, from Eastern Europe in the 1930s, and from Asia in the 1970s. In Africa the challenge of eradicating famine remains. Over time, countries have tended to converge with respect to some aspects of performance more than others. There has been a particularly strong tendency toward convergence in indicators of basic health. Large falls in infant mortality have been achieved by many countries—even those with very low incomes. The countries now classified as developing have better standards of basic health than the industrial countries did when they were at the corresponding level of income. The same holds for literacy, although less so. Convergence in per capita income has been much more disappointing.

Despite the dramatic progress in some countries, the differences in per capita incomes are vast across countries and regions. Table 1.1 shows the great strides that have been made in raising incomes around the world. But it also shows the great income differences and the lack of progress in many parts of the world.

Economic theory suggests that productivity and per capita incomes would converge across countries over time, assuming that the countries which are now developing get access to the new technol-

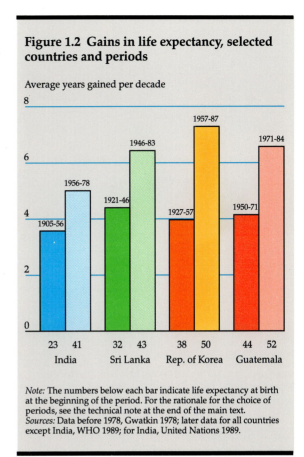

Figure 1.2 Gains in life expectancy, selected countries and periods

Average years gained per decade

Note: The numbers below each bar indicate life expectancy at birth at the beginning of the period. For the rationale for the choice of periods, see the technical note at the end of the main text.
Sources: Data before 1978, Gwatkin 1978; later data for all countries except India, WHO 1989; for India, United Nations 1989.

ogy introduced by the industrial countries (see Chapter 2). There is evidence that this has happened in the industrial countries. With interruptions caused by war, the variation in their per capita incomes has declined steadily over the past century. This convergence began with the industrial revolution. In the nineteenth century, Australia, Canada, Japan, the United States, and Western Europe began to industrialize and to grow at an accelerating rate. Some other nations followed in the early twentieth century. But by 1945, most of the world had failed to make much progress.

Asia, the world's most populous region, has recently begun to catch up—in some cases, at a spectacular rate. But Sub-Saharan Africa has seen its per capita incomes fall in real terms since 1973. In 1950 the region's per capita income was 11 percent of the industrial-country average; now it is 5 percent. Latin America has also slipped, especially since 1980. There are disparities within groups of countries, too. They are growing among the less advanced economies as a whole, and especially in East and South Asia.

Extraordinary progress is possible even when countries seem doomed to fail. Forty-three years

Table 1.1 Historical trends in GDP per capita
(1980 international dollars)

Region or group	1830	1913	1950	1973	1989	Growth rate 1913–50	Growth rate 1950–89
Asia	375 (40)	510 (23)	487 (15)	1215 (16)	2,812 (28)	−0.1	3.6
Latin America	.. ..	1,092 (49)	1,729 (52)	2,969 (40)	3,164 (31)	1.2	1.2
Sub-Saharan Africa	.. ..	.. ..	348 (11)	558 (8)	513 (5)	..	0.8
Europe, Middle East, and North Africa	.. ..	.. ..	940 (29)	2,017 (27)	2,576 (26)	..	2.0
Eastern Europe	600 (64)	1,263 (57)	2,128 (65)	4,658 (63)	5,618 (56)	1.4	2.0
Developing economies	.. ..	701 (32)	839 (25)	1,599 (22)	2,796 (28)	..	2.7
OECD members	935	2,220	3,298	7,396	10,104	1.1	2.3

Note: Data presented are simple averages of GDP per capita. Numbers in parentheses are regional GDP per capita as a percentage of GDP in the OECD economies. Regional groupings include only non-high-income countries. Hungary is included in Eastern Europe group, not in Europe, Middle East, and North Africa.
Sources: For 1830–1965, Maddison, background paper. Data for 1950–65 for Africa and the Middle East are based on OECD; data after 1965 are based on growth rates from the World Bank data base. Benchmark values are 1980 international dollar estimates from Maddison, background paper, if available; from Summers and Heston 1984, otherwise.

ago an influential government report in an important developing country observed that labor today shunned hard, productive jobs and sought easy, merchant-like work. The report showed that workers' productivity had fallen, wages were too high, and enterprises were inefficient and heavily subsidized. The country had virtually priced itself out of international markets and faced a severe competitive threat from newly industrializing China and India. It was overpopulated and becoming more so. This would be the last opportunity, concluded the prime minister in July 1947, to discover whether his country would be able to stand on its own two feet or become a permanent burden for the rest of the world. That country was Japan. The central question of this Report is why countries like Japan have succeeded so spectacularly while others have failed.

The setting for development

The key to global development has been the diffusion of technological progress. New technology has allowed resources to be used more productively, causing incomes to rise and the quality of life to improve. Scientific and medical innovation has proceeded at a breathtaking pace during the past two hundred years (Box 1.1).

Using new technologies effectively has often required adaptation and innovation in economic institutions, and occasionally political and social institutions, too. New means of transport extended markets and thereby increased the division of labor, leading, as Adam Smith observed, to more specialization: goods and labor were traded for money instead of bartered, and so on. Today, creating and strengthening market institutions is the biggest task for the former socialist countries of Europe and for many of the developing countries.

Global integration

Trade was crucial in the spread of technology. Countries have usually developed more quickly as part of the world economy than in isolation, although protection has stimulated growth in some instances. Historically, trade wars have retarded global development.

The Great Depression and its aftermath are perhaps the clearest example of this. The collapse of the post World War I trading system did not trigger the Great Depression, but it did contribute to its depth, spread, and duration. The stock market crash of October 1929 caused demand and trade to slump. After the failure to reach a cooperative trade agreement in 1929, the United States raised

Box 1.1 Innovations that changed the world

During the past two hundred years, a series of major scientific and technological advances have dramatically changed the course of development.

Health and medicine

In the nineteenth century, improved nutrition played the lead role in increasing people's life expectancy and in reducing infant mortality rates. In this century progress has come from the medical sciences. Jenner's smallpox vaccine (1790) opened the way for the vaccination of cholera, typhoid, and anthrax. Pasteur established the relationship between microbes and immunity (1880). Half a century later came Fleming's discovery of penicillin (1929), its clinical application (1941), and the development of other antibiotics. As a result, the morbidity rate of tuberculosis in the United States, for example, declined from 79 per 100,000 in 1939 to 9 in 1988. Widespread immunization programs have contributed to dramatically reduced infant mortality rates, which are estimated to have declined in low-income economies from 124 per 1,000 live births in 1965 to 72 in 1985.

Food production

Steady increases in food production in the nineteenth century, followed by more dramatic increases in the twentieth, made possible some remarkable improvements in people's nutrition. The green revolution in the 1960s and 1970s was possible because high-yielding hybrid varieties of wheat and maize, dwarf varieties of rice, and chemical fertilizers and pesticides were introduced. India doubled its average yield of wheat within a few years after the introduction of these improvements in 1966–67. In China, where rural reforms provided added flexibility in farming practices, new grain varieties and farming techniques made it possible to support 22 percent of the world's population on 7 percent of its arable land.

Transport, energy, and communications

The industrial revolution in Europe began with inventions that augmented labor with machinery and new sources of energy. After Savery's steam engine (1698) and Newcomen's improved engine (1712), Watt's more efficient engines (1770 and 1796) brought steam into wide use. The production and transport of coal grew quickly. Next came improvements in oil refining (1850s), then a method of drilling for oil. The internal combustion engine (1876) and the technologies for electricity generation and transmission (1886) were part of the same progression, transforming old industries and launching new ones. Transportation was revolutionized along the way, with the steamship and the locomotive (1830s), the automobile (1885), and the airplane (1903). Harbors, highways, railways, and airports brought trade to the remotest of places.

The telegraph (1844), telephone (1876), radio (1895), and television (1925) changed the way people interact. With the electronic computer (1924), communication satellites (1960), and fiber optics (1977), information is now transmitted and processed at breathtaking speed, yet at practical cost.

tariffs in the Smoot-Hawley Act of 1930. America's trading partners retaliated. World trade fell by two-thirds—from $3 billion in October 1929 to $1 billion in July 1932. Some of the contraction was the result of the Depression, but the hostility toward trade caused damage that took decades to repair.

The deterioration of the climate for trade in 1929 had followed a long period of peacetime market integration. Britain had entered the nineteenth century with an unwieldy system of tariffs and customs laws accumulated over five hundred years. The transition to liberal trade was not easy. High duties on grain imports (the Corn Laws) assured landlords relative prosperity, while consumers paid high prices and export-oriented manufacturing was stifled. In 1845, when the potato crop failed in Ireland, mass starvation followed. This disaster paved the way for the repeal of the Corn Laws, and Britain moved to a more liberal trade regime. Other countries followed. Expanding agricultural markets lessened protectionist pressures, and the period from 1848 to 1873 became one of freer trade throughout Europe.

This process of international integration was reinforced by integration within countries. Innovations in transport were crucial. Accelerating market integration, along with new manufacturing technologies, led to rapid increases in productivity.

Though this shift toward international integration undoubtedly spurred development, it also exposed countries to external economic shocks, and hence to occasional setbacks. Dramatically lower freight rates for shipping appear to have caused profits and wages to fall, but wages fell less so the cost of labor rose in real terms. Cheap grain from North America, Argentina, Australia, and the Ukraine was brought to Europe. Many countries raised their tariffs, on manufactures as well as

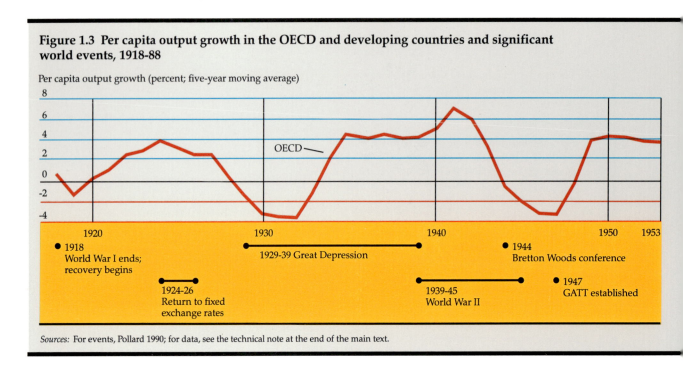

Figure 1.3 Per capita output growth in the OECD and developing countries and significant world events, 1918-88

Per capita output growth (percent; five-year moving average)

OECD

1920 · 1918 World War I ends; recovery begins

1924-26 Return to fixed exchange rates

1930 1929-39 Great Depression

1940 1939-45 World War II

1944 Bretton Woods conference

1947 GATT established

1950 1953

Sources: For events, Pollard 1990; for data, see the technical note at the end of the main text.

food. By 1913, the average tariff on manufactures was 20 percent in France, 18 percent in Italy, and 13 percent in Germany. Meanwhile, however, the first great global boom in trade had pulled many developing, primary-product exporters along. Argentina had grown so fast that by the 1920s its per capita income was 80 percent of Britain's.

Foreign trade was financed in the late nineteenth century by a surge of foreign lending from Europe, to the newly settled countries of the temperate zones and to czarist Russia. Technological breakthroughs in chemicals, electrical products, and automobiles—sometimes called a second industrial revolution—added new products sought in import markets. British foreign lending in 1913 reached half of national saving and 5 percent of national income. World War I cost continental Europe much of its productive labor power and physical capital (Figure 1.3). Farm output had expanded significantly outside Europe during the war. So the gradual recovery of European agriculture lowered prices after 1925. Prices collapsed after the October 1929 crash. The period from 1918 to 1925 was one of great instability in exchange rates, tariffs, trade agreements, and regulations.

The Great Depression and World War II shattered the global economy and badly shook the confidence of the developing countries, especially in Latin America, in trade as an engine of growth. The need for international agreements on trade and currencies was greater than ever before. The

Monetary and Financial Conference of the United and Associated Nations at Bretton Woods in July 1944 set out to create "a world in which countries did not close their eyes to the repercussions of their actions on others" (Robinson 1975). The conference led to new rules and institutions for international monetary and exchange relations (under the International Monetary Fund), long-term capital flows for reconstruction and development (under the World Bank), and international trade (eventually embodied in the General Agreement on Tariffs and Trade, GATT). Even before these institutions were fully operational, the Marshall Plan supported postwar reconstruction in Western Europe; productivity missions from the United States toured Europe and Japan, helping to develop trade relations and to spread information on technology.

The Soviet Union decided not to join the Bretton Woods framework and formed a parallel international system. Eastern European nations nationalized their economies and adopted Soviet-style central planning. The Council for Mutual Economic Assistance (CMEA) was set up to coordinate their economic activities.

The Marshall Plan sponsored the formation of the European Payments Union, creating the institutional basis for free trade within Western Europe. The GATT spurred the move toward broader multilateral trade agreements. The formation of the European Economic Community (EEC) in

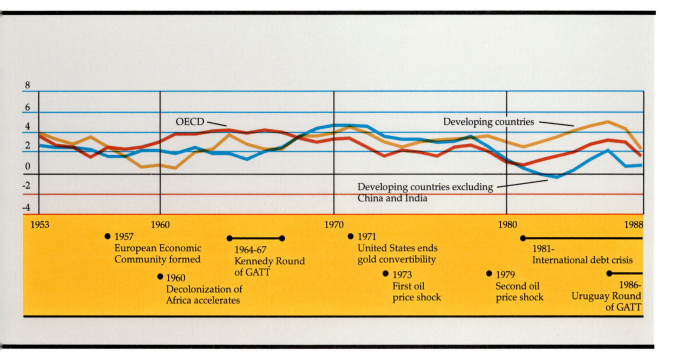

8				
6				
4	OECD		Developing countries	
2				
0				
-2		Developing countries excluding	
-4		China and India	

1953　　　　　1960　　　　　　　　　　1970　　　　　　　　　1980　　　　　1988

● 1957
European Economic
Community formed

● 1960
Decolonization of
Africa accelerates

1964-67
Kennedy Round
of GATT

● 1971
United States ends
gold convertibility

● 1973
First oil
price shock

● 1979
Second oil
price shock

1981-
International debt crisis

1986-
Uruguay Round
of GATT

1957, the formation of the OECD, and successive rounds of GATT agreements all pushed the same way. Investment in Europe and Japan increased to record levels as these countries sought to catch up technologically with the United States. Economic growth between World War II and the early 1970s was faster than ever before. The developing countries, many of which were newly created nations, joined this growing global system but with varying degrees of commitment. East Asia embraced trade with enthusiasm; South Asia, Africa, and Latin America were more reluctant.

After supporting unprecedented growth in trade and global integration for nearly three decades (Figure 1.4), the international framework shifted in the 1970s. Fixed exchange rates became insupportable, and the United States suspended the convertibility of the dollar in 1971. In 1973 EEC governments floated major European currencies. The shock induced by the decision of the members of the Organization of Petroleum Exporting Countries (OPEC) to raise oil prices disrupted international trade and capital flows. The trade system came under great stress. A slide toward protection began that still threatens the liberal trading order established after 1945.

That is the background against which the governments of developing countries must choose their trade policies. Today more than 4 billion people, or nearly 80 percent of the world's population, live in developing countries. Their share in global output is less than 20 percent; their share in world trade is 17 percent. As a group, these economies still have a long way to go before they are fully integrated with the global economy.

Figure 1.4 The share of exports in GDP, selected country groups, 1900-86
(percent)

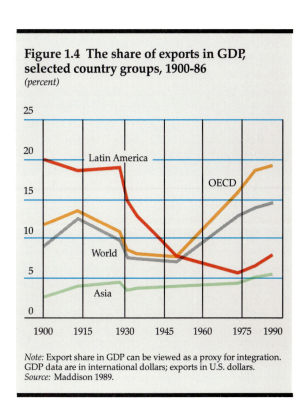

Note: Export share in GDP can be viewed as a proxy for integration. GDP data are in international dollars; exports in U.S. dollars.
Source: Maddison 1989.

Despite the revival of protectionism since the 1970s, the world economy remains highly integrated. This, as history has shown, exposes countries to external shocks. The shocks of the 1970s and 1980s have been severe. The collapse of the Bretton Woods system, sharp rises in food and other commodity prices, and soaring oil prices in 1973–74 and 1979–80 affected nearly every economy. In the aftermath of the second oil price shock, the United States adopted a mix of monetary and fiscal policies in the early 1980s that pushed interest rates high worldwide. For oil-importing developing countries, the scale of the shocks of the 1970s varied, but in most was less than 10 percent of GDP. However, the terms of trade and interest rate effects grew in the 1980s. In Sub-Saharan Africa and Latin America the combined effects were estimated to average more than 10 percent of GDP—larger than in other developing regions.

Although policies in the industrial countries contributed to the quick recovery from the recession after the 1973-74 oil price shock, they also led to high rates of inflation later in the decade. Many industrial countries followed an accommodating monetary policy which resulted in low and, in some countries, even negative real interest rates during the 1970s. Large international capital flows resulted from the recycling of surpluses of oil exporters. But the upswing came to an abrupt halt with the second oil price shock in 1979–80 and the sharp tightening of monetary policy in the large industrial countries. Between the late 1970s and the early 1980s, the real dollar London interbank offered rate (LIBOR) rose from −1 percent to 6 percent, growth and trade sharply decelerated, and the prices of oil and other commodities declined. Exporters of these categories, and those who depend on worker remittances derived from these exports, suffered setbacks. There was little cooperation in forming policies among the large industrial countries.

A debt problem that would be transmitted worldwide unfolded in the 1970s as many developing countries borrowed to increase consumption, invest in doubtful projects, and finance imported oil (which was then subsidized). The volume of international bank lending increased by nearly 800 percent during the decade, to about $800 billion. Most commercial lenders to developing countries did little to investigate how loans were used, relying instead on sovereign guaran-

tees. The productivity of investment in low- and middle-income countries may have fallen by a third between the 1960s and the 1970s. Their external debt grew from $63 billion in 1970 to $562 billion in 1980.

The debt crisis emerged as the world recession, high real interest rates, and terms of trade shocks of the early 1980s caused acute debt-servicing problems for severely indebted nations. Interest payments owed by the developing countries grew 40 percent during the period 1980–83 to $64 billion. That was about 3.2 percent of their GNP, compared with less than 1 percent only a few years earlier. Mexico declared a debt moratorium in 1982. Many other countries were forced into debt restructuring agreements with official creditors and commercial banks. By 1982, commercial banks had virtually ended their voluntary lending to most developing countries. Aggregate net financial transfers to developing nations (disbursements of long-term loans minus total debt service) swung from a net inflow of $36 billion in 1981 to a net outflow of $30 billion in 1989. In severely indebted countries, investment fell sharply; this weakened the recovery when the international environment later improved. In the 1980s, real GDP growth slowed in Sub-Saharan Africa, Latin America, and the Middle East, North Africa, and Eastern Europe (Figure 1.5).

Economic growth accelerated in the industrial countries in the second half of the 1980s. Less regulation and lower taxes, combined with the falling price of oil in 1986, expansionary monetary policies, and greater policy cooperation, led to increased activity. Low inflation, moderate wage increases, and high business profits spurred private investment, especially in Japan and Europe. A number of developing countries at this time had strong trade linkages in manufactures and comparatively stable macroeconomic climates. They were able to take advantage of the industrial countries' recovery, and raised their growth rates.

Greater integration in the 1980s led trade and financial flows to grow faster than output. But it was another decade prone to shocks, making the task of adjustment for most developing countries all the harder. There were wide swings in exchange rates, and international interest rates were erratic. The U.S. current account balance swung from a $7 billion surplus in 1981 to a $162 billion deficit in 1986, gradually declining to about $110 billion in 1989. (The United States absorbed about 23 percent of the merchandise exports from developing countries in 1989—more than the combined

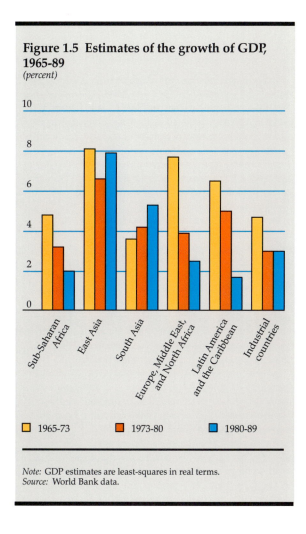

Figure 1.5 Estimates of the growth of GDP, 1965-89
(percent)

Legend:
- 1965-73
- 1973-80
- 1980-89

Categories (left to right): Sub-Saharan Africa, East Asia, South Asia, Europe, Middle East, and North Africa, Latin America and the Caribbean, Industrial countries

Note: GDP estimates are least-squares in real terms.
Source: World Bank data.

flow to Japan, Germany, and France.) In recent years, this deficit is estimated to have absorbed an average of 4–5 percent of the world's savings. Meanwhile, debt overhang and a sharp decline in financial flows to developing countries led the combined current account deficit of these countries to decline from about $70 billion in 1980 to $50 billion in 1989.

Succeeding in an integrated world

Even in the face of the negative external shocks of the past twenty years, some economies performed remarkably well—notably those in East Asia. But most have struggled, especially during the past decade. Often, this was not for want of effort. Many developing countries modified their economic policies when their debt troubles mounted. in the early 1980s. The need for such adjustment grew in 1982 with the deep recession in the industrial countries and a steep decline in the real prices

of primary commodities. Many governments cut their budget deficits, altered certain relative prices (the real exchange rate, the real interest rate, and the internal terms of trade between agriculture and industry), and restructured their activities. A number also replaced quantitative trade restrictions with tariffs and reformed their tariff structures. Balance of payments deficits fell sharply. Despite much progress, however, fiscal imbalances remain. Deficits have often been reduced by cutting public investment rather than by containing current expenditures or reforming taxes to increase revenues.

The new economic climate has posed challenges in industrial countries as well. Structural rigidities, energy price controls, misaligned exchange rates, and trade barriers prevented adjustment and slowed recovery in the 1970s and early 1980s. Policy then began to shift. Macroeconomic management focused on the fight against inflation (although monetary policies became more accommodating as inflationary pressures eased in the latter half of the 1980s). Fiscal and regulatory policies emphasized supply-side incentives; taxes on both household income and business profits came down. Most countries began reducing the role of the public sector. Major structural reforms included the privatization of publicly owned enterprises and the liberalization of product, labor, and financial markets.

During the 1980s, the backwardness of the command economies contrasted sharply with the rapid technological advance in the market-oriented economies of Asia and the West. Economic performance deteriorated in the Soviet Union (Box 1.2) and other East Bloc economies. Some countries, notably the former German Democratic Republic and Poland, have undertaken extremely bold reforms. Economic conditions in nearly all these economies are grave, and projections suggest that the bottom of the decline still lies ahead.

Recent developments

A seven-year expansion in the world economy came almost to a halt in 1990. Signs of slowing economic activity in a number of large industrial countries became evident as monetary policies were tightened in response to production at near-capacity levels and rising inflation. The slowdown became more widespread and pronounced with the Gulf crisis in August 1990. Increased uncertainty had adverse effects on consumer and business confidence, which in turn led to markedly

Box 1.2 The Soviet economic crisis

Mikhail Gorbachev, after sounding a cry of alarm when he rose to leadership in 1985, used three words repeatedly in his call for reform: perestroika (restructuring), uskoreniye (acceleration of growth), and glasnost (openness). The economy was in trouble, and corrective measures had been postponed for too long. He pointed out that the Soviet Union produced more shoes and far more steel than the United States, but the quality of the shoes was poor and the use of steel wasteful.

Was this a short-term crisis? Or was it more deeply seated? Clearly not the former, as President Gorbachev recently pronounced: "Today, when we talk about radical restructuring of economic management, it is vital to recall what the real situation was in our country back in the late 1970s and early 1980s. By that time the rates of economic growth had fallen so low, as to virtually signify stagnation." A sharp drop in industrial production had been accompanied by the exhaustion of natural resources in populated regions and by the increasing obsolescence of plant and equipment. Death rates and infant mortality rates were rising.

Between 1985 and 1987 perestroika was put in place to retool and modernize industry and to increase the attention to quality control. Accompanying measures included improving worker initiative and making the bureaucracy more accountable. Despite some initial success, however, reforms did not address underlying systemic problems.

Uskoreniye proved elusive. Real output stagnated, and the fiscal deficit rose from 2.5 percent of GDP to 8.5 percent.

The program's failure spurred more serious efforts to reform the economy in 1987 and 1988. The material allocation system was scrapped. Prices were allowed to move in a freely negotiated range. The soft budget constraint was hardened. Cooperative enterprises were encouraged, and private family enterprises were legalized. Foreign trade was decentralized, and a currency retention scheme was introduced along with a system of differentiated exchange rates and limited foreign currency auctions.

Because the measures were introduced piecemeal, they had the opposite of their intended effect. Imports from the convertible currency area grew strongly, while manufactured exports scarcely changed. Increases in enterprise autonomy were circumscribed by the system of state orders, which covered most of industrial output. The dismantling of the traditional system of planning began, but the inflexible and distorted official price system—and the state distribution agency—were left largely intact. Throughout the late 1980s, the capital stock and labor force declined.

In 1990, net material product—according to official estimates—declined by 4 percent, and inflation was running at 12 percent. The traditional centrally planned system had largely collapsed, but a functioning market system had not yet replaced it.

Transforming the Soviet economy will be difficult. It will require many of the actions discussed in this Report: stabilizing the macroeconomy, reforming prices in a context of greater domestic and international competition, and reforming property rights and government institutions.

---

lower growth of consumer spending and business investment in the industrial countries. The financial requirements of the unification of Germany and war-related reconstruction in the Middle East exerted upward pressures on short-term interest rates in Germany and Japan despite the economic slowdown in 1990 and early 1991. Real GDP growth in the industrial countries slowed to about 2.6 percent in 1990, compared with 3.3 percent in 1989 and 4.5 percent in 1988.

Canada, the United Kingdom, and the United States have been in recession. Growth has also slowed elsewhere in western Europe. Equity prices in Japan have fallen by about 50 percent, and the quality of commercial bank portfolios in both Japan and the United States has deteriorated. Although the slowdown of the industrial economies is likely to be short-lived and shallow, the recovery is expected to be only gradual. The finan-

cial problems of the private sector in several large economies will continue to hamper growth. Output in the industrial countries is expected to expand by less than 2 percent in 1991.

In the developing countries, real GDP growth declined from 4.3 percent in 1988 to 2.9 percent in 1989 and to only 2.2 percent in 1990, the lowest since 1982. The main reasons—in addition to continuing macroeconomic instability and domestic policy weaknesses—were falling non-oil commodity prices, high international (nondollar) interest rates, and slower growth in world trade.

Oil prices rose from less than $20 a barrel (Brent crude grade) in July 1990 to $35–40 after Iraq's August invasion of Kuwait and the subsequent U.N. embargo on oil exports from Iraq and Kuwait. By the end of the war and the freeing of Kuwait in early 1991, oil prices had declined to about $20 a barrel. If prices remain in that range, the effect of the 1990 oil price shock on the industrial economies will be small and short-lived. For the industrial economies as a group, the terms of trade loss of the 1990 shock is estimated to be one-third that of the 1973–74 shock and only one-sixth that of 1979–80.

By contrast, the consequences for Eastern Europe have been severe because countries there have begun to pay for oil with hard currency. For oil-importing developing countries as a group, the effect of the increase in the oil price on the current account balance is estimated to have been about 7 percent of their combined exports. In addition, the Arab Republic of Egypt, Jordan, and Turkey have had extensive economic relationships with Iraq and Kuwait. These and other countries—Bangladesh, India, Morocco, Pakistan, the Philippines, Sri Lanka, and Sudan—have to pay higher interest rates on debt service, and have lost trade and service contracts and workers' remittances. Revenues from tourism have also fallen sharply.

Output contracted sharply in the Middle East, Eastern Europe, and (because of a severe recession in Brazil) Latin America. Growth also slowed in Sub-Saharan Africa. However, in countries covered by the Special Program for Assistance to Africa, which have been implementing reforms, output grew faster than the population. In Asia, because of the improved performance of China and some of the newly industrializing economies (NIEs) in the region, the growth rate accelerated to 3.5 percentage points more than the average for the developing countries as a whole. Output growth in the developing countries is expected to recover somewhat in 1991, to about 3 percent. Nevertheless, by early 1991 conditions were still deteriorating in many countries—especially those most affected by the Gulf War.

Prospects for world development

Many factors will have an important bearing on the global climate for development in the coming years: the growth of world trade, the policies adopted by the industrial countries, the state of the international capital markets, and so on. In every case the degree of uncertainty is large (see Box 1.3). To arrive at a view about the prospects for growth in the developing countries, judgments need to be made (either explicitly or implicitly) for each of these external factors. Without knowing anything else about the outlook, it is clear that there will always be a premium on economic flexibility. Countries that can respond easily to any of a range of outcomes are likely to fare best.

World trade

The Uruguay Round of GATT talks, begun in 1986, continued into 1991. These talks are the first to include developing countries as main participants. If the Uruguay Round succeeds, it will lead to better market access for industrial and developing countries; lower tariffs worldwide; significant cuts in agricultural subsidies; more discipline in the use of industrial subsidies; and the extension of multilateral arrangements to services, trade-related investment rules, and intellectual property rights. The most difficult of these areas has been agriculture. There are large differences between the negotiating positions of the United States and the European Community on the size and speed of cuts in export subsidies, domestic price supports, and import barriers. Aside from agriculture, however, progress has been made, notably in textiles and clothing, services, tariff cuts, trade-related investment rules and intellectual property rights, and dispute settlement. A successful outcome to the talks is critical for the world trading system. A good agreement will greatly improve the prospects for the developing countries.

EUROPEAN INTEGRATION. As the European Community dismantles national barriers to the free movement of goods, services, labor, and capital, it could become the world's single biggest market. Over five to seven years, according to the European Commission, the region's aggregate GDP could jump by 4.5 to 7 percent as a result of integration alone. Project 1992 also involves steps toward monetary union, which may lead to a single currency for Europe. This, combined with the effects of market unification, could increase long-term growth in western Europe by about 1 percentage point a year.

THE RISE OF EAST ASIA. Between 1965 and 1988, the East Asian economies increased their share of world GDP from 5 to 20 percent and of world manufactures exports from 10 to 23 percent. Japan has emerged as the second largest economy in the world, whereas a number of developing economies in the region have joined the ranks of the high-income economies. By the end of the 1980s, the four NIEs of East Asia accounted for half the manufactured exports of developing countries. The region's financial power had grown commensurately. At the regional level, closer economic relations developed within the Association of Southeast Asian Nations. A new Asia-Pacific Economic

Box 1.3   The climate for development in the 1990s

	Pessimistic	Optimistic
World trade	GATT negotiations collapse; unilateral policies by large industrial countries lead to trade wars; trade declines overall, though by less within regional blocs.	GATT makes real progress; regional GATT-compatible agreements produce dramatically greater integration in Europe, Asia, and the Western Hemisphere; world trade expands rapidly.
Capital flows	International capital markets are overcautious, and transfers to developing countries fail to pick up.	Capital flows to the developing countries resume; greater confidence spurs direct foreign investment.
World finance	Major institutions fail in Japan and the United States, leading to high risk premiums, low investment, a prolonged economic slowdown, and possibly higher inflation; the debt crisis continues to impede growth in the developing regions.	Major institutions muddle through; financial reforms and regulatory changes reduce systemic risks; economic recovery is rapid; Brady Initiative and its successors gradually reduce developing- country debt burdens.
Industrial-country policy	Large industrial countries fail to cooperate; they follow poor macroeconomic policies, and financial instability and low growth result.	Macroeconomic policies of the large industrial countries stabilize financial markets and lead to sustained growth.
Security	The decline of the superpowers leads to regional crises and ethnic strife within and among countries; arms races divert economic resources; terrorism, drugs, and poverty undermine internal security.	End of cold war reduces tensions among superpowers; new international security arrangements are developed through a strengthened United Nations.
Technology	Technologies required for competitive products become more and more sophisticated and labor-saving; technology flows are restricted by protectionist policies and firm strategies; developing-country advantages resulting from cheap labor and raw materials diminish.	New technologies improve health and productivity (especially in agriculture); multinationals develop wider global production networks; computers reduce advantages of large markets; better communications make it easier for countries with adequate human capital to catch up in productivity.
Energy	Oil prices remain volatile because of ongoing political and social instability in the Middle East, which continues to be the main supplier of oil.	New political arrangements in the Middle East, combined with constructive dialogue between producers and consumers of petroleum, lead to a period of unusual stability in real oil prices.
Environment	Damage to the environment mounts, with economic repercussions; global resources dwindle; the frequency of local environmental disasters increases.	Environmental ill-effects prove less costly and less immediate than predicted; new national and international policies take adequate steps to protect scarce resources.

Cooperation group, loosely resembling the OECD, began annual ministerial meetings; its members are Japan, the United States, and ten other Pacific Rim nations.

COOPERATION IN THE WESTERN HEMISPHERE. With the United States–Canada Free Trade Agreement in effect, the United States declared an "En-terprises for the Americas Initiative" to improve trading relationships throughout the Americas. Mexico and the United States may enter "fast track" negotiations on a free trade area; any accord would be a first for countries with such large income differences.

How far do all these developments signal a breakdown in the open trading order of the postwar years? How will the trading prospects of many low-income countries be affected? The answer is unclear. Some of the recent trade initiatives have strong regional dimensions, but none so far has involved raising external barriers. In the end the outcome will depend on whether the extra trade created by regional integration will outweigh the trade diverted by it. If the Uruguay Round collapses, the risk that the regional groups will turn inward is far greater.

International capital flows and finance

In the 1980s, international capital flowed mainly among the industrial countries. Several large countries, including the United States, became net capital importers; that is, their domestic investment exceeded their national savings (Table 1.2). Developing countries were bypassed by international lenders and investors, mainly because of their high external debts and deteriorating economic and political conditions. During the decade, aggregate net resource transfers to these countries shifted from positive to negative. The investment-output ratios of the low- and middle-income countries fell in the 1980s and have not recovered.

SAVINGS-INVESTMENT BALANCES. The pattern of savings-investment balances across broad country groups is not likely to depart over the medium term from the broad trend established in the past few years. A shrinking U.S. current account deficit and higher oil revenues for oil-exporting countries may be offset by more imports, reconstruction costs, and military spending in the Gulf. Lower

private and public savings in Japan, and falling current account surpluses in the Asian NIEs (because of exchange rate appreciation and slower growth in world trade) will also help to reduce the imbalances of the 1980s. Germany's current account surplus will decline as unification increases investment demand. And the demand for international credit and investment in Eastern Europe and the Middle East may rise just as the industrial economies recover from the slowdown of 1990–91. All this implies that international interest rates are likely to remain high over the medium term.

The current account deficit of many developing countries may therefore rise at a very moderate pace—from $51 billion or 1.8 percent of GNP in 1989 to about $70 billion in 1995 and about $90 billion by 2000, averaging 1.5–2.0 percent of GNP over the 1990s. As debt repayments reduce interest payments on existing debt, new net flows will cause interest payments to rise. Outflows on factor services will also rise because the higher stock of direct foreign investment will expand the flow of remittances. By the mid-1990s the severely indebted developing countries could still be exporting more goods and nonfactor services than they import, although the balance should narrow significantly. The current pattern of net capital flows—which resembles that of the 1960s in the relative importance of official flows, direct investment, and private lending—might prevail well into the 1990s. High international interest rates, together with only a modest growth of international financial flows to the developing countries in the next several years, could slow development. The baseline projections, however, forecast an acceler-

Table 1.2 Global savings and investment
(percentage of world GDP, unless noted)

Category and group	1970–73	1974–80	1981–85	1986–88	Level in 1988 (billions of dollars)
Gross national savings					
High-income OECD members	16.5	16.2	14.6	16.3	2,997
(United States)	(5.2)	(4.8)	(4.9)	(3.8)	(664)
Other high-income economies[a]	0.8	1.3	1.2	1.0	175
Low- and middle-income economies	4.1	6.1	6.3	5.0	875
World total[b]	21.4	23.6	22.1	22.3	4,048
Gross domestic investment					
High-income OECD members	16.0	16.1	14.5	16.2	2,981
(United States)	(5.0)	(4.6)	(5.0)	(4.4)	(740)
Other high-income economies[a]	0.7	0.9	1.0	0.8	151
Low- and middle-income economies	4.6	6.0	5.6	4.5	781
World total[b]	21.2	23.0	21.1	21.5	3,913

a. Derived as a residual; high-income countries minus OECD.
b. World savings and investment differ because of discrepancy in world current accounts.
Source: World Bank data.

Table 1.3 Aggregate long-term net resource flows to developing countries, 1980–95

Component	Level (billions of dollars)				Share (percent)		
	1980	1986	1989	1995a	1980	1989	1995a
Net flowsb	82.8	51.2	63.3	103	100.0	100.0	100.0
Official grants	12.5	14.0	18.6	25	15.1	29.4	24.3
Official loans							
(net)	20.1	19.6	18.0	31	24.3	28.4	30.1
Bilateral	12.2	6.3	6.1	10	14.7	9.6	9.7
Multilateral	7.9	13.3	11.9	21	9.5	18.8	20.4
Private flows	50.2	17.6	26.7	47	60.6	42.2	45.6
Private loans	41.1	8.1	4.3	12	49.6	6.8	11.6
Direct foreign							
investment	9.1	9.5	22.4	35	11.0	35.3	34.0

a. Projections.
b. Excluding IMF transfers.
Source: World Bank 1990d.

ation of developing-country growth rates from those of the 1980s on the premises of increased domestic savings and a greater efficiency of investment (Table 1.3).

EXTERNAL DEBT. The international strategy for dealing with the more than $1.3 trillion in outstanding developing-country debt (this figure includes the debts of Eastern Europe) reached a turning point in 1988 and 1989. The emphasis shifted from debt rescheduling to the reduction of debt and debt service. Using debt buybacks, reduced interest rates, exchanges of debt at a discount for new secured debt, and so on, Brady Initiative agreements to reduce commercial debt and debt service have already reduced debt in Costa Rica, Mexico, and the Philippines by $9.5 billion. New debt reduction and rescheduling mechanisms for the official debt of low-income countries, adopted at the Toronto economic summit of June 1988, have been now applied in nineteen countries. These cover $5.8 billion, or 11 percent of bilateral official debt. Despite this new strategy, the debt crisis continues to dampen prospects for many of the forty-six severely indebted countries (see Chapter 8).

AID. Official development assistance (ODA) on highly concessional terms, representing about 90 percent of all grants and net lending from official sources, is the principal form of resource transfer to the poorest countries. In 1989 it accounted for nearly two-thirds of new resource flows to low-income countries and four-fifths of the flows to the poorest countries. In Sub-Saharan Africa, net flows of ODA were 8 percent of GNP, or $28 per capita, in 1989 (WDI, table 20).

The volume of aid extended by member governments of the Development Assistance Committee

(DAC) of the OECD bilaterally and through multilateral channels rose by an annual average of about 3 percent in real terms in the 1980s. That was in line with the growth of their economies. In 1989 the ratio of aid to GNP ranged from 0.15 for the United States to 0.32 for Japan, 0.78 for France, and 0.94 for Denmark and the Netherlands (WDI, table 19). Although some DAC governments (Denmark, France, Italy, Norway, Sweden, and Switzerland) increased their aid as a share of GNP, the amount of aid fell as a share of GNP for several large contributors (Germany, the United Kingdom, and the United States). As a result, the DAC countries' aid-GNP ratio remained constant at 0.35 percent throughout the 1980s. As the decade progressed and many developing countries experienced economic distress, however, it became an objective to make aid more effective. There was a growing awareness of the limitations of government in promoting growth. This led aid-granting and developing-country governments alike to recognize the role of the private sector and to stress the importance of better domestic policies. More and more, aid-granting countries will take effectiveness into account when setting their aid budgets. An adequate volume of aid is essential.

DIRECT FOREIGN INVESTMENT. Flows of direct foreign investment (DFI) are likely to grow in response to policy reforms. However, they will probably remain concentrated in globally integrated, middle-income countries with well-developed infrastructure. In 1989, about 70 percent of DFI flows to developing countries came from Japan (18 percent), the United Kingdom (20 percent), and the United States (32 percent). Just twenty developing economies, mainly in Asia and Latin America, accounted for 90 percent of the net flows between 1981 and 1990. The economic reconstruction of

Eastern Europe and the USSR will increase the competition for DFI. Nevertheless, for the smaller, reforming developing countries even modest increases in DFI flows can have a measurable effect on growth.

FINANCIAL INSTITUTIONS. The financial situations of some of the biggest banks and insurance companies of the United States and Japan have been weakened by rising interest rates, falling share and real estate prices, and bad investments. A ratio of market capitalization to assets of 8 percent is to be applied to all international banks by December 1992, as agreed in the Basle Accord. As these institutions struggle to raise capital, they are cutting back on new lending. Japan and the United States appear determined to contain the problem by bolstering deposit insurance and restructuring failed institutions. But the credit markets, already influenced by the financing requirements of Eastern Europe and the Middle East, are bound to be affected. Upward pressure on interest rates will remain for the medium term.

OECD POLICY. The macroeconomic policies of the industrial countries affect the external climate for development in a variety of ways. Most important, perhaps, by promoting steady and noninflationary growth at home they can improve the outlook for developing-country exports.

The industrial countries' macroeconomic policies also influence the demand for, and supply of, global savings, and thereby the level of world interest rates. Conversely, financial integration has made the task of setting national macroeconomic policy much more complicated. Diverging or inconsistent policies have often been the main cause of volatility in financial markets. To counter this, the Group of Seven industrial countries (G-7) have in recent years achieved a greater degree of policy cooperation, which can be credited with some of the equilibrating adjustments among the main exchange rates since 1985. But coordination of interest rate changes and intervention in the currency markets may not always be sufficient, and occasionally may even be counterproductive. Pooling information on broader aspects of macroeconomic policy, notably on projected fiscal imbalances, would be helpful.

An uncertain world

The global trading and financial systems are the most obvious and familiar aspects of the economic climate with which the developing countries will have to contend. But there is a long list of other uncertainties. In each case, it is easy to imagine outcomes that might greatly help the development effort—and others that might cripple it.

SECURITY. East-West political tensions have eased. In itself, the end of the cold war should improve the prospects for global growth. But this is also an opportunity to make significant cuts in U.S. and Soviet military spending. New treaties and shifting alliances are rapidly reducing conventional forces in Europe. By 1994, the weapons of the former Warsaw Pact members will number at most one-third of their 1988 levels. Savings from western military budgets might persuade governments that their earlier commitments to increase aid to the developing countries can now be met. But aid from the Soviet Union to its friends in the developing world is sure to be tightly squeezed. The Soviet Union's acute economic difficulties have already caused severe disruption to its trade with developing countries such as India. A political breakdown is imaginable that might send a flood of refugees into the countries of Eastern Europe, which already face the formidable problems of economic transition.

Military spending is about 5 percent of GNP in the industrial countries as well as the developing countries. But military spending is about half of the combined spending on health and education in the industrial countries, whereas these two magnitudes are about the same in developing countries. Large military spending has undoubtedly claimed scarce resources, and probably slowed growth in the developing world. Perhaps, on the one hand, there will now be fewer conflicts reflecting cold war ideologies. On the other hand, superpower disengagement could encourage some developing countries to build and exercise greater military power. More states may assert their regional ambitions. Ethnic tensions within countries could aggravate these trends, as could new conflicts over regional resources such as water and oil.

POLITICAL CONSIDERATIONS. The 1980s witnessed political reforms and shifts to participatory forms of government in many parts of the world. In recently published work, scholars and policymakers have placed greater stress on personal freedom and pluralist government, not only as values in their own right, but also as factors that are associated with development. Whatever the merits of such arguments, fairness and pluralism loom ever larger in the aid-granting countries' consideration of aid effectiveness and aid priorities.

ADVANCES IN TECHNOLOGY. Because most innovations originate in industrial countries, and because research tends to focus on problems of local concern, technical advances may systematically favor industrial-country producers and consumers. Industry studies suggest that new technology may have reduced the competitive disadvantage of industrial-country manufacturers. Some firms in traditionally labor-intensive subsectors (for example, textiles, clothing, and shoes) are beginning to reopen operations in high-wage countries.

Although differences between low- and high-wage producers may have narrowed in some industries, advances in communications and transport have shifted the advantage to production chains that combine operations in industrial and developing countries. Assembly and other labor-intensive processes can be efficiently located, where wages are low. New trends in automation, multipurpose plants, and modular product design are reducing the minimum economic size of production units. This will make it easier to establish facilities in smaller, specialized markets.

New technology offers the possibility of entirely new products and processes, including some that could dramatically improve the lives of the world's poor. Past breakthroughs in medicine and agricultural genetics had precisely such effects; advances in biotechnology could soon make farmers in developing countries much more productive. At the same time, however, advances in the materials sciences may displace raw materials produced by developing countries. Innovation could reduce the demand for petroleum, feedstocks, and metals, shifting input requirements toward commonly available materials.

THE ENERGY OUTLOOK. The global demand for energy is expected to increase by about 2 percent a year in the 1990s. Demand will grow fastest in the developing countries, where continuing urbanization will raise the demand for petroleum in residential use and power generation. Increases in industrial-country demand for petroleum will be mainly the result of its use in automobiles and other forms of transport. Natural gas will expand further as a major energy source—especially in developing countries and the USSR, where safety and environmental concerns will cause a shift away from nuclear power.

In the short term, oil prices will be influenced by security and other considerations in the Gulf area, and by the ability of OPEC to exert its influence. In the medium term, petroleum production from non-OPEC sources will level off by the mid-1990s. The Gulf will continue to be the major supplier of oil; indeed its share of world oil production will rise from 36 percent in 1989 to 43 percent in 2000. There is likely to be a moderate rise in the real price of petroleum in the medium term. In some countries, domestic prices could rise more rapidly if environmental concerns lead to higher energy taxes. The range of domestic energy prices is extremely wide. In 1989 gasoline prices in the United States and a number of developing countries were only a fraction of those in western Europe.

ENVIRONMENTAL DAMAGE. Widespread misuse of resources ranges from the overexploitation of fishery, land, and forests to local and international pollution of the environment. Studies in Germany, the Netherlands, and the United States have found that environmental damage from air, water, and noise pollution amounts to between 0.5 and 2.5 percent of GNP annually. This exceeds the estimated cost of pollution controls. The harm (including that caused by climate change) may be greater in the developing world. The annual cost of deforestation is estimated at 6–9 percent of GNP in Ethiopia and 5.7 percent of GDP in Burkina Faso. Estimates of the costs of substantially limiting pollution are generally much smaller—typically about 1–2 percent of GNP in industrial countries.

Long-term growth and environmental conservation need not be mutually exclusive, although well-designed environmental policies may reduce short-term economic growth as conventionally measured. Such policies make sense nonetheless. They would increase economic welfare and be far more efficient than strategies expressly designed to limit economic growth. Some harmful activities, however, cannot be monitored. And in other cases a straightforward technical solution is precluded by political considerations; examples include protection of the oceans and the atmosphere.

Experience in combining greater regard for the environment with continued economic growth is limited, but encouraging. The industrial countries reduced their energy demand per dollar of GNP by 23 percent between 1970 and 1987. Controls have successfully reduced many sorts of pollution at only a small cost, if any, in growth as conventionally measured. Emissions of sulphur oxides per dollar of GNP, for example, have been cut by more than half in virtually every industrial country. But much remains to be done. In the United States, where energy prices are low, consumption per capita is more than twice as high as in Japan. Reducing the demand for energy will require both a shift to energy-efficient outputs and energy conservation through higher prices. There can be no question that greater efforts to protect the environment are needed, but the exact scale of the undertaking is, and probably will remain, uncertain. So this is yet another variable in the situation that will confront the developing countries over the coming years.

Quantitative global scenarios for the 1990s

Long-term projections have serious limitations. This is particularly true just now, with so many uncertainties in the world economy. Accordingly, the projections published in *World Development Report*s have become more guarded in recent years (Box 1.4). The two central scenarios presented here reflect some of the doubts concerning the global economic background. The baseline scenario assumes moderately favorable external conditions, and the downside scenario assumes moderately unfavorable conditions (Table 1.4). (Extreme scenarios, resulting either in very high or very low growth for the world economy during a decade, although plausible, are considered unlikely.) The downside scenario does not allow for major adverse events—a financial crisis, a precipitous rise in energy prices, or a trade war. The baseline case assumes that there will be moderate progress in

domestic-policy reform in many of the developing countries. Variations of this baseline case are also considered by taking the external setting to be fixed while exploring different assumptions about domestic policy in the developing countries (Chapter 8). Unsurprisingly, very good policies yield considerably higher growth rates, whereas backsliding leads to much slower growth than in the baseline.

The baseline scenario makes the following assumptions. The average price of oil will follow a gently upward path in real terms. The United States will reduce its structural fiscal deficit. The recession in the United States and some other industrial countries will be mild and short-lived. Growth in Europe and Japan, after a moderate slowdown in the short run, will remain relatively strong as policy reforms lead to faster growth in productivity. Real interest rates will remain high for the medium term. The Uruguay Round will make substantial progress in key areas of negotiations, but not in agriculture. Project 1992 will yield a significant long-term growth dividend for Europe. Net inflows of capital into developing countries will gradually expand. Most developing countries will continue to implement policy reforms.

The assumptions of the downside scenario differ as follows. The price of oil will be somewhat higher. The Uruguay Round will drag on inconclusively, producing no medium-term benefits in expanded trade. Financial difficulties in the United

Table 1.4 The international economic climate in the 1990s: a comparison of recent and projected indicators
(average annual percentage change, unless noted)

| | | Recent experience | | Projections for the 1990s | | | | | |
Indicator	Trend 1965–89	1980–89	1990	World Bank baseline, 1990–2000	World Bank downside, 1990–2000	IMF baseline, 1991–96	Project LINK, 1991–95	WEFA Group, 1991–95	DRI, 1991–95
High-income OECD members									
Real GDP	3.1	3.1	2.6	2.9	2.2	3.1	2.8	3.2	3.1
Inflation[a]	6.6	3.8	3.7	3.6	4.3	3.4	3.4	4.4	3.3
Interest rate (percent)									
Nominal[b]	8.6	10.2	8.4	7.4	9.6	..	7.7[c]	8.6	7.9[c]
Real[d]	3.1	5.8	4.3	3.4	5.1	3.9	4.0[c]	4.3	4.9[c]
World trade[e]	4.1	4.1	5.0	5.8	4.5	..	5.6	4.3	..
Real price of oil[f]	9.3	−10.1	22.2	−0.6	0.9	−3.0	0.9	0.8	−2.0

a. GDP deflators in local currency for World Bank and IMF projections; for others, inflation is measured by consumption price deflator.
b. Six-month LIBOR on dollar deposits.
c. U.S. three-month Treasury bill rate; the real rate is the Treasury bill rate deflated by the U.S. GNP deflator; DRI projections are for the U.S. long-term government bond yield deflated by the U.S. GNP deflator.
d. LIBOR deflated by U.S. inflation rate (percentage change in the GNP deflator).
e. World volume of exports.
f. Average OPEC price of oil deflated by the manufactures unit value exported by industrial countries; Project LINK's is the average price for Saudi Arabian exports deflated by the GNP deflator.
Sources: World Bank data; IMF 1991; WEFA Group 1991; DRI/McGraw-Hill 1990; Project LINK 1991.

Box 1.4   How well did early *World Development Reports* foresee growth in the 1980s?

World Development Reports of a decade ago—and the predictions by the rest of the international community—were generally too hopeful about growth in the 1980s. The Reports' high-case scenario—with good policies and a return everywhere to the strong performance of 1960–78—proved far too optimistic. The low-case scenario was much closer to the mark for both industrial and developing economies.

The projections for the 1980s made in the Reports between 1979 and 1982 reveal two trends (see Box figure 1.4). First, as the world economy moved into deep recession, both the high- and low-case projections for the 1980s were revised downward. The revisions for Sub-Saharan Africa were fairly significant, which mainly reflected the sharp economic deterioration there. Second, even the low-case projections were too

Box figure 1.4   The World Bank's long-term projections of average GDP growth for the decade of the 1980s compared with outcomes
(percent)

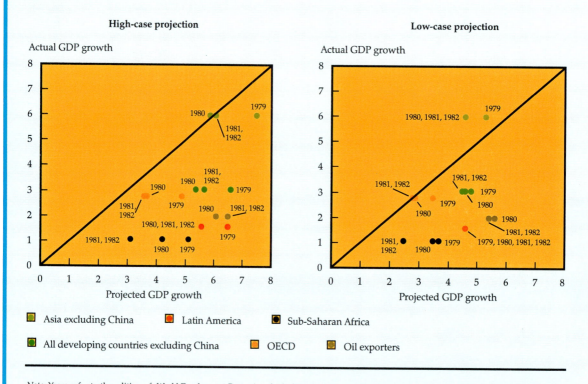

Note: Years refer to the edition of *World Development Report* in which the projection was published. If outcomes matched projections exactly, the data would fall along the diagonal line. Points below the line indicate optimistic projections; points above, pessimistic ones. For more information on the projections and outcomes, see the technical note at the end of the main text.
Source: World Bank data.

States and Japan will push risk premiums higher than in the baseline. That, together with a greater perception of financial risk and uncertainty, will depress private investment and cause slower productivity growth in the G-7 countries. Net capital flows to developing countries will grow more slowly, with private flows playing a negligible role. Most developing countries will continue economic reform, but at a slower pace than in the baseline.

Quite different outcomes, obviously, are possible. The GATT talks might succeed in all the areas of negotiations, including agriculture. World trade could then expand by 7 percent or more a year starting in the mid-1990s—faster than in recent years (but still below the 9 percent annual average

optimistic for Latin America and the oil-exporting countries but somewhat pessimistic for Asia.

Why the errors? World trade grew at 4.7 percent a year in the 1980s, not at the high case's 5.7 percent. Real interest rates, high in 1979–81, were expected to come down quickly (they didn't), and large inflows of capital were expected to flow into developing regions (they didn't). Nor did the projections look for a sharp decline in the oil prices.

The 1982 Report assumed that by 1990 (in the low case), the total external financing of the low- and middle-income countries as a group would be $147 billion—with $19.5 billion in direct foreign investment, $54.5 billion in official development assistance, and $74 billion in commercial flows. Instead, the estimated net external financing (excluding China) in 1990 was $63 billion, 43 percent of the assumed level. And ODA was only about 0.35 percent of the OECD countries' GNP, not the 0.7 percent targeted a decade before.

These assumptions about capital flows to the developing countries in the 1980s were based on an optimistic projection of global saving for 1990. The OECD was expected to run a current account surplus of $55 billion in 1990, and the high-income oil exporters were to have a large combined surplus throughout the 1980s. Instead, the OECD had a $90 billion deficit in 1990, whereas the large oil-exporting developing countries were in deficit for much of the 1980s and only recently moved into a small surplus. Although the early Reports recognized the potential severity of the debt crisis, they did not foresee the large negative transfer of resources from developing countries after the mid-1980s.

Perhaps most important, many assumptions about the domestic policies that underlie the developing countries' projections were not satisfied. For example, one cause of the poor performance of Latin America in the early 1980s was domestic policy weakness—leading to large fiscal deficits. In contrast, the better domestic policies of Asian economies in the 1980s moved their economic performance fairly close to the high case.

The Reports are careful to state that their projections are *not* to be seen as "precise forecasts for the future." Those projections are nevertheless often taken as indicating the World Bank's ability to map the growth paths of member countries.

of the 1960s). Eliminating Multifibre Arrangement restrictions and lowering agricultural subsidies in industrial countries could mean significant gains for the developing countries. Alternatively, the impetus to faster growth could come from faster expansion of intraregional trade in the Western Hemisphere, Europe, and the Pacific Basin. Because many companies established by foreign in-

vestments are trade-intensive, the recent acceleration of such investment could generate further trade growth later on.

If, however, Project 1992 leads to more protection in Europe, and other regions retaliate, the growth of world output might decline. Losses resulting from a trade war, compared with a projection assuming liberalization, could amount to 3–4 percent of world output. Industrial-country restrictions on imports reduce the GNP of the developing countries by 3–4 percent; the harm is greater for major exporters of manufactures.

Alternative projections

The *baseline scenario* suggests that the growth in some developing regions may be disappointing over the next few years. The average increase in output of 4.9 percent a year masks big differences among regions (Table 1.5). High real interest rates in the industrial countries will hurt all the developing countries; a continuation of negative transfers will restrain growth in the highly indebted ones. But some of the countries that did badly in the 1980s are now implementing major policy reforms; more countries should see their per capita growth rates rise significantly in the medium term. The countries that have so far failed to introduce reforms are likely to fall further behind.

The average growth of per capita income in the severely indebted middle-income countries may climb to 2.0 percent a year. That compares with an average of -0.5 percent a year in the 1980s. The projection assumes that positive net financial transfers to several countries in the group will resume in the medium term, although in the aggregate they will remain negative for some time. Some of the large economies that have embarked on wide-ranging reform (Brazil, Mexico, and Venezuela) may be able to achieve a significantly faster growth rate than projected by the mid-1990s.

The Asian NIEs should continue growing at rates significantly above average for developing countries, albeit more slowly than in the 1980s. By the year 2000 some current NIEs should have joined the ranks of the industrial economies. Under the assumption that they adopt favorable domestic policies, China and India are also expected to grow faster than the average for developing countries.

The economic situation in many poor countries, however, could remain precarious. Average per capita incomes in Sub-Saharan Africa are expected to grow less than 1 percent a year in the first half of the 1990s, and somewhat faster later. Even by 2000

Table 1.5 Real GDP and real GDP per capita growth rates for low- and middle-income economies, 1965–2000
(annual percentage change, unless noted)

Region or group	GDP, 1989 (billions of dollars)	Population, 1989 (millions)	Real GDP growth			Real GDP per capita growth		
			Trend, 1965–89	Projection for 1990s		Trend, 1965–89	Projection for 1990s	
				Baseline	Downside		Baseline	Downside
All low- and middle-income economies	3,303	4,053	4.7	4.9	4.1	2.5	2.9	2.2
Region								
Sub-Saharan Africa	171	480	3.2	3.6	3.5	0.4	0.5	0.3
Excluding Nigeria	142	367	3.3	3.6	3.1	0.4	0.4	0.0
Asia								
East Asia	895	1,552	7.2	6.7	5.6	5.2	5.3	4.2
South Asia	351	1,131	4.2	4.7	4.2	1.8	2.6	2.1
Europe, Middle East, and North Africa	828	433	4.2	3.6	3.2	2.2	1.8	1.4
Latin America and the Caribbean	964	421	4.3	3.8	3.1	1.8	2.0	1.3
Income group								
Low-income economies	996	2,948	5.1	5.5	4.8	2.9	3.5	2.9
Middle-income economies	2,308	1,105	4.5	4.5	3.7	2.5	2.6	1.9

Note: For group totals, see the technical note at the end of the main text.
Source: World Bank data.

average incomes in Africa will be less than in 1980. In some thirty countries undergoing major reform, however, the quality of investment projects is improving, external financial support is available, and both output growth and investment are higher than the average for Sub-Saharan Africa. Some of these countries could also benefit indirectly from Project 1992 (because of the expected higher level of demand for commodities in Europe).

Growth prospects in Eastern Europe crucially depend upon how well governments manage the transition to a market economy. The baseline projections show a slow pace of growth in the short to medium term but significantly faster growth after the mid-1990s. Prospects for the large oil producers in North Africa and the Middle East depend not only on the success of their economic reforms but also on oil prices. The baseline projections indicate that these countries could grow at a modest pace of 3.5–4.0 percent a year.

In the *downside scenario*, the average growth of the industrial countries is lower in the 1990s by 0.7 percentage point. Real interest rates are assumed to rise sharply (Table 1.4). Output growth in the developing countries is about 1.1 percentage points lower in East Asia, 0.7 points lower in Latin America, and 0.5 points lower in South Asia and Sub-Saharan Africa (excluding Nigeria). Oil importers fare worse than these averages, because oil prices are high in the downside scenario. For the developing countries as a group, the average rate of GDP growth is similar to the 1980s.

More extreme scenarios, although plausible, are unlikely. But a ''low case'' scenario, based on great turbulence in the trading and financial systems and highly unstable oil prices, could result in a 1.7 percentage point drop from the baseline in the average industrial-country growth rate and a 2.0 percentage point drop in the developing-country growth rate during the 1990s. Alternatively, a ''high case'' scenario could result in 1.1 percentage points higher growth in the industrial countries than the baseline and 1.6 percentage points higher average growth in the developing countries.

Domestic reform or external conditions: which matters more?

The projections in Table 1.5 assume that only the external environment changes. They do not consider the effect of policy and institutional changes in the developing countries. How much of a difference might reform make? This is an extremely difficult question to answer quantitatively, as opposed to qualitatively. Estimates based on the work of the World Bank's country economists, presented in Chapter 8, show that international conditions are important, and that domestic policies and institutions are even a greater factor in long-term growth. Estimates for forty countries suggest that, on average, better domestic policies could raise GDP growth by twice as much as better external factors. What are the appropriate policies and institutions? Answering this question in qualitative terms is the task of the rest of this Report.

Paths to development

Economic development is defined in this Report as a sustainable increase in living standards that encompass material consumption, education, health, and environmental protection. Development in a broader sense is understood to include other important and related attributes as well, notably more equality of opportunity, and political freedom and civil liberties. The overall goal of development is therefore to increase the economic, political, and civil rights of all people across gender, ethnic groups, religions, races, regions, and countries. This goal has not changed substantially since the early 1950s, when most of the developing world emerged from colonialism.

Thinking on development has undergone a sea change during the past forty years. The change is by no means total, nor is there universal agreement on what it takes for a country to develop. But the early faith in the ability of the state to direct development has given way to a greater reliance on markets. Inward-oriented strategies are more and more being replaced by outward-oriented ones. Discriminatory taxes on agriculture to fund industry are no longer the norm.

In recent years many countries have implemented market-oriented reforms. With these changes has come a growing recognition that development is a multidimensional process, within which price reforms, investment, and institution-building are complementary. Success depends on getting many things right.

Several countries have achieved rapid development in the postwar period. For the most part, they have two features in common: they invested in the education of men and women and in physical capital; and they achieved high productivity from these investments by giving markets, competition, and trade leading roles. New ideas, progress in technology, and pressures to achieve efficiency thus were nourished by their economies.

The extent and efficiency of the state's involvement in the economy has been critical. One lesson is that it is better for the state to focus on areas where it complements and supports the private sector (by providing, for example, information, infrastructure, health, research, and education) than on areas where it supplants the private sector (by, for example, producing cement and steel, or running airlines and hotels). A second lesson is that the quality of government matters as much as the quantity. Many economic, sociopolitical, and historical factors play a role in government. History shows that civil and political liberties—goals in themselves—need not impede economic development. And in achieving several developmental goals, civil and political liberties appear to help.

The evolution of approaches to development

Economists have traditionally considered an increase in per capita income to be a good proxy for other attributes of development. But the weakness of income growth as an indicator is that it may mask the real changes in welfare for large parts of the poor population. Improvements in meeting the basic needs for food, education, health care, equality of opportunity, civil liberties, and environmental protection are not captured by statistics on income growth.

Policymakers in most developing countries have long recognized that development encompasses more than rapid income growth. They have often differed, however, about priorities. India's economic plans, for example, assumed that income growth by itself would fail to reach many of the poor. Much stress was placed on measures to tackle poverty directly. A different emphasis is seen in Malaysia's policy documents: ''For operational purposes, therefore, rapid economic growth of the country is a necessary condition for the success of the New Economic Policy. It is only through such growth that the objectives of the NEP can be achieved without any particular group in Malaysian society experiencing any loss or feeling any sense of deprivation'' (Malaysia 1973).

Although different cultures place different values on the various elements of development, broadly defined, most seek improvement in every dimension. Many of the indicators used to measure progress (infant mortality, school enrollment, gender equality in education, indexes of political freedom, and so on) are correlated with income per capita. But the correlation is imperfect. All these factors need to be assessed independently of economic growth.

Structural transformation

Development has almost always involved a shift in the sectoral composition of output. Agriculture's share in production and employment—which is typically high in the early stages—begins to decline, and that of manufacturing industry to increase. The share of the industrial sector in GDP in low-income countries increased from 27 percent in 1965 to 34 percent in 1988, whereas that of agriculture fell from 42 to 31 percent. There are similar shifts in the sectoral shares of employment (Figure 2.1), although agriculture remains the biggest employer in many developing countries. The next stage in this sectoral evolution is usually a shift toward services.

As in industrial countries, population growth in the countries now classified as developing was fueled first by rapidly falling mortality rates which were the result of better living conditions. Although rising incomes and falling mortality provide incentives for lowering fertility and slower population growth, this demographic transition does not always happen in an orderly way. The population of the developing world grows about 2 percent a year, which is more than twice the growth rate in industrial countries. This rate has declined somewhat in the 1980s from the previous two decades, but with important regional differences: East Asia has experienced a sharp decline; Sub-Saharan Africa, an increase.

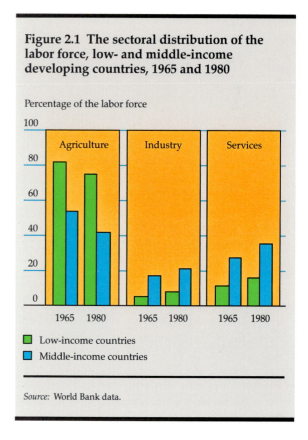

Figure 2.1 The sectoral distribution of the labor force, low- and middle-income developing countries, 1965 and 1980

Percentage of the labor force

Source: World Bank data.

Rapid agricultural growth has generally been associated with successful industrialization and sustained gains in overall output and productivity. Growth in output and productivity are usually lower where agricultural growth is low. Of sixty-eight developing countries for which the World Bank has reliable data, thirty experienced agricultural growth rates of more than 3 percent a year during the past twenty-five years. All thirty had a GDP growth rate of at least 2.5 percent, and two-thirds of the countries whose agricultural sector grew fast also experienced very rapid economic growth (exceeding 5 percent).

Growth in agricultural yields has usually been essential for growth in agricultural output. Hence higher yields are also positively associated with growth in overall output (Table 2.1). Technological progress is one of the factors that have raised the productivity of land and labor, enabling a smaller agricultural labor force to meet the domestic and external demand for farm products. In order to speed the development process, some countries have implicitly or explicitly taxed agriculture as a means to promote industry. This has generally not worked well. Instead, policies consistent with rising agricultural productivity have proved a firmer foundation for industrialization (Chapter 4).

Falling costs in various industries have enabled countries to diversify their production structures, enter new production lines, and compete successfully in world markets. Rapidly growing urban centers are usually part of this pattern. In the industrial countries, nearly 80 percent of people live in urban areas. In the developing countries, the urban share of the population has doubled in the past thirty years to more than 40 percent. Government strategies have directly or indirectly affected this transition. Excessive industrial protection; import-substitution; and a pro-urban bias in pricing, taxes, and subsidies have often encouraged an inefficient pattern of production and urbanization. In many countries, pressures on urban infrastructure have increased without any corresponding economic gain.

Changes in development thought

When many developing countries achieved independence, their leaders were concerned with both political and economic development. Their political goal was national unity and identity. Their primary economic goal was the rapid structural transformation of backward agrarian economies into modern industrial ones.

The dominant paradigm of that time recognized four main issues in development, and recommended policies to address them:

• *Physical capital.* It was a goal of policy to increase saving and investment and thus the rapid accumulation of capital.

• *Agriculture.* The farm sector was seen as a source of resources for industrial investment. Policies to protect industry turned the terms of trade against agriculture.

• *Trade.* Policymakers felt that import substitution was necessary for development. It was also feared that integration with the global economy might destabilize development. The response usually was import protection.

• *Market failure.* It was assumed that in the early stages of development markets could not be relied upon, and that the state would be able to direct the development process.

The major development institutions (the United Nations and its agencies, including the World Bank, and several bilateral aid agencies that form part of Official Development Assistance) supported these views with varying degrees of enthusiasm. By the early 1980s the dominant paradigm had shifted.

CAPITAL FORMATION. A lack of physical capital, especially infrastructure, was initially thought to be the critical constraint on development (Mandelbaum 1945; Rosenstein-Rodan 1943; Nurske 1952; Lewis 1954, 1955). Domestic capital formation was a primary concern. As a leading development economist put it, the "central problem in the theory of economic development is to understand the process by which a community which was previously saving 4 or 5 percent of its income or less converts itself into an economy where voluntary saving is about 12 to 15 percent of national income or more" (Lewis 1954).

Table 2.1 The growth of agricultural productivity and the nonagricultural sectors, 1960–88

Growth of agricultural yield per hectare	Average nonagricultural growth rate					
	More than 4 percent		2–4 percent		Less than 2 percent	
More than 2.5 percent	China Cameroon Egypt, Arab Rep. of Korea, Rep. of	Mexico Pakistan Panama Syrian Arab Rep. Turkey	Burundi Colombia Costa Rica	Hungary Nicaragua Philippines Yugoslavia	Liberia	
1–2.5 percent	Brazil Côte d'Ivoire Congo	Indonesia Thailand	Bangladesh El Salvador Greece India Mali	Malawi Mauritania Morocco Sri Lanka Togo	Zambia	
Less than 1 percent	Rwanda		Argentina Bolivia Ethiopia Nigeria	Peru Sudan Senegal Zimbabwe	Central African Rep. Ghana	Tanzania Uganda Zaire

Note: The nonagricultural growth rate is calculated as the weighted average of the growth rates of industry and services, with the weights being the share of each in GDP. Calculations are from national accounts data for all countries for which data are available and for which the initial share of agriculture in GDP in the 1960s was more than 10 percent.
Source: World Bank data.

One influential model also stressed a foreign exchange constraint—that is, the difficulty of financing import needs by means of exports (Chenery and Bruno 1962; Little 1982; Bacha 1984). This so-called two-gap model of the domestic saving and foreign exchange constraints to growth guided external aid and lending agencies in judging the extra resources that developing countries would need to finance imports and investment.

Later the contribution that human capital makes to development came to be emphasized. The role of human capital was especially clear in the experience of the East Asian economies. They invested heavily in education and skills. Research on the productivity of education has elucidated the link between human capital and development (Schultz 1961; Becker 1964). Accumulation of human capital emerges from all this work as one of the most powerful engines of development.

INCENTIVES FOR AGRICULTURE AND INDUSTRY. Often, promoting industry meant neglecting agriculture—or worse. Two assumptions appeared to justify transferring resources, through implicit or explicit taxes, from the farm sector to industry. One was that the supply of unemployed or underemployed agricultural workers was abundant. The other was that farmers were unresponsive to changes in price. Together these implied that the loss of agricultural output caused by taxing the sector would be small. ''If these surplus workers were withdrawn from agriculture and absorbed into other occupations, farm output would not suffer, while the whole new output would be a net addition to the community's income. The economic case for the industrialization of densely populated backward countries rests upon this mass phenomenon of disguised rural unemployment'' (Mandelbaum 1945). But with time, the damaging effects of policies discriminating against agriculture have come to be widely recognized.

FOREIGN TRADE. For years the conventional wisdom was that trade had only a small and possibly detrimental role in development. The declining growth in trade volumes—3.5 percent a year from 1850 to 1913, which fell to 0.5 percent a year during the period 1913-48—and the worsening terms of trade for primary commodities seemed to mean that trade could not be relied on as a source of growth (Prebisch 1959; Singer 1949). An approach based on import-substitution would allow domestic industry to grow, conserve scarce foreign capital, decrease external dependency, and strengthen nationhood. Although domestic enterprises would

fail if exposed to international markets, protection would give them a guaranteed domestic market in which to grow; later they would be able to compete. The costs of this protection of infant industry in misallocated resources were perceived to be minimal; once the infants grew to adulthood, rapid learning-by-doing was expected to emerge and guide the economy to profitable growth.

In many countries the bias against exports was reinforced by the desire to achieve self-sufficiency in food, which was often a top priority. Rather few economists recognized the role of trade liberalization for development early on (see Haberler 1959), but with the accumulation of case study evidence this recognition spread (Balassa and Associates 1971; Krueger 1978).

THE ROLE OF THE STATE. The success of state planning in achieving rapid industrialization in the Soviet Union (for so it was perceived) greatly influenced policymakers in the 1950s. Its avowedly egalitarian character was also appealing. The staggering human costs of this transition became apparent only much later. Moreover, policymakers viewed the economic collapse of the Great Depression of the 1930s as evidence of widespread market failures. The subsequent recovery was attributed to government intervention (a view supported by the Keynesian revolution in macroeconomics). Government allocation of scarce resources and the rationing of essential consumer goods during World War II seemed to confirm the effectiveness of state intervention.

Domestic conditions at home in most developing countries also encouraged a major role for the state. Illiteracy was widespread, and many policymakers believed that development would have to be directed by ''the best and the brightest.'' The idea that the state should occupy the ''commanding heights'' of the economy also began to take hold. Soon, along with redistributing assets and income, alleviating poverty, and meeting basic needs, the state became directly involved in producing goods for investment and consumption.

Even in the 1950s, some questioned whether the state was competent to do all this. ''The adequate performance of these functions exceeds the resources of governments of all under-developed countries. . . . We are faced with the paradoxical situation that governments engage in ambitious tasks when they are unable to fulfill even the elementary and necessary functions of government'' (Bauer 1958). The balanced growth approach ''requires huge amounts of precisely those abilities which we have identified as likely to be very limited in supply in underdeveloped countries" (Hirschman 1958). But even the skeptics supported government involvement in production. The state was expected to initiate growth by creating incentives and pressures for further action, and then to stand ready "to react to, and to alleviate, these pressures in a variety of areas" (Hirschman 1958). Others went further: "Apparently, nobody in the advanced countries sees any other way out of the difficulties, which are mounting in the under-developed countries, than the socialistic one, however differently one's attitude may be towards the economic problems at home" (Myrdal 1956).

Growth theories

Classical economic analysis envisaged that per capita output would be stationary as the rate of profit declined with diminishing improvements in productivity. The neoclassical tradition also incorporated the idea of falling marginal product of inputs, so that sustained growth was possible only through exogenous technological change (Solow 1957). If countries have access to the same technology, therefore, growth rates would be expected to converge across countries. The recent record of industrial countries offers support for convergence.

The growth rates of developing countries, however, have diverged (Chapter 1). At first look, this seems to be at odds with the expectation of convergence. But in practice, technological change has not been equal nor has it been exogenously transmitted in most developing countries, because of import and other restrictions. Furthermore, even if all economies have access to the same technology, national growth rates can differ if human capital and the incentives to adopt new technology differ across countries. The "new" growth theories note that technological change is endogenous, and that education and knowledge produce positive externalities or increasing returns (Romer 1986; Lucas 1988).

Accordingly, a big push in an economy open to foreign technology can yield large gains—an idea generally put forward early on. The Cambridge model of the 1940s and 1950s assumed that output would grow in proportion to reproducible inputs, or capital. Rosenstein-Rodan (1943) postulated the big push by which an economy propels itself into self-sustaining industrialization and rapid growth. Rostow (1960) envisaged a takeoff from a stationary state to per capita growth.

Thus investment policies that encourage externality-generating activities (improvements in edu-

cation) or introduce increasing returns (improvements in physical infrastructure) can be good for growth. Also important are complementary policies that facilitate the spread of knowledge and that permit free entry and exit of firms—and free mobility of people, capital, and technology.

Linkages in development

Education, technology, and openness have complex relations to development. They enable economies to respond not only to price signals but also to new ideas. This link between knowledge and growth has been important in East Asia for the past forty years and in Scandinavia, especially between 1860 and 1950 (Box 2.1). It was recognized in the literature early on. "It is not enough that knowledge should grow; it should also be diffused, and applied in practice. The rate at which knowledge is taken up depends partly on the receptiveness of the people to new ideas, and partly on the extent to which institutions make it profitable to acquire and apply new ideas . . . New ideas will be accepted most rapidly in those societies where people are accustomed to a variety of opinion, or to change . . . A country which is isolated, homogeneous, proud, and authoritarian is by contrast unlikely to absorb new ideas quickly when it meets them" (Lewis 1955).

The green revolution in agriculture, which above all included the spread of new, high-yielding varieties of wheat and rice, is an example of the interaction between new technology and education. The new varieties were developed by scientists in Mexico and the Philippines with assistance from the Rockefeller Foundation. To gain access to these technologies, domestic economies needed to be receptive. In order for them to be absorbed, adapted, improved, and disseminated, domestic research and local technologies had to be strengthened. Countries in South Asia did these tasks reasonably well, and farm yields there doubled and tripled. Wealth and the ability to bear risk were important, but the most critical factor in adopting the technology was the ability of farmers to make use of new information.

Openness encourages the flow of technologies from industrial countries to developing countries; education encourages the adoption, adaptation, and diffusion of technology. Differences in the rate of technology adoption and economic growth among countries are in large part the result of differences in education. "The worldwide spread of modern economic growth has depended chiefly on the diffusion of a body of knowledge concern-

Box 2.1 Scandinavian models of development

Denmark, Finland, Iceland, Norway, and Sweden have successfully combined private ownership and market competition with government actions—to ensure an egalitarian income distribution, provide insurance against loss of income caused by disabilities, and address market failures. These activities of government, which were of limited importance before World War II, expanded rapidly thereafter. The high spending of the welfare state required the high incomes of the postwar era.

The early period: mid-1800s to World War II

The Scandinavian countries started industrialization in the mid-1800s and late 1800s. Security for property rights and trade reforms were important conditions for growth. Governments generally did not restrict the workings of the market, and financial institutions and ownership structures were allowed to develop with little state interference.

Literacy was already very high when industrialization began in the last century. Substantial attention was given to primary and general education, including women's education, as well as to technical and mercantile education in trade schools and universities. The government focused on building the infrastructure for development, which included legal and administrative frameworks and transport.

The later period: after World War II

Scandinavia is rightly acclaimed for having reached an advanced phase of welfare. But some characteristics of the welfare state have had costs that could have been avoided with difficult policies. First, in an attempt to keep down the cost of capital, financial markets were heavily regulated after the war. This, however, limited the access of smaller firms and entrepreneurs to capital. It has also discouraged the adaptation to the financial innovations abroad. (These markets were deregulated during the 1980s.)

Second, policies guaranteeing low unemployment and the public sector's larger and larger share in employment have in the long term seriously weakened the discipline of the market on union wage demands. This has resulted in high labor costs and lower profits and investment. Privatizing certain public services—now under consideration—may strengthen discipline in the labor market.

Third, the high marginal tax rates for most of the labor force are a burden on growth. In response, Sweden is embarking on a program of tax reform to alleviate the distortions in the choice between work and leisure and to shrink parallel, underground labor markets.

Scandinavia's pragmatic willingness to avoid conflict and to seek consensus in political and economic life has certainly shaped development there in important ways. Although it is impossible to say if the search for consensus has contributed much to growth, it has molded Scandinavia's special combination of private and public activity.

ing new production techniques . . . the more schooling of appropriate content that a nation's population had, the easier it is to master the new technological knowledge becoming available'' (Easterlin 1981). Equally essential is the freedom of individuals and firms to borrow foreign technology, learn from foreign ideas, and buy foreign goods. The more open the economy, the greater the returns to education and to physical investments.

Another important link connects macroeconomic stability to the success of microeconomic policies. Countries with low inflation and sustainable external balances have been far more successful in achieving lasting growth.

Finally, human development and poverty alleviation, on the one hand, and economic growth, on the other, seem to reinforce each other. Human development and poverty alleviation have always been development goals in the eyes of policymakers and planners. Their methods, however,

have varied, and have ranged from government interventions to market solutions. Elements of both are needed: market-oriented policies to support growth, together with well-targeted social programs.

Aggregate outcomes in development

Incomes and welfare have improved substantially in the postwar era. In low- and middle-income countries, output has grown at an average annual rate of nearly 5 percent since 1965, with output per capita growing at 2.5 percent. Social progress has also been strong. Secondary school enrollment has nearly doubled since 1965, to about 40 percent. Infant mortality seems to have fallen substantially, from an estimated 124 deaths per thousand births in 1965 to 72 in 1988.

Not all countries have achieved the same successes. The rate of GDP growth has varied substantially from region to region. Incomes improved consistently in East Asia; performance also improved in South Asia, but more slowly and patchily. In other regions, income growth deteriorated. Since 1960, per capita real incomes have surged in Japan, the Republic of Korea, and Singapore; stagnated in Argentina, Jamaica, and Peru; and dropped in Ghana, Nigeria, and Zambia (Figure 2.2).

The rates of saving and investment rose in many countries. India consistently saved more than 20 percent of its income in the 1970s and 1980s. In 1988, Brazil saved 28 percent of its income; China, 37 percent; Côte d'Ivoire, 22 percent; and Kenya, 22 percent. Investment as a share of income averaged 26 percent for developing countries in 1988. But again, country differences were substantial. Investment shares were about 4 percent in Bolivia, Sudan, and Zaire and about 30 percent in the Republic of Korea, Portugal, and Venezuela.

The growth of trade in low- and middle-income countries was strong as a whole; exports expanded by almost 5.3 percent during the period 1965–89. Brazil, China, Korea, and Turkey were among the strongest performers. But many countries fared poorly, particularly in Sub-Saharan Africa, where real exports plummeted in the 1980s (Figure 2.3). In all developing countries, the share of exports in output increased from about 13 to 23 percent in this period—a trend dominated by East Asia, where the share increased from 8 to 30 percent.

Government involvement in the economy also varied greatly. The share of public employment in the formal nonagricultural sector in 1980 was estimated to be more than 70 percent in Benin, Ghana, India, Tanzania, and Zambia, and less

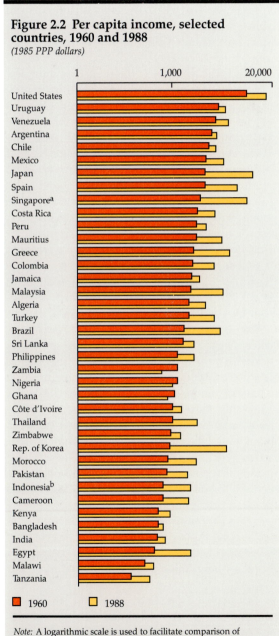

Figure 2.2 Per capita income, selected countries, 1960 and 1988
(1985 PPP dollars)

■ 1960   □ 1988

Note: A logarithmic scale is used to facilitate comparison of countries with high and low per capita income. Countries were selected, based on data availability, to provide a balanced sample in terms of population size and regional distribution.
a. Data are for 1960 and 1985.
b. Data are for 1962 and 1988.
Source: Summers and Heston 1991.

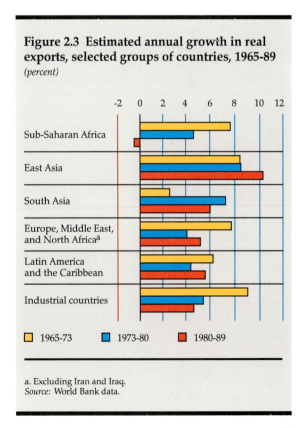

Figure 2.3 Estimated annual growth in real exports, selected groups of countries, 1965-89
(percent)

□ 1965-73   ■ 1973-80   ■ 1980-89

a. Excluding Iran and Iraq.
Source: World Bank data.

than 25 percent in Argentina, Guatemala, and Korea (Heller and Tait 1984). In some countries, public consumption has averaged more than 15 percent of output, which implies that the wages of public employees may have absorbed more than a third of nonagricultural output.

Highlights of economy experiences

Much can be learned about the effectiveness of different development strategies from the experiences of individual economies. The following paragraphs highlight the recent stories of development in China, India, Nigeria, Brazil, Argentina, Malaysia, Sri Lanka, Korea, other East Asian newly industrializing economies, and the OECD economies. The subject of regional variations in income within economies is also raised.

- *China.* From 1950 to 1978 the Chinese economy was centrally planned in most respects. The defects of such a highly centralized administrative system became clear, despite the progress in infrastructure and resource mobilization, "it makes productive enterprises subordinate to administrative organs . . . [and] involves excessive command planning from above and is too rigid" (Hsu 1982). So structural reforms were introduced in 1978. The most striking were rural reforms that introduced price and ownership incentives to farmers. Real farm prices have increased by 50 percent, and the agricultural growth rate rose from 2.5 percent in 1965–78 to 7.2 percent in 1978–88.

- *India.* The government has been actively involved in the production process, regulating "the scale, technology, and location of any investment project other than relatively small ones . . . a chaotic incentive structure and the unleashing of rapacious rent-seeking were the inevitable outcomes" (Srinivasan 1990). This extensive government involvement was accompanied by macroeconomic stability in the 1960s and 1970s, but growth was slow nonetheless. During the period 1960–79, the growth of per capita income averaged 1 percent a year. Absolute poverty declined from about 55 percent in the early 1960s to only 45 percent in the mid-1980s. Since the late 1970s, some industries have been deregulated. The exchange rate, whose real value relative to the dollar was the same in 1955 and 1980, has depreciated in real terms. These partial reforms contributed to an acceleration in the per capita growth rate to about 3 percent in the 1980s.

- *Nigeria.* A telling statistic about this oil exporter is that its per capita growth rate, which av-

eraged 1.1 percent a year in the period 1960–73, declined 2.8 percent a year after the oil price increase of 1973. Public spending was largely responsible for the decline. Between 1973 and 1981, public employment tripled from 0.5 to 1.5 million. Government expenditure rose fivefold between 1972 and 1974 and accounted for almost 80 percent of total oil revenue. Public investment increased from 5 percent of GDP in 1974 to 17 percent in 1977, and accounted for more than half of total investment in that year. The budget turned from surplus to a deficit averaging 24 percent of retained revenue in 1975–78 (Bevan, Collier, and Gunning, forthcoming).

- *Brazil.* This country is often cited as an example of the success of good import substitution policies. For almost three decades (between 1960 and 1987) its average growth rate was an impressive 6.6 percent a year. What is revealing about the miracle years of 1967 to 1979, however, is that rapid growth was preceded and accompanied by economic reform. Before 1967, classic stabilization measures (tight credit and budget controls) were applied to bring down inflation. In 1967, a new tariff law reduced protection to domestic manufacturing from 58 to 30 percent. In 1968, a crawling peg exchange rate replaced the multiple exchange rate system. These policies produced a surge in export volume of more than 10 percent a year between 1964 and 1980, and an annual rate of growth of 9.4 percent (Maddison and Associates, forthcoming).

- *Argentina.* At the turn of this century, Argentina's per capita income was comparable to those of Australia and Canada. But since the 1940s the country has suffered chronic macroeconomic instability and slow growth. Inflation and repeated failures to stabilize the financial environment have discouraged domestic savings and investment. Without macroeconomic stabilization, Argentina has had difficulty adjusting to shocks to its terms of trade, a problem compounded by high levels of protection. These continuous macroeconomic failures largely explain the decline in Argentina's growth rate, which has fallen from an average of 4 percent a year in the period 1960–73 to 0.8 percent in 1973–87.

- *Malaysia and Sri Lanka.* In 1960, these two countries had similar per capita incomes, education levels, infant mortality rates, ethnic diversity, and economic structures. Since then they have followed different development strategies. Even after the reforms of 1978, Sri Lanka remained less open than Malaysia. Agricultural taxation has been lower in Malaysia too: taxation of rubber exports has averaged less than 30 percent, compared with more than 60 percent in Sri Lanka. During the period 1960–78, Malaysia grew at 7.0 percent and Sri Lanka at 4.4 percent. Productivity growth has averaged 1.5 percent in Malaysia and 0 percent in Sri Lanka. Between 1960 and 1988, infant mortality rates dropped from an estimated 70 per thousand in both countries, to about 15 in Malaysia and about 30 in Sri Lanka. The share of the poor in Malaysia's population is estimated to have been reduced from about 37 percent in 1973 to 15 percent in 1987; in Sri Lanka it fell from 37 to 27 percent between 1963 and 1981.

• *Republic of Korea*. Undoubtedly, this economy is an example of spectacularly rapid development. But analysts differ as to the causes. The growth rate during the period 1960–87 in Korea was 9.0 percent. Social indicators have also improved rapidly. Korea continued its import substitution approach in the 1960s. A strong export drive was also launched in the 1960s. After experiencing economic difficulties in the late 1970s, Korea pursued a more and more liberal approach in the 1980s. During the period 1960–87, the annual growth of total factor productivity (TFP) was an estimated 1.7 percent in Korea. Income distribution compares very favorably with that of other developing economies, though it is estimated to have worsened.

• *Other East Asian economies*. The economies of Hong Kong and Singapore have also achieved enviable success. So has Taiwan, China, which during the period 1960–87 grew 9.5 percent. This economy opened up early, initiating new policies in 1958–59 that "reversed the import-substitution strategy [and] reoriented the economy to the world market" (Myers 1990). Income distribution compares favorably with that in other economies, and it has improved.

The government of Singapore has been considerably more interventionist than the government of Hong Kong. During the period 1960–87, growth rates were 8.8 percent in Singapore and 8.6 percent in Hong Kong, whereas productivity grew by 1.7 percent in Singapore and by 3.1 percent in Hong Kong.

These East Asian economies have performed exceedingly well for long periods of time. Although they differ in many important respects, they all share several features: high and rising levels of education, and an outward orientation. But these economies raise important questions about the proper roles of state and market. Hong Kong followed a relatively free-market approach.

The other economies were relatively more interventionist. Japan and Korea followed policies of protection for infant industries and of credit subsidies. Why, in these cases, did interventionist policies succeed when they so often failed elsewhere? Some economists argue that intervention worked because markets were still freer than in other economies. Some go so far as to argue that intervention set the East Asian economies back, that they would have done even better without it. Other economists say that the secret is to intervene competently. But this begs the key question: what is the difference between competent and incompetent intervention?

The issue remains controversial, but three propositions now command quite wide support. First, government intervention in these economies was subjected to international competition and market-related checks and balances. These governments did not avoid the discipline of market forces. When protection failed, it was promptly removed—difficult to do, and most unusual. Second, governments were careful to offset the bias against exports that is usually a feature of trade protection. Their trade regimes, in other words, remained highly outward-oriented. Third, intervention in the market in these East Asian economies was, in an overall sense, more moderate than in most other developing economies. These and other institutional features seem to distinguish the East Asian economies, including Japan (see Box 2.2). Interventions in trade and industry are further discussed in Chapter 5.

• *OECD countries*. During the past three decades, the OECD countries have experienced solid growth, averaging about 3 percent a year, and with less country-by-country variation than among the developing countries (Harberger 1984). The fastest-growing advanced economy has been Japan; its output increased by 6.5 percent a year between 1965 and 1980. Two features of this experience stand out: first, rapid technological progress, supported by a strong outward orientation; second, a rise in saving rates, supported by moderate fiscal policies. Often the government's budget was in surplus. This stimulated saving and investment and created opportunities to cut taxes. Germany's postwar growth (3.5 percent during the period 1965–80) was export-oriented, with low inflation and a realistic exchange rate that ensured international competitiveness. By and large, organized labor supported the government's growth-oriented policies. Economies of scale, learning by doing, and the restructuring of industry led to

Box 2.2 What's behind the Japanese miracle?

Exceptional investments in people, physical assets, and technology are generally considered the main reasons for Japan's success, as elaborated on elsewhere in this Report. The institutional and policy factors that created the climate for these large investments and their productivity are still debated.

The bureaucrats?

Some see the Japanese miracle as the result of bureaucrats in the Ministry of International Trade and Industry (MITI) guiding firms' production and investment decisions. Since the 1930s at least, Japanese bureaucrats have influenced manufacturers' decisions. They have eased their access to capital and to foreign technology. They have granted subsidies, trade barriers, and tax breaks. They have formulated plans to allocate production. And they have sanctioned cartels. As industrial consultants who can persuade their clients to follow their advice, MITI's officials have a close relationship with manufacturers.

The size of interventions?

By any measure—the size of government expenditures or taxes, government-induced macroeconomic disturbances, controls on prices, the role of state-owned enterprises in manufacturing, or restrictions on private sector activities—the role of government in Japan's economy is small. Moreover, of the nearly half million Japanese manufacturing firms in the 1950s, most were small and medium-size—accounting for half the value added in manufacturing (60 percent in the late 1970s).

Institutions?

Traditional Japanese views on rights and appropriate behavior have affected the resolution of conflicts—and the relations between workers and managers, between large firms and subcontractors, and between government agencies, producers, and producers' associations. For example, norms of behavior toward authority, which encourage a free flow of information between workers and supervisors, and a consensus-building approach in conflict resolution have allowed better quality control in mass assembly.

All three

Each explanation probably captures an aspect of reality. But it is difficult to draw lessons for other countries from an institutional explanation of Japan's success—except to note that bureaucrats did not try to fight market trends. Instead, they tried to anticipate those trends, and they retreated when they were wrong. The market was a disciplining factor.

---

rapid advances in productivity. In Britain, economic growth in the 1960s and 1970s was slower because of high inflation, troubled labor relations, an overvalued exchange rate, frequent balance of payments problems, low corporate profits, and too little investment. Growth improved during the 1980s.

• *Regional differences in income within countries.* Data on average incomes for countries conceal regional variations in incomes, especially in large countries. Variations in *nominal* income, or output, per capita originating from region to region are substantial in several large countries, including Brazil, China, India, Indonesia, and Nigeria (see the maps for examples). Differences in expenditures, as well as differences in *real* terms—that is, after correcting for regional price differences—are expected to be less (see below). Within China, the per capita nominal income in the eastern region (which contains 29 percent of the population) was estimated to be 50 percent higher than in the southern region (43 percent of the population) in

1987. The average per capita income in the western region of India (14 percent of the population) was about 60 percent higher than in the eastern region (22 percent of the population) in 1986–87. In Indonesia, the per capita output in Sumatra (20 percent of the population) was estimated to be 36 percent more than in Java (60 percent of the population) in 1988. According to available data, this difference is virtually eliminated if income from oil is excluded, or if expenditures are compared. Within Nigeria, the eastern region was estimated to have a 70 percent higher per capita income (also including oil income) than the northern region in 1981.

Variations in nominal income, however, are biased upward because costs of living are typically higher in the wealthier regions. But data for cost of living adjustments are scarce. Where the adjustments were possible, in the case of Brazil, differences do diminish (in real terms). In 1980 the southeastern region of Brazil (with about 40 percent of the people) had an estimated per capita nominal income more than three times that of the northeastern region (30 percent of the people). According to an estimate for 1975, when measured in *real terms*, the southeastern region's income was twice, rather than three times, that of the northeastern region.

The evidence from industrial countries shows smaller regional differences in nominal terms. In the United States, the Middle Atlantic region (15 percent of the population) had a 16 percent higher nominal per capita income in 1988 than the South Atlantic region (17 percent of the population). The differences were estimated to have narrowed in the past three decades. Adequate comparisons of trends in regional inequalities in the developing countries, however, are constrained by lack of data; the available data do not show any clear reduction in regional inequalities.

The various economy experiences, though highly suggestive, need to be analyzed more carefully if they are to yield systematic evidence. A larger number of countries must be compared with

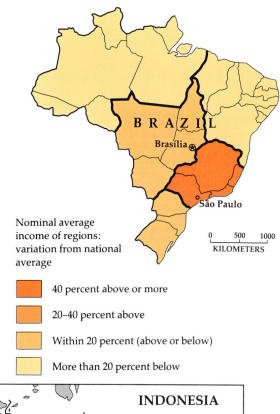

Nominal average income of regions: variation from national average

■ 40 percent above or more

■ 20–40 percent above

■ Within 20 percent (above or below)

□ More than 20 percent below

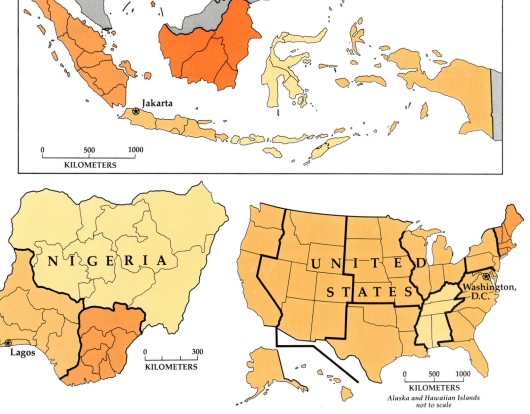

Note: Regional estimates include income from oil production, especially important in Indonesia and Nigeria.
Sources: Indonesia income data from Biro Pusat Statistik 1989; Nigeria data from World Bank; Brazil data from IBGE 1987; United States data from U.S. Department of Commerce, Bureau of the Census 1990.

Box 2.3   Total factor productivity in economic growth

An important advance in economics of the past fifty years has been to identify and measure total factor productivity, which measures changes in output per unit of all inputs combined. Before, most analysis of productivity focused on the growth of labor productivity, and to a lesser degree, on the growth of the average productivity of capital.

Observe the following differences. The total output of the United States in the first part of the twentieth century grew at about 3 percent a year. Its capital stock also grew at about 3 percent, whereas the labor input (measured in worker-hours) grew at only about 1 percent a year. In the capital-labor mix, capital accounted for about one-third, and labor, two-thirds. So inputs were rising about 1.7 percent a year: two-thirds times 1 percent plus one-third times 3 percent. Total factor productivity, or the residual, thus accounted for 1.3 percent in output growth: 3 percent (the rate of growth of output) minus 1.7 percent (the growth rate of inputs).

The early calculations of total factor productivity for different countries led to the conclusion—surprising at the time—that about half of growth in output was due to the residual, which was quickly baptized as technical change. What makes up the residual? Technological innovations have no doubt generated some improvements in total factor productivity. But the main additional element is in the quality of labor. If the additions to the labor force are more productive than the existing force, they will add more to output than they would

under the formula based on labor's share. And the extra contribution from upgrading the quality of labor ends up in the residual.

Adjusting for labor quality makes it easy to identify the residual with technical change—defined very broadly. Technical change includes such obvious innovations as the mechanical cotton picker, the pneumatic tire, the hand-held calculator, the personal computer, the fork-lift truck, and the containerized shipping system.

But technical change also includes numerous ways of reducing real costs. These costs may fall as more discipline is instilled in the work force by a more demanding manager—or as the work force becomes more productive because a too-demanding manager has been fired. An assembly line might be made more productive simply by straightening it out—or a farm by introducing a different fertilizer. Productivity may also be increased by, for example, installing a facsimile machine, closing down unprofitable branches, or buying longer-lasting tires for trucks.

The way to understand more about what makes up the residual is to study the growth of total factor productivity in detail—product by product, industry by industry, sector by sector. Even with close study not every source of cost reduction can be identified, but the most important ones surely can. This identification alone reveals the kaleidoscopic sources of growth encompassed in the residual.

---

one another in an econometric framework that ensures consistency of treatment. Then it may be possible to infer the factors that fuel development.

The determinants of the growth of income

Comparative studies were pioneered by the International Labour Organisation in the early 1970s (Meier and Seers 1984), in the trade studies of Little, Scitovsky, and Scott (1970), and by studies done under the sponsorship of the National Bureau of Economic Research (Bhagwati 1978; Krueger 1978). Since then, further studies have accumulated rapidly. They include recent work at the World Bank (where five large multicountry studies have covered approximately sixty countries), other agencies of the United Nations, and the World Institute for Development Economics Research.

Two of the main conclusions of this body of research are as follows. First, sustained development in many countries, notably the Scandinavian

countries after 1870 and the East Asian economies after World War II, can be largely explained by education (and the associated quality of institutions) and by policies promoting outward orientation and competition. Outward orientation boosts growth and productivity. Import substitution policies have generally had disappointing results. Protected infant industries have rarely grown up, while the anti-export bias from protection has impeded the growth of exports. Further, these policies have lowered agricultural incentives. Second, severe and prolonged macroeconomic imbalances hurt investment and growth. Private investment is hampered because public borrowing and debt crowd it out and investors are uncertain about the future of the economy.

Another method of analyzing the growth process is to estimate the contribution that capital and labor make to growth. Patterns of experience across countries can be examined through a comparative study of large groups of countries and of econometric analyses of the data derived from them. One result applies to both industrial and developing countries. The sum of the contributions of the factors of production fails to account for overall growth. The so-called residual in the estimated production function, or total factor productivity, accounts for the rest. It captures the efficiency with which inputs are used (Box 2.3).

The empirical literature on the determinants of economic growth in industrial countries is voluminous (Denison 1962; Jorgensen and Griliches 1967; Maddison 1981). Similar work for developing countries has been less comparable, however, because of data problems. Data on inputs are generally unavailable. Estimates of human and capital stock are vital for this sort of analysis.

For this Report, a consistent set of data for output, capital stock, labor force, arable land, and years of education of the working population has been constructed. For GDP growth, national accounts data have been used. Their limitations need to be borne in mind (Box 2.4). Estimates of physical and human capital were prepared for sixty-eight countries. The group includes some of what are now high-income countries (Japan, Greece, Spain, and Portugal), but none of the results is sensitive to their inclusion. Of the other countries, twenty-seven are in Africa; fifteen in Latin America; nine in East Asia; eight in Europe, the Middle East, and North Africa; and four in South Asia.

The contribution of capital and labor

For the sample of developing countries used, the estimated elasticity of output to capital for the 1960–87 period is about 0.4; for every 1 percent capital increases, output increases by about 0.4 percent. Under assumptions of perfect competition in product and factor markets, this elasticity reflects the share of capital in the economy. For industrial countries, this share has indeed been estimated at between 0.25 and 0.4 percent. The estimated elasticity of output to labor is about 0.45 percent. This elasticity is somewhat lower than that of industrial countries; estimates for the United States put the figure between 0.6 and 0.75 percent. The much lower levels of education in developing countries probably account for much of this difference.

The contribution of education

Many studies document the high returns on investment in education. In past studies of growth, education has been roughly proxied by literacy rates, or by primary school enrollment ratios. Research for this Report suggests that increasing the average amount of education of the labor force by one year raises GDP by 9 percent. This holds for the first three years of education; that is, three years of education as compared with none raises GDP by 27 percent. The return to an additional year of schooling then diminishes to about 4 percent a year—or a total of 12 percent for the next three years. These results are consistent with earlier studies.

Almost everywhere, growth rates fell after 1973 (Table 2.2). Two possible causes were examined: slower growth of inputs, particularly capital, and slower growth in the efficiency with which the inputs were used. Slowing growth of the capital

Table 2.2 The growth of GDP, inputs, and TFP

(percent)

Region, group, or economy	GDP 1960–73	GDP 1973–87[a]	GDP 1960–87[a]	Capital 1960–73	Capital 1973–87[a]	Capital 1960–87[a]	Labor 1960–73	Labor 1973–87[a]	Labor 1960–87[a]	TFP 1960–73	TFP 1973–87[a]	TFP 1960–87[a]
Developing economies												
Africa	4.0	2.6	3.3	6.3	6.3	6.3	2.1	2.3	2.2	0.7	−0.7	0.0
East Asia	7.5	6.5	6.8	9.8	10.7	10.2	2.8	2.6	2.6	2.6	1.3	1.9
Europe, Middle East, and North Africa	5.8	4.2	5.0	7.7	7.5	7.6	1.4	1.9	1.7	2.2	0.6	1.4
Latin America	5.1	2.3	3.6	7.4	5.6	6.3	2.5	2.8	2.6	1.3	−1.1	0.0
South Asia	3.8	5.0	4.4	8.0	7.2	7.7	1.8	2.3	2.1	0.0	1.2	0.6
Sixty-eight economies	5.1	3.5	4.2	7.4	7.1	7.2	2.2	2.4	2.3	1.3	−0.2	0.6
Industrial economies												
France	5.5	2.1	3.9	5.7	3.8	4.8	0.4	−1.0	−0.2	2.3	0.9	1.7
Germany[b]	4.3	1.8	3.1	5.3	3.0	4.2	−0.3	−0.9	−0.6	1.9	0.9	1.4
United Kingdom	3.3	1.3	2.4	3.6	2.6	3.1	0.1	−0.5	−0.2	1.7	0.6	1.2
United States	3.7	2.2	3.0	3.8	2.8	3.4	1.8	1.9	1.8	1.0	−0.1	0.5

Note: Estimates for developing countries are based on a sample of sixty-eight economies; see the technical note at the end of the main text.
a. Until 1985 for industrial economies.
b. The Federal Republic of Germany before reunification with the former German Democratic Republic.
Sources: World Bank data; Boskin and Lau 1990.

Box 2.4 Measurement informs policy—or does it?

The demand for economic data in policy analysis has intensified since Simon Kuznets pioneered national income accounting in the 1920s. With Keynes's macroeconomic models and Leontief's input-output models, the data, analytical tools, and computing capabilities have mushroomed. But serious problems of data and measurement still plague quantitative economic analysis.

Dubious quality

In many countries, estimates of agricultural production are not based on reliable estimates of crop area and yields. Estimates of industrial production are based on partial coverage of enterprises, ignoring for the most part small-scale production units. Measures such as national savings, investment, and consumption are indirectly estimated, derived as the difference between two other magnitudes, which are themselves subject to error.

There are serious gaps in the data on literacy, school enrollment, poverty levels, and nutritional levels. Reliable estimates of life expectancy at birth—based on recent censuses—and measures of births and deaths are only available for thirty countries for the years after 1980 (Box table 2.4). Only twenty-seven countries have series for more than one period. Thus, most of the available estimates are based on assumptions about mortality.

Poor comparability

GDP measures pose important problems in comparability across countries and over time. Among the major hurdles are price changes accompanying quality changes, changes in relative prices, the choice of base periods, and the extent of coverage of economic activity. The conventional use of official exchange rates introduces biases during periods of volatile exchange rates. Purchasing power parities (PPPs) generally yield a more accurate measure of output by comparing the value of a specified basket of goods and services in the domestic market, expressed in national currency, with the value of the same basket in foreign currency.

Own-account consumption and subsistence production are often inadequately measured, if at all. Even with imputations, the pricing of such volumes is less than satisfactory. Multiple exchange rates, enforced through rationing or other means, distort GDP measures because the prices used do not reflect true values. Parallel or underground market activities lead to incentives for evading taxes; these activities are not captured fully in GDP. If the share of such activities in measured GDP changes over time, estimated growth rates based on measured GDP will be off the mark.

Externalities associated with resource overuse and environmental degradation present another difficult issue for proper accounting. If an economy overuses its environmental resources and if market prices do not fully reflect this use, conventional GDP measures overstate the capability of the economy to sustain the flow of goods and services.

Tenuous policy inferences

Can we infer, from an observed positive association between policies and performance, that performance responds to policy? Econometric tests of causality often cannot be applied with the available data—not to mention the complex problems of interpreting the results of such tests or of drawing statistical inferences from them. Policy conclusions based on analyses of meager data sets can be seriously biased. Ultimately, it is a matter of judgment whether an observed association between policy and performance is causal or simply the result of both being driven by a third set of unobserved (or latent) variables.

Implications for analysis

These cautionary remarks should not lead us to abandon quantitative analysis. Nor do they relieve us of the responsibility of deriving policy lessons from such analysis. We have no serious alternative to empirically based analysis for policymaking. Judgments will have to be made. And insights from analytical descriptions of economic history will have to be combined imaginatively with purely econometric analysis. This Report reflects the results of such an effort. Although there can be no finality about its conclusions, it does represent a careful assessment of the available evidence.

Box table 2.4 The availability of relatively reliable data for selected social indicators in developing economies

(number of countries or areas)

Region, total number of economies	Number with data on life expectancy at birth				Number with data on infant mortality rate				Number with data on probability of dying by age 5			
	Total	Before 1975	1975–79	1980–	Total	Before 1975	1975–79	1980–	Total	Before 1975	1975–79	1980–
Africa, 50	16	9	4	3	36	11	10	15	35	12	10	13
Latin America, 27	24	5	3	16	26	1	3	22	26	2	4	20
Asia and Oceania, 40	20	1	8	11	27	3	9	15	27	3	10	14
Total, 117	60	15	15	30	89	15	22	52	88	17	24	47

Source: United Nations 1990c.

stock is not, it seems, to blame. It grew on average by slightly more than 7 percent a year before and after 1973. Even in Africa, the rate of capital formation was 6.3 percent a year in both periods.

With certain technical caveats, if input growth was broadly unchanged in the second period and output growth declined, then growth in the productivity of input use must have fallen. The data support this view—strikingly so (Table 2.3). Variations in productivity growth reflect changes in resource allocation, technologies, and dynamic comparative advantage. Slower TFP growth points to diminishing advances in technology, fewer improvements in the efficiency of input use, or both.

Since 1960, growth in productivity has accounted for a relatively small proportion of output growth for most developing countries. The exception is East Asia, where the share is more than 25 percent. For the industrial economies, productivity growth has been much more important. A recent study of the United States suggests that technical progress alone accounts for more than 50 percent of output growth since 1945 and labor force growth for 27 percent (Boskin and Lau 1990). Another draws this conclusion: ''a major difference between [developing and developed countries] seems to be that growth in the former is largely accounted for by the accumulation of inputs rather than the growing efficiency in their deployment'' (Chenery and Srinivasan 1988).

The small role that productivity growth plays on average in developing countries is unlikely to be explained by lower rates of technological change. In East Asia, productivity increased at 2.6 percent a year for the period 1960–73, about the same as in the industrial countries. The importance of productivity growth, despite its small share, is indicated by the fact that differences in it account for more than half of the variation in growth rates across countries. Economic policy, as this Report will explain, goes a long way to explain these differences.

The association between productivity growth and aggregate growth is strong and positive (Figure 2.4). It holds across regions and in different periods. In the period 1973–87, the average decline in growth rates (about 1.5 percent) is exactly matched by the decline in TFP growth (Table 2.2). Historical data for Japan also support this strong association between economic growth and productivity growth (Ohkawa and Rosovski 1973). During periods of rapid growth, such as 1912–18 or 1931–38, TFP grew as well (at 2.1 percent a year in the period 1912–18 and at 3.8 percent a year in

Table 2.3 Percentage share of output growth accounted for by factor input growth, sample of world economies, 1960–87

Region or group and period	Capital	Labor	TFP
1960–73			
Africa	59	22	17
East Asia	50	16	35
Europe, Middle East, and North Africa	51	10	38
Latin America	55	20	25
South Asia	81	20	0
Total	56	18	26
1973–87			
Africa	92	37	−27
East Asia	62	17	20
Europe, Middle East, and North Africa	68	19	14
Latin America	94	51	−48
South Asia	55	19	24
Total	76	28	−6
1960–87			
Africa	73	28	0
East Asia	57	16	28
Europe, Middle East, and North Africa	58	14	28
Latin America	67	30	0
South Asia	67	20	14
Total	65	23	14
Selected industrial countries, 1960–85			
France	27	−5	78
Germany[a]	23	−10	87
Japan	36	5	59
United Kingdom	27	−5	78
United States	23	27	50

Note: For economy classifications and estimates, see the technical note at the end of the main text.
a. The Federal Republic of Germany before reunification with the former German Democratic Republic.
Sources: For developing economies, World Bank data. For industrial economies, Boskin and Lau 1990.

1931–38). During periods of slow growth, productivity stagnated or declined (it fell by 0.2 percent during the period 1918–31). In the period 1960–73, output grew at 9.2 percent and productivity at 3.4 percent. In the period 1973–87, output grew at 3.7 percent and productivity at 0.8 percent.

The contribution of domestic policy

Policies can affect both the quantity of inputs and their productivity. A policy of import substitution, for example, may increase investment but decrease efficiency and technological progress, and hence productivity. It can be argued that an import tariff has only a once and for all effect on efficiency and does not affect the rate of technical progress.

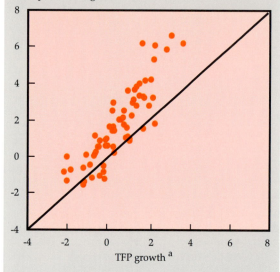

Figure 2.4 The average annual growth of per capita income and productivity, selected economies, 1960-87
(percent)

a. The unexplained residual of GDP growth after controlling for growth in conventional inputs (labor, capital, land).
Source: World Bank data.

Alternatively, it has been claimed that tariffs make it harder to adopt new technology and therefore slow the growth of productivity. Theory, therefore, is ambiguous. Evidence from country studies brings out the aspects of policy that affect productivity, which are further discussed in Chapters 3 and 7. Three suggestive overall findings are mentioned here.

First, the contribution of additional education in raising total output and productivity has already been noted. In addition to this effect, the level of education (as opposed to changes in the kind of education) of the population also seems important. A three-year-higher initial level of education is associated with an increase of 0.4 percent in the annual growth rate (or 11 percent extra output during a twenty-seven-year period).

Second, openness and competition are associated with growth in productivity. This holds for the various measures of openness used in this Report, including the two used in this chapter: movements in the domestic prices of traded goods toward international prices, and changes in trade shares. The more detailed review in Chapters 4

and 5 confirms this positive association between openness and competition, on the one hand, and growth, on the other. Other studies have found similar results.

Third, macroeconomic instability diminishes the return on investment and the growth of output, as country studies have suggested (see Chapters 4 and 6). This is only weakly supported by one proxy used in the cross-country estimation, the foreign exchange premium. Finally, the data suggest that an increase in the share of government consumption in GDP results in a decline in productivity growth later on. This is consistent with the results of other studies (Barro, forthcoming).

The evidence suggests that good policies—assumed to be reflected by alternative measures—and investments, both physical and human, are complementary. Both better policies and more education contribute to growth. Furthermore, they seem to interact. Thus, the effect on growth of better policy and more education together is greater than that of each separately (Table 2.4). Similar results are obtained for changes in education and for investment.

These results appear fairly robust for alternative groupings of countries and measures of policy. The variables under consideration may not be independent sources of good performance; causality has not been established, and variables omitted from the analysis may be affecting the results. But the evidence still suggests that simultaneous efforts to improve policy and to augment human and physical capital can have exceptionally high returns.

The effects of external factors

The terms of trade facing developing countries, growth in the OECD countries, international interest rates, and capital flows are just some of the external factors that can affect development. The importance of these factors for the aggregate prospects for development is discussed throughout this Report (see Chapters 1, 5, 6, and 8; also see Dell and Lawrence 1980). But can they account for *differences* in performance among individual countries? A study of thirty-three developing countries did not find a statistical association between differences in growth rates and the magnitude of external shocks (Mitra and Associates 1991).

Capital flows are another external factor that affects development. Concessional aid is an important source of financing for low-income countries, and its volume makes a difference to these coun-

Table 2.4 Interaction of policy with education and investment, 1965–87

Interacting variables	Average GDP growth	Average TFP growth	Probability of higher than median GDP growth	Probability of higher than median TFP growth
Policy "distortion" [a] *and education* [b]				
Low distortion and high education level	5.5	1.40	63.7	53.9
Low distortion and low education level	3.8	0.25	52.0	49.9*
High distortion and high education level	3.8	0.00	35.7	38.1
High distortion and low education level	3.1	−0.40	42.0	46.0*
Policy "distortion" [a] *and change in education* [c]				
Low distortion and high rate of increase in education	5.3	1.30	57.0	54.3
Low distortion and low rate of increase in education	4.0	0.40	55.1	48.8*
High distortion and high rate of increase in education	3.5	−0.16	35.0	39.7
High distortion and low rate of increase in education	3.4	−0.19	39.2	44.7*
Policy "distortion" [a] *and investment* [d]				
Low distortion and high investment	5.2	0.91	73.6	56.5
Low distortion and low investment	3.5	0.75	35.6	46.4*
High distortion and high investment	4.6	0.07	53.8	44.0
High distortion and low investment	2.6	−0.36	26.7	41.2*

Note: All results are significant at the 5 percent level unless marked with an asterisk (*), in which case they are not significant.

a. High distortion here is reflected by a foreign exchange premium of more than 30 percent; low distortion, a premium of 30 percent or less. See the technical note at the end of the main text.

b. Education is measured by the average years of schooling, excluding postsecondary schooling, of the population age fifteen to sixty-four. High education is defined here as more than 3.5 years; low education, 3.5 years or less.

c. Five-year increase (above or below the median).

d. Investment rate as a share of GDP (above or below the median).

Sources: For foreign exchange premium, International Currency Analysis, Inc., various years. For all other variables, World Bank data.

tries. At the same time, the efficiency with which aid is used matters, and improvements in both the quality and quantity of aid are needed. Efficiency, in turn, depends on the policies of lenders and borrowers alike (Box 2.5). Overall assessments of aid effectiveness are inconclusive, but country studies yield four important lessons that can strengthen the effectiveness of aid. First, aid often serves multiple objectives. When it is determined primarily by political considerations, special care is needed to ensure that its economic effects are satisfactory. Second, foreign assistance can reinforce good domestic policies as well as bad ones, and in the final analysis, efforts to support good policies are crucial. Third, a country's capacity to absorb aid depends on its human, financial, and administrative capabilities. Strengthening these capabilities must be a priority. Fourth, stability in the volume of funding and transparency of conditions on the aid help its recipients put it to better use.

Components of overall development

Meeting basic needs is an important part of economic development. The governments of many developing countries have made it a priority. India's first prime minister, while introducing the country's third five-year plan in 1960, stated: "It is said that the national income over the First and Second Plans has gone up by 42 percent and the per capita income by 20 percent. A legitimate query is where has this gone . . . I can see that people are better-fed and better clothed, they build brick houses . . . But some people probably have hardly benefited." (India 1964). Meeting basic needs requires both economic growth and a range of well-targeted social programs.

Several studies using household data show that social spending can significantly improve the welfare of households. Yet only a few studies have examined the effects of social spending using aggregate data. It would be especially helpful to know whether social spending or overall growth in incomes was the more effective way to improve social welfare. Several indicators are typically used to measure welfare: life expectancy, infant mortality, and school enrollment, none of which is devoid of drawbacks.

Data for public expenditures, income growth, and the educational status of adult females were examined for their effects on infant mortality and secondary school enrollment. The results from these cross-country analyses are mixed (Chapter 3). Evidence in this Report and in other studies stresses the importance of well-designed social spending for development. Greater efficiency in the delivery of services and more accurate targeting are recurring themes (Sen and Drèze 1990).

Box 2.5 The contribution of aid

When aid can be ineffective

Sometimes aid can permit countries to postpone improving macroeconomic management and mobilizing domestic resources. External agencies continued to provide aid to Tanzania while the country experimented with disastrous rural policies and institutions. The ready availability of foreign assistance to Pakistan—largely for political reasons—enabled it to postpone fiscal reform. Sometimes aid can strengthen lobbies that have a strong vested interest in a distorted policy framework and so make policy reform more difficult.

Aid at times can replace domestic saving and flows of trade, direct foreign investment, and commercial capital as the main sources for investment and technology development. Several countries have allowed food aid to depress agricultural prices. They have also postponed critical investments in rural infrastructure and ignored the need to build agricultural institutions.

Aid is sometimes turned on and off in response to the political and strategic agenda of bilateral funding agencies, making resource flows unpredictable. This resource instability can result in interruptions in development programs, as in Egypt, India, and Pakistan.

Uncoordinated and competing bilateral agencies can transfer incompatible technologies and deliver conflicting projects and advice. These problems of bilateral aid arise partly from the widespread practice of tying aid to the purchase of equipment, shipping, and technical advice from agency sources, which substantially reduces net resource transfers. In Pakistan, for example, the cost of using agency shipping lines to transport aid-funded procurements (often a substantial proportion of total project costs) was 50–115 percent higher than the cheapest alternative.

Swings in policy advice from funding agencies can add to the cost of aid for developing countries. Many recipients, advised to dismantle industrial protection and marketing boards, complain that agencies had encouraged these strategies in the 1960s and 1970s, when import substitution and regulation were in vogue. Agencies can often adjust rapidly to the changing thinking on development, but recipients of aid need more time to adjust because of their weak administrative structures.

When aid is effective

Aid improves the credibility of economic reform by providing assistance in the design of reform packages and by holding down the cost. Structural adjustment lending has triggered and helped sustain reforms in many countries that have been committed to reform, including Chile, Mexico, and Turkey. In the Republic of Korea, the infrastructure and education projects of the 1950s helped the economic takeoff that followed the reforms of the early 1960s. Humanitarian relief is another unassailable reason for aid.

Aid provides external resources for investment and finances projects that could not be undertaken with commercial capital because of debt overhang or a long project gestation period. Aid discussions also inform industrial countries about reforms in developing countries. This knowledge improves the developing countries' access to capital and direct foreign investment and, as in the cases of Korea, Malaysia, and Thailand, helps them become commercial borrowers.

Project assistance helps expand much-needed infrastructure—roads, railways, ports, and power generating facilities. It also builds technical expertise in project evaluation, monitoring, and implementation. Aid also contributes to personnel training and institution building (for example, in Korea, Pakistan, Thailand, Colombia, and Mexico). In addition, information on best practices—such as Bangladesh's Grameen Bank, Bolivia's Emergency Social Fund, and Jamaica's Food Stamp Scheme—helps recipients tailor practices to their circumstances and avoid mistakes.

Domestic policies, institutions, and administrative capacity also vitally affect the success of project aid. An excellent example of their contribution to the effectiveness of project aid is the green revolution in South Asia in the 1960s. It was successful both because of technology transfers, research, and infrastructure financed by aid and because of the responsiveness of domestic institutions.

Aid can support better economic and social policies. External aid and finance agencies are more and more sensitive to a project's effects on the environment and on social conditions. The emphasis on policies has also resulted in successful programs to reduce poverty, for example, in Bolivia, Côte d'Ivoire, and Malaysia. In Pakistan, concern with low achievements in education and health is prompting more lending for human resources to complement efforts to alleviate poverty.

The results are quite clear about the importance of educating women. The educational status of adult women is by far the most important variable explaining changes in infant mortality and secondary school enrollments (see Figure 2.5). An extra year of education for women is associated with a drop of 2 percentage points in the rate of infant mortality. Household-level studies have reported even larger reductions of 5–10 percentage points.

As noted at the outset, overall development includes more than economic variables: it includes noneconomic features which enrich the quality of life. Some noneconomic variables are associated with economic development, although lines of causation are generally difficult to establish. For example, some of the economic and social indicators discussed above are positively associated with noneconomic components of development, such as civil and political liberties (Box 2.6).

Equity is a separate concern in its own right. It has two aspects: income distribution and the incidence of poverty. There is no clear link, in either direction, between growth and changes in income distribution (see Chapter 7). But economic growth is strongly associated with a reduction in the incidence of poverty. A review of twenty developing countries found that growth was associated with an improvement in absolute poverty in all but one country (and the exception had negative per capita growth during the period considered). Lal and Myint (in preparation) find the same effect in their detailed country studies. *World Development Report 1990* also found strong evidence that growth reduces absolute poverty.

The way forward

Perhaps the clearest lesson from work on development during the past thirty years is that there is a premium on pragmatism and an open mind. Ideas that were once the conventional wisdom, and which guided governments and multilateral institutions in forming their approaches to development, have now been largely set aside. New ideas stress prices as signals; trade and competition as links to technological progress; and effective government as a scarce resource, to be employed sparingly and only where most needed.

In development, generalizations can be as rash as unbending commitments to theories. Quantitative evidence of the sort reviewed in this chapter is suggestive, but no more. There is no magic cure for economic backwardness. There is more than one way to succeed—if only because there are

Figure 2.5 Female educational attainment and decline in infant mortality, selected economies, 1960-87

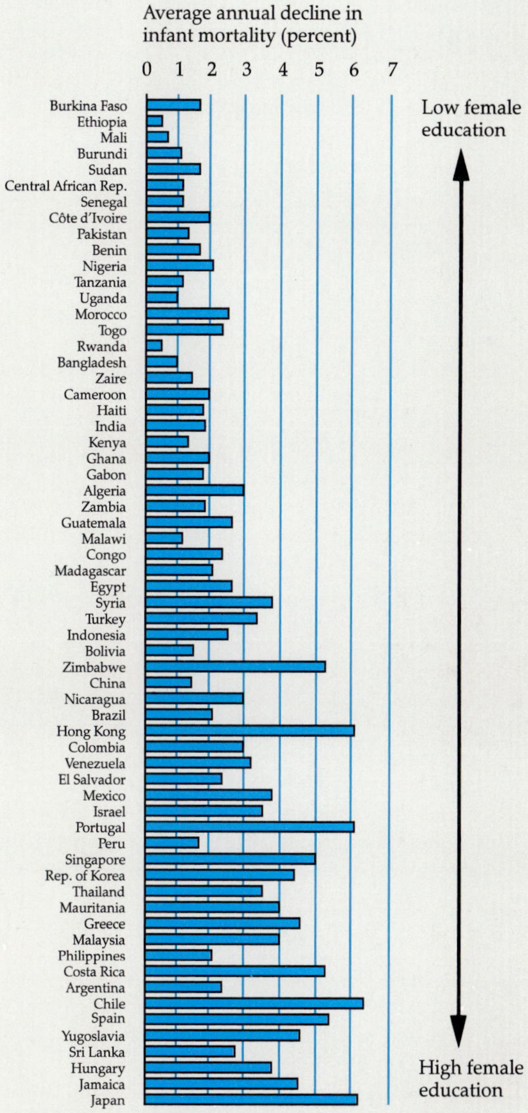

Average annual decline in infant mortality (percent)

Note: Economies are listed in ascending order by level of female education, defined as the average years of schooling, excluding postsecondary schooling, of females age fifteen to sixty-four. For the method of estimation, see the technical note at the end of the main text.
Source: World Bank data.

many different sorts of success. And success needs to be evaluated according to the various dimensions of development, not just income growth.

The fastest-growing economies of the sixty-eight analyzed are the four newly industrializing economies of East Asia. The best performer in terms of

Box 2.6 Noneconomic components of development: liberties

What connection, if any, is there between economic development and liberties, one of the noneconomic components of overall development? One possibility is that a free press and open public debate might expose actions by the government or the private sector that might otherwise hold development back. A free press and expanding flow of information often spur social and economic progress. India's free press can plausibly be credited with preventing famines, because it forced the government to act promptly. But it can also be said that freedoms in general make it harder for government to take tough but necessary decisions. The latter view is often advanced to explain the success of countries such as the Republic of Korea (with its "good" authoritarian rule) in contrast to countries such as India (where liberties and policy weaknesses may have gone together).

To examine this further, data on political and civil liberties were taken from *Freedom in the World* (Gastil 1989). This survey has been undertaken every year but one since 1973. It ranks countries according to thirty specific tests under two criteria: political rights, defined as "rights to participate meaningfully in the political process"; and civil liberties, or the "rights to free expression, to organize or demonstrate, as well as rights to a degree of autonomy such as is provided by freedom of religion, education, travel, and other personal rights." The resulting index is highly correlated with another constructed by Humana (UNDP 1991). All such measures are crude. They cannot support firm conclusions. However, the results are interesting. There is a strong relation between income growth, education levels, and declines in infant mortality; between female education levels, and changes therein, with infant mortality decline; and between political and civil liberties and achievements in male and female education and infant mortality decline (Box table 2.6).

The results of regression analysis do not go as far as to suggest that liberties contribute positively to income growth, but they imply that they do not hold growth back. Some studies find that the relationship between freedom and growth is ambiguous (Grier and Tullock 1989). Dasgupta (1990) reports a clearer effect for 1970–80, finding that "political and civil rights are positively and significantly correlated with real national income per head and its growth." Scully (1988) also reports a positive effect.

Finally, after controlling for income growth and regional effects, liberties appear to be strongly and positively associated with measures of welfare improvements such as women's education, overall education, and infant mortality declines (Box figure 2.6). These results do not show the lines of causation, but they suggest that these important components of overall development go together.

Box figure 2.6 The association between political and civil liberties and women's education, selected economies, 1973-86

Ratio of female to male educational attainment

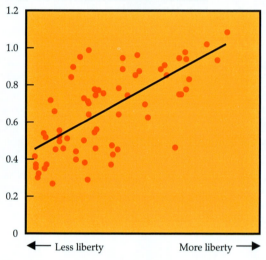

Note: Data are period averages for a sample of sixty-seven economies; data for 1974 were unavailable. Educational attainment is defined as the average years of schooling, excluding postsecondary schooling, of the population age fifteen to sixty-four. For the method of estimation, see the technical note at the end of the main text.
Sources: For data on political and civil liberties, Gastil 1987; for data on education, World Bank.

Box table 2.6 Correlation matrix for measures of overall development, 1973–87

Measure	1	2	3	4	5	6	7	8
1. Growth	1.00	0.30	0.12*	0.23	0.31	0.42	0.37	0.19*
2. Decline in infant mortality[a]		1.00	0.27	0.41	0.29	0.67	0.71	0.59
3. Change in education			1.00	0.92	−0.18*	0.30	0.25	0.32*
4. Change in female education				1.00	0.22	0.52	0.48	0.28
5. Change in female-male education gap					1.00	0.55	0.56	0.39
6. Education level						1.00	0.98	0.57
7. Female education level							1.00	0.63
8. Political and civil liberties								1.00

Note: Numbers are period averages; data are for a sample of sixty-eight economies. All correlation coefficients are statistically significant at least at the 10 percent level, except for those marked with an asterisk (*).
a. Because of low data quality, these data cover only the period 1973–84.
Sources: For political and civil liberties, Gastil 1989. For others, World Bank data.

progress on infant mortality is Chile, along with Japan. Jamaica and Japan score highest on education (although Costa Rica and Venezuela are better with regard to gender equality). Costa Rica, along with Japan, ranks highest in political and civil liberties. Some of the poorest performers in the economic sphere also fared badly in some of the noneconomic aspects.

The statistical research therefore shows that the various measures of development are linked, more closely in some cases than in others. But there are always exceptions. If indicators are ranked, then Algeria, Brazil, and Gabon are in the top one-third ranked by income, but half way down the rankings for infant mortality and education. Pakistan also scores well on income growth, but consider-

ably less well on gender equality in education. In a spirit of pragmatism and open-mindedness, it is right to conclude that income growth has been overemphasized as a measure of welfare, but also that income growth usually does not militate against success in the other dimensions.

The challenge for governments is to translate the broad lessons of development experience into policies that work. To help in this task, the next four chapters of this Report examine different areas of policy—human capital, domestic markets, foreign trade, and macroeconomic policy—in detail. In each case the Report asks: What have governments done, and what appears to have worked best?

Investing in people

If you plan for a year, plant a seed. If for ten years, plant a tree. If for a hundred years, teach the people. When you sow a seed once, you will reap a single harvest. When you teach the people, you will reap a hundred harvests.

—K'UAN-TZU, 551–479 B.C.

In the past century, vast progress has been achieved in human welfare—the ultimate goal of development. This advance has usually taken place hand in hand with economic growth. Even where growth lagged, however, the quality of life improved. Governments have played a leading role. Public spending on classrooms and textbooks, safe drinking water and sanitation, nutrition and immunization programs, and family planning clinics have been critical, especially for the world's poor. But the demands of the future require better targeting, new and more efficient methods of delivery, fewer regressive subsidies, and closer partnership with the private sector in the provision of certain services.

During times of economic hardship, such as the 1980s, tough choices need to be made, and short-term gains in economic growth need to be balanced against long-term threats to human development and the quality of life. One lesson from the past is that the economies—such as Japan and the Republic of Korea—which committed themselves to education and training made great strides in both human development and economic growth. Equally, however, investing in education buys no guarantee of faster growth. When econ-

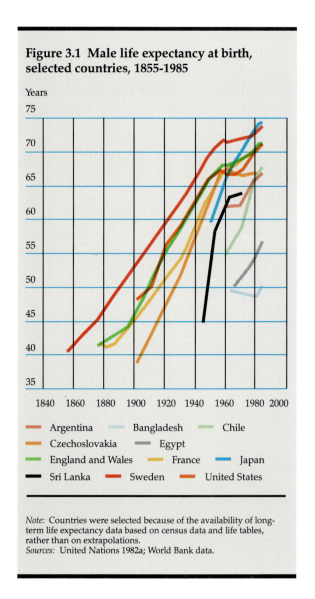

Figure 3.1 Male life expectancy at birth, selected countries, 1855-1985

Note: Countries were selected because of the availability of long-term life expectancy data based on census data and life tables, rather than on extrapolations.
Sources: United Nations 1982a; World Bank data.

The age-standardized death rate in the United States declined from 40 per thousand in 1700 to 5 in 1980. During the same period, the British death rate fell from 28 to 7 per thousand. Life expectancy at age 10 years for a U.S. native-born white male increased from about 50 years in 1700 to 57 in 1925, whereas British males started at a lower life expectancy of 39 and achieved 54 in 1925. The causes of these changes remain controversial. They have been widely attributed to improvements in medical technology and expansion of hospital services. Considerable evidence points to the important role disease control has played in increasing life expectancy. Others have argued that improvement in nutrition was the principal factor and that the decline in rural mortality before 1920 is largely attributable to the rising living standards of the rural population.

Recent studies have strengthened the nutrition argument. For national populations in North America and Europe, average adult height has been found to be highly correlated with life expectancy. Americans were found to have achieved modern heights by the mid-eighteenth century and to have reached levels of life expectancy that were not attained by the general population of England or even by the British peerage until the first quarter of the twentieth century. One of the reasons given for this difference is the higher average meat consumption by Americans, even in middle of the eighteenth century.

The studies have found that improvements in nutritional status accounted for as much as four-tenths of the secular decline in mortality rates, with nearly all of this effect concentrated on infant mortality. Data from eight European countries from 1880 to 1970 reveal that a 1 percent increase in height was associated with a 5 percent decline in crude mortality rates, and a three times larger decline in infant mortality. Increases in height accounted for 39 percent of the decline in the infant mortality rate, whereas growth in per capita income accounted for 27 percent, and the remaining 33 percent was attributable to unmeasured factors. Moreover, using a body mass index in addition to height at maturity as an indicator of nutritional level appears to explain most of the decline in mortality rates in England, France, and Sweden between 1775 and 1875, and about half the mortality decline between 1875 and 1975.

Eliminating chronic malnutrition may not depend solely on agricultural production. Famines have coexisted with surpluses, the result not of natural calamities or inadequate farm technology but of a sharp loss in purchasing power of a section of the population and failures in the system of food distribution. The English experience during the period 1600–40 showed that hunger could also be avoided by appropriate government policies on food inventories and food prices in times of shortage, combined with advances in agricultural technologies.

omies are badly managed, investments in people may go to waste. The Philippines had great promise in the 1950s; its per capita income and literacy rate were almost as high as in Korea. Today it lags behind the other economies of Southeast Asia—a result of highly protectionist industrial policies and years of authoritarian rule, which squandered foreign borrowings and undermined domestic entrepreneurship.

Welfare and growth

In 1890, Alfred Marshall wrote that "health and strength, physical, mental, and moral . . . are the basis of industrial wealth; while conversely the chief importance of material wealth lies in the fact that when wisely used, it increases the health and strength, physical, mental, and moral, of the human race." The historical experience of nations bears witness to this statement.

Health

Better diets, housing, and control of communicable diseases have raised the quality of life everywhere. By reducing illness, these improvements have increased people's alertness, capacity for learning, and ability to cope with and enjoy life. By prolonging life, they have made investments in knowledge and skills even more worthwhile. And the benefits of good health flow well into the future: a mother's good health strongly influences the early physical and mental development of her children.

Between 1880 and 1985, average life expectancy at birth of males in industrial countries rose by twenty-five to thirty years (Figure 3.1 and Box 3.1); female life expectancy rose even faster. Similar increases in life expectancy have been achieved more quickly and at lower levels of income in some developing countries since the 1940s. Average male

Table 3.1 The economic burden of adult illness, selected countries and years

Country and year	Days ill (past month)[a]	Work days absent (past month)[a]	Potential income loss (percentage of normal earnings)[b]
Ghana, 1988/89	3.6	1.3	6.4
Côte d'Ivoire, 1987	2.6	1.3	6.4
Mauritania, 1988	2.1	1.6	6.5
Indonesia, 1978	1.0	0.6	2.5
Philippines (Bicol region), 1978	0.9	0.6	2.5
Bolivia (urban), 1990	..	1.2	4.4
Peru, 1985/86	4.5	0.9	3.1
Jamaica, 1989	1.2	0.5	2.1
United States, 1988[c]	..	0.3	1.5

Note: Countries were selected on the basis of data availability.
a. To calculate these numbers for the eight developing countries, the probability of being ill (or absent from work) was multiplied by the number of days ill (or work days lost because of illness) in the month before the survey.
b. Potential income loss is the probable number of days of absence from work as a percentage of reported normal days at work.
c. For the United States, data are reported for the number of restricted-activity days resulting from illness in the population aged eighteen to forty-four years.
Sources: For the United States, U.S. Department of Health and Human Services 1989. For other countries, household surveys; see the Chapter 3 section on adult illness in the technical note at the end of the main text.

life expectancy increased in Japan from about 60 years in 1950 to 75 years in 1985, surpassing levels in other industrial countries; in Sri Lanka it increased from 45 years in 1945 to 64 years in 1971. Many factors have contributed to these improvements. For example, UNICEF (1991) estimates that vaccines given to children in developing countries in the past ten years have prevented 1.6 million polio cases. The percentage of developing-country households with access to safe water (vital in the control of infectious diseases) rose from a mean of 48 percent in 1975 to 57 percent in 1985. The improvements in life expectancy, however, have been distributed unevenly: life expectancy (at fifteen) in the poorest countries is still as much as twenty years less than in other developing countries. In developing countries, about 25 million children and young adults die each year—most from preventable causes. About 1.5 billion people still lack basic health care (UNDP 1991).

Better health is desirable as an end in itself. But it also brings substantial economic benefits—releasing resources that can then be used to achieve other development goals. Better health and nutrition raise workers' productivity, decrease the number of days they are ill, and prolong their potential working lives. By reducing morbidity and debility, the malaria eradication program in Sri Lanka in the 1940s and 1950s led to a 10 percent rise in incomes. In Sierra Leone, a 10 percent increase in the caloric intake of farm workers consuming 1,500 calories a day raised output by 5 percent. Similar results have been found among Kenyan road construction workers with a daily intake of 2,000 calories.

Household survey data from nine countries suggest that the economic effects of illness may be substantial. An average adult worker in Peru might expect to be ill 4.5 days a month and miss about one day of work as a result; in Ghana the corresponding figures were 3.6 and 1.3 days (Table 3.1). In the United States, workers aged between eighteen and forty-four years miss, on average, one-quarter of a day's work a month.

The potential income loss from illness in eight developing countries averages 2.1–6.5 percent of yearly earnings. Reducing illness could raise GDP accordingly. Averting illness obviously requires resources, but these figures suggest that it might yield a large benefit even in narrow economic terms, in addition to its human benefits. There are complications. These estimates assume that other household members will not compensate by working more. Yet potential loss of earnings is only a partial measure of output loss. The full cost would include the value of lost nonmarket work (such as child care and food preparation), forgone earnings of other household members, costs of treatment, and so on. On the whole, the strictly economic case for effective efforts to improve health is strong.

Health and nutrition also have long-run effects on productivity and output because they influence a child's ability and motivation to learn. Disease and malnutrition in infancy may retard mental development, and illness and temporary hunger may reduce children's ability to concentrate and keep them away from school. Among Nepalese children, height-for-age, a measure of nutritional history, was found to be the most important factor, after family income, in explaining grade or school enrollment and attainment. In the Philippines, weight-for-height was a significant predictor of performance in mathematics achievement tests among urban school children. These effects, in turn, influence adult productivity. Studies in south India and the Philippines suggest that the long-run effects of nutrition on wages can be large and positive.

Education

By improving people's ability to acquire and use information, education deepens their understanding of themselves and the world, enriches their

---

Box 3.2 Educating women: a key to development

When schools open their doors wider to girls and women, the benefits from education multiply. Consider the scatter plots in Box figure 3.2, which show primary school enrollment rates of males in 1965 compared with infant mortality and fertility rates in 1985. The scatter plots confirm the expected negative correlation between education and infant mortality and fertility; they suggest that raising a country's education level (here represented by male enrollment rates) can improve the health and life expectancy of children and create incentives for reducing family size. But in the group of countries with a large gender gap (represented by the top trend line in each plot)—where the enrollment ratio of girls is only three-fourths or less that of boys—infant mortality and total fertility rates

are higher at every level of male enrollment. Countries which achieved near universal primary education for boys in 1965 but in which enrollment rates for girls lag far behind have about twice the infant mortality and fertility rates in 1985 of countries with a smaller gender gap.

This illustrates a point confirmed by other studies: failing to raise women's level of education closer to men's detracts from the social benefits of raising men's. If the cost of increasing enrollment rates rises as a country approaches universal enrollment, then it may be more cost-effective to spend the additional resources on girls who have lower enrollment rates than on boys.

Box figure 3.2 The effect of the gender gap in education on infant mortality and total fertility, 1985

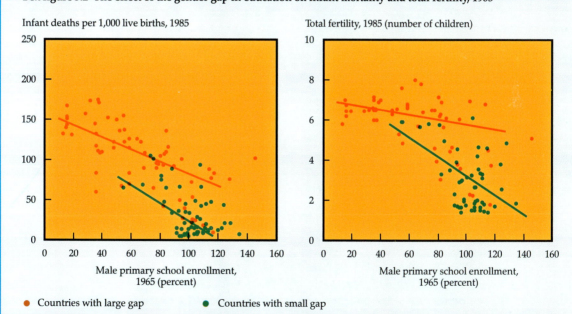

Note: The figure assumes that primary school enrollment affects infant mortality twenty years later. The gender gap in education is the ratio of female to male enrollment at the primary school level.
Source: King and Hill, forthcoming.

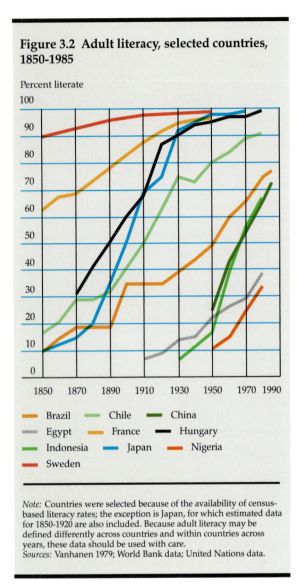

Figure 3.2 Adult literacy, selected countries, 1850-1985

Percent literate

Legend:
- Brazil
- Chile
- China
- Egypt
- France
- Hungary
- Indonesia
- Japan
- Nigeria
- Sweden

Note: Countries were selected because of the availability of census-based literacy rates; the exception is Japan, for which estimated data for 1850-1920 are also included. Because adult literacy may be defined differently across countries and within countries across years, these data should be used with care.
Sources: Vanhanen 1979; World Bank data; United Nations data.

minds by broadening their experiences, and improves the choices they make as consumers, producers, and citizens. Education strengthens their ability to meet their wants and those of their family by increasing their productivity, and their potential to achieve a higher standard of living. By improving people's confidence and their ability to create and innovate, it multiplies their opportunities for personal and social achievement.

Consider the evidence on the benefits of women's education (Box 3.2). Better-educated women, who are more informed about the value of health care and personal hygiene, tend to be less affected by the absence of community health programs and tend to use them more frequently when they are available. In Nigeria and the Philippines, studies suggest that the mother's education is so

important in determining child mortality that it makes up for the absence of medical facilities in the community (Barrera 1990; Caldwell 1979). Other studies have found that if women are better educated, couples are more likely to use contraception.

A century and a half ago, the countries that are now industrialized achieved levels of literacy higher than those in many developing countries in Africa and Asia today (Figure 3.2). But literacy rates have also risen rapidly in some developing countries. Two striking examples are Chile, which reached a literacy level comparable to that of industrial countries at a lower level of income, and Indonesia, where adult literacy rose from just 17 percent in 1950 to 67 percent in 1980. Governments everywhere have declared universal literacy to be a principal goal.

An increase in formal schooling accounts for most of the literacy gains in the developing world in the past three decades. Even in low-income countries, primary school enrollments have outpaced the growth of the youth population, and gross enrollment rates (excluding China and India) rose from 38 percent in 1960 to 76 percent in 1987. But countries have not progressed at the same rate. More than 1 billion adults are still illiterate in the developing world (UNDP 1991). Some countries in Sub-Saharan Africa have extremely low enrollment rates—Burkina Faso, Ethiopia, Guinea, Mali, Niger, and Somalia enrolled only 20–40 percent of children in 1987—and enrollment rates stagnated or fell in the 1980s in other countries that had been performing well. For example, gross primary enrollment rates fell from 93 percent in 1980 to 66 percent in 1987 in Tanzania, and from 94 to 76 percent in Zaire. Moreover, within countries, wide disparities persist. Among women, only one out of two is literate in Asia and only one out of three in Sub-Saharan Africa. The gaps between majority and minority groups and between rural and urban populations also remain large.

Again, progress on education is to be sought mainly as an end in itself. But the evidence that education promotes economic growth, and thus puts other goals of development within reach, is firm. A one-year increase in schooling can augment wages by more than 10 percent after allowing for other factors (Table 3.2). An additional year of schooling has raised farm output by nearly 2 percent in the Republic of Korea and 5 percent in Malaysia. And in family-owned enterprises in urban Peru, education appears to be more critical to earnings than physical capital.

Table 3.2 The effect of an additional year of schooling on wages and farm output, selected countries and years

Country and year	Percentage increase in wages		Percentage increase in farm output	Sources
	Male	Female		
Côte d'Ivoire, 1987	12 P			van der Gaag and Vijverberg 1987
	21 S			
Ghana, 1988/89	5			Glewwe 1990
Korea, Rep. of, 1976, 1974	6		2	Lee 1981, Jamison and Lau 1982
Indonesia, 1986	8	12 S		Behrman and Deolalikar 1988
France, 1987		11		Riboud 1985
Peru, 1986	13	12 P	3	King 1989, Jacoby 1989
	8	8 S		
Malaysia, 1987	16	18	5	Jamison and Lau 1982, World Bank data
Nicaragua (urban), 1985	10	13		Behrman and Blau 1985
Philippines, 1980		18		Griffin 1987
Spain, 1979		10		Hernandez-Iglesias and Riboud 1985
Thailand, 1986; 1973	17	13 P	3	Schultz, forthcoming; Jamison and Lau 1982
	7	25 S		
United States, 1967				Smith 1979
Whites	6	7		
Blacks	5	11		

P, primary school level.
S, secondary school level.
Note: These results were all estimated controlling for other factors such as work experience and other individual characteristics. In most cases, the estimated effects have also been corrected for any statistical bias resulting from selecting a sample of wage earners only. The estimates for Côte d'Ivoire, Ghana, and Korea pertain to combined samples of men and women.

Education affects productivity and growth through several channels. A better-educated person absorbs new information faster and applies unfamiliar inputs and new processes more effectively. When a new product or process is introduced, much needs to be learned about how it works and how it applies to specific circumstances and environments. In the dynamic and uncertain environment of technological change, more highly educated workers have a big advantage. In Peru, if farmers had an additional year of schooling, it increased their probability of adopting modern farm technology by 45 percent. In Thailand, farmers with four years of schooling were three times more likely to use new chemical inputs than farmers with one to three years of schooling.

Japan's rapid industrialization after the Meiji Restoration was fueled by its aggressive accumulation of technical skills, which in turn was based on its already high level of literacy and a strong commitment to education, especially the training of engineers (Box 3.3). Korea's relatively strong base of human capital in the early 1960s speeded its own industrialization. This accumulation of human capital started during the period 1910–45, with substantial on-the-job training and foreign technical assistance. Important education programs were launched during the late 1940s and 1950s, focusing on universal primary education and adult literacy; higher education was also expanded, and many students were sent overseas for technical and advanced training (Pack and Westphal 1986).

Contrary to popular belief, education appears to promote entrepreneurship at least as powerfully as cultural factors—important though these have sometimes been. Legal restrictions on the ownership of land forced the Jews of medieval Europe into commerce; and cultural taboos often create economic opportunities for ethnic minorities (migrant Hakka Chinese dominate northern India's leather-tanning industry, which is thought to be polluting by high-caste Hindus; Basu, forthcoming). But, more generally, entrepreneurship is a matter of skills, not cultural inheritance. That is why entrepreneurship may be one of the most important channels through which education raises economic productivity.

In market economies entrepreneurs are the link between innovation and production. They perceive new economic opportunities, take risks, and change their methods of production and distribution. Entrepreneurial ability has been characterized as a combination of moderate risk-taking, individual responsibility, long-range planning, and organizational ability. Education promotes all four. In a study of entrepreneurs in northern Thailand, 40 percent had a university degree. In Malaysia, even when ethnicity and family wealth are controlled for, entrepreneurs in larger enterprises are more educated than entrepreneurs in smaller firms. In Bolivia, Côte d'Ivoire, Ghana, and Peru, entrepreneurs—defined narrowly as persons who own a nonfarm enterprise with at least one hired worker—are not more educated than wage employees; but, as in Malaysia, enterprise size is positively associated with the entrepreneur's years of education (Figure 3.3).

Population

The decline in death rates from about thirty per thousand in 1945 to about ten per thousand in 1988—a decline that has outweighed the decrease in fertility rates during that period—has fueled rapid population growth in the developing world. The world's population has doubled since 1950, and the share of the world's population living in the poorest developing regions rose from two-thirds in 1950 to three-fourths in 1985. The average population growth rate in developing regions increased to more than 2 percent in the period 1950–75 (Figure 3.4). It has since dropped in Latin America and steadied in Asia as a whole; but it will continue to rise in Africa during the next two decades, despite initial signs of declining fertility in Botswana, Kenya, and Zimbabwe.

Rapid population growth has caused serious concern about the outlook for economic growth, human development, and the environment in developing countries. Although not a threat in every country, for many developing countries it is a critical issue. For example, in some countries, high fertility rates and poverty together form a vicious circle that threatens the welfare—or even survival—of the population, especially children. Through malnutrition and disease, poverty leads to more infant and child deaths, which in turn induce couples to have more children to guarantee the survival of some. At the same time, high birth rates have been shown to be associated with higher infant and maternal deaths.

Although mortality rates still differ widely among countries, differences in population growth are mainly the result of differences in fertility rates. Fertility reflects decisions made by individuals, which raises the question of how such decisions can come to be detrimental to society as a whole. Why should the social costs and benefits of having children differ from the private costs and benefits? It has often been argued that rapid population growth promotes development because a large population makes it possible to achieve scale economies in production. But removing barriers to international trade means that a country's own population is no longer a barrier to achieving economies of scale. The small industrializing countries of Asia demonstrate this benefit from trade. Singapore, with a population of 2.7 million, annually exports about $35 million worth of manufactured exports—about twice as much as does Brazil, with a population of 147 million.

The effect of population growth on the natural environment is another source of divergence between private and social costs (Box 3.4). The pressure of population can raise agricultural demand, leading in turn to the abuse of marginal land and other natural resources. The annual rate of deforestation in the 1980s was 0.5–2.3 percent in Brazil and 0.4 percent in Bolivia, whereas extensive deforestation in Nepal is thought to have caused land erosion and floods in Bangladesh and India. Although many parts of Sub-Saharan Africa still have large areas of potentially cultivable lands and relatively low population densities, a rapidly expanding population moving into the tropical forests already poses environmental problems. Côte d'Ivoire is said to have an annual deforestation rate of 6–16 percent; its forests could disappear in less than twenty years.

Policies to slow population would help to ease the long-term threat to the natural environment from global warming and other ecological problems. But these dangers reflect other pressures, too: the widespread use of natural-resource-intensive technologies; ineffective regulation of common-property resources; land tenure systems that do not secure long-term rights to land use; and policies that distort the prices of nonrenewable resources. Action on such matters must be a priority for governments everywhere.

Population growth may exacerbate other market failures besides the depletion of resources. The congestion of urban areas is one. Here, again, population control needs to be accompanied by other measures: better city planning, rural development, traffic control, and so on. Universal education helps motivate people to limit the number of children they have and to improve the quality of their children's lives; it is one of the most effective population-control policies.

Challenges in human development

The agenda for human development differs widely from country to country. Egypt's most pressing

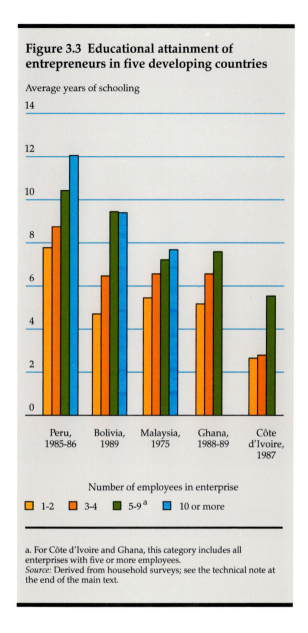

Figure 3.3 Educational attainment of entrepreneurs in five developing countries

Average years of schooling

Number of employees in enterprise

◻ 1-2   ◼ 3-4   ◼ 5-9[a]   ◼ 10 or more

a. For Côte d'Ivoire and Ghana, this category includes all enterprises with five or more employees.
Source: Derived from household surveys; see the technical note at the end of the main text.

concerns will not be the same as Thailand's or Turkey's—although all three are lower-middle-income countries with roughly the same population. Despite the diversity, however, most countries have the following goals in common: to slow population growth, to improve health and nutrition, to build technical capacity, and to reduce poverty.

Slowing population growth

Family planning has been promoted by external aid and finance agencies as a means to control overall population growth. This approach has been accepted by some governments. But others have reacted negatively to the idea of population

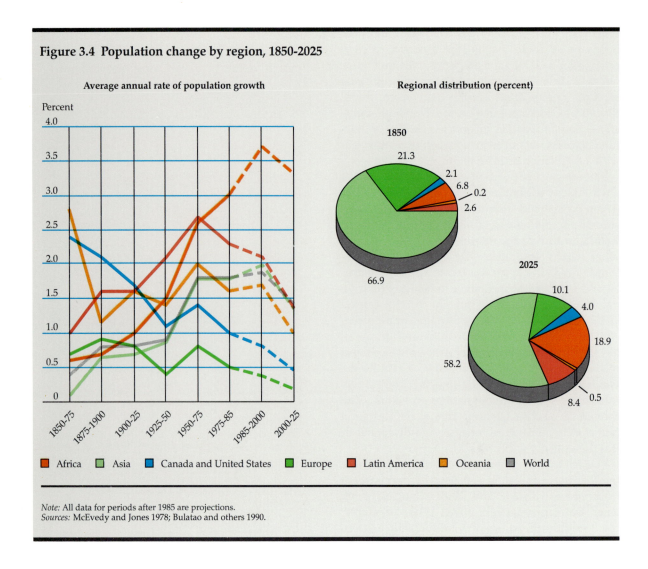

Figure 3.4 Population change by region, 1850-2025

Average annual rate of population growth

Regional distribution (percent)

Note: All data for periods after 1985 are projections.
Sources: McEvedy and Jones 1978; Bulatao and others 1990.

control as an end in itself, preferring instead to view family planning programs as a way to enable couples (especially women) to exercise choice, to improve the health of mothers and children, or to reduce poverty.

Urbanization and economic growth in developing countries both tend to reduce population growth. They make caring for many children more difficult or more expensive; they encourage parents to spend more on educating each child rather than on supporting a bigger family. In general, high-income countries have low fertility rates and high levels of education and health; low-income countries have high fertility rates and low levels of education and health. In India, farm households in higher-growth areas, which were exposed to the new technologies of the green revolution, had fewer children and gave them significantly more schooling than did those in other areas .

But income growth is neither necessary nor sufficient to control population. Family planning programs can work. The implementation of these programs has contributed significantly to the decline of fertility in low-income countries such as Indonesia and Sri Lanka. Thailand has successfully reduced its population growth rate from 3.1 percent in the 1960s to 1.9 percent in the period 1980-89, and the total fertility rate declined from 6.3 children in 1965 to 2.5 in 1989. Family planning can also have additional effects on child survival by improving maternal health or increasing resources available per child. Studies have found that a doubling of government expenditures per capita on family planning programs in urban areas would reduce infant mortality by 3 percent in Colombia, and that a 20 percent rise in the proportion of villages with a family planning clinic would reduce infant mortality by more than 4 percent in India.

Box 3.4 Population, agriculture, and environment in Sub-Saharan Africa

Rapid population growth, agricultural stagnation, and environmental degradation are closely interrelated and mutually reinforcing. Until recently, it was generally believed that controlling population was not a priority in Sub-Saharan Africa, where population density is low and land is abundant. However, population density and land availability vary greatly across countries in the region. Countries with low per capita arable land and high population growth, such as Burundi, Ethiopia, Ghana, Kenya, Nigeria, Rwanda, and Togo, are experiencing an economic and environmental crisis of agricultural stagnation, deforestation, land degradation, and desertification. Per capita arable land declined from 0.5 hectare per person in 1965 to 0.3 in 1987. The traditional system of shifting cultivation is under stress as land has become more scarce, and fallow periods are gradually being reduced. In Kenya, Lesotho, Liberia, Mauritania, and Rwanda, fallow periods are no longer sufficient to allow soil fertility to be restored, and crop yields have fallen as a result. People are forced to migrate onto marginal land in semi-arid areas and into tropical forests to establish new farms, so population pressure is causing not only soil degradation, but also deforestation, desertification, and falling agricultural output.

The pressure on land has been exacerbated by people's needs to gather fuelwood and graze their livestock. Fuelwood accounts for about 80 percent of energy needs in Sub-Saharan Africa, and it is in very short supply. As the situation worsens, farmers have to burn animal dung and crop residues instead of using them to enrich the soil. With an estimated 160 million head of cattle in Africa, overgrazing is acute. More than one-quarter of Sub-Saharan Africa's land area of 750 million hectares is moderately to very severely desertified. The agricultural potential in these areas may have been lost for years.

Agricultural stagnation and environmental degradation also affect population growth. High infant and child mortality rates caused by food shortage and malnutrition induce men and women to have more children, partly to ensure that some survive to support them in old age. Fertility is high in the region, at 6.6 children for an average woman, compared with 4 in other developing countries. To break this vicious circle, policies are urgently needed to control population; increase agricultural productivity without damaging the environment; and reduce malnutrition, poverty, and infant and child mortality.

Contraceptive use has been lowest, and fertility rates highest, in Sub-Saharan Africa. A compelling reason for trying to slow population growth in the region is the already mounting cost of providing basic health care and schooling, services that need to be not merely maintained but greatly improved. However, the trends in African population growth are not well understood. Low contraceptive use has been attributed to ignorance: only about half of Africa's women have heard of a way to prevent pregnancy, compared with 85–95 percent in other regions. But evidence also shows that African women, on average, want larger families—between six and nine children—than women in other regions. This suggests that even more information and family planning services might make little difference to begin with. Recent surveys, however, indicate that a growing proportion of women want no more children. In the 1970s, only 16 percent of Kenyan women wanted no more children, according to the World Fertility Survey; in 1989, 49 percent gave that answer, according to the most recent Demographic and Health Survey. The same trend is appearing in other countries. This may indicate that the region has reached a demographic turning point, but it is too early to tell.

Improving health and nutrition

In this Report, infant mortality and life expectancy at birth have so far received the most attention as measures of social welfare. This is partly because of the availability of data. However, it should not distract attention from the chronic deprivation and morbidity of living children and adults. Two tasks are urgent: to provide nutrition to improve the mental and physical well-being of children and adults; and to improve the control and treatment of disease.

Undernutrition and micronutrient malnutrition affect the more than 1 billion people who live in poverty in developing countries. In infants and pre-adolescent children, micronutrient deficiencies have been associated with stunted growth, mental retardation, and learning disabilities. In adults, they cause a higher incidence of disease and worsen performance at work. Preventive and curative approaches to the problem have been tried. The best techniques vary according to cir-

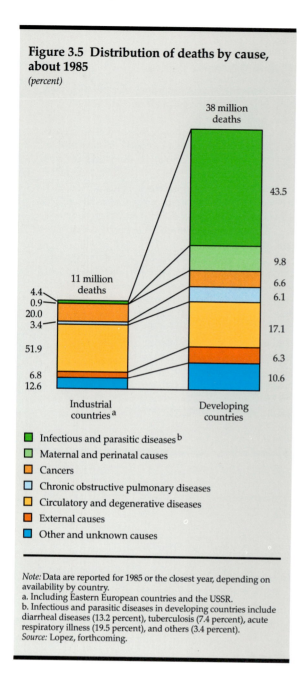

Figure 3.5 Distribution of deaths by cause, about 1985

(percent)

38 million deaths

43.5

9.8

6.6

6.1

17.1

6.3

10.6

11 million deaths

4.4
0.9
20.0
3.4

51.9

6.8
12.6

Industrial countries [a]

Developing countries

- ■ Infectious and parasitic diseases [b]
- ■ Maternal and perinatal causes
- ■ Cancers
- ■ Chronic obstructive pulmonary diseases
- ■ Circulatory and degenerative diseases
- ■ External causes
- ■ Other and unknown causes

Note: Data are reported for 1985 or the closest year, depending on availability by country.
a. Including Eastern European countries and the USSR.
b. Infectious and parasitic diseases in developing countries include diarrheal diseases (13.2 percent), tuberculosis (7.4 percent), acute respiratory illness (19.5 percent), and others (3.4 percent).
Source: Lopez, forthcoming.

cumstances. One lesson, however, is that education about nutrition is important. Failure to educate the public is a major reason why diet-fortification programs in some Latin American countries have failed. A second lesson is that nutritional initiatives can be carried out by all sorts of different institutions. For example, schools can be used to deliver micronutrients to children as well as to the general community.

The appropriate methods for treating and controlling disease will again vary from case to case. In the developing countries as a whole, infectious and parasitic diseases account for almost half of all deaths, nearly all of which are children under five years; in the industrial countries, circulatory and degenerative diseases are the main killers, accounting for more than half of all deaths (Figure 3.5). When a new disease such as AIDS erupts, however, these patterns can shift dramatically (Box 3.5).

Among developing countries, epidemiological profiles vary widely—because of different levels of government efforts to control communicable diseases, different fertility rates, and many other factors that alter the risks of various diseases. For example, the profiles of Brazil, China, and the Republic of Korea have more and more resembled those of wealthier, industrial countries. In Brazil, rapid urbanization and industrialization in the 1970s were accompanied by an increase in the number of traffic-related deaths and industrial injuries; cardiovascular diseases have become the leading cause of death, accounting for a third of the deaths in the country as a whole and even higher proportions in urban areas. In China, industries are exposing the population to severe environmental pollution. In some parts of the country, exposures to lead and dust are sixty to eighty times the maximum allowable limits; mercury concentration in the air is twelve times the limit; and noise pollution is bad enough to have caused hearing loss among workers. In Korea, rapid industrial growth and urbanization have also changed lifestyles and shifted the epidemiological profile. In the 1980s, the main causes of deaths were cancer, heart disease and stroke, and injuries from accidents and violence; these accounted for 60 percent of deaths in 1987.

What is the best way to improve developing-country health care? In particular, how much should be spent on preventive, as opposed to curative, care? WHO and UNICEF estimate that nearly 43 percent of the 14.6 million child deaths each year could be prevented through vaccinations (at an average cost of $13 per child) or low-cost interventions such as oral rehydration therapy (at $2 to $3 per child per year). A recent World Bank study (Jamison and Mosley, forthcoming) ranked various policies by cost-effectiveness (as measured by cost per year of healthy life saved). One conclusion is that measles immunization programs and programs to reduce perinatal mortality are very cost-effective. With such measures, an extra year of healthy life costs just $5. The appropriate balance of spending between preventive and curative care depends, however, not only on cost but also on reach. Health promotion and disease prevention are generally neglected in favor of expensive treatments that reach relatively few and are often ineffective, such as for many kinds of cancers. Immunization programs still deserve priority in low-income countries. Programs for family planning, nutrition education and supplementation, and perinatal care are also highly cost-effective. Once these needs have been met, however, the presumption in favor of preventive over curative programs is weaker. Tuberculosis treatment programs, for example, have proved cost-effective.

Box 3.5 AIDS in developing countries

Acquired Immune Deficiency Syndrome (AIDS) is a fatal disease which strikes an adult on average eight or ten years after being infected by the human immunodeficiency virus (HIV). Since 1985, the cumulative number of persons infected with HIV has risen worldwide from 2.5 million to between 8 and 10 million, and in Africa from 1.5 million to about 5.5 million. By the year 2000, the World Health Organization estimates that 25 to 30 million adults worldwide will have been infected with HIV. The share of developing countries has grown from 50 percent in 1985 to 66 percent now, and is expected to increase to 75 percent in the year 2000 and to 80–90 percent by 2010. Infection rates among adults in several large African capital cities and even in some rural areas are already 25 percent and are expected to climb to this level in other cities over the next ten years. Because every 10 percent increase in the infection rate increases annual mortality by at least 5 per thousand, previously high levels of adult mortality are tripling and quadrupling in these areas. Outside Africa, new infections appear to be rising most rapidly in Asia.

This human tragedy is imposing a potentially crippling burden on Africa's peoples, economies, and already inadequate health care systems. It is a human and economic disaster of staggering dimensions. Infections strike adults in the prime of life, plus up to one-third of all children born to infected mothers. By 1992, the total number of infected children in Africa alone is expected to reach 1 million, and many more will become orphans. In contrast to malaria and other causes of excess adult mortality in developing countries, AIDS does not spare the elite. In some African cities, relatively well-educated and more productive workers are infected in disproportionately large numbers (Box figure 3.5). The epidemic is therefore likely to have a detectable, and possibly substantial, effect on per capita income growth and welfare for years to come. Moreover, AIDS patients fortunate enough to be admitted to hospitals will occupy places thereby denied to others, many with conditions that would otherwise have been curable. They will require long hospital stays, expensive drugs, and the time of skilled staff. In some central African capitals, more than 50 percent of admissions to hospitals are now AIDS cases. The direct costs of treatment have also been estimated to be quite high, ranging from 78 to 932 percent of per capita GNP in Zaire and from 36 to 218 percent of per capita GNP in Tanzania, depending on the type of treatment used.

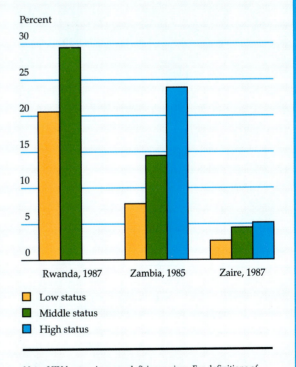

Box figure 3.5 HIV infection rate and socioeconomic status in selected urban samples, Sub-Saharan Africa

Percent

- Low status
- Middle status
- High status

Note: HIV, human immunodeficiency virus. For definitions of socioeconomic status and the samples used, see the Chapter 3 section on AIDS in the technical note at the end of the main text.
Sources: Bugingo and others 1987; Melbye, Nselesani, and Bayley 1986; Ndilu 1988.

Building technical capacity

Building and strengthening technical capacity—the ability of people to use new and existing technologies—is necessary for economic growth. A major technological change in the workplace in recent years is the use of computers, even in jobs usually regarded as requiring less skill. This has profound implications for education needs. It calls for learning primarily through symbols rather than visual observation, and for problem-solving in dynamic situations. To meet these needs, the government could play two roles: expand and improve the quality of primary and secondary education, and create incentives to increase the supply of and demand for more specialized technical training.

Many developing countries are expected to be able to achieve universal primary education by the year 2000. But making this expansion in enrollment worthwhile requires improvements in the quality of education. A large proportion of students who complete primary education in low-income countries fail to reach national or international standards of achievement in mathematics, science, and reading. Industrial countries too must continually improve and update their educational systems as rapid changes in technology make failures to learn more costly. The perceived decline in the competitiveness of U.S. industry has been attributed to a decline in the quality of the technical preparation of students relative to other industrial countries. A 1986 survey of adults aged 21–25 found that 20 percent had not achieved an eighth-grade reading level, whereas many job manuals require tenth- to twelfth-grade skills. And although only 1 percent were unable to perform simple arithmetic operations, 35 percent were not able to answer questions involving simple quantitative problem-solving.

Beyond the basics, what is the right educational base for rapid economic growth? In lower-middle-income developing countries where workers already are assembling electronic devices for international markets, skill needs will change quickly as trade and employment patterns shift and technology advances. Managerial and advanced technical skills will be crucial for exploiting new opportunities and technologies. The newly industrialized, export-oriented countries will have different needs—in particular, indigenous technological innovation to maintain their competitiveness. This will require investing in research and development, but it will also depend on achieving even higher standards of general education. There may be a conflict between the goals of greater breadth in the education of scientists and technologists and of specialization in certain fields of study. In particular, where the number of scientists and technicians is small, specialization may be premature. Science research is also important in the long term, but it must be tied closely to production on the shop floor if it is to have a significant and immediate effect on productivity.

Estimates of the social returns from investing in education indicate that the strongest case for public support of education is at the primary level in low-income countries—this meets the goal of promoting equity as well as that of raising productivity. These results do not mean that investments in higher education are unimportant. Educated, well-trained people can provide the leadership needed in agriculture, the emerging industrial sector, and government. The public cost of such investments may be too high, however, especially when it drains resources from primary education and other basic social services, for which government support is essential. Governments will need to be more selective in choosing which level of education or training to improve, which costs to meet (for example, academic materials rather than boarding expenses), and whom to subsidize.

Reducing poverty

More than 1 billion people in the developing world today live in poverty. *World Development Report 1990* concluded that this number could be reduced by a strategy of both labor-intensive economic growth and efficient social spending. Economic growth is necessary to reduce poverty, but experience shows that it is insufficient. Social expenditures on health care and schooling expand opportunities for the poor, but again may not be enough. Even in countries where basic social welfare indicators have improved, segments of the population remain relatively underserved. In Brazil, more than 10 percent of infants born in the northeastern region do not reach their first birthday, a higher infant mortality rate than that in many African and Asian countries. In Peru, the infant mortality rate in the Andean provinces is five times or more the rate in Lima. And the health problems of the female population are exceptionally acute in Bangladesh, Bhutan, Nepal, and Pakistan. The life expectancy at birth of girls in these countries is lower than that of boys; in other low-income countries, women live longer than men. These countries are different because families spend more on their sons than on their daughters.

Safety nets are needed to protect the most vulnerable groups: the unemployed, the disabled, the aged, and (often) women, who all lack access to public programs that are tied to employment; and the poor, who suffer most when times are hard. Guaranteeing food security through food-price subsidies, food rations, or food supplementation schemes meets basic needs, provided the measures are well targeted. Carefully targeted income-support programs for the elderly or the infirm provide safety nets for people who are otherwise hard to reach. Public employment programs, such as those used in South Asian countries, build and maintain infrastructure that could benefit the poor while cushioning their incomes during spells of unemployment.

Public policy

The queen of Travancore in what is now the state of Kerala, India, announced in 1817 that "the State shall defray the entire cost of the education of its people in order that there may be no backwardness in the spread of enlightenment among them, that by diffusion of education they become better subjects and public servants." Most governments would agree that public policy must play the leading role not just in education, but in social services generally. Not only the quantity but also the quality of public expenditure is important. How successful has public policy been in these areas during recent decades?

The correlations of income growth and government spending with social indicators were assessed for this Report using cross-country, time-series data. The limitations of the quality of data and aggregative analysis were fully recognized. With these caveats, it was found that for industrial countries, income growth, not government spending, explains improvements in infant survival and secondary enrollment. This is unsurprising. These countries had already achieved high levels in these two indicators by 1960; changes in their social spending since then have been geared to other objectives. The results for developing countries, however, were mixed. According to one model, a 10 percent increase in health spending reduces infant mortality by 0.8 percent, and a 10-percent increase in income decreases infant mortality by 1.1 percent. Using a different model, only the income effect remains statistically significant. A 10 percent increase in private income is associated with a fall of 0.5 percent infant mortality. Similarly mixed results were found for secondary school enrollment (see the Chapter 3 section on public spending in the technical note at the end of the main text).

In countries with high infant mortality, an additional dollar of public health spending per capita would be associated with a decrease in infant mortality rate of 16 per thousand, if the government expenditure were twice as efficient. Note that, in these countries, average health spending per capita is very much lower than the average for countries with low mortality (about $1 per capita compared with about $20). Thus, a large percentage increase translates into a modest increase in money terms—but with substantial effects on mortality.

Many well-designed and well-targeted programs have worked—and not necessarily with a heavy drain on public resources. In the health sector, the eradication of malnutrition and greater availability of health facilities reduced mortality rates. Chile's infant mortality dropped from 120 per thousand in the 1960s to 19 in 1989, and the percentage share of malnourished children declined from 37 to 7.5 percent. Nutritional programs for children and pregnant women as well as an improvement in the country's basic health infrastructure contributed to this steady progress. China reduced infant mortality significantly from an estimated 265 per thousand in 1950 to 44 in 1981 (Ahmad and Wang 1991), a decline attributable to a broad, publicly financed disease-prevention strategy, coupled with accessible and affordable primary care as well as income growth. Lower mortality rates in Kerala than in the equally densely populated state of West Bengal in India could not be explained by the difference in their per capita incomes, income and asset distributions, and extent of industrialization or urbanization. They do seem to be attributable to the wider distribution and greater utilization of health facilities in rural areas of Kerala. Another study found that 73 percent of the decline in infant mortality in Costa Rica during the period 1972–80 could be explained by the greater availability of primary care facilities (rural and community health programs and vaccination campaigns) and secondary care (such as clinics), after controlling for income growth.

Similarly, in education, a labor retraining program in Mexico in the 1980s was successful in upgrading the skills of tens of thousands of workers, increasing productivity and alleviating poverty among them. In Peru's push to expand primary enrollment since the 1950s, government programs played a key role by building more schools in rural areas and by increasing the supply of textbooks. This narrowed the gap in access to schools between rural and urban residents.

Where more public spending is warranted, it

needs to be better targeted. Government spending is not always efficient or equitable. Many countries spend a disproportionate share of their education budgets on higher education; students from upper-income groups benefit most. In Chile, Costa Rica, the Dominican Republic, and Uruguay, the top income quintile has received more than half the higher education subsidies, the bottom quintile less than one-tenth. In Bangladesh, India, Nepal, and Papua New Guinea, the best-educated 10 percent have received more than half of what the government has spent on education; in Bangladesh, the worst case, the top 10 percent get 72 percent of the education budget.

In health, an emphasis on expensive hospital and other kinds of elaborate curative care instead of inexpensive, preventive care means that basic health indicators show a smaller improvement. Public spending for hospital care is high in Brazil, at 78 percent of total health expenditures in 1986, compared with spending for immunization, prenatal care, and control of communicable diseases. Côte d'Ivoire's infant mortality rate is higher than that of other countries in the region with similar or lower income levels and smaller health budgets. This has also been attributed to its emphasis on hospital care, which draws resources away from rural primary care facilities that are understaffed, lack essential inputs, and often run without supervision.

The evidence also shows that many programs have been ineffective. Despite the remarkable rise in primary school enrollment, a large proportion of pupils have failed to achieve functional literacy and numeracy. This is frequently attributed to poor teacher preparation and shortages of learning materials. An Indonesian study found that the average primary school teacher had mastered only 45 percent of the subject matter in science subjects, and that most textbooks were out of date. Public health facilities in some countries are underused, even in areas with high mortality and morbidity. The decline in outpatient attendance in Ghana has been blamed on the shortage of essential drugs and other medical supplies, and on poor staff morale caused by falling real wages. Capital investments in the social sectors are often rendered ineffective by a failure to provide for current spending on essential inputs. Governments often seem unable to set standards, monitor quality, and target programs accurately.

Providing resources

Social programs have come under severe financial pressure in the past decade. Regional averages conceal this; they show a rising, or at least constant, share of education and health expenditures to GDP during the period 1975–85 (Table 3.3). But in about half of the countries for which data are available, public expenditures for education and health as a percentage of GDP fell between 1980 and 1985. In the fewer countries that have more recent expenditure data, the decline was even larger after 1985. In many cases this will have meant a falling standard of provision—but not always. For example, spending on health was cut in Chile during the country's difficult macroeconomic adjustment, but real per capita resources for primary health care and nutrition increased.

Table 3.3 Government expenditures for education and health as a percentage of GDP, 1975, 1980, and 1985

Region or group	Education			Number of countries with declining expenditures, 1980–85[a]		Health			Number of countries with declining expenditures, 1980–85[a]	
	1975	1980	1985			1975	1980	1985		
Industrial countries	6.0	5.9	5.5	12	(21)	3.3	3.4	4.0	8	(18)
Central and West Asia	3.9	4.1	4.4	4	(13)	1.1	1.1	1.4	5	(8)
South Asia	2.0	2.4	3.1	0	(4)	0.7	0.8	0.7	2	(4)
East Asia	2.8	2.9	3.1	0	(9)	0.9	0.9	1.0	2	(6)
North Africa	6.0	5.7	6.9	1	(5)	1.5	1.5	1.4	2	(3)
Sub-Saharan Africa	4.2	4.6	5.0	13	(23)	1.1	1.3	1.2	6	(10)
Latin America and the Caribbean	4.2	4.6	4.4	13	(24)	1.7	2.3	2.2	5	(13)
Eastern Europe	4.9	4.8	4.7	4	(7)	..	0.9	1.1	1	(2)
Total				47	(106)				31	(64)

Note: The numbers of countries with data for 1975, 1980, and 1985 are in parentheses. For purposes of comparability across countries, data are taken only from consolidated budget accounts; countries that report only budgetary central government expenditure are not included. Government social spending before 1975 is reported by a much smaller number of countries and is therefore not shown.
a. Number of countries in which public education (health) expenditures as a percentage of GDP declined between 1980 and 1985.
Sources: IMF data; Unesco data.

It often makes sense to shelter some social programs from short-term economic pressures for the sake of long-term investments in social welfare. But the state's role need not be limited to financing and provision. By setting and enforcing standards of provision, and by otherwise influencing the private sector, it can widen its role even in the face of tight budgets. For some publicly provided services, it may be appropriate to charge users. Other services can often be provided by the private sector, though governments will need to establish safety nets for the poor. Such measures will conserve scarce public funds and promote efficiency at the same time.

ALTERNATIVE FINANCING SCHEMES. Most developing countries already have a fee-for-service private health care system; introducing elements of cost recovery into the public health system therefore ought to be feasible. The government's share in total spending in the social sectors has been substantial, especially in education, but households have also borne part of the cost (Table 3.4). In the Republic of Korea, for instance, spending on public health as a proportion of GDP has been rising, but the role of the government is still small compared with the private sector's. The government concentrates on preventive care for rural residents and the poor. User charges have risen as insurance coverage broadened and firms increased the subsidy for their employees' health care. Since 1980, Zimbabwe has made impressive progress in health care, especially in rural areas, through increases in public spending and a broadening base of finance. By source of funds, the private sector covered 35 percent of costs in 1988 (50 percent in 1985, according to United Nations data); this includes costs met from private insurance, industry, and out-of-pocket spending. The diversity of providers of services and sources of funding has increased the ability of the government to maintain services despite economic pressure (Box 3.6).

Many other financing options besides fee-for-service are available. Health insurance systems can play a useful role. Although broad insurance coverage may not be currently attainable in most developing countries, limited health insurance is feasible. Brazil, Korea, and Mexico demonstrate that the coverage of health insurance can be gradually expanded—in Brazil and Mexico, from a third or less of the population to nearly 100 percent in 15–20 years; in Korea, from less than a tenth of the population in 1977 to 47 percent in 1986. Many other developing countries are experimenting with private health insurance plans as a way to meet

Table 3.4 The government share in total education and health expenditures
(percent)

Country and year	Education	Health
Low-income countries		
Tanzania, 1975	..	57.0
India, 1980	45.4	20.2
Ghana, 1975	..	60.2
Sri Lanka, 1988	73.1	44.5
Sudan, 1980	..	17.2
Sierra Leone, 1985	..	40.5
Average	..	39.9
Middle-income countries		
Zimbabwe, 1985	69.0	50.2
Honduras, 1985	..	21.2
Thailand, 1988	..	13.6
Ecuador, 1985	..	24.1
Colombia, 1985	73.0	20.3
Peru, 1985	..	27.4
Jordan, 1985	57.5	27.0
Fiji, 1985	..	67.4
Malta, 1988	94.1	60.3
Venezuela, 1980	..	44.4
Korea, Rep. of, 1988	..	4.2
Greece, 1985	88.0	44.6
Iran, Islamic Rep. of, 1975	..	43.3
Average	..	34.5
Average for sixteen high-income countries, mid-1980s[a]	88.5	58.2

Note: Countries were selected on the basis of data availability. Data are for 1975 or the latest year available.
a. Presented for purposes of comparison.
Source: United Nations 1990b.

future demands for health care, especially expensive curative care. There are concerns, however, about equity (because these plans generally start in the formal employment sector) and the risk that costs will rise too quickly (because consumers and health care providers lack incentives to economize).

In education, several countries have encouraged community participation and parental support at the primary level. Korea's experience in promoting primary education in the 1950s shows that this need not create inequities. Students and parents covered 71 percent of the costs of constructing and operating schools, learning materials, and transportation, and the central and local governments financed teacher salaries and the remaining expenses. Later, when the central government financed a larger share, local sources continued to provide about one-fourth of the cost of local education. Zimbabwe's success in expanding education in the 1980s was built on a strong partnership between the public and private sectors. Government schools were built by local groups and par-

Box 3.6 The role of international aid in the social sectors

In the 1980s, the share of education and health in bilateral aid to developing countries fell from 18 percent to 16.3 percent, and in multilateral aid from 14 percent in 1985 to 12 percent in 1988. Nearly 10 percent of bilateral aid and 5 percent of multilateral aid were allocated to education, which represented an average annual funding of $4.3 billion. Five to 6 percent of bilateral aid and 8 to 9 percent of multilateral aid was spent on health and population programs, with an average annual flow of $2.7 billion (Box table 3.6).

Evidence suggests that aid has not been allocated to priority areas. More than 95 percent of education assistance was targeted to the secondary and higher levels of education, rather than to the primary level. Moreover, the bulk of aid given to primary education was not allocated to increasing the supply of critical resources for learning, such as teaching materials and teacher training, which have been found to be the most cost-effective. In low-income countries, quantitative expansion has been the focus; buildings, furniture, and equipment accounted for 57.8 percent of all aid. Only 1.5 percent of total aid is given for primary health care, and only 1.3 for population assistance.

Box table 3.6 International aid for the social sectors, 1980–88
(percent)

Source and type of aid	1980–81[a]	1983–84	1985–86	1987	1988
Bilateral[b]					
Education	12.7	11.9	10.9	10.6	11.0
Health and population	5.5	5.1	5.3	5.2	5.3
Total	18.2	17.0	16.2	15.8	16.3
Multilateral[c]					
Education	..	..	5.0	4.3	4.3
Health and population	..	..	8.9	7.8	7.8
Total	..	..	13.9	12.1	12.1

a. Data not available for 1982.
b. Bilateral aid, which accounts for about three-fourths of total aid for the period 1980–88, includes aid from member countries of the Development Assistance Committee of the OECD: Australia, Austria, Belgium, Canada, Denmark, Finland, France, Germany, Ireland, Italy, Japan, Netherlands, New Zealand, Norway, Sweden, Switzerland, United Kingdom, and United States.
c. Multilateral aid includes aid from international organizations such as the European Community, the World Bank, and various other U.N. agencies.
Source: OECD 1980 through 1989.

---

ents' associations; the government paid for maintenance and repair, staff salaries, instructional materials, and operational expenses. Other schools were established and maintained by nongovernmental or local government organizations: the central government paid a grant for each enrolled student and covered up to one-fourth of the total costs of building.

NONGOVERNMENTAL PROVISION OF SOCIAL SERVICES. It is always important to ask whether governments have the capacity to implement their social programs. In some cases, large and complex programs could overextend the government's planning and administrative resources. Relying for some services on nongovernmental organizations, both nonprofit and for-profit, helps to broaden access to adequate schooling and health care. Private, nonprofit providers tend to be smaller and more flexible in their planning and budgeting; the government, constrained by civil service laws and employees' unions, is less able to change ineffective programs. Allowing private organizations to provide services under controversial programs—such as family planning in some Latin American countries—enables the government to keep its distance while still ensuring that services are available.

Cooperation between the public and private sectors may be particularly appropriate if nongovernmental providers are experienced and efficient and if the government has been unable to expand rapidly enough to satisfy demand. In Rwanda, religious missions, which have traditionally provided most health care services, are reimbursed by the government for 86 percent of staff salaries; these missions continue to provide 40 percent of health services. The governments of Zambia and Zimbabwe also cover a substantial part of mission expenditures on health services. As with other goods and services, competition among for-profit providers in the social sectors is important to ensure efficiency in the delivery of services. Any public subsidies to the for-profit sector (whether in the form of tax breaks or import subsidies) are best linked to the quality of services provided.

Past increases in literacy, numeracy, and technical skills have been achieved not only through formal schooling, but also in many other ways. These range from village literacy projects to national campaigns, from agricultural extension services to firm-based training and technical assistance. All these lend themselves well to community support and private sector provision. There are lessons here for building technical capacity in the future. Japan and Germany developed successful training systems, voluntarily provided by firms that recognize training on the job to be particularly important when the pace of technical change is rapid. In several developing countries, private firms also played an active role, but the incentives to provide job training were shaped by policy. In Brazil, firms that develop their own in-service training are entitled to deductions from a payroll tax; this program has been used to develop and run a national system of youth apprenticeships since the late 1950s. It is said that the program has enabled Brazil to meet the needs of firms and national goals for training, as well. In Nigeria, a 1 percent payroll tax levied in 1971 was also meant to encourage more employer-sponsored training. Firm-sponsored training programs, however, were slow in coming. The tax program has now become a financing mechanism for establishing vocational training centers.

THE ROLE OF THE POLICY CLIMATE. Human development does not depend solely on the policies of education and health ministries. Other enabling policies are also important. Expanding work opportunities for women and providing day care services for mothers create incentives for women to stay in school longer. Family planning programs have been most successful in countries that have seen improvements in the education and work opportunities of women. Clean water and improved waste disposal are important for controlling the spread of communicable diseases. Environmental regulations limiting air pollution and the disposal of toxic chemicals have long-run health benefits.

Finally, economic growth is crucial. Countries with high growth rates between 1975 and 1985 have infant mortality rates that are 15 percent lower than countries that had an average annual growth rate lower than 5 percent. The overall stance of policy also influences the productivity of social investments. The performance of World Bank investment projects in the social sectors is associated not only with the project design and institutional arrangements, but also with the overall economic policy framework. Policies that encourage innovation and investment and that increase the demand for workers who are better educated and better trained provide the crucial conditions for development. In India, returns on investments in schooling were higher in areas that were able to adopt the modern high-yielding grain varieties of the green revolution, and investments in schooling in those areas also increased. In the United States, firms with newer physical capital, especially in the high technology industries, hired more educated workers and also spent more on in-house training.

Deteriorating macroeconomic conditions (high inflation and interest rates that discourage investments) and restrictive labor market policies discourage innovation and entrepreneurship (see Chapter 4). East European countries generally have higher education levels than countries with similar levels of income. The region's rigid labor markets and restricted wage differentials have, however, led labor to be allocated inefficiently and investments in skills to be wasted. The established systems for training and education cannot respond to the new demands. In Hungary, apprenticeship training provides narrow occupational training in obsolete skills; people trained in management, commerce, and high technology industrial skills appear to be in short supply.

Greater mobility in the domestic labor market, by increasing the rate of return for the most highly educated and trained technicians and scientists, promotes efficient transfers of technology and skills and reduces the "brain drain." Laws that restricted labor mobility in pre-reform China and the Soviet Union are still in place. Radical market-oriented reforms are urgently needed in both countries. Employers need greater control of salary scales, promotion policies, and hiring and firing. If China's new labor contract system, established in 1986, were extended to permanent workers, it could transform labor relations and productivity. Labor exchanges have placed more than 6 million workers in new enterprises in China since 1988; this will improve labor mobility and lead to better allocation of investments in skills. A national social security system that does not tie workers to a specific place of employment will further encourage mobility.

Investing in people

Development requires a careful balancing of the roles of the government and the private sector across a broad range of policies. In social spending, there are large, and largely unexploited, opportunities for a more successful partnership between public and private providers. But in this area, more than in any other except macroeconomic policy, the state usually is cast in the leading role. Governments need to make a clear commitment to this task, and put it among their highest priorities. The evidence shows that investing heavily in people makes sense not just in human terms, but also in hard-headed economic terms.

The climate for enterprise

Sustained growth requires more than a high rate of capital formation. It requires using that capital productively, which in turn requires the right market incentives, the right institutions, and the right supportive investments—three key ingredients of productivity.

Above all, appropriate market incentives are necessary. Getting price signals right, and creating a climate which allows businesses to respond to them, can raise the rate of return on investments by half—even double it, where distortions had been particularly large (as indicated by the statistical analysis later in this chapter). That difference in the productivity of investments can make a difference of 1 to 2 percentage points in the annual growth rate of GNP per capita. It can help to transform a stagnating economy into a vigorously expanding one.

But market incentives are not enough on their own. If farms and firms are to respond to appropriate signals, they need access to information and markets, and the ability to transact at acceptable costs. Often these conditions are not met, sometimes because of misguided government interventions. But inappropriate interventions are not always the culprit; the absence of public institutions and investments frequently prepetuates market failure. Markets for goods, inputs, labor, and capital need to be better integrated; from the farm to the town, from the city to the market abroad. And information is often poorly transmitted, even when there is appropriate pricing. Entrepreneurs need access to appropriate infrastructure and to research and extension services; these foster the integration of markets and help to spread new technology. Businesses also need a legal and con-

tractual framework for their activities—one that protects property rights, facilitates transactions, allows competitive market forces to determine prices and wages, and lets firms enter and exit.

The public sector can play a crucial role in lowering the transaction costs to farms and firms by supporting them with investments and institutions. When this happens, the economic rate of return of projects is higher. Public investments and institutions are needed to foster competition. To that end, there is also scope for promoting more private sector provision of goods and services that are usually publicly provided: power and telecommunications, small-scale and rural credit, research and development, and agricultural extension. Good government policies, institutions, and investments are vital. But the key to rapid development is the entrepreneur. Governments need to serve enterprise, large and small, not supplant it.

Entrepreneurs unleashed

Irene Dufu, a Ghanaian nurse turned business woman, shows what access to resources in a more and more competitive economy can do to spark the entrepreneurial spirit. She registered her fishing company—Cactus Enterprise Ltd.—in Tema, Ghana, in 1978, having started operations informally two years earlier. She began with a small wooden vessel and a crew of twelve. Today she employs sixty-five fishermen on three boats. Her turnover in 1989 was more than $1.2 million.

What was Mrs. Dufu's route to success? While serving as a nursing officer at the Accra military hospital, she was approached by a group of artisan fishermen from a village where her father had served as regent. These fishermen were seeking a loan to buy new canoes. They were illiterate and lacked collateral, so the banks had turned them down. Mrs. Dufu received a loan on their behalf, using her house as security. The fishermen repaid it in six months. This started Mrs. Dufu thinking about a career switch. Salaries in the army and public enterprises were not keeping pace with the rapidly rising cost of living, and she had three children to educate. Many successful trading businesses and bus transport companies in Ghana are owned by women. Why not go into fishing and marketing on her own? With an end-of-service gratuity from the army, she bought a truck, which she then used as collateral for a loan to purchase a secondhand wooden fishing boat. Then she recruited a captain with a nose for tracking down shoal movements and a crew willing to spend weeks at sea.

She found she could compete with the state-owned fishing company, selling cheaper yet still enjoying good margins. She then bought and repaired an inexpensive tuna ship which allowed her to break into the market for canned tuna, supplying a U.S. company. Since the liberalization of Ghana's foreign exchange market in 1987, Mrs. Dufu has been able to keep a foreign exchange account, making it easier to raise the money to buy and repair the two secondhand vessels. Refitting the engine in one boat will need to wait, however. Ghanaian banks give priority to government borrowing: only 10 percent of overall credit was allocated to the private sector in 1989. Despite the credit constraints, Mrs. Dufu is contributing to Ghana's economic resurgence.

Yoon Soo Chu shows what a modest start, hard work, and several doses of learning-by-failing can do in an enabling policy and institutional environment. In 1977 Chu and his small team of engineers were given 15 square feet in the corner of an old lab in the electronics division of a conglomerate in the Republic of Korea. It seemed absurd that a tiny and spartan laboratory in Korea could challenge giant U.S. and Japanese corporations. But Chu also knew that his senior managers wanted to produce microwave ovens. Soon he had gathered the world's top oven models and was choosing the best parts of each for his prototype. After a year Chu was ready to test a prototype. He pushed the "on" button: the plastic in the cavity melted. So Chu spent many more eighty-hour weeks to come up with a new design. This time, the stir shaft melted. The Japanese and Americans were selling more than 4 million microwave ovens a year, and Chu did not have a working prototype.

By June 1978 he was ready with a new version. Nothing melted. Chu's managers at the conglomerate approved a makeshift production line. Soon three ovens a day were being produced. Four years later microwave production topped 200,000 units a year. By the late 1980s, production exceeded 1 million units. Among U.S. buyers nowadays, the odds are more than one in five that their microwave was designed by Mr. Chu and produced on that assembly line. The conglomerate's emphasis on quality control and its in-depth knowledge of the market account for this startling success. Chu and other engineers often travel abroad to understand design and marketing better. And as elsewhere in Korea, everybody works hard: eleven hours a day, twenty-seven days a month, managers and workers alike.

The Patels of Tanzania started Afro Cooling to manufacture car radiators. They bought the technology from an Indian firm that had been making radiators for twenty-five years and had adapted the technology to Indian needs. Production started in 1979 with the help of twelve expatriate experts—who had left by 1983. Afro Cooling's production increased steadily thereafter, when trade reforms began. The firm is efficient. It uses labor-intensive techniques and simple equipment, but it emphasizes strict quality control. Its managers and skilled workers have assimilated the technology of a labor-intensive engineering product, and adapted it. They marketed their products aggressively at home and overseas—even during times of economic decline and unhelpful economic policies. Despite the recent import liberalization, they continue to dominate the local market for radiators. They have diversified into industrial coolers and heat exchangers. They export nearly half of their production.

In varied settings and circumstances, Dufu, Chu, and Patel illustrate the power of entrepreneurship: the ability to seize new and often risky opportunities and to adapt, innovate, and expand. Countless other cases are less encouraging.

The Morogoro Shoe Company, a parastatal in Tanzania, started business in 1980 with World Bank financing. It was to be one of the largest shoe factories in the world, and to export more than 80 percent of its production. But the factory was badly designed and built; problems have plagued it from the beginning. Capacity use has averaged less than 4 percent. It has not exported a single pair of shoes. The company has had inadequate management, bad product design, and nonexistent quality control. It produces negative value added at world prices. It cost the economy half a million dollars a year in the mid-1980s to keep the firm in business—not counting the interest and principal on $40 million of capital costs.

The conditions for success and failure can be seen in these contrasting examples. Although they are only illustrative (and need to be complemented by the analysis given below), these cases are suggestive: success requires an appropriate set of signals to provide entrepreneurs with the incentives to embark on productive and profitable activities. Then entrepreneurs must be able to respond to these signals. For this, they need skills—which is why education is so important. But they also need access to information and markets; knowledge about appropriate technological choices and best practices; and access to credit, inputs, and outlets for their products.

Morogoro Shoe is not alone—anything but. It is possible to find ''value subtracting'' firms in all continents; they range from Polish shipyards to Chinese car plants. They can be found in the public as well as private sectors. For Morogoro Shoe, access to potential markets and investment finance was not a problem. But the other conditions for success were not met. Heavily restricted trade, a distorted pricing regime, and an overvalued exchange rate destroyed the incentive to export and hence to be competitive. The result is an extreme case, but not an uncommon one. As reviewed in Chapter 2, the aggregate cross-country evidence mirrors the lessons from these individual cases. Respectable levels of investment per se have not automatically ensured high GDP growth; investment also needs to be productive.

Enterprise in agriculture

A clear lesson of experience is that high productivity in agriculture is especially important for industrialization and growth—and is feasible. As industrialization gets under way, manufacturing firms depend heavily on rural demand for their products, on agricultural products as inputs for processing, and on agricultural exports to generate foreign exchange. An explicit push for industrialization at the expense of agriculture has often undermined agricultural incentives, largely via the indirect and direct taxation of the agricultural sector. This was often justified by mistakenly viewing agriculture as having low potential for productivity growth and technological progress, in contrast with industry. Coupled with agricultural export pessimism, these meant that the establishment of appropriate incentives and institutions in agriculture was neglected.

The effects of inappropriate exchange rate, trade, and pricing policies have been devastating for agriculture: market signals become so distorted that farmers receive only a fraction of the value (or border price) of the commodities they produce (often between 25 and 50 percent), while the inputs and goods they consume become scarcer and more expensive.

Policies outside agriculture—such as those affecting trade and industry—have often imposed a ''tax'' on the farmer and hampered agricultural growth at least as much as sector-specific price and

tax policies have done. Import restrictions and high tariffs to protect industry reduce the availability of agricultural inputs and increase their prices. They also push up the prices of urban-produced and of imported goods consumed in the rural areas. And an overvalued exchange rate, which reduces producer prices for agricultural exports, usually coexists with restrictive trade policies. Excessive government spending (often including subsidies to industry) further contributes to the currency overvaluation, imposes an inflation tax on rural incomes, and crowds out resources from agriculture. Worse still, direct agricultural policies, such as low producer prices (to channel subsidized food to urban consumers) often compound the negative incentives originating in nonagricultural sectors.

What does all this mean for the beleaguered farmer? A recent study of eighteen developing countries reveals the extent of the biases against agriculture and their adverse effects on agricultural performance. The largest agricultural losses—measured by the difference between the actual and the potential rate of agricultural growth—are found for the ''extreme discriminators'' in the sample: Côte d'Ivoire, Ghana, and Zambia. Government policies implicitly taxed the farmer by more than 50 percent, resulting in the lowering of their crop prices by more than half in twenty-five years. Ten other countries, classified ''representative discriminators,'' set an average implicit ''tax'' of more than 35 percent on agriculture. These, too, incurred large losses in agricultural value added. By contrast, agricultural losses were small or nonexistent for the countries that discriminated mildly or not at all: Brazil, Chile, the Republic of Korea, Malaysia, and Portugal.

An extensive empirical literature confirms that farmers respond very significantly to government policies: when the prospects for farm profits are good, they innovate, adapt technologies, improve existing practices, and increase production. But in assessing the farmer's response to policy conditions, all factors affecting farm profits need to be considered, not just pricing. And the effects of policies on individual crops need to be distinguished from their effects on aggregate agricultural output.

The crop-specific supply response to improved pricing incentives can be very large, even in the short term. For milk for instance, the response to better prices to farmers can be almost instantaneous: it can involve no more than changing the feed mix. For annual crops the response can be especially strong: Tanzania's cotton production doubled within a year when producer prices were substantially increased in 1986/87. Agricultural export crops can also react quickly to changes in prices and exchange rates very significantly in the short term, much like individual crops. Agricultural export response to incentives has in fact been estimated to be even higher than the response for all exports.

When policy conditions have been very bad, leaving factors of production substantially underutilized, even the aggregate agricultural supply response to improved prices can be impressive in the short term. In Ghana, before the reforms in the early 1980s, cocoa prices paid to farmers were so low that crops were left to rot; improved pricing resulted in large production increases that boosted overall agricultural output.

However, where excess capacity is not so large the aggregate supply response to reform, though positive, is often limited in the very short term—in contrast to the crop-specific response. Aggregate output can grow only if inefficiencies are reduced, more resources are devoted to agriculture, or technology changes. But it takes time to improve established practices, adopt new techniques, and to overcome constraints of labor, capital, and land. With time, laborers migrate, and also farmers can adjust the mix of crops, use additional factors of production, and improve techniques. Five to ten years after a one-time increase in agricultural prices, overall farm production can increase significantly—often by a percentage similar to, or even larger than, the price increase itself.

Implementing an integrated package of reforms in the exchange rate, agricultural pricing, and public expenditure policies can result in a substantial production response for the overall sector. When comparing the performance of Sub-Saharan African countries that implemented reforms with those that did not, a slight difference between the two groups began to emerge in the early 1980s, when the reforms were initiated. The differences between the two groups increased over time; by the late 1980s the agricultural growth rate was more than 2.5 percentage points higher for the reforming group—suggesting the responsiveness of Africa's agriculture to policy changes.

To strengthen and sustain the farmers' response to changed incentives, complementary institutions and investments are essential. Farmers require knowledge about improved practices to minimize waste and better utilize the resources at their disposal. They also need to learn about new technologies and to get access to markets, storage facilities, credit, and inputs. Further, farming is inherently a risky business because of weather, pests, disease, and volatility in input supplies and prices. Governments can help by providing research and extension services, secure land-tenure arrangements, better education, and physical infrastructure such as roads and irrigation.

These complementary factors are not fully independent of economic policies. Appropriate pricing promotes institutional change and investment, both public and private. When pricing is right and agroclimatic conditions are appropriate, farmers demand additional infrastructure, extension, and credit services; research institutions intensify efforts to develop and adapt varieties highly beneficial to farmers; and private traders and moneylenders proliferate. Some of the demand for these services is met by farmer groups themselves and by other private enterprises, and some by policymakers approving public programs where supply response is expected to be particularly high. But when the public sector plays a fuller complementary part and anticipates the demand for public services, the eventual supply response can be greater and can come sooner.

China's experience shows the power of the interaction between price incentives and a supportive institutional setting. Extensive crop-breeding work had been done since the 1950s; the number of extension-service stations increased from a few hundred to more than 17,000 in 1979. But output only accelerated after 1979, when prices were raised substantially and the "household responsibility system" was introduced. This gave households control over the land they occupied and let them keep their net income. Output growth accelerated from about 3 percent a year during the period 1965–80 to more than 6 percent during 1980–88.

Investing in research and extension

Agricultural research and extension have a substantial public good component: as a result, the government's role in their promotion has long been recognized. Research resulting in a new pattern of crop rotation, for instance, can be used by one farmer without reducing its availability to others (it is thus a "nonrival" or public good); it would also be difficult and costly for the private sector to exclude farmers that do not pay for such research from using the new information. It is therefore hard for private researchers to appropriate enough of the rewards to make their investment worthwhile. And once new techniques are developed and available, farmers need to be acquainted with the technologies, and shown how to get the most out of them. That is the role of extension services. Experience shows that both these forms of agricultural investment can pay.

RESEARCH. A combination of international and indigenous agricultural research is crucial for the development and adaptation of new techniques and varieties suitable to the crops and agroclimatic systems of the developing world. The returns on investing in research and development (R&D) in agriculture can be very high—often between 30 and 60 percent, according to many crop-specific studies. Examples include research on maize in Peru, rubber in Malaysia, and wheat in Chile and Pakistan. Such high returns suggest that too little is still being invested in these activities—despite the substantial increase in spending and scientific effort during the past thirty years.

Private R&D has grown in recent years, but it rarely exceeds 10 percent of national spending on agricultural research. This is not just because it is difficult to capture the returns. Governments often restrict and regulate private R&D. Pakistan, for instance, did not allow private companies to do research on plant breeding in the past. Restrictions on buying plant and animal germplasm, equipment, and scientific expertise from abroad have further hampered private efforts in some countries. India restricted imports of grandparent stock of commercial poultry to encourage local breeding and production of chicks; the Philippines, in contrast, encouraged technology transfers by private companies through tax incentives for R&D. As a result, feed-efficient hybrid poultry has been adopted more rapidly in the Philippines than in India.

In some applied areas, there are incentives to do private research when the results can be embodied in naturally protected or patented proprietary products. But private incentives are weak in basic biological and physical research, and in generic and applied research when results cannot be patented, or protected by intellectual property laws.

Innovative farmers, both wealthy and poor, experiment with new techniques and often allocate a small portion of their plot for informal trials of new technology. But they rarely conduct formal research because the farm is generally too small to capture more than a small share of the potential benefits from the farmers' own research. Even a private firm in the technology-supply industry (for example, a seed company) may be too small to appropriate a significant share of the benefits from its own research. It will rely instead on improved varieties from public research, whether domestically or internationally funded (Box 4.1).

Biotechnology research has barely begun in the developing countries. It promises to improve the tolerance of crops and animals to stresses and pests; increase the efficiency with which plants and livestock use nutrients; and relieve the present biological constraints on higher yields. Equally important, it may reduce the need for agrichemicals, which would be beneficial for the environment. Although the scope of the green revolution was limited (it focused on just a few crops, which responded to irrigation), the biorevolution

Box 4.1 A different sort of enterprise: Gurdev Khush breeds super rice at the International Rice Research Institute

In Asia rice is the main source of calories for 2.7 billion people. A crucial achievement of the green revolution has been to increase rice production in the past twenty-five years faster than Asia's population has grown. During this time, the real price of rice has been halved, and the disastrous famines predicted by so many people never happened. The first high-yielding variety of rice for the tropics, IR8, was made available in 1966 by the International Rice Research Institute, based in the Philippines. A cross between a dwarf Chinese rice and an Indonesian variety, IR8 changed the architecture of the rice plant. Improved varieties, such as IR36, have been developed since then, permitting up to three crops a year. It is now the most widely grown crop variety in the world. Gurdev Khush, IRRI's chief plant breeder and the creator of IR36, believes that existing techniques could be used to increase rice production by 25–30 percent during the next decade.

But to meet the growing demands for the next century, Khush and his colleagues is breeding a new super rice, capable of feeding many more mouths from less land. It will look very different from existing varieties: sturdier stems, dark green leaves, more vigorous roots, and genetic resistance to a multitude of diseases and insects. Farmers will be able to get a higher yield from seeding it directly, rather than by transplanting seedlings, which is what makes rice farming so laborious now. It is expected to produce 13–15 tons per hectare from each crop, compared with a maximum output of current varieties of 8–9 tons. Biotechnology may hold the key to developing this new variety.

Food production in Africa will have to grow by at least 4 percent a year from 1990 to 2020 to meet the growing demands of the region's people. In 1988 the World Bank launched an African Agricultural Services Initiative to improve agricultural performance by helping to develop and disseminate new technology, and by encouraging the better use of the technology that already exists—suited to the prevailing farming conditions. For instance, dissemination of a technology requiring extensive weeding would only be advocated in settings where labor constraints are not prevalent.

The initiative concentrates on establishing national T&V-type extension services, and on strengthening research, infrastructure, and supplies of credit and inputs. Improvement of economic policy is a vital component. The initiative provides resources, including the stationing of technical staff in nonexecutive positions in Africa. It differs from earlier programs because it encompasses all agricultural services and because the services provided will be managed by local staff, not expatriates. Accordingly, great emphasis is placed on training managers and on working with farmers. Further, the initiative envisages expanding the role of farmers' groups and of the private sector in the management and provision of extension and other support services.

can reach the entire rural population. Thus it holds promise for all continents.

It is possible, however, that as a result of biotechnological advances some commodities produced for export in developing countries may be displaced by new products from industrial countries and that very different patterns of agricultural production and trade may emerge. Yet the benefits of biotechnology research for the developing world may still outweigh the costs, particularly if domestic response to changing circumstances is flexible, and the new techniques developed in industrial countries are shared with developing countries. In low-income economies such as those in Africa, improved indigenous scientific education and agricultural training programs will be needed to help adapt and spread the new technologies. It will be some time, though, before new varieties to suit the developing countries are ready: up to five years for potato and rice (Box 4.1); five to ten years for banana, cassava, and coffee; and ten or more years for coconut, oil palm, and wheat.

EXTENSION. Publicly provided extension services can be successful. A review of almost fifty public sector extension programs in the developing world showed a significantly positive effect in most of them. But public programs have also failed. Success usually requires an appropriate set of complementary agricultural policies—not to mention having new technologies and better practices to extend. Often extension systems have failed to offer new techniques or have extended technologies without taking account of the specific agroclimatic and resource constraints facing different farm systems or areas—so, for instance, costly fertilizer and labor-saving technologies are extended in labor-abundant, low-yield areas.

Just as important for successful extension is the presence of a political, managerial, and budgetary commitment. Budgetary crises too often leave extension workers on the payroll but without funds for daily subsistence and fuel while on the road. The quality of rural infrastructure matters. So do the skills and experience of extension staff, who frequently know less than farmers about appropriate practices.

Farmer participation, particularly in program development and feedback, significantly improves the chances that an extension program will succeed. Interaction with farmers is part of the training and visit (T&V) approach to extension. This attempts to strike a balance between delivery (focusing on the professionalism of staff, who work full time on extension services under a single line of command) and feedback (through regular visits to the farmers, with the extension worker spending a large part of the day in the farmer's field). Success has not been universal, in part because the farmer's feedback has been insufficiently emphasized, yet the T&V system appears to have raised production in a variety of settings. In some African countries, T&V, though not without its problems, has brought better management and discipline where once there was duplication of effort and lack of direction. External agencies such as the World Bank have become more and more committed to the support of this structured approach (Box 4.2).

The private sector is too little used as an avenue for providing extension services. The experiences of coffee growers in Colombia and cattle ranchers in Argentina show that in commercial agriculture regional or crop-specific associations can function effectively, spreading the costs and benefits of extension among their members. In Kenya, veterinary services are provided through a mixture of public and private farmer support. Traders, seed suppliers, and agroprocessors often provide extension services. In Thailand, a diversified commercial agricultural enterprise improved the quality and quantity of the crops it procured for processing by establishing its own extension services to farmers. It began by recruiting extension agents from the graduates of agricultural extension schools. After this approach failed, the company hired farmers instead, who were paid to provide part-time extension to other farmers. The program is now successful. A large food-product multinational has set up its own extension service in Costa Rica; this has successfully disseminated better techniques for growing pineapples. Such examples illustrate that, as restrictions on private initiative in trading, marketing, and production are removed, and as the commercialization of agriculture widens, the private sector can play a larger role in extension services.

Credit and marketing

The private sector can also be a provider of agricultural credit.

Banco del Desarrollo in Santiago, Chile, is a hybrid between a profit-oriented credit union and a church-supported nongovernmental organization (NGO). It traditionally offers consumer and small-scale manufacturing and agricultural credit to low-income families. Since late 1989, microenterprise credits, averaging $50 each, have been offered on a pilot basis for food production, textiles, and services. The interest rates are based on the cost of funds. The recipients of these credits are normally considered uncreditworthy, but Banco del Desarrollo gets around this by lending to members of a group of four or five borrowers who unconditionally guarantee each other's promissory notes. The group thus provides implicit appraisal and supervision. After one year of operations, only 3.5 percent of loans were nonperforming.

Banco del Desarrollo is not the only institution to combine credit to the poor with financial discipline. Before it was nationalized in 1969, the Syndicate Bank in India was a pioneer in lending to very small operators, such as roadside sellers of vegetables. Nowadays Grameen Bank in Bangladesh, ADEMI in the Dominican Republic, and BKK and Kupedes in Indonesia are successfully reaching farmers and other small-scale operators while maintaining financial viability. But such institutions are rare.

Formal banking institutions usually require collateral, such as equipment, land, or even livestock. But because poor households usually lack such assets, they generally have no access to formal credit. The cost of informal credit from moneylenders can be high; real interest rates often exceed 80 percent. Loans are scarce or expensive when lenders lack information about borrowers and face difficulties in enforcing repayment. Gathering information on borrowers can be costly. In rural Pakistan moneylenders devote an average of one day per applicant to obtaining information, and reject one applicant in two.

Informal finance for the poor farmer can also come from a range of other sources: family, friends, traders, and loan associations. Rotating fund associations are common in rural areas; they are a main source of credit in Asia and Africa, where powerful social sanctions, including rejection by the community, help to enforce repayment. In northern Nigeria and in many areas of China, there are active loan markets that do not require collateral. Information and enforcement rely on kinship and village sanctions. But because lenders operate within a limited geographical area and the demand for credit is seasonal, such arrangements can break down. Local credit markets collapsed in Thailand during a regional drought.

These private credit institutions are evidently partial and imperfect. This may justify intervention: the government, it is argued, can overcome market failure because it has the power to enforce repayment. This may be so in principle, but rarely in practice. Governments often find it politically impossible to enforce lending terms. In India, politicians compete with each other by promising, if elected, to have such debts forgiven. And there have been many other problems. Governments have proved far less skillful in collecting and assessing information than lenders who know the community well. Cheap public credit in rural areas has largely failed to reach poor farmers. Public credit programs have often run into financial difficulties early on; frequently they have collapsed or become a drain on the government budget.

What then is the role for public policy? To begin with, a stable macroeconomy and a nondistorting regulatory framework are preconditions for developing the financial sector. The emergence of an independent, solvent, and competitive banking sector, which is free to set market-clearing interest rates, and not unduly influenced by pressures to lend from the public sector or politicians, improves the mobilization and allocation of credit. It can often improve allocation by shifting resources from some large, unproductive state-owned enterprises to efficient private activities, including farms.

But even a healthy financial sector will not always ensure an adequate supply of credit to the small farmer. To increase the supply, governments can foster the development of credit institutions and markets. For instance, modifications to the law of contract can make it easier for traders to extend credit, by allowing them to deduct repayments from the value of the crop. Improving the security of land tenure creates collateral in some settings. Public spending on rural infrastructure promotes competition in credit (and other) markets. Improving the literacy and numeracy of the poor makes them more creditworthy.

This illustrates an important point: an efficient intervention in one market often helps another market to work better as well. Policy toward risk in agriculture is another example. Public crop-insurance and price-stabilization programs have not been very effective in reducing risks or reaching the poor, and have proven costly. A better way for the government to lessen the risks faced by farmers is to let markets work and to facilitate the emergence of private programs, both domestically and externally, such as improving access to international commodity futures markets for private traders, millers, and farm associations. Equally important in order to lower risk is to invest in infrastructure, including public utilities, storage facilities and irrigation. In India, for instance, erratic electricity supplies for irrigation have often hurt farm productivity. If the public sector's electricity producers could be made more efficient, one source of risk for farmers would be removed.

Access to wider markets is essential if farmers are to adopt new technology and raise their productivity. Government has a role here, too. Infrastructure is again critical, as is a policy and regulatory environment that allows the private sector to flourish. But as in the case of credit and insurance, direct public involvement has often failed in marketing. State monopolies in agriculture have often paid farmers too little and too late, in order to finance their own inefficient operations and subsidize urban consumers. The consequences for the government's budget, for farmers' incomes, and for agricultural production have often been disastrous (Box 4.3).

Empowering the manufacturer

In coping with their economic environment, industrial firms have many advantages over farms. They tend to be larger, fewer in number, and less dispersed, so their transactions costs are not so great. They are less subject to uncontrollable risks, such as the weather. And they often have more assets, making credit easier to get. All this means that firms are better placed than farms to embark on investments in information and technology and to reap their benefits. In other ways, however, factories and farms have much in common. Factories also need infrastructure (roads, ports, water, and electricity). Very small enterprises may find it difficult to borrow. Above all, firms are just as vulnerable to harmful regulatory policies.

In 1978, a major expansion of India's Sindri Fertilizer Company was designed to produce 2,000 tons of ammonia and urea a day. Regulations required the firm to buy a high proportion of locally made equipment for the new complex, including turbo-compressors never previously manufactured domestically. The equipment did not work and had to be rebuilt; then it kept breaking down. Utility companies with exclusive licenses for local distribution could not provide reliable supplies of electricity. When problems with the railway system reduced the plant's petroleum supplies, the government refused to authorize fuel imports to meet its requirements. Converting to other fuels more than doubled production costs. Union pressures led to chronic overstaffing. Of the plant's 8,000 workers, only 4,400 were directly productive. In its first eighteen months, the new facility operated at 33 percent of capacity for eight and was closed for ten. Its rate of return was negative.

In contrast, a competitive domestic environment allowed Tomás Gómez in Chile to thrive. He started a very small business in the late 1970s, producing leather shoes in two rooms in Santiago. Competition in the domestic industry was fierce, so the company had to be efficient to survive; but an overvalued exchange rate and high tariffs on competing imports discouraged exports. Following the external trade liberalization of the early 1980s, potential importers visited Chile and placed orders with the company. Mr. Gómez devoted 20 percent of his production to exports. Today he exports 80 percent of his production, worth $2.5 million a year, or almost one-tenth of the country's exports of shoes. He employs 350 workers in a large and modern factory.

Industrial regulation

A good rationale exists for various industrial regulations. Rules on health standards, environmental

Box 4.3 Parastatal marketing institutions and producer prices: impairing competition and incentives to farmers

State enterprises in agriculture were created in many countries during colonial times to regulate small growers and protect European farmers against competition. They have expanded over the past three decades and now monopolize many markets for agricultural inputs, outputs, services, and trade. Agricultural prices are commonly set either by the parastatals themselves or by legislation much below their international levels. Often one price is set throughout the country and throughout the year. Maintaining the same prices year round, irrespective of the proximity of the harvest or the state of stocks, discourages the private sector from holding supplies in reserve and building private storage facilities. Year-round uniform pricing encourages consumption and discourages production off-season, when the full cost of providing the product (growing it plus storing it for a long period) is highest. And when producers are paid the same price throughout the country, production close to consumption or shipment centers is usually discouraged.

Agricultural marketing institutions have also been plagued by corruption: funds are "lost" and supplies "leak" to the parallel market. Poor forecasting of crops, excessive accumulation of stocks, and selling at the wrong times have often destabilized the very markets the institutions are intended to stabilize. And political constraints have led to overstaffing and waste.

All these defects have made the agricultural parastatals a heavy drain on public sector finances (Box table 4.3).

Box table 4.3 Losses from the marketing of parastatal agricultural products, selected countries and periods

Country and period	Products	Transfers as percentage of current government expenditure	Transfers and credit as percentage of GNP
China, 1988	Grains	10.5	2.0
India, 1984–85	Grains	4.6	0.5
Gambia, 1982–87	Groundnuts	10.8	2.8
Mali, 1982–85	Grains	8.8	1.3
Mexico, 1982–85	Milk, grains, oilseeds	3.5	..
Tanzania, 1980–81	All crops	12.4	1.7
Zambia, 1980–86	Maize, fertilizer, cotton	4.0	3.2
Zimbabwe, 1983–87	All crops	5.6	4.6

Source: Knudsen and others 1991.

protection, worker safety, as well as rules to protect consumers and producers from restrictive or monopolistic practices, are part of the legal and institutional framework that any economy needs. All too often, however, governments in developing countries have failed to provide or enforce such rules. Instead, they have regulated purely economic aspects of firms' behavior, hampering competition and often causing high costs in lost output and income.

The main "anticompetitive" weapons in the domestic regulatory arsenal have included (a) entry barriers, such as establishment and capacity licensing, exclusivity arrangements, and other market reservation policies often used to promote state enterprises or protect powerful interests; (b) exit barriers, such as weak enforcement or a lack of appropriate laws; (c) price controls, ostensibly to protect consumers; (d) canalization or confinement policies, which give only specific firms the right to buy and sell certain goods according to centralized guidelines and priorities; and (e) ad-

ministratively regulated allocation of key resources, such as credit and even physical inputs.

Barriers to entry and exit can do enormous harm. In Argentina, large subsidies that favored well entrenched firms discouraged new entrants. Industrial concentration has risen while smaller firms have lost market share. Exit barriers such as the inability to take firms to court or to liquidate them—the norm for parastatals in Africa, China, and Eastern Europe—encourage unprofitable and inefficient firms and, again, discourage new entrants. This also hampers the introduction of new technologies, because inefficient production lines and obsolete plants can stay in business.

Large and expanding firms are not always beneficiaries of government policies. The emergence of large, efficient private corporations, which are important conduits for technology transfer and industrial modernization in countries such as Brazil and the Republic of Korea, has been obstructed in other developing countries by regulatory restrictions. Where the government has allocated industrial capacity, reserved subsectors to state enterprises, and decided on plant locations, firms have failed to expand and thus to benefit from scale economies and greater specialization (Box 4.4). In Pakistan, capacity licensing prevents producers from reaching an efficient scale of production. In the cotton-spinning industry, licensing requirements keep mills to an average size of 15,000 spindles; the most efficient scale is almost twice that.

More difficult to quantify, yet equally damaging, are the extra transactions costs caused by a regulatory maze. For large firms the constraints of restrictive regulatory and domestic trade policies is not so much the explicit exclusion from access to resources, as it is the waste of effort associated with manipulating the rationing and licensing system. Further, under restrictive trade practices benefits accrue to large firms from manipulation of the system itself, rather than from the innovation, adoption of new technologies, and efficient production that would be demanded from the rigor of competitive markets—at home and abroad.

Internal and external restrictions often exist side by side, compounding each other's adverse effects on technological progress and industrial productivity. However, the neglect of internal regulatory reform in many countries—which often entails reforming institutions—has meant that domestic deregulation has not always proceeded apace with external trade openness. As a result, anticompetitive regulatory policies can be present in economies that are open to foreign trade, as in some African countries. Their external liberalization programs still left elaborate licensing, internal trade restrictions, and regulatory systems in place; this hampers competition and dampens the response to liberalization. Despite increased openness to external trade in Malawi, investment response has been limited: regulatory barriers continue to block entry in key industries, such as textiles.

Labor-market regulation

The goal of government regulation of labor markets usually is to protect individual welfare, not to influence the pattern of industrial development. Restrictions on child labor, working hours, and health and safety risks at work all fit this goal.

Box 4.4   The payoffs from regulatory reform: India and Indonesia

India's strategy for industrialization has been based on import substitution and an unusually comprehensive and restrictive regime of regulation in domestic markets. In eleven subsectors that produce about 50 percent of Indian manufacturing output, the main results of this strategy have been that: (a) A few large firms dominate, while medium-size producers are "squeezed out." (b) Average plant sizes are below economic scales of production for most products. (c) Protected firms have captive markets and thus garner high rents: net pretax profits in India's manufacturing sector were on average 20.8 percent of value added in 1982, compared with 3.5 percent in the Republic of Korea in 1981. (d) Technological innovation is slow. Total factor productivity in these industries fell by more than 1 percent a year between 1966 and 1980.

Unsurprisingly, India's international competitiveness has suffered. Is manufactured exports as a share of developing countries' manufactured exports has declined, and its share of manufacturing in GDP has not increased since 1978. Other results are harder to quantify: transaction costs are high; and resources are diverted by excessive administration, by unproductive rent-seeking, and by uncertainty and delays.

In Indonesia, the private sector has also been hindered by regulation. Until 1988, domestic and foreign investment was restricted to certain areas; there were capacity limits and ceilings on the number of permitted projects. Before starting operations, even approved indigenous firms had to obtain import and export licenses, a domestic trading license, land rights, a permanent operating license, and storage and location permits. All this often took two years. Total factor productivity fell by 2.5 percent in the mid-1980s.

In India, recent partial reforms proved successful. Industrial licensing has been eased since the mid 1980s, as have some import controls on some raw materials and intermediate goods. These changes, though modest, have nonetheless had a positive effect. Competition has squeezed the profits of large firms (the top 100 firms reported a drop of about 24.3 percent in 1986–87 despite a 9 percent rise in sales), and many new, smaller firms have been created.

In Indonesia reform has been more comprehensive: foreign investors are now able to acquire firms in priority areas as long as 20 percent of the equity is domestically owned; rules on domestic investment have been significantly relaxed. Private investment grew in 1989; the growth of total factor productivity has been positive in recent years; and the average rate of return on investment increased from 13 percent in the period 1982–85 to 22 percent in 1986–88.

With the same goal in view, however, many governments also regulate wages and job security—and these policies, although well-intentioned, often have the perverse effect of reducing incomes and employment.

Minimum-wages rules and wage indexation increase the cost of hiring workers. This leads firms to adopt an input mix that employs fewer people and more capital. This can result in unemployed or underemployed labor. Meanwhile the unwarranted shift toward capital intensity will make the economy less productive.

The precise effects vary. Some countries in Africa and Asia rarely enforce their labor regulations, often because it would be too costly to do so. Only the more visible firms—those employing a large number of workers—may have to comply, because small and medium-size enterprises find it easy and advantageous to evade the regulations. In contrast, labor regulations in much of Latin America (for example, in Uruguay and, until recently, Chile and Colombia) appear to have directly influenced resource allocation and employment, because the modern sector consists mainly of large and visible enterprises. In Chile in the early 1980s, low aggregate demand combined with labor market rigidities, such as minimum wages and lack of wage flexibility in the protected formal sector, accounted for an open unemployment rate that exceeded 20 percent.

Most economies have a mandatory minimum wage. But during the 1980s it fell significantly in real terms in many developing countries. Only when labor in the protected formal sector wields significant power, distortions and inequities in the wage structure are likely to remain. In Brazil, wage indexation has been used to maintain real wages in the formal sector, interfering with structural adjustment and resource allocation, and contributing to income disparities.

Employment regulations, such as job-security laws, can undermine the link between pay and performance and also lead employers to hire fewer permanent workers. In Senegal, tight rules on dismissals virtually guarantee employment; unsurprisingly, many workers are poorly motivated, and firms are wary of increasing employment. In China, employment regulations have fulfilled social objectives by maintaining high levels of urban employment, but the economic costs have been high. Although overall reform has helped, workers are still not allowed to move freely and seek out jobs in which their skills are most needed and rewarded. Overemployment in state enterprises is substantial, and inefficient enterprises are not liquidated because bankruptcy laws are not enforced. This impairs labor allocation still further. Ultimately, the expansion of productive employment opportunities is slowed as a result of employment regulations that were originally intended to help workers.

The minimal use of labor regulations in the Republic of Korea and other East Asian economies has not impeded rapid growth in employment and real wages. Working hours in Korean manufacturing, including overtime, which is often mandatory, are the longest in the world. But since the mid-1960s growth in manufacturing wages and employment has exceeded 8 percent a year—faster than in any other economy (Table 4.1).

A government's policies toward its own public employees can have a big effect on the economy, partly because of the sheer size of the public sector in many developing countries, partly because of the importance of the services that public workers provide. In Ghana, government employment grew by 15 percent a year between 1975 and 1982, even though real GNP per capita was falling, reducing resources available for maintaining real wage levels and for financing other recurrent costs. Indeed, governments have tried to protect public employment in the face of economic and financial hardships in many African and some Asian and Latin American countries. The result has generally been a steep decline in the real wage of public workers. Financial stringency has led governments to use fewer highly skilled staff and to economize on inputs. Hence agricultural extension workers without fuel for their vehicles; hence corridors crowded with idle messengers and tea servers; and so on. Low wages have led to wide-

Table 4.1 Annual percentage growth rates of real earnings, employment, and labor productivity in manufacturing, selected economies and periods

Economy and period	Earnings	Employment	Productivity
Brazil, 1965–85	1.7	4.6	4.7
Colombia, 1966–84	0.8	3.1	2.1
Japan, 1950–70	5.4	4.6	6.9
Korea, Rep. of, 1966–84	8.1	8.2	7.3
Portugal, 1966–84	0.7	2.1	0.9
Turkey, 1966–84	3.0	5.0	2.1
Yugoslavia, 1965–85	1.3	4.2	1.9
Taiwan, China, 1966–85	6.4	6.7	7.0

Source: Lindauer 1989.

Box 4.5   Tax reform

Taxes provide revenues to finance public spending and influence savings, investment allocations, and the structure of production. The level of revenue collection helps to determine whether a country can finance public sector capital formation, maintain its infrastructure, and provide for an adequate level of health and education services. In general, income taxes, taxes on foreign trade, and taxes on goods and services (sales and excise taxes) each account for about one-third of revenues. Although tax patterns differ across countries, tax-to-GDP ratios in developing countries are in the 10–20 percent range, about half of the levels of the industrial countries, whereas expenditure levels are in the 20–30 percent range—much closer to the levels of industrial countries. Many tax systems in developing countries do a poor job of collecting revenue and introduce large distortions into the economy. Weak tax administration leads to widespread tax evasion, which also fosters income inequality.

The objective of tax reforms is to raise revenue and reduce the costs of tax-induced distortions. Recent reforms have emphasized revenue adequacy, horizontal equity, simplicity and neutrality, and compatibility between the tax system and administrative capacity. A main objective has been to broaden the tax base so that the tax structure can be simplified and the tax rates lowered, thereby reducing tax-induced distortions and evasion. For taxes on goods and services, base broadening implies a shift from trade taxes to consumption taxes, such as a value added tax—setting the central rate in the range of 10–20 percent. For income taxes, this can be achieved by reducing exemptions and lowering the top marginal rates to between 30 and 50 percent. Further, selective excise taxes on luxuries and nonessentials can simultaneously enhance revenues and increase the progressivity of the tax system—without significant efficiency losses.

Comprehensive tax reform can work. In Jamaica, Malawi, and Mexico, tax reforms have limited the use of selective tax breaks and have also raised revenues by widening the tax base rather than by increasing the tax rate. In countries such as Indonesia, a value added tax has been effective in raising revenue and reducing distortions. By replacing cascading sales taxes, it has removed the burden of double taxation on final goods and of indirect taxation on exports and investment.

---

spread absenteeism, petty corruption, moonlighting, and a general breakdown in morale and discipline. All this goes on to reduce the productivity of the private sector, too, because the quality of the social and physical infrastructure and other public services deteriorates.

Taxation and productivity

Governments need to tax households and business to finance their spending. But taxes have an economic cost. Taxes on commodities or expenditures (such as a sales tax) lower incentives to work; tax exemptions or taxes that vary across categories also distort the incentives to invest and produce particular goods. High taxation of the final product of an enterprise significantly reduces the private return to the investor; the investor will often choose a different project or decide not to invest at all.

It is difficult to estimate the economywide efficiency loss caused by the overall rate of domestic taxation. But it is clear that highly unequal and discretionary tax rates can be extremely damaging. Governments in many developing countries lack the administrative capacity to apply their tax systems to a broad base of taxpayers. To raise a given amount of revenue, therefore, tax rates must be higher. This increases the disincentives faced by the taxed and widens the distorting gap between the taxed and the untaxed. In Sri Lanka, for instance, growing enterprises that become limited liability corporations have faced very large increases in tax obligations. As a result, small- and medium-size firms limit their effort at expansion, and the emergence of large, dynamic, national firms is hampered.

Recent experience suggests, however, that tax distortions can be reduced and that the multiple objectives of revenue, economic efficiency, equity, and administrative effectiveness are attainable—through a systemic approach to tariff and tax reform. Reductions in customs tariffs to promote efficiency gains is more sustainable when domestic taxation is simultaneously broadened to maintain revenue targets. Improvements in tax administration, reductions in tax exemptions to the nonpoor, and simplification of the tax structure are key components of revenue and efficiency-enhancing tax reforms. Developing countries such as Colombia, Indonesia, Korea, Malawi, Mexico, and Turkey have revamped their tax systems through a comprehensive approach to reform (Box 4.5).

Evidence on the productivity of investment projects

A policy climate that promotes enterprise—by letting price signals be seen and acted upon—can radically increase the productivity of investments. The experiences of the World Bank and International Finance Corporation (IFC) as lenders in support of public and private investment projects confirm this.

World Bank and IFC projects are evaluated after their completion using standard cost-benefit methods. For 1,200 of these projects—implemented during the past twenty years—economic rates of return (ERRs), which measure the contribution of the project to the economy (or its productivity), have been compared with various indexes of market distortion. (For a discussion of how ERRs are computed and of the analytical methods used in this section, see the Chapter 4 portion of the technical note at the end of the main text.)

The indicators of distortion look, for instance, at trade (how high are tariffs and how prevalent are nontariff barriers?), the value of currency (how big is the premium on foreign currency in the parallel market?), interest rates (are real rates negative or positive?), and the public sector's financial demands (how big is the government's budget deficit?). By every measure, ERRs are highest in undistorted markets, and lowest in distorted markets.

Projects implemented in an undistorted policy climate can have, on average, an ERR that is at least 5 percentage points higher than in a distorted climate (Table 4.2). To put this finding another way, with a few exceptions, undistorted policies makes an investment at least one and a half times as productive. The implication for growth is striking: a difference in the ERR of 5 percentage points, if achieved across the economy, would translate into a difference in the annual rate of GDP growth per capita of more than 1 percentage point every year.

In broad terms, the result holds for different measures of distortion, and across sectors of the economy. The premium on the parallel-market foreign exchange rate captures distortions caused not only by exchange rate policies, but also by other policies affecting the economic agent's demand for parallel market transactions, such as trade restrictions, taxes and regulations, constraints on capital flows, and macroeconomic and political instability. This indicator is highly correlated with ERRs. Where the official exchange rate is close to equilibrium levels—as approximated by virtually no premium on the parallel-market exchange rate—the average ERR for public projects exceeds 18 percent. Where the premium exceeds 200 percent, the ERR is less than 9 percent. For agriculture, industry, and nontradables (transport, housing, public utilities, and energy), the average ERR of public and private sector projects combined is between 5

Table 4.2 Economic policies and average economic rates of return for projects financed by the World Bank and the IFC, 1968–89

(percent)

Policy distortion index	All projects	All public projects	Public agricultural projects	Public industrial projects	Public projects in nontradable sectors	All private projects
Trade restrictiveness						
High	13.2	13.6	12.1	INSF	14.6	9.5
Moderate	15.0	15.4	15.4	INSF	16.0	10.7
Low	19.0	19.3	14.3	INSF	24.3	17.1
Foreign exchange premium						
High (200 or more)	8.2	7.2	3.2	INSF	11.5	INSF
Moderate (20–200)	14.4	14.9	11.9	13.7	17.2	10.3
Low (less than 20)	17.7	18.0	16.6	16.6	19.3	15.2
Real interest rate						
Negative	15.0	15.4	12.7	12.7	17.9	11.0
Positive	17.3	17.5	17.0	17.8	17.9	15.6
Fiscal deficit[a]						
High (8 or more)	13.4	13.7	11.7	10.3	16.6	10.7
Moderate (4–8)	14.8	15.1	12.2	21.0	16.8	12.2
Low (less than 4)	17.8	18.1	18.6	14.1	18.2	14.3

Note: INSF, insufficient number of observations (less than 10) to make inferences.
a. Percentage of GDP.
Source: World Bank data.

and 13 percentage points higher when the premium is small then when it is large (Figure 4.1). Projects in the nontradables sector are, it seems, just as vulnerable to a bad economic climate as the others.

Trade restrictions were measured using a yearly index of tariff and nontariff barriers in thirty-two countries. The pattern of the results is roughly the same, and it applies to private sector projects as well as to public sector ones (Figure 4.2). Private projects can readily go wrong if policy conditions are distorted (Box 4.6). Using budget deficits or interest rates as measures of distortion, the story is similar, although their overall effects on ERRs are not as large.

But there is more to success than a good envi-

Figure 4.2 Rates of return for projects financed by the World Bank and the IFC under varying degrees of trade restrictiveness, 1977-88

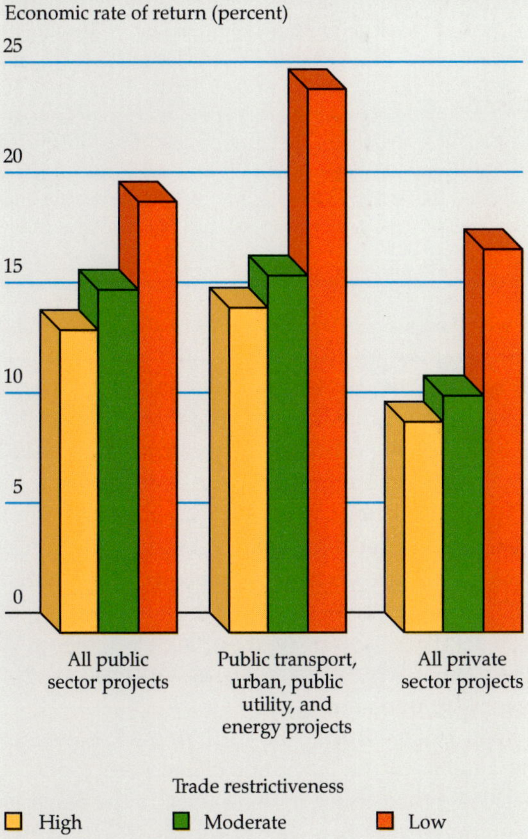

Economic rate of return (percent)

Trade restrictiveness

☐ High   ■ Moderate   ■ Low

Note: For the definition of trade restrictiveness, see the technical note at the end of the main text. Calculated for 530 public and private projects.
Sources: World Bank data; Halevi, Thomas, and Stanton, background paper.

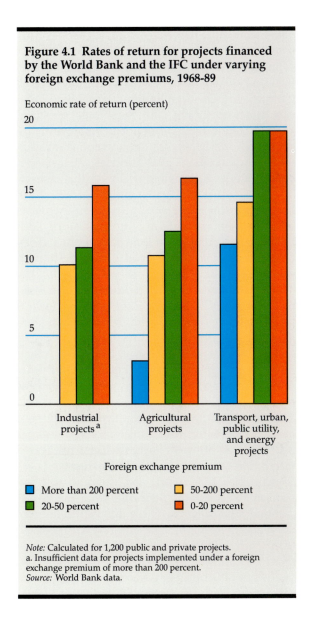

Figure 4.1 Rates of return for projects financed by the World Bank and the IFC under varying foreign exchange premiums, 1968-89

Economic rate of return (percent)

Foreign exchange premium

■ More than 200 percent   ☐ 50-200 percent
■ 20-50 percent   ■ 0-20 percent

Note: Calculated for 1,200 public and private projects.
a. Insufficient data for projects implemented under a foreign exchange premium of more than 200 percent.
Source: World Bank data.

ronment. The Tanzanian firms of Afro Cooling and Morogoro Shoe show that firms can perform very differently even in the same policy and national setting. The analysis of the Bank- and IFC-financed investment projects reveals a wide variation in ERRs even within the same country, ranging from negative to highly positive ERRs—exceeding 50 percent. Only some of that variation can be attributed to the economic climate.

The background research done for this Report makes it possible to be more precise. Under relatively undistorted conditions, as measured by low parallel premiums, the probability that a project will be an extreme failure (that is, have a negative

83

Box 4.6 Wrong incentives often make private projects go under

When market incentives are inappropriate, and complementary investments and institutions absent, private sector projects will tend to be inefficient. During the late 1970s, millions of dollars were invested in a private meat-production company in a developing economy. The enterprise was designed to process 40,000 head of cattle a year and export 80 percent of its production of frozen meat. Export demand did not materialize: an overvalued currency made the foreign selling price too high. Export taxes and wholesale-price controls on domestic sales lowered the firm's revenue even further. Meanwhile the firm paid market prices for its inputs, which were not controlled. It tried to circumvent the wholesale-price restrictions by setting up its own retail shops, but the required licenses were never granted. Poor public services made matters worse: the parastatal electricity company was unable to provide adequate supplies. The firm bought a standby generator, but it was unable to purchase enough diesel fuel because its administrative allocation of foreign exchange was too small. The enterprise's purchases of cattle for processing never reached 10 percent of capacity: it lost money steadily before closing in the early 1980s.

ERR) is less than 10 percent; under more distorted conditions, the probability of failing altogether is nearly three times larger. Conversely, the probability of a very successful project (one with an ERR of 20 percent or more), is twice as likely in an undistorted climate than for projects implemented in a more distorted one. But even with undistorted policies, a merely satisfactory project (one with an ERR of 10 percent or more) is not assured; the probability is about 70 percent. This raises the question of why many projects are unsatisfactory even with undistorted policies.

One reason is that the indicators that measure the quality of the economic climate are partial, at best. The four policy indexes used in the research, even taken together, do not capture the quality of economic institutions (such as the legal and regulatory framework) and of complementary public investments. And possibly the biggest reason for variability in ERRs, even after accounting for the policy climate, is simply that some firms will always be more successful than others: success resides in firm-specific factors such as skill, drive, determination, willingness to take risks, a measure of luck, and an ability to learn from mistakes—witness Chu in Korea.

The importance of institution-building

The World Bank's experience with investment projects also points to the importance of institutions—contractual arrangements (including, for instance, land-tenure systems and rules on entry and exit), property rights, norms of behavior, and the organizational structures at the project level. Implementing an investment project is often, in itself, an exercise in institution-building. Each project has its own institutional objectives, such as better techniques of management, higher technical standards, and adequate accounting procedures.

But lack of competent managers and inadequate technical skills and accounting procedures are all too common. Of seven hundred World Bank projects reviewed in the late 1980s, only one-third were judged to have substantially attained the institutional objective of strengthening project-related organizations and agencies; almost one-quarter showed negligible results in this respect. The weaknesses of implementing agencies have been especially important in agricultural projects in Africa, all the more so in complex ventures such as integrated rural development programs. They help to explain why the record of many such projects is not good.

The data show that the productivity of investments is much higher when the project's institutional objectives are achieved. Before implementation, the *expected* ERR for the appraised public sector projects was, on average, 22 percent. When institutional objectives had been attained *after* project implementation, the reestimated ERR turned out to exceed 20 percent—that is, it was close to expectations. This contrasts sharply with public projects for which institutional objectives had not been attained; in those cases the reestimated ERRs averaged less than 10 percent.

Difficulties in recruiting and retaining qualified staff greatly affect the performance of the implementing organizations. These difficulties, in turn, often are the result of labor and financial policies. Many such policies are external to the firm, such as limits on hiring skilled personnel in response to budgetary difficulties in government or legislative constraints on shedding unproductive labor.

Others are internal to the state organization itself—weak pay incentives, for instance, or underfinancing the costs of operation and maintenance. Sometimes the private sector has responded to these failures with innovative approaches of its own. These have demonstrated the benefits of involving local people—through NGOs and community groups—in designing and implementing projects. Community participation has proved successful in improving project effectiveness and promoting institution-building in many different settings. Water supply projects in Malawi are a typical example (Box 4.7).

Supportive public investments in infrastructure

Investments in infrastructure help to reduce costs, integrate markets, and disseminate information. As a result they make entrepreneurs more productive. In Nigeria, for instance, the costs of weak infrastructure for manufacturing enterprises are very high. Every firm of more than fifty employees that was surveyed had its own standby generator despite being connected to the power grid; altogether, firms had invested an average of $130,000

each in their own power supplies. They also invest in private boreholes because of the unreliable water supply, and employ messenger motorcycles or radio transmitters because telephones and postal services do not work. The cost of such private facilities ranged between 10 and 25 percent of the value of all the firms' equipment. This clearly reduces the productivity of each firm—but the effects can be broader. Weak infrastructure can alter the character of a country's development. In Thailand, for instance, regional cities have stayed small, and industrial growth has been held back by poor transport and by the absence of an infrastructure for technology, information, and business services.

Infrastructure is at least partly a public good. It is not easily divisible, so it is difficult to exclude nonpayers; it is often subject to economies of scale, resulting in natural monopolies. The private sector is thus unlikely to produce enough; the public production and provision of many infrastructure services are required for development.

The ERR evidence from the World Bank's and IFC's projects provides evidence that public investments matter. The productivity of projects in agriculture and industry increases significantly as

---

Box 4.7 Participation enhances project efficiency and benefits the poor

In 1968, a community of 2,000 people in Malawi started work on a novel water supply system. Community members began the planning, construction, and operation of their own water supply and distribution. Field staff for the project were recruited locally; traditional community groups formed the basis for water committees; government support was limited. Virtually all of the more than 6,000 standpipes installed nationwide are still in working order. More than 1 million Malawians have high-quality, reliable, and convenient water through systems that they themselves built, own, and maintain.

An analysis of rural and urban development over thirty years found high correlations between project performance and levels of participation. A survey of twenty-five World Bank agricultural projects evaluated five to ten years after completion found that participation was an important determinant in project performance and sustainability. In one World Bank project, Peruvian farmers in San Lorenzo formed thirty-two community groups and successfully took over all aspects of an irrigation project that had been designed and run by the national government. During a ten-year period in the Philippines, the National Irrigation Ad-

ministration shifted from a top-down management approach to heavy reliance on local farmers in the design, operation, and maintenance of local irrigation systems. The canals and structures worked better, rice yields were 20 percent higher, and the irrigated area 35 percent greater, than in a control group without participation.

Agricultural extension, rural infrastructure, urban upgrading, and the social sectors also benefit from the involvement of community groups. In Kenya, participation-based agricultural extension among local groups of women farmers doubled the number of farmers reached and promoted the adoption of new techniques. In a mountainous district in Nepal, local communities efficiently managed the construction of sixty-two suspension bridges. But not all projects have high returns from popular participation. Large-scale infrastructure and dam construction, for example, cannot benefit from the expertise and supervision of local community groups. Nevertheless, public discussion and evaluation of such projects by directly affected communities helps to identify potential environmental damage and economic dislocation.

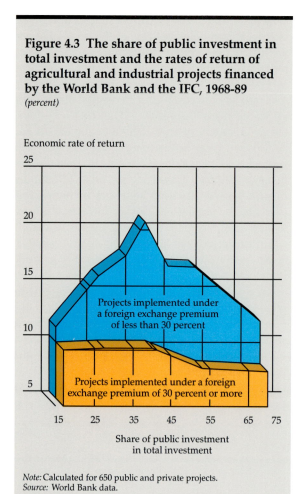

Figure 4.3 The share of public investment in total investment and the rates of return of agricultural and industrial projects financed by the World Bank and the IFC, 1968-89
(percent)

Economic rate of return

Projects implemented under a foreign exchange premium of less than 30 percent

Projects implemented under a foreign exchange premium of 30 percent or more

Share of public investment
in total investment

Note: Calculated for 650 public and private projects.
Source: World Bank data.

the share of overall public investments in GDP grows—up to a point. On average, the ERR increases by more than 6 percent as the share of public investment in GDP is raised from 5 to 10 percent, but as the share of public investment continues to increase the ERR tapers off and then declines.

Thus, although identifying country-specific turning points in the relation between public investment and ERRs is difficult on the basis of this evidence, the data suggest that striking an appropriate balance is important. This is also seen when the relative importance of public and private investment is analyzed by plotting the share of public investment in total investment (rather than GDP) against the projects' ERRs. Assume that the policy climate is good—as measured by a low currency overvaluation. For projects in the tradables sectors, the ERR is significantly higher when public investments are neither very low nor very high

as a share of total (Figure 4.3). Interestingly, if the policy climate is bad, the ERR of these projects is very low regardless of the share of public investment in total investment. Put differently, the results suggest that there is a strong interaction between policies and complementary public investments: the effects of enhancing the latter are substantial only when policies are appropriate; and the beneficial effects of improved policies are much larger when an appropriately balanced public investment program is present.

A subsectoral decomposition of World Bank projects indicate that investments in transport are highly productive. In good economic climates, the ERRs for public transportation projects have averaged more than 25 percent; this is considerably higher than the average returns from other public or private projects.

The strong case for public investment, however, need not preclude more private participation. Carefully regulated private monopolies can be efficient providers of infrastructure. Africa provides recent examples of successful private sector provision: private bus operators in Ghana, for instance, or private contractors for water supply and refuse collection in Togo. Private participation works well in Thailand's power sector, and in the Chilean, Czech, Hungarian, and Turkish telecommunications systems. Power and telecommunications have in fact recently seen a big increase in private activity. Technological advances have reduced the scale of efficient investments in these sectors and radically altered their monopoly characteristics, especially in telecommunications. Competing firms can now serve the same population.

Implications for policy

The quality of policies can make a big difference to the productivity of investment projects. But how quickly will the productivity of investments change as a result of improvements in policies? Even radical reforms may not succeed in raising ERRs overnight. Some benefits should come quickly; for instance, stronger price incentives can have a rapid effect on annual crop yields, and hence on the returns from existing irrigation systems. For other projects, however, the need to restructure them—or to start anew—will delay some of the benefits.

Overall, then, improving economic conditions will take time. But significant benefits should be visible in a few years. The evidence from the World Bank's and IFC's projects suggests that better conditions can pay off handsomely within the time it takes to complete a new project.

Table 4.3 compares the ERRs on the projects according to (a) the policy climate before they were initiated and (b) the climate when they were completed. Projects that were identified in a distorted climate but completed in an undistorted one show an average ERR of almost 18 percent. This is the same high average ERR as for projects initiated and completed in an undistorted environment. In other words, it is never too late to improve a distorted climate. Conversely, projects identified and prepared in an undistorted climate but completed in a distorted one—that is, cases in which markets became more distorted while the project was under way—show a much lower return.

The parallel-market foreign currency exchange premium is used as the measure of distortion in Table 4.3. Improving the policy climate even in this narrow sense usually requires changes not just in the exchange rate but in other aspects of policy. More generally, better policies also mean fewer distortions in the other three measures introduced above: trade restrictions, interest rates, and macroeconomic stability. The next two chapters pursue these themes. Chapter 5 looks in much more detail at the importance of openness to the international economy; Chapter 6 deals with macroeconomic policy and the financial sector.

The case for openness to trade and for prudent macroeconomic policies is gaining wider acceptance. The need for domestic liberalization—for the reform of ill-advised programs of regulation and licensing—is sometimes forgotten in the process. It deserves to be emphasized; a competitive domestic economy is all too important. Restructuring the regulatory framework, which requires institution-building and legal reform, is often more difficult technically and delicate politically. It is indispensable nonetheless. Entry to and exit from activities should be easy for workers, entrepreneurs, and capital. Institutions that establish secure property rights and legal remedies should be strengthened, so that entrepreneurs can manage their risks, gain access to credit, and lower their transaction costs. Institutions that promote the ac-

Table 4.3 Average economic rates of return for projects financed by the World Bank and the IFC under varying initial and final foreign exchange premiums, 1968–89
(percent)

Premiums before project start[a]	ERR under varying premiums at project completion[b]	
	More than 30	Less than 30
More than 30	11.7	17.8
Less than 30	13.2	17.7

Note: The number in each cell is the average of the ERRs of public and private sector projects.
a. Average foreign exchange premiums during the year of project appraisal, which takes place about a year before project implementation starts.
b. Three-year average of the foreign exchange premiums at about the time of project completion.
Source: World Bank data.

quisition of skill and access to technology are also extremely important.

An enabling economic climate, complemented by institutional development and investments, will not always prevent market failure. But, as in the cases of small-scale credit and crop insurance, the government cannot be expected to deal with market failures whenever they arise. In recognizing their limitations, governments should encourage the private production or provision of public goods and services, and also involve NGOs and the local users of the services and investments in their design and implementation.

This has implications, too, for the aid community in general and the World Bank in particular. First, it pays to limit public sector investment and institutional support to areas that help foster competition and the private sector, rather than crowd it out. Second, external aid and lending agencies should promote the involvement of private sector and local communities in decisions about the provision of public services. Third, aid is likely to work much better when used for projects undertaken in competitive and market-oriented climates. And finally, external agency support for improvements in the policy climate pays off. Perhaps the most powerful rationale for supporting structural reforms is that they raise the productivity of investments—public and private.

Integration with the global economy

Openness—the free flow of goods, capital, people, and knowledge—transmits technology and generates economic growth across nations. Two hundred years ago, imports of machinery and the emigration of skilled workers helped carry the industrial revolution from Britain to Europe. Japan and the United States were both highly successful at borrowing established technology and exploiting linkages with more advanced industrial countries to become major players in world markets. In the past forty years, East Asia has grown rapidly through the expansion of trade.

The linkages between openness and technological change are twofold. First, increasing global competition raises the demand for new technology. Second, the supply of new technology for industrializing countries is determined largely by the degree to which they are integrated with the global economy. New products and processes are transmitted through imported inputs and capital goods, sold directly through licensing agreements, and transmitted through direct foreign investment or export contacts with foreign buyers. Yet a market-friendly approach also requires government action to help producers master new technology. Governments must ensure the educational base, which is essential for developing technological capability; promote competition; coordinate efforts for quality control; and protect intellectual property rights.

Flows of capital and skilled workers across nations continue to provide an important avenue for technology transfer. The East Asian countries have successfully assimilated technology by sending students abroad, exploiting linkages with overseas nationals, and encouraging exchanges with re-

search centers. Direct foreign investment (DFI) has contributed to technology transfer and fostered export growth in economies such as Brazil and Mexico. Yet the gains from foreign investment depend critically on the policy climate. DFI in a protected sector, for example, is likely to generate net losses instead of welfare gains.

By increasing competition and expanding access to technology, trade generates benefits which may even exceed the gains from improved resource allocation. Yet almost all industrial and developing countries have restricted trade to promote industry and raise revenue. In retrospect, these objectives would have been better attained in other ways. Where protection accompanied rapid development, as in East Asia, competition was maintained in external and domestic markets. These countries preserved incentives for technological change by using export success as a yardstick for performance. Trade intervention was also moderate and restricted in time, minimizing costly distortions from protection.

Channels of technology transfer

Technology is the knowledge that leads to improved machinery, products, and processes. Additions to this knowledge reduce the real cost of production and lead to the introduction of new products. Technology also includes the knowledge embodied in management know-how. Chapter 2 showed that growth in productivity, the best proxy for technological change, has accounted for as much as 30 percent of GDP growth in the East Asian countries.

Integration with the global trading system affects technological change in two ways. First, it improves the *supply* of new technology. Second, it raises the *demand* for new technology.

Supply-side channels

Technology is embodied in imported inputs and capital goods, sold directly through licensing agreements, and transmitted through direct foreign investment, labor movements, or contacts with foreign buyers. In all these ways, openness increases the supply of new products and processes.

TRADE. Technology is embodied in many kinds of imported inputs—ranging from capital equipment and turnkey plants to sophisticated components for electronic assembly. One explanation for the observed relation between high trade shares and GDP growth is that increasing trade allows countries to import capital goods. A comparison of

foreign technology imports by Argentina, Brazil, India, the Republic of Korea, and Mexico in the 1960s and 1970s shows that Korea relied extensively on imports of embodied technology. In 1985, India increased access to imported capital goods and components for the electronics sector, and it liberalized restrictions on the entry and exit of firms. Since then, out-of-factory prices have fallen as much as 60 percent for some products, and exports of electronics have increased.

The second source of technology transfer from trade occurs through exporting (Box 5.1). Exposure to international markets keeps exporters informed of new products, and foreign buyers are an important source of information that can be used to upgrade technology. In a survey of 113 Korean export enterprises in the 1970s, 20 percent of the firms cited contacts with foreign buyers and suppliers as important; only 8 percent considered licenses and technical agreements important. From contacts with foreign buyers, firms received blue-

---

Box 5.1 Export takeoffs: two success stories

The two stories below suggest that successful entry into export markets requires a combination of access to information, the appropriate incentive structure, and domestic entrepreneurship.

Garment exports in Bali, Indonesia

Foreign exchange earnings in the Bali garment industry increased from less than $3 million in 1975 to more than $65 million in 1987. The industry began in the early 1970s as a tourist-oriented sales effort by local businesses and expatriates who financed their travels by returning home with suitcases full of clothing. These expatriates, who generally had little business experience, provided limited but inexpensive capital, foreign contacts, and international mobility. Several of these early joint ventures were quickly replicated once their profitability was demonstrated.

A recession in 1981 led many local producers to reevaluate their informal relationships with local expatriates and turn to more highly skilled foreign partners, who were drawn to Bali by its new reputation as a profitable production site. By 1986 Bali had a sufficiently strong reputation as a boutique supplier that many foreign buyers were willing to purchase garments under more arms-length arrangements. Yet stricter enforcement of established immigration laws, which regulate the employment of expatriates, seems to have contributed to a temporary slowdown in the improvement of the quality of garment exports.

Rice exports in Viet Nam

In the mid-1980s, Viet Nam was a net importer of rice and requested international food aid several times during the decade to avert famine. By 1989, it had become the third largest exporter of rice, following the United States and Thailand. Rice trade shifted from net imports of 280,000 tons in 1988 to net exports of nearly 1.5 million tons in 1989, representing one-third of total hard currency exports.

No major change in weather accounted for this reversal in performance. Rather, a series of interrelated policy reforms transformed Viet Nam from a net importer to a net exporter of rice. During 1988 and 1989, agriculture was decollectivized and rice returned to family-farm production. Price controls were eliminated, and a large real devaluation of the currency in 1989 strengthened financial incentives to export. Finally, trade institutions were reorganized to eliminate state monopolies in imports and exports, which introduced competition among the mostly state-owned trading companies.

The lessons from these two case studies are quite different. Traditional reforms (price decontrol, privatization, and devaluation) transformed Viet Nam from a net importer to a net exporter of rice. In Bali, access to information on international markets, technical management, and capital provided the vital push.

prints and specifications, information on the production techniques and technical specifications of competing products, and feedback on the design, quality, and technical performance of exported products. China's heavy reliance on foreign trade corporations to mediate trade arrangements between Chinese enterprises and world markets has lessened the degree to which exporters have gained access to free technical assistance. Recent reforms, however, have greatly increased the involvement of manufacturing enterprises in trade and should facilitate technology transfer.

BUYING TECHNOLOGY THROUGH LICENSING. Concern about the monopoly power of technology suppliers, combined with balance of payments problems, led many developing countries to control the flow of disembodied technology and restrict royalty payments in the 1960s and 1970s. In India, restrictions on the size and time allowed for making royalty payments encouraged suppliers to favor lump-sum transfers. Yet by discouraging long-term relationships between suppliers and buyers, this form of payment made suppliers less responsible for ensuring successful technology transfer. Other countries sought to limit payments for technology imports by restricting access to several firms, which in turn discouraged competition. In contrast, Japan's Ministry of International Trade and Industry (MITI) reinforced interfirm rivalry by making sure that foreign technologies were available to a number of domestic firms.

Trade flows and the licensing of foreign technologies allow countries to avoid the cost of duplicating established technologies. Restrictive policies on technology imports in Brazil, China, and India have frequently led to intensive scientific activity that could have been accelerated through greater use of established technologies developed abroad.

The demand for technology

In a more competitive environment, firms respond to international competition by trying more and more to minimize costs. This may simply lead to better use of established technology, or to efforts to acquire and adapt new technology. In Turkey, which liberalized trade and reformed its financial sector during the 1980s, the private sector has accelerated technology imports—embodied in machinery that is available through licenses or technical agreements—as well as the purchase of designs and know-how.

By distorting relative prices, protection has often led to the costly adoption of capital-intensive techniques in economies with abundant labor. In Côte d'Ivoire, the textile sector was developed in the 1960s primarily through direct foreign investment, which was induced by income tax and import duty exemptions, interest subsidies, high tariffs, and restrictive import licensing. Subsidized credit, by lowering the cost of capital, led to more capital-intensive plants. Firms' choice of sophisticated technology, which required a high level of expatriate employment, also inflated their wage bill. These high production costs were passed on to consumers in a protected market. In contrast, the textile industry in Japan developed as a highly labor-intensive sector, using imported secondhand machinery modified to substitute labor for capital. In Japan and the Republic of Korea, the technology for textile production became capital-intensive only when relative prices changed and labor became the scarce factor.

An escalated tariff structure can also affect the choice of technology. In the Philippines, as in many other countries, the more processed the product, the higher its import duties. This has encouraged assembly and packing operations that are heavily dependent on imported materials and equipment. Typically, governments respond with local-content regulations requiring finished products to contain a certain share of domestically produced components. Local content rules are often applied across the board, without regard for comparative advantage, further reducing the competitiveness of the assembled products.

Export competition, like import competition, also forces firms to the forefront of technological developments. One of Brazil's vehicle-components firms, Metal Leve, entered the international market in 1965 to use up excess capacity and exploit fiscal and credit incentives. The entrepreneurial ability of the firm's leadership and the firm's entry into international markets created a dynamic process of technological change and expanding export shares, driven by foreign demand for high quality. Exporting also strengthens the incentive to adopt new technology by increasing the returns from innovation through expanded market opportunities. In the computer industry, for instance, firms must target global markets from the beginning in order to make their investments profitable.

Government technology policy

One of the clearest lessons of Japanese and East Asian experience is the value of a strategy of importing, and building on, established technology from abroad. Countries which rely on imported technology have generally made very strong internal efforts to diffuse and develop technology. This ability to select, diffuse, and build on imported technology—sometimes referred to as technological capability—is also determined by policy action in several areas, in addition to openness. One of these is education (discussed in detail in Chapter 3). The others are domestic competition (also discussed in Chapter 4), the macroeconomic framework (discussed in detail in Chapter 6), information services, norms and standards, intellectual property, and research and development.

DOMESTIC COMPETITION. Innovation and the diffusion of technology are promoted by domestic competition, especially if the domestic market is large. One study of the United States in the early nineteenth century showed that as navigable inland waterways expanded, patent activity increased. Access to larger markets and more regional competition sped up the pace of innovation. A recent study of successful industries in six European countries, Japan, Korea, Singapore, and the United States found that domestic competition was a key to global success (Porter 1990). In Japan, almost every sector that became a major exporter on world markets had numerous domestic competitors—the machine tool industry alone has more than 100 manufacturers. Domestic competition is important even in industries with substantial economies of scale (for example, the chemical industry in Germany, the car and truck industries in Sweden, and pharmaceuticals in Switzerland).

Barriers to internal competition—licensing restrictions limiting entry, pricing policies, and bankruptcy or labor laws regulating exit, in addition to tariffs and nontariff barriers—often discourage technological change (see Chapter 4). In India's fertilizer sector, where competition has been virtually eliminated by government controls on entry and by pricing policies which pass on higher costs, older plants using obsolete processes survive despite operating at less than 30 percent capacity. In Europe's computer industry, sheltered national markets were handed over to "national champion" firms that never left their protected markets.

Yet market-friendly government policies may mean more than removing barriers to internal competition. Governments may need to use antitrust provisions to ensure that producers and distributors do not collude or exploit monopoly power. Import competition generally provides a powerful check on collusive practices, but it may not be sufficient if import distributers have monopoly power or goods are nontraded. In the United States, all recent antitrust cases involved nontradable goods such as trucking and dentistry services. Yet poorly designed antitrust policies can be "captured" by the very interests that they are supposed to regulate—as in India. A simple antitrust code which only prohibits price-fixing and other clearly restrictive practices is a good approach. Policies which go further—such as restricting mergers or joint-ventures—may increase competition but could hurt efficiency if scale economies are important.

THE MACROECONOMIC FRAMEWORK. The macroeconomic framework affects the pace and choice of technology transfer through its effect on interest rates, exchange rates, and the availability of foreign exchange. High national saving rates and capital formation in the Republic of Korea and Japan were associated with a fast diffusion of technology in that the cost of capital declined and the turnover of the capital stock accelerated. Studies have shown a strong association between equipment investment and economic growth for the industrial countries; Chapter 2 showed that a rapidly increasing capital stock has contributed a significant share to GDP growth in developing countries since 1960.

An unstable macroeconomic framework generally results in foreign exchange rationing, which, for instance, leads to restrictions on royalty payments for technology licenses. Particularly in the less industrialized countries, where a large share of technology is transferred either in the form of capital-goods imports or licenses, foreign exchange restrictions are likely to be a significant deterrent to technology development.

An overvalued exchange rate can also distort the process of choosing technology by lowering the cost of imported machinery and biasing the pattern of development toward capital-intensive growth. If the cost of capital is either too high (as in India, which imposes high tariffs on capital-goods imports) or too low (as in Ghana, the Philippines, and Tanzania during the 1950s) the speed of technology transfer and the benefits from imported technology under local conditions will decline.

INFORMATION SERVICES. Government agencies and industry associations can make a valuable contribution by coordinating the exchange of information among technology importers, which in turn encourages the standardization of components and devices. Government agencies have, however, had mixed success in getting information to exporters of manufactures. Exporters need detailed information on production specifications and marketing options—which the public sector usually lacks the expertise to provide. To increase the efficiency of public information services, they could be sold. This would oblige the supplier to find information worth paying for. Such services also need to be judged against performance standards. For example, services designed to promote manufactured exports could be evaluated through changes in export shares. In the East Asian economies, trade promotion agencies only became successful after a long build-up of experience by private suppliers, private associations, and small units of government officials who promoted trade. Governments should encourage competition between public and private sector providers of information by eliminating restrictions on entry of private and foreign suppliers of consultancy services.

NORMS AND STANDARDS. A strong central system of metrology, norms, standards, testing, and quality control helps an economy to upgrade and diffuse technology. In economies as diverse as the Republic of Korea and Turkey, testing and quality control services have contributed to export success and created incentives to invest in upgrading. Experience, however, suggests three important considerations. First, unless there is vigorous competition so that inferior products cannot easily be sold, quality control services will not be supplied. Second, entry into this sector should not be restricted to public organizations. These services are successfully provided by domestic and foreign firms in a number of industrializing countries. Third, an economy's standards should conform to international specifications. Otherwise, country-specific standards can become a form of protection. Moreover, cooperative standards also help prevent monopolies. Industrial countries can play an important role in disseminating technology by encouraging open standards, which allow firms to link products as well as communication between machines without special equipment or permission. Korea made use of open standards for personal computers to launch their exports.

INTELLECTUAL PROPERTY. Most industrializing countries—especially the least industrialized—are engaged in adapting and diffusing products and processes developed in the industrial countries. Consequently, until now, increased patent protec-

tion has been perceived in industrializing countries as benefiting foreign companies more than domestic industry. Patent protection can promote the development of innovative technology by domestic firms and the transfer of existing technology from industrial countries. But it can also raise the cost of using newly patented technology. Yet for the newly industrializing economies—which are now reaching the technology frontier in several areas—the gains from greater protection of intellectual property may soon become important. Historically, industrial nations strengthened their intellectual property protection as they developed. Even industrializing economies are capable of quickly reversing their attitudes. A resolution by the Food and Agriculture Organization (FAO) mandating that germplast be available at no cost to all countries was supported by developing countries in 1983. By 1985, however, many of these countries wanted to protect the new crop varieties they had developed. They joined the United States in its reservations against the FAO proposal, which was defeated.

Better protection of intellectual property is rapidly becoming a central issue for other reasons. The changing nature of technology is making it more difficult to assimilate new developments by copying imported products—leading more firms to seek licensing arrangements. Industrial countries which view unauthorized copying in the context of trade losses are pressing for greater patent and trademark protection in industrializing countries. By leveraging the issue in the context of bilateral trade negotiations, including potential trade retaliation, the United States and the European Community (EC) have been instrumental in strengthening the patent laws in Korea and Mexico.

Yet multilateral agreements negotiated through the GATT and the World Intellectual Property Organization would be preferable to case by case bilateral efforts. This would provide a more comprehensive global approach and would minimize the threat of trade retaliation. Intellectual property protection is most critical for areas in which industrializing countries would benefit from industrial country research, such as the prevention of tropical diseases. Research in industrializing countries is often based on extensions of established designs and processes, which could also be protected. Access to licenses for foreign innovations could also be actively promoted. Industries in developing countries could seek to limit restrictive clauses in their international licensing agreements, such as those which ban exports.

RESEARCH AND DEVELOPMENT. In agriculture, the rate of return on publicly sponsored crop research has typically ranged between 30 and 60 percent (see Chapter 4). Yet the returns from publicly sponsored research in industry have probably not been so high. Studies suggest that Japanese success in developing new technologies results more from improving incentives to private industry than from expanding government-subsidized programs.

Governments in developing countries often spend a large share of the resources available for technology transfer on national research and development institutions. In many cases, as in India and Thailand, they have had little effect. Particularly in low-income countries, a large share of research and development could better be used to assimilate and monitor technology development abroad. Yet government-sponsored R&D centers are more likely to follow the interests of their staff in basic research. The Republic of Korea has made such centers more accountable to their users by forcing them to increase share of revenues from private contracts.

TECHNOLOGY TRANSFER: AN ASSESSMENT. Is openness equally important at all levels of development? In Africa, strong protection of industry and reliance on public enterprises discouraged competition, leading to low rates of productivity growth. Countries of all income levels could create the demand for new technology by fostering competition and building the educational base needed to absorb changes in the marketplace. There is a critical need for broadly based primary and secondary education, combined with on-the-job training programs. In 1986, only 20 percent of the school-age population (13 percent for women) were enrolled in secondary schools in Sub-Saharan Africa. Despite heavily subsidized university education, Africa has skill shortages in science, engineering, auditing, and higher-level accounting and management. Low-income countries also need to encourage partnerships with firms which have gained experience in adapting technology and marketing. The recent export success of Mauritius in garments may be traced to a combination of favorable policies, a well-educated labor force, and a large influx of direct investment from Hong Kong.

The recent acceleration of technical change in old and new fields such as microelectronics, telecommunications, and biotechnology is creating a more and more complex, competitive world in which adopting and adapting new technology is even more important. Successful policies will encourage both the most efficient use of established technology and its rapid diffusion through internal and external competition. Governments can improve technological capability best by providing education, fostering domestic and external competition, and encouraging the development of information services and quality control.

Labor flows and direct foreign investment

International flows of capital and labor affect growth and welfare in two ways. First, foreign inflows can finance domestic investment and help economies adjust to temporary shocks. (Official and commercial inflows are discussed in Chapters 4 and 6; this chapter looks primarily at the potential for foreign investment as a new source of additional capital, in light of the dwindling supply of commercial flows.) Second, foreign investment and labor migration are potentially important avenues for transferring technology. But the gains from foreign investment depend on the policy climate. Greater foreign investment in a protected domestic market could hinder development rather than promote it.

Labor movements

Migration, transfers of skilled personnel, and returning workers from abroad all contribute to the diffusion of technology. After legal barriers were removed from the emigration of skilled workers in the United Kingdom (1825) and exports of machinery (1842), British entrepreneurs and workers helped to develop railways and coal mining in Europe and elsewhere. In the period after World War II, large numbers of foreign students received science and engineering training in the United States and then returned abroad to use—and diffuse—their knowledge. In Pakistan, a cottage industry in soccer ball exports was initiated by a Kashmiri immigrant from India, who had studied the sports equipment business in Germany.

Labor mobility provides other benefits apart from technology embodied in migrating workers. It is another avenue for reducing the disparity in incomes worldwide. In several industrial countries, such as Norway and Sweden, high unemployment accompanied the transition from agriculture to manufacturing. Emigration helped to relieve population pressure in those countries: 25 percent of the Swedish population emigrated to the United States between 1865 and 1920. Higher labor mobility could improve welfare for labor-scarce regions as well. The trade-increasing potential of regional integration plans put forth by such bodies as the Caribbean Community (CARICOM) and the Central African Customs and Economic Union (UDEAC) is likely to be limited. Yet these plans could alleviate unemployment or shortages of skilled labor in member countries if they permit greater labor mobility.

Looser immigration and emigration policies in both industrial and developing economies are likely to lead to global gains in human welfare. One cost, however, is the loss of skilled and highly trained people emigrating to industrial countries— the brain drain. In Bangladesh, the share of professionals emigrating abroad was so large that it is believed to have contributed to shortages in some professional categories. After completing their education, 63 percent of students from the Republic of Korea, 49 percent from Jordan, and 33 percent from Greece remained in the United States between 1962 and 1976.

The net losses from brain drain may be mitigated by other factors. Net remittances from migrants in France, Germany, Kuwait, Saudi Arabia, and some other countries are often high. Migrants send back from 10 to 50 percent of every dollar earned. In addition, emigrating workers may contribute to the diffusion of new ideas and technologies, either when they return home or simply by facilitating the exchange of information. In sum, the net losses from emigration of skilled workers are not clear. Governments can mitigate these

costs by eliminating subsidies to those who can afford higher education, or to those who are likely to move abroad. Governments may also wish to tax the incomes of skilled emigrants, especially if they remain citizens of their home countries.

Technological change and direct foreign investment

After 1945, direct foreign investment was a major conduit for know-how between the United States and Europe. Case studies of Hong Kong and Mexico show that the presence of foreign firms has increased the diffusion of technology and improved the efficiency of local firms. In Brazil, a large share of manufactured exports originates from firms with foreign investment. Evidence from Côte d'Ivoire and Venezuela suggests that foreign-owned manufacturing firms are more productive and that joint ventures export a higher share of total output than domestically owned firms (Table 5.1). This is true even after capital intensity and firm size are taken into account. It seems plausible that a foreign presence could raise the productivity of firms that remain wholly domestically owned. For the three countries shown in Table 5.1, however, the evidence on this is inconclusive.

The diffusion of management and marketing skills is likely to be as important as the transfer of product and process technologies. In Bali, Indonesia, and Taiwan, China, foreign investment has generated positive spillovers by overcoming the informational costs of entering world markets. Because foreign firms already have marketing link-

Table 5.1 The relative performance of foreign firms in manufacturing, selected countries and years

Country	Relative output per worker of foreign relative to domestic firms[a]		Net foreign exchange earnings as share of sales (percent)[b]		
	Firms with majority foreign ownership	Firms with minority foreign ownership	Firms with majority foreign ownership	Firms with minority foreign ownership	Domestic firms
Côte d'Ivoire					
1976	4.2	3.8	3	37	−8
1987	2.2	2.1	8	28	18
Venezuela					
1976	0.9	1.4	. .	. .	. .
1988	1.3	1.2	−13	36	−11
Morocco					
1985	0.7	0.6	14	13	21
1986	0.7	0.6	17	16	21
1987	0.9	0.8	18	17	24
1988	0.8	0.7	22	16	28

Note: All averages weighted using firm sales. Foreign firms are defined as all firms of which at least 5 percent of assets are foreign owned.
a. Ratio of foreign firm to domestic firm productivity (output per worker).
b. Equal to exports minus imported inputs divided by sales. For Morocco, equal to exports divided by sales because no data were collected on imported inputs.
Source: World Bank data.

ages, know-how, and production experience, some host economies have actively encouraged global exporters to establish production units in their country. Economies which have exploited the linkages of foreign firms with global markets include Ireland, Malta, Mauritius, and Singapore.

Despite its significant role for diffusing technology, direct foreign investment in an economy with highly distorted policies is likely to generate net losses for the host country instead of welfare gains. In Côte d'Ivoire (as mentioned above in this chapter), selective protection and subsidies to multinational textile firms led to inefficient production. Another study found that more than a third of foreign investment projects earned negative returns for the host country because of import protection. As shown in Table 5.1, majority-owned foreign firms generated less foreign exchange than joint ventures or domestic firms. In all three countries, much of the manufacturing sector has been protected, so both foreign and domestic firms have concentrated on the domestic market. In addition, both Morocco (for phosphates) and Venezuela (for petroleum and aluminum) imposed restrictions on foreign ownership in sectors with high export earnings. Following the trade reform which began in Morocco in 1984, however, productivity and export sales increased faster in the foreign firms than in their domestic counterparts (Table 5.1).

Host countries can maximize potential gains from DFI with evenly enforced investment codes, a low level of protection, and a minimal reliance on income tax breaks or credit subsidies to foreign firms. Taxes which restrict repatriation of profits also discourage direct investment. To reduce the possibility that multinationals could exploit their advantages in information and charge higher prices, host countries can encourage competition between foreign firms and avoid granting exclusive privileges to any one foreign investor. In Turkey, for example, liberalization of foreign investment has created competition among local joint ventures and licensees to upgrade the national automobile sector. It is best for local and foreign firms to face equal tax policies: a lower uniform tax rate is preferable to a schedule that discriminates for or against multinationals.

Foreign investors are also likely to prefer a clear regulatory system. A World Bank study of forty-four international mining companies found that most of the companies surveyed preferred working within the bounds of a clearly defined investment and corporate tax code to negotiating individual agreements on tax breaks or subsidies. The

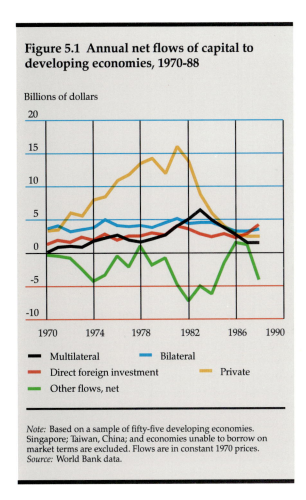

Figure 5.1 Annual net flows of capital to developing economies, 1970-88

Billions of dollars

Multilateral — Bilateral — Direct foreign investment — Private — Other flows, net

Note: Based on a sample of fifty-five developing economies. Singapore; Taiwan, China; and economies unable to borrow on market terms are excluded. Flows are in constant 1970 prices.
Source: World Bank data.

three countries considered most attractive for mineral investment—Botswana, Chile, and Papua New Guinea—have quite high tax rates by developing-country standards.

Aggregate flows of direct foreign investment and growth

The fall in access to commercial bank lending for developing countries has increased the attractiveness of direct foreign investment. In 1988, DFI surpassed all other forms of lending as a source of foreign capital to developing countries (Figure 5.1; see also Table 1.3).

Although DFI grew at a slower rate than commercial flows, averaging 6 percent annually in real terms from 1970 to 1989, it fluctuated much less than private flows. After a steady upward trend in the 1970s, DFI dropped off between 1981 and 1986, recovering to its 1981 level in 1988. But the aggregate picture hides significant differences in the growth of these flows to various regions. In real terms DFI increased 12 percent a year between

Table 5.2 Investment, growth, and net flows of capital, 1970–89
(percentage of GDP)

Period and correlation	Official flows / GDP[a]	Direct foreign investment / GDP	Private flows / GDP
Between domestic investment / GDP and flows			
1970–75	0.14	0.50*	0.45*
1975–82	0.13	0.26*	0.26*
1982–89	0.10	0.24	0.24
1970–89	0.16	0.39*	0.31*
Between GDP growth and flows			
1970–75	0.34*	0.52*	0.21
1975–82	0.17	0.24	0.23
1982–89	−0.07	0.15	−0.05
1970–89	0.16	0.33*	−0.02

* Statistically significant at the 5 percent level.
Note: All values shown are period averages for sixty countries.
a. Official flows include bilateral and multilateral flows.
Source: World Bank debt reporting service.

1970 and 1989 in Asia, compared with 3 percent in Latin America and a decrease in Africa.

Apart from potential gains through technology transfer, DFI generates employment, accounting for as much as 60 percent of manufacturing employment in some economies, such as Singapore. As DFI in industrializing countries continues to shift into services, its favorable effect on employment is likely to rise. DFI also shifts the burden of risk for an investment from domestic to foreign investors. Repayments are linked to the profitability of the underlying investment, whereas under debt financing the borrowed funds must be serviced regardless of the project's success. Table 5.2 shows that DFI is the only capital inflow that was strongly associated with higher GDP growth during the period 1970–89, although the direction of causation is not clear. If DFI is likely to promote growth, the converse is also true.

Prospects for enhanced flows of DFI to developing countries in the 1990s remain uncertain. One study estimates that the share of developing countries in global foreign investment flows declined in the 1980s from 26 to 21 percent. In addition, DFI in developing countries is highly concentrated: in the 1980s, fifteen countries attracted 75 percent of all investment. DFI cannot be viewed as a substitute for commercial lending or official flows; it is at best a complement. The flow and effectiveness of DFI will be improved by adequate domestic and official financing by organizations such as the World Bank to support the expansion of infrastructure, health care, and education.

To sum up, direct foreign investment is a potentially important source of capital to supplement domestic investment, technology transfer, and employment generation. Yet the evidence on technology transfer through DFI is mixed. The extent to which foreign inflows contribute to growth depends largely on the effectiveness of host-country policies. The scope for increased inflows of DFI to developing countries will also be determined by industrial-country policies. Regional integration has made Europe even more attractive to foreign investment, which will discourage flows to the developing countries. In general, increasing protection in industrial countries diverts DFI from other destinations and makes developing countries less attractive as sites for export-oriented foreign investment.

Trade policy and economic growth

When developing countries establish open trading regimes, they attract DFI for the right reason: foreign investors see opportunities to create internationally competitive businesses. But the gains from liberal trade go far beyond this. Trade restrictions distort the allocation of investment and encourage lobbying by private interests and governments. Consumers pay the costs of restrictive trade policies, while protected sectors gain. In the United States, one study estimated that the cost to consumers of restraints on imports of Japanese automobiles was between $93,000 and $250,000 for each job saved.

Dispersion in the level of protection can lead to significant distortions, even if the average level of protection is low. Buyers of inputs from protected sectors—such as automobile producers who must purchase locally made steel in Brazil, India, or Pakistan—are at a disadvantage in world markets. In the United States, manufacturers of personal computers complain that duties on components reduce their international competitiveness. But if policymakers protect final products instead and allow inputs to be imported duty-free, then the so-called effective protection for these products is often much higher than indicated by official tariff levels.

High tariffs often invite discretionary enforcement: in many countries, official levels of protection are high but actual tariff collections are low. Brazil's import-weighted statutory tariff level for

---

Box 5.2 Protection in industrial countries: a historical perspective

Centuries before the industrial revolution, countries had learned to protect domestic markets. Beginning in the thirteenth century, England enacted a series of laws that restricted the type and origin of fabrics which could be worn. Although some laws had a social objective—to identify social classes through their costumes—the basis for others was clearly economic. In addition to laws against imports of French products, the British also protected producers against countries such as India. British producers in the seventeenth century succeeded in getting a law passed which prohibited importing or wearing silk and calicoes from China, India, and Persia. Restrictions on imported calicoes provided an impetus to England's calico-printing, silk, and cotton-linen industries.

Yet a comparison of protection levels in industrial countries during the past two hundred years with those prevailing in developing countries today (Box table 5.2) shows that average levels of protection in industrial countries never reached the level of protection presently found in developing countries. In 1820, the average level of tariffs on manufactures for seven countries was 22 percent. Although industrial countries did benefit from higher natural protection before transport costs declined, the average tariff for twelve industrial countries ranged from 11 to 32 percent from 1820 to 1980. For example, in Japan low tariffs were mandated through foreign treaties until 1899. Once these restraints were removed, rates seldom rose above 10–15 percent until 1911. Even after 1911, the overall level of tariffs never exceeded 20 percent. In contrast, the average tariff on manufactures in developing countries is 34 percent (Table 5.3).

Box table 5.2 Tariff rates in industrial countries, 1820–1987
(unweighted average percentages)

Kind of goods and country or region	1820	1875	1913	1925	1930[a]	1950	1987
Manufactures							
Austria	. .	15–20	18	16	24	18	9
Belgium	7	9–10	9	15	14	11	7
Denmark	30	15–20	14	10	. .	3	. .
France	. .	12–15	20	21	30	18	7
Germany	10	4–6	13	20	21	26	7
Italy	. .	8–10	18	22	46	25	7
Netherlands	7	3–5	4	6	. .	11	7
Spain	. .	15–20	41	41	63	. .	. .
Sweden	. .	3–5	20	16	21	9	5
Switzerland	10	4–6	9	14	19	. .	3
United Kingdom	50	0	. .	5	. .	23	7
United States	40	40–50	25	37	48	14	7
Average	22	11–14	17	19	32	16	7
All goods							
Australia	. .	. .	16	18	14	17	. .
Canada	. .	14	17	14	13	9	6
Japan	. .	4	20	13	19	4	8
United States	45[b]	41	40	38	45	13	6
Average	. .	6	23	21	23	11	7

a. For manufactures, the average is for 1931 instead of 1930.
b. Data are for 1821 instead of 1820.
Sources: For 1820 and 1875 (average tariff on duties), Bairoch 1976. For 1987, GATT data reported in Kelly and others 1988. For other years: for the United States (ratio of customs revenues to dutiable imports), U.S. Department of Commerce 1975; for Japan (ratio of customs revenues to dutiable imports), Ohkawa, Shinohara, and Umemura 1979; for Canada and Australia (ratio of customs revenues to dutiable imports), Mitchell 1983; for 1913 and 1925 (average statutory tariffs), League of Nations 1927.

the private sector was 40 percent in 1985, yet total customs revenues as a share of import volumes were only 6 percent. Exemptions (including those for public sector firms) explain a significant part of the discrepancy. In many countries such exemptions are often granted ad hoc, giving politicians a powerful tool for illicit gain.

Freer trade is even more desirable when domestic markets are dominated by only a few firms. In Pakistan, where the domestic market is too small to sustain many bicycle manufacturers, imports could spur competition to improve product quality and lower prices. Evidence on profit margins from countries as diverse as Chile, Colombia, Côte d'Ivoire, Morocco, and Venezuela suggests that imports are an important source of competition. In markets that require large production volumes for efficiency, trade leads to consolidation of output and allows specialization in production. Under free trade, Venezuela would not be able to support fifteen auto assembly firms.

By affecting the nature of inputs as well as production processes, trade could generate gains which greatly exceed the short-term benefits from improved resource reallocation (Grossman and Helpman, forthcoming). Access to better-quality inputs is likely to improve productivity and accelerate output growth. Exporters and importers learn about new products and processes arising from international advances in technology. Larger markets, which provide greater returns from research efforts and increase competition, motivate producers to develop or adapt new technology. Yet it is sometimes argued that monopoly profits are necessary to reward producers for investing in research and adapting imported technology to local conditions. If domestic investors cannot fully appropriate the gains from innovation or adaptation, they will underinvest in technology. In industry, however, many efforts to apply and diffuse knowledge require in-house technical expertise and may therefore be fully captured by the firm. What does the historical evidence suggest about the relation between protectionist systems and technological change? The answer seems to be that openness has generally promoted faster growth.

The evidence on trade

As industrial countries developed, they relied less on protection than do most countries developing today. Since the beginning of the nineteenth century, tariffs in industrial countries have averaged less than 25 percent (Box 5.2). In 1987, the average tariff in developing countries was more than 30

Table 5.3 Tariffs and nontariff barriers in developing countries, 1987

Region	Manufactures		All goods	
	Tariffs	NTBs	Tariffs	NTBs
East Asia	22	20	21	22
South Asia	81	47	77	48
Europe, Middle East and North Africa	26	31	24	32
Africa	30	30	33	30
Latin America and the Caribbean	34	20	33	21
Average	34	27	32	28

Note: NTBs, nontariff barriers. Data are unweighted tariff averages.
Source: UNCTAD 1987, based on eighty-two individual country sources. For Republic of Korea, World Bank estimates.

percent, and that was after a decade of extensive reforms (UNCTAD 1987). Tariff protection in South Asia is more than twice as great as the historical average for industrial countries.

Industrial countries rarely used nontariff measures during industrialization, although lately this has been changing—witness the increase in voluntary export agreements for autos and steel and the Multifibre Arrangement (MFA) for textiles. Yet for a sample of eighty-two developing countries, nontariff barriers were applied to 28 percent of all imports in 1987 (Table 5.3). Overall, the evidence suggests that the industrial countries grew with somewhat lower tariffs and substantially fewer nontariff barriers than those employed today by developing countries.

Studies which measure the short-term (static) gains from moving to freer trade find that the gains vary from less than 1 percent to as high as 6 percent of GDP. The gains are larger still if domestic markets are dominated by only a few producers, or if there are economies of scale in production. These studies, however, only measure changes at one point in time; they are not designed to analyze the potential linkages between trade policies and long-term growth.

Most of the studies which have analyzed GDP growth and openness to trade have found a positive relation (Box 5.3). Figure 5.2 also shows that there is a positive association between productivity growth and trade and exchange rate policy, using seven different measures of openness. The accumulated evidence suggests that the long-run gains from increased competition and the spillover of technology are likely to be much greater than the short-term gains.

Yet a degree of skepticism is warranted for two reasons. First, most studies examine the relation between economic growth and trade volumes, not

In this chapter, openness means access not only to goods, but also to services, technology, foreign investment, and capital flows. Neutrality in trade policy means that incentives are neutral between saving a unit of foreign exchange through import substitution and earning a unit of foreign exchange through exports. Price comparisons between goods sold in domestic and international markets provide one measure of neutrality. If domestic markets are competitive, price comparisons incorporate the effect of the trade and exchange rate policies that affect domestic prices: tariffs, quotas, different exchange rates for imports and exports, and subsidies. But information on relative prices is often unavailable, so many other proxies are used instead (for examples, see Barro, forthcoming).

The simplest measures of trade orientation are based on actual trade flows, such as imports plus exports as a share of GDP. (For an overview of the literature on openness and growth, see the background papers by Dollar, Harrison, and Jen.) Most of these measures show a positive association with GDP growth, even after controlling for other factors. Unfortunately, they are at best an imperfect proxy for *trade policy*. Other factors, such as country size or foreign capital inflows, also affect trade: for example, large countries tend to have smaller trade shares. One improvement over this approach is to use the deviation of actual from predicted trade flows, based on variables such as country size (Balassa 1985; Syrquin and Chenery 1989).

The use of administrative data, which include tariffs and nontariff barriers, are difficult to aggregate into an overall index. Coverage ratios for nontariff barriers cause the greatest difficulty. Because the coverage ratio

indicates the percentage of imports covered by trade barriers, an extremely effective barrier that excludes almost all imports in one category would receive little weight. Most studies based on these direct measures of policy find a positive relation between trade and growth (for example, Heitger 1986).

Microeconomic studies also have generally shown a positive association between increased exports and productivity growth. However, the relation between imports and productivity growth is sometimes positive and sometimes negative. (For the work summarized in the last two sentences, see both Nishimizu and Page 1990 and Tybout 1991.) Empirical work has been unable to distinguish between the expected positive effect of imports on productivity growth in the long run and the fact that imports are initially drawn to sectors with low productivity in which a country does not have an international advantage.

Another difficulty in measuring the effect of trade policies on growth is that trade policy itself may be a function of other variables, including growth. Studies that have tried to identify the causal relation between GDP growth and growth in exports or imports have had mixed results (for example, Hsiao 1987; Jung and Marshall 1985).

The majority of the evidence now available shows a positive relation between openness—however measured—and growth. Yet the difficulties in isolating the impact of trade *policies* per se and establishing causality suggest that the debate is not fully resolved. More effort needs to be devoted to gathering detailed data on quotas and tariffs for developing countries.

policies; this is partly because measuring "policy" poses difficult questions. Some East Asian economies have achieved high shares of trade in GNP with trade policy intervention. Nevertheless, more recent studies have tried to identify the effect of trade policies in their own right, using information on tariffs, quotas, and relative prices. These still show a positive relation between openness and growth.

Second, interpreting the observed correlation between trade policies and growth is difficult. Policies that are not directly concerned with trade (macroeconomic policy, measures to promote domestic competition, and so on) may be responsible both for superior export performance and for high GDP growth. Moreover, it is difficult to establish the direction of causality between trade policies and growth.

Intervention and growth

The evidence supports two broad conclusions. First, there is a general statistical association between less intervention and lower price distortions on the one hand and higher productivity growth on the other. Second, there is considerable variation in country experience—hence the dispersion of points around the general trends in Figure 5.2. In part, this is because openness is only one factor which explains productivity growth; this Report also documents the importance of establishing macroeconomic stability, providing social services, and fostering a productive climate for enterprises. Yet it is also true that such countries as Korea achieved high rates of export growth in conjunction with selective protection. Why is intervention more risky on average? Why are there exceptions?

Figure 5.2 Openness and growth in productivity: partial correlations for developing countries, 1960-88

(percent)

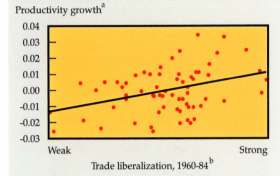

Productivity growth[a]

Weak — Strong

Trade liberalization, 1960-84[b]

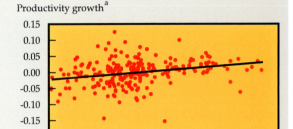

Productivity growth[a]

Weak — Strong

Trade liberalization, 1978-88[b]

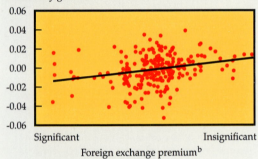

Productivity growth[a]

Significant — Insignificant

Foreign exchange premium[b]

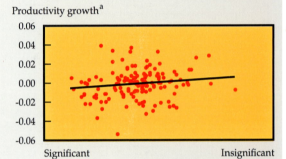

Productivity growth[a]

Significant — Insignificant

Price distortion[b, c]

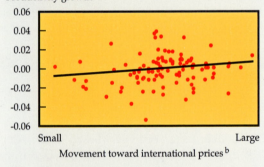

Productivity growth[a]

Small — Large

Movement toward international prices[b]

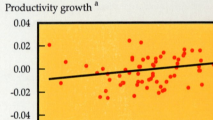

Productivity growth[a]

Significant — Insignificant

Bias against agriculture[b]

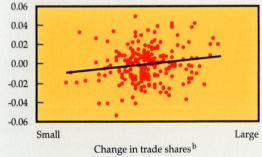

Productivity growth[a]

Small — Large

Change in trade shares[b]

Note: The measures of trade liberalization, foreign exchange premium, price distortion, and change in trade shares are significant at the 5 percent level in a regression of GDP growth on openness, input growth (capital, labor, education, and land), and dummy country variables. The measure of bias against agriculture is significant at the 10 percent level. Data are averages for 1960-66, 1967-73, 1974-81, and 1982-88, except for the trade liberalization index for 1978-88, which uses annual data because of the shortened period. The number of countries sampled ranges from sixty to eighteen.

a. Unexplained residual of GDP growth, after controlling for input growth and country effects.

b. This represents a proxy for trade and exchange rate policy, after controlling for input growth and country effects.

c. The relative price of consumer goods is purged of its nontraded component by taking the residual from a regression of this price index on urbanization, land, and population. See also Dollar, forthcoming.

Source: See the technical note at the end of the main text.

From a purely practical point of view, government intervention in trade is risky for several reasons. Countries often underestimate how difficult it can be to offset trade-induced distortions. A duty drawback scheme to reimburse exporters for tariffs paid on inputs is a second-best measure to attack distortions caused by protection. To ensure that incentives to produce for domestic and export markets are truly equal, exporters must also be compensated for any tariffs on their products (which shift incentives toward producing for the domestic market) and the exchange rate overvaluation that arises with protection. One study of Latin American countries found that export subsidies offset only a small fraction of the anti-export bias arising from tariffs and distorted exchange rates. In addition, countries which provide export subsidies become vulnerable to countervailing duties (imposed mainly by the United States) if they have signed the GATT subsidies agreement.

In many countries, the costs of failures in implementation have exceeded gains there might have been from correcting market failures. In Argentina and Côte d'Ivoire, efforts to distribute export credits to offset trade and exchange rate distortions were short-lived. Subsidies create financing problems and are often allocated to favored groups or sectors. In Costa Rica, subsidies for nontraditional exports were 5 percent of total central government expenditures in 1990; 80 percent of these subsidies were received by fewer than 20 firms. Korea, which tied credits and subsidies to successful export performance, also made mistakes: the drive to establish heavy industry through widespread subsidies in the 1970s was at best only a partial success. Often, policies designed as short-term measures to give domestic industries a chance to grow or restructure are never dismantled. The main arguments for and against intervention are reviewed in Box 5.4.

What distinguishes the countries which intervened in trade and yet were also able to grow rapidly? First, the successful interventionists preserved incentives for technological change by maintaining international and domestic competition and imposing performance requirements in return for any credit subsidies, import protection, or restrictions on domestic entry. In Japan and Korea, subsidies and protection were strictly tied to achieving export success within a defined period. Companies which did not perform well were allowed to fold. In the Japanese synthetic fiber industry, MITI helped firms obtain licenses from several different national sources to ensure new

entry—which resulted in excess capacity and ruthless competition.

Successful intervention has also been tempered by a flexible, highly pragmatic approach. The ability to terminate special treatment when intervention fails is critical. In 1980, Korea quickly reversed its 1970s policies of broad support—through protection and subsidies—for the development of heavy industry. In contrast, many industrializing countries have continued to subsidize ailing public sector firms and have restricted exit by poor performers.

Second, their intervention was moderate in the sense that it did not lead to large price distortions. Botswana, Canada, and Malaysia used relatively low tariffs and avoided nonprice measures such as quotas to diversify production. Measures of effective protection for Korea suggest that relative prices never became significantly distorted in favor of production for the domestic market (Westphal 1990). In part, price distortions were minimized in some of the East Asian economies because of their orientation toward global markets. Their commitment to world markets provided an external check on interventionist policies—guiding policy on exchange rates, protection, and subsidies.

In practice, few economies have successfully used infant industry protection to create viable, internationally competitive industries. The cost of government failures has been shouldered most often by the agricultural sector and by the consumers who pay higher prices for low-quality products. If governments do intervene, the guiding principles should be (a) to impose competition by fostering outward orientation and domestic competition, (b) to intervene at the source of the distortion (for example, to subsidize education rather than use protection when the problem is lack of human capital), and (c) to intervene only through nondiscretionary, time-bound policies that do not encourage rent-seeking. Economies which do choose to use trade protection should use low tariffs instead of nontariff barriers such as quotas or price controls.

Conditions for success in trade reform

In recent years a growing number of developing countries have embarked on programs of trade policy reform. Where these programs have been maintained, they have generally succeeded—that is, both trade and overall output appear to have expanded as a result. But in many cases programs

Box 5.4 Should states intervene in trade or shouldn't they?

Arguments for intervention

• Selective state intervention has figured prominently in two of the impressive success stories of development: Japan and the Republic of Korea. Both countries employed taxes and subsidies, directed credit, restrictions on firm entry and exit, and trade protection to encourage domestic industry. In other countries, including resource-rich Canada, Malaysia, and Botswana, moderate intervention supported diversification of the export base and helped new industries get established (Lewis 1988). In Canada, moderate tariffs (10–30 percent) protected industry into the early twentieth century. The government did not use quotas or exchange controls, however, nor attempt to prevent the decline of uneconomic industries. In 1988, manufactures exceeded 50 percent of total exports. Malaysia has also employed modest tariff protection, but it has used exchange controls and import sparingly. Manufactures rose from 6 percent of exports in 1965 to 46 percent in 1988. In Botswana, which has one of the highest GDP growth rates in the world for the postwar period, the value of manufactured exports surpassed that of beef exports in the mid-1980s. At independence beef products had provided almost all of Botswana's export earnings. Although skillful management of the mining sector has been critical to success, modest use of import restrictions promoted both manufactured and horticultural production, with protection conditional on production at import-equivalent prices.

• A long-term decline in the terms of trade for nonfuel commodities, combined with more inelastic demand for some of these products, suggests that countries could well boost export earnings by diversifying into manufactures. In the past, government intervention was sometimes necessary because producers lacked the information or expertise needed to enter industrial production (for example, Brazil, Korea, and Turkey).

• A wide range of market failures, from lack of information to incomplete capital markets, could justify an industrial policy. High rates of return on innovation in agriculture and industry suggest that private agents

may be underinvesting in research and development. For industry, less evidence is available, but several studies on industrial development of computers and computerized axial tomography scanners in the United States suggest that consumer benefits from innovations have greatly exceeded research costs. An often-mentioned failure concerns industrywide learning by doing. In principle, governments could use subsidies instead of protection to encourage domestic producers to learn by doing or enter markets with high setup costs. In practice, protection has been a more popular tool because it is more practical administratively and financially.

• A recent argument for trade intervention calls for using trade policy as a strategic tool to give domestic firms an edge in global markets (Helpman and Krugman 1989; Brander and Spencer 1985). When large oligopolies compete in world markets, governments might want to subsidize national firms to shift oligopoly profits to them. Similarly, a government could try to subsidize the entry of national firms into global markets with scale economies that preclude more than a few players.

Arguments against intervention

• The high costs of intervention in trade policy have been documented by a number of studies (Balassa and Associates 1971; Bhagwati 1978). Even in the Republic of Korea, some prominent import-substituting projects were costly failures. The ''Big Push'' to develop heavy industry in 1973–79 contributed to real appreciation of the exchange rate, loss of competitiveness, and distortions in financial markets (Collins 1990). GNP growth in Korea fell to −4.8 percent in 1980. It turned around again to 6 percent in 1981–82 following devaluation, liberalization of price and import controls, and tax reform. Where interventions have been successful, the evidence suggests that countries do better if the interventions result in neutral incentives. Success also depends on a time limit for the interventions. But most countries do not have the administrative capacity to collect all the information needed to ensure that inter-

---

have been only partly maintained, and often they have collapsed altogether. How far can countries and the international community (which also has a stake in these reforms) improve the chances that trade liberalization will succeed?

One study of thirty-six trade reforms in nineteen developing countries between 1945 and 1984 found that only fifteen of the reforms were fully sustained, nine were partially sustained, and twelve collapsed (Papageorgiou, Michaely, and

Choksi 1990). A study of trade reforms which accompanied World Bank loans in the 1980s found that many countries realigned their exchange rates and offset biases against exporters, and converted quotas to tariffs. Only a few of the countries examined, however, reduced their tariffs substantially. Evidence suggests the merits of phasing out quantitative restrictions rapidly, and reducing tariffs to reasonably low and uniform levels, such as a range of 15–25 percent. Experience supports a substan-

ventions result in neutral incentives. And protected sectors may continue to lobby for protection of infant industries long after they mature. Europe and Japan provide examples from the industrial countries of the difficulty of trying to dismantle protection of agriculture.

• Efforts to encourage diversification out of commodities and into industry have often resulted in high levels of protection for manufacturing sectors. In the process, many countries undermined their agricultural base and created industrial sectors that depended on indefinite protection for survival (for example, Argentina, Egypt, and India).

• In practice, trade policy is generally not a desirable instrument for encouraging domestic industry. Although protection may encourage learning by doing—by promoting production—and draw more workers to the protected sector, relative prices become distorted in favor of production for domestic markets. To offset the anti-export bias, additional measures are necessary, often resulting in a labyrinth of interventions.

• The case for strategic subsidies to help national firms in developing countries compete on world markets is weak (Bhagwati 1989). Apart from a few isolated cases—such as the Brazilian aircraft industry—producers are more likely to have oligopoly power in home than in global markets. That makes protection even more costly than in the perfectly competitive case. If other countries retaliate by subsidizing their national firms, everyone may be worse off. Studies of the gains from promoting entry by domestic firms into world markets have shown the gains to be small or nonexistent (Grossman 1989). A study of the Brazilian aircraft industry found no welfare gains from subsidizing exports, in part because other countries also subsidized entry (Baldwin and Flam 1989). A study of the global rivalry between a large U.S. airplane manufacturer and a large European one estimated that government subsidies imposed a considerable welfare cost on the United States and brought little (if any) welfare gain to Europe (Baldwin and Krugman 1987).

tial and comprehensive reform within, say, five years, with major and decisive actions in the first year.

Despite these difficulties in implementing reform and sustaining it once introduced, liberalizing countries outperformed the others. A study of developing countries in the 1980s found that, holding other factors, countries that implemented trade reforms experienced a higher annual increase in GDP growth (Thomas and Nash, forth-

coming). Growth rates for reforming countries were higher even when other effects were taken into account, including external financing, changes in the terms of trade, movements in the real exchange rate, and faster growth in the OECD countries.

Microeconomic aspects

Successful reforms have usually reduced the coverage of quantitative restrictions and the level and dispersion of tariffs. Quantitative restrictions may be phased out in various ways. Where product quotas are used, the quota ceiling can be gradually raised until the quota becomes redundant, a method used by Australia, the EC, and New Zealand. Where import licenses are used, licensing can be phased out by reducing the number of products to which licenses apply, making the licenses transferable, and shifting to "negative lists," which permit unrestricted imports of all products not listed.

Tariffs may be reduced either by making equally proportional cuts in all tariffs or by reducing the top rate to a target level, which is gradually lowered. A nonuniform tariff structure may in principle generate more revenue, with higher tariffs on goods with the most inflexible demand. Designing such a system, however, requires massive amounts of information and could also adversely affect income distribution. Equally important, nonuniform tariffs are subject to lobbying pressures, raise administrative difficulties, and introduce the perception of inequity. Next to a no-tariff system, the best practical policy is to establish a relatively low uniform tariff structure and a duty-drawback program for exporters.

Reforms to promote a more competitive domestic economy (discussed in Chapter 4) are crucial. Restrictions on market entry or exit, price and production controls, or regulations that reduce competition in the nontradables sector may dampen the expected supply response to trade reforms. In Mexico, entry barriers made it difficult for firms to respond to the new incentives. Until recently, regulations in the transport sector steeply increased the cost of shipping products to ports or the U.S. border. Regulations inhibiting exit by insolvent companies (such as bankruptcy laws and institutional or political constraints) also prevent improvements in the structure of production under trade reforms. Restrictions on exit partly explain the failure of earlier trade liberalization attempts in Poland and Yugoslavia. Such cases confirm one of

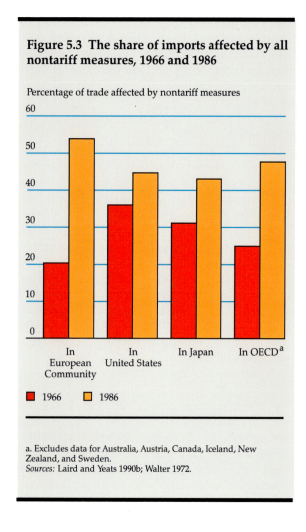

Figure 5.3 The share of imports affected by all nontariff measures, 1966 and 1986

Percentage of trade affected by nontariff measures

In European Community · In United States · In Japan · In OECD[a]

■ 1966   ■ 1986

a. Excludes data for Australia, Austria, Canada, Iceland, New Zealand, and Sweden.
Sources: Laird and Yeats 1990b; Walter 1972.

the main themes of this Report: success in one aspect of reform requires complementary efforts in others.

The macroeconomic context

This point applies to macroeconomic policy with equal, if not greater, force. Large fiscal deficits and money financing of those deficits worsen the external balance and generate inflation, frequently leading to losses in reserves. If the nominal exchange rate is not allowed to adjust, foreign exchange shortages often oblige the government to return to licensing, higher protection, and trade restrictions.

Although tariffs are a much more distortionary means of raising revenue than sales taxes or value added taxes, administrative weaknesses in many countries lead them to rely heavily on trade taxes as a revenue source.

The effect of liberalization on revenues depends

on the mix of policies. Governments need to assess the potential revenue effect of reforms. A switching from quantitative restrictions to tariffs can be undertaken under almost any fiscal situation. Tariff reductions, however, need to be accompanied by measures to convert remaining quotas to tariffs, together with a reduction in tariff exemptions. Declines in tariff revenue—if expenditures cannot be reduced—may need to be compensated for with other measures. Reformers have improved tax administration and collection (in Ghana, Pakistan, and Thailand); increased rates and coverage of sales and excise taxes (in Malawi, Mauritius, Mexico, and the Philippines); introduced a value added tax (in Jamaica, Morocco, and Turkey); or increased the price of public sector output and services.

The timing of compensatory revenue measures is of critical importance. Although trade reform in both Mexico and Morocco led to a decline in trade tax revenues, Mexico cushioned the loss through higher revenues from a value added tax instituted before the reform. Morocco, however, rolled back some of its tariff reforms initiated in 1984 when implementation difficulties with its new value added tax and the collapse of world phosphate prices added to its revenue problems.

A World Bank study of nineteen trade-reforming countries found that appreciation of the real exchange rate was often associated with the collapse of a reform episode. Trying to implement trade reforms when the exchange rate is grossly overvalued will make balance of payments problems worse and is likely to sabotage the reform effort. As controls on imports are relaxed, a real depreciation will increase the prices of tradables, making export production more attractive and temporarily dampening the impact of competition for producers of import-competing goods. (The role of macroeconomic policy in development is discussed in detail in Chapter 6.)

Political-economy considerations

Even the best-conceived trade reform may fail because of problems which are not purely economic. Those who stand to lose from a trade reform are generally more organized and politically powerful than those who stand to gain, such as consumers at large or rural agricultural interests. Reform also threatens vested interests within government, from protected state enterprises to trade regulators who derive rents from the status quo to politicians who seek to cultivate support. Getting the pace and sequencing of reform right can help to overcome such difficulties. (Chapter 7 returns to these issues in the art of reform.)

The global climate for trade

Industrial-country protection

Trade reform in developing countries is much more likely to go ahead if success in trade is not punished. During the past several decades, average tariffs in industrial countries have been reduced to less than 6 percent. But the use of other protective measures such as quotas, subsidies, voluntary export restraints, and countervailing and anti-dumping measures, has risen alarmingly since the 1960s. Increased protection is largely the result of greater competition on world markets, exacerbated by the inability of the GATT to control nontariff barriers. Between 1966 and 1986, the share of imports affected by all nontariff measures increased by more than 20 percent for the United States, almost 40 percent for Japan, and 160 percent for the EC (Figure 5.3). By 1986, 21 percent of imports from developing countries to the OECD were covered by so-called hard-core nontariff barriers: quotas, voluntary export restraints, the MFA, and other highly restrictive measures (Figure 5.4). This number does not even include other restrictions such as price restraints or health and safety regulations. If these measures were included, the share of trade covered by nontariff barriers in industrial countries could be equal to the 28 percent of trade covered by all nontariff measures in developing countries in 1987.

Subsidies to agriculture increased by 80 percent in the United States, by 60 percent in Canada, and by 21 percent in Japan between 1980 and 1985, while the number of countervailing and anti-dumping cases filed by Australia, Canada, the EC, and the United States more than doubled. New evidence suggests that anti-dumping and subsidy investigations are being used as a threat against foreign imports, even when the countervailing and anti-dumping duties are not applied. Since the mid-1980s, industrial countries have done almost nothing to roll back the accumulated protection. The increasing use of such measures by industrial countries during the past 30 years provides a disturbing precedent for retaliatory action and for the enactment of similar measures by developing countries.

Laird and Yeats (1987) estimated that the cost (in 1990 dollars) to developing economies in terms of forgone exports was $55 billion in 1980—almost

Figure 5.4 Hard-core nontariff measures applied against industrial and developing countries, 1986

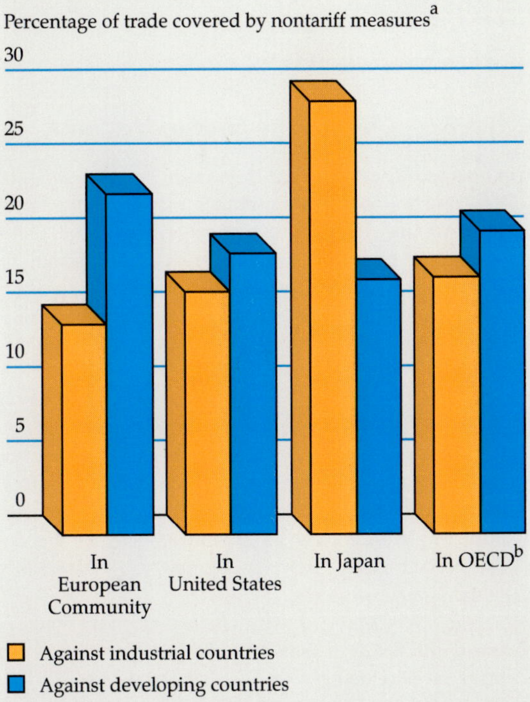

Percentage of trade covered by nontariff measures[a]

a. Calculated using 1981 trade weights. Hard-core nontariff measures include quotas, voluntary export restraints, the Multifibre Arrangement, and other highly restrictive measures.
b. Excludes data for Australia, Austria, Canada, Iceland, New Zealand, and Sweden.
Source: Laird and Yeats 1990a.

equal to the value of total official development assistance in that year. Action by developing economies to reform their trade policies must be met by equal efforts to reduce protection in the industrial world. But developing economies should not slow their own reform efforts simply because of rising protection in industrial ones. The four East Asian NIEs were able to increase their share in total world trade and manufactured exports more than eightfold between 1965 and 1989, despite rising protection in industrial countries. The scope for increased trade in manufactures for the rest of the industrializing economies remains significant: they accounted for only 5 percent of manufactured exports in 1988. Can they too continue to benefit from trading opportunities despite declining terms of trade for commodities?

105

The evidence in Box 5.5 shows a relatively small decline in primary commodity prices in relation to manufacturers during the course of this century.

Nevertheless, falling primary commodity prices since the 1970s and volatility in these markets pose serious problems for low-income primary producers. The solution is not an easy one. If countries produce a large share of world exports (such

---

Box 5.5 Commodity price movements

Can a country still benefit from trade if a large share of its exports is primary products? In the 1950s, Raoul Prebisch and Hans Singer suggested that the gains from trade for developing countries would decline as the price of commodity exports relative to manufactures imports fell. The Prebisch-Singer hypothesis provided a rationale for import-substituting industrialization. The evidence is not persuasive.

Between 1900 and 1986, nonfuel commodity terms of trade declined by an average of 0.6 percent a year (Box figure 5.5a). If we choose a different period, however, the decline is much smaller. Between 1920 and 1986, the terms of trade fell less than 0.3 percent a year. In addition, these figures are likely to overstate the decline because they ignore improvements in the quality of manufactured goods.

Many developing countries have diversified their exports: the share of manufacturing in the nonfuel exports of developing countries increased from 15 percent in 1963 to 62 percent in 1987 (Balassa, background paper). In addition, small exporters of commodities such as coffee or cocoa have probably benefited from improved terms of trade as grain import prices have declined. Consequently, the terms of trade for developing countries have probably fallen by much less than the nonfuel commodity decline.

Nor do changing prices take into account offsetting increases in trade volumes. Despite significant declines in the relative price of nonfuel commodities since 1973, revenues from commodities have stayed relatively constant in relation to those from manufactures. Export volumes from developing countries over this period nearly doubled, offsetting the declining terms of trade (Box figure 5.5b). Because of differences in domestic policy, some countries did much less well than others: nonfuel commodity export revenues fell 50 percent in South Asia and increased by about the same amount in East Asia.

Box figure 5.5a Nonfuel primary commodities versus manufactures: relative price index, 1900-90

Index: 1977-79 = 100

Note: The manufactures price index used is the U.S. wholesale price index.
Sources: World Bank data; Grilli and Yang 1988.

Box figure 5.5b Trends in exports and the terms of trade of developing countries, 1965-88

Index: 1965 = 100

Note: Barter terms of trade are the weighted export unit values of primary commodities deflated by the weighted import unit values of each region. The barter terms of trade multipled by the actual volume of exports yields the income terms of trade. Data are based on a sample of ninety developing countries.
Source: World Bank data.

as coffee or cocoa) or if increasing export volumes from some groups of exporters depress prices, a case could be made for controlling production through export taxes. In practice, however, attempts to stabilize international or domestic producer prices have not met with much success. In many cases, the implicit tax on agriculture is too high because of a combination of export taxes and the protection of manufacturing. Although new financial instruments designed to hedge commodity price risk hold promise, their use has been limited because many poor countries pose an unacceptable credit risk for commercial financing.

Yet both developing and industrial countries have recourse to policies which can make a significant difference (see also Box 5.4). In some low- and middle-income countries during the 1970s, inappropriate policies led to losses in market share and greater dependence on a few primary commodity exports. Industrial countries, which impose greater protection for goods at a higher stage of processing, discourage the development of local processing capacity for industrializing countries.

Regional trading blocs

The unification of Europe in 1992, the United States-Canada free trade agreement in 1989, and the proposed inclusion of Mexico in the United States-Canada agreement could herald a new era of regional trading blocs. Although such blocs may constitute a step toward global free trade, it remains to be seen whether they will support or hinder the goal of a more open global trading system.

In principle, the formation of a trading bloc leads to net gains for its members when goods which were domestically produced are now imported from lower-cost partners. Other potential sources of gain include economies of scale and in-

creased competition from larger markets, particularly in countries with emerging infant industries and low domestic demand. Yet a trading bloc may also lead to losses if members replace lower-priced goods from outside the bloc with more expensive goods produced by other members. Even if a regional trading bloc can be designed to generate net gains for its members, these gains are exceeded by the benefits from unilateral trade reform.

What about primary product exporters? The evidence presented in Box 5.5 shows that primary product exporters also stand to gain from rising exports.

The historical evidence (Table 5.4) suggests that regional blocs in all but the EC have not generated a large share of total trade in the post-World War II period. Why? In a number of cases (CARICOM and the Central American Common Market in Central America; UDEAC in Africa) intraregional conflicts have made it difficult to liberate internal trade. In many blocs, such as the Andean Pact, participants sought to rationalize production by allocating specific markets to designated producers instead of allowing the competitive process to determine the allocation of production. These designated producers were not necessarily the most efficient; nor were tariffs low enough in relation to the rest of the world to provide external competition. Consequently, the expected benefits from rationalization of production or increased competition have been limited. Developing-country trading blocs have often imposed high tariffs or quotas against nonmembers, increasing the likelihood that net losses from the bloc will exceed gains. In addition, except in the EC, trading opportunities and pro-competitive effects have been limited by the small size of regional markets in comparison with the rest of the world. Finally, regional trading blocs have frequently produced

Table 5.4 Intraunion trade as a percentage of total exports, 1960–87

Economic union	1960	1970	1976	1980	1983	1987
European Community[a]	34.6	48.9	..	52.8	52.4	58.8
Association of South-East Pacific States	21.7	14.7	13.9	17.8	23.1	17.7
Central African Customs and Economic Union	1.6	3.4	3.9	4.1	2.0	0.9
Central American Common Market	7.5	26.8	21.6	22.0	21.8	11.9
Caribbean Community	4.5	7.3	6.7	6.4	9.3	6.3
LAIA–Latin American Free Trade Area	7.7	10.2	12.8	13.5	10.2	11.3
Andean Group	0.7	2.3	4.2	3.5	4.3	3.2
West African Economic Community	2.0	9.1	6.7	6.9	11.6	7.7
Economic Community of West African States	1.2	2.1	3.1	3.9	4.1	5.5
Economic Community of the Great Lake Countries	0.0	0.2	0.2	0.2	0.2	..
Mano River Union	0.0	0.1	0.2	0.1	0.1	..
Regional Cooperation for Development	..	1.0	0.8	5.3	8.5	5.2

a. Includes the original six members up to 1970 and nine after 1980.
Source: Lächler 1989.

similar products, limiting the opportunity to exploit differences in skills or endowments.

Do trading agreements between industrial and developing countries show more promise? Larger markets and greater differences in the structure of production could in principle generate greater gains for the participants. But such a strategy could also undermine the GATT and the multilateral trade system, and thus reduce the incentives of partners within such blocs to move toward global free trade. Other countries, reacting to the formation of such blocs, may set up their own network of trading blocs. Such a system is likely to reinforce current protectionist trends, and it could be a blow to developing countries' efforts to reform trade.

Unilateral trade liberalization and multilateral efforts to free up global trade are preferable to the formation of trading blocs; however, steps can be taken to maximize the gains from such unions. First, members should commit themselves to multilateral reform and the GATT. The EC, for example, continued to participate in multilateral trade negotiations in the post-World War II period at a pace similar to other industrial countries (except in agriculture). Second, the external tariffs set by regional blocs should be reduced or limited to those of the most open member; meanwhile, internal efforts should concentrate on freeing up trade and ending efforts to allocate production. Third, participants should continue to move toward freer trade through unilateral reforms. Postponing reforms to win agreement with other members of the trading bloc will greatly increase the costs of such arrangements.

Trade routes to growth

Openness to trade has improved resource allocation, increased competition and product specialization, and provided a broad avenue for technology transfer. Ironically, greater competition and a more integrated world have also resulted in a global trading system which is now poised at a critical juncture. The world faces two important trade challenges in the 1990s. First, regional trading arrangements must be carefully managed to ensure that multilateral commitments are strengthened, not forgotten. Second, and even more urgent, the Uruguay Round of trade talks must be revived. However difficult, all participants must reach agreement to open up agriculture, expand the GATT to eliminate quantity restrictions (on autos, steel, and textiles), and restrict the use of so-called fair trade legislation (anti-dumping and subsidy measures). In this, the developing countries can play a key role; in their own interests, they should press for free trade and continue to reform their own trading systems. The industrial countries of today grew prosperous through trade. No effort should be spared to ensure that the developing countries can follow that same path to progress.

The macroeconomic foundation

The experience of the 1970s and 1980s indicates that macroeconomic stability is necessary for sustainable growth. Sound fiscal and monetary policies create a hospitable climate for private investment and thus promote productivity. The previous chapters have shown that macroeconomic stability certainly does not by itself lead to development—but without it all other efforts are likely to be in vain.

Countries often experience external or internal macroeconomic shocks. Flexibility in adjusting quickly to the fiscal and monetary problems that these shocks cause is crucial if growth is to be sustained. Lack of adjustment may result in high inflation, an overvalued exchange rate, and a balance of payments crisis. These lead in turn to low investment and slow growth. The contrast is illustrated by comparing the experience of the East Asian economies in the 1970s and 1980s with that of Latin America in the past decade. For a country experiencing significant domestic and external imbalances, a credible reduction in the fiscal deficit is almost always necessary to reduce inflation, and an appropriate exchange rate is needed to reduce the balance of payments deficit.

These macroeconomic prescriptions may seem straightforward, but putting them into practice rarely is. The pace and sequencing of macroeconomic stabilization policies are difficult issues in their own right. The task is all the more demanding when macroeconomic reform is merely an element of a broader program of economic reform—as this Report says it usually needs to be. Potential conflicts among various reforms need to be minimized, and complementarities need to be taken advantage of. (The purely economic aspects

of program design will be addressed later in this chapter. Some of the political difficulties raised by reform, and how they can be overcome, will be examined in Chapter 7.)

In many developing countries, long-term growth requires a higher level of investment. Countries that lack access to adequate supplies of foreign savings will find this difficult to finance. They must do all they can to encourage domestic saving. A stable macroeconomy can help greatly; it is likely to promote saving and investment alike. The microeconomic reforms suggested elsewhere in the Report should then help to ensure that these bigger volumes of investment are used more productively.

Good macroeconomic policies will also make it easier to attract foreign savings. External debt will, however, remain an obstacle to growth in many countries. A heavy burden of debt service preempts resources that could otherwise be used for domestic investment; it also acts as a disincentive for investment because it makes firms anxious about future exchange rate devaluation and higher levels of taxation. Debt and debt service reduction, in parallel with the necessary policy changes, can smooth the path of reform, improve the program's credibility with private investors, and contribute to fiscal adjustment.

Policies to promote stability and growth

The adverse macroeconomic shocks of the early 1980s led to sharp declines in growth rates, and many countries have since been slow to recover. As a result, much more attention has recently been paid to the relation between macroeconomic policy

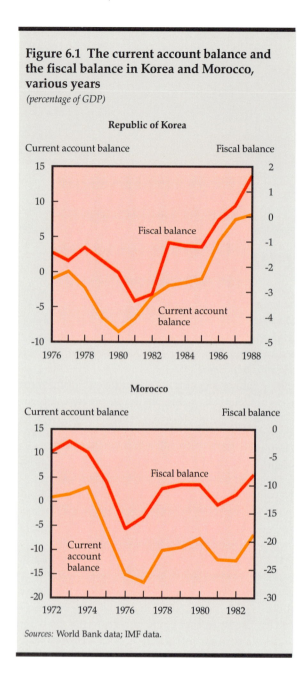

Figure 6.1 The current account balance and the fiscal balance in Korea and Morocco, various years
(percentage of GDP)

Republic of Korea

Morocco

Sources: World Bank data; IMF data.

ing on how they are financed, the rate of inflation (Figure 6.2). Monetary policy in developing countries largely follows fiscal policy. In many countries the absence of well-developed capital markets limits the instruments of monetary policy to credit controls, interest rate ceilings, and changes in reserve requirements. The degree of central bank autonomy may affect the conduct of monetary policy: money creation is in many cases the residual source of financing, so if the central bank is obliged to finance a big deficit it may be unable to implement a restrictive monetary policy targeted at controlling inflation.

The mode of deficit financing is crucial. When a deficit is financed by printing more money than the public wants to hold, prices will rise. Inflation may bring a reduction in private wealth insofar as the value of financial assets may be eroded—the so-called inflation tax. But this effect is likely to be short-lived and to diminish as inflationary expectations strengthen; the longer the experience of inflation, the less economic agents will be willing to hold the non-interest-bearing assets on which the "tax" is levied. Moreover, if real tax revenues also fall with inflation because of delays in collection, the deficit will widen; that will cause faster money creation and even higher inflation. After a certain point, therefore, high inflation may actually reduce the inflation tax. This appears to have occurred in Ghana, Malawi, and Zaire between the periods 1973–78 and 1978–83, and in Chile between 1963–73 and 1973–78.

When budget deficits are financed by excessive domestic borrowing, they can lead to higher interest rates that crowd out the private sector. There are limits to a rapid accumulation of domestic debt; at some point, the public will be unwilling to hold more debt or will do so only at higher interest rates, further increasing the cost of debt service, as happened in Argentina and Brazil. Eventually deficits must be brought down with cuts in spending, or through higher taxes. Otherwise inflationary financing of the deficit is inevitable.

Inflation and growth

Countries with different rates of inflation have been able to achieve long periods of growth. But high and unstable inflation—and high inflation is usually unstable—is likely to reduce growth by creating an unstable economic climate, causing distortions in relative prices, and absorbing resources. Inflation requires frequent price adjustments. These tend to blur the information

and growth. The lesson is that durable growth requires sustainable policies—ones that do not give rise to accelerating inflation or unfinanceable current account deficits. Macroeconomic stability must be a top priority.

Fiscal and monetary policy

A prudent fiscal policy is the foundation of a stable macroeconomy. Taxes and public spending affect resource allocation, and fiscal deficits affect both the balance of payments (Figure 6.1) and, depend-

embodied in relative prices. Entrepreneurial effort is diverted from production and investment decisions to short-term financial matters. Distortions in key prices such as the real interest rate and the real exchange rate are also likely to hamper growth. Corrective inflation (the increase in prices needed to achieve a change in relative prices that represents an adjustment to a real shock) can be more efficiently achieved when inflation is low and is expected to remain that way.

Inflation may also worsen the distribution of income by harming low-income groups (which tend to hold a larger share of their assets as cash balances) more than other groups. High rates of inflation, as in Argentina, Brazil, and until recently Israel, can also lead to nonproductive expansion of the financial system. The demand for financial-intermediation services rises with the public's attempt to protect the real value of its assets. Banks proliferate, trying to capture the part of the inflation tax that falls on non-interest-bearing deposits. In Brazil, the financial sector's share of GDP doubled between 1975 and 1987, a waste of resources caused by a demand for services that existed only because of high inflation.

Exchange rate policy

A competitive real exchange rate is necessary to support the expansion of the export sector and to avoid the emergence of balance of payments difficulties that might lead to calls for import restrictions. Countries that have allowed their real exchange rate to become grossly overvalued have experienced both a slowing of the expansion of their export sector and capital flight. Exchange rate overvaluation retards growth and has contributed to the decline of the agricultural sector and the deterioration of the external position of many African countries.

The equilibrium real exchange rate is not fixed for all time; its level depends on the terms of trade, real interest rates abroad, the outlook for capital flows, the level of import tariffs, the extent of capital market controls, and the composition of government spending. Correcting external imbalances generally requires adjusting the exchange rate toward its equilibrium level to redirect resources to the tradable goods sector and to reduce spending. In the short run, most of any nominal devaluation is also a real devaluation. If it is to endure, this real devaluation has to be supported by anti-inflationary policies, including in many cases lower fiscal deficits. Evidence shows that a real depreciation is

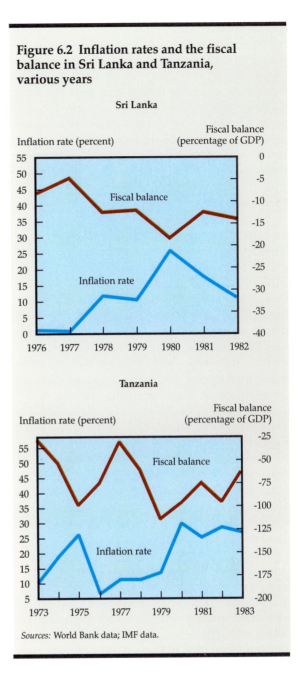

Figure 6.2 Inflation rates and the fiscal balance in Sri Lanka and Tanzania, various years

Sri Lanka

Sources: World Bank data; IMF data.

eroded rather quickly when fiscal and monetary policies are lax or price indexation is widespread.

A fixed exchange rate has sometimes been used to control inflation, serving as a nominal anchor for domestic policies and demonstrating the authorities' commitment to low inflation. In this case, exchange rate policy takes priority; other policies should adjust to support it.

Does this approach work? The argument, as advanced for some countries in Latin America, is that it restores the credibility of the government's commitment to reduce inflation. But as the experience of Argentina, Brazil, and Israel shows, the fixed exchange rate will not be sustainable unless the macroeconomic fundamentals are right (that is, unless the fiscal deficit has been cut). India, Pakistan, and Thailand have maintained a fixed exchange rate for long periods of time, but this seems to have been a by-product of low inflation, rather than a means of achieving it. Inflation continued to be relatively low even after their commitment to a fixed exchange rate was abandoned.

Booms and busts

No country is ever in a stable equilibrium. Economies are always adjusting to internal and external shocks. The past two decades have been unusually turbulent. Two oil price shocks and a debt crisis have rocked the world economy, and sharp fluctuations in commodity prices have had enormous effects on large producers. For some, these shocks were favorable; for others, unfavorable. Countries varied in their response. Following favorable shifts in their terms of trade, many countries pursued unsustainable policies, financing them with the windfall gains of positive shocks or external borrowing. In other countries the origin of the boom was internal; an increase in government spending, for example. The short-term effect of such booms depended on how the additional spending was divided between tradable and nontradable goods, whereas the medium-term effect depended on whether the additional spending was directed to consumption or investment.

Boom and bust episodes show it is important to pursue policies that do not give rise to large macroeconomic imbalances, to adjust quickly, and to respond cautiously to shifts in terms of trade. There is an important distinction between terms of trade shocks that give rise to a permanent change in wealth and those that do not. The windfalls from temporary changes in terms of trade should be saved. It is difficult, however, to determine a priori whether a shock will be permanent or temporary. Prudence calls for treating all favorable shocks as temporary, at least until the dust settles.

External booms

Favorable shifts in the terms of trade induced a big increase in government spending in, for instance, Mexico and Nigeria and fueled domestic booms that were already under way in Côte d'Ivoire and Morocco. Mexico grew rapidly after increases in government expenditures following major oil discoveries in 1977 and the second oil price shock.

The fiscal deficit doubled, reaching 17.2 percent of GDP in 1982, and foreign debt accumulated rapidly, setting the stage for the debt crisis of that year. Nigeria's response to the oil windfall was to increase government spending by more than the rise in revenues; the resulting fiscal deficit was financed with external borrowing and the inflation tax. The response to the second oil price boom was similar (large budget deficits and a continuing overvaluation of the currency), except that the mix of public spending shifted further toward consumption.

The investment boom in Côte d'Ivoire began with a series of sugar projects; increases in world coffee prices led to further expansion. Between 1974 and 1978, the investment-to-GDP ratio increased 10 percentage points. But even when the terms of trade began to decline, investment expansion continued, financed by domestic and external borrowing, and debt accumulated rapidly. Morocco's economy experienced two large shocks in 1974 when the price of world phosphates quintupled and military spending increased rapidly because of the conflict in the Western Sahara. In 1974–77, an ambitious investment program financed with external borrowing increased the investment-to-GDP ratio by 11 percentage points. The budget deficit tripled to 11.7 percent of GNP; however, monetary discipline cushioned the inflationary effect of these policies.

Commodity booms increase spending, raise the price of nontraded goods relative to that of traded goods, and shift capital and labor to the expanding sector. The real exchange rate appreciates, squeezing the nonboom tradables sector in a phenomenon known as "Dutch disease." When booms are temporary, a devaluation may be necessary. Indonesia, for example, devalued the rupiah in November 1978 to prevent a real appreciation of the currency. This prevented a decline in the farm sector and helped to increase Indonesia's share in world agricultural exports. Nigeria, in contrast, failed to offset the appreciation of its currency between 1974 and 1984; large premiums were charged in the parallel currency market, and foreign exchange was rationed. The oil price boom, together with poor marketing and pricing policies, disrupted the farm sector, causing a steep decline in the production of traditional cash crops and heavy migration to the cities.

Internal booms

Internal booms usually result from excessive government spending, as in Brazil in the 1970s, or from a surge in private spending in response to changes in policy, as in Chile in 1980–81. Easy access to external financing sustained the increases in spending, but excessive borrowing created a balance of payments crisis later. Between the two oil price shocks, Brazil substantially increased its public investment, largely in public enterprises.

Countries such as Colombia experienced more moderate domestic booms but did not experience debt crises because they borrowed abroad more modestly or at low interest rates. The end of Colombia's coffee boom in the 1970s was followed by a large increase in public investment, particularly in the energy sector, that raised the current account deficit to 10.8 percent of GDP by 1983. Colombia avoided a debt crisis because its debt was small to begin with, because the authorities borrowed cautiously, and because the response to macroeconomic imbalances was swift. The lesson of such episodes is that countries should try to keep their spending consistent with their permanent income.

Busts

The good times generally ended with a reversal in the terms of trade or a cutoff in external financing. In several countries the landing was hard. In Mexico, prosperity ended abruptly in 1982, with lower oil prices, higher interest rates, and massive capital flight. Mexico's creditors refused to roll over the country's short-term debt, and the country suspended interest payments. The next four years saw high inflation and a decline of 10 percent in per capita income. Turkey lost its access to external financing in 1977. In the next three years, GDP stagnated, investment and consumption declined, unemployment increased rapidly, and inflation reached 100 percent. In Chile's bust of 1982, GDP fell by 14 percent (Figure 6.3).

These cases show how large the costs of unsustainable polices can be. That is why it is far better, whenever possible, to anticipate rather than react to emerging macroeconomic imbalances; the transition to a sustainable path will then be far less painful. Fiscal adjustment can be more moderate, making it easier to protect investment in infrastructure, education, and health from cuts.

From stabilization to growth

In the 1980s many countries embarked on programs of stabilization and structural reform. Stabilization policies work mainly on the demand side to reduce inflation and external deficits (though

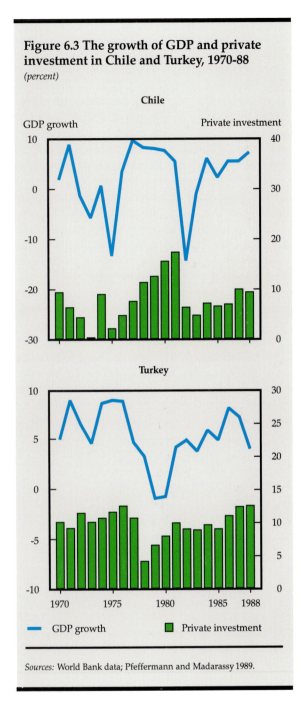

Figure 6.3 The growth of GDP and private investment in Chile and Turkey, 1970-88
(percent)

Sources: World Bank data; Pfeffermann and Madarassy 1989.

they also have supply-side effects). Structural policies are concerned with the supply side; they address the efficiency of resource use, emphasizing reforms in specific sectors—especially trade, finance, and industry. It is possible to postpone structural reforms during stabilization, but the converse is rarely true: structural reforms are unlikely to succeed unless they are preceded or accompanied by stabilization. Similarly, stabilization is unlikely to be sustainable without structural reforms.

113

Adjustment programs—usually supported by the International Monetary Fund (IMF) and the World Bank—address internal and external imbalances and, in varying degrees, incentives and institutions. In the short run, stabilization can lower output growth. The benefits take a lot longer to come through, as do the gains from structural reform. Several studies have found a strong association between adjustment programs and improvements in the balance of payments, but the effects on growth are less clear. One study found a negative effect on growth immediately after a program; but, for countries where programs had been in place for three or more years, several Bank studies have found a positive effect on growth (Box 6.1).

Adjustment programs very often include measures to reduce the fiscal deficit. Some countries have cut their primary deficits (which exclude interest outlays) by as much as 10 percent of GDP. The composition of the reduction varies from case to case. Ghana, Jamaica, and Mexico, for instance, reduced both current and capital outlays; Côte d'Ivoire and Indonesia cut mainly capital spending; Morocco cut mainly current spending. In many countries macroeconomic stability has been an elusive goal. In Brazil and Argentina, the inability to reduce the fiscal deficit has been a major cause for the failure of several stabilization attempts.

Fiscal reform often involves difficult trade-offs. Cutting capital spending may create less political resistance than cutting current spending (mainly wages and subsidies). Abolishing inefficient investment projects is fine, but cuts in productive investment in infrastructure and education, for example, are likely to hurt long-term growth. All sorts of spending should be reviewed; dispensing with some programs, especially in military spending, will do much less harm than dispensing with others. On the revenue side, tax reform has a role to play. Exemptions, inefficient tax collection, narrow bases, and low compliance all mean that high tax rates are needed to raise relatively little revenue. In Pakistan, for instance, the agricultural sector (one-fifth of GDP) is exempted altogether from direct income taxes; there are many exemptions for industry, too.

A further complication for many countries' adjustment was the burden of public debt. Although domestic and foreign public debt often grew si-

---

Box 6.1   What the assessments of adjustment programs say about income performance

Since the early 1980s, many developing countries have launched economic adjustment programs. These programs—usually supported by the IMF and the World Bank—address internal and external imbalances and, to varying degrees, incentives and institutions.

Have they succeeded? Answering this question is not straightforward. Changes in external factors may affect performance during the course of an adjustment program. Even without such changes, it may be difficult to say how the economy would have performed if the program had not been implemented. And the mere fact that a program is supported by the IMF or World Bank does not necessarily mean that policy reforms have been pushed through.

Adjustment programs usually include stabilization measures as well as structural reforms. In the short run, stabilization may lower output growth. The efficiency gains and growth in output that are expected from structural reforms typically take much longer.

Several assessments examined performance before and after an IMF program but without controlling for external factors or estimating a counterfactual scenario. These studies found improvements in the balance of payments, but the evidence on growth and inflation was inconclusive.

Other assessments compared changes in the performance of countries that had programs with changes in a control group of nonprogram countries. These studies found improvements in the balance of payments in the program countries relative to the control group, but no conclusive evidence on growth. Another study found moderate improvements in economic performance. The drawback of this approach is that unless the two groups share the same initial conditions, the group participating in the program or receiving a loan may not represent a random sample of the overall set of countries.

A third approach is to construct a counterfactual scenario, guided by the country's history of similar macroeconomic imbalances. Studies of this kind have found a strong association between the program or loan and improvements in the balance of payments, a negative effect on investments, but little effect on growth. Khan (1990) found a negative effect on growth immediately after the program. World Bank studies have found a positive effect on growth, but only for early loan recipients (countries for which three or more years had elapsed since initiating the reform).

multaneously, the underlying processes were different. Domestic debt expanded with the shift from external to internal financing; public external debt grew as government guarantees were extended to public enterprises, and as private debt, amortization, and interest payments were rescheduled. This shift of external liabilities to the public sector further weakened the fiscal position. In Turkey, continued deficits and the shift to more costly domestic financing helped to increase the public debt from about 12 percent of GDP in 1980–81 to 30 percent in 1987–88. And there is another dilemma: when the external debt is a public liability, devaluation may be in conflict with fiscal adjustment. In Turkey a real depreciation of the currency improved the current account position, but it increased interest payments denominated in domestic currency and hence the fiscal deficit.

The social effects of adjustment

Labor markets play an important role in determining the outcome of adjustment. Downward flexibility of real wages will cushion the effect on output and employment of policies that are intended to reduce domestic absorption. The evidence suggests that real wages are in fact flexible. In Bolivia, Chile, and Ghana, real wages declined significantly during adjustment. However, when labor markets bear a disproportionate share of the adjustment burden, the fall in real wages may cause an excessive decline in aggregate demand, which in turn may jeopardize the recovery of output. In Malaysia in the mid-1980s, changes in the exchange rate, interest rate, and commodity prices all helped to cushion the effect of adjustment on real wages and employment. As a result, the subsequent recovery was faster.

Recently attention has focused on the short-run effect of adjustment on the poor. Fiscal consolidation often involves cuts in government programs and a temporary rise in unemployment. Different groups are affected in different ways by fiscal cuts. The needs of the persistently poor and the newly poor (those who lost jobs as a result of adjustment) are not the same; nor are those of urban and rural households. Special programs, as in Bolivia and Ghana, can include temporary measures to protect the groups that are most at risk. This is a worthy goal in its own right, but it may also help to maintain political support for adjustment.

The evidence on countries that undertook strong programs does not point to a clear relation between adjustment and changes in employment or the social indicators. The social effect of new

policies may take longer to emerge than the relatively short period considered in most studies. A review of the trends in social indicators shows that most countries made progress in the 1980s, although progress was slowest in the countries where the indicators were poor to begin with. Lack of good data, and the difficulty of projecting what would have happened if adjustment had not been undertaken, make most evaluations of the effects of adjustment inconclusive.

The art of reform

The scope of the economic reforms that are needed in the developing world varies widely. Some countries urgently need to rationalize prices and incentives; others need to privatize state-owned enterprises or invest in education, health, and infrastructure. Everywhere such measures need to be grounded in macroeconomic stability. Experience shows that the surest path to development is to improve policies in all these respects. But how are such diverse elements to be combined? In what order should reforms be undertaken, and how quickly? There are few hard rules, but history does suggest some general principles.

Reforms have to deal with trade-offs among policies—the so-called competition of instruments problem. For example, reform of the financial sector often calls for distressed financial institutions to be restructured; in the short run, this may raise public spending and make it harder to cut the budget deficit. Adopting positive real interest rates will lower the burden of credit subsidies but increase the cost of servicing domestic debt. Lower tariffs may initially reduce government revenues (as in Mexico and Morocco), whereas shifting from quantitative restrictions to tariffs will generally raise them (as in Indonesia and Peru); the net effect may be a bigger fiscal deficit. These trade-offs make it harder for governments to adopt programs which, taken as a whole, appear to add up. Yet it is essential that programs not merely add up, but are seen to do so.

Many reform programs have successfully dealt with conflicts and tradeoffs. But reforms have also failed. In Tanzania in 1977, in the aftermath of a coffee boom, import controls and foreign exchange licensing were removed without complementary changes in exchange rates and macroeconomic policy. Within months, the balance of payments turned sharply negative and the country lost most of its foreign exchange reserves. The reforms were abandoned, leaving the external sector more restrictive than before. Zambia in 1985 adopted an ambitious program to cut public expenditure, auction foreign exchange, and reduce subsidies to urban consumers amid significant internal political opposition within the government. A year later, however, the price of copper, the dominant export, fell sharply while the country's fiscal and monetary situation deteriorated. Consumer subsidies on some food staples were removed overnight while stockpiles of others were not at hand. Urban unrest followed, and the government, strongly dependent on urban political support, reversed the reforms.

Credibility

If reform is to succeed, investment must respond. Expectations are crucial. The private sector may choose to wait and see, and let the government prove its commitment to the new policies. But this may be a vicious circle, because if it takes too long to restore confidence and investment, the program may fail for that reason alone. If the reforms are credible, however, additional transfers of resources from abroad will raise confidence and fuel an even greater investment recovery than the program was counting on.

Credibility can be improved by first achieving macroeconomic stability. This may reduce the extent of the competition of instruments problem. Even then, in countries with a record of aborted programs, the private sector may be rightly skeptical about the government's bold new initiatives. The longer the history of high inflation and unsuccessful remedies, the harder the task—witness Argentina and Brazil, as compared with Chile and Mexico. Often, the government has no choice but to rebuild its reputation, and then guard it jealously. In this respect, it is important not to promise too much. It may also be necessary for policy to "overshoot" (as Poland's arguably did in the currency devaluation of January 1990), to prove that this time the reformers really do mean business.

Macroeconomic stability

Low inflation is vital not just because it makes the reform program more credible, but also because without it other elements of the program will be directly undermined. Macroeconomic instability contributed, for instance, to the failure of several trade reforms. Reforming the trade regime usually calls for a real devaluation of the currency in response to the effects of reductions in tariffs and nontariff barriers. An expansionary fiscal policy, however, contributes to a currency appreciation,

adding pressures for a reversal of the reforms. Expansionary monetary and fiscal policies are the single greatest threat to trade reform.

Macroeconomic stability also makes reform of the financial sector more likely to succeed, and thus supports the development of capital markets that can foster private investment. The aim of financial reform is to increase savings and to see them used more efficiently. In many cases it involves removing interest rate ceilings to achieve positive real interest rates, and abolishing regulations that affect the size and allocation of bank credit. Close links with world financial markets require domestic interest rates to be high enough relative to international rates for investors to keep their financial assets in the country. For this to work, macroeconomic stability and strong bank supervision both need to be in place. Otherwise, expectations of inflation, exchange rate devaluation, or government borrowing may push real interest rates too high, increasing the fiscal deficit and contributing to further macroeconomic instability. Excessively high interest rates and inadequate supervision of the banking system (especially in the presence of deposit insurance) may cause defaults and instability in credit markets. In Argentina, Chile, the Philippines, Turkey, and Uruguay, rapid interest rate liberalization under conditions of macroeconomic instability and inadequate bank supervision led to financial crises that severely damaged their economies.

Timing

The timing of reforms involves political considerations. New governments are in a strong position to initiate reforms: they are less obligated to defend the status quo, and their clients and opponents may not yet be well organized. Economic crisis also improves the conditions for reform by strengthening coalitions that favor reform and helping to subordinate special interests. (These issues are further discussed in Chapter 7.) Economic and political crises are opportunities for radical change. In Indonesia, reformers designed their plan for liberalization (complete with estimates of effective protection) well before the crisis of 1983. When the choice came to implement it, the homework had already been done.

Speed

Should reform be gradual or "shock therapy"? Some principles are set out in Box 6.2. Gradualism may sometimes be justified when reform faces par-

Box 6.2 The speed of reform

The case for gradualism

- Gradualism in implementing reforms is defined here to mean that reform is spread out over more than two years. Indonesia, the Republic of Korea, Mauritius, Morocco, and Turkey have used a gradual approach. Trade liberalization through the GATT was also a steady but gradual process.

- In an economy with rigid prices and wages or other structural distortions that prevent optimal adjustment, shock therapy may have perverse effects. If the policy shift is sudden, potentially viable factories may collapse and potentially productive employees may be dismissed from their jobs. In such a distorted climate, a gradual policy change may reduce the overall costs of adjustment by spreading out the adjustment over time. If there are imperfections in the market that prevent private economic agents from choosing the most appropriate pace of adjustment, gradualism in policy reform may have the same effect by allowing agents to spread out the costs of adjustment.

- Gradualism allows for midcourse adjustment. As reforms occur under distorted economic conditions, there is considerable uncertainty about the outcome of any specific reform. Structural reforms, no matter how ambitious, will not eradicate all market failures and distortions. Unexpected interactions between reforms and any remaining market failures could lead to disappointing results.

- Gradualism allows for political fine-tuning. Policymakers have time to learn about the probable gainers and losers and to forestall opposition. Policymakers can defuse potential opponents by giving them something they want from reform and can mollify losers through temporary transfers that help them thorough the transition.

- Gradualism may be the preferred approach to reform when there is a substantial administrative constraint or when new institutions have to be built. If capital markets are not well developed, for instance, a rush to privatize may result in an underpricing of assets and less than optimal allocation.

The case for shock treatment

- Shock treatment implies that reforms are implemented quickly in a concentrated period lasting less than two years. Bolivia, Ghana, Mexico, and Poland introduced reforms to eliminate substantial distortions during a short period. Chile carried out most reforms, and Mexico liberalized trade rapidly.

- If reform improves welfare, the optimal policy is to implement the program rapidly so that the welfare gain is achieved as quickly as possible. It may be that adjustment costs increase more than proportionately with the length of time taken to implement a reform. Although it might then make sense for the private sector to spread the *adjustment* over time, it does not follow that *policy reform* itself must be introduced gradually. Indeed, the cost of relocating labor and capital may often be less when the relocation is spread over time. Workers have time to acquire new skills, capital can be allowed to become obsolete, and factories can be reconfigured or modernized.

- Concerns with the cost of adjustment should affect the speed of reform only when inefficiencies prevent the private sector from adjusting at a socially optimal rate. But these inefficiencies can work both ways. When reforms lack credibility or capital markets work poorly, adjustment may be too slow from a social perspective—making a case for even more drastic reform than otherwise.

- Rapid action can improve the political sustainability of reform if it prevents a joint assault by special interest groups against changes that are in the general interest. Bold changes are especially necessary if a government lacks credibility. In countries where policies have vacillated and reform programs have come and gone, private agents are likely to respond sluggishly to the announcement of yet another reform package—especially if it is gradual. A conclusive reform can help to reshape expectations about the government's commitment and so contribute to its success.

- Adjustment usually occurs in a climate of crisis. Governments do well to capitalize on the broad, potentially short-lived mandate for reform that crisis confers by front loading the reform program.

ticularly large economic uncertainties. And, by their nature, some reforms take longer than others: price reforms can be done quickly, but new institutions (such as contract laws) take time to develop. Many gradual reforms have worked.

But some gradual reforms (for example, in Japan, the Republic of Korea, and Thailand) may have succeeded because they took place in rela-

tively strong and stable economies. In general, the analytical case for speed is strong. Often, erring on the side of speed appears to be best because swift actions bring the benefits of reform more quickly. Speed also makes sense if the political opportunity for reform is unlikely to last. Gradualism may not be feasible for economies in acute crisis or for governments with limited credibility.

Scope

Comprehensive packages of reform exploit the complementarities stressed throughout this Report and therefore promise the greatest benefits. The dangers of partial reform are all too clear. Stabilization has caused stagnation for lack of policies to promote investment (Bolivia and the Philippines in the 1980s); trade liberalization has failed in economies with distorted factor markets, macroeconomic instability, and inappropriate exchange rate policies (Argentina, Brazil, and Sri Lanka in the 1960s; Peru, the Philippines, Portugal, Turkey, and Uruguay in the 1970s); domestic deregulation or privatization has created monopolies in the absence of trade reforms that check domestic market power (Poland and Togo in the 1980s); financial sector reform failed because of high inflation (Argentina in the 1970s, Israel in the early 1980s, and Turkey in the early 1980s). In all these cases, broader programs attacking interrelated ills would have been more likely to succeed.

Sequencing

To achieve these benefits, it might seem that reforms should be implemented simultaneously. Often, this is indeed desirable. Import liberalization, for example, makes domestic producers more efficient. But the reallocation of resources may be hampered by controls and other rigidities in the financial markets or elsewhere. In this case deregulation should proceed at roughly the same pace as trade reform, so that the program raises output rather than unemployment and financial speculation. Equally, introducing domestic reforms without liberalizing import policy can cause even more resources to be misallocated in highly protected sectors.

Because it may not be practical to implement reforms simultaneously, the need for sequencing is implied. Effective sequencing usually calls for strong initial steps against the most costly distortions, taking care to avoid back-and-forth movements of resources. This suggests the following order for reform. At the outset comes macroeconomic stabilization, which can either precede or accompany structural reform. Many kinds of structural reform (the substitution of quantitative restrictions by tariffs, for example) complement stabilization. Next comes the liberalization of product markets, including deregulatory reform. It would be preferable not to delay domestic reforms until after trade reform. In the area of the liberalization of the external sector, the trade account best precedes the capital account. Asset markets adjust faster than goods markets, so the premature deregulation of capital flows can lead to speculation and financial instability.

It would be fair to criticize this as a counsel of perfection. Political considerations, and a host of other factors, both economic and noneconomic, interfere with a reforming government's planning. But in broad terms, this approach to reform avoids many of the obstacles that have driven governments off course during the past twenty years.

Investment and saving

Comprehensive programs of economic reform are the key, for many countries, to increasing both the quantity and quality of saving and investment. During the 1980s, saving and investment declined in the middle-income countries. Gross investment, which had averaged about 26 percent of GDP in the period 1974–80, declined by 3 percentage points. Lower foreign saving accounted for two-thirds of the decline in total saving. Investment remained fairly stable in low-income countries (excluding China and India) because higher foreign saving compensated for lower domestic saving (Table 6.1). The reduction in investment reflects in part the decline in public investment, which was inevitable for many countries where unsustainable expansion in public investment had taken place, usually in the latter part of the 1970s.

During the past two decades, both the aggregate level of investment and the private and public shares have varied significantly across countries and over time. For example, the relative stability of both public and private investment and the high level of the latter in the Republic of Korea contrast sharply with the declining trends and low private investment in Argentina, the wide fluctuations of private investment in Jamaica, and the dramatic turnaround in the composition of investment in Côte d'Ivoire (Figure 6.4). Such vast differences in investment behavior raise questions about what determines private investment and what role government policy plays in raising it.

The quantity and quality of investment

Countries that have kept inflation low and real interest rates moderate, and that have allowed sufficient credit to flow to the private sector, have been more likely to have high levels of private investment as a share of GDP. A large external debt

Table 6.1 Investment and saving, 1965–89
(percentage of GDP)

Economy group	Gross domestic investment			Foreign savings[a]			Gross national savings[b]		
	1965–73	1974–80	1981–89	1965–73	1974–80	1981–89	1965–73	1974–80	1981–89
Low-income	19.6	24.4	26.4	1.2	1.1	3.4	18.4	23.3	23.0
China	24.8	31.0	34.9	−0.3	−0.1	5.5	25.2	31.1	34.4
India	17.1	21.3	23.9	1.7	1.1	3.6	15.3	20.3	20.4
Indonesia	13.7	23.6	29.5	2.6	−3.0	2.7	11.1	26.7	26.9
Kenya	21.0	24.1	23.7	4.4	8.9	7.1	16.6	15.2	16.6
Nigeria	14.1	22.2	12.0	4.3	−1.3	2.7	9.7	23.5	9.3
Low-income, excluding									
China and India	14.1	19.6	19.1	2.8	2.3	6.2	11.3	17.2	12.9
Middle-income	21.6	26.4	23.2	3.0	5.3	3.4	18.1	21.0	19.7
Brazil	20.5	23.8	19.8	1.9	4.6	1.8	18.5	19.2	18.0
Korea, Rep. of	23.3	30.0	29.8	8.2	7.1	0.8	15.1	22.9	29.0
Morocco	14.3	26.0	24.4	2.7	14.5	13.0	11.7	11.5	11.4
Malaysia	21.2	27.3	30.7	−1.5	−1.2	3.3	22.7	28.5	27.4
Philippines	20.5	29.3	20.1	1.4	5.4	2.4	19.0	23.9	17.7
Thailand	23.9	26.6	25.8	2.4	5.1	4.2	21.5	21.5	21.6

a. Gross domestic investment minus gross national savings.
b. Excludes net transfers from abroad.
Source: World Bank data.

and wide policy swings that raise the variability of output and the real exchange rate deter private investment. And to the extent that public and private investment are complementary, cuts in public investment have also contributed to the decline of private investment.

FINANCIAL CONDITIONS. Statistically, cross-country differences in macroeconomic conditions explain differences in investment quite well. This is presumably because variability in output makes investors wary, and more likely to postpone projects. Inflation increases the riskiness of long-term projects and distorts information about relative prices, and so it may also dampen private investment. Macroeconomic stability increases confidence and thereby fosters private investment.

Macroeconomic policy also affects investment by influencing the quantity of credit available for the private sector's use. Evidence supports the hypothesis that credit flows have a positive and statistically significant effect on private investment. Because interest rate ceilings are an important tool of monetary policy for many developing countries, the quantity rather than the price of credit becomes the relevant variable for investment decisions. Tighter monetary policy or a change in the composition of credit that favors the public sector reduces private investment. When bank loans are a main source of financing, which is often the case, lower government borrowing releases resources for private investment.

In general, countries with positive real flows of credit to the private sector, such as Colombia, Indonesia, Korea, and Thailand, have also had stable levels of investment. Investment has tended to decline in countries where the flow of private sector credit was negative. Even without widespread credit rationing, not all firms are able to borrow as much as they would like. This is particularly true in the absence of adequate collateral and an efficient system to settle disputes, when credit allocation is linked to a firm's reputation rather than to the rate of return of the project. In Egypt, where credit availability is important to investment decisions, government borrowing seems to have crowded out less well-known firms, but not those with well-established reputations.

Cross-country evidence also suggests that high real interest rates reduce private investment. Investment decisions depend on the internal rate of return on investment (the marginal efficiency of capital) and the cost of capital. The cost of capital depends partly on the mix of financing, bonds, equity, and bank borrowing. Because bank borrowing represents a main source of financing, an increase in its cost relative to the marginal efficiency of capital will reduce investment. This interest rate effect is likely to be stronger in countries which have well-developed financial markets and which use open market operations, rather than credit ceilings, to control the money supply.

In principle, a real currency depreciation has an ambiguous effect on investment. It may reduce it

Figure 6.4 Differing patterns of private and public investment in four countries, 1970-88
(percentage of GDP)

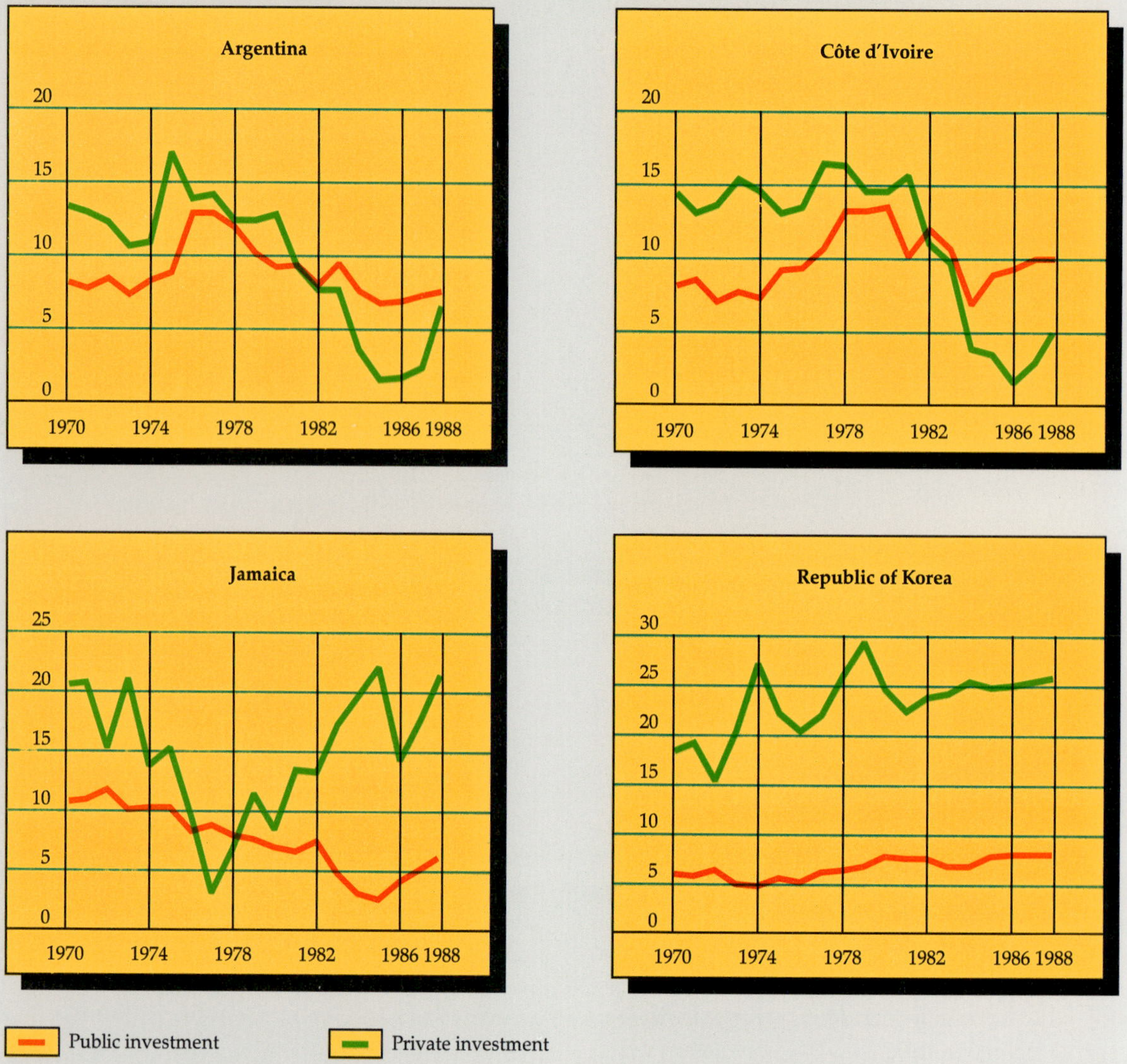

Argentina

Côte d'Ivoire

Jamaica

Republic of Korea

■— Public investment   ■— Private investment

Source: World Bank data.

by increasing the cost of imported intermediate inputs and capital goods, and by reducing the quantity of credit in real terms, as prices rise following the depreciation. But it may also encourage investment by improving profitability in the traded goods sector and, sometimes, by increasing the supply of foreign exchange, which can be used to pay for additional imports of capital goods.

One study found that a real devaluation may in practice reduce investment in the short run, especially if it lowers output. (In that case investment would fall unless all the burden of adjusting to changes in relative prices fell on private and public consumption.) In the medium term, however, and if the real devaluation is expected to last, investment is likely to rise, in part as a result of the sustained improvement in the profitability of exports. In Chile and Indonesia, investment fell in the short term in response to large real devaluations but recovered in the medium term with the expansion of the traded goods sector. Recovery took about five years in Chile and three years in

Indonesia. The negative effects of a devaluation may persist longer in low-income countries because of a slower supply response.

Evidence suggests that countries with a heavy debt burden have lower investment ratios. A large debt is likely to be associated with external credit rationing or high risk premiums, which reduce private investment. The debt overhang also acts as an implicit tax; it discourages investment because it implies that eventually some combination of higher taxes, currency depreciation, and lower domestic demand will be required to effect the required external transfer.

PUBLIC AND PRIVATE INVESTMENT. Several countries have achieved fiscal adjustment, in part by cutting public investment or postponing capital outlays. Cuts in health care, education, and infrastructure programs may slow private investment and growth in the medium term. But public investment can lower private capital formation if it uses scarce resources or if its output competes directly with private goods. The complementary and crowding-out effects of public investment are not incompatible. In the short run, the financing of public infrastructure may increase interest rates or reduce credit to the private sector and so crowd out private investment. In the medium term, however, it can increase productivity and private investment. The evidence on the net effect is inconclusive, mainly for lack of data. Some recent research, however, does suggest that public and private investment are complementary. Other cross-country work suggests that investments in infrastructure (as opposed to, for example, investments in state-owned enterprises or military hardware) are especially likely to promote private investment.

This is plausible. Studies of individual countries show that firms' operating costs rise and investment falls when infrastructure is weak. Government investment in infrastructure seems to have promoted private investment in Egypt, for instance. In Korea, public investment appears to have a positive effect on private investment in both the short and long runs. An implication of these results is that capital outlays on infrastructure should continue during periods of fiscal adjustment; they are more likely than other types of public investment to complement and increase private investment.

THE COMPOSITION OF PRIVATE INVESTMENT. Private investment consists of both equipment and structures. Some degree of complementarity should exist between the two, but at the margin it is likely that they make different contributions to growth. Equipment investment (mainly machinery) appears to be more closely associated with productivity growth than the rest. Discrimination against capital goods (through high tariffs or taxes) will increase their price and reduce the share in total investment of investment in equipment. This matters because new equipment is likely to embody new technology and to bring important external economies.

Determinants of saving

Individuals save to smooth their consumption over time. Their saving rate depends on current income, expected lifetime income, and the expected return on savings. Saving patterns change over an individual's lifetime, with the peak coming during a person's prime earning years. The larger the fraction of income received by workers at the peak of their earnings, the higher the overall saving rate. Demographic factors also influence saving: the lower the dependency ratio (the proportion of the population below fifteen and above sixty-five years old), the higher the saving rate. Faster-growing economies also tend to have higher saving rates because the gap between the lifetime income of active workers and that of retired workers is large, and because the aggregate saving rate moves closer to the saving rate of active workers. Faster growth is the best way to increase saving. These factors seem to explain the high rate of saving in Japan (Box 6.3).

In many developing countries, agriculture accounts for a significant part of household income. Agriculture—and the income derived from it—is subject to considerable uncertainty, which can spread to other economic activities closely linked to agriculture. At the same time, imperfections in financial markets may prevent households from borrowing against future income. All this makes the rate of saving more responsive to changes in expectations about future income; and the more uncertain the future, the larger will be the demand for savings as a "buffer stock."

Evidence shows a strong correlation between growth rates and saving rates. Changes in the growth rate explain most of the fluctuations in the saving rate in the Republic of Korea, for instance. As the economy expanded rapidly, Korea's national saving increased from less than 10 percent of GNP in the mid-1960s to 32.8 percent in 1986. Variability in income growth rates is also related to variability in saving. Indonesia and Myanmar had

Box 6.3 Determinants of household saving in Japan

Household saving in Japan is higher than in most other countries. During the period 1970–86, it was 23 percent of household income; in the United States, 14.3 percent; in the United Kingdom, 10.4 percent; and in Sweden, 7.8 percent.

Some of these differences can be explained by conceptual discrepancies. The procedures used to calculate saving rates in the United States and Japan differ in three main ways. First, depreciation is evaluated at historical cost in Japan but at replacement cost in the United States. Second, capital transfers are excluded from both savings and disposable income in Japan but are included in the United States. Third, interest paid by households to businesses or foreigners is excluded from personal income in Japan but is included in the United States. An adjustment for these factors would lower Japanese household saving by 3–4 percentage points. Other differences affecting cross-country comparisons are the treatment of consumer durables, private pensions and life insurance, and social security funds. After all such adjustments, Japanese saving remains high.

Various explanations have been advanced: (a) cultural factors, such as the Confucian heritage, a high degree of risk-aversion, the weakness of demonstration effects, and the prevalence of intergenerational transfers; (b) demographic and socioeconomic factors, such as the age structure of the population, the distribution of income, and the high labor force participation of the aged; (c) institutional factors, such as the bonus system and the unavailability of consumer credit; (d) government policies, including tax breaks for savings (until recently) and a low level of social security benefits; and (e) economic factors, such as rapid rates of growth, and high and rising land and housing prices.

A review of the literature on saving in Japan suggests that the low proportion of the aged, the country's growth rate, and the bonus system can each account for 2–3 percentage points of the gap between Japan's saving rate and other countries. Other factors which may have in the past contributed to the high saving rate (such as tradition, tax breaks for savings, the underdeveloped social security system, the extended family, and the unavailability of consumer credit) are becoming less important. As Japan's demographic structure becomes similar to that of other countries, its household saving rate is likely to decline.

---

variable and sometimes negative real growth rates during the 1960s, and low and variable saving rates. In recent years, however, as real growth rates stabilized, both countries experienced a rapid increase in saving rates.

THE ROLE OF THE FINANCIAL SECTOR. Because few developing countries have easy access to external savings, most of any increase in investment will have to be financed domestically. The financial sector can play an important role by increasing the efficiency of the transformation of savings into investment. Evidence suggests that distortions of this sector that result in negative real interest rates are associated with low growth. Negative real interest rates may reduce aggregate savings, diminish the savings available for investment, and distort its allocation among investment alternatives. Financial reform, when well-managed, usually leads to moderately positive real interest rates. The net effect of higher real interest rates is ambiguous in principle. The empirical evidence suggests that an increase in the real interest rate has a positive, though small, effect on saving. Positive real interest may also increase the share of savings channeled through the financial system. Once that system works reasonably efficiently, this is also desirable.

Government policies can do little in the short run to influence the demographic and cultural factors that affect private saving. In the absence of capital inflows from abroad, therefore, the increase in savings needed to finance higher investment will require higher public saving—that is, smaller public deficits.

PUBLIC SAVING. The effect on private saving of higher public saving depends on how that increase is achieved—through lower expenditures or higher taxes. A World Bank study of a sample of developing countries found that less than half of the increase in public saving obtained by cutting government consumption will be offset by lower private saving; in the case of a tax increase, slightly more of the increase in public saving will be offset. Permanent changes in taxation and spending have a smaller effect on private saving than do temporary measures, because most households are likely to adjust saving rather than consumption when they believe measures are temporary. Reducing government deficits appears to be the best way to increase national saving.

Global economic conditions

The world recession of 1980–83 and the increase in international interest rates showed how great an effect macroeconomic developments in the industrial countries can have on developing countries. The developing world's exporters of manufactured goods appear to be most sensitive to fluctuations in industrial countries' growth—more so than the countries that export mainly primary goods. Also, Asian and Latin American countries with close trade links to the United States benefited more from its 1983–84 expansion in demand for imports than many African countries, which had stronger links with the European markets.

The importance of financial markets in transmitting the effects of industrial countries' policies increased with the integration of world markets and the accumulation of external debt by developing countries. After 1979–80, when interest rates became more volatile, several Latin American countries with a high proportion of floating rate debt suffered a sharp increase in debt service payments. The consequent balance of payments problems were further compounded by the effects of the world recession and the reduction in the availability of external financing.

How important are external factors for developing countries? World Bank simulations suggest that, other things being equal, an increase of 1 percentage point in the growth of the OECD could raise the developing countries' growth over the long term by 0.7 percent. Conversely, a 1 percentage point increase in LIBOR could reduce growth by 0.2 percentage point. A 1 percent increase in the growth of the OECD is also estimated to lead to a 0.2 percent increase in exports from developing countries. These effects, however, vary across countries, depending on their trade patterns and the structure of their external debt.

The role of external factors needs to be stressed. In the short term, unfavorable external shocks, higher interest rates, a decline in the terms of trade, or inadequate external flows may derail the implementation of any well-designed adjustment program. Over the long term, a strong world economy could encourage the adoption of economic reforms. This would improve domestic efficiency and ensure that countries would fully benefit from the continued expansion of global markets. Although the quality of economic management is what matters most, global economic conditions are important in shaping the outlook for developing countries.

External resources and growth

External resources enable developing countries to raise their growth rate by financing additional investment or smoothing adjustment to external shocks. External finance could in principle help an economy out of a low-growth trap, enabling it to "take off" despite structural or political limitations to increased domestic saving. Concessional aid enables countries to alleviate poverty and increase long-run growth. Industrial countries share the responsibility for ensuring that capital flows are used to aid, rather than hinder, development. For concessional flows to be effective, external aid and finance agencies must coordinate their programs and design projects which carefully evaluate the needs and administrative capabilities of the countries they assist. These agencies must also end policies such as the tying of aid.

The debt crisis illustrates the costs of misused capital flows. The returns from foreign inflows and the ability to repay foreign borrowing depend on the efficiency of those investments, which in turn vary with country policies. In many countries during the 1970s, investment was channeled to public sector undertakings which had low rates of return. Particularly in the late 1970s and early 1980s, some developing countries used external financing to maintain unsustainable levels of consumption in the face of shortfalls in export revenues or shifts in terms of trade. In other cases, alongside macroeconomic mismanagement, external borrowing financed capital flight (Box 6.4).

A significant share of foreign capital may be used to finance consumption instead of investment, reducing the long-run effect of inflows on growth. Although a fraction of inflows will always translate into consumption increases, even without domestic distortions, a recent study found that for some countries, the share of external transfers used in consumption has been exceedingly high. The additional consumption spending from an additional dollar of foreign loans in the 1960s and 1970s was 88 cents for Bolivia, and 99 cents for Colombia. Yet in the Republic of Korea, which increased domestic savings from 6 percent in the early 1960s to 30 percent by the mid-1980s, foreign savings were largely channeled to investment. Many studies, however, have found that foreign capital inflows—especially before the late 1970s and early 1980s—have been positively associated with an increasing share of domestic investment in GDP.

Despite the cost of using foreign inflows to post-

Box 6.4 Capital flight

Capital flight is an elusive concept. Statistically, it is hard to distinguish from the normal capital flows generated by trade relations and by growing world financial integration. Some authors define it as capital that leaves a country in response to perceptions of abnormal risk at home. Capital flight has also been defined as that part of foreign assets that does not yield an investment income recorded in balance of payment statistics. Alternatively, it can be defined as all capital outflow, because any outflow entails some loss for the domestic economy. So defined, capital flight can be measured as the stock of external assets acquired by residents or as net short-term capital outflows from the nonbank private sector (hot money). The error and omissions entry of the balance of payments is usually incorporated in these measurements under the assumption that a large part of capital flight consists of illegal transactions that appear only in this item. When capital flight takes the form of underinvoicing of exports and overinvoicing of imports, it will not be captured in balance of payments entries. None of these definitions is entirely satisfactory, and all of them pose measurement problems. At best, they provide only a range of estimates.

The extent of capital flight has varied widely. For the period 1980–84 it has been estimated at about $16–17 billion for Argentina, $40 billion for Mexico, and $27 billion for Venezuela. In some years, capital flight in Argentina and Venezuela was equivalent to half savings in those countries. In Brazil capital flight has been relatively small, but it seems to have increased during the late 1980s.

Capital flight, however defined or measured, is above all a symptom of macroeconomic mismanagement—in many instances compounded by political instability. As investors choose from among domestic financial assets, inflation hedges (consumer durables or land), and foreign assets, they make their decisions on the basis of domestic inflation and interest rates, foreign interest rates, and the expected rate of depreciation of the currency. If investors fear a devaluation, they will move their funds abroad to avoid a capital loss. Similarly, high inflation rates and repressive financial policies that keep real interest rates too low will encourage residents to invest abroad or to stockpile.

Because capital flight generally occurs during a period of scarce foreign capital inflows, it imposes heavy costs on an economy. As a symptom of macroeconomic mismanagement, it also increases domestic instability—both financially (because hot money flows can impede the pursuit of domestic economic objectives) and politically (because it reduces the political legitimacy of efforts to service external debt). Capital flight also harms domestic growth by diverting savings out of the country. It shrinks the tax base, which reduces government income and shifts more of the burden onto low-income citizens. And it contributes to the debt problem by increasing the cost of borrowing (which rises with the amount borrowed), reducing the resources available to repay debt.

Reversing capital flight requires restoring confidence in the economy and the government through a resumption of growth and the adoption of sustainable policies. Unfortunately, it is much easier for a government to lose credibility than to regain it.

pone adjusting to permanent shocks, access to capital has been nevertheless essential in some countries to successfully cope with short-term shocks. Korea (following its economic crisis in 1980), Turkey (during 1980–82), and Indonesia (during the mid-1960s) all received capital inflows while implementing adjustment. Because all three faced their economic problems before the 1982 debt crisis, they had the enormous advantage of continued access to capital inflows and favorable borrowing conditions during the adjustment period.

To facilitate adjustment to shocks, the World Bank introduced adjustment loans in 1980. These loans, which accounted for about 25 percent of total World Bank lending by the end of the 1980s, were intended to provide balance of payment support for macroeconomic stabilization and long-term structural reforms in trade, domestic and labor markets, financial markets, and public sector management. By allowing expenditures to be higher than otherwise, the loans were intended to cushion the short-run adjustment costs to output, employment, and consumption. The evidence suggests that such lending was reasonably successful in allowing countries to improve their balance of payments position, and that a majority of participants adhered to agreed policy reforms. Although the evidence is not conclusive, early loan recipients were more likely to show a positive growth effect (see Box 6.1). But the share of investment in GDP has not recovered for many countries.

A legacy of debt

The period of abundant inflows of financial resources to the developing world came to an abrupt

Table 6.2 Indicators of external debt for developing economies, 1970–89
(average percentage for period)

Economy group	Total external debt[a]			Interest payments[b]			Net transfers[a]		
	1970–75	1976–82	1983–89	1970–75	1976–82	1983–89	1970–75	1976–82	1983–89
Low-income	10.2	14.8	28.5	2.9	4.3	9.8	1.1	1.2	0.7
Low-income, excluding China and India	20.5	28.5	60.7	2.9	5.3	11.8	2.7	2.4	1.0
Middle-income	18.6	34.6	54.9	5.1	11.0	15.4	1.9	1.9	−2.7
Argentina	20.1	46.1	80.3	14.1	17.9	41.6	−0.3	2.7	−5.4
Brazil	16.3	28.2	42.0	12.1	28.5	30.3	3.3	0.8	−2.5
Morocco	18.6	55.1	109.5	2.8	13.0	17.1	1.8	6.8	−1.7
Philippines	20.7	45.8	79.2	4.2	14.1	20.5	1.2	1.8	−3.4

Note: Variables are yearly averages calculated for the period; economy averages are weighted using the share of GNP in 1981.
a. As a share of GNP.
b. As a share of total export receipts.
Source: World Bank data.

end in 1982, setting off the debt crisis. With the crisis, increased private flows went primarily to meet the debt servicing needs of debtor countries, and little additional capital was available for investment and sustained growth. As the crisis persisted throughout the 1980s, many debtor countries began to experience a reversal in resource transfers (Table 6.2), lower investment and growth, and higher inflation. Contributing to the crisis was a complex brew of policy error (large fiscal deficits, overvaluation, and a bias against exports), external shocks (rapid increases in world interest rates, falling commodities prices, and world recession), and the overly expansionary lending policies of 1979–81.

Net transfers to developing countries became negative in the second half of the 1980s (Figure 6.5). Principal and interest arrears (a form of implicit financing) reached about 6.9 percent of developing-country debt in 1989. Current account deficits fell from 3 percent of GNP in 1980 to less than 1 percent in 1987–89 as developing countries began to export more goods and nonfactor services than they received. Direct foreign investment has increased substantially from the level of the early 1980s, in part as a result of debt swaps. Most of the expansion in DFI has been concentrated in East Asia; China, Indonesia, Korea, Malaysia, and Thailand account for about one-fourth of foreign investment in developing countries. Any expansion of DFI in other countries is likely to depend on their political and macroeconomic stability, and on their rules on taxes and remitted profits.

Most of the low-income countries' debt is owed to official creditors, bilateral and multilateral; a large part of the stock of private export credits is also officially guaranteed. At the end of 1989 the debt of the severely indebted low-income countries was equivalent to their combined GNP. Official creditors have engaged in debt forgiveness and rescheduling, and they have provided new flows at highly concessional terms. Otherwise these countries would have had to devote more than half of their export earnings to servicing debt; in fact less than half of the scheduled amount was paid. Debt relief has been concentrated on official debt. Bilateral creditors have rescheduled under the Paris Club arrangements, offering highly concessional conditions—the so-called Toronto terms. Under these terms, bilateral official creditors who have extended nonconcessional loans may choose between canceling one third of the consolidated amount, adopting the longer repayment used for concessional debt (twenty-five years' maturity and a grace period of fourteen years), or cutting the interest rate. The debtors concerned are likely to require further debt and debt service reduction if they are to achieve higher investment and growth.

For commercial debt, under the Brady Initiative, official creditors have offered to support debt and debt service reduction for countries that adopt adjustment programs and take measures to encourage direct foreign investment and the repatriation of capital. Reductions take place through debt buybacks—the exchange of old debt for new par-value bonds at a reduced interest rate or for discounted, partially collateralized bonds.

Several countries, starting with Chile in 1985, have used debt-equity swaps to reduce their external debt and encourage direct foreign investment. When the buyback is financed by selling stock in publicly owned enterprises, there is no fiscal effect; the government already owns the asset. But when the operation involves swapping public debt for private assets, the government needs to raise money to acquire the private assets. How it is done matters. Argentina, Brazil, and Mexico suspended their formal swap programs in 1989 in part because of concerns about their inflationary effects; this is particularly strong when the central bank prints money to retire the debt. Some new swap programs are linked to privatization efforts; for instance, those for the telephone company and pub-

lic airline in Argentina. Mexico's new swap program is restricted to state-owned enterprises, infrastructure, and other development projects. Other types of debt swaps have also been introduced: debt-for-trade swaps in Peru and Yugoslavia, and debt-for-nature and debt-for-health swaps in other countries.

By 1990, new debt agreements based on the Brady Initiative had been implemented in Costa Rica, Mexico, and the Philippines, and negotiations were under way in Morocco, Uruguay, and Venezuela. In addition to their direct economic effects, these agreements have favorably influenced expectations. Following Mexico's announcement of an agreement in July 1989, real interest rates declined substantially and capital inflows rose (Box 6.5). The Brady Initiative also led to a significant rise in the price of debt in the secondary market. It stabilized after the announcement of the initiative in March 1989 and then began to rise in the four countries with Brady plans. The price continued to fall for other countries that continued to accumulate arrears, such as Argentina and Brazil. When other policies are adequate, debt relief may provide the right spark for an economic recovery and improve incentives for reform. Peru's recent experience clearly illustrates that stopping debt service does not solve the stabilization problem, and the experiences of Argentina and Brazil show that reducing the fiscal deficit remains the crux of the matter. The failures of Argentina and Brazil to reach debt settlements deepened the skepticism about the likelihood of success of their stabilization efforts. The experiences of Chile, Mexico, and Venezuela show how debt renegotiation can support domestic policies by increasing overall confidence and encouraging the return of expatriated capital.

Despite progress, the debt crisis continues to threaten development. Factors that could sustain and augment progress include the implementation of strong, credible adjustment programs in highly indebted countries; expanded country coverage of commercial debt and debt service reduction; more concessional rescheduling for the poorest debtor countries; and a reduction of the stock of debt owed to bilateral agencies. Private lending is likely to grow only modestly as commercial banks rebuild their capital. Yet additional private financing could take the form of repatriation of assets through instruments such as project and trade-linked finance, direct foreign investment, joint ventures, and debt and equity issues abroad. Official flows are likely to grow somewhat faster than

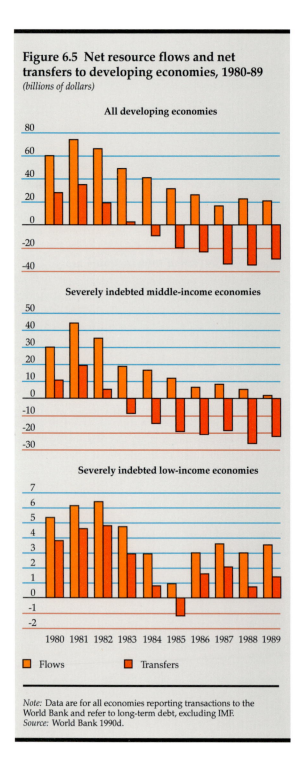

Figure 6.5 Net resource flows and net transfers to developing economies, 1980-89
(billions of dollars)

Note: Data are for all economies reporting transactions to the World Bank and refer to long-term debt, excluding IMF.
Source: World Bank 1990d.

Box 6.5 The 1990 Mexican debt agreement

Since the 1982 debt crisis, Mexico has negotiated rescheduling and new money packages in 1983–84 and in 1986–87. These agreements, which involved complex negotiations, failed to provide medium-term relief on the external front. In 1985 Mexico introduced important reforms of external trade and of the financial sector, privatized many state-owned enterprises, and overhauled regulations on direct foreign investment. Despite these efforts, external debt continued to cloud the horizon. Large external transfers created uncertainty about future exchange rate and tax policies. To prevent capital flight, Mexico had to pay very high real interest rates on its domestic debt, which increased its fiscal deficit and threatened the substantial fiscal reforms that had been undertaken in recent years. Medium-term debt relief seemed to be the missing ingredient for the success of the reform effort.

In March 1990, Mexico and its commercial creditors implemented a debt restructuring agreement. Banks could chose from a menu of options that included new money and two facilities for reducing debt and debt service: an exchange of discount bonds against outstanding debt, or an exchange of bonds against outstanding debt without any discount (par bond) but bearing a fixed interest rate. About 13 percent of creditors chose the new-money option, 40 percent chose the discount bond (at 65 percent of par), and 47 percent chose the par bond at 6.25 percent interest. Bonds are to be paid in a single installment at the end of 2019. Their principal is secured by the pledge of U.S. Treasury zero-coupon bonds, and the interest payments are secured for eighteen months. The collateral funds were drawn from country reserves and loans from the IMF, World Bank, and Japan. Participating banks were eligible to take part in a new debt-equity swap program linked to the privatization of public enterprises.

The debt-restructuring agreement is expected to reduce Mexico's net transfers abroad by about $4 billion a year during the period 1989–94. About half the reduction comes from the rescheduling of amortization. These reductions will improve Mexico's fiscal position and should have a beneficial effect on growth. The agreement has also altered expectations by diminishing the uncertainty about future exchange rate and tax policies. Following announcement of the agreement in July 1989, real interest rates declined substantially and capital inflows revived.

the industrial countries' income, with multilateral institutions remaining as the link between the international capital markets and many developing countries. Whether net transfers grow either in the form of new lending or debt reduction is likely to depend on whether countries adopt policies to maintain macroeconomic stability and improve their creditworthiness.

Rethinking the state

The important thing for government is not to do things which individuals are doing already, and to do them a little better or a little worse; but to do those things which at present are not done at all.

—JOHN MAYNARD KEYNES,
"The End of Laissez-Faire"

The agenda for reform that has emerged in the course of this Report calls for governments to intervene less in certain areas and more in others—for the state to let markets work where they can, and to step in promptly and effectively where they cannot. In many countries this calls for a stronger orientation toward the market and a more focused and efficient public sector role. History suggests that this is the surest path to faster growth in productivity, rising incomes, and sustained economic development.

Judging by their recent activities, many governments in industrial and developing countries have come around to this view. But economic policy cannot be implemented in laboratories; it has to be made to work in the real world. Reformers face a variety of political constraints on their actions. In many developing countries, one of the obstacles to reform has been its political costs, actual or potential. Political instability and other political considerations go a long way toward explaining why, in the first place, many of these countries adopted, to their economic disadvantage, the policies they did. And they underline the difficulty many countries face in changing course swiftly. So it is important to ask whether sufficiently broad support for the sorts of reforms that have been recommended can

be built. It has often been argued, for instance, that democracy and structural adjustment do not mix well. Is this true?

Governments also have other objectives in addition to faster economic growth. Employment generation is a related goal. Most think it right to alter the distribution of income in helping the poor or in improving equity. How is this best achieved? Do such policies serve the goal of faster economic growth, or act as an additional constraint? And in the narrower economic domain, how is the public sector's performance to be improved? These questions also are all part of reconsidering the role of government in development.

The political economy of development

Political instability is a fact of life in many countries. The past forty years have seen scores of racial, tribal, communal, and guerrilla wars. Coups d'état have occurred in many of the Latin American countries (except in Mexico, Costa Rica, and a few of the Caribbean island nations); in many North African and Middle Eastern countries (for example, Algeria, Egypt, the Islamic Republic of Iran, Iraq, Lebanon, Libya, the Syrian Arab Republic, and Turkey); and in many parts of Asia and Sub-Saharan Africa. Since 1948, there has been at least one coup attempt per developing country every five years (Table 7.1).

And there is more to political stability than merely avoiding coups. Separatist movements, regional rivalries, ethnic frictions, and other sometimes violent social conflicts can plague even the most secure executive. Repressive governments can create a semblance of stability even when they entirely lack popular support, as Eastern Europe showed until recently. In 1987, roughly half of the world's governments were not democratic (Figure 7.1), whereas about three-fifths of nonindustrial countries fell into that category.

Social consensus helps governments to establish legitimate authority to govern. Without this authority, even the most basic functions such as taxation and allocation of public spending can become problematic. When it began its modernization in the second half of the nineteenth century, Japan's per capita income was the lowest among the countries which are today classified as industrialized. However, the country was already politically well-developed, and this was undoubtedly a great asset. The government was not democratically elected, but it was perceived to be legitimate by the population; it had a strong administration and a broad tax base. All this helped it to undertake its major reforms after the Meiji Restoration in 1868.

As the industrial countries have discovered in the course of their history, economic modernization creates new sources of wealth. This can shake the coalition on which traditional social order was established. A transition of this sort affects many developing countries today. Fragile social consensus, entrenched special interests, and weak administrative capacity have influenced their choice of economic policies, and the outcomes.

To a large extent, governments everywhere tend to tailor economic policies to balance conflicting interests. Political rather than economic considerations explain why the governments of many OECD countries intervene in support of ailing industries or regions. The resurgence of protectionism among OECD countries in the 1980s, the problems encountered in the current round of GATT negotiations, and the slow pace at which some industrial countries addressed their macroeconomic imbalances in the 1970s and 1980s highlight how, even in societies with secure institutions, much-needed economic reforms can be blocked.

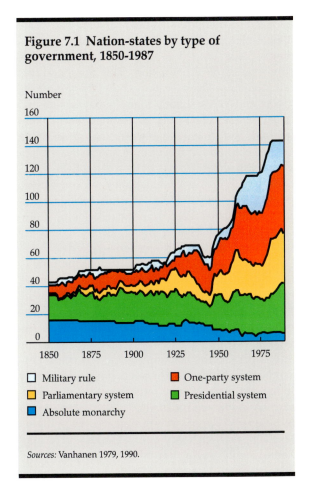

Figure 7.1 Nation-states by type of government, 1850-1987

Sources: Vanhanen 1979, 1990.

Constituencies and interventions

In many developing countries, political and economic instability have put the social consensus under strain. Such difficulties are hardly new. For many years they have tended to subordinate economic policy to the task of securing the support of influential groups for the government. The crude policy instruments which many governments often have as a result of these skewed priorities, combined with their often-weak administrative ca-

Table 7.1 Irregular executive transfers: average occurrence per country, 1948–82

Income group	1948–52	1953–58	1959–64	1965–70	1971–76	1977–82
Low-income	1.0 (21)	1.1 (24)	1.2 (39)	1.4 (51)	1.3 (53)	0.9 (55)
Middle-income	1.6 (30)	1.7 (32)	1.4 (41)	0.8 (47)	0.9 (51)	0.6 (55)
High-income	0.0 (23)	0.2 (23)	0.1 (24)	0.2 (25)	0.1 (28)	0.1 (28)

Note: Number of countries considered is in parentheses. Both successful and unsuccessful executive transfers are included. Irregular successful executive transfers are changes in the office of the national executive from one leader to another, outside conventional legal or customary procedures for transferring power. Unsuccessful irregular executive transfers are failed attempts at such irregular transfers. Countries are ranked according to their per capita income in 1988.
Sources: Taylor and Jodice 1983; data base supplied by the Inter-University Consortium of Political and Social Research. Income group classifications are from the World Bank.

pacity, have compounded the problem—and made it potentially more damaging. Typically, governments have tended to centralize economic resources and decisionmaking. This tendency was reinforced by the prevailing belief in the 1950s, 1960s, and 1970s, among many policymakers and development economists, and sometimes in external aid and finance agencies, that developing countries could not rely upon markets and the private sector alone to develop their industries.

In the 1950s and 1960s, utilities, oil companies, plantations, and assorted manufacturing industries were nationalized in many developing countries, including Algeria, Brazil, Chile, Egypt, Sri Lanka, and Tunisia. Governments regarded themselves as too weak administratively at the time to tax and regulate private enterprises at arms' length. The nationalization of the major private Bolivian mining companies in 1952 followed decades of attempts by governments to tax the families that owned the mines. An inability to regulate and supervise the banking system led many governments to nationalize banks or intervene directly in the allocation of credit. Interventions in agriculture have followed a similar pattern. Farming in Sub-Saharan Africa, for example, has been highly taxed through currency overvaluation, state marketing boards paying low procurement prices, and export taxes.

In many developing countries, it is common to find tariffs, tax incentives, or special regulations designed to protect special-interest groups. In some cases, "predatory" states have designed policies and programs to transfer resources to very narrowly defined interest groups, and they have resorted to coercion when the legitimacy of such policies was questioned. The strength of urban interests in Latin American and Africa helps to explain why the industrialization strategies adopted by many countries in these regions were strongly biased against farming.

Many governments have assumed the role of employer of last resort, partly as a result of concerns about the social and political implications of unemployment. Until recently, university graduates had guaranteed employment in government in several Sub-Saharan African countries. In the Gambia, the civil service doubled between 1974 and 1984. The central governments of Argentina and Sri Lanka reckon that a fifth of their staffs are redundant; Brazil's government puts the figure at half.

State-owned enterprises (SOEs) have been used to create employment (though seldom for the poorest), raise incomes in certain regions, or meet the demands of powerful groups such as the military. In the 1970s and early 1980s, the Sri Lankan government built several textile factories and sugar refineries in backward areas with high rural unemployment. In Argentina throughout the 1970s, industries run by the military were highly protected.

Programs of public expenditure have financed the underpricing of utilities—water, electricity, telecommunications, railway, or city transport—and supported untargeted food subsidies. Most staple foods in Egypt and Mexico were subsidized until recently, as was wheat flour in Brazil. These subsidies usually benefited the politically active urban population at the expense of the agricultural areas where most of the poor live. Uneconomic public investment projects are often politically motivated: a very large power project in Zaire, for instance, was intended to improve the government's control over an unruly region. In some such cases, corruption in the execution of expenditures is also a problem (see below), sometimes involving foreign suppliers.

The costs

By the 1980s, persistent difficulties in financing external and public sector deficits made the costs of these interventions plain to see. When the supply of external finance dwindled after 1982, demands for special treatment outran the economy's capacity to deliver.

Buying support at the cost of economic efficiency was, in the end, self-defeating. Governments reacted to mounting civil service wage bills by letting nominal wages lag behind inflation; this generated the resentment of public servants and led to low morale and poor service. Together with discretionary interventions, their situation fueled corruption. Then, in some countries, corruption brought the government down. The hope of employment in government induced migration from rural to urban areas, aggravating the problem of urban unemployment. Underpriced and overstaffed utilities meant poor services—chronic power cuts, silent telephones, bad public transport. This caused further dissatisfaction. More generally, this highly interventionist approach slowed growth, which in many countries again undermined political stability.

Piecemeal interventions also made it harder to establish essential public institutions. For instance, direct control of the financial system meant there was no effort to build capacity in banking supervision. High tariffs and the inflation tax made it less necessary to broaden tax bases. The expansion of agricultural state banks, which was intended to make credit widely available to farmers, made it less urgent to develop cadastres and clarify ownership rights—that is, to address the underlying reasons for the high cost of rural credit. Meanwhile, in many developing countries the agricultural banks have failed to deliver, so farmers are as badly off as before.

Market failure and government failure

As the earlier chapters of this Report made clear, intervention by the public sector is not undesirable in itself. On the contrary, many sorts of intervention are essential if economies are to achieve their full potential. An abbreviated list of indispensable interventions would include the maintenance of law and order, the provision of public goods, investments in human capital, the construction and repair of physical infrastructure, and the protection of the environment. In all these areas (and arguably more) markets ''fail'' and the government must step in. But the countless cases of unsuccessful intervention suggest the need for caution. Markets fail, but so do governments. To justify intervention it is not enough to know that the market is failing; it is also necessary to be confident that the government can do better.

Governments are prone to fail, at least in economic terms, for a variety of reasons. As noted above, economic goals may not be their highest priority. A combination of political objectives and constraints and weak administration may lead governments to intervene in ways that are economically harmful. Also, the consequences of economic interventions are difficult to predict. For instance, in the 1950s many Latin American countries protected their industries to (among other things) reduce their dependence on imports. Later it became evident that they had increased their dependence, because the new urban manufacturing sector that evolved under protection relied heavily on imported inputs and machinery.

Private firms are not always better at making decisions or predicting their consequences. But tests of performance are usually clearer to private firms, which enables them to take corrective action faster. Furthermore, without the help of the government, it is harder for private firms to shift the costs of their mistakes onto taxpayers.

Another difficulty is that government intervention creates vested interests which make it difficult to change the policy. Not all interventions need to be reversed: investments in infrastructure, for example, can generate enough resources to cover their costs. But protection for manufacturing in the early stages of industrialization can only succeed, if at all, as long as it is temporary. Once protection is granted, however, it is exceptionally difficult to remove.

Protection creates rents: owners of some labor, capital, or land obtain higher returns than they would in the absence of intervention. This draws new resources to the protected industry until, at the margin, the rents disappear. Removing the protection penalizes not only the owners who first received the rents as a windfall, but also those who came later, seeking normal returns. Removing the tariff, in this case, can force into loss the firms that gained least. Thus, even when protection has not been created by industrial interests, protection creates industrial interests. These then become a formidable obstacle to liberalization.

Corruption

Excessive intervention breeds corruption. Again, the problem is by no means confined to governments, or to the developing countries. In some countries, it has grown to alarming and destructive proportions.

Corruption weakens a government's ability to carry out its functions efficiently. Bribery, nepotism, and venality can cripple administration and dilute equity from the provision of government services—and thus also undermine social cohesiveness. Corruption was identified as a serious problem in ancient China and India, in the Ottoman Empire in the fourteenth century, in England in the early 1800s. Every other year a scandal is a reminder that it continues in Europe, Japan, and the United States. Corruption has also contributed to the fate of many governments: it was a major justification for the military overthrow of the Ghanaian civilian government in 1981 and the Nigerian one in 1983; an important theme in the 1982 Mexican presidential campaign; a major reason for the fall of the government in the Philippines in 1986; and a problem the authorities consider of the utmost gravity in the USSR.

Corruption manifests itself in a variety of ways. A common one is bribery of customs officials, who then allow in illegal imports, or legal imports at below-legal duties, or expedite clearance procedures. This has been a serious problem in nu-

Box 7.1 Fighting corruption

Being a tax official in the Philippines Bureau of Internal Revenue (BIR) in the early 1970s was so lucrative that jobs and transfers to the bureau were sold. Manila's most "extensive, expensive, and lavish assortment of cars" was in the BIR's parking lot. Then-president Ferdinand Marcos's New Society, announced in 1972, aimed to alleviate poverty and fight corruption, a fight that intensified in 1975 when 2,000 government officials suspected of improper conduct were fired. In that sweep, the BIR's commissioner was replaced by Justice Efren Plana.

Problems

After a few months, Plana identified a number of serious problems. Chief among these were practices whereby officials would require payments to process a tax matter, provide a record, or make a routine clearance; accept bribes to lower tax assessments or stop the harassment of taxpayers with no tax obligations; embezzle funds; illegally print fiscal labels and stamps; succumb to cash, nepotism, and influence for personnel decisions, such as transfers and appointments; and break down the internal auditing systems (officials in charge of investigating others routinely accepted bribes from those being investigated).

The bureau was virtually free of corruption when Plana left it in 1980 to become deputy minister of finance and, shortly thereafter, a justice of the supreme court.

Solutions

Plana's success was based on six innovations. First, supervision and auditing were improved by using a group of highly skilled outsiders teamed with irreproachable incumbent senior officials. Second, administrative systems were introduced to monitor performance on the basis of objective criteria such as the number of tax assessments and taxes collected. Third, about 100 high-level corrupt agents were punished by being dismissed or reorganized. Fourth, tax laws were simplified to make them more efficient and reduce the discretion left to tax officials. Fifth, control systems were tightened—tax payments began to take place through banks rather than tax agents, and confirmation letters were sent to check tax-payers' payments. Sixth, personnel practices were improved. Recruitment became meritocratic, an antinepotism regulation forbade the appointment of even distant relatives, and promotions were based on performance. But these achievements—in a country where corruption remained widespread—did not last. In the early 1980s, nepotism became a problem once again, and tax assessments and tax collections dropped significantly.

merous countries: in the United States at the turn of the century, in Singapore in the 1960s, in Indonesia in the 1970s, and in Cameroon in the 1980s. Police indulgence of extortion and other crimes in Hong Kong led to the creation of an anticorruption office in the 1970s. In the late 1970s, an inquiry in Massachusetts revealed that 76 percent of a sample of public buildings had at least one "structural" defect that could not have occurred without inspectors' complacency. Two-thirds of the names on the civil service roster in 1978 in Zaire were fictitious. These and less malign forms of corruption—absenteeism, moonlighting, or lack of dedication—undercut public administration.

Corruption can seldom be reduced unless its larger underlying causes are addressed. It flourishes in situations where domestic and international competition is suppressed, rules and regulations are excessive and discretionary, civil servants are underpaid, or the organization they serve has unclear or conflicting objectives. In Cameroon, obtaining all the authorizations and permits necessary to start a new business takes two years even

for a well-connected businessman; the law requires twenty-four different steps involving twenty separate offices. Anticorruption campaigns are periodically undertaken, sometimes with success (Box 7.1). But often the root causes remain: weak agencies fighting market forces with controls society considers excessive, discretionary, or illogical.

Remedies: democracy and institutions?

Authoritarianism often has been seen as a useful, if regrettable, expedient for effective policymaking in the face of political instability. A strongly held view from the 1950s through the 1970s was that development policies took time to bear fruit, and that this was inconsistent with the politics of short-term electoral cycles. Democracies were seen as having a built-in inclination toward populist policies (Box 7.2). Benevolent authoritarian regimes (led by philosopher-despots) were needed, it was argued, to push through unpopular reforms and tame an unruly or otherwise ineffective administration. Economies managed with varying degrees of authoritarianism have made progress at different times in the past, for example, Brazil, Chile, Spain, and some of the East Asian economies. Yet at the same time, some democracies—old ones as in India or new ones as in the Philippines—have been unable so far to make rapid progress.

During the 1980s, however, severe disenchantment with authoritarian regimes set in. Now it is better understood that such regimes are no less likely to yield to the interests of narrow constituencies. Few authoritarian regimes, in fact, have been economically enlightened. Some of the East Asian NIEs are the exceptions, not the rule. Dictatorships have proven disastrous for development in many economies—in Eastern Europe, Argentina, Central African Republic, Haiti, Myanmar, Nicaragua, Peru, Uganda, and Zaire, to name only a few.

Democracies, conversely, could make reform more feasible in several ways. Political checks and balances, a free press, and open debate on the costs and benefits of government policy could give a wider public a stake in reform. The need to pro-

duce good results in order to be reelected could help, rather than hinder, economic change: it increases governments' incentives to perform well and keeps predatory behavior in check.

Experience allows no hard and fast conclusion. Peru is going through one of the worst economic crises in its history, mostly as a result of policies implemented in the late 1980s by a democratically elected government. Bolivia has been unable to improve its government's administrative capacity despite almost a decade of democracy. Literacy rates in China in 1950 were similar to those in India, and four decades later they are twice as high. Yet India is one of the oldest and most sophisticated democracies in the developing world.

Democratic governments are not necessarily more adept at managing reform, either. Transitional democratic governments, perhaps because their political base is still fluid, appear to be particularly vulnerable (Tables 7.2 and 7.3). Democratic governments have a better record than authoritarian governments in countries that are not politically polarized; the reverse seems to be true in polarized societies. On the whole, the evidence suggests that the democratic-authoritarian distinc-

Box 7.2 Populist experiments

The populist experiments in Latin America—Allende in Chile (1971–73), Peron in Argentina (1946–49), and Garcia in Peru (1985–88)—are extreme examples of the interaction between political and economic processes. Populist policies have emphasized growth and short-run distributional goals, brushing aside the risks of inflation and excessive deficits and ignoring external constraints and the responses of firms and households to their aggressive anti-market policies. Addressing poverty and income distribution issues, which populist regimes viewed as the source of social conflict and political instability, could not be done, however, through unsustainable economic policies.

In a typical populist cycle, the new administration sets in motion a marked shift in policies. Excess capacity and the availability of foreign reserves at first support higher output growth, which in many cases is accompanied by an increase in real wages. Inflation is kept low with the help of price controls. But bottlenecks soon appear as a result of the strong expansion in domestic demand; because of dwindling foreign reserves, these cannot be bypassed by increasing imports. Shortages, accelerating inflation, and declining reserves lead to capital flight and the demonetization of the economy. The budget deficit worsens as

subsidies increase, and taxes decline in real terms. In this unsustainable position, the government is forced to devalue the currency and cut subsidies. Inflation accelerates and real wages fall.

The Chilean experience of 1970–73 clearly illustrates this sequence of events. To achieve rapid growth and improve the living conditions of low-income groups, the government stepped up public spending. Public sector wages were increased, adding to the fiscal deficit. Agrarian reform was intensified, and the mining and banking sectors as well as parts of the industrial sector were nationalized. The combination of price controls and expansionary demand policies fueled repressed inflation; the parallel market flourished. Foreign reserves were so low that it was impossible to meet the surge in demand by increasing imports. By 1972, the government was forced to devalue the escudo and adjust public sector prices. It was unable to control wages, however. Between 1970 and 1973, inflation increased from 35 percent to about 600 percent a year, and the fiscal deficit jumped from 2.7 to 24.7 percent of GDP. GDP growth accelerated to 9 percent in 1971 but turned negative in 1972 and 1973, when output fell by 5.6 percent.

Table 7.2 The success of economies with differing political systems in implementing an IMF adjustment program
(percent)

Percentage of adjustment years	Continuous democratic systems	Continuous authoritarian systems	Transitional democratic systems
In which fiscal deficits fell	49	50	25
In which expenditures as percentage of GDP fell	38	46	29
In which credit expansion slowed	61	62	43

Note: Based on reform episodes in seventeen countries from the 1950s through the 1980s.
Source: Haggard and Kaufman 1990.

Table 7.3 The success of economies with differing political systems in controlling rapid inflation

Measure	Democratic systems	Authoritarian systems
Percentage of inflation episodes which ended in stabilization		
In nonpolarized environments	75	62
In polarized environments	29	67
Percentage of adjustment programs that led to breakdown of system twelve months or less after program started	11	14

Note: Based on 114 standby arrangements from 1954 to 1984 signed by nine Latin American countries.
Source: Remmer 1986.

tion itself fails to explain adequately whether or not countries initiate reform, implement it effectively, or survive its political fallout.

But as indicated in Chapter 2, there is suggestive evidence that links features of democratic systems positively with overall aspects of development and welfare. A further result emerges from the empirical literature on the relation between economic performance and political systems: by developing human resources and, more particularly, by investing in education, countries have been found to strengthen the basis for open political systems. Some studies suggest that for a given level of income, improvements in social indicators are associated with freedom and liberty. Other studies suggest that political instability declines not only as income rises but also as education improves—although further research is necessary to confirm this finding.

Institutions and development

Another approach to the problems of political instability, fragile social consensus, and weak governance is to build more effective institutions. This is an extremely broad concept. It encompasses the public bodies through which the state discharges its most fundamental responsibilities: maintaining law and order, investing in essential infrastructure, raising taxes to finance such activities, and so on. But the idea goes further. It extends to the conventions that govern the way people deal with each other: property rights, contracts, and norms of conduct. The discussion of how society's institutions affect economic performance has been one of the liveliest in the economic literature in the past two decades. Although understanding of these issues is far from complete, it is clear that a primary task of institutional development is to improve allocative efficiency and reduce transactions costs—the costs of people dealing with people (Box 7.3).

People's values and ideologies affect institutions, and these in turn affect the economy. Analyzing the role in development of such factors as culture, religion, law, and politics has a strong intellectual foundation in the work of Hayek, Hegel, Marx, and Weber. Centralized political institutions backed by a strong bureaucracy are argued to have stifled entrepreneurship and productivity growth in ancient China—even though technologically the country was far ahead of what is now the West. At the level of organizations, recent research suggests that the superior performance of Japanese manufacturing results (among other factors) from norms of behavior that promote the flow of information between workers and supervisors; these lower firms' internal transactions costs and help them adapt to markets demanding high-quality products with short life cycles. Another study has found that when workers in the United States get a share of their firm's profits, it seems to have a favorable effect on their productivity.

Often, the institutions of government can affect economic performance more directly. Fiscal deficits have led to very high inflation in Latin America but not in South Asia, where central banks are more independent. Credit programs for small and medium-size industries have been much more successful in Sri Lanka—where they have been implemented by a competent and motivated civil service relatively independent of political interference—than in Bangladesh. For the same reason, rural development programs have enhanced productivity in some parts of South Asia, but less so in

Box 7.3 The contribution of institutional innovations to development

Over the centuries, market-mediated transactions have been a major force in institutional development, which in turn has been a major force in economic development. As markets have expanded, market participants spontaneously have defined rights, formulated contracts, and evolved norms of behavior with a view to improving the efficiency of their interactions.

The letter of credit, a contract that emerged in the Middle Ages in Italy, increased the scope of exchange and contributed to the expansion of international trade. By better defining creditors' rights in regard to a firm's assets, public liability companies—an innovation in late-eighteenth-century England—allowed firms to take risks and attract resources to activities that otherwise could not have developed. Since the 1970s, leasing contracts have allowed enterprises to reduce the risks associated with large investments in equipment. In Bangladesh, the Grameen Bank found innovative ways to lend to low-income groups while keeping defaults low. This was achieved by establishing contracts that made the community, not only the borrower, responsible for payments.

Behavior also adapts to market needs and influences transactions costs. Stealing and trading have the same linguistic root in various languages because of the dishonesty of early traders. Only after markets become established, transactions become regular, and competition increases do traders have an incentive to establish and maintain their reputation. Traders in industrial market economies are more honest not only because sanctions are administered more efficiently, but also because a good reputation reduces transactions costs.

Norms of behavior not yet adapted to the needs of a modern economy substantially increase transactions costs. Pilferage is serious in the ports cities of many developing countries partly because stevedores are more loyal to their families, clans, or tribes than to the organization employing them. Not pilfering and being honest deprives their families of a source of additional income—behavior families would consider dishonest.

Africa and Latin America. State-owned enterprises have been efficient in Singapore and Taiwan, China, where they were subject to competition and their access to the budget was restricted—but not in Argentina, Bolivia, and Nigeria.

In many instances, the state has stimulated growth by restructuring institutions: the abolition of feudal arrangements and the standardization of currency, taxes, weights and measures, and internal tariffs in revolutionary France in the 1790s; patent laws in nineteenth-century Europe and the United States; the integration of customs, commercial, and civil and commercial law in both Germany and Italy in the nineteenth century; the modernization of Meiji Japan in the second half of the 1800s, and that of Turkey in the early part of this century; Brazil's company-law reforms in the early 1970s; the creation of stock exchanges in East Asia and the economic integration of Western Europe after 1945. All of these depended on state action. They molded the framework of enterprise in ways which increased entrepreneurial security and eased the flow of resources and people. In most developing countries, strengthening or creating institutions remains a difficult but necessary task (Box 7.4).

Supporting institutional development requires a state with well-developed administrative structures and agencies responsive to markets' needs.

The political weaknesses of developing countries are often, however, manifested in the efficiency of their bureaucracies. By itself, an efficient bureaucracy does not guarantee successful development, nor can it substitute for market forces. As indicated above, it can even retard development. Nonetheless, an efficient bureaucracy enables governments to govern. It was key to the survival of ancient civilizations such as Egypt (3000 B.C.) and China—where the well-structured bureaucracy which had existed since at least 200 B.C. was still operating less than a hundred years ago. The basic principles of bureaucracy were already well understood by the ancient Chinese. The civil servants, the mandarins, were recruited by competitive examination. There were systems of promotion, career patterns, and job security. Serving the state was a privilege reserved only for those with demonstrated talents. Building efficient bureaucracies was also an essential step in the process of nation-making in Europe—but remains a priority in many developing countries.

Nongovernmental organizations

Nongovernmental organizations (NGOs) have become an important force in the development process which, to some extent, has mitigated the costs of developing countries' institutional weaknesses, which often include administrative shortcomings

Box 7.4 Setting priorities for institutional development: easier said than done

The priorities for institutional development naturally vary with a country's history, culture, economic policies, and stage of development. For most of Eastern Europe, the priority is to establish the institutions necessary for a market economy to function efficiently: property rights, corporate and bankruptcy laws, commercial courts, banking legislation, and stock exchanges. For low-income Africa and Latin America, the priority is to improve the management of the public sector, a goal that often requires a simultaneous reduction in the size of the government and a strengthening of its capacity.

Elsewhere priorities may be less clear-cut. Particular countries have their own accomplishments and needs:

• In South Asia and some parts of Latin America, training and visit programs have had a strong effect on agricultural productivity.

• In Sri Lanka, a recent change in civil courts procedures has greatly improved the workings of bankruptcy laws and reduced financial intermediation costs, after several years of complaints from the banking community.

• In Brazil, mechanisms are being devised to improve the flow of information among universities, research institutes, and industry—making research more responsive to industry's needs.

• In Malaysia, a recently created government bond-rating system is expected to reduce private firms' financing costs significantly.

• In northern Brazil, Egypt, India, Indonesia, and Sri Lanka, the improvement of cadastres and land titling is overdue and could greatly improve the efficiency of rural credit markets and reduce the generally extremely high costs of rural credit.

• In many countries, better banking supervision is important for successful financial liberalization.

Identifying institutional needs is not easy, however. First, institutions essential in industrial societies may prove superfluous in developing countries. Stock exchanges, treasury-bill markets, credit-rating bureaus, land-titling offices, and metrology and standards bureaus are expensive to set up, and it is difficult to decide whether they are being developed ahead of market needs. Second, some institutions are unproductive in the presence of systemwide problems. For instance, an underpaid civil service renders most public institutions a hindrance rather than a help to markets. Poorly planned public spending deprives institutions of current inputs and reduces their efficiency. Third, there are no simple indicators of institutional needs and priorities. There is scope, however, to develop quantitative indicators of the efficiency of public institutions; for example, how long does it take to register a business, obtain a passport, clear customs, get an import license, or pay taxes?

---

and an inability to carry out efficiently essential development tasks, such as providing social services or protecting the environment. In response, NGOs have grown rapidly in recent years, both in numbers and in the volume of resources they mobilize. In 1987, NGOs transferred about $5.5 billion from industrial to developing countries—nearly $1 billion more than the International Development Association.

Most of NGOs' resources (about 60 percent) are raised by themselves. The rest ($2.2 billion in 1987) are from official aid agencies, which channel funds through NGOs because such organizations are more effective in bringing about popular participation, in working at the grassroots level, and in operating in remote areas. NGOs have also been important in sensitizing governments and international aid and finance agencies to the social and environmental aspects of development. In addition, in many countries, they have taken the lead on controversial development issues such as family planning. Although many developing-country governments are suspicious about some NGOs' self-appointed role as agents of change, governments of countries such as Bolivia, Egypt, India, Jordan, Mexico, the Philippines, Togo, and Uganda are seeking ways to encourage more NGO action.

NGOs vary in coverage and effectiveness. In Bangladesh, NGOs specialized in health and family planning reach only one-sixth of the country's 80,000 villages. Many small NGOs' managerial capacity needs to be developed before they can be effective. For others, little is known about fundraising costs. In addition, even the most effective NGOs cannot fulfill all the gaps left by the commercial and public sectors. Aside from their growing numbers and the volume of resources they mobilize, the importance of NGOs lies in their ability to involve communities and grassroots organizations more effectively in the development process and in addressing poverty.

Equity and redistribution

Governments have always been concerned with equity. Income transfers in OECD countries (excluding interest payments but including social security payments) amount to 40 percent of government expenditure and are as high as 20–30 percent of GDP in Austria, France, Germany, the Netherlands, and Sweden. A better distribution of income may facilitate economic management. Political scientists have suggested that mechanisms to redistribute income by sharing the benefits of growth more equally have helped some OECD governments to diffuse opposition against market-oriented reforms; the short-term victims of change are cushioned.

An analysis of thirty-two countries (twenty-five developing and seven OECD countries) showed that the higher the risk of term of trade shocks that a nation faces in international markets, the more likely it is to increase trade barriers. It also showed that the larger its social-insurance programs, the less likely it is that the government will be protectionist (Bates, Brock, and Tiefenthaler 1991). Other recent research suggests that wage negotiations through nonmarket mechanisms (negotiations between unions, industrialists, and governments) that take equity into account may explain the relatively low unemployment in the Nordic countries (Jackman, Pissarides, and Savouri 1990). Some economists have also suggested that the relatively egalitarian distributions of income in Asia allowed countries there to adjust to the external shocks of the 1970s more rapidly than their Latin American counterparts.

Despite such evidence, greater equality of income is still considered by some to be inimical to growth. Increasing the capital stock, it is argued, requires high saving rates; this in turn implies a distribution of income that is tilted toward the (high-saving) rich. The Republic of Korea's tax reform of 1973 largely excluded capital income (interests, dividends, capital gains, and other returns on assets) from the tax base. The conventional wisdom among industrial countries as well as policymakers in developing countries has been that things ought to be done "one at a time": first, economic growth; second, social equity; third, civil and political liberties.

In fact, there is no evidence that saving is positively related to income inequality or that income inequality leads to higher growth. If anything, it seems that inequality is associated with slower growth (Figure 7.2). The notion of a trade-off be-

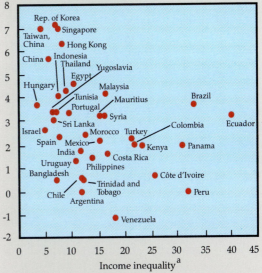

Figure 7.2 Income inequality and the growth of GDP in selected economies, 1965-89

GDP growth per capita (percent)

a. The ratio of the income shares of the richest 20 percent and poorest 20 percent of the population. Data on income distribution are from surveys conducted mainly in the late 1960s and early 1970s.
Sources: World Bank data; Berg and Sachs 1988.

tween growth and equity, which helped to entrench antigrowth policies in socialist economies and antiequity policies in conservative ones, has been further discredited by the many economies that consistently outperform the rest on both counts: Costa Rica, Indonesia, Japan, Korea, Malaysia (Box 7.5), and the Scandinavian economies.

Greater equality is not achieved through income transfers—except in the case of safety nets for vulnerable, small, and well-targeted groups of the population. *World Development Report 1990* showed that the pattern of development has strong distributional implications. Industrial protection and discriminatory taxes on farming help to explain why income inequality is more severe in Latin America than in Asia. The bulk of developing countries' revenues generally consist of indirect taxes, which are generally less progressive than income taxes. Subsidies for capital (in the form of tax incentives, subsidized credit, or currency over-valuation) invariably lead to more capital-intensive modes of production, and thus worsen distribution.

Another lesson is that public expenditure can have powerful redistributive effects. Various

Box 7.5 The politics of inclusion: Malaysia and Sri Lanka

Similar starts

Both Malaysia and Sri Lanka were British colonies—until 1963 and 1948, respectively. Both had well-developed, export-oriented, tree-crop plantations in the 1960s—rubber and palm oil in Malaysia, rubber and tea in Sri Lanka. Both had sophisticated bureaucracies. Both had advanced democratic political institutions. And both had relatively well-educated populations, with 90 percent primary school enrollment. Both countries also had problems caused by the presence of highly differentiated ethnic groups, with a majority that was economically underprivileged but politically dominant. In Malaysia, Bumiputras (Malays and other sons of the soil) accounted for 55 percent of the population, Chinese 35 percent, and Indians 10 percent. In Sri Lanka, Sinhalese accounted for 72 percent of the population, Tamils 18 percent, and other groups 10 percent. Both countries adopted discriminatory policies specifically to improve the lot of the majority groups (legislatively in Malaysia and de facto in Sri Lanka).

Both countries used public enterprises not only in the plantation sector, but also in other areas such as airlines, cement, banks, and manufacturing. They supported rice farmers through subsidized fertilizer, credit, and irrigation. They gave preferred access to public employment and public procurement to the majority ethnic group. And they emphasized education and health services for all—but biased higher education in favor of the majority.

Different results

In the early 1960s, Malaysia's per capita income (at $320) was twice Sri Lanka's. Three decades later, Malaysia's per capita income is five times Sri Lanka's. Malaysia has also contained conflict among its ethnic groups without serious violence. By contrast, since 1983, ethnic and regional conflicts in Sri Lanka have

claimed tens of thousands of lives. The cost of destroyed infrastructure and forgone income from disrupted economic activities has been estimated to be close to two-thirds of GDP. In addition to its superior growth, Malaysia has reduced the incidence of poverty from 50 percent in 1970 to 10 percent today—and reduced the inequalities between and within ethnic groups.

Reasons for the difference

Unlike Sri Lanka (until 1977, when the economy was liberalized) Malaysia's authorities adjusted the anti-growth elements of their policies—such as foreign investment and industrial licensing rules—when growth rates faltered. Trade policies were kept open, with moderate tariff levels (although, in selected important cases, highly effective protection was retained). Private enterprises did not need permits to expand production or invest. Nor were they harassed by currency controls, extensive quantitative trade restrictions, or the threat of nationalization without compensation. Minority businesses that were discriminated against in domestic markets were thus not shut out from business opportunities abroad. They could use their income to buy abroad goods and services (such as education) that were being denied them at home.

Sri Lanka's heavy regulatory framework before 1977 gave ample opportunities for discretion and discrimination. Economic controls ended up becoming controls on individuals—despite Sri Lanka's democratic traditions. Travel was restricted because of exchange controls, and simple business transactions (such as obtaining a permit to invest, to import, or to expand production) often ended up being highly politicized. The perception was that government could influence, and was influencing, the distribution of assets among ethnic groups.

---

studies have found that education is the most important single variable influencing income inequality. Investments in education, health, and nutrition—if well-designed and -implemented—can improve distribution and at the same time promote development in other ways. The reform programs of the 1980s and 1990s thus have emphasized more and more the need to protect social programs during fiscal adjustment.

When markets work well, greater equity often comes naturally. For instance, labor markets are fragmented in many countries. People with similar attributes are unable to obtain similar rewards or employment: sex, ethnicity, location, and industrial occupation consistently appear as determi-

nants of wages, regardless of productivity. Helping women to participate in labor markets has been an important reason for the improving distribution of income in Malaysia and Indonesia. Government spending on improving infrastructure and the delivery of social services has traditionally been the main mechanism to integrate markets, and this remains of major importance. A variety of other public programs that can reduce inequalities while improving allocative efficiency and spurring growth—for example, programs designed to improve access to infrastructure, credit, and land.

Land reform often seems to have raised the incomes of the poor. China, Japan, and Korea are all regarded as outstanding examples of economies that have succeeded at land reform. The evidence on its effect on agricultural efficiency is more mixed, however. It is hard to separate the effects of land redistribution from the effects of the complementary investments and institutions oriented toward increasing agricultural productivity that have typically accompanied land reform. There does appear to be evidence, however, that the social stability resulting from land reform has contributed to faster growth.

For all these reasons, efforts to improve equity can sit comfortably within reform programs aimed at promoting growth. It is clear, however, that market-distorting and overzealous redistribution can quickly pose overwhelming financial problems. For example, the cost of food subsidies in Brazil in the late 1970s, and more recently in Egypt, ballooned as international food prices went up. Subsidies to protect declining industries have to rise continuously to achieve the same effect, because maintaining preference requires that dynamism elsewhere in the economy must be offset. In Europe, for instance, maintaining farm incomes relative to other incomes has become more and more expensive because of faster growth in other sectors.

Also, crude transfers through market-distorting interventions almost always end up worsening the distribution of income rather than improving it. Fertilizer subsidies in Bangladesh, Brazil, Ecuador, Egypt, India, and Pakistan accrue mainly either to fertilizer manufacturers or to better-off farmers. The large subsidy on wheat in the 1970s in Brazil reduced the demand for beans grown by small farmers. Production of beans declined. Farmers sold their land and migrated to the cities, where they increased the demand for subsidized wheat. Rich commercial farmers bought the migrants' land at distress prices.

Reforming the public sector

In about the fourteenth century, an Arabic treatise argued: ''Commercial activity on the part of the ruler is harmful to his subjects and ruinous to the tax revenue . . . crowds out competitors; dictates prices for materials and products which could lead to the financial ruin of many businesses. When the ruler's attacks on property are extensive and general, affecting all means of making a livelihood, the slackening of business activity too becomes general'' (Ibn Khaldun 1981). One of the most striking legacies of the 1980s is the rediscovery of these ancient truths. Many governments are reconsider-

ing their involvement in the economy, reviewing their spending priorities, and undertaking fewer commercial activities. For this reappraisal to succeed, the administrative capacity of the state will need to be improved—and governments will have to cope with opposition from the vested interests created by decades of excessive intervention.

Rationalizing public expenditure

Government expenditure accounts for slightly more than 20 percent of GDP in low-income countries, and close to 30 percent in middle-income ones. These ratios are much lower than in industrial countries today, but much higher than in industrial countries at a comparable stage of development (Tables 7.4 and 7.5). The evidence suggests that many of the developing countries' public spending programs provide very low returns.

PUBLIC INVESTMENT. The quality of public investment significantly depends on the quality of the economic climate (see Chapter 4). But some developing countries are experiencing economic difficulties because the projects themselves, very often financed with the support of external agencies, were ill-advised. A loss-making silver-smelting plant in Bolivia, a value-subtracting shoe fac-

Table 7.4 Percentage share of government expenditure in GNP or GDP, industrial countries, 1880–1985

Year	France	Germany	Japan	Sweden	United Kingdom	United States
1880[a]	15	10	11	6	10	8
1929[a]	19	31	19	8	24	10
1960[b]	35	32	18	31	32	28
1985[b]	52	47	33	65	48	37

a. GNP.
b. GDP.
Source: World Bank, various years.

Table 7.5 Percentage share of government expenditure and consumption in GNP or GDP, industrial and developing countries, 1972 and 1986

Economy group	Expenditure[a]		Consumption[b]	
	1972	1986	1972	1986
Low-income	19	23	12	13
Lower-middle-income	15	27	11	14
Upper-middle-income	25	27	12	14
Industrial market	28	40	14	19

a. GNP.
b. GDP.
Source: World Bank, various years.

tory in Tanzania, and irrigation systems with low rates of return in Sri Lanka are only a few of countless possible examples. The costs can be considerable. In Zaire, the hydropower and transmission-line project that was mentioned earlier in this chapter cost almost $3 billion in 1990 prices—about a third of the country's external debt. The project has never operated at more than 30 percent of its capacity, and it is now in the midst of extensive rehabilitation, although it began operating only in 1982. This is an extreme case, but unproductive projects on a less spectacular scale are all too common.

WAGES AND THE CIVIL SERVICE. Wage bills are a large part of government expenditure in most countries. Before the reform programs, the wage bill absorbed more than 60 percent of current revenues in the Central African Republic—and more than 40 percent in the Gambia. The tendency to overstaff and underpay that in the last few decades has prevailed in many developing countries means that much of this spending is wasted. The problem of poor motivation has often been compounded by ill-defined career structures, and by politicized recruitment and senior appointments. In some countries the institutional structures and systems originally established to staff and operate the civil service have collapsed. In Uganda, a civil service census turned up not only numerous nonexistent workers but also entire nonexistent schools.

As a result, in Latin America, South Asia, and Africa, civil service reform has become a high priority for many governments. Civil service reform programs generally have three components. The first is a retrenchment effort to downsize the civil services to more manageable numbers of employees. The second is pay and grading restructuring to increase incentives, reduce moonlighting and corruption, and provide a better framework for career development. The third is institutional rebuilding to create the control structures and operating procedures needed to manage a modern and efficient civil service.

Most civil service reform programs have moved on all fronts simultaneously. The more successful African programs have cut back on the numbers of public employees (Ghana, the Gambia, and Guinea). But their progress has been limited to improved pay structures and some reform of institutional structures. No African country's ongoing reform program has completely rebuilt its civil service structures. The Ghanaian program, in opera-

tion since 1985 and probably the farthest-reaching, has yet to establish an effective system to control recruitment.

None of the programs now under way appears to embrace a serious examination of government functions to determine which can be privatized, delegated to the local community, or stopped altogether. Given the need for smaller, more efficient public sectors and a more dynamic private sector, future civil service reform efforts would definitely benefit from tackling such larger issues.

SUBSIDIES AND TRANSFERS. Expenditure on subsidies and transfers accounts for about 3 percent of GDP on average for a large sample of countries. It is difficult to generalize about them because they are one of the most heterogeneous categories of spending. Moreover, reporting systems are weak in most countries. The real cost of subsidies and transfers could easily be twice what is on the books. Subsidies often result from government interventions in prices, and they may apply to all manner of goods and services: wheat in Egypt and the Soviet Union; bus travel in Sri Lanka; fertilizer in Bangladesh, Ecuador, and India; and so on. Transfers are usually made to state-owned enterprises. They become necessary either because the SOEs are inefficient, or because price controls and other restrictions force them to operate at a loss. These transfers, however, are generally insufficient to meet the enterprises' needs for capital investment; as a result, standards of service have deteriorated dramatically in some countries. The telephone system and railways in Argentina and the bus service in Egypt, for instance, have suffered from far too little investment.

MILITARY SPENDING. The world spends $1,000 billion on the military every year. In the late 1980s, military expenditure totaled $860 billion a year in high-income countries and $170 billion a year in developing ones. Of this $170 billion, $38 billion was spent on imports of arms, mostly from industrial countries.

If global military expenditure were reduced, the world would undoubtedly be a better place. But is this realistic? Humanity is no stranger to wars and conflicts—twentieth-century humanity least of all (Box 7.6). The recent war in the Gulf region; ensuing conflicts there; continued violence in Afghanistan, Angola, Central America, and Indochina; civil wars in Ethiopia, Mozambique, Somalia, and Sudan; and the snail's pace of superpower disarmament—all make it only too clear how difficult progress toward lasting peace will be.

Unsurprisingly, military spending is higher in the developing countries that face external or internal threats. Military spending is more than 10 percent of GDP in several countries. After the ethnic conflict that erupted in 1983, Sri Lanka's military expenditure has increased from less than 1

Box 7.6 War and development

The two world wars involved unprecedented numbers of nations and resulted in unprecedented loss of life. But regional wars and civil upheavals since 1945 have also claimed lives and have devastated individual countries, many of them in the developing world (Box table 7.6). The commonly reported estimates of 450,000 deaths in the Iran-Iraq conflict equal about 1 percent of those countries' combined populations at the start of the conflict in 1979. The 2 million losses in the Ethiopian Civil War constitute more than 7 percent of the country's 1974 population.

Battlefield death tolls underestimate war's impact. War makes heavy claims on the most productive workers. In World War I, only 4.5 percent of Germany's fatalities were more than forty years old; 63 percent were between ages twenty and thirty. In addition, soldiers are not the only ones to die. Civilians succumb directly fighting and from war-related famine and disease; military mobilization results in lower birth rates. Totaled this way, the loss of life during the period 1914–21 (which includes the Soviet civil war) may exceed 60 million. Only about 8 million of these were mobilized men.

The costs of fighting involve more than the cost of bullets, uniforms, and equipment. The 1969 Soccer War between Honduras and El Salvador lasted just 100 hours. About 2,000 people died. But 100,000 people became refugees. The fighting destroyed half of El Sal-

vador's oil refining and storage facilities and paralyzed the Central American Common Market. Military expenditure and forgone output during the first five years of the Iran-Iraq conflict cost more than $400 billion. The cost by the end of the war in 1988 was much higher. Economic disruption is similarly severe in civil wars. The conflict in northern Ethiopia's Eritrea territory has cut the labor force; bombs and mines have caused farmers to avoid some land, thus effectively taking it out of production—40 percent of land was estimated to have been left idle in 1987, which partly explains the food shortfalls in the region.

Inevitably, war retards development. The combined costs of replacing lost equipment, providing health care for the wounded, and enduring lower productivity are paid long after armistice. In the Nigerian Civil War of 1967–70, the government sought to finance the war without triggering high inflation or causing deterioration in the balance of payments. It restricted bank credit to restrain internal demand; it raised taxes, cut capital investment, and sharply decreased nondefense expenditures, including those for general administration, social and community welfare, and economic services. But because of the high cost of importing weapons and of forgone exports, these policies could not prevent the deterioration of Nigeria's balance of payments position.

Box table 7.6 Deaths during wars, 1900–89

Period	Number of wars		Deaths during international wars (thousands)			Deaths during civil wars (thousands)			Total deaths as percentage of world population
	Civil	International	Civilian	Military	Total[a]	Civilian	Military	Total[a]	
1900–09	10	6	230	12	243	25	139	166	0.02
1910–19	15	9	7,045	13,470	20,556	1,140	139	1,327	1.13
1920–29	11	8	21	42	109	39	111	371	0.02
1930–39	11	8	933	838	1,770	646	1,109	1,796	0.17
1940–49	13	7	20,176	19,110	39,285	1,007	5	2,182	1.70
1950–59	20	5	1,073	1,926	3,031	1,571	253	1,879	0.17
1960–69	12	9	622	605	1,256	1,827	1,222	3,301	0.13
1970–79	18	7	639	606	1,246	3,543	1,236	4,957	0.16
1980–89	29	6	702	931	1,733	1,899	179	2,081	0.08
1900–89	141	63	31,440	37,539	69,229	11,697	4,393	18,059	. .

Note: All but 11,000 of the war deaths following 1949 took place in developing countries. All numbers are estimates and are subject to significant error. Domestic conflicts are not always clearly definable as civil wars, and thus coverage of these statistics varies among studies. A variety of civil disruptions are excluded. For example, estimated deaths during purges and collectivization in the Soviet Union during the 1930s, which range from 5 to 20 million people, are not included. Figures for deaths resulting from other such events after World War II are also excluded because of poor data. Rough estimates for these range up to 15 million. Also, some wars are counted as civil even when foreign intervention occurred. Deaths during the Korean War, deaths during the Viet Nam War for the 1965–75 period, and the war in Afghanistan for the 1978–89 period are included under international wars.
a. Totals include total estimated deaths. When breakdowns are unavailable, deaths are omitted from civilian and military subcategories. Totals may also differ as a result of rounding. Deaths were prorated when reporting periods spanned more than one decade.
Sources: Sivard 1988, 1989.

Table 7.6 Public expenditure on the military compared with that on social sectors, 1986
(percentage of GNP)

Military expenditure	Expenditure on health and education			
	1–1.9	2–4.9	5–9.9	10 and above
Less than 1		Brazil Ghana Mexico Niger	Barbados Cyprus Gambia	Costa Rica Luxembourg
1–1.9	Nigeria Paraguay	Argentina Bangladesh Cameroon Colombia Dominican Rep. Ecuador Guatemala Haiti Nepal Philippines Romania Rwanda Sierra Leone	Algeria Central African Rep. Côte d'Ivoire Fiji Jamaica Malta Papua New Guinea Swaziland Trinidad and Tobago Venezuela	Austria Finland Ireland Japan Switzerland
2–4.9	Uganda Zaire	Burundi Benin Bolivia Burkina Faso El Salvador Guinea India Indonesia Mali Myanmar Turkey Uruguay	Bulgaria Chile Congo Czechoslovakia Gabon German Dem. Rep. Hungary Italy Kenya Lesotho Liberia Madagascar Malawi Mauritania Poland Senegal Somalia South Africa Spain Tanzania Thailand Togo Yugoslavia Zambia	Australia Belgium Botswana Canada Denmark France Germany, Fed. Rep. Netherlands New Zealand Norway Panama Portugal Sweden
5–9.9		Chad China Pakistan Peru Sri Lanka Sudan United Arab Emirates	Bahrain Cuba Egypt Ethiopia Greece Honduras Korea, Rep. of Kuwait Malaysia Morocco Singapore Tunisia United States Yemen, Arab Rep.	United Kingdom Zimbabwe
10 and above		Angola Iraq	Iran, I.R. of Israel Jordan Oman Syria USSR Yemen, P.D.R.	Guyana Libya Nicaragua Saudi Arabia

Note: The ranges given in this table are illustrative of the differences in expenditures in the different categories; they are not necessarily indicative of precise differences across countries because of some differences in the definition of the categories. The estimates of social expenditure do not cover those by local bodies.
Source: Sivard 1989.

percent of GDP to about 5 percent. Many poor countries expend more on the military than on social sectors (Table 7.6). During the past three decades, military and civilian regimes appear to have spent roughly the same share of their GDP on their armed forces.

In high-income countries, military spending has been increasing at the same rate as GDP. In developing countries, military expenditure has been declining—from 6–7 percent of GDP in the late 1970s to about 5 percent in the second half of the 1980s. This was mainly the result of a drastic reduction of military spending in the Middle East (especially in Syria and Egypt) and in Latin America (after the fiscal crisis of the 1980s). But 5 percent of GDP is still an enormous sum; in many countries it would be more than enough to double government spending on infrastructure or on health and education.

Governments need to take every possible step to reduce military expenditure. Costa Rica is an outstanding example of a government which decided to reduce military spending and focus its efforts on the provision of health and education—an approach which improved equity and achieved a degree of political stability unusual in the developing world. Costa Rica's poor soils and sparse natural resources meant, however, that the country had few enemies; its experience may not be easy to replicate.

Many countries have to deal with bigger internal and external threats than those facing Costa Rica; even so, these threats hardly justify the sums being spent today on armed might. Aid and finance agencies are entitled to ask whether it makes sense to help governments whose first priority is not to develop but to add to their military strength.

Privatizing and reforming state-owned enterprises

In the 1980s and 1990s so far, transferring state-owned enterprises to the private sector has been an important government objective both in OECD countries such as New Zealand and the United Kingdom, and in developing countries such as Argentina, Brazil, Chile, Ghana, the Republic of Korea, Malaysia, Mexico, Nigeria, Togo, and Turkey. In most of these countries, privatization has meant much more than merely transferring assets to the private sector. It has been part of a broader exercise aimed at stabilizing and liberalizing the economy on several fronts—regulation, prices, trade, the financial sector. Governments have consciously set out to redefine the economic role of the state. As part of this shift, they have curtailed the SOEs' privileged access to the budget or credit system, tariff or nontariff protection for their products, and regulatory protection from private competitors. They have signaled a new determination not to pursue narrow distributional goals at the expense of efficiency.

Many countries have taken the view that unless privatization were part of such a broad program of reform, it would be an empty gesture. It would merely transfer the control of rents from the public to the private sector. There have been variants on this general approach. In China, deregulation has been accompanied by new institutional arrangements that allow the government to retain ownership while improving the enterprises' efficiency. In Argentina, and in Mexico to a lesser extent, privatization with heavy foreign participation has been used to reduce external debt and increase investment in basic infrastructure, such as energy and telecommunications. In Argentina and Brazil, revenues from privatization are also expected to contribute significantly to balancing the fiscal deficit.

PROBLEMS OF IMPLEMENTATION. Privatization has proven to be an arduous exercise, however. Thin markets for domestic capital, adverse economic conditions, and the resistance of trade unions and civil servants have slowed the process

virtually everywhere. Except for relatively advanced economies such as Argentina, Brazil, and Mexico, the infrastructure of privatization—lawyers, accountants, merchant bankers, and entrepreneurs—is largely missing in most developing countries. The need to build up this infrastructure is particularly acute in Eastern Europe, where it is difficult even to find qualified individuals to serve as directors of companies. Departments competent to handle privatization must be created, then adequately staffed and funded: a challenge in itself during times of financial stringency.

Legal issues also complicate privatization. In Mexico, constitutional amendments had to be passed in 1983 before privatization could go forward. In Turkey, sales were canceled when the courts deemed them illegal. In socialist economies, laws must be passed defining property rights, legalizing private ownership, establishing guidelines for articles of incorporation, and protecting minority shareholder interests; all these are necessary if the legality of a private purchase of a company is to be established. Similarly, the legality of the seller must be established. Contrary to popular belief, governments in socialist countries did not hold clear titles to firms. In some instances, assets were nationalized shortly after World War II, but the promised compensation, which would have legalized the nationalizations, was never made. Czechoslovakia and the former German Democratic Republic established new laws granting previous owners priority rights to compensation or the return of their original property. Uncertainty over whether there is a prior claim on the firm's assets has made many potential investors wary of privatization.

Previous attempts at decentralization in socialist economies had given workers in many enterprises rights that traditionally belong to shareholders in Western countries. Workers' councils in Poland have the right to decide on mergers and enterprise dissolution, asset sales, and appointment of chief executive officers; in Yugoslavia, workers' rights are codified even more extensively. In addition, state-owned assets are one of the few positive legacies of years of communist rule; the people insist on a fair distribution of this wealth as partial compensation for the suffering of the past. As a result, there is strong resistance to passing it into the hands of the old communist *nomenklatura*—the managerial class, linked through party ties, who ran the economy. Yet this group is among the richest, and it has the best information on the real worth of enterprises and the business connections to make firms run. These is a fear that an open market sale of assets will restore the *nomenklatura* to its earlier dominance.

The experience of the former German Democratic Republic suggests that, even under favorable financial, legal, and technical conditions, selling enterprises will take some time. The 9,000 state enterprises to be privatized in eastern Germany correspond to about 30,000–40,000 firms in a market economy. Even though state enterprise sales by Germany's privatization agency (Treuhandanstalt) have now reached 300 per month (compared with 25 per month during ten years in the British privatization program), it will take years to complete the process. Uncertainty about the value of the companies was initially so great that purchase prices were to be settled later by arbitration. Although asset and enterprise values are now clearer, price contingency clauses are being included in most sales contracts to enforce commitments by buyers.

Overall economic conditions, political considerations, and technical aspects of the process also complicate privatization. In Chile, some of the firms privatized during the period 1974–78 were renationalized within a few years to salvage them from the bankruptcies that followed the deep economic crisis. In the mid-1980s in Nepal, a privatization was reversed because of opposition to the transfer of the enterprise to a minority ethnic group. In Bangladesh, unresolved questions of share pricing and debt overhang led privatized firms to neglect investment in maintenance and new capacity. Instead, the firms concentrated on generating immediate cash flow—and much of the efficiency gains expected from privatization evaporated. In the former German Democratic Republic and Hungary, the first heads of the privatization agencies resigned within a year; in Argentina, alleged corruption in some privatizations led to a cabinet reshuffle. Even where privatization has encountered fewer setbacks, achievements have often been modest. In Mexico, for instance, two-thirds of SOEs have been privatized—but these sales account for less than 20 percent of the SOEs' total assets.

A REVOLUTION NONETHELESS. The recent change in government thinking on privatization has been, despite such difficulties, extraordinary. Much of what has been achieved would have been unthinkable ten years ago. In Argentina, the government has privatized two television stations, and awarded sales contracts for the telephone company, the national airline, some components of the national petroleum company, and the main distributor of electricity. More privatizations are expected in the near future. In Chile, privatizations have reversed the emergency nationalizations of the preceding years; sectors traditionally dominated by the government, such as steel, petroleum, and telecommunications, may be privatized in the near future.

In Côte d'Ivoire, the private sector, already involved in water supply, is also going into power generation; in Togo, textile firms have been sold to foreign investors. More privatizations are expected soon in Brazil, Peru, Sri Lanka, and Turkey. Liquidations of nonviable SOEs are going ahead in several African countries.

The first phase of drafting and implementing new legal statutes has been largely completed in Czechoslovakia, Hungary, Poland, and Yugoslavia. Czechoslovakia and Poland seem committed to a quicker pace of privatization and to the creation of a broader shareholding base. Hungary has opted to go more slowly; it is creating joint-stock companies whose shares are deposited with a state holding company until the enterprises can be valued and sold through public offerings. It expects to privatize about two hundred companies in this way during 1991.

In Poland most shops, gas stations, and trucks are already owner-operated, and a significant portion of housing is now private. Typically, the assets have been leased, not bought outright. Auctions of small assets, coordinated by the central authorities, have already started in Czechoslovakia. For the larger firms, programs of ''free'' distribution of shares are being planned to accelerate privatization. The Polish plan calls for the conversion of several hundred large firms into joint-stock companies, with most shares allotted to workers, pension funds, banks, and other financial intermediaries (acting as trust funds for the population at large); the remaining shares will be sold to private investors. Similar arrangements may be worked out in Czechoslovakia.

LESSONS. Privatization is necessary and highly desirable, even though difficult and time-consuming. It is not to be undertaken as end in itself, but as a means to an end: to use resources more efficiently. Removing price distortions and controls as quickly as possible is essential for that purpose. Unless prices are true indicators of costs and consumer demand, the true profitability of an enterprise can not be known, so its asset cannot be properly valued. Selling the enterprise at an appropriate price may be impossible, and meanwhile managers will be unable to make informed decisions on investment and production. Letting the price system work as it should means removing distortions such as price controls, distorted transfer prices between enterprises, subsidized loans, and preferential access to the budget and credit system; it also means getting macroeconomic policy right, and that includes avoiding an overvalued exchange rate.

It would be difficult to privatize all SOEs in the near future even if governments wanted to. Meanwhile efforts to raise productivity cannot wait. Governments need not hesitate to liquidate inherently unprofitable enterprises, and the remaining SOEs can be managed much more effectively. Soft budget constraints, interference in management and recruitment, and restrictions on competition (either in product or factor markets) need to be reduced or eliminated. Efficient state enterprises are to be found in many economies: for instance, Brazil, Ethiopia, France, Italy, Korea, Malaysia, and Singapore. These show that SOEs can be run as efficient commercial concerns responsive to consumers. In many developing countries, improving the performance of SOEs is as urgent as privatization in its own right.

The challenge of reform

The challenge for governments is to implement reforms in the face of sometimes trenchant political opposition. Structural reforms may hurt powerful interests. Streamlining the civil service threatens urban workers with unemployment, especially in Africa, where the public sector often employs up to half the salaried work force. Groups that can organize against reform have to be reckoned with; the beneficiaries are often dispersed and unorganized, making it difficult for the government to count on their support.

Box 7.7 From a centrally planned to a market economy

Transforming a centrally planned economy into a market economy requires complex and unprecedented reforms. There is no experience to guide transitions of the current magnitude. And most countries in transition are simultaneously creating a new political order. There is relatively little disagreement that the transitions have to be made, but there is much controversy about the theory, timing, scope, speed, and sequencing of reforms.

Three sets of issues arise. One concerns the economic implications of a policy sequence: will one kind of reform achieve its objectives while other economic distortions remain? Another question is political: will mounting opposition derail reforms scheduled near the end of the sequence? Finally, there is technical feasibility. New legal, accounting, and financial systems will require greater technical expertise and longer gestation periods than reforms that include only price deregulation.

One school of reform proposals puts change in ownership at the head of the sequence before or alongside changes that address macroeconomic stability and markets. The rationale is partly political. With early privatization, there is less risk that the economy will remain state-controlled and greater pressure for complementary market-oriented reforms. But another school of thought begins with macroeconomic and market-building reforms: it leaves privatization—at least for large state enterprises—to a second stage. (Under both proposals some agricultural, retail, and residential assets would be privatized early.) The rationale is that private ownership requires financial institutions, experience, and expertise that do not yet exist in the transitional economies. Without this infrastructure, rapid privatization could lead to widespread corruption and economic and political chaos. Within each school there are further differences on the proper order for addressing particular distortions.

No single reform sequence will fit all the transitional economies. Reform histories vary; unlike others, Hungary has had more than two decades of experience with decentralized economic decisions. Macroeconomic conditions range from great instability (the Soviet Union) to relative stability (Czechoslovakia). Private sector activity has been relatively higher in predominantly agricultural countries such as China and Viet Nam but negligible in more industrialized nations.

A preferred sequencing (Box figure 7.7) would include early steps to stabilize the macroeconomy and deregulate domestic- and external-sector prices to give clear, accurate signals for economic activity and for the valuation of enterprises. These steps would be accompanied and followed by intense efforts to rationalize enterprises, improve economic decisionmaking, reform trade policy, and build managerial skills and a strong financial sector. Privatization of large state enterprises would become the next priority. Protection

Box 7.7 *(continued)*

would be cut and the economy would be opened to foreign competition on a firm, preannounced schedule—first in goods and later in capital markets. Institution building would be a basic theme from the start and at all levels: the legal contractual system, the structure of ownership, and the roles of key organizations in the economy would require reform and restructuring.

Large-scale privatization would not be at the head of the sequence, but to address the risk in delaying it, there would be early legal commitments (the distribution of shares) that would guarantee private ownership within a reasonable time. The program would be fast, in that each type of reform would move at the maximum rate consistent with developing institutional ca-

pacities. Indeed, a three-to-five-year time span seems optimistic in light of the progress achieved so far in the transitional economies.

Reforms will surely involve painful adjustments. Inflation and unemployment will worsen as price controls are removed and the real economic losses of some activities are revealed. Political opposition may mount with these developments and with the rise in income inequality that comes after radical change in the incentive structure. But progress in exports and the availability of consumer goods could soon follow. And, given the relatively strong human resource endowments in Eastern Europe, prospects for growth could be excellent.

Box figure 7.7 The phasing of reform

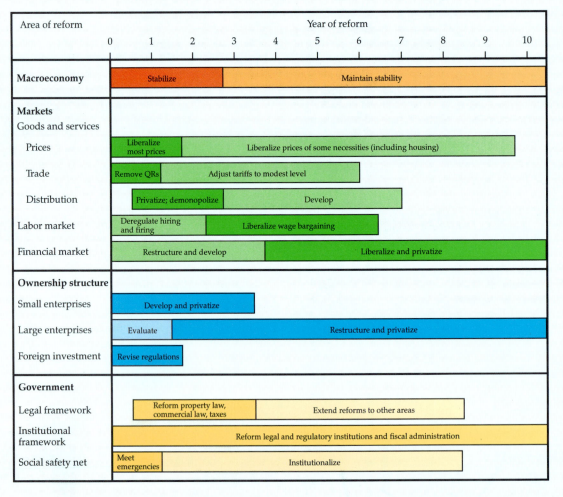

Note: Darker shading indicates intensive action. QRs, quantitative restrictions.

If output responds quickly to a program of reforms, support for the program will increase and the changes can be consolidated. Rapid growth in exports bolstered reforms in Indonesia, Korea, and Turkey. Strong export growth can also help to prevent policy reversals caused by balance of payments problems and dwindling foreign exchange reserves. Reforms that improve the investment climate are more likely to be sustained because new investors will add to the forces in support. Expanding output and investment would enlarge the tax base, raise tax revenues, and reduce the budget deficit. All this argues for reforms that are bold enough to elicit a prompt supply-side response. Timid programs are unlikely to win converts to the cause of reform. Many reformers in Eastern Europe have taken these lessons to heart (Box 7.7).

Despite the political difficulties, many governments have shown great ingenuity in implementing controversial reforms. For instance, the governments of Bolivia, Ghana, Korea, and Mexico strived to convince the public of the costs of inaction and to explain the thinking behind their reforms. International diplomacy can lend credibility to the cause. Agreements with the EEC helped Greece, Israel, Portugal, and Spain adopt trade reforms in the 1960s; accession to the GATT helped Mexico in 1986. Some governments have negotiated social pacts to distribute the burden of adjustment equitably between labor and business, as in Mexico in the 1980s and Israel in 1986. In Chile in the early 1980s and Sri Lanka in the mid-1980s, the success of trade liberalization gradually changed the orientation of the manufacturers' association from import substitution to export promotion. In general, governments committed to addressing their societies' problems have rarely lost power because of this determination.

Of course, there are limits to persuasion. Often, it seems, reform can be born only of a full-blown economic or political crisis. Examples range from Meiji Japan to contemporary Argentina, Ghana, Peru, and Poland. Sometimes, even in the face of economic collapse, reform is blocked by the government's key supporters. In such cases, external lenders and aid agencies face an extremely uncomfortable fact: despite the country's need of external resources, such support may do more harm than good by helping to keep the anti-reform administration in power.

In countries that are not paralyzed by political forces, and where reform can go forward, the task for external aid and finance agencies is to promote it. They can do this by avoiding support for unproductive activities or for new projects that would be implemented under severely distorted conditions. In many countries, external agencies must help to strengthen the public institutions without which development assistance is likely to be ineffectual. Reform sometimes imposes heavy costs on those least able to bear them: the poor. Well-designed safety nets (such as the emergency adjustment funds introduced in Bolivia and Ghana in the 1980s) can help the most vulnerable and, in doing so, broaden the constituency for development.

Reform will remain a formidable task, requiring political courage and economic vision. Combining the many different elements described here and in other chapters is, in itself, enormously difficult. The appropriate combination of factors will vary from country to country, according to circumstances. And even when reform is well-designed, governments are sure to encounter unforeseen setbacks, some of them entirely beyond their control. Development is indeed a challenge—but, as history tells us, one that can be met.

Priorities for action

The past forty years have witnessed many cases of remarkably rapid economic advance among the countries of the developing world—so rapid that some countries are on the point of "graduating" to the ranks of the high-income industrial countries. Most developing countries have made progress at a slower pace. Even so, in comparison with the industrial countries at a comparable stage of development, these countries have still done well, and their standards of living have improved greatly. Unfortunately, however, in some countries, especially in Sub-Saharan Africa, development is moving too slowly to make much difference in people's lives. For them, better economic performance is not merely very desirable. It is literally a matter of life and death.

This wide range of experience has told us much, though by no means everything, about what works in development and what does not. Development has emerged as a fragile and multidimensional process. It depends on complex interactions among institutions, policies, and the global economic climate. There have been no shortcuts. Neither forced modernization of industry nor massive inflows of external resources led to the gains expected a generation ago. But steady—even exceptional—progress has come through actions that foster competitive markets, private initiative, and investment in physical and human capital.

It is true that many countries must overcome tremendous obstacles—adverse natural conditions, poor infrastructure, weak administrative capacity, entrenched special interests, and inadequate financial resources. Experience is nevertheless turning policy reform into the art of the possible. Comprehensive, market-friendly reforms have succeeded under varied economic and political conditions.

The progress of development in the 1990s will depend on concerted action by the global community, including industrial and developing countries and external finance agencies. Their joint task is to foster a global economic climate that promotes the exchange of goods, knowledge, and capital. It is the particular responsibility of the industrial countries and the finance agencies to

• Defend and extend the liberal order of international trade established after 1945

• Ease the flow of capital across borders

• Pursue domestic economic policies that promote global saving and steady, noninflationary growth

• Support the transfer of technology

• Protect the environment and conserve energy.

In discharging these responsibilities, the industrial countries will be directly furthering their own interests. At the same time, they will be laying the foundation for more rapid advance in the developing world.

As important as these actions by the industrial countries are, the future of the developing countries is largely in their own hands. Even if the industrial countries fail to play their part, the developing countries can do much to move forward more quickly. It would be a tragic mistake for them to use the weaknesses of economic policy in the industrial countries as a reason to delay essential economic reforms. The right strategy for the developing countries, whether external conditions are supportive or not, is to

• Invest in people, including education, health, and population control

• Help domestic markets to work well by fostering competition and investing in infrastructure

• Liberalize trade and foreign investment

• Avoid excessive fiscal deficits and high inflation.

These elements of the development strategy interact (see Figure 4 in the Overview). Investing in people spurs productivity all the more powerfully in an economy that already has undistorted domestic markets; at the same time, efficient domestic markets increase the returns from education and therefore make an expansion of investment in education easier to bring about. A stable macroeconomy makes it easier to withstand the external shocks that linkages to the global economy cause from time to time; conversely, global linkages provide access to foreign capital, which makes it easier to maintain domestic macroeconomic stability in the face of internal shocks.

Perhaps the most fruitful interaction is between efficient domestic markets and the global economy. Efficient markets attract foreign investment, which boosts productivity. At the same time, trading links to the outside world let countries pursue their international comparative advantage; that helps the domestic economy use its resources even more efficiently.

In many cases, there will be conflicts among policies as well as complementarities. Investing in education cannot be allowed to expand public spending in a way that threatens macroeconomic stability. In some countries there is a similar conflict between liberalizing trade and prudent macroeconomic policy: lower tariffs, unless offset by additional resource mobilization, may reduce government revenues and increase public deficits.

To implement a market-friendly development strategy while overcoming such conflicts requires, in many countries, reconsidering the role of the state. Many governments lack the administrative capacity to do as much as they might wish. Yet careful intervention is sometimes essential for development to occur. If governments are to do more in such areas (notably, providing better education and infrastructure) they must do less in others (especially micro-managing trade and industry). Administrative constraints aside, such a realignment would be highly desirable in any case. The resources for more public spending where it is essential can be found by cutting spending where it is wasted.

Military spending is a particular concern for all countries, rich and poor alike. Can recent declines in defense spending in developing countries be sustained? The present vacuum in security arrangements and the repercussions of the conflict in the Gulf region make the answer uncertain. It could take very little to shift the dynamics of regional relations toward either new arms races or mutual restraint. An important complicating factor is that weapons producers will bid aggressively for developing-country business as their markets in the OECD countries and the Eastern Bloc become less lucrative. Developing countries and external aid and finance agencies would do well to tilt incentives the other way by discouraging arms production and promoting nonproliferation.

The social and political dimensions of development—poverty alleviation, social justice, political and civil liberties, popular participation, and decentralization—have been receiving more and more attention from the development community. Two recent publications have addressed the implications of a socially responsible development strategy for industrial and developing countries alike (UNDP 1990; World Bank 1990c). For the world community, new challenges lie ahead: to act on the findings of these and similar studies and measure performance such as the disparity between spending on education and health and spending on arms. Similarly, strategies will need to be designed and implemented to accelerate development for the most disadvantaged classes and communities—again, in many industrial countries as well as in the developing world.

The challenge of development is formidable indeed. No more important task confronts the human race. Enough has been learned, however, to justify some confidence about the future. The strategy outlined in this Report draws on this experience. The measures suggested are not a counsel of perfection. As many countries have shown, they are a workable program.

Tasks for global action

This Report has stressed that favorable international conditions can make rapid economic development all the more possible. Industrial countries, with only one-fifth of the global population, account for four-fifths of world output, more than four-fifths of world trade, and almost all exports of capital and technology. Their effect on development grows as more developing countries turn outward. The prospects for global economic growth and rapid development will be strongly influenced by how industrial countries perform.

Global trade

The world trading system is facing its biggest test in more than forty years. The global trade talks need to be revived, and the protectionism that has grown in recent years cut down. Quantitative barriers and subsidies in labor-intensive industries are particularly damaging to development: studies suggest that higher export earnings from ending these restrictions would exceed the value of average annual aid flows from OECD countries. Trade liberalization by OECD countries could roughly double developing-country exports of clothing and textiles. A 50 percent reduction in OECD agricultural protection could raise export revenues of developing countries by 2–40 percent. Commodity exporters would gain if the tilt in the industrial countries' protective structure against processed commodities were removed. OECD reforms in trade policy would have a significant positive effect on growth and employment in developing countries. They would also redirect some foreign investment to developing countries as investors lost sheltered domestic markets in industrial countries.

The stalemate in the global trade negotiations—coupled with growing regional linkages among the world's economies—may lead to new regional trading arrangements centered on Europe, Japan, and the United States. If these blocs fall into conflict, the world economy will lose much. At the same time, it may be easier to liberalize trade regionally rather than globally, and regional agreements may provide new momentum for liberalization worldwide. To be constructive, the regional arrangements need to be compatible with the GATT. They also need to be designed to create new opportunities for trade (through low internal and external barriers) without diverting trade away from partners outside the region (through large differences between internal and external barriers).

Capital flows and finance

Despite encouraging signs, the problem of external debt continues to depress the prospects for the severely indebted countries. The Brady Initiative to reduce commercial debt and debt service marked an important departure, but so far it has produced results in only a handful of middle-income countries that have relatively strong economic prospects. Debt relief has been modest—on average much smaller than the market discount on

debt at the time negotiations were started. The Toronto plan to reduce bilateral official debt was another breakthrough. But even if Toronto terms were extended to all the official debt of the severely indebted low-income countries (excluding Nigeria), the remaining scheduled debt service would be more than twice the actual debt service paid in 1990. Thus these and new debt-reducing initiatives will need to be strengthened and supplemented in the new decade. In addition, the nonofficial debt of low-income countries remains to be addressed.

The agreements concluded so far have increased the debt exposure of the IMF and the World Bank relative to that of commercial banks. Because of the impact of the debt crisis on private sector lending to the developing world, bilateral and multilateral grants and loans will most likely contribute more than half of all resource flows to developing countries in the 1990s. An adequate volume of these flows is therefore crucial. The quality of these flows could be raised through increased coordination among aid and finance agencies; more effective support for market-oriented policy measures (providing greater support for fewer but more ambitious reforms); stronger emphasis on supporting private sector initiatives; greater attention to environmental policies; and features that "insure" debt-creating flows against price and interest rate volatility. When funds are channeled to finance imports (whether inputs or generalized balance of payments support), more fungibility will be needed. Tying aid funds to imports from particular countries greatly reduces their value; tying them to particular beneficiaries impedes the working of domestic market forces.

Economic policies

Industrial and developing countries both benefit from an ample supply of world savings, from steady economic growth in the OECD countries, from sound financial markets, and from prices, exchange rates, and interest rates that are free from shocks induced by policy. Industrial-country policies to increase private and public savings can supply the capital for new investment opportunities worldwide—such as in Eastern Europe, in the Soviet Union, and for rebuilding the economies of the Middle East. Policies that promote steady growth in the OECD countries will be helpful to developing-country prospects for exports and growth. As suggested in Figure 8.1, the growth rates of industrial countries and developing countries track each other fairly well. At the same time, disciplined monetary expansion and firm prudential regulation of capital markets can in turn reduce the volatility of prices, exchange rates, and interest rates—all important for flows of international trade and capital and thus for the prospects of developing countries.

Technology

The price of imported technology is likely to rise for most developing countries, as industrial countries seek greater returns from innovation in such important fields as information technology, biotechnology, and new materials technology. As enforcement of patents increases, the use of licensing agreements will rise. Nevertheless, more rapid technological diffusion can occur through international action. Critical steps include multilateral agreements on intellectual property rights through the GATT and the World Intellectual Property Organization; international agreements that ensure developing-country access to licenses for foreign innovation; and limits on restrictive licensing clauses that ban or restrict exports. Encouraging firms in industrial countries to form alliances with producers in developing countries can promote better access to established technologies and foster new products and materials that are adaptable worldwide.

The global environment

Stewardship of the global environment calls for bold leadership in both industrial and developing countries. The problems are unprecedented—they involve great uncertainty, risks of future catastrophe, and large distributional effects, both within and across countries. An international consensus will have to be forged and maintained on extremely controversial issues, including protection of the ozone layer and potential global warming. Need all countries share the burden of protecting the environment equally? Or might developing countries bear a smaller share of present costs because they contributed less to the stock of accumulated pollutants? International tensions could also intensify over environmental spillovers, as in the case of rivers shared by several countries (the Nile, for example, is essential to Egypt, Ethiopia, and Sudan).

The main priority worldwide is to establish incentives, regulations, and safeguards that lead to a proper allocation of resources for environmental

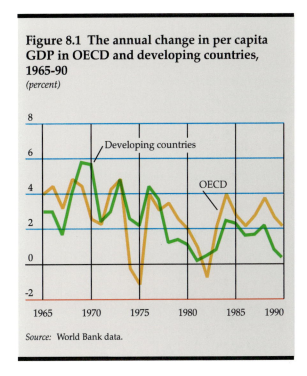

Figure 8.1 The annual change in per capita GDP in OECD and developing countries, 1965-90
(percent)

Source: World Bank data.

maintenance and energy conservation. Degradation of rivers in Eastern Europe and deforestation in Africa illustrate the dangers of poor or nonexistent environmental policies. Often, a first step is to eliminate subsidies for activities that harm the environment, including the colonization of forests that have poor soils and the excessive use of pesticides and fertilizer in agriculture. Removing such distortions improves economic efficiency (even as conventionally measured) while preserving the environment. If pollution is taxed and regulated, concern for environmental and energy conservation can be incorporated into public and private decisionmaking. It is also important to establish clear property rights: owners have a stake in preserving a resource. In some cases property rights can be vested in the state, with charges for the use of environmental resources, as in extractive reserves in the Amazon.

The global community is recognizing that economic development and environmental conservation need not be mutually exclusive: a wide range of environmental actions have high returns. They justify far stronger policies than those currently in force. International initiatives designed to support lending to protect the global commons—such as the new Global Environment Facility of the World Bank, the United Nations Development Programme, and the United Nations Environment

151

Programme—will be important in building an international consensus. *World Development Report 1992* will have the environment as its theme.

Specific actions that work

Many of the problems countries face in the 1990s have been solved somewhere, somehow, during the last forty years. Experience can point to solutions that are likely to work in the future. The strategy recommended in these pages is a practical one, grounded as securely in experience as in economic principles. Reforms can encounter difficulties of design and implementation (Box 8.1). But they have worked in various country contexts. To show that the lessons add up to a workable program, the Report concludes with examples of market-friendly reforms that have worked, and of

---

Box 8.1   For policymakers everywhere: seven lessons in reform

Successes provide the dos, failures the don'ts. The specifics of reform programs may vary across different regions and stages of development. But here are seven general pitfalls to be avoided—or, on the flip side, seven lessons for stronger efforts and better results.

• *Lack of ownership undercuts the program.* Programs initiated primarily because of the external financing that supported them, not because of conviction about their benefits, have often withered away for lack of government commitment to carrying them through. For a program to be viewed as a country's own, nationals need to participate in its design and development. Building an internal consensus is critical.

• *Flip-flops in reform hurt credibility.* Flexibility in policymaking is important. But when policies have been reversed capriciously—for example, when a tariff reform was soon followed by an import surcharge—the private sector has adopted a wait-and-see attitude. Rather than responding energetically to a new reform, private agents act tentatively, if at all. Flexibility is important, yet bold, seemingly irreversible steps by the government build confidence. They are especially needed in countries with a record of policy reversals.

• *Institutional demands must not be glossed over.* In many countries, ambitious changes could not be followed through because the country lacked trained personnel and adequate institutions—an independent judiciary, clearly defined and enforced property rights, and a strong central bank. Reform is a complex process of interwoven tasks, and there need to be mechanisms for interministerial coordination in order to carry them out. The development of institutional capacity needs to be emphasized from the outset, because institution-building takes time and results will not be immediate. In the meantime, it helps to implement actions that economize on scarce capabilities—such as deregulating domestic markets, liberalizing agricultural marketing, and removing quantitative restrictions.

• *Attention to macroeconomic instability is fundamental.* Continuing fiscal imbalances can derail reforms. Severe macroeconomic instability has caused more than one trade and financial liberalization program to fail. In highly inflationary settings, upfront and drastic reduc-

tion of the fiscal deficit is paramount. Many structural reforms can help: liberalizing agricultural marketing, switching from quantitative restrictions to tariffs, privatizing loss-making state enterprises, and improving tax administration.

• *Vulnerable people must not be forgotten.* The social costs of inaction are generally much larger than those of adjusting, but it is necessary to cushion the effect of adjustment on the most adversely affected groups. Cutbacks in public spending can hurt vulnerable groups. Reforms that allow agricultural prices to rise help poor farmers, but often hurt the rural landless and urban poor. Thus special programs of assistance to the poor are needed during the reform. Attention to politically powerful groups is also often necessary to sustain the changes. And programs to compensate and retrain discharged civil servants are often needed when the public sector retrenches.

• *Partial attempts often fail.* Partial efforts have been ineffective. When domestic deregulation did not accompany external liberalization, investment and output responded slowly. And when trade reform did not accompany domestic deregulation, investment went to the wrong sectors. When tariff reduction was not complemented by a broadening of the domestic tax base and a reduction in tax exemptions and subsidies, fiscal imbalances emerged, threatening the trade liberalization. There is thus a premium on simultaneously taking complementary actions.

• *It pays to be realistic.* Policymakers and external agencies need to be realistic in preparing the financing plan to support the reforms. Many countries may also need to reassign funds from low-priority to high-priority areas, for example, by switching some expenditures from the military to infrastructure and social programs. Realism also applies to expectations about what the reform is going to achieve. It pays not to promise too much too soon, yet to be loud and clear about the importance of reforming—and to contrast the outcome of reform with the alternative outcome of not reforming. Realistic expectations about the benefits and costs of the changes make the sustainability of the program more likely.

opportunities to make reform work again in the future.

Investing in people

Few policies promote development as powerfully as effective investment in human resources. An estimated 80 percent of the world's population lives in the developing countries—a proportion that is rising. Crucial issues in many of these countries include expanding primary education, alleviating poverty, and controlling population growth through better education, health care, and family planning. Opportunities exist to improve primary schools in Bangladesh, to reduce poverty in Bolivia through local action, and to fight poverty with population policies in the Sahel and elsewhere.

Extending and improving primary education. *Bangladesh has few resources except its people—much like Japan a hundred years ago. Yet more than two-thirds of its adults are illiterate, a consequence of historically low school enrollment. Primary school enrollment is currently only 59 percent (49 percent for females), and the quality of education is poor. Teachers are often inadequately trained and supervised; they spend relatively few hours with students and have insufficient classroom materials. Only one-quarter of those children who start primary school complete it. Recently, Bangladesh has developed a comprehensive reform program. It will provide new low-cost classrooms, an innovative curriculum for students who do not go beyond primary school, and new teacher training institutions. There will be more women teachers, and all teachers will have greater autonomy. These steps will receive considerable external support but will also require larger government expenditures. Although many resources must be committed to relief and reconstruction because of the recent cyclone, long-term investments in primary education remain crucial. To date, Bangladesh has spent only 1.7 percent of GNP on education (compared with 3 percent for the poorest fourth of developing countries as a group); furthermore, secondary and college education have claimed a large share of this budget.*

Alleviating poverty through local action. *To protect the poor during the economic recovery of the mid-1980s, the government of Bolivia initiated an emergency social fund to finance small, technically simple projects formulated and implemented by a variety of public, private, and voluntary organizations. A new social investment fund, also responding to local requests, will extend coverage of health, education, and sanitation services to the poorest Bolivian communities. NGOs and local authorities will develop and implement projects under competitive bidding. In La Paz, for example, health*

centers and water supply and sewerage facilities are being planned in neighborhoods of rural migrants. In high-poverty areas with no access to health and education services, established organizations will be encouraged to expand their activity in the underserved community. To minimize costs and ensure project sustainability, appraisal criteria will be rigorous, including economic analysis and recovery of operating costs if appropriate. Such community-based programs can address the current needs of the poor and encourage the institution-building that leads to sustained poverty reduction.

Fighting poverty with population policies. *In the Sahel, resources are thinly stretched. Even with much aid, there is too little for an adequate standard of living—and much too little to finance human and physical investments. Yet fertility rates are among the world's highest, and the population is growing ever faster (2.2 percent a year in the 1960s, 2.9 percent in 1987). Investments in human resources are thus inadequate: primary school enrollments are half as high as in the average low-income country. In parallel with development agencies, the governments of the Sahel need to act decisively to lower population growth. The scope for progress is great: the proportion of women using contraceptives is extremely low compared with such African countries as Botswana and Zimbabwe. Agency assistance for population control programs is likely to be available.*

Making markets work

To promote efficiency in the domestic economy, governments need to strengthen price signals, deregulate markets, and upgrade infrastructural investments and key institutions. Opportunities include providing infrastructure in Nigeria, improving industrial markets in India, revitalizing financial markets in Ghana, and establishing a new legal framework in Hungary.

Providing infrastructure. *Poorly designed and maintained infrastructure has hindered growth in Nigeria. Firms have been forced into private provision, unproductive factor substitution, and output reduction. Telecommunications services are unacceptably poor, with one telephone line per 500 inhabitants (50 percent of the average for Sub-Saharan Africa); firms depend on private radios and messengers for basic communications. Many infrastructure deficiencies are the result of rapid population increases in urban centers and of inappropriate pricing policies. In Lagos, as the population grew by more than 3 million during two decades, water was freely provided; inadequate government financing prevented expansion of the service. National priorities include improving both the physical and communications* infrastructure as well as the financial planning and management of infrastructure projects. Nigeria is initiating a long-term venture to decentralize infrastructure services and to mobilize the private sector. Selected merchant banks are already working with state and local governments to reappraise, cofinance, and supervise urban infrastructural development. This will include rehabiliting and maintaining roads, water supply, solid waste disposal, and sanitation services. The national telecommunications network is being commercialized. Investments will be directed toward improving the utilization of facilities and expanding them in high-demand areas. These reforms will promote the expansion of output throughout the Nigerian economy.

Improving industrial markets. India's industry has never achieved its potential. Manufacturing accounts for a smaller share of GDP than in comparable countries. Along with highly protective trade policies, excessive regulation is to blame. Throughout the mid-1980s in many subsectors, an industrial license was required to establish a new plant, to expand output by more than 5 percent in a year or 25 percent in five years, to manufacture a new product, or to relocate. Plants remain uneconomically small, product mixes do not match demand, technical progress is slow, and capacity is underused. Recent experience with partial liberalization—including relaxation of restrictions against entry and expansion, and foreign technology diversification—has been positive. Excessive regulation remains. It includes barriers to adjustment and exit, and labor rules that protect a small number of privileged workers. Liberalizing trade would complement deregulation, lowering the overall cost structure and checking excessive profits in the monopolized sectors. These objectives will not be achieved easily because the government will have to overcome the opposition of protected enterprises and the regulatory bureaucracy. But past successes indicate that further deregulation could attract reasonable public support.

Revitalizing financial markets. Ghana needs to invigorate its financial sector. The country's remarkable 1983 Economic Recovery Program stabilized its economy and removed many structural distortions. But private investment is still only 6 percent of GDP. Credit has been an important constraint. Until 1989 the state-run banking system functioned under strict credit limits for reasons of macroeconomic stability. Sixty percent of the system's assets are nonperforming loans inherited from the crisis of the mid-1980s; this "credit" cannot be shifted to profitable projects. Poor performance has made bankers excessively risk-averse and encouraged large transfers of savings outside the banking system. Revitalized financial institutions and markets could go a long way toward providing capital for private investment.

This could be achieved by shifting monetary control to indirect methods and by clearing the banks' balance sheets. Permitting new kinds of instruments and financial intermediaries would promote the growth of competitive financial markets, encouraging bankers and producers to take advantage of the economic recovery.

Establishing a new legal framework. In Eastern Europe, Hungary has the most experience of markets and private ownership. Yet its legal system has many gaps. Most of the basic laws are recent: a company law (1989) provides for limited liability organization; a transformation act (amended in 1990) spells out how state companies are to be turned into joint-stock companies; and a securities act (1990) provides rules for the issuance of securities. Hungary has no act to determine rights over real estate, and there is no incentive to take companies to bankruptcy under current laws. Accounting practices differ from the West's (the country's outputs and inputs are not valued at market levels, which makes it nearly impossible to estimate enterprise assets). A new law in 1991 will require international accounting standards. An autonomous central bank is being introduced. Hungary needs experience with these new institutions. For example, an important public offering had to be halted recently because no clear provisions had been made for distributing shares when the offering was oversubscribed. To establish confidence, the stock exchange needs a track record, and the legal system a body of precedents. All this will take time. Hungary will need to train thousands of accountants, bank staff and regulators, lawyers, investment bankers, and others with related skills.

Opening up to trade and technology

Experience shows that policies for openness are crucial for rapid growth. Equally important are domestic efforts to improve the productivity of agricultural and manufacturing exports. The need to remain competitive is no less important for commodity exports than for manufacturing. Institutional reforms can also strengthen links with the global economy. Opportunities include liberalizing trade in Pakistan and building institutions for technological development in Thailand.

Liberalizing trade. Trade reform in Pakistan could invigorate industry and lift a long-standing constraint on growth—a shortage of foreign exchange that is caused by a persistent anti-export bias. Until recently, imports have been restricted by quotas and exports by product- and firm-specific output licensing. Thus Pakistan's exports still consist largely of primary commodities (cotton and rice) which have volatile prices and uncertain growth prospects. Trade reforms are urgently needed to make exporting attractive relative to import substitution. Pakistan is now beginning such reforms. Under the first phase of its program, protection is being shifted from nontariff barriers to tariffs. Because many nominal protection rates will remain above 100 percent and the rate structure will remain highly dispersed, a sequence of tariff reductions will then be required to reduce protection and make the overall level of protection more neutral. Because import taxes are a large share of total tax revenues, domestic tax reforms are needed as well. A realistic exchange rate policy, coupled with fiscal and monetary discipline, is also needed to complete Pakistan's shift to an outward-looking strategy.

Building institutions for technological development. For countries such as Thailand that have established global links in a wide range of manufactured products, the next task is to strengthen technological linkages: to develop institutions that foster the absorption, adaptation, and diffusion of technology. Much of Thailand's technology trade is now conducted by subsidiaries of foreign firms; the country's capacities to absorb and generate technology have not yet caught up with its competitive trading position. Technological inflows could be strengthened by reducing duties on imported capital goods. Technology diffusion could be encouraged by eliminating the anti-subcontracting bias of tax policy. Externalities in the absorption and diffusion of technology, particularly in agriculture, also justify public investments in Thailand's technological capabilities. Government institutions and private providers that offer industrial extension (in technology search, assessment, negotiation, design) should be strengthened, and public research (in universities and other institutes) should be redirected toward commercial needs. Coherent systems of standards, testing, and certification also need to be developed. Finally, there are strong reasons to invest in human capital, especially in science and technology training, secondary education, and international exchanges in engineering and science.

Fostering macroeconomic stability

Low and stable inflation, which can only come from financial discipline in the public sector, is the best foundation for successful microeconomic reform. It enables prices to do their job as signals for resource allocation, and it strengthens the incentives for saving and investment. Examples of stabilization are Indonesia and Mexico.

Stabilization as a prelude to growth: Indonesia. In 1967 Indonesia's Suharto government inherited an extensively nationalized, highly regulated, unstable economy. It gradually rationalized economic management during the next fifteen years, but strong economic growth came mainly from rising oil revenues. After 1983, spurred by declining oil prices, Indonesia has implemented ambitious adjustment measures and policy reforms.

Macroeconomic reforms in 1983 focused on devaluation, the reduction of the government's investment program, tax reforms, and deregulation of interest rates. There was a second major devaluation in 1986 and a new, flexible exchange rate management program in 1989. Microeconomic reforms began with bank deregulation and some liberalization of foreign investment. Starting in 1986, the authorities streamlined the investment-approval process; the Investment Priority List was later replaced by a short negative list. The government also deregulated key industries such as plastics and shipping. Trade policies also needed reform: the import-licensing system had put restrictions on more than 1,500 categories. In 1985, customs administration was contracted to a Swiss surveillance company, and dismantling of quantitative barriers began in 1986. Within two years the share of imports subject to controls fell from 43 to 21 percent.

The early phases of adjustment, which concentrated on macroeconomic stabilization, dampened economic activity, but growth was strong by 1987. Indonesia grew by nearly 7 percent in 1989, and investment recovered. Non-oil exports paid for 86 percent of imports, compared with 29 percent in 1981–82. A former minister who oversaw the reforms attributes their success to the extended period of weakness in oil prices which forced the government to pursue a consistent policy that eventually won popular support.

Stabilization as the prelude to growth: Mexico. In the 1960s, Mexico grew rapidly under the early stages of an import substitution strategy. By 1976, it faced large fiscal and balance of payments deficits and worsening inflation. These troubles receded with large discoveries of oil and heavy external borrowing. But within a few years Mexico's debt more than quintupled, setting the stage for the collapse of credit and the sharp economic decline of 1982–83.

Mexico has turned the corner on these difficulties. Macroeconomic reforms began in 1983, when an IMF-supported stabilization program halved the fiscal deficit. By 1987, however, inflation was rising again because of declining oil prices, rising interest payments, and a rapidly expanding fiscal deficit. The government responded by negotiating an ''Economic Solidarity'' pact with labor, farming, and business interests in order to contain basic prices and wages, and by adopting forceful fiscal and exchange rate reforms. As a result, between 1987 and 1989 the fiscal deficit declined from 16 to 3 percent of GDP, and the annual inflation rate from 159 to 20 percent.

Microeconomic reforms have concentrated on reducing government involvement in the economy. The number of SOEs has been reduced from 1,100 in 1982 to 350 in 1990 through mergers, liquidations, and sales; the huge state telephone and steel monopolies are also scheduled for sale. Recently, the government deregulated large, politically sensitive industries such as tortilla manufacturing and trucking; liberalized key prices; and has begun to restructure ownership rights in agriculture and to reprivatize banking. Major external-sector reforms began in 1985. Mexico acceded to the GATT, eliminated more than three-quarters of its import-license restrictions, lowered average tariffs by half, developed favorable regulations for export processing, and substantially reduced export taxes and restrictions on fruits and vegetables. By 1987, exports of manufactures overtook oil exports. The rules governing foreign investment were substantially liberalized in 1989; negotiations continue on a free trade agreement with the United States.

The reforms are beginning to bear fruit. GDP growth climbed into the 2–4 percent range in 1989 and 1990 and is projected to rise to 5 percent in 1991. Inflation is under control and real wages, which had fallen by more than 40 percent in the 1980s, are growing. The strategy of reform was shaped by Mexico's broadly based, single-party system. Relatively conservative policies were followed, but the burden of adjustment was distributed across different economic groups. Mexico's close relations with the United States also helped by increasing the return from outward orientation and by facilitating the renegotiation of Mexico's staggering debt.

Environmental policies

Water pollution and land degradation have grave local consequences. Deforestation and air pollution have effects worldwide. These and other problems need to be addressed through more effective policies. Issues include reducing water pollution in Indonesia and preserving the Amazon rainforests.

Reducing water pollution. In Indonesia, worsening water pollution has been caused by neglect of the environment during economic growth. Only 40 percent of Java's population has access to safe water; the eight major rivers on the northern coast are seriously polluted; and groundwater withdrawal has caused saline intrusion into the aquifers that provide water for domestic use. In Jakarta it costs $20–$30 million a year simply to boil water for home use. Costs associated with illness and with reduced property values, although unquantified, are undoubtedly high. With urban and industrial uses of water expected to grow at rapid rates, large shortages are forecast within a decade or so. Solutions involve systematic attention to efficiency (40 percent of municipal water is ''lost''), stiff fines for polluters, and appropriate fees for irrigation (farmers now pay for only 13 percent of irrigation costs). Indonesia has been slow to address these problems because the mechanisms of water resource administration are still evolving. Autonomous river basin authorities could provide a better framework for planning, coordination, and monitoring. Clean water will not come cheap; it is estimated that $1 billion will be needed to meet the water supply needs of Jakarta alone.

Preserving the global commons. The Amazon rainforests of Brazil, Colombia, Ecuador, and Peru are a world resource—a symbol of the global environmental challenges of the 1990s. Thirty thousand species of plants live in the rainforests. But the Amazon's deforested area has grown from 1 percent in 1975 to 8 percent in 1990. It is now larger than France. The entire world is threatened by the loss of biodiversity and increased carbon emissions. In Brazil, deforestation was encouraged because of massive road building in the Amazon, tax incentives, and demographic pressures. Much new action is needed to discourage nutrient mining—the one-time extraction of the nutrients of the forest canopy and soil—and to encourage sustainable, forest-based activities. Road construction needs to be evaluated in terms of global as well as local costs and benefits. Strong agroecological zoning can establish large, protected reserves and prevent the granting of titles on poor soils. Initiatives in this direction are currently mired in complex local politics. Compensation will be required to create incentives for local action, to relieve the financial burden on poor farmers, and to offset the opposition of ranching and logging interests. Because benefits will accrue worldwide, international support will be both necessary and appropriate.

Implications of good policies

What would happen if the world community implemented policies in the spirit of those outlined above? No one can know for sure, but some broad estimates are possible based on the projections of several country models at the World Bank, which assess long-term growth under different assumptions about country policies and international conditions. These models reflect a wide range of country-specific data and assumptions. Their results need to be interpreted cautiously, but nevertheless provide illustrative magnitudes for the changes that are possible.

The results suggest the importance of both the global context and domestic action for long-term growth (Table 8.1). The global economic climate

Table 8.1 Changes in GDP growth rates relative to the central case, 1990–2000
(percentage deviation)

Domestic policies	Global economic climate		
	Poor	*Good*	*Very good*
Very good	1.0	1.5	2.0
Good	−1.0	Central case	0.5
Poor	−3.0	−2.0	−1.0

Note: The changes in the growth rate given in each cell are unweighted deviations from the ''central case.'' The figures are rounded.
Source: World Bank data; see the technical note at the end of the main text.

makes a difference. Compared with the baseline scenario (a good global economic climate), favorable external conditions could raise growth by 0.5–1 percentage point a year. This is significant. The variation in growth rates attributed to different domestic actions could be even larger. Holding the global situation constant, the difference between good and poor domestic policies would yield on average 1.5–2 percentage points growth per year—on average, about twice the improvement from better external conditions. Given the uncertainty about the quality of the global economy, countries that can adapt their domestic policies flexibly to changing circumstances will be at a great advantage. Even if global conditions are inhospitable, the reward for good domestic policies is very high.

What are the long-term implications of these projections? Holding the external context fixed to its baseline path, the projections say that the difference between poor and very good policies is worth, on average, 3.5 percentage points of growth a year. After ten years, with compounding, a country with very good policies would be more than 40 percent better off than another that started with the same income but pursued poor policies. If that growth advantage were sustained, the first country would have twice the income of the second after twenty years—which would make a crucial difference in poverty reduction.

A global challenge

In the time it takes to read this paragraph, roughly a hundred children will be born—six in industrial countries and ninety-four in developing countries. Here lies the global challenge. No matter what the outlook in the industrial economies, the world's long-term prosperity and security—by sheer force of numbers—depend on development.

Development is better understood today than before. The institutions of market economies have proven more complex than the textbooks suggest, especially when interactions with political, social, and environmental processes are taken into account. Nonetheless, sound general principles have emerged to guide policy.

Despite the uncertain outlook for the 1990s, a measure of optimism is justified now that more and more countries are opting for a market-friendly approach. With strong international cooperation, the opportunities for development will be brighter. There is more agreement today than at any time in recent history about what needs to be done and how to do it. What remains is to put these ideas into practice everywhere.

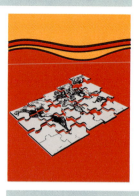

Technical note

Chapter 1

Data and definitions. The historical section of this chapter uses data on GDP and GDP per capita for the period 1700–1988 (for Table 1.1 and Figures 1.1 and 1.3) which are based on a 41-economy sample (with a combined population of 3.99 billion people in 1988) along with aggregate figures on Eastern Europe from Maddison, background paper (covering 310 million people). The sample, along with Maddison's data on Eastern Europe, thus covers roughly 86 percent of the world's population. Economies are classified as OECD, Eastern Europe, and developing. The developing economies are further grouped by geographical region: Latin America; South Asia; East Asia; Africa; and Europe, Middle East, and North Africa (non-OECD, non-Eastern Europe). The economies included in each group are as follows. OECD: Australia, Austria, Belgium, Canada, Denmark, Finland, France, Germany, Italy, Japan, Netherlands, Norway, Sweden, Switzerland, United Kingdom, United States. Eastern Europe (Maddison): Czechoslovakia, Hungary, USSR. Latin America: Argentina, Brazil, Chile, Colombia, Mexico, Peru. South Asia: Bangladesh, India, Pakistan. East Asia: China; Indonesia; Philippines; Republic of Korea; Thailand; Taiwan, China. Africa: Ethiopia, French Africa (aggregate for Benin, Burkina Faso, Cameroon, Central African Republic, Chad, Congo, Côte d'Ivoire, Gabon, Madagascar, Mali, Mauritania, Niger, Senegal, Togo), Kenya, Nigeria, Tanzania. Europe, Middle East, and North Africa: Algeria, Arab Republic of Egypt, Islamic Republic of Iran, Morocco, Syria, Turkey, Yugoslavia. The term "four newly industrializing economies of East Asia" refers to Hong Kong; the Republic of Korea; Singapore; and Taiwan, China.

Statistical methods. Data are based on a benchmark of 1980 dollars as determined by the International Comparison Project (ICP), if available, or on a benchmark of Maddison estimates of 1980 ICP dollars for others. For countries not in the ICP-Maddison sample (Algeria, Ethiopia, Islamic Republic of Iran, Morocco, Syria, and other African countries), estimates are from a computer data base (copyright 1987 and 1988 by Prospect Research Corporation) developed by Robert Summers and Alan Heston. GDP volume estimates for 1830–1965 are taken from Maddison (1981, 1989), and Maddison and Associates, (forthcoming) for the ICP-Maddison sample countries. The volume series is spliced to a World Bank data base GDP volume series at 1965. GDP volume indexes for 1950-65 are taken from OECD 1968 for the non-ICP-Maddison sample countries. These indexes are also spliced to World Bank data starting in 1965.

World Development Report forecasts. Box 1.4 uses projections for average real GDP growth over the decade of the 1980s as reported in the *World Development Reports* of 1979, 1980, 1981, and 1982. The projections for the developing regions are based on the country classifications used in those Reports at the time of their publication. Because the World Bank's regional country classifications have changed during the past ten years, an attempt has been made to plot the "outcomes" (actual growth performance in the 1980s) on the basis of the original classifications. Therefore, the growth rate averages, as plotted in the box figure, may differ from the regional averages that are presented elsewhere in this report. The plotted growth rates for both the projections and outcomes are based on GDP in constant price and dollar exchange rates that were used in the Reports cited above. Because the World Bank's country classification for the Europe, Middle East, and North Africa region has changed significantly, an analytical group, "oil exporters," is plotted in its place.

Figures. Figure 1.1 is based on data taken from the sample described above, with the exception of the United Kingdom. Estimates for the United Kingdom for the years before 1830 are extrapolated backward from the sample data using growth rates from Crafts 1981. The starting date for the United Kingdom coincides with estimates of the beginning of the industrial revolution. Some economic historians view the time around 1840 as the beginning of a period of acceleration in U.S. per capita income growth. The conclusion of Japan's deflationary period in 1885–86 is seen by some as the beginning of modern economic growth in that country. For other countries shown in the figure, periods of continuous growth based on 5-year, center-weighted, moving averages of GDP per capita were used to identify the shortest doubling periods that excluded cyclical macroeconomic effects.

Figure 1.2 uses life expectancy estimates from Gwatkin 1978 for years before 1978 and from WHO 1989 for 1978 onward. Limited data availability prevented the identification of a sample with the same life expectancies at the beginning of each noted period. Instead, starting point life expectancies are provided and sample countries are presented in the order of starting life expectancy and chronology (which coincide). Breaking points between periods were determined by the availability of intermediate-year survey data. Figure 1.3 presents timeline data that are 5-year, center-weighted moving averages for a 41-country sample. Data are weighted by GDP. Averages for OECD- and developing-country groups are derived by dividing the total GDP for the group (aggregated at 1980 international dollars) by the total population of the group. Figure 1.5 uses statistics from a World Bank data base based on a 130-country sample. Group averages are GDP weighted.

Chapter 2

Data selection. This chapter uses data from a sample of 68 economies in 5 regions: 27 in Sub-Saharan Africa, 10 in East Asia, 15 in Latin America, 12 in Europe, Middle East, and North Africa (from which Pakistan is excluded), and 4 in South Asia (with which Pakistan is included). The selection of this sample was determined solely by the availability of the required data. The following developing countries with populations of more than 10 million in 1988 did not meet the data criteria: Ecuador, Iran, Iraq, Myanmar, Nepal, Saudi Arabia, South Africa, and Viet Nam.

Statistical methods. Most variables are from a World Bank data base and are self-explanatory. Physical and human capital series, however, do not exist as such. Lau, Jamison, and Louat 1991 suggested a method to overcome this difficulty by computing these stocks from annual capital investment and educational enrollment data. The chapter expands their method and applies it to a larger set of countries.

A growth accounting approach is used. Variables are defined as follows. Variables related to output

and inputs: change of GDP in 1980 dollars, zy; change in utilized capital (through the use of instrumental variables), zk; change in agricultural land, zh; change in labor force, zl; average level of education (in years of primary and secondary schooling) for the population 15–64 years of age in 1960, e_{60}; change in education if education level ranges from 0 to 3, de_{03}; change in education if education level ranges from 3 to 9, de_{39}. Variables related to openness: price of tradables relative to the U.S. level, zp_{tr}; change in price of tradables if price level is below U.S. level, zp_{tr1}; change in price of tradables if price level is above U.S. level, zp_{tr2}; change of price level of tradables in direction of U.S. price level (under an assumption of symmetrical response; that is, zp_{tr1} minus zp_{tr2}), zp_{tr}; product of change of price of tradables in direction of U.S. price level and level of education (that is, zp_{tr} times e), zp_{tre}; and a dummy for missing data on zp_{tr}, $mvpt$. The growth of total factor productivity (the component of zy not explained by zk, zl, or zh) was calculated as the residual between the actual zy and predicted zy using the estimated coefficients on zk, zl, and zh obtained by regression 1 in Note table 2.1 for the sample of 68 countries.

In Table 2.4, the use of the foreign exchange premium as a proxy for policy distortions allows for the

Note table 2.1 Regressions of selected factors in GDP growth, 1960–87

Variable	(1)	(2)	(3)	(4)	(5)
zk	0.38	0.38	0.38	0.38	0.38
	(17.7)	(17.6)	(17.6)	(17.6)	(17.6)
zl	0.44	0.46	0.046	0.45	0.45
	(3.6)	(3.8)	(3.8)	(3.7)	(3.8)
zh	0.04	0.04	0.04	0.04	0.04
	(1.3)	(1.4)	(1.4)	(1.4)	(1.4)
de_{03}	0.09	0.09	0.09	0.09	0.09
	(2.5)	(2.6)	(2.6)	(2.6)	(2.6)
de_{39}	0.04	0.04	0.04	0.04	0.04
	(1.9)	(2.0)	(2.0)	(2.0)	(2.0)
e_{60} (*100)	0.13	0.16	0.16	0.17	0.17
	(1.5)	(1.8)	(1.8)	(1.9)	(1.9)
zp_{tr1}		0.04			
		(2.0)			
zp_{tr2}		−0.03			
		(−1.2)			
zp_{tr}			0.04	−0.02	
			(2.3)	(−0.6)	
zp_{tre}				0.01	0.01
				(1.6)	(2.7)
$mvpt$		0.004	0.004	0.004	0.004
		(1.3)	(1.3)	(1.3)	(1.3)
R^2	0.2256				
n	1,826	1,826	1,826	1,826	1,826

Note: Numbers in parentheses are t-statistics.
All regressions include dummies for regions (Africa; East Asia; Europe, Middle East, and North Africa; Latin America and the Caribbean; South Asia) and for time (1960–73 and 1974–87).
All data are annual. All changes are differences of log levels except for education levels (which are differences of levels).

Note table 2.2 Dependent variable: change in infant mortality

Independent variable	(1)	(2)	(3)
Growth in private income	−0.024	−0.029	−0.032
	(−2.3)	(−3.6)	(−3.4)
Growth in health expenditure			
General government	−0.002	−0.002	−0.004
	(−0.1)	(−0.1)	(−0.3)
Consolidated central government	0.001	0.001	0.001
	(0.1)	(0.1)	(0.1)
Budgetary central government	0.003	0.002	0.001
	(0.4)	(0.3)	(0.2)
Gastil's index		0.002	0.001
		(4.6)	(2.0)
Female education			−0.004
			(−5.7)

Note: t-statistics in parentheses. Continent dummies are included. All changes are first differences in logs.

largest number of observations. The use of two indexes of trade liberalization (Papageorgiou, Michaely, and Choksi 1990; Thomas, Halevi, and Stanton, background paper) and of yearly changes in education yielded results consistent with those shown in Table 2.4.

The effect of "liberty" on infant mortality decline. For regressions on 247 annual country observations for which Gastil's liberty index (political and civil liberties), education data, and reliable infant mortality data are available (1973–84), see Note table 2.2. Because Gastil's index goes from 2 (best) to 14 (worst) (his two indexes of political and civil liberties, which each run from 1 [best] to 7 [worst], have been added together), the positive coefficient on this index implies that political and civil liberties have a negative and significant effect on infant mortality.

Income differences. The analysis in the maps and the text section on regional differences in income within countries is based on the following definitions of regions. Brazil: the southeastern region includes the states of Minas Gerais, Espírito Santo, Rio de Janeiro, and São Paulo; the northeastern region includes Maranhão, Piauí, Ceará, Rio Grande do Norte, Paraíba, Pernambuco, Alagoas, Sergipe, and Bahia. China: the eastern region comprises of the provinces of Anhui, Fujian, Jiangsu, Jiangxi, Shandong, Shanghai, and Zhejiang; the south and southwest region here includes Henan, Hubei, Hunan, Guangdong, Guangxi, Sichuan, Guizhou, and Yunnan. India: the eastern region consists of the states of Bihar, Orissa, and West Bengal; the western region includes Daman, Diu, Goa, Gujrat, and Maharashtra. Nigeria: the eastern region includes the provinces of Anambra, Benue, Cross River, Imo, and Rivers; the northern region includes Bauchi, Borno, Gongola, Kaduna, Kano, Plateau, Sokoto, and Niger. United States: the Middle Atlantic region includes the states of New Jersey, New York, and Pennsylvania; the South Atlantic region includes Georgia, North Carolina, South Carolina, Virginia, and West Virginia.

In Box figure 2.5, years of education is computed separately for males and females from primary and secondary school enrollment. Enrollment series are generally available from 1960 onward; in some countries, however, it was also possible to find data from 1950 to 1960. These series are projected backward in order to get series from 1902 onward. Finally, the total number of person-school-years in the working-age population is computed by the perpetual inventory method, and mean years of schooling are obtained by dividing this total number by the size of the working-age population for each period.

Chapter 3

Data for the two cross-sectional analyses. The analyses of the economic burden of adult illness (Table 3.1) and of the education of entrepreneurs (Figure 3.3) are based on several household surveys, including Living Standards Measurement Surveys in six countries conducted in the late 1980s, the 1975/76 Malaysia Family Life Survey, the 1978 Bicol (Philippines) Multipurpose Survey, and the 1978 Indonesian Socioeconomic Survey. These surveys are nationally representative random samples, with the exception of the Philippine and Bolivia (urban only) surveys. For details, see the two background papers by King, Rosenzweig, and Wang.

The economic burden of adult illness. The analysis examined the incidence of illness among adults between ages 20 and 59 years (in the month before the survey), and the duration of illness and absence from work of those who were ill. Self-reported illness may be affected by several factors other than health status, including wages, the possibility of work-sharing arrangements among family members, and the availability of paid sick leave. Sensitivity analyses, however, do not show statistically significant association of self-reported illness or absence from work to daily earnings or whether the worker was entitled to paid sick leave or social security. The number of days lost due to illness was then evaluated at the reported daily earnings of workers. Results show that potential income loss could be substantial comparing with workers' normal income.

Education of entrepreneurs. Figure 3.3 is supported by statistically robust results from multivariate analyses. One background analysis consisted of multinomial logit regressions on occupational choice of adults. Given the choice of being an entrepreneur and undertaking appropriate statistical corrections for possible sample selection bias, the size of the enterprise was found to be positively associated with the education of the entrepreneur. These results took account of the entrepreneurs' age, sex, and place of residence; for Malaysia, ethnicity and inherited wealth were also controlled for.

AIDS in developing countries. Box figure 3.5 is based on studies of urban samples from three countries. In Rwanda, the sample consisted of 1,255 urban adults from a national sample; in Zambia, 1,078 patients, blood donors, and staff of an urban hospital; and in Zaire, 5,951 employees of an urban textile factory. Low, middle, and high socioeconomic status are defined, respectively, as: for Rwanda, primary education or less, more than primary education, and no definition; for Zambia, 0–4 years of education, 5–9 years, and 10 or more years; and for Zaire, workers, foremen, and executives.

Public spending and social indicators. The analyses of the relative effect of income growth and changes in public spending in the social sectors on changes in infant mortality rates and school enrollment rates were based on two studies which used different econometric models and measures of income: (a) a fixed-effect model with GDP and time dummies, estimated using quinquennial time-series data for 124 countries (see Note table 3.1) (King and Rosenzweig, background paper); (b) a first-difference model with a variable reflecting private income growth (GDP mi-

Note table 3.1 The effect of income and social expenditures on infant mortality; a fixed-effect model

Independent variable[a]	Coefficient	t
GDP	−0.0000367	−2.954
Health1	−0.0011655	−1.069
Health2	0.0035853	0.836
Educ1	−0.0007568	−0.702
Educ2	−0.0039422	−1.287
Interactions with variable for developing economies		
GDP	0.0000008	0.057
Health1	−0.0148330	−5.826
Health2	−0.0701540	−1.748
Educ1	0.0010280	0.504
Educ2	0.0209830	2.401

Note: Number of observations = 409; adjusted R^2 = 0.9990. Health1 and Educ1 are expenditure data for the consolidated central government accounts; Health2 and Educ2 are derived from budgetary central government accounts. These data are expressed as per capita spending. The infant mortality rates (IMR) were first transformed as log (IMR/1 − IMR). All variables are then defined as the differences from the country means.
a. Time dummy variables and dummies for missing variables are omitted from the table.
Sources: Government expenditures are IMF data and Unesco data; GDP data are from Summers and Heston's (1988) estimates of internationally comparable real product; infant mortality rates are from a World Bank data base, checked against the data survey by Hill and Pebley 1989. See King and Rosenzweig, background paper.

Note table 3.2 The effect of income and social expenditures on infant mortality; a first-difference model

Independent variable	Coefficient	t
Intercept	−0.024752	−20.63
Private income	−0.049862	−4.04
Government health expenditure		
General government	−0.026073	−1.33
Consolidated central	−0.003557	−0.45
Budgetary central	−0.004220	−0.50

Note: All variables, including the dependent, infant mortality rate (IMR), are defined as the log-differences between *t* and *t* − 1. Private income is measured by GDP, minus total government expenditure.
Sources: World Bank data; IMF data. See Bhalla and Gill, background paper.

nus total government expenditure) and using an annual time-series data for 68 economies (see Note table 3.2) (Bhalla and Gill, background paper). Using model a, the elasticity of IMR with respect to public spending is −0.08, and income elasticity is −0.11. Using model b, the elasticity of IMR with respect to private income is −0.05.

Chapter 4

Data and definitions. The last sections of the chapter analyze the productivity of projects utilizing the data on reappraised economic rate of return (ERR) for 1,200 projects in the public and private sectors. The analysis is based on a background paper by Kaufmann. The ERR data originate in the Operations Evaluation Department of the World Bank and the Evaluation Unit of the IFC. Reappraisal of a project takes place within one year of project completion, and the ERR evaluation is then performed according to the standard Squire–van der Tak methodology. The ERR on an investment project is a commonly used productivity indicator measuring the economic contribution of the investment project to the overall economy. It is calculated by measuring a project's benefits and costs, which are adjusted utilizing border and shadow prices to capture opportunity costs. The ERR is the discount rate at which the project's net present value of the stream of benefits and costs is set to zero. An ERR for the project of less than 10 percent implies that each dollar invested in plant and machinery yields annual economic benefits of less than 10 cents per dollar invested—a return that is lower than alternative investment opportunities and does not compare favorably with that on investments in less risky financial instruments. When the net economic benefits are significant, the ERR will exceed the 10–15 percent range.

The average ERR on all evaluated projects has been about 15 percent, but the variation has been large, ranging from negative values to ERRs of more than 50 percent. Similarly, policy performance has varied enormously across countries and over time. Various country- and year-specific policy variables measuring policy distortions were gathered independently and incorporated into the statistical analysis to determine whether policy-related factors explained differences in the performance of projects. The results are summarized in Table 4.2.

The projects reviewed began as early as the mid-1960s; evaluation took place 1973–89. These projects were implemented in 58 developing economies. For these economies, independent information was available on at least one macro-financial variable (real interest rate, fiscal deficit) or a variable measuring trade restrictions. In addition, data on foreign exchange rate premiums were gathered for each country and year. Thus, each project ERR was correlated with at least two policy indexes.

Table 4.2 presents average ERRs for various values of the four policy indexes: (a) real interest rates, from a World Bank data base; (b) IMF data on central government fiscal deficits; (c) the Halevi-Thomas (Thomas, Halevi, and Stanton, background paper) index of trade restrictiveness/openness, ranging from one (most restrictive) to five (most open), for 32 countries for which comparable published information on tariff and nontariff barriers was available from Bank documents; and (d) the parallel exchange rate premiums (sources were International Currency Analysis, Inc., various years, for the parallel rate and IMF data for the official exchange rate. In addition, as background, other policy indexes were collected and correlated with ERRs, including a measure of distortion in the relative price of tradables (from Dollar, forthcoming) and a second trade liberalization index (from Papageorgiou, Michaely, and Choksi 1990).

Statistical methods. For the overall sample, the simple correlations between each policy index and the project ERRs are of the right sign and statistically significant. For most sectoral and public-private breakdowns, the significance of the correlations between the different policy indexes and sectoral ERRs is maintained, although for selected subsamples (such as between the fiscal deficit and the ERR of nontradables) the simple correlations are not statistically significant.

To explore causality, a variety of controlling variables were obtained for most countries, which made multivariate analysis possible. A tobit procedure was utilized (instead of ordinary least-squares) to address the censoring in the data at an ERR of -5 percent. The ERR of each project is the unit of observation for the dependent variable in the multivariate analysis. Country- and year-specific policy and structural variables were used as independent variables. In addition

to the policy indexes, controlling variables in the analysis included, among others, the economywide capital-labor ratio; years of education; degree of institutional complexity of the project; GDP growth rate; and external terms of trade changes. Alternative specifications, including dummy variables to control for country-specific and year-specific effects, were also estimated.

Results. Estimates of the various specifications indicate an economic and statistically significant effect of policy indexes on ERRs, controlling for other factors. The parallel exchange rate premiums and trade restrictiveness variables remain significant across specifications even when combined with each other in the same specification. And the magnitudes of the coefficients are large, which suggests increases in ERRs of 8–10 percentage points (or more) when large improvements in the parallel premiums and trade regime take place. In contrast, when included along the parallel premiums and trade restrictiveness variables, the real interest rate variable loses all economic and statistical significance. The fiscal deficit variable is significant in the single-policy specification and in some combined-policy specifications. Further, a number of additional sensitivity tests were performed by segmenting the sample by time periods and country sizes; the results were not altered.

To test the effect of public sector investments on the productivity of projects in agriculture and industry, two variables were related to ERRs: public investment as a share of GDP, and public investment as a share of total investment in the economy (drawn from a World Bank data base). Figure 4.3 shows the simple ERR averages for each range of the public investment over total investment variable, after the sample is segmented for low and high parallel premiums, respectively. Multivariate tobit analysis was also carried out to control for other structural and policy-related variables. The public investment variables were specified as kink-linear, to allow for a breaking point and separate slopes for the lower and higher ranges of the variable. This permitted testing the hypothesis that the effect of complementary public investments is different when an increase takes place at relatively low levels of public investments than at high levels.

The results of both types of specifications (public investment as a share of GDP, and public investment as a share of total investment) supported the hypothesis that increases in the share of overall public investments improve the ERR of tradable projects, up to a point. For the public investment in total investment specification, the effect of an increase in the share is positive up to a share of 40–45 percent, and negative thereafter, the coefficients being large and statistically significant.

Data and definitions. Figure 5.2 is based on a background paper by Harrison, which draws on a cross-country, time-series data set assembled by the core team for *World Development Report 1991.* Seven proxies for trade and exchange rate policies were used to test the statistical relationship between openness and growth. The first, index of trade liberalization, 1960–84, measures the degree of trade liberalization using data on exchange rate and commercial policies (source: Papageorgiou, Michaely, and Choksi 1990). Although this measure is not comparable across countries, country dummies included in the regressions should control for differences in measurement. The second, index of trade liberalization, 1978–88, measures the movement toward liberalization for 30 countries for the period 1978-88. The index was calculated using country sources on tariffs and nontariff barriers (source: Thomas, Halevi, and Stanton, background paper). The third, foreign exchange premium, measures the deviation of the black market rate from the official exchange rate (source: International Currency Analysis, Inc., various years). The fourth, change in trade shares, measures the ratio of exports and imports to GDP (source: World Bank data). The fifth, movement toward international prices, was derived from the relative price of a country's tradables, which was computed using current and constant national accounts price indexes. The variable is based on a benchmark of the relative price of consumption goods for 1980 from Summers and Heston 1988. It is then transformed to measure the movement toward unity. The sixth, index of price

distortion, is a modified version of the index used in Dollar (forthcoming). The relative price of consumption goods from Summers and Heston is "purged" of its nontraded component by taking the residual from a regression of this index on urbanization, land, and population. The seventh, bias against agriculture, measures the indirect bias against agriculture from industrial sector protection and overvaluation of the exchange rate. (source: Schiff and Valdés, forthcoming).

Statistical methods. The effects of these seven variables on GDP growth were separately tested, controlling for other effects such as input growth (capital, labor, education, land) and country differences. Annual observations were available for time periods which ranged from 1960–87 for trade shares to 1978–88 for the Halevi-Thomas trade liberalization index (Thomas, Halevi, and Stanton, background paper). The number of countries available for each index varies, ranging from 60 (for trade shares) to 19.

Results. Note table 5.1 shows the results for different period averages. Although the annual data were used for the estimates presented in columns 1 and 2, cyclical fluctuations could in theory lead to spurious correlations between the policy variables and GDP growth. Consequently, six- or seven-year averages were also used. Period averages were computed for 1960–66, 1967–73, 1974–81, and 1982–88. These results are given in columns 3 and 4. Finally, averages for the entire period were also computed, reported in columns 5 and 6. With the exception of the foreign exchange premium and changes in trade shares—which do suggest that greater openness positively affects growth—the other variables are not significant

Note table 5.1 Effects of openness on growth: synthesis of findings

Openness variable	Annual data		Six-year averages		Entire period averages	
	Levels (1)	Changes (2)	Levels (3)	Changes (4)	Levels (5)	Changes (6)
Trade liberalization index						
1960–84	>0*	>0	>0**	>0	<0	>0
1978–88	>0**	>0	..	..	<0	>0
Foreign exchange premium[a]	>0**	>0**	>0**	>0	>0**	>0
Trade shares	>0	>0*	<0	>0**	>0	>0**
Price distortion measure[a]	>0**	<0	>0**	>0**	<0	>0
Movement toward world prices	..	>0**	..	>0	..	>0
Bias against agriculture[a]	>0*	>0	>0*	>0**	>0	>0

** Significant at the 5 percent level.
 * Significant at the 10 percent level.
Note: All regressions except entire period average include country dummies.
a. For purposes of comparison, a value of ''>0'' indicates that more openness (less distortion) positively affects growth. Consequently, for the foreign exchange premium, price distortion measures, and bias against agriculture, the table shows ''>0'' when a higher level of distortion negatively affects growth.

when long-term averages are used. Trade policies in developing countries have varied too much during the 1960–87 period to make long-term averages very meaningful. This analysis draws more from variations in trade policy over time *for the same country* rather than exploiting differences across countries.

The annual data and six-year averages do indicate a robust relation between openness and growth. All variables which are statistically significant show a positive relation between openness and growth—in levels or differences, annually, or over several years.

Although the partial correlations presented in Figure 5.2 are all statistically significant, the amount of variation explained by the openness variable varies. The R^2 on the partial correlations ranged from 0.03 to 0.30, indicating that although trade policy is important, much variation in growth rates is still unexplained, even after accounting for education, labor, land, and capital stock.

Direct foreign investment. The chapter's discussion of direct foreign investment in manufacturing uses data for Côte d'Ivoire, Morocco, and Venezuela to compare the relative performance of domestic and foreign firms in the manufacturing sector. Relative levels of labor productivity as well as export orientation were compared for domestic firms, joint ventures (minority foreign ownership), and majority-owned foreign firms. Means were computed, weighted by the share of each firm in total sectoral output. Because labor productivity or export orientation could be higher simply because of capital intensity or the size of the firm, means were also computed controlling for the capital-labor ratio and firm size, but the results remained unchanged.

The possibility that domestic firms benefit from a significant foreign presence, generating so-called technological spillover effects, was also analyzed. The possibility of ''spillover'' was tested by deriving a production function for domestic firms and measuring the effect of foreign firms on the growth in productivity of domestic firms. Foreign presence was measured by the share of foreign investment in the sector. The evidence suggests few spillovers.

Chapter 7

Types of government. Figure 7.1 is based on Vanhanen 1979, 1990. The data base created from these sources contains time series for 145 countries from 1850 to 1987 (although many countries in the sample did not gain independent governments until after World War II). The classification of one-party states differs from Vanhanen's in that it includes countries in which a single party receives more than 95 percent of the vote, as well as countries that have one party by law. This correlates, in general, with Vanhanen's ranking of ''index of democratization'' (a combination of vote received by the largest party and the percentage of

population participating in the vote) using a cutoff of 10 percent in the index of democratization.

Income distribution. The data on income distribution in Figure 7.2 are from Sachs 1989, with additions of United Nations and World Bank data. Income inequality is defined as the ratio of the income shares of the highest and lowest quintiles. Per capita GDP growth statistics are World Bank data calculated using the ordinary least-squares method for 1965–89. Other variables are also from a World Bank data base. The statistical work was conducted using both levels and growth of education stock and per capita GDP. Continental dummy variables were included.

One set of regressions tested the hypothesis that income inequality matters for the rate of growth a country can achieve. In this regression it appears that high inequality is associated with lower growth. With continental dummies, however, the result does not hold up. The second set of regressions tested the hypothesis that the level of income inequality is influenced by education and per capita GDP. The level of both education and per capita GDP are associated with lower income inequality. Without continental dummies, the growth of per capita GDP appears to be associated with lower income inequality. This result, however, disappears with the inclusion of continental dummies. In sum, the relation between growth and income inequality is weak, and the direction is ambiguous.

Chapter 8

The estimates in Table 8.1 are based on model simulations by the World Bank's country economists for a sample of 40 countries, taking into account domestic policies and external economic conditions. The estimates in the table are based on an unweighted average of deviations (in percent per year) under the specified scenario from the growth rate projected in the ''central case.'' For each country, the central case is based on good domestic policies and external economic conditions as depicted by the baseline scenarios described in Chapter 1.

The results should be regarded as very rough estimates and are to be interpreted only as illustrative. The number of countries considered for calculating the averages varies from cell to cell because not all country-specific exercises considered all combinations of domestic policy stance and external economic conditions. In addition, the external conditions assumed under the ''poor'' and ''very good'' case scenarios are country-specific; for example, higher international oil prices may have been considered as part of a ''very good'' case scenario for an oil-exporting country but as part of a ''poor'' case scenario for an oil-importing country. Conversely, the key assumptions for the baseline scenario for the external economic conditions are uniform across countries.

Bibliographical note

This Report has drawn on a wide range of World Bank sources—including country economic, sector, and project work, and research papers—and on numerous outside sources. The principal sources are noted below, and also listed in two groups: background papers commissioned for this Report and a selected bibliography. Some of the background papers will be available through the Policy, Research, and External Affairs Working Paper series. These, as well as the documents in the selected bibliography with World Bank departmental origins, are available through the Report office. The views they express are not necessarily those of the World Bank or of this Report.

In view of the breadth of the Report's subject, the core team consulted a wide range of people inside and outside the Bank—inevitably too many to mention here, but to whom the team is grateful. Extensive written comments were provided by Jean Baneth, Charles Blitzer, Javed Burki, Partha Dasgupta, Albert Fishlow, Mark Gersovitz, A. O. Hirschman, Paul Isenman, Pierre Landell-Mills, Enrique Lerdau, Paul Meo, Costas Michalopolous, John Nash, Arvind Panagariya, Anandarup Ray, Joanne Salop, Ibrahim Shihata, Andrei Shleifer, Ernest Stern, Paul Streeten, and Oktay Yenal. Extensive comments were provided by many on the staff of the International Monetary Fund; in the Country Economics, External Affairs, Planning and Budgeting, Policy and Review, and Resource Mobilization departments and the Economic Development Institute of the World Bank; and on the staffs of *World Development Report 1990* and *World Development Report 1992*. There was especially close collaboration with Francisco Aguirre-Sacasa, Shaida Badiee, Meta de Coquereaumont, Dennis de Tray, Parvez Hasan, Johannes Linn, Stephen O'Brien, Robert Picciotto, D. C. Rao, Bruce Ross-Larson, Miguel Schloss, Lyn Squire, Andrew Steer, and Wilfried Thalwitz. Many provided valuable comments

on the Report's outline and the Overview. The Report benefited from regional, Bankwide management discussions, from visiting seminar speakers, from presentations outside the Bank, and from discussions with the Operational Vice Presidents. Useful contributions were received from the Executive Directors. Assistance was provided by Judy Baker, Jennifer Keller, Francis Ng, and Rebecca Sugui.

Chapter 1

This chapter benefited from the advice of many experts, including Irma Adelman, Ramesh Chander, Charles Kindleberger, Angus Maddison, Douglass North, Jeffrey Williamson, John Williamson, and Shahid Yusuf. Paul Armington, Norman Hicks, Robert E. Lucas, Jr., Desmond McCarthy, Vikram Nehru, Chukwuma Obidegwu, Hans Singer, and Mark Sundberg provided helpful comments on contemporary economic conditions, and the staff of the Systems and Socio-Economic Data divisions of the International Economics Department on data and computing. Box 1.2 draws on materials from Katsenelinboigen 1990, Nove 1989, and IMF and others 1990. Robert Lynn helped with the statistical analysis in Box 1.6. Data on contemporary economic conditions in this chapter were drawn from various IMF, OECD, and World Bank sources as well as from *The Economist*, *New York Times*, and *Washington Post*. Robert Lynn and Abdel-Illah Stambouli provided help with the work on projections and scenarios.

Chapter 2

Numerous World Bank and academic studies were consulted. The method for constructing physical and human capital stock was initially developed by Lawrence Lau, Dean Jamison, and Frederic Louat 1991. Box 2.1 is based on a background paper by Clas Wihl-

165

borg. Box 2.2 draws on Friedman 1988. Box 2.3 is taken from a background paper by Arnold Harberger. Box 2.5 is based on a paper by Ijaz Nabi. Various background papers were consulted, as were Bevan, Collier, and Gunning, forthcoming; Lal and Myint, in preparation; and Maddison and Associates, forthcoming. Helpful comments were made by Gary Becker, Armeane Choksi, Jaime de Melo, William Easterly, Anne O. Krueger, Lawrence Lau, Robert Z. Lawrence, Paul Romer, Marcelo Selowsky, Shekhar Shah, and George S. Tolley.

Chapter 3

This chapter draws extensively on World Bank documents and academic publications. It also benefited from the comments of World Bank staff who work on the social sectors and experts outside the World Bank. Mark Rosenzweig collaborated on the analyses of illness, education of entrepreneurs, and the effect of public expenditures on basic indicators of social welfare. The analysis of the effect of public spending in the social sectors used estimates of internationally comparable real product from Summers and Heston 1988, and infant mortality rates were checked against the data survey by Hill and Pebley 1989. Box 3.1 draws from Fogel 1986, 1990, and McKeown 1976. Box 3.2 is based on the work on women's education in developing countries by King and Hill, forthcoming. Box 3.3 is drawn from Broadbridge 1989, Emi 1968, and Morishima 1982. Box 3.4 is based on Cleaver and Schreiber 1991 and United Nations 1990c. Box 3.5 was drafted by Joseph Kutzin with additional data from Jill Armstrong; it draws from Over and Kutzin 1990 and WHO 1991. Box 3.6 is based on data from OECD 1980 through 1989; Lockheed and Verspoor, forthcoming; and *World Development Report 1990*. The population working group of the World Bank's Population and Human Resources Department provided some data on health and population. Jere Behrman, Fred Golladay, Ravi Kanbur, Douglas H. Keare, Kye Woo Lee, and William McGreevey provided extensive comments.

Chapter 4

This chapter draws heavily on the academic literature, and on World Bank reports, project evaluation data from the Bank's Operations Evaluation Department and from the IFC, and internal documents. The sources for the analysis of economic rates of return for projects financed by the Bank and IFC are given in the technical note. The discussion on agriculture draws on an extensive review of the literature and in particular from Schiff and Valdés, forthcoming; Binswanger 1990; Feder, Just, and Zilberman 1982;

Hoff and Stiglitz 1990; and Ruttan, background paper. The section on industrial and labor regulations draws in part from Lindauer 1989 and López, background paper. The entrepreneurship story of Mr. Chu in the Republic of Korea is drawn from Magaziner and Patinkin 1989; the other stories are from Bank and IFC reports, and were complemented by staff interview notes. Box 4.1 is excerpted by permission from "The Future Written in a Grain of Rice," *The Economist* 318, 7697 (March 9–15, 1991): 83-84. Box 4.2 is from World Bank 1990a. Box 4.3 is from Knudsen and others 1991. Box 4.4 is from Bank reports on India and Indonesia. Box 4.5 draws from Thirsk 1991, and Shirazi and Shah, forthcoming. The discussion of infrastructure benefited from an essay by Attila Karaosmanoglu. The data on parallel premiums were prepared by Felicia Yesari. Jock Anderson, Paul Ballard, Peter Hazell, David Lindauer, Guy Pfeffermann, Sarath Rajapatirana, and Enrique Rueda Sabater provided extensive comments.

Chapter 5

This chapter draws heavily on World Bank documents, operational experience, and academic sources. In addition to World Bank data and numerous outside sources, the discussion on technology incorporates examples from Rosenberg and Frischtak 1985 and Evenson and Ranis 1990. The discussion of intellectual property protection is based primarily on Mansfield 1989; discussions with Claudio Frischtak; and Nogués 1990. The analysis of the role of government intervention is based on a variety of sources, but benefited greatly from Westphal 1990 and Grossman 1989. The discussion of trade reform draws primarily from Thomas and Nash, forthcoming, and Papageorgiou, Michaely, and Choksi 1990. Box 5.1 is based on Wheeler, Cole, and Irianiwati 1990 and material provided by David Dollar. Table 5.1 draws on three census data sets analyzed with the assistance of Mona Haddad and Brian Aitken. The data on aggregate capital flows used in Figure 5.1 and Table 5.2 were collected for this chapter by David McMurray. Box figures 5.5a and 5.5b are based on data provided by Ron Duncan, who also commented on the analysis. Michele DeNevers, Ashoka Mody, and Lant Pritchett provided extensive comments.

Chapter 6

This chapter draws on a range of World Bank, IMF, and academic sources. The material in the section on booms and busts draws extensively on the country studies of the World Bank Research project on Macroeconomic Policies, Crisis, and Growth in the Long Run and on Corden 1991. Box 6.1 draws on Goldstein and Montiel 1986 and World Bank, various years. Box 6.2 is based on Rodrik 1989, World Bank 1990c, and Webb and Shariff 1990. Box 6.3 draws on Kawasaki 1990 and Horioka 1990. Box 6.4 is based on Cuddington 1986, Dooley 1986, and Edwards and Tabellini 1989. Box 6.5 is based on van Wijnbergen 1990. Edgardo Barandiaran, Max Corden, Wafik Grais, Ejaz Ghani, and Kazi Matin made extensive comments.

Chapter 7

This chapter draws on extensive academic literature, operational experience, and World Bank internal documents. The section on the political economy of development is based on Taylor and Jodice 1983, Ohkawa and Rosovsky 1973, Eckaus 1986, Finger 1990, Roubini and Sachs 1989, O'Donnell 1988, Bates 1981, Londregan and Poole 1989, Hoff and Stiglitz 1990, Krueger 1990, and Wolf 1987. Lant Pritchett also made a valuable contribution to this section. Klitgaard 1988 is the main source for the section on corruption. The section on democracies draws from Nunberg 1990, Weede 1983, Lipset, Seong, and Torres 1991, and Grier and Tullock 1989. The section on institutions is based on, among others, Hicks 1969, Matthews 1986, Nellis 1989, North 1991, Hagen 1962, Perkins 1967, Blinder 1990, Aoki 1990, Friedman 1988, and Supple 1971. The section on holding society together was drafted in collaboration with Homi Kharas, who also drafted the Malaysia portion of Box 7.5. Dilesh Jayanntha provided valuable comments on the Sri Lanka portion of that box. This section also draws on Cameron 1984, Espig-Andersen and Korpi 1984, Hirschman 1990, Fields 1991, Sachs 1985 and 1989, Berg and Sachs 1988, and Jackman, Pissarides, and Savouri 1990. The section on reforming the public sector is based on numerous internal Bank documents as well as on Lindauer and Valenchik 1990. The discussion on military expenditures is based on data from U.S. Arms Control and Disarmament Agency 1986, Sivard 1989, and UNDP 1990. Roger Sullivan drafted the section on wage expenditures and civil service reform, drawing from operational experience, several internal Bank documents, and Merode, forthcoming. The section on state-owned enterprises, privatization, and reform is based on operational experience, a vast literature, and published documents, particularly Kjellström 1990 and Michalet 1989. Homi Kharas drafted the discussion of Eastern European countries. Haggard and Kaufman 1990 and Remmer 1986 were the primary sources for the section on the political economy of reform. Box 7.1 is based on Klitgaard 1988; Box 7.2 on Dornbusch and Edwards 1989; Box 7.6 on work by Jack Hamilton; and Box 7.7 on Fischer and Gelb, forthcoming, Hinds 1990; and Kornai 1990. Box figure 7.7 is based

on work by Alan Gelb and Cheryl Gray in the Socialist Economies Unit of the World Bank's Country Economics Department. Detailed comments were received from Robert Bates, Jessica P. Einhorn, Gerald Pohl, Geoffrey Lamb, and Mary Shirley.

Chapter 8

Sources for the section on priorities for global action include Bhagwati 1989; Chipman 1991; World Bank 1990d; *World Development Report 1990*; and a background paper by Pearce. The section on specific actions that can work is based on World Bank 1989a; Brimble and Dahlman 1990; Kalter and Khor 1990; and World Bank internal documents. Detailed comments were received from Kemal Dervis, Harinder Kohli, Dani Leipziger, Rachel McCulloch, Joan Nelson, and Dani Rodrik.

Background papers

Adelman, Irma. "Long-Term Economic Development."

Austin, Gareth. "Government Intervention, Political Systems, and Economic Performance in Sub-Saharan Africa: A Historical Perspective."

Balassa, Bela. "Trends in Developing Country Exports, 1963-88."

Bhalla, Surjit, and Indermit Gill. "Social Expenditure Policies and Welfare Achievement in Developing Countries."

Bhalla, Surjit, and Lawrence J. Lau. "Openness, Technological Progress, and Economic Growth in Developing Countries."

Chhibber, Ajay, and Mansoor Dailami. "Public Policy and Private Investment: Recent Evidence on Key Selected Issues."

Coutinho, Rui, and Gianpiero Gallo. "Public and Private Investment in Developing Countries: Some Cross-Country Evidence."

———. "The Impact of Adjustment Programs: A Survey."

Dasgupta, Partha. "The State and the Idea of Well-Being."

Dollar, David. "Outward Orientation and Growth: An Empirical Study Using a Price-Based Measure of Openness."

Easterly, William, "How Does Growth Begin? Models of Endogenous Development."

Elias, Victor J. "The Role of Total Factor Productivity on Economic Growth."

Fardoust, Shahrokh. "The World Economy in Transition: Recent History and Outlook for the World Economy."

Fernandez-Arias, Eduardo. "External Finance and Economic Growth: Theory and Evidence."

Finger, J. Michael. "That Old GATT Magic No More Cast Its Spell: How the Uruguay Round Failed."

Fischer, Stanley, and Vinod Thomas. "Policies for Economic Development."

Hamilton, J. M. "War and Development."

Harberger, Arnold C. "Reflections on the Growth Process."

Harrison, Ann E. "Openness and Growth: A Cross-Country, Time-Series Analysis for Developing Countries."

———. "Are There Technology Spillovers from Foreign Investment? Micro Evidence from Panel Data."

Hunter, Janet E. "The Japanese Experience of Economic Development."

Jen, Stephen Yung-li. "Outward Orientation and Economic Performance in Developing Countries: A Survey."

Kaufmann, Daniel. "Determinants of the Productivity of Projects in Developing Countries: Evidence from 1,200 Projects."

———. "The Forgotten Rationale for Policy Reform: The Productivity of Investment."

King, Elizabeth M., and Mark R. Rosenzweig. "Do Public Expenditures Promote Human Development? Results from a Fixed-Effect Model."

King, Elizabeth M., Mark R. Rosenzweig, and Yan Wang. "Assessing the Economic Burden of Illness: Evidence from Eight Countries".

———. "Human Capital and Entreprenuership: Evidence from Five Countries".

Lall, Sanjaya. "Technological Development and Industrialization."

Leff, Nathaniel H. "Direct Foreign Investment, Multinational Corporations, and Developing Countries: Risk, Returns, and Growth."

López, Ramón. "On Microeconomic Distortions as Determinants of the Social Efficiency of Investment and Technological Change."

Maddison, Angus. "World Economic Growth: The Lessons of Long-Run Experience."

Meyers, Kenneth. "The Importance of Long Term Factors in Development."

Newport, Ian, and Zoe Kolovou. "Legal Systems."

North, Douglass C. "Institutions and Economic Development."

Pearce, David. "Environment and Development: An Overview."

Pillai, P. P. "The Kerala Model of Development."

Ruttan, Vernon W. "The Role of Governments in Promoting Technical Change in Agriculture in Developing Countries."

Shleifer, Andrei. "Externalities and Economic Growth: Lessons from Recent Work."

Singer, H. W. "Multilateralism and Nationalism in the Shadow of the Debt Crisis."

Srinivasan, T. N. "Development Thought, Strategy, and Policy: Then and Now."

Thirsk, Wayne. "Tax Distortions and Tax Reform in Developing Countries."

Thomas, Vinod, Nadav Halevi, and Julie Stanton. "Does Policy Reform Improve Performance?"

Wihlborg, Clas. "The Scandinavian Models for Development and Welfare."

World Bank. "Bilateral Development Aid Strategies in the 1980s." Replenishment Operations Division, Resource Mobilization Department.

Selected bibliography

Abbreviations used, in addition to those identified in the text: LSMS, Living Standards Measurement Study. MADIA, Managing Agricultural Development in Africa. NBER, National Bureau of Economic Research. PPR, Policy, Planning, and Research, World Bank. PRE, Policy, Research, and External Affairs, World Bank.

Ahmad, Ehtisham, and Yan Wang. 1991. "Inequality and Poverty in China: Institutional Change and Public Policy, 1978–1988." *World Bank Economic Review* 5, 2: 231–58.

Alesina, Alberto, and Lawrence H. Summers. 1990. "Central Bank Independence and Macroeconomic Performance: Some Comparative Evidence." Discussion Paper 1496. Harvard University, Cambridge, Mass.

Aoki, Masahiko. 1990. "Toward an Economic Model of the Japanese Firm." *Journal of Economic Literature* 28, 1: 1–28.

Ayal, Eliezer B., and Luechai Chulasai. 1988. "Entrepreneurship in the Towns of Northern Thailand." *Journal of Development Planning* 18: 251–63.

Bacha, Edmar L. 1984. "Growth with Limited Supplies of Foreign Exchange: A Reappraisal of the Two-Gap Model." In Moshe Syrquin, L. Taylor, and Larry Westphal, eds., *Economic Structure and Performance*. New York: Academic Press.

Bairoch, Paul. 1976. *Commerce extérieur et développement économique de l'Europe au XIXe siècle.* Paris: Moufon.

Bairoch, Paul, and Maurice Levy-Leboyer. 1981. *Disparities in Economic Development since the Industrial Revolution.* London: Macmillan.

Balassa, Bela. 1985. "Exports, Policy Choices, and Economic Growth in Developing Countries after the 1973 Oil Shock." *Journal of Development Economics* 18: 23–35.

Balassa, Bela, and Associates. 1971. *The Structure of Protection in Developing Countries.* Baltimore, Md.: Johns Hopkins University Press.

Baldwin, Richard E., and Harry Flam. 1989. "Strategic Trade Policies in the Market for 30–40 Seat Commuter Aircraft." Seminar Paper 431. Institute for International Economic Studies, University of Stockholm, Sweden.

Baldwin, Richard E., and Paul Krugman. 1987. "Industrial Policy and International Competition in Wide-Bodied Aircraft." In Richard E. Baldwin, ed., *Trade Policy Issues and Empirical Analysis*. Chicago: University of Chicago Press.

Bapna, S. L. 1980. *Aggregate Supply Response of Crops in a Developing Region*. New Delhi: Sultan Chand.

Baran, Paul. 1957. *The Political Economy of Growth*. New York: Monthly Review Press.

Barlow, Robin. 1967. "The Economic Effects of Malaria Eradication." *American Economic Review: Papers and Proceedings* 57 (May): 130–48.

Barrera, Albino. 1990. "The Role of Maternal Schooling and Its Interaction with Public Health Programs in Child Health Production." *Journal of Development Economics* 32: 69–91.

Barro, Robert. Forthcoming. "Economic Growth in a Cross Section of Countries." *Quarterly Journal of Economics*.

Bartel, Ann P., and Frank R. Lichtenberg. 1987. "The Comparative Advantage of Educated Workers in Implementing New Technology." *Review of Economics and Statistics* 54, 1: 1–11.

Basu, Ellen. Forthcoming. *Blood, Sweat, and Mahjong: Family and Pariah Enterprise in an Overseas Chinese Community*. Ithaca, N.Y.: Cornell University Press.

Bates, Robert H. 1981. *Markets and States in Tropical Africa*. Berkeley: University of California Press.

Bates, Robert, Philip Brock, and Jill Tiefenthaler. 1991. "Risk and Trade Regimes: Another Explanation." *International Organization* 45, 1: 1–18.

Bauer, P. T. 1958. *Some Economic Aspects and Problems of Under-Developed Countries*. Bombay: Forum of Free Enterprise.

Baumol, William J., Sue Anne Batey Blackman, and Edward N. Wolff. 1989. *Productivity and American Leadership*. Cambridge, Mass.: MIT Press.

Becker, Gary. 1964. *Human Capital*. New York: Columbia University Press.

Behrman, Jere R., and David M. Blau. 1985. "Human Capital and Earnings Distributions in a Developing Country: The Case of Prerevolutionary Nicaragua." *Economic Development and Cultural Change* 34: 1–31.

Behrman, Jere R., and Anil B. Deolalikar. 1988. "School Repetition Dropouts and the Returns to School: The Case of Indonesia." University of Pennsylvania, Philadelphia.

Berg, Andrew, and Jeffrey Sachs. 1988. "The Debt Crisis: Structural Explanation of Country Performance." NBER Working Paper 2607. Cambridge, Mass.

Bernstein, Jeffrey I., and M. Ishaq Nadiri. 1988. "Interindustry R&D Spillovers, Rates of Return, and Production in High-Technology Industries." *American Economic Review: Papers and Proceedings* 78, 2: 429–34.

Bevan, David, Paul Collier, and Jan Gunning. Forthcoming. *The Political Economy of Poverty, Equity and Growth: Indonesia and Nigeria*. New York: Oxford University Press.

Bhagwati, Jagdish. 1978. *Foreign Trade Regimes and Economic Development: Anatomy and Consequences of Exchange Control*. Cambridge, Mass.: Ballinger.

———. 1989. "Is Free Trade Passe after All?" *Weltwirtschaftliches Archiv* 125, 1: 17–44.

Bhalla, Surjit. Forthcoming. "The Role of Welfare Policies and Income Growth in Improving Living Standards in India and Sri Lanka." PRE Working Paper. World Bank, Office of the Vice President, Development Economics, Washington, D.C.

Binswanger, Hans. 1990. "The Policy Response of Agriculture." *Proceedings of the World Bank Annual Conference on Development Economics 1989*: 231–58.

Birkhaeuser, Dean, Robert E. Evenson, and Gershon Feder. 1989. "The Economic Impact of Agricultural Extension: A Review." Yale University, Economic Growth Center Discussion Paper 567, New Haven, Conn.

Biro Pusat Statistik. 1989. *National Income of Indonesia 1983–88*. Jakarta.

Blejer, Mario, and Mohsin S. Khan. 1984. "Government Policy and Private Investment in Developing Countries." *IMF Staff Papers* 31, 2: 379–403.

Blinder, Alan S. 1990. "Pay, Participation, and Productivity." *Brookings Review* 8, 1: 33–38.

Boskin, Michael J., and Lawrence J. Lau. 1990. *Post-War Economic Growth in the Group-of-Five Countries: A New Analysis*. Center for Economic Policy Research Publication 217. Stanford, Calif.: Stanford University, Department of Economics.

Brander, James A., and Barbara J. Spencer. 1985. "Export Subsidies and International Market Share Rivalry." *Journal of International Economics* 18, 2: 83–100.

Brimble, Peter, and Carl J. Dahlman. 1990. "Thailand: Technology Strategy and Policy for Sustained Industrialization." World Bank, Industry and Energy Department, Industry Series Working Paper 24, Washington, D.C.

Broadbridge, Seymour A., 1989. "Aspects of Economic and Social Policy in Japan, 1868-1945." In Peter Mathias and Sidney Pollard, eds., *The Cambridge Economic History of Europe*, vol. 8. Cambridge, U.K.: Cambridge University Press.

Bugingo, G., A. Ntilivamunda, D. Nzaramba, P. Van de Perre, A. Ndikuyeze, S. Munyantore, A. Mutwewingabo, and C. Bizimungu. 1987. "Etude sur la Séropositivité Liée à l'Infection au Virus de l'Immunodeficience Humaine au Rwanda." *Revue Médicale Rwandaise* 20: 37–42.

Bourguignon, François, and Christian Morrison. 1989. *External Trade and Income Distribution.* Paris: Development Centre of OECD.

Buiter, Willem H. 1988. "Some Thoughts on the Role of Fiscal Policy in Stabilization and Structural Adjustment in Developing Countries." Background paper for *World Development Report 1988.* World Bank, Office of the Vice President, Development Economics, Washington, D.C.

Bulatao, Rodolfo A., Eduard Bos, Patience W. Stephens, and My T. Vu. 1990. *World Population Projections, 1989–90 Edition: Short- and Long-Term Estimates.* Baltimore, Md.: Johns Hopkins University Press.

Caldwell, John. 1979. "Education as a Factor in Mortality Decline: An Examination of Nigerian Data." *Population Studies* 33, 3 (Nov.): 395–414.

Calmfors, Lars, and Ragnar Nymoen. 1990. "Real Wage Adjustment and Employment Policies in the Nordic Countries." *Economic Policy* 11 (Oct.): 397–448.

Cameron, David R. 1984. "Social Democracy, Corporatism, Labor Quiescence, and the Representation of Economic Interest in Advanced Capitalist Society." In John H. Goldthorpe, ed., *Order and Conflict in Contemporary Capitalism.* Oxford, U.K.: Clarendon Press.

Cardoso, Eliana, and Albert Fishlow. "Latin American Economic Development: 1950–1980." NBER Working Paper 3161. Cambridge, Mass.

Cassen, Robert, and Associates. 1987. *Does Aid Work?* New York: Oxford University Press.

Cavallo, Domingo, and Yair Mundlak. 1982. "Agriculture and Economic Growth in an Open Economy: The Case of Argentina." International Food Policy Research Institute Report 36. Washington, D.C.

Chenery, Hollis, and Michael Bruno. 1962. "Development Alternatives in an Open Economy: the Case of Israel." *Economic Journal* 72, 285: 79–103.

Chenery, Hollis, Sherman Robinson, and Moshe Syrquin. 1986. *Industrialization and Growth: A Comparative Study.* New York: Oxford University Press.

Chenery, Hollis, and T. N. Srinivasan. 1988. *The Handbook of Development Economics.* 2 vols. New York: North-Holland.

Chhibber, Ajay, and Nemat Shafik. 1990. "Does Devaluation Hurt Private Investment? The Indonesian Case." PRE Working Paper 418. World Bank, Office of the Vice President for Development Economics, Washington, D.C.

China, State Statistical Bureau. 1988. *Statistical Yearbook of China 1987.* Hong Kong: Longman.
————. 1989. *Statistical Yearbook of China 1989.* Beijing: China Statistical Press.

Chipman, John. 1991. "Third World Politics and Security in the 1990s: 'The World Forgetting, By the World Forgot?'" *Washington Quarterly* 14, 1: 151–68.

Cho, Yoon-Je Cho, and Deena Khatkhate. 1989. *Lessons of Financial Liberalization in Asia: A Comparative Study.* World Bank Discussion Paper 50. Washington, D.C.

Chudnovsky, Daniel. 1990. "North-South Technology Transfer Revisited: Research Issues for the 1990s." International Development Research Centre, Ottawa, Canada.

Cipolla, Carlo. 1978. *The Economic History of World Population.* 7th ed. Harmondsworth, U.K.: Penguin.

Cleaver, Kevin. 1985. *The Impact of Price and Exchange Rate Policies on Agriculture in Sub-Saharan Africa.* World Bank Staff Working Paper 728. Washington, D.C.

Cleaver, Kevin, and Gotz Schreiber. 1991. "The Population, Environment, and Agriculture Nexus in Sub-Saharan Africa." World Bank, Western Africa Department, Washington, D.C.

Collins, Susan M. 1990. "Lessons from Korean Economic Growth." *American Economic Review: Papers and Proceedings* 80, 2: 104–07.

Commission on Health Research for Development. 1990. *Health Research: Essential Link to Equity in Development.* New York: Oxford University Press.

Corbo, Vittorio, and Patricio Rojas. 1991. "World Bank-Supported Adjustment Programs. Country Performance and Effectiveness." PRE Working Paper 623. World Bank, Country Economics Department, Washington, D.C.

Corbo, Vittorio, and Klaus Schmidt-Hebbel. 1990. "Public Policies and Saving in Developing Countries." World Bank, Country Economics Department, Washington, D.C.

Corden, W. Max. 1991. "Macroeconomic Policies and Growth: Some Lessons of Experience." *Proceedings of the World Bank Annual Conference on Development Economics 1990*: 59–84.

Crafts, N. C. R. 1981. "The Eighteenth Century: A Survey." In Floud and McCloskey 1981.

Cuddington, John T. 1987. "Economic Determinants of Capital Flight: An Econometric Investigation." In Donald R. Lessard and John Williamson, eds., *Capital Flight: The Problem and Policy Responses.* Washington, D.C.: Institute for International Economics.

Culpeper, Roy, and Michel Hardy. 1990. "Private Foreign Investment and Development: A Partnership for the 1990s?" North-South Institute, Ottawa, Canada.

Cumby, Robert, and R. Levich. 1987. "On the Definition and Magnitude of Recent Capital Flight." In Donald R. Lessard and John Williamson, eds., *Capital Flight: The Problem and Policy Responses*. Washington, D.C.: Institute for International Economics.

Cummings, Dianne, Dale Cummings, and Zvi Jorgenson. 1980. "Economic Growth, 1947–73: An International Comparison." In John Kendrick and Beatrice Vaccara, eds., *New Developments in Productivity Measurement*. Chicago: University of Chicago Press.

Dahlman, Carl J., and Ousa Sananikone. 1990. "Technology Strategy in the Economy of Taiwan: Exploiting Foreign Linkages and Investing in Local Capability." World Bank, International Economics Department, Washington, D.C.

Dasgupta, Partha. 1990. "Well-Being and the Extent of Its Realization in Developing Countries." *Economic Journal* 100, 4: supplement.

Deaton, Angus. 1989. "Saving and Liquidity Constraints." NBER Working Paper 3196. Cambridge, Mass.

Dell, Sidney, and Roger Lawrence. 1980. *The Balance of Payments Adjustment Process in Developing Countries*. Elmsford, N.Y.: Pergamon.

De Long, J. Bradford, and Lawrence H. Summers. Forthcoming. "Equipment Investment and Economic Growth." *Quarterly Journal of Economics*.

Denison, Edward F. 1962. *The Sources of Economic Growth in the United States and the Alternatives before Us*. New York: Committee for Economic Development.

Dervis, Kemal, and Peter A. Petri. 1987. *The Macroeconomics of Successful Development: What Are the Lessons?* NBER Macroeconomics Annual. Cambridge, Mass.: MIT Press.

Deolalikar, Anil B. 1988. "Nutrition and Labor Productivity in Agriculture: Estimates for Rural South India." *Review of Economics and Statistics* 70, 3 (August): 406–13.

Dollar, David. Forthcoming. "Outward-Oriented Developing Economies Really Do Grow More Rapidly: Evidence from 95 LDCs, 1976–85." *Economic Development and Cultural Change*.

Dooley, Michael P. 1986. "Country-Specific Risk Premiums, Capital Flight, and Net Investment Income Payments in Selected Developing Countries." International Monetary Fund, Washington, D.C.

Dornbusch, Rudiger, and Sebastian Edwards. 1989. "The Macroeconomics of Populism in Latin America." PPR Working Paper 316. World Bank, Country Economics Department, Washington, D.C.

Douglas, Roger. 1990. "The Politics of Successful Structural Reform." *Policy* 6, 1: 2–6.

DRI/McGraw-Hill. 1990. *World Markets: Executive Summary*. 4th quarter. Lexington, Mass.

Easterlin, Richard. 1981. "Why Isn't the Whole World Developed?" *Journal of Economic History* 41, 1: 1–17.

Eckaus, R. S. 1986. *Some Temporal Aspects of Development: A Survey*. World Bank Staff Working Paper 626. Washington, D.C.

Edwards, Sebastian. 1989. "Real Exchange Rates in the Developing Countries: Concepts and Measurement." NBER Working Paper 2950. Cambridge, Mass.

Edwards, Sebastian, and Guido Tabellini. 1990. "The Political Economy of Fiscal Policy and Inflation in Developing Countries: An Empirical Analysis." University of California, Los Angeles.

Eichengreen, Barry, and Richard Portes. 1989. "Dealing with Debt: The 1930s and the 1980s." PPR Working Paper 259. World Bank, International Economics Department, Washington, D.C.

Emi, Koichi. 1968. "Economic Development and Educational Investment in the Meiji Era." In Unesco, *Readings in the Economics of Education*. Paris.

Ernst, Dieter, and David O'Connor. 1990. "Technological Capabilities, New Technologies, and Latecomer Industrialisation: An Agenda for the 1990s." Paris: Development Centre of OECD.

Esman, Milton J., and Norman T. Uphoff. 1984. *Local Organizations: Intermediaries in Rural Development*. Ithaca, N.Y.: Cornell University Press.

Espig-Andersen, Gosta, and Walter Korpi. 1984. *Social Policy as Class Politics in Post War Capitalism: Scandinavia, Austria, and Germany*. London: Oxford University Press.

Evans, Peter B. 1989. "Predatory, Developmental, and Other Apparatuses: A Comparative Political Economy Perspective of the Third World State." *Sociological Forum* 4: 561–87.

Evenson, Robert E., and Gustav Ranis, eds. 1990. *Science and Technology: Lessons for Development Policy*. Boulder, Colo.: Westview.

Faini, Riccardo, and Jaime de Melo. 1990. "Adjustment, Investment, and the Real Exchange Rate in Developing Countries." PRE Working Paper 473. World Bank, Country Economics Department, Washington, D.C.

Fardoust, Shahrokh, and Ashok Dhareshwar. 1990. *A Long-Term Outlook for the World Economy: Issues and Projections for the 1990s*. Policy and Research Series 12. Washington, D.C.: World Bank.

Feder, Gershon, Richard Just, and David Zilberman. 1982. *Adoption of Agricultural Innovation in Developing Countries: A Survey*. World Bank Staff Working Paper 542. Washington, D.C.

Fields, Gary S. 1991. "Growth and Income Distribution." In Psacharopoulos 1991.

Findlay, Ronald. 1990. "The New Political Economy: Its Explanatory Power for LDCs." *Economics and Politics* 2, 2: 193–221.

171

Finger, J. Michael. 1990. "The GATT as International Discipline over Trade Restrictions: A Public Choice Approach." PRE Working Paper 402. World Bank, Country Economics Department, Washington, D.C.

Finger, J. Michael, and Patrick A. Messerlin. 1989. *The Effects of Industrial Countries' Policies on Developing Countries*. Washington, D.C.: World Bank.

Finsterbusch, Kurt, and Warren A. Van Wicklin III. 1989. "Beneficiary Participation in Development Projects: Empirical Tests of Popular Theories." *Economic Development and Cultural Change* 37, 3: 573–93.

Fischer, Stanley. 1989. "Economic Development and the Debt Crisis." PPR Working Paper 17. World Bank, Office of the Vice President, Development Economics, Washington, D.C.

Fischer, Stanley, and Alan Gelb. Forthcoming. "Issues in Socialist Economy Reform." *Journal of Economic Perspectives*.

Floud, Roderick, and Donald McCloskey. 1981. *The Economic History of Britain since 1700*. Cambridge, U.K.: Cambridge University Press.

Fogel, Robert W. 1986. "Nutrition and the Decline in Mortality since 1700: Some Additional Preliminary Findings." *Studies in Income and Wealth* 51: 439–555.

———. 1990. "Second Thoughts on the European Escape from Hunger: Famines, Chronic Malnutrition, and Mortality." University of Chicago, Chicago, Ill.

Friedman, David. 1988. *The Misunderstood Miracle*. Ithaca, N.Y.: Cornell University Press.

Frimpong-Ansah, J. H. 1989. "The Challenges to Private Entrepreneurship in Sub-Saharan Africa." *Tanzania Journal of Economics* 1, 1: 19–46.

Frischtak, Claudio R., Bita Hadjimichael, and Ulrich Zachau. 1989. *Competition Policies for Industrializing Countries*. Policy and Research Series 7. Washington, D.C.: World Bank.

Gastil, Raymond. 1989. *Freedom in the World*. New York: Freedom House.

GATT (General Agreement on Tariffs and Trade). 1990. *International Trade 89–90*. Vol. 2. Geneva.

Gelb, Alan H. 1989. "Financial Policies, Growth, and Efficiency." PPR Working Paper 202. World Bank, Country Economics Department, Washington, D.C.

Gerschenkron, Alexander. 1968. *Continuity in History and Other Essays*. Cambridge, Mass.: Harvard University Press.

Glewwe, Paul. 1990. "Schooling, Skills, and the Returns to Education: An Econometric Exploration Using Data from Ghana." World Bank, Population and Human Resources Department, Washington, D.C. Processed.

Goldstein, Morris, and Peter Montiel. 1986. "Evaluating Fund Stabilization Programs with Multi-country Data: Some Methodological Pitfalls." *IMF Staff Papers* 33, 2: 304–44.

Greene, Joshua, and Delano Villanueva. 1990. "Private Investment in Developing Countries: An Empirical Analysis." IMF Working Paper 40. Washington, D.C.

Grier, Kevin B., and Gordon Tullock. 1989. "An Empirical Analysis of Cross-National Economic Growth, 1951–80." *Journal of Monetary Economics* 24: 259–76.

Griffin, Charles G. 1987. "Methods for Estimating the Value of Time with an Application to the Philippines." University of Oregon, Eugene.

Grilli, Enzo R., and Maw Cheng Yang. 1988. "Primary Commodity Prices, Manufactured Goods Prices, and the Terms of Trade of Developing Countries: What the Long Run Shows." *World Bank Economic Review* 2, 1: 1–47.

Grossman, Gene M. 1989. "Promoting New Industrial Activities: A Survey of Recent Arguments and Evidence." Princeton University, Princeton, N.J.

Grossman, Gene M., and Elhanan Helpman. Forthcoming. *Innovation and Growth: Technological Competition in the Global Economy*. Cambridge, Mass.: MIT Press.

Gwatkin, Davidson R. 1978. "The End of An Era." Overseas Development Council, Washington, D.C.

Haberler, Gottfried. 1959. *International Trade and Economic Development*. Cairo: National Bank of Egypt.

Haddad, Lawrence, and Howarth E. Bouis. 1989. "The Impact of Nutritional Status on Agricultural Productivity: Wage Evidence from the Philippines." Development Economics Research Centre, University of Warwick, U.K.

Hagen, Everett. 1962. *On the Theory of Social Change*. Homewood, Ill.: Dorsey.

Haggard, Stephen, and Robert Kaufman. 1990. "The Political Economy of Inflation and Stabilization in Middle-Income Countries." PRE Working Paper 444. World Bank, Country Economics Department, Washington, D.C.

Halstead, Scott B., Julia A. Walsh, and Kenneth S. Warren, eds. 1985. *Good Health at Low Cost*. New York: Rockefeller Foundation.

Harberger, Arnold, ed. 1984. *World Economic Growth*. San Francisco, Calif.: ICS Press.

Hazell, Peter, Carlos Pomareda, and Alberto Valdés. 1986. *Crop Insurance for Agricultural Development: Issues and Experience*. Baltimore, Md.: Johns Hopkins University Press.

Heggie, Ian G. 1989. "Reforming Transport Policy." *Finance and Development* 2, 6: 42–44.

Heitger, Bernhard. 1986. "Import Protection and Export Performance: Their Impact on Economic Growth." *Weltwirtschaftliches Archiv* 260 (July): 1–19.

Heller, Peter, and Alan Tait. 1984. *Government Employment and Pay: Some International Comparisons.* IMF Occasional Paper 24. Washington, D.C.

Helpman, Elhanan, and Paul R. Krugman. 1989. *Trade Policy and Market Structure.* Cambridge, Mass.: MIT Press.

Hernandez-Iglesias, Feliciano, and Michelle Riboud. 1985. ''Trends in Labor Force Participation of Spanish Women: An Interpretive Essay.'' *Journal of Labor Economics* 3, 1, part 2 (January): S201–17.

Hicks, John. 1969. *A Theory of Economic History.* New York: Oxford University Press.

Hill, Kenneth, and Anne R. Pebley. 1989. ''Child Mortality in the Developing World.'' *Population and Development Review* 15, 4: 657–87.

Hinds, Manuel. 1990. ''Issues in the Introduction of Market Forces in Eastern European Economies.'' World Bank, Europe, Middle East and North Africa Technical Department, Washington, D.C.

Hirschman, A. O. 1958. *The Strategy of Economic Development,* New Haven, Conn.: Yale University Press.

———. 1990. ''The Case Against 'One Thing at a Time'.'' *World Development* 18, 8: 1119–22.

Hoff, Karla, and Joseph Stiglitz. 1990. ''Introduction: Imperfect Information and Rural Credit Markets— Puzzles and Policy Perspectives.'' *World Bank Economic Review* 4, 3: 235–50.

Horioka, Charles Yuji. 1990. ''Why Is Japan's Household Saving Rate So High? A Literature Survey.'' *Journal of the Japanese and International Economies* 4: 49–92.

Hsiao, M. W. 1987. ''Tests of Causality and Exogeneity between Exports and Economic Growth: The Case of the Asian NICs.'' *Journal of Economic Development* 12, 2: 143–59.

Hsu, Ti-hsia. 1982. *China's Search for Economic Growth: The Chinese Economy since 1949,* China Studies Series. Beijing: New World Press.

Huntington, S. P. 1968. *Political Order in Changing Societies.* New Haven, Conn.: Yale University Press.

Hwa, Erh-Cheng. 1983. *The Contribution of Agriculture to Economic Growth: Some Empirical Evidence.* World Bank Staff Working Paper 619. Washington, D.C.

IBGE (Brazilian Institute of Geography and Statistics). 1987. *Estatísticas Históricas do Brasil.* Vol. 3, *Séries Econômicas. Demográficas e Sociais de 1500 a 1985.* Séries Estatísticas Retrospectivas. Rio de Janeiro.

Ibn Khaldun. 1981. *The Mugaddimah: An Introduction to History.* (Originally published in about the 14th century.) Edited and abridged by N. Dawood. Princeton, N.J.: Princeton University Press.

ILO (International Labour Office). 1970. *Toward Full Employment: A Programme for Colombia.* Geneva.

———. 1971. *Matching Employment Opportunities and Expectations: A Programme of Action for Ceylon.* Geneva.

IMF (International Monetary Fund). 1990. *World Economic Outlook.* Oct. Washington, D.C.

———. 1991. *World Economic Outlook.* April. Washington, D.C.

IMF, World Bank, Organisation for Economic Co-operation and Development, and European Bank for Reconstruction and Development. 1990. *The Economy of the USSR: A Study Undertaken in Response to a Request by the Houston Summit: Summary and Recommendations.* Washington, D.C.: World Bank.

India, Planning Commission. 1964. *Report of the Committee on Distribution of Income and Levels of Living.* Vol. 1. New Delhi.

International Currency Analysis, Inc. Various years. *World Currency Yearbook.* New York.

Jackman, Richard, Christopher Pissarides, and Savvas Savouri. 1990. ''Labour Market Policies and Unemployment in the OECD.'' *Economic Policy* 11 (Oct.): 449–90.

Jacoby, Hanan. 1989. ''The Returns to Education in the Agriculture of the Peruvian Sierra.'' World Bank, Population and Human Resources Department, Washington, D.C.

Jamison, Dean T., and Lawrence Lau. 1982. *Farmer Education and Farm Efficiency.* Baltimore, Md.: Johns Hopkins University Press.

Jamison, Dean T., and W. Henry Mosley, eds. Forthcoming. *Disease Control Priorities in Developing Countries.* New York: Oxford University Press.

Johnson, Dale, and Ronald Lee, eds. 1987. *Population Growth and Economic Development: Issues and Evidence.* Madison: University of Wisconsin Press.

Jorgensen, Dale, and Zvi Griliches. 1967. ''The Explanation of Productivity Change.'' *Review of Economic Studies* 34, 99: 249–83.

Jung, W., and P. Marshall. 1985. ''Exports, Growth, and Causality in Developing Countries.'' *Journal of Development Economics* 14, May--June: 241–50.

Kalter, Eliot, and Hoe Ee Khor. 1990. ''Mexico's Experience with Adjustment.'' *Finance and Development* 27: 22–25.

Katsenelinboigen, Aron J. 1990. *The Soviet Union, Empire, Nation and System.* New Brunswick, N.J.: Transaction.

Kawasaki, Kenichi. 1990. ''The Saving Behavior of Japanese Households.'' OECD Working Paper 73. Paris, France.

Kazushi, Ohkawa, and Henry Rosovsky. 1973. *Japanese Economic Growth.* Stanford, Calif.: Stanford University Press.

Keesing, Donald B., and Andrew Singer. 1990. ''Development Assistance Gone Wrong: Why Support Services Have Failed to Expand Exports.'' PRE Working Paper 543. World Bank, Country Economics Department, Washington, D.C.

Kelly, Margaret, Naheed Kirmani, Miranda Xafa, Clemens Boonekamp, and Peter Winglee. 1988. *Issues and Developments in International Trade Policy.* IMF Occasional Paper 63. Washington, D.C.

Keynes, John Maynard. 1972. "The End of Laissez-Faire" (1926). In *The Collected Writings of John Maynard Keynes.* New York: St. Martin's Press.

Khan, Mohsin S. 1990. "The Macroeconomic Effects of Fund-Supported Adjustment Programs." *IMF Staff Papers* 37, 2: 195–231.

Killick, Anthony. 1989. *A Reaction Too Far.* London: Overseas Development Institute.

Kim, Young-Ju. 1987. *Health Care Financing in Korea.* Seoul, Republic of Korea: Social Development Planning Division, Economic Planning Board.

King, Elizabeth M. 1989. *Does Education Pay in the Labor Market? The Labor Force Participation, Occupation, and Earnings of Peruvian Women.* LSMS Working Paper 67. Washington, D.C.: World Bank.

King, Elizabeth, and M. Anne Hill, eds. Forthcoming. *Women's Education in Developing Countries.* Baltimore, Md.: Johns Hopkins University Press.

Kjellström, Sven. 1990. "Privatization in Turkey." World Bank, Europe, Middle East, and North Africa Country Department I, Washington, D.C.

Klitgaard, Robert. 1988. *Controlling Corruption.* Berkeley: University of California Press.

Knudsen, Odin, John Nash, James Bovard, Bruce L. Gardner, and Alan Winters. 1991. *Redefining the Role of Government in Agriculture in the 1990s.* World Bank Discussion Paper 105. Washington, D.C.

Kornai, Janos. 1990. *The Road to a Free Economy: Shifting from a Socialist System: the Example of Hungary.* New York: Norton.

Korten, Frances F., and Robert Y. Sly, Jr. 1988. *Transforming a Bureaucracy: The Experience of the Philippine National Irrigation Administration.* West Hartford, Conn.: Kumarian Press.

Krueger, Anne. 1978. *Liberalization Attempts and Consequences.* Cambridge, Mass.: Ballinger.

———. 1990. "Government Failures in Development." *Journal of Economic Perspectives* 4, 3: 9–23.

Krueger, Anne O., Constantine Michalopoulos, and Vernon Ruttan. 1989. *Aid and Development,* Baltimore, Md.: Johns Hopkins University Press.

Kuznets, Simon. 1971. *The Economic Growth of Nations.* Cambridge, Mass.: Harvard University Press.

Lächler, Ulrich. 1989. "Regional Integration and Economic Development." World Bank, Industry and Energy Department, Industry Series Working Paper 14, Washington, D.C.

Laird, Samuel, and Alexander Yeats. 1987. "Empirical Evidence Concerning the Magnitude and Effects of Developing Country Tariff Escalation." *Developing Economies* 25, 2: 99–123.

———. 1990a. *Quantitative Methods for Trade-Barrier Analysis.* New York: Macmillan.

———. 1990b. "Trends in Nontariff Barriers [in German]." *Weltwirtschaftliches Archiv* 126, 2: 300–25.

Lal, Deepak, and Hla Myint, eds. In preparation. *The Political Economy of Poverty, Equity, and Growth.* New York: Oxford University Press.

Lau, Lawrence, Dean T. Jamison, and Frederic F. Louat. 1991. "Education and Productivity in Developing Countries: An Aggregate Function Approach." PRE Working Paper 612. Background paper for *World Development Report 1990.* World Bank, Office of the Vice President, Development Economics, Washington, D.C.

Lau, Lawrence, and Lawrence Klein. 1990. *Models of Development.* San Francisco: ICS Press.

League of Nations. 1927. *Tariff Level Indices.* Geneva: International Economic Conference, Economic and Financial Section.

Lee, Kye-Woo. 1981. "Equity and an Alternative Education Method: A Korean Case Study." *Comparative Education Review* 25, 1: 45–63.

Lee, Kyu Sik, and Alex Anas. 1990. "The Costs of Infrastructural Deficiencies in Nigeria." World Bank, Infrastructure and Urban Development Department, Washington, D.C.

Lele, Uma, and Robert E. Christiansen. 1990. *Markets, Marketing Boards, and Cooperatives in Africa: Issues in Adjustment Policy.* MADIA Discussion Paper 11. Washington, D.C.: World Bank.

Lele, Uma, and Ijaz Nabi. 1991. *Transitions in Development: The Role of Aid and Commercial Flows.* San Francisco, Calif.: ICS Press.

Levin, Henry M., Ernesto Pollit, Ray Galloway, and Judith McGuire. Forthcoming. "Micronutrient Deficiency Disorders." In Jamison and Mosley, forthcoming.

Levy, Brian. 1991. "Obstacles to Developing Small and Medium-Sized Enterprises." PRE Working Paper 588. World Bank, Country Economics Department, Washington, D.C.

Lewis, W. Arthur. 1954. "Economic Development with Unlimited Supplies of Labor." *Manchester School of Economic and Social Studies* 22, 2: 139–91.

———. 1955. *The Theory of Economic Growth.* Homewood, Ill.: Irwin.

Lewis, John P., and contributors. 1986. *Development Strategies Reconsidered.* U.S.–Third World Policy Perspectives 5. Washington, D.C.: Overseas Development Council.

Lewis, Stephen R., Jr. 1988. "Primary Exporting Countries." In Chenery and Srinivasan 1988.

Lindauer, David L. 1989. "Labor Market Performance and Worker Welfare in Korea." Paper presented at the Conference on Economic and Social Change in the Republic of Korea, Newport, R.I.

Lindauer, D. L., and A. D. Valenchik. 1990. "The Growth of Government Spending in Developing Countries: A Review of Trends, Causes, and Consequences." Development Discussion Paper 353. Harvard University, Institute for International Development, Cambridge, Mass.

Lipset, Seymour Martin, Kyoung-Ryung Seong, and John Charles Torres. 1991. "A Comparative Analysis of the Social Requisites of Democracy." Hoover Institution, Stanford, Calif.

Little, I. M. D. 1982. *Economic Development: Theory, Policy, and International Relations.* New York: Basic Books.

Little, I. M. D., Tibor Scitovsky, and Maurice Scott. 1970. *Industry and Trade in Some Developing Countries: A Comparative Study.* London: Oxford University Press.

Liu, Lili. 1990. "Entry/Exit, Learning, and Productivity Change: Evidence from Chile." World Bank, Country Economics Department, Washington, D.C.

Lockheed, Marlaine, and Adriaan Verspoor. Forthcoming. *Improving Primary Education in Developing Countries.* New York: Oxford University Press.

Londregran, John B., and Keith T. Poole. 1989. "Poverty, the Coup Trap, and the Seizure of Executive Power." Working Paper 36-88-89. Carnegie Mellon University, Graduate School of Industrial Administration, Pittsburgh, Pa.

Lopez, Alan D. Forthcoming. "Causes of Death in the Industrialized and the Developing Countries: Estimates for 1985." In Jamison and Mosley, forthcoming.

López, Ramón, and Luis Riveros. 1989. "Macroeconomic Adjustment and the Labor Market in Four Latin American Countries." PPR Working Paper 335. World Bank, Country Economics Department, Washington, D.C.

Lucas, Robert E. 1988. "On the Mechanics of Economic Development." *Journal of Monetary Economics* 22: 2–42.

Maasland, Anne, and Jacques van der Gaag. 1990. "World Bank–Supported Adjustment Programs and Living Conditions." Paper prepared for the Conference on Adjustment Lending: Policies for the Recovery of Growth, World Bank, Washington, D.C., Sept. 13–14.

McEvedy, Colin, and Richard Jones. 1978. *Atlas of World Population History.* New York: Facts on File.

McKeown, Thomas. 1976. *The Modern Rise of Population.* New York: Academic Press.

Maddison, Angus. 1981. *Les phases du développement capitaliste.* Paris: Economica.

———. 1989. *The World Economy in the 20th Century.* Paris: Development Centre of OECD.

Maddison, Angus, and Associates. Forthcoming. *The Political Economy of Poverty, Equity, and Growth: Brazil and Mexico.* New York: Oxford University Press.

Magaziner, Ira C., and M. Patinkin. 1989. "Fast Heat: How Korea Won the Microwave War." *Harvard Business Review* 67 (Jan.–Feb.): 83–92.

Mahar, Dennis J. 1989. *Government Policies and Deforestation in Brazil's Amazon Region.* Washington, D.C.: World Bank.

Malaysia, Government of. 1973. *Mid-Term Review of Second Malaysia Plan 1971–1975.* Kuala Lumpur: Government Press.

Mandelbaum, K. 1945. *The Industrialization of Underdeveloped Areas.* Oxford, U.K.: Blackwell.

Mansfield, Edwin. 1989. "Protection of Intellectual Property Rights in Developing Countries." IFC, Economics Department, Washington, D.C.

Marsden, Keith. 1990. *African Entrepreneurs—Pioneers in Development.* IFC Discussion Paper 9. Washington, D.C.

Marshall, Alfred. 1930. *The Principles of Economics.* 8th ed. (orig. pub. 1890). London: Macmillan.

Matthews, R. C. O. 1986. "The Economics of Institutions and the Sources of Growth." *Economic Journal* 96: 903–18.

Meier, Gerald M., and Dudley Seers, eds. 1984. *Pioneers in Development.* New York: Oxford University Press.

Melbye, Mads, E. K. Nselesani, and Anne Bayley. 1986. "Evidence for Heterosexual Transmission and Clinical Manifestations of Human Immunodeficiency Virus Infection and Related Conditions in Lusaka, Zambia." *Lancet* 2: 1113–15.

Merode, Louis de. Forthcoming. "Civil Service Pay and Employment Reform in Africa: Selected Implementation Experiences." World Bank, Africa Technical Department, Washington, D.C.

Michalet, Charles Albert. 1989. "Le Rééquilibrage entre le secteur public et le secteur privé: le cas du Mexique." OECD, Paris.

Middleton, John, Adrian Ziderman, and Arvil Van Adams. 1990. "Vocational Education and Training in Developing Countries: Policies for Flexibility, Efficiency, and Quality." World Bank, Population and Human Resources Department, Washington, D.C.

Mitchell, B. R. 1983. *International Historical Statistics: The Americas and Australasia.* Detroit, Mich.: Gale Research Co.

Mitra, Pradeep, and Associates. 1991. "Adjustment in Oil Importing Developing Countries: 1973, 1979, 1990." World Bank, Asia Country Department 1, Washington, D.C.

Mody, Ashoka. 1989. *New Environment for Intellectual Property.* World Bank, Industry and Energy Department, Industry Series Working Paper 10, Washington, D.C.

Moock, Peter R., and Joanne Leslie. 1986. "Childhood Malnutrition and Schooling in the Terai Region of Nepal." *Journal of Development Economics* 20, 1: 33–52.

Moock, Peter, Philip Musgrove, and Morton Stelcner. 1989. "Education and Earnings in Peru's Informal Nonfarm Family Enterprises." PPR Working Paper 236. World Bank, Population and Human Resources Department, Washington, D.C.

Morawetz, David. 1977. *Twenty-five years of Economic Development*. Baltimore, Md.: Johns Hopkins University Press.

Morishima, Michio. 1982. *Why Has Japan "Succeeded": Western Technology and the Japanese Ethos*. Cambridge, U.K.: Cambridge University Press.

Mowery, David C., and Nathan Rosenberg. 1989. *Technology and the Pursuit of Economic Growth*. New York: Cambridge University Press.

Myers, R. H. 1990. "The Economic Development of the Republic of China on Taiwan, 1965–81." In Lau and Klein 1990.

Myrdal, Gunnar. 1956. *Development and Underdevelopment*. Cairo: National Bank of Egypt.

Nafziger, E. Wayne. 1988. "Society and the Entrepreneur." *Journal of Development Planning* 18: 127–52.

Nag, Moni. 1985. "The Impact of Social and Economic Development on Mortality: A Comparative Study of Kerala and West Bengal." In Halstead, Walsh, and Warren 1985.

Nagle, William J., and Sanjoy Ghose. 1990. "Community Participation in World Bank Supported Projects." World Bank, Strategic Planning and Review Department, Washington, D.C.

Nam, Sang-Woo. 1990. "A Sectoral Accounting Approach to National Savings Applied to Korea." *Journal of Development Economics* 33: 31–52.

Ndilu, Mibandumba. 1988. "Medical, Social, and Economic Impact of HIV Infection in a Large African Factory." Abstract 9583 (poster), Fourth International Conference on AIDS, Stockholm, Sweden.

Nehru, Jawaharlal. 1946. *The Discovery of India*. New York: John Day.

Nellis, John. 1989. "Public Enterprise Reform in Adjustment Lending." PRE Working Paper 233. World Bank, Country Economics Department, Washington, D.C.

Nelson, Joan M., ed. 1990. *Economic Crisis and Policy Choice: The Politics of Economic Adjustment in the Developing Countries*. Princeton, N.J.: Princeton University Press.

Nelson, Joan M., and John Waterbury. 1989. *Fragile Coalitions: The Politics of Economic Adjustment*. U.S.–Third World Policy Perspectives 12. New Brunswick, N.J.: Transaction.

Nishimizu, Mieko, and John M. Page, Jr. 1990. "Trade Policy, Market Orientation, and Productivity Change in Industry." In Jaime de Melo and André Sapir, eds., *Trade Theory and Economic Reform: North, South, and East*. Cambridge, Mass.: Blackwell.

Nogués, Julio. 1990. "The Role of Trade Arrangements in the Formation of Developing Countries' Trade Policies". World Bank, Latin American and Caribbean Technical Department, Washington, D.C.

North, Douglas. 1991. "Institutions." *Journal of Economic Perspectives* 5, 1: 97–112.

Nove, Alec. 1989. *An Economic History of the U.S.S.R.* 2d ed. London: Penguin Books.

Nunberg, Barbara. 1990. "Bolivia: A Review of Public Pay and Employment Issues." World Bank, Country Economics Department, Washington, D.C.

Nurske, Ragnar. 1952. "Some International Aspects of the Problem of Development." *American Economic Review: Papers and Proceedings* 42, 2: 571–82.

O'Donnell, Guillermo. 1988. "State and Alliances in Argentina, 1956–76." In Robert H. Bates, ed., *Toward a Political Economy of Development*. Berkeley: University of California Press.

OECD (Organisation for Economic Co-operation and Development). 1968. *National Accounts of Less Developed Countries 1950/66*. Paris.

———. 1980 through 1989. *Development Co-operation* (title varies; annual report). Paris.

Ohkawa, Kazushi, and Henry Rosovsky. 1973. *Japanese Economic Growth: Trend Acceleration in the Twentieth Century*. Stanford, Calif.: Stanford University Press.

Ohkawa, Kazushi, Miyohei Shinohara, and Mataji Umemura, eds. 1979. "Estimates of Long-Term Economic Statistics of Japan since 1868." In Ippei Yamazawa and Yuzo Yamamoto, eds., *Foreign Trade and Balance of Payments*. Vol. 14. Tokyo: Toyo Keizai Shinposha.

Over, Mead, and Joseph Kutzin. 1990. "The Direct and Indirect Costs of HIV Infection: Two African Case Studies." *Postgraduate Doctor Middle East* 13, 11: 632–38.

Pack, Howard, and L. E. Westphal. 1986. "Industrial Strategy and Technological Change: Theory versus Reality." *Journal of Development Economics* 21: 87–128.

Papageorgiou, Demetrios, Michael Michaely, and Armeane M. Choksi. 1990. *Liberalizing Foreign Trade in Developing Countries: Lessons of Experience*. Washington, D.C.: World Bank.

Park, Yung Chul. 1990. "Development Lessons from Asia: The Role of Government in South Korea and Taiwan." *American Economic Review: Papers and Proceedings* 80, 2: 118–21.

Perkins, Dwight. 1967. "Government as an Obstacle to Industrialization: The Case of Nineteenth Century China." *Journal of Economic History* 27: 478–92.

Pfeffermann, Guy P., and Andrea Madarassy. 1989. *Trends in Private Investment in Thirty Developing Countries.* IFC Discussion Paper 6. Washington, D.C.

Pindyck, Robert. "Irreversibility, Uncertainty, and Investment." PPR Working Paper 294. World Bank, Country Economics Department, Washington, D.C.

Pinstrup-Andersen, Per, Maurice Jarmitto, and Frances Stewart. 1987. "The Impact on Government Expenditure." In Giovanni A. Cornia and Richard Jolly, eds., *Adjustment with a Human Face.* Oxford, U.K.: Clarendon Press for UNICEF.

Polak, Jacques. 1989. *Financial Policies and Development.* Paris: Development Centre of OECD.

Pollard, Sidney. 1990. *Wealth and Poverty: An Economic History of the Twentieth Century.* New York: Oxford University Press.

Porter, Michael E. 1990. *The Competitive Advantage of Nations.* New York: Free Press.

Pradhan, B. K., D. K. Ratha, and Atul Sarma. 1990. "Complementarity between Public and Private Investment in India." *Journal of Development Economics* 33: 101–16.

Prebisch, Raul. 1959. "Commercial Policy in Underdeveloped Countries." *American Economic Review: Papers and Proceedings* 49, 2: 251–73.

Preble, Elizabeth. 1990. "The Impact of HIV/AIDS on African Children." *Social Science and Medicine* 31, 6: 671–80.

Project LINK. 1991. "World Outlook." March. Philadelphia: University of Pennsylvania.

Psacharopoulos, George. 1991. *Essays on Poverty, Equity, and Growth.* Elmsford, N.Y.: Pergamon.

Psacharopoulos, George, and Maureen Woodhall. 1985. *Education for Development: An Analysis of Investment Choices.* New York: Oxford University Press.

Ranis, Gustav, and T. Paul Schultz. 1988. *The State of Development Economics.* New York: Blackwell.

Rao, J. Mohan. 1989. "Agricultural Supply Response: A Survey." *Agricultural Economics* 3 (March): 1–22.

Reisen, Helmut. 1989. *Public Debt, External Competitiveness, and Fiscal Discipline in Developing Countries.* Princeton Studies in International Finance 66. Princeton, N.J.: Princeton University, Department of Economics.

Remmer, Karen L. 1986. "The Politics of Stabilization: IMF Stand-by Programs in Latin America, 1954–84." *Comparative Politics*, Oct.: 1–24.

Rhee, Yung Whee, and Thérèse Bélot. 1989. "Export Catalysts in Low-Income Countries." World Bank, Industry and Energy Department, Industry Series Working Paper 5, Washington, D.C.

Ribe, Helena, Soniya Carvalho, Roberto Liebenthal, Peter Nicholas, and Elaine Zuckerman. 1990. *How Adjustment Programs Can Help the Poor: The World Bank's Experience.* World Bank Discussion Paper 71. Washington, D.C.

Riboud, Michelle. 1985. "An Analysis of Women's Labor Force Participation in France: Cross-Section Estimates and Time-Series Evidence". *Journal of Labor Economics* 3, 1, part 2 (January): S177–200.

Robinson, Austin. 1975. "A Personal View." In Milo Keynes, ed., *Essays on John Maynard Keynes.* New York: Cambridge University Press.

Rodriguez, Carlos Alfredo. 1989. "Macroeconomic Policies for Structural Adjustment." PPR Working Paper 247. World Bank, Country Economics Department, Washington, D.C.

Rodrik, Dani. 1989. "Credibility of Trade Reform: A Policy Maker's Guide." *World Economy* 12, 1: 1–16.

Romer, Paul M. 1986. "Increasing Returns and Long-Run Growth." *Journal of Political Economy* 94: 1002–37.

Rosenberg, Nathan, and Claudio Frischtak, eds. 1985. *International Technology Transfer: Concepts, Measures, and Comparisons.* New York: Praeger.

Rosenstein-Rodan, Paul N. 1943. "Problems of Industrialization in Eastern and South-Eastern Europe." *Economic Journal* 53: 202–11.

Rosenzweig, Mark R. 1990. "Population Growth and Human Capital Investments: Theory and Evidence." *Journal of Political Economy* 98: 538–70.

Rosero-Bixby, Luis. 1985. "Infant Mortality Decline in Costa Rica." In Halstead, Walsh, and Warren 1985.

Rostow, W. W. 1960. *The Stages of Economic Growth.* Cambridge, U.K.: Cambridge University Press.

Roubini, Nouriel, and Jeffrey Sachs. 1989. "Government Spending and Budget Deficits in the Industrial Economies." *Economic Policy* 8: 99–127.

Sachs, Jeffrey D. 1985. *External Debt and Macroeconomic Performance in Latin America and East Asia.* Brookings Papers on Economic Activity 2. Washington, D.C.: Brookings Institution.

———. 1989. Social Conflict and Populist Policies in Latin America. NBER Working Paper 2897. Cambridge, Mass.

Schiff, Maurice, and Alberto Valdés. Forthcoming. *The Political Economy of Agricultural Pricing Policy.* Vol. 4, *A Synthesis of the Economics in Developing Countries.* Baltimore, Md.: Johns Hopkins University Press.

Schultz, T. Paul. Forthcoming. "The Benefits of Educating Women." In King and Hill, forthcoming.

Schultz, Theodore W. 1961. "Investment in Human Capital." *American Economic Review* 51, 1: 1–17.

———. 1964. *Transforming Traditional Agriculture.* New Haven, Conn.: Yale University Press.

———. 1978. *Distortions of Agricultural Incentives.* Bloomington: Indiana University Press.

Schweitzer, Julian. 1990. "Transition in Eastern Europe: The Social Dimension." *Finance & Development* 27 (Dec.): 6–8.

Scitovsky, Tibor. 1990. "Economic Development in Taiwan and South Korea, 1965–81." In Lau and Klein 1990.

Scully, Gerald W. 1988. "The Institutional Framework and Economic Development." *Journal of Political Economy* 96, 3: 652–62.

Sen, Amartya. 1983. "Development: Which Way Now?" *Economic Journal* 93 (Dec.): 745–62.

Sen, Amartya Kumar, and Jean Drèze. 1990. *Hunger and Public Action*. New York: Oxford University Press.

Serven, Luis, and Andrés Solimano. 1990. "Private Investment and Macroeconomic Adjustment. An Overview." PPR Working Paper 339. World Bank, Country Economics Department, Washington, D.C.

Shafik, Nemat. 1990. "Modeling Investment Behavior in Developing Countries. An Application to Egypt." PPR Working Paper 452. World Bank, International Economics Department, Washington, D.C.

Shihata, Ibrahim. Forthcoming. *The World Bank in a Changing World: Selected Essays.* London: Kluwer.

Shirazi, Javad Khalilzadeh, and Anwar M. Shah, eds. Forthcoming. *Tax Policy in Developing Countries.* World Bank Symposium. Washington, D.C.

Simon, Julian. 1982. *The Ultimate Resource.* Princeton, N.J.: Princeton University Press.

Singer, Hans. 1949. "Economic Progress in Underdeveloped Countries." *Social Research* 16: 1–11.

Singh, Inderjit. 1990. *The Great Ascent: The Rural Poor in South Asia.* Baltimore, Md.: Johns Hopkins University Press.

Sivard, Ruth Leger. 1988. *World Military and Social Expenditures 1987–88.* 12th ed. Washington, D.C.: World Priorities.

———. 1989. *World Military and Social Expenditures 1989.* 13th ed. Washington, D.C.: World Priorities.

Smith, James P. 1979. "The Distribution of Family Earnings." *Journal of Political Economy* 87, 5, part 2 (Oct.): S163–92.

Sokoloff, Kenneth L. 1988. "Inventive Activity in Early Industrial America: Evidence from Patent Records, 1790–1846." *Journal of Economic History* 48, 4: 813–50.

Solow, Robert M. 1957. "Technical Change and the Aggregate Production Function." *Review of Economics and Statistics* 39: 312–20.

South Commission. 1990. *The Challenge to the South.* London: Oxford University Press.

Srinivasan, T. N. 1990. "External Sector in Development: China and India, 1950–89." *American Economic Review: Papers and Proceedings* 80, 2: 113–17.

Stern, N. H. 1989. "The Economics of Development: A Survey." *Economic Journal* 99: 597–685.

Strauss, John. 1986. "Does Better Nutrition Raise Farm Productivity?" *Journal of Political Economy* 94 (April): 297–320.

Summers, Robert, and Alan Heston. 1984. "Improved International Comparisons of Real Product and Its Composition, 1950–1980." *Review of Income and Wealth* 30, 2: 207–62.

———. 1988. "A New Set of International Comparisons of Real Product and Rice Levels: Estimates for 130 Countries, 1950–1985." *Review of Income and Wealth*, March: 1–24.

———. 1991. "The Penn World Table (Mark V): An Expanded Set of International Comparisons, 1950–1988." *Quarterly Journal of Economics* 106, 2.

Sundararajan V., and Subhash Thakur. 1980. "Public Investment, Crowding Out, and Growth: A Dynamic Model Applied to India and Korea." *IMF Staff Papers* 27: 814–55.

Supple, Barry. 1971. "The State and the Industrial Revolution, 1700–1914." In Carlo M. Cipolla, ed., *The Fontana Economic History of Europe.* Vol. 3, *The Industrial Revolution.* Glasgow, U.K.: Collins.

Syrquin, Moshe, and Hollis Chenery. 1989. "Three Decades of Industrialization." *World Bank Economic Review* 3, 2: 145–81.

Tan, Jee-Peng, and Alain Mingat. 1991. "Educational Development in Asia: A Comparative Study Focusing on Cost and Financial Issues." World Bank, Asia Regional Office, Washington, D.C.

Tanzi, Vito. 1990. "The IMF and Tax Reform." IMF Working Paper 90/39. Washington, D.C.

Taylor, Charles, and David Jodice. 1983. *World Handbook of Political and Social Indicators.* New Haven, Conn.: Yale University Press.

Terrell, Katherine, and Jan Svejnar. 1990. "How Industry-Labor Relations and Government Policies Affect Senegal's Economic Performance." World Bank, Country Economics Department, Washington, D.C.

Thirsk, Wayne. 1991. "Lessons from Tax Reform: An Overview." PPR Working Paper 576. World Bank, Country Economics Department, Washington, D.C.

Thomas, Vinod, and John Nash. Forthcoming. *Best Practices in Trade Policy Reform.* New York: Oxford University Press.

Tybout, James. 1991. "Researching the Trade-Productivity Link: New Directions." PRE Discussion Paper. World Bank, Country Economics Department, Washington, D.C.

Udry, Christopher. 1990. "Credit Markets in Northern Nigeria: Credit as Insurance in a Rural Economy." *World Bank Economic Review* 4, 3: 251–70.

UNCTAD (United Nations Conference on Trade and Development). 1987. *Handbook of Trade Control Measures of Developing Countries.* Geneva.

UNDP (United Nations Development Programme). 1990. *Human Development Report 1990*. New York: Oxford University Press.

———. 1991. *Human Development Report 1991*. New York: Oxford University Press.

UNICEF (United Nations Children's Fund). 1991. *The State of the World's Children 1991*. Oxford, U.K.: Oxford University Press.

United Nations. 1982a. "Demographic Indicators of Countries: Estimates and Projections as Assessed in 1980." *Population Study* 82.

———. 1982b. "Infant Mortality: World Estimates and Projections, 1950–2025." *Population Bulletin of the United Nations* 14: 31–53.

———. 1982c. "Levels and Trends in Mortality since 1950." *Population Study* 72.

———. 1984. *1982 Yearbook of International Trade Statistics*. Vol. 2, *Trade by Commodity*. New York.

———. 1989. *1987 Demographic Yearbook*. New York.

———. 1990a. *The Global State of Hunger and Malnutrition: 1990 Report*. New York.

———. 1990b. *National Accounts Statistics*. New York.

———. 1990c. *World Population Trends and Policies: 1989 Monitoring Report*. New York.

———. 1990d. *World Resources, 1990–91*. New York: Oxford University Press.

———. 1991. *World Population Trends and Policies: 1990 Monitoring Report*. New York.

U.S. Arms Control and Disarmament Agency. 1986. *World Military Expenditures and Arms Transfers*. Washington, D.C.: U.S. Government Printing Office.

U.S. Congress, Office of Technology Assessment. 1990. *Worker Training: Competing in the New International Economy*. Washington, D.C.: U.S. Government Printing Office.

———. 1991. *Energy in Developing Countries*. Washington, D.C.: U.S. Government Printing Office.

U.S. Department of Commerce, Bureau of the Census. 1975. *Historical Statistics from Colonial Times to the Present*. Washington, D.C.: U.S. Government Printing Office.

———. 1990. *Statistical Abstract of the United States*. Washington, D.C.: U.S. Government Printing Office.

U.S. Department of Health and Human Services. 1989. *Vital and Health Statistics* (Current Estimates from the National Health Interview Survey, 1988). Washington, D.C.: National Center for Health Statistics.

van der Gaag, Jacques, and Wim Vijverberg. 1987. "Wage Determinants in Côte d'Ivoire: Experience, Credentials, and Human Capital." *Economic Development and Cultural Change* 37, 2 (January): 371–81.

Vanhanen, Tatu. 1979. *Power and the Means of Power*. Ann Arbor, Mich.: University Microfilms International.

———. 1990. *The Process of Democratization*. New York: Taylor and Francis.

van Wijnbergen, Sweder. 1990. "Mexico's External Debt Restructuring in 1989–90." PPR Working Paper 424. World Bank, Latin America and the Caribbean Country Department II. Washington, D.C.

Villanueva, Delano, and Abbas Mirakhor. 1990. "Interest Rate Policies, Stabilization, and Bank Supervision in Developing Countries: Strategies for Financial Reforms." IMF Working Paper 90/8. Washington, D.C.

Walter, Ingo. 1972. "Nontariff Protection among Industrial Countries: Some Preliminary Evidence." *Economia Internazionale* 25: 335–54.

Webb, Steven B., and Karim Shariff. 1990. "Designing and Implementing Adjustment Programs." World Bank, Country Economics Department, Washington, D.C.

Weede, Erich. 1983. "The Impact of Democracy on Economic Growth: Some Evidence from Cross-National Analysis." *Kykloos* 36, 1: 21–39.

WEFA Group. 1991. *World Economic Outlook*. Vol. 1. Philadelphia, Pa.

Westphal, Larry E. 1990. "Industrial Policy in an Export-Propelled Economy: Lessons from South Korea's Experience." *Journal of Economic Perspectives* 4, 3: 41–59.

Wheeler, David. 1984. *Human Resource Policies, Economic Growth, and Demographic Change in Developing Countries*. Oxford, U.K.: Clarendon Press.

Wheeler, David, William Cole, and Lisana Irianiwati. 1990. "Made in Bali: A Tale of Indonesian Export Success." World Bank, International Economics Department, Washington, D.C.

WHO (World Health Organization). 1989. *1989 World Health Statistics*. Geneva.

———. 1991. "Current and Future Dimensions of the HIV/AIDS Pandemic: A Capsule Summary." GPA/SFI. Geneva.

Winkler, Donald R. 1989. "Decentralization in Education: An Economic Perspective." PRE Working Paper 143. World Bank, Population and Human Resources Department, Washington, D.C.

Wolf, Martin. 1987. "Differential and More Favorable Treatment of Developing Countries and the International Trading System." *World Bank Economic Review* 1, 4: 647–68.

World Bank. 1987. "Tanzania: An Agenda for Industrial Recovery." Southern Africa Department, Washington, D.C.

———. 1988. *Adjustment Lending: An Evaluation of Ten Years of Experience*. Policy and Research Series 1. Washington, D.C.

———. 1989a. *India: An Industrializing Economy in Transition*. Country Study. Washington, D.C.

———. 1989b. *Project Performance Results for 1987.* Operations Evaluation Study. Washington, D.C.

———. 1989c. ''Strengthening Trade Policy Reform.'' Country Economics Department, Washington, D.C.

———. 1989d. *Sub-Saharan Africa: From Crisis to Sustainable Growth.* Washington, D.C.

———. 1990a. *Agricultural Extension: The Next Step.* Agriculture and Rural Development Department, Policy and Research Series 13. Washington, D.C.

———. 1990b. *Adjustment Lending Policies for Sustainable Growth.* Policy and Research Series 14. Washington, D.C.

———. 1990d. *World Debt Tables, 1990-91 Edition: External Debt of Developing Countries.* Washington, D.C.

———. 1990e. *World Tables, 1989–90 Edition.* Baltimore, Md.: Johns Hopkins University Press.

———. 1991a. *Global Economic Prospects and the Developing Countries.* 1991 edition. Washington, D.C.

———. 1991b. *Price Prospects for Major Primary Commodities.* Washington, D.C.

———. Various years. *World Development Report.* New York: Oxford University Press.

World Institute for Development Economics Research. Various years. *Research for Action.* Helsinki.

Statistical appendix

The tables in this statistical appendix present summary data on population, national accounts, trade, and external debt of low- and middle-income economies, high-income economies, and the world as a group. Readers should refer to the "Definitions and data notes" for an explanation of the country groups and to the technical notes of the World Development Indicators for definitions of the concepts used.

Table A.1 Population (mid-year) and average annual growth

	Population (millions)				Average annual growth (percent)			
Country group	1965	1973	1980	1990	1965–73	1973–80	1980–90	1990–2000[a]
Low- and middle-income economies	2,394	2,911	3,370	4,138	2.5	2.1	2.1	1.9
Low-income economies	1,743	2,129	2,456	3,013	2.5	2.0	2.1	1.9
Middle-income economies	650	782	914	1,125	2.3	2.3	2.1	1.9
Severely indebted middle-income economies	323	392	459	565	2.4	2.3	2.1	1.8
Sub-Saharan Africa	244	301	364	496	2.6	2.7	3.2	3.2
East Asia	972	1,195	1,346	1,580	2.6	1.7	1.6	1.4
South Asia	645	781	922	1,156	2.4	2.4	2.3	1.9
Europe, Middle East, and North Africa	273	315	361	440	1.8	2.0	2.0	2.0
Latin America and the Caribbean	240	295	349	430	2.6	2.4	2.1	1.8
High-income economies	680	736	780	835	1.0	0.8	0.7	0.6
OECD members	649	698	733	776	0.9	0.7	0.6	0.5
Other economies	254	277	296	324	1.1	1.0	0.9	0.7
World	3,328	3,924	4,446	5,298	2.1	1.8	1.8	1.6
Oil exporters (excluding USSR)	127	158	197	274	2.8	3.1	3.4	3.1

a. Projections. For the assumptions used in the projections, see the technical notes for Table 26 in the World Development Indicators.

Table A.2 GNP, population, GNP per capita, and growth of GNP per capita

Country group	1989 GNP (billions of dollars)	1989 population (millions)	1989 GNP per capita (dollars)	Average annual growth of GNP per capita (percent) 1965–73	1973–80	1980–89	1988	1989	1990[a]
Low- and middle-income economies	3,232	4,053	800	4.2	2.5	1.5	1.4	1.4	0.0
Low-income economies	981	2,948	330	2.4	2.1	4.1	3.4	3.3	3.2
Middle-income economies	2,253	1,105	2,040	5.2	2.3	0.5	0.6	0.6	-1.1
Severely indebted middle-income economies	958	554	1,720	4.8	2.9	-0.3	-0.7	-1.3	-3.4
Sub-Saharan Africa	162	480	340	1.7	0.6	-1.2	-3.1	0.0	. .
East Asia	841	1,552	540	5.2	4.7	6.3	9.5	2.2	6.4
South Asia	367	1,131	320	1.2	1.9	2.9	6.7	0.0	3.1
Europe, Middle East, and North Africa	944	433	2,180	. .	1.8	0.4	0.0	-0.5	. .
Latin America and the Caribbean	823	421	1,950	4.7	2.3	-0.5	-1.7	-1.2	-2.4
High-income economies	15,230	831	18,330	3.7	2.3	2.3	3.7	2.7	2.1
OECD members	14,748	773	19,090	3.8	2.3	2.4	3.7	2.8	2.1
Other economies	. .	323	. .	. .	. .	. .	. .	. .	. .
World	20,736	5,206	3,980	2.8	1.5	1.2	2.4	1.5	1.7
Oil exporters (excluding USSR)	478	553	. .	6.0	1.0	-2.5	-2.1	-1.1	. .

a. Preliminary data.

Table A.3 Composition of GDP
(billions of dollars)

Country group and indicator	1965	1973	1980	1985	1986	1987	1988	1989	1990[a]
Low- and middle-income economies									
GDP	389	867	2,430	2,550	2,655	2,745	3,030	3,303	3,476
Total consumption	309	660	1,807	1,938	2,024	2,051	2,237	2,451	. .
Gross domestic investment	80	201	657	604	653	679	781	859	. .
Net exports	0	6	-34	8	-22	16	12	-6	. .
Low-income economies									
GDP	169	315	790	828	793	821	931	996	974
Total consumption	138	241	588	632	602	605	683	736	. .
Gross domestic investment	32	71	202	223	220	234	272	283	. .
Net exports	-1	3	0	-28	-29	-17	-25	-23	. .
Middle-income economies									
GDP	215	549	1,640	1,722	1,862	1,924	2,099	2,308	. .
Total consumption	167	415	1,218	1,304	1,424	1,448	1,555	1,716	. .
Gross domestic investment	46	129	456	380	432	445	509	576	. .
Net exports	2	5	-34	37	6	31	36	16	. .
Severely indebted middle-income economies									
GDP	114	290	810	788	810	850	962	1,091	1,210
Total consumption	89	228	624	606	643	656	733	842	. .
Gross domestic investment	24	61	205	151	155	178	210	226	. .
Net exports	1	0	-19	30	12	16	19	23	. .
Sub-Saharan Africa									
GDP	31	69	225	198	168	151	164	171	180
Total consumption	26	55	177	172	148	129	143	146	152
Gross domestic investment	4	12	45	24	25	24	26	26	28
Net exports	0	1	3	1	-5	-2	-4	-1	-0
East Asia									
GDP	91	206	547	589	585	644	780	895	892
Total consumption	70	148	379	406	395	416	504	588	. .
Gross domestic investment	20	56	166	191	189	212	262	307	. .
Net exports	1	2	1	-9	1	16	14	1	. .

Table A.3 *(continued)*

Country group and indicator	1965	1973	1980	1985	1986	1987	1988	1989	1990[a]
South Asia									
GDP	69	97	220	277	295	328	350	351	374
Total consumption	60	81	184	225	239	268	285	289	313
Gross domestic investment	12	17	49	65	67	71	79	76	79
Net exports	-2	-1	-12	-13	-12	-11	-14	-13	-17
Europe, Middle East, and North Africa									
GDP	81	206	644	749	858	810	808	828	. .
Total consumption	62	148	463	566	652	614	590	598	. .
Gross domestic investment	18	52	200	191	240	206	219	242	. .
Net exports	1	6	-18	-8	-33	-10	-0	-12	. .
Latin America and the Caribbean									
GDP	100	254	714	681	689	731	838	964	. .
Total consumption	78	201	550	528	551	563	641	746	. .
Gross domestic investment	20	54	173	121	122	149	175	188	. .
Net exports	1	-0	-10	33	16	19	22	30	. .
High-income economies									
GDP	1,434	3,401	8,096	9,156	11,130	12,924	14,504	15,021	. .
Total consumption	1,185	2,595	6,256	7,321	8,848	10,224	11,302	11,658	. .
Gross domestic investment	240	774	1,787	1,802	2,211	2,640	3,130	3,286	. .
Net exports	9	27	-9	23	71	51	67	63	. .
OECD members									
GDP	1,413	3,335	7,775	8,835	10,804	12,541	14,073	14,537	. .
Total consumption	1,169	2,551	6,076	7,079	8,592	9,934	10,977	11,298	. .
Gross domestic investment	235	757	1,707	1,733	2,141	2,557	3,029	3,176	. .
Net exports	9	27	-9	23	71	51	67	63	. .
Other economies									
GDP	. .	. .	. .	. .	. .	. .	. .	. .	. .
Total consumption	. .	. .	. .	. .	. .	. .	. .	. .	. .
Gross domestic investment	. .	. .	. .	. .	. .	. .	. .	. .	. .
Net exports	. .	. .	. .	. .	. .	. .	. .	. .	. .
World									
GDP	2,044	4,790	11,796	13,067	15,411	17,522	19,570	20,443	. .
Total consumption	1,678	3,658	9,087	10,334	12,164	13,748	15,126	15,736	. .
Gross domestic investment	358	1,098	2,738	2,696	3,210	3,720	4,385	4,658	. .
Net exports	8	35	-29	37	37	55	59	49	. .
Oil exporters (excluding USSR)									
GDP	35	109	550	609	582	460	466	465	. .
Total consumption	25	66	320	475	469	344	352	330	. .
Gross domestic investment	7	26	143	118	139	105	112	112	. .
Net exports	3	16	87	16	-26	11	2	23	. .

Note: Components may not sum to totals because of rounding. Net exports include goods and nonfactor services.   a. Preliminary data.

Table A.4 Consumption, investment, and saving
(percentage of GDP)

Country group and indicator	1965	1973	1980	1985	1987	1988	1989
Low- and middle-income economies							
Total consumption	79.5	76.1	74.4	76.0	74.7	73.8	74.2
Gross domestic investment	20.5	23.2	27.0	23.7	24.7	25.8	26.0
Gross national savings	18.8	21.7	23.9	21.1	22.6	23.5	22.9
Low-income economies							
Total consumption	81.5	76.7	74.4	76.4	73.7	73.4	73.9
Gross domestic investment	19.0	22.5	25.5	26.9	28.4	29.2	28.5
Gross national savings	18.1	21.0	24.6	22.4	24.9	25.1	24.5
Middle-income economies							
Total consumption	77.7	75.6	74.3	75.8	75.2	74.1	74.4
Gross domestic investment	21.5	23.5	27.8	22.1	23.1	24.2	24.9
Gross national savings	19.5	22.2	23.6	20.5	21.5	22.7	..
Severely indebted middle-income economies							
Total consumption	78.2	78.8	77.0	76.9	77.2	76.2	77.2
Gross domestic investment	20.8	21.1	25.3	19.2	20.9	21.9	20.7
Gross national savings	18.9	18.6	20.2	17.6	18.2	19.4	17.6
Sub-Saharan Africa							
Total consumption	84.8	80.1	78.6	87.2	85.7	87.0	85.7
Gross domestic investment	13.9	17.8	20.0	12.1	15.9	15.7	15.1
Gross national savings	13.0	16.1	18.0	9.4	9.8	7.7	8.9
East Asia							
Total consumption	77.0	71.9	69.4	69.0	64.6	64.5	65.6
Gross domestic investment	22.3	27.2	30.4	32.5	33.0	33.6	34.2
Gross national savings	22.8	25.5	29.4	29.2	33.7	34.0	33.1
South Asia							
Total consumption	86.0	83.6	83.4	81.2	81.9	81.5	82.2
Gross domestic investment	16.8	17.0	22.0	23.6	21.6	22.5	21.6
Gross national savings	13.5	16.0	16.7	17.9	17.1	17.3	16.5
Europe, Middle East, and North Africa							
Total consumption	76.3	71.9	71.8	75.6	75.8	73.0	72.2
Gross domestic investment	22.4	25.2	31.0	25.5	25.4	27.1	29.2
Gross national savings	18.9	25.2	26.9	22.4	22.2	25.0	..
Latin America and the Caribbean							
Total consumption	78.6	78.9	77.1	77.5	77.0	76.5	77.4
Gross domestic investment	20.3	21.2	24.3	17.7	20.4	20.9	19.5
Gross national savings	19.0	19.0	20.4	17.2	18.4	18.9	17.2
High-income economies							
Total consumption	82.7	76.3	77.3	80.0	79.1	77.9	77.6
Gross domestic investment	16.7	22.7	22.1	19.7	20.4	21.6	21.9
Gross national savings	17.7	24.1	23.3	20.5	21.1	22.2	22.6
OECD members							
Total consumption	82.8	76.5	78.2	80.1	79.2	78.0	77.7
Gross domestic investment	16.6	22.7	22.0	19.6	20.4	21.5	21.8
Gross national savings	17.7	24.1	22.4	20.2	20.9	22.1	22.4
Other economies							
Total consumption	..	..	..	..	..	..	..
Gross domestic investment	..	..	..	..	..	..	..
Gross national savings	..	..	..	..	..	..	..
World							
Total consumption	82.0	76.3	76.6	79.1	78.5	77.3	77.1
Gross domestic investment	17.5	22.9	23.2	20.6	21.2	22.3	22.6
Gross national savings	17.9	23.7	23.4	20.6	21.3	22.3	22.5
Oil exporters (excl. USSR)							
Total consumption	72.1	61.1	58.2	78.0	74.8	75.5	71.0
Gross domestic investment	20.1	24.2	25.9	19.4	22.9	24.1	24.1
Gross national savings	19.9	33.7	41.1	22.8	26.5	24.2	..

Table A.5 Investment, saving, and current account balance before official transfers
(percentage of GNP)

Country	Gross domestic investment			Gross national savings			Balance of payments: current account balance (before official transfers)		
	1965–73	1973–80	1980–89	1965–73[a]	1973–80	1980–89	1965–73	1973–80	1980–89
Latin America and the Caribbean									
*Argentina	19.7	23.4	15.5	20.1	. .	15.5	0.4	. .	−4.3
*Bolivia	25.4	24.9	12.2	21.3	18.5	12.2	−4.1	−6.4	−10.2
*Brazil	21.3	24.0	21.5	19.1	19.3	21.5	−2.1	−4.6	−1.8
*Chile	14.3	17.3	18.1	11.9	12.1	18.1	−2.4	−5.2	−8.4
Colombia	18.9	18.8	20.4	15.8	19.0	20.4	−3.2	0.2	−3.0
*Costa Rica	21.8	25.5	27.4	13.0	13.8	27.4	−8.8	−11.7	−10.3
*Ecuador	19.0	26.7	23.2	12.7	21.2	23.2	−6.2	−5.5	−6.6
Guatemala	13.3	18.7	13.5	11.6	16.4	13.5	−1.7	−2.3	−4.2
*Honduras	18.6	24.9	17.0	14.0	14.7	7.4	−4.6	−10.2	−9.6
Jamaica	32.0	20.2	25.2	23.7	13.6	25.2	−8.4	−6.6	−10.2
*Mexico	20.6	24.2	23.1	14.9	20.2	23.1	−5.7	−4.0	−1.8
*Peru	24.1	23.9	26.2	20.9	19.7	26.2	−3.2	−4.2	−4.2
*Uruguay	12.0	15.7	12.3	12.0	11.3	12.3	−0.0	−4.4	−2.3
*Venezuela	31.1	34.2	22.0	31.9	35.8	22.0	0.8	1.6	1.6
Sub-Saharan Africa									
Cameroon	16.6	21.8	23.7	. .	17.0	23.7	. .	−4.8	−4.6
*Congo, People's Rep.	29.3	34.0	*38.2*	4.2	10.4	*38.2*	−25.2	−23.6	*−13.8*
*Côte d'Ivoire	22.8	29.1	18.3	. .	16.8	18.3	. .	−12.3	−11.0
Ethiopia	12.8	9.5	12.8	11.0	6.9	12.8	−1.8	−2.5	−7.5
Ghana	12.3	8.7	. .	8.7	6.9	. .	−3.6	−1.8	−5.2
Kenya	22.6	26.0	25.4	17.2	16.3	25.4	−5.5	−9.7	−7.4
Liberia	19.1	28.7	. .	. .	27.5	. .	. .	−1.2	. .
Malawi	20.0	29.6	19.2	. .	10.8	19.2	. .	−18.8	−13.0
Niger	9.7	23.8	15.8	. .	10.0	15.8	. .	−13.8	−13.3
Nigeria	16.3	22.8	13.8	11.8	24.4	13.8	−4.5	1.6	−1.4
*Senegal	14.7	17.5	16.0	. .	4.2	16.0	. .	−13.3	−14.8
Sierra Leone	13.8	14.1	13.4	9.7	−1.0	. .	−4.1	−15.1	. .
Sudan	11.9	16.3	13.0	11.0	9.6	13.0	−0.9	−6.8	−10.2
Tanzania	19.9	23.9	. .	17.1	14.1	. .	−2.8	−9.8	−9.7
Zaire	9.8	9.7	9.4	14.2	5.3	9.4	4.5	−4.4	−7.0
Zambia	31.9	28.5	17.2	34.3	19.9	17.2	2.4	−8.6	−12.2
East Asia									
Indonesia	15.8	24.5	30.4	13.7	24.6	30.4	−2.1	0.1	−2.8
Korea, Rep.	23.9	31.2	31.2	17.6	25.9	31.2	−6.3	−5.3	1.6
Malaysia	22.3	28.7	32.2	22.6	29.4	32.2	0.2	0.6	−2.9
Papua New Guinea	27.8	22.0	26.2	. .	11.7	26.2	. .	−10.3	−20.7
*Philippines	20.6	29.1	21.7	19.7	24.3	21.7	−1.0	−4.8	−4.1
Thailand	24.3	26.9	26.7	22.1	21.9	26.7	−2.1	−5.0	−4.1
South Asia									
India	17.2	21.3	23.9	15.8	21.0	23.9	−1.4	−0.3	−2.4
Pakistan	16.1	17.5	18.8	. .	11.7	18.8	. .	−5.8	−4.0
Sri Lanka	15.8	20.6	25.8	11.2	13.4	25.8	−4.6	−7.2	−10.2
Europe, Middle East, and North Africa									
Algeria	32.6	44.6	35.2	30.5	39.0	35.2	−2.2	−5.6	−0.8
*Egypt, Arab Rep.	14.0	29.3	27.9	9.3	18.2	27.9	−4.7	−11.1	−11.7
*Hungary	. .	32.0	*27.9*	. .	32.0	27.9	. .	. .	. .
*Morocco	15.1	25.9	25.3	13.6	16.8	25.3	−1.5	−9.0	−6.1
*Poland	. .	. .	*28.3*	. .	. .	28.3	. .	−5.6	−2.9
Portugal	26.6	29.7	30.4	. .	29.7	30.4	. .	. .	. .
Tunisia	23.3	29.9	27.5	17.8	23.2	27.5	−5.5	−6.7	−5.6
Turkey	18.5	21.8	22.8	16.0	18.1	22.8	−2.5	−3.7	−2.1
Yugoslavia	29.9	35.6	38.2	27.1	32.9	38.2	−2.7	−2.7	. .

Note: Asterisks indicate severely indebted middle-income economies. Figures in italics are for years other than specified.   a. Excludes transfers, 1965–69.

Table A.6 GDP and growth rates

Country group	1989 GDP (billions of dollars)	Average annual growth of GDP (percent)						
		1965–73	1973–80	1980–89	1987	1988	1989	1990[a]
Low- and middle-income economies	3,303	6.5	4.7	3.8	3.8	4.3	2.9	2.3
Low-income economies	996	5.3	4.5	6.2	5.9	8.1	4.1	4.5
Middle-income economies	2,308	7.0	4.7	2.9	2.9	2.7	2.4	1.1
Severely indebted middle-income economies	1,091	6.4	5.2	1.9	2.8	1.3	1.3	–1.6
Sub-Saharan Africa	171	4.8	3.2	2.1	0.2	2.9	2.9	1.5
East Asia	895	8.1	6.6	7.9	8.9	9.7	5.5	6.7
South Asia	351	3.6	4.2	5.1	4.3	8.2	4.5	4.2
Europe, Middle East, and North Africa	828	7.7	3.9	2.9	1.2	2.1	1.5	–0.8
Latin America and the Caribbean	964	6.5	5.0	1.6	3.1	0.5	1.3	–0.7
High-income economies	15,021	4.8	3.1	3.0	3.5	4.4	3.4	2.6
OECD members	14,537	4.7	3.0	3.0	3.4	4.4	3.3	2.6
Other economies	..	..	..	..	..	..	..	..
World	20,443	5.0	3.3	3.1	3.5	4.4	3.3	2.5
Oil exporters (excluding USSR)	..	8.3	3.7	0.8	–0.3	2.5	2.2	..

a. Preliminary data.

Table A.7 Structure of production
(percentage of GDP)

Country group	1965		1973		1980		1985		1987		1988		1989[a]	
	Agri- culture	Indus- try	Agri- culture	Indus- try	Agri- culture	Indus- try	Agri- culture	Indus- try	Agri- culture	Indus- try	Agri- culture	Indus- try	Agri- culture	Indus- try
Low- and middle-income economies	31	31	24	34	19	38	19	36	18	36	18	36	19	38
Low-income economies	44	28	38	32	33	37	33	33	31	33	31	34	32	37
Middle-income economies	19	34	15	35	12	39	12	37	13	37	12	37	12	36
Severely indebted middle-income economies	17	33	14	33	11	37	11	36	11	36	11	36	..	..
Sub-Saharan Africa	41	20	31	25	28	32	33	26	30	25	31	24	32	27
East Asia	42	35	35	40	29	44	27	41	25	42	24	43	24	44
South Asia	44	21	43	19	35	22	31	24	29	24	30	23	32	26
Europe, Middle East, and North Africa	..	..	16		13	41	14	37	15	37	15	35	15	..
Latin America and the Caribbean	16	33	12	33	10	37	10	37	10	37	10	37	..	..
High-income economies	5	42	4	37	3	37	3	34	3	31	..	..	..	..
OECD members	5	43	4	37	3	36	3	34	3	31	..	..	..	..
Other economies	..	..	..	..	..	..	..	..	..	..	..	..	..	..
World	10	40	8	37	7	37	6	35	5	32	..	..	..	..
Oil exporters (excluding USSR)	..	..	13	48	10	54	14	38	13	35	14	35	14	35

a. Preliminary data.

Table A.8 GDP by sector growth rates
(average annual percentage change)

Country group	Agriculture			Industry			Services		
	1965–73	1973–80	1980–89	1965–73	1973–80	1980–89	1965–73	1973–80	1980–89
Low- and middle-income economies	3.1	2.5	3.3	8.3	4.9	4.5	7.3	6.4	3.5
Low-income economies	2.9	2.1	4.0	8.8	6.6	8.6	5.8	5.5	6.2
Middle-income economies	3.3	3.0	2.6	8.1	4.4	3.0	7.7	6.6	2.8
Severely indebted middle-income economies	2.8	3.2	2.1	7.4	5.9	1.5	7.3	5.9	1.9
Sub-Saharan Africa	2.4	1.1	2.0	10.4	4.3	0.7	3.4	4.2	2.3
East Asia	3.2	2.5	5.2	12.4	9.4	10.4	9.8	7.2	7.7
South Asia	3.1	2.2	2.9	3.9	5.5	6.7	4.0	5.3	6.3
Europe, Middle East, and North Africa	. .	. .	2.9	. .	. .	3.1	. .	. .	2.7
Latin America and the Caribbean	2.8	3.3	1.9	7.5	5.4	1.6	7.5	5.8	1.6
High-income economies	. .	−2.3	1.5	10.9	1.9	2.1	12.6	0.7	3.1
OECD members	. .	−2.5	1.3	10.9	1.7	2.2	12.6	0.6	3.1
Other economies	. .	. .	. .	. .	. .	. .	. .	. .	. .
World	2.4	0.2	2.6	10.6	2.3	2.4	12.1	1.2	3.2
Oil exporters (excluding USSR)	4.1	2.7	5.4	9.8	1.4	−1.1	7.9	9.8	1.9

Table A.9 Growth of export volume
(average annual percentage change)

Country and commodity group	1965–73	1973–80	1980–87	1987	1988	1989
Low- and middle-income economies	5.1	3.5	4.6	10.9	9.8	4.9
Primary goods	4.0	1.2	2.8	4.1	4.1	2.7
Food	2.5	4.9	3.4	11.6	−5.1	. .
Fuels	5.3	−0.8	1.8	−4.2	7.2	. .
Nonfood primary	2.4	3.1	0.3	−3.1	8.6	. .
Metals and minerals	5.4	7.3	1.3	8.6	−0.4	. .
Manufactures	10.9	13.0	7.0	20.4	14.7	2.4
Low-income economies	10.4	3.5	4.2	7.7	9.1	6.0
Primary goods	12.7	1.4	0.8	−3.2	0.1	5.1
Food	0.6	3.9	3.7	7.1	−3.3	. .
Fuels	23.6	−0.1	−0.5	−7.0	6.3	. .
Nonfood primary	6.4	2.6	−0.3	−10.0	−4.9	. .
Metals and minerals	6.6	5.6	−1.6	10.7	−5.7	. .
Manufactures	. .	10.3	10.2	21.6	18.9	8.6
Middle-income economies	3.9	3.5	4.7	11.9	10.0	4.5
Primary goods	2.1	1.2	3.6	6.7	5.6	1.9
Food	3.0	5.3	3.3	13.1	−5.6	. .
Fuels	1.8	−1.2	2.9	−2.9	7.7	. .
Nonfood primary	1.3	3.2	0.6	−0.5	13.7	. .
Metals and minerals	5.0	8.1	2.2	8.1	1.1	. .
Manufactures	14.7	13.9	6.0	20.0	13.2	. .
Severely indebted middle-income economies	0.6	2.8	3.6	8.2	12.1	−0.6
Primary goods	−1.4	0.9	2.5	4.1	. .	−1.4
Manufactures	15.6	10.9	7.4	20.7	23.9	−4.9
Sub-Saharan Africa	14.2	−0.2	−1.8	6.0	2.7	0.9
Primary goods	14.7	−0.8	−2.0	2.4	4.4	. .
Manufactures	5.8	9.7	2.4	28.4	−9.2	. .
East Asia	10.6	9.4	9.6	13.2	11.4	6.3
Primary goods	8.4	5.0	4.6	−3.3	−0.8	. .
Manufactures	28.3	17.1	13.8	25.0	18.2	0.7
South Asia	−0.2	4.5	5.4	12.0	6.8	10.6
Primary goods	−1.9	2.1	3.7	−5.3	−2.2	. .
Manufactures	1.1	6.3	6.2	22.8	11.1	. .

Table A.9 Growth of export volume (continued)

Country and commodity group	1965–73	1973–80	1980–87	1987	1988	1989
Europe, Middle East, and North Africa	..	-0.6	4.8	11.2	10.4	3.0
Primary goods	..	..	..	..	..	..
Manufactures	..	..	..	..	..	..
Latin America and the Caribbean	-0.4	2.2	3.4	9.0	10.5	2.0
Primary goods	-1.9	0.2	2.3	5.6	4.9	4.5
Manufactures	16.7	9.5	6.1	17.1	25.0	-4.6
High-income economies	10.1	5.2	3.4	5.0	5.7	2.4
Primary goods	8.8	3.8	1.4	4.0	-1.3	-0.4
Food	6.2	8.0	4.3	17.5	-2.5	..
Fuels	13.4	1.0	-2.7	-9.4	10.1	..
Nonfood primary	4.2	4.7	3.3	2.9	-11.8	..
Metals and minerals	8.2	9.8	1.6	-2.4	-12.9	..
Manufactures	10.7	5.6	4.0	5.3	7.6	2.8
OECD members	9.5	5.4	3.8	5.5	5.2	2.1
Primary goods	5.7	6.4	4.1	10.5	-4.0	-0.9
Food	6.2	8.0	4.2	17.8	-2.5	..
Fuels	8.4	3.7	4.5	5.5	3.7	..
Nonfood primary	2.9	6.2	3.6	4.5	-11.6	..
Metals and minerals	8.2	9.7	1.5	-3.1	-13.9	..
Manufactures	10.6	5.2	3.7	4.4	7.5	2.7
Other economies	..	..	..	..	..	..
World	9.2	4.9	3.6	6.0	6.4	2.8
Primary goods	6.9	2.8	1.9	4.0	0.4	0.4
Food	4.9	7.0	4.1	15.8	-3.2	..
Fuels	9.8	0.3	-1.2	-7.6	9.1	..
Nonfood primary	3.7	4.1	2.5	1.2	-6.4	..
Metals and minerals	7.3	9.1	1.6	0.6	-9.3	..
Manufactures	10.7	6.2	4.2	6.7	8.3	2.7
Oil exporters (excl. USSR)	8.2	-1.8	-6.2	-9.6	17.7	7.3
Primary goods	8.2	-1.1	-6.8	-9.9	17.4	..
Food	-5.6	-5.7	-1.7	-26.3	17.7	..
Fuels	8.8	-0.8	-7.5	-17.0	15.5	..
Nonfood primary	6.6	-2.5	-19.8	32.7	42.2	..
Metals and minerals	..	8.3	1.6	20.6	-10.0	..
Manufactures	..	15.5	6.5	-3.9	22.4	..

Table A.10 Change in export prices and terms of trade
(average annual percentage change)

Country group	1965–73	1973–80	1980–87	1987	1988	1989
Export prices						
Low- and middle-income economies	6.1	14.7	-4.6	8.5	3.0	2.1
Primary goods	5.8	18.5	-6.9	9.5	0.4	..
Food	5.9	8.3	-2.7	-7.4	15.1	..
Fuels	9.0	29.5	-9.7	23.4	-14.3	..
Nonfood primary	3.1	9.8	-3.9	22.6	20.1	..
Metals and minerals	2.7	4.0	-3.3	11.7	31.6	..
Manufactures	5.8	6.8	-0.9	6.0	6.5	5.6
High-income OECD members	4.8	10.3	0.4	11.8	8.4	5.3
Primary goods	6.1	8.6	-4.1	3.7	16.0	8.2
Food	6.1	5.1	-3.5	-1.4	17.0	..
Fuels	6.7	19.4	-6.8	-1.8	-11.1	..
Nonfood primary	4.3	6.7	-3.1	9.6	26.0	..
Metals and minerals	2.2	4.6	-2.4	19.0	47.5	..
Manufactures	4.6	10.7	1.8	13.9	6.5	4.7
Terms of trade						
Low- and middle-income economies	0.1	2.1	-3.7	0.3	-2.0	0.9
Middle-income economies	1.0	1.9	-3.8	0.2	-2.0	0.2
Severely indebted middle-income economies	2.8	0.5	-2.8	0.5	-1.2	8.0
Sub-Saharan Africa	-6.7	5.4	-5.7	0.6	-5.4	1.2
East Asia	3.3	0.3	-2.3	-0.5	1.2	2.5
South Asia	3.3	-3.1	1.3	0.6	1.8	-1.8
Europe, Middle East, and North Africa	..	5.7	-4.3	3.3	-9.7	-6.0
Latin America and the Caribbean	3.1	1.2	-3.9	-3.9	2.2	7.2
High-income economies	-1.3	-2.2	0.3	-0.1	0.0	-0.1
OECD members	-1.1	-3.3	1.4	-0.4	0.5	-0.4
Other economies	..	..	..	..	..	..
World	-0.9	-1.5	-0.4	0.1	-0.4	0.1
Oil exporters (excl. USSR)	..	13.5	-9.0	21.1	-22.5	6.6

Table A.11 Growth of long-term debt of low- and middle-income economies
(average annual percentage change, nominal)

Country group	1970–73	1973–80	1980–87	1988	1989	1990
Low- and middle-income economies						
Debt outstanding and disbursed	17.9	22.6	15.0	−2.1	−0.1	5.0
Official	15.2	18.0	18.5	0.8	4.0	12.1
Private	20.7	26.1	12.9	−4.4	−3.5	−1.4
Low-income economies						
Debt outstanding and disbursed	16.7	16.5	18.3	5.5	5.5	8.8
Official	14.7	14.1	17.5	4.3	6.8	12.0
Private	26.0	23.8	20.0	7.7	3.3	2.8
Middle-income economies						
Debt outstanding and disbursed	18.4	24.7	14.2	−4.6	−2.2	3.5
Official	15.6	21.2	19.1	−1.2	2.3	12.2
Private	20.0	26.5	12.0	−6.6	−5.0	−2.4
Severely indebted middle-income economies						
Debt outstanding and disbursed	16.8	25.2	16.2	−4.8	−2.4	3.5
Official	12.6	22.0	25.4	0.1	3.5	17.9
Private	18.6	26.5	12.9	−7.6	−6.1	−6.2
Sub-Saharan Africa						
Debt outstanding and disbursed	20.1	23.9	18.1	1.7	4.2	10.7
Official	17.1	22.4	22.0	2.1	8.7	14.2
Private	25.5	26.2	12.6	0.9	−5.1	2.4
East Asia						
Debt outstanding and disbursed	23.4	22.7	17.9	−0.7	−0.0	6.7
Official	26.5	17.9	20.3	1.7	1.4	13.4
Private	20.7	26.6	16.5	−2.5	−1.1	1.4
South Asia						
Debt outstanding and disbursed	11.6	11.2	15.5	5.9	7.9	8.9
Official	12.3	10.4	12.1	4.1	6.5	8.7
Private	1.5	24.5	33.9	11.4	11.8	9.6
Europe, Middle East, and North Africa						
Debt outstanding and disbursed	22.3	31.1	13.4	−2.0	1.1	8.7
Official	16.3	26.7	17.3	−2.4	1.4	11.8
Private	32.2	35.8	9.7	−1.5	0.8	5.1
Latin America and the Caribbean						
Debt outstanding and disbursed	16.8	21.6	14.3	−5.6	−4.2	−1.3
Official	11.6	15.2	21.3	1.2	3.8	12.1
Private	18.9	23.5	12.7	−7.9	−7.2	−7.0

Table A.12 Composition of debt outstanding

(percentage of total long-term debt)

	Debt from official sources			Debt from private sources			Debt at floating rate		
	1970–72	1980–82	1989	1970–72	1980–82	1989	1973–75	1980–82	1989
Latin America and the Caribbean									
*Argentina	12.6	9.0	18.6	87.4	91.0	81.4	6.6	29.2	80.4
*Bolivia	58.2	49.3	81.7	41.8	50.7	18.3	7.3	28.4	24.2
*Brazil	30.7	11.9	27.0	69.3	88.1	73.0	26.1	46.0	66.3
*Chile	46.0	11.1	32.9	54.0	88.9	67.1	8.3	23.4	53.9
Colombia	68.1	46.1	52.6	31.9	53.9	47.4	5.4	33.7	42.2
*Costa Rica	39.8	36.8	52.6	60.2	63.2	47.4	15.5	42.4	43.7
*Ecuador	51.4	29.5	38.6	48.6	70.5	61.4	8.2	37.2	63.3
Guatemala	47.5	71.0	76.0	52.5	29.0	24.0	3.5	5.6	10.3
*Honduras	73.8	62.6	81.4	26.3	37.4	18.6	1.8	18.9	19.0
Jamaica	7.4	68.3	83.9	92.6	31.7	16.1	4.7	17.3	23.8
*Mexico	19.5	10.9	20.9	80.5	89.1	79.1	31.8	61.4	75.3
*Nicaragua	65.3	58.0	82.3	34.7	42.0	17.7	44.2	42.1	18.4
*Peru	15.6	39.4	46.7	84.4	60.6	53.3	16.1	22.9	28.7
*Uruguay	44.2	21.1	23.2	55.8	78.9	76.8	10.1	28.5	70.4
*Venezuela	30.8	3.6	3.2	69.2	96.4	96.8	17.2	57.8	73.9
Sub-Saharan Africa									
Cameroon	82.2	56.6	72.7	17.8	43.4	27.3	1.8	11.3	9.7
*Congo, People's Rep.	86.5	45.3	58.4	13.5	54.7	41.6	0.0	15.1	31.7
*Côte d'Ivoire	51.6	24.3	41.1	48.4	75.7	58.9	19.1	36.9	35.4
Ethiopia	87.3	90.9	87.5	12.7	9.1	12.5	1.5	2.1	5.2
Ghana	58.0	90.3	91.9	41.9	9.7	8.2	0.0	0.0	1.4
Kenya	58.3	54.8	72.5	41.7	45.2	27.5	2.1	10.1	3.7
Liberia	81.1	74.0	82.8	19.0	25.9	17.2	0.0	16.9	11.3
Malawi	85.8	72.2	95.1	14.2	27.8	4.9	2.3	21.9	3.7
Niger	97.0	41.0	73.9	2.9	59.0	26.1	0.0	13.4	7.7
Nigeria	68.8	15.1	47.6	31.2	84.9	52.4	0.7	48.0	37.8
*Senegal	63.2	69.1	93.9	36.8	30.9	6.1	24.5	9.4	1.5
Sierra Leone	60.6	67.4	82.7	39.4	32.6	17.3	3.8	0.0	1.2
Sudan	86.9	75.1	78.4	13.1	24.9	21.6	2.2	9.6	14.2
Tanzania	61.0	75.5	94.5	39.0	24.5	5.5	0.4	0.3	2.4
Zaire	42.5	65.9	89.2	57.5	34.1	10.8	32.8	11.9	5.3
Zambia	22.0	69.7	86.1	78.0	30.3	14.0	20.7	10.2	14.3
East Asia									
Indonesia	72.3	51.7	61.0	27.7	48.3	39.0	4.9	15.1	27.8
Korea, Rep.	35.2	34.3	37.3	64.8	65.7	62.7	11.8	29.0	20.2
Malaysia	51.0	21.9	23.6	49.0	78.1	76.4	17.4	36.7	43.9
Papua New Guinea	6.1	23.4	34.8	93.8	76.6	65.2	0.0	22.9	16.4
*Philippines	22.6	31.4	53.0	77.4	68.6	47.0	7.2	24.1	41.6
Thailand	40.1	39.1	42.5	59.9	60.9	57.5	0.4	22.4	24.9
South Asia									
India	95.1	83.9	59.3	4.9	16.1	40.7	0.0	3.0	16.7
Pakistan	90.5	92.6	93.9	9.5	7.4	6.1	0.0	3.2	10.6
Sri Lanka	81.6	79.5	85.1	18.4	20.5	14.9	0.0	12.9	3.5
Europe, Middle East, and North Africa									
Algeria	48.3	22.4	28.5	51.7	77.6	71.5	33.9	23.4	32.3
*Egypt, Arab Rep.	70.9	82.4	82.3	29.1	17.6	17.7	2.1	2.5	8.9
*Hungary	0.0	12.1	11.7	0.0	87.9	88.3	0.0	81.3	64.4
*Morocco	79.1	55.9	76.6	20.9	44.1	23.4	2.7	27.2	39.7
*Poland	92.3	36.6	68.5	7.7	63.4	31.5	11.3	47.0	64.0
Portugal	29.3	24.7	19.7	70.7	75.3	80.3	0.0	33.9	29.8
Tunisia	71.4	60.1	72.2	28.6	39.9	27.8	0.0	13.6	19.4
Turkey	92.2	63.3	46.8	7.8	36.7	53.2	0.8	23.0	29.8
Yugoslavia	37.5	23.6	37.5	62.5	76.4	62.5	3.2	10.1	55.8

Note: Asterisks indicate severely indebted middle-income economies.

World Development Indicators

Contents

Key

In each table, economies are listed within their groups in ascending order of GNP per capita, except those for which no GNP per capita can be calculated. These are italicized, in alphabetical order, at the end of their group. The ranking below refers to the order in the tables.

The key has been expanded this year to give the dates of the most recent population censuses and official population estimates (as reported in the UN's *Population and Vital Statistics Report,* January 1991), and related demographic surveys. It also includes the years or periods for which estimates have been made from the most recent demographic surveys (as reported by the UN Population Division's PRED Bank database). This information is included to demonstrate that demographic indicators are derived from sources that are sometimes old and because the currentness of these sources can be a reflection of the overall quality of a country's indicators. Beyond these years, demographic estimates—whether official or not—may be derived from other sources, such as registration data, or may be generated by projec-

tion models, interpolation routines, or other methods. World Bank estimates and projections reported in the following tables are partly based on the sources in this table (using a different methodology from that of the UN); asterisks indicate where sources of later date are used. Further explanations of Bank estimates are given in *World Population Projections, 1989–90 Edition*.

Figures in colored bands in the tables are summary measures for groups of economies.

The letter *w* means weighted average; *m*, median value; *t*, total.

All growth rates are in real terms.

The data cutoff date is April 30, 1991.

The symbol .. means not available.

The numbers 0 and 0.0 mean zero or less than half the unit shown.

A blank means not applicable.

Figures in italics indicate data that are for years or periods other than those specified.

The symbol † indicates economies classified by the United Nations or otherwise regarded by their authorities as developing.

	Country ranking in tables	Population census	Official population estimate	Life expectancy	Infant mortality	Total fertility
Afghanistan	35	1979	1989			1976–80
Algeria	78	1987	1987	1983	1983	1984
Angola	42	1970	1975			1984
Argentina	76	1980	1990	1979–81	1983	1976–80
Australia	107	1986	1990	1986*	1986*	1984*
Austria	113	1981	1989	1986*	1987*	1986*
Bangladesh	5	1981	1989	1981	1981*	1986*
Belgium	112	1981	1988	1984*	1987*	1986*
Benin	25	1979	1989		1977–81	1976–80
Bhutan	36	1969*	1980			1984
Bolivia	43	1976	1989	1970–75	1972*	1976–80*
Botswana	68	1981	1989		1979*	1984*
Brazil	85	1980	1990	1976–80	1975*	1981–86*
Bulgaria	79	1985	1988	1985*	1987*	1985*
Burkina Faso	18	1985	1990		1971	1960–61
Burundi	10	1979	1989	1970–71	1984*	1981–86*
Cameroon	57	1976*	1989	1958–65	1974–78	1976–80
Canada	116	1986	1989	1985*	1986*	1986*
Central African Rep.	26	1975*	1986		1970	1966–70
Chad	9	1964	1978			1963–64

	Country ranking in tables	Population census	Official population estimate	Life expectancy	Infant mortality	Total fertility
Chile	71	1982	1989	1981–83	1986	1986
China	21	1990	1990	1981	1981*	1986*
Colombia	63	1985	1988	1983	1983*	1981–86*
Congo, People's Rep.	55	1984	1984		1970	1984
Costa Rica	72	1984	1989	1979–81	1982–84*	1984*
Côte d'Ivoire	49	1975*	1983		1977–81	1975–80
Czechoslovakia	92	1980	1990	1986*	1987*	1985*
Denmark	118	1981	1990	1985–86*	1986*	1986*
Dominican Rep.	50	1981	1988	1980	1981–86*	1981–86*
Ecuador	59	1982	1989	1982	1982*	1981–86*
Egypt, Arab Rep.	44	1986	1989	1975–77	1984–86*	1984*
El Salvador	62	1971	1989	1970–72	1970–72*	1985*
Ethiopia	2	1984	1990			1981
Finland	121	1985	1990	1986*	1986*	1985*
France	114	1990	1990	1986*	1987*	1986*
Gabon	89	1961*	1985			1960–61
Germany	117	1987	1989	1986*	1986*	1986*
Ghana	27	1984	1987		1984*	1981–86*
Greece	97	1981	1989	1980*	1986*	1985*
Guatemala	54	1981	1990	1980–82	1980–82*	1985*
Guinea	30	1983	1988			1954–55
Haiti	22	1982	1989	1970–71	1980*	1983*
Honduras	53	1974*	1989	1973–75	1977–79*	1981*
†Hong Kong	104	1986	1989	1985–86	1985–86*	1985*
Hungary	86	1980	1990	1986*	1987*	1985*
India	20	1981*	1989	1981–83	1981–83	1984*
Indonesia	33	1980*	1989	1971–80	1976*	1981–86*
Iran, Islamic Rep.	90	1986	1990	1973–76	1973–76*	1971–75*
Iraq	98	1987	1987		1970	1971–75
Ireland	101	1986	1990	1985*	1986*	1986*
†Israel	103	1983	1990	1983*	1986*	1986*
Italy	109	1981	1990	1983*	1986*	1985*
Jamaica	65	1982	1989	1969–71	1976–78	1982
Japan	123	1985	1989	1986*	1986*	1986*
Jordan	69	1979	1976	1979	1978	1981–86
Kampuchea, Dem.	37	1962	1969			1982
Kenya	23	1979*	1989	1975	1975*	1984*
Korea, Rep.	94	1985	1990	1978–79	1971–75*	1985*
†Kuwait	111	1985	1989	1984–85	1984–85	1985
Lao PDR	6	1985	1985		*	*
Lebanon	80	1970	1970	1970		1966–70
Lesotho	32	1976*	1989	1975	1975	1976–80
Liberia	38	1984	1989		1981–86*	1981–86*
Libya	96	1984	1989		1969	1971–75
Madagascar	12	1974–75	1985			1976–80
Malawi	7	1987	1989	1966–77	1974	1984
Malaysia	77	1980	1989	1971–81	1971–81	1984
Mali	16	1987	1989		1984*	1981–86*
Mauritania	34	1977*	1977		1975	1976–80*
Mauritius	74	1983	1989	1983	1984–86	1985
Mexico	75	1990	1990	1979–81	1979–81*	1986*
Mongolia	81	1989	1989		*	*
Morocco	51	1982	1982	1972*	1980*	1981–85*
Mozambique	1	1980	1989		1975	1976–80
Myanmar	39	1983	1987		*	1982*
Namibia	60	1970	1970		*	*
Nepal	8	1981	1989	1974–76	1972–76*	1985*
Netherlands	110	1971*	1990	1985*	1987*	1986*
New Zealand	106	1986	1990	1985*	1986*	1985*
Nicaragua	82	1971	1986		*	*

	Country ranking in tables	Population census	Official population estimate	Life expectancy	Infant mortality	Total fertility
Niger	17	1988	1988			1960
Nigeria	13	1963	1988		*	1976–80*
Norway	122	1980	1990	1984–85*	1986*	1985*
Oman	95		1985		1985	
Pakistan	24	1981	1990	1972–81	1972–81*	1985
Panama	70	1980	1990	1970–80	1985–87	1986
Papua New Guinea	52	1980	1989			1976–80
Paraguay	61	1982	1989	1982	1978*	1986*
Peru	58	1981	1990	1972	1981–86*	1981–86*
Philippines	48	1980*	1989	1979–81	1979–81*	1984*
Poland	73	1978	1989	1986*	1987*	1986*
Portugal	93	1981	1989	1986*	1986*	1985*
Romania	99	1977	1990	1984*	1985*	1985*
Rwanda	19	1978	1985		1980	1981–86
†Saudi Arabia	100	1974	1989			
Senegal	45	1988	1988	1970–71	1981–85*	1981–86*
Sierra Leone	11	1985	1985	1964–73	1971	1971–75
†Singapore	105	1980	1989	1984–86*	1986–87*	1986*
Somalia	4	1975*	1975			1976–80
South Africa	84	1985	1985	1970	1980	
Spain	102	1981	1990	1980–81*	1985*	1984*
Sri Lanka	31	1981	1989	1980–81	1982–83*	1981–86*
Sudan	40	1983	1983		*	1976–80*
Sweden	120	1985	1990	1986*	1987*	1986*
Switzerland	124	1980	1989	1985–86*	1987*	1985*
Syrian Arab Rep.	56	1981	1989	1976–78	1976–78	1976–80
Tanzania	3	1978*	1989	1975	1975	1976–80
Thailand	64	1980	1989	1979–81	1983*	1981–86*
Togo	28	1981	1988		1969*	1971–75*
Trinidad and Tobago	91	1980	1988	1979–81	1981–83*	1981–86*
Tunisia	66	1984	1986	1968–69	1981*	1984*
Turkey	67	1985	1989	1970–80	1976*	1983*
Uganda	14	1980	1980		*	1969*
†United Arab Emirates	115	1980*	1983		1975	1981
United Kingdom	108	1981	1989	1983–85*	1987*	1986*
United States	119	1980*	1989	1986*	1987*	1986*
Uruguay	87	1985	1989	1974–76	1985	1976–80
Venezuela	83	1981	1989	1981	1981	1986
Viet Nam	41	1989	1989		*	*
Yemen, Rep.	46				*	1981*
Yugoslavia	88	1981	1990	1984–85*	1987*	1983*
Zaire	15	1984	1989		1972*	1971–75*
Zambia	29	1980	1989		1970	1976–80
Zimbabwe	47	1982	1989		1980*	1984*

*Asterisks indicate that sources of later date are used.

Note: Economies with populations of less than 1 million are included only as part of the country groups in the main tables, but are shown in greater detail in Box A.1. Other economies not listed in the main tables nor in Box A.1, but also included in the aggregates, are shown in greater detail in Box A.2. For data comparability and coverage throughout the tables, see the technical notes.

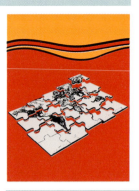

Introduction

The World Development Indicators provide information on the main features of social and economic development. Most of the data collected by the World Bank are on the low- and middle-income economies. Because comparable data for high-income economies are readily available, these are also included here. Additional information may be found in other World Bank publications, notably the *World Bank Atlas*, *World Tables*, *World Debt Tables*, and *Social Indicators of Development*. These data are now also available on diskette, in the World Bank's ☆STARS☆ retrieval system.

In these notes the term ''country'' does not imply political independence but may refer to any territory whose authorities present for it separate social or economic statistics. The World Bank's main classification criterion for certain operational and analytical purposes is gross national product (GNP) per capita, and economies are presented in these tables in ascending order of GNP per capita. Other analytical and geographical criteria are also used for classification, and in this edition there are two changes in the country groups. Replacing the former group *total reporting economies* is the new classification *world*, and replacing the former *non-reporting nonmember economies* is the group *other economies*. These changes have been made possible by the greater availability of data during the past year. Like all the other country groups in the tables, the categories include countries with populations of less than 1 million in addition to the 124 countries listed. The definitions and data notes at the beginning of the main Report provide a detailed description of the country groups.

Although every effort has been made to standardize the data, full comparability cannot be en-

sured, and care must be taken in interpreting the indicators. The statistics are drawn from the sources thought to be most authoritative, but the data are subject to considerable margins of error. Variations in national statistical practices also reduce the comparability of data, which should thus be construed only as indicating trends and characterizing major differences among economies, rather than taken as precise quantitative indications of those differences.

The indicators in Table 1 give a summary profile of economies. Data in the other tables fall into the following broad areas: production, domestic absorption, fiscal and monetary accounts, core international transactions, external finance, and human and natural resources.

In this edition, a new table on the environment has been added, and changes have been made to the external debt tables and the table on urbanization. Methodological revisions in the underlying constant price economic data have also been made; this affects the growth rates derived from the basic time series data. These changes are described briefly below, and more fully in the technical notes.

The new table—Table 33, Forests, protected areas, and water—is based mainly on data from *World Resources 1990–91* published by the World Resources Institute. The table includes indicators on forested areas, deforestation, protected land areas, and the supply and use of internal renewable water resources. All economies face the challenge of using natural resources in a way that will both provide for current needs and preserve them to assure sustainable development. Yet little attention has been paid internationally—and in most cases, nationally—to the indicators needed to monitor and evaluate such environmental issues. As a result, the indicators available today, including those in Table 33, are untried and probably less reliable than the other socioeconomic indicators reported in this publication. Nonetheless, a start must be made, if only to demonstrate the need for better global monitoring procedures.

Several tables on external debt have been rearranged to reflect new material in the World Bank publication *World Debt Tables*. Table 23, Aggregate net resource flows and net transfers, highlights the importance of official grants and net foreign direct investment in net resource flows. Other additions to the external debt tables include additional debt service ratios.

Data supplied by the UN Population Division on the population of capital cities and the percentage of population residing in cities of 1 million or more in 1990 have been added to Table 31, Urbanization. The previous series covering large cities had not been updated in recent years and has now been dropped.

Data on external debt are compiled directly by the Bank on the basis of reports from developing member countries through the Debtor Reporting System. Other data are drawn mainly from the United Nations and its specialized agencies, the International Monetary Fund, and country reports to the World Bank. Bank staff estimates are also used to improve currency or consistency. For most countries, national accounts estimates are obtained from member governments through World Bank economic missions. In some instances these are adjusted by Bank staff to conform to international definitions and concepts to provide better consistency and to incorporate latest estimates.

For ease of reference, only ratios and rates of growth are usually shown; absolute values are generally available from other World Bank publications, notably the 1991 edition of the *World Tables*. Most growth rates are calculated for two periods, 1965–80 and 1980–89, and are computed, unless otherwise noted, by using the least-squares regression method. Because this method takes into account all observations in a period, the resulting growth rates reflect general trends that are not unduly influenced by exceptional values, particularly at the end points. To exclude the effects of inflation, constant price economic indicators are used in calculating growth rates. Details of this methodology are given at the beginning of the technical notes. Data in italics indicate that they are for years or periods other than those specified—up to two

years earlier for economic indicators and up to three years on either side for social indicators, since the latter tend to be collected less regularly and change less dramatically over short periods of time. All dollar figures are US dollars unless otherwise stated. The various methods used for converting from national currency figures are described in the technical notes.

The Bank continually reviews methodologies in an effort to improve the international comparability and analytical significance of the indicators. Differences between data in this year's and last year's edition reflect not only updates for the countries but also revisions to historical series and changes in methodology. The main methodological change in this edition is that 1987 prices are used for economic indicators; indexes and growth rates calculated from constant price data may therefore differ from those of earlier editions. This process is described more fully in the technical notes.

As in the Report itself, the main criterion used to classify economies in the World Development Indicators is GNP per capita. These income groups broadly distinguish countries at different stages of economic development. Many of the economies are further classified by geographical location. Other classifications include severely indebted middle-income economies and all oil exporters. For a list of countries in each group, see the Definitions and data notes. The major classifications used in the tables this year are 41 low-income economies with per capita incomes of $580 or less in 1989, 58 middle-income economies with per capita incomes of $581 to $5,999, and 25 high-income economies. Four new Bank members are included in the middle-income category: Bulgaria, Czechoslovakia, Mongolia, and Namibia. Data for a group labeled "other economies," which includes Albania, Cuba, the Democratic People's Republic of Korea, and the USSR, are shown only as aggregates in the main tables because of paucity of data, differences in methods of computing national income, and difficulties of conversion. Some selected indicators for these countries, however, and for the former German Democratic Republic, are included in Box A.2 of the technical notes.

Economies with populations of less than 1 million are also not shown separately in the main tables, but basic indicators for these countries and territories, and for Puerto Rico, are in a separate table in Box A.1 of the technical notes.

The summary measures in the colored bands are totals (indicated by *t*), weighted averages (*w*), or median values (*m*) calculated for groups of economies. Countries for which individual estimates are not shown, because of size, nonreporting, or insufficient history, have been included by assuming they follow the trend of reporting countries during such periods. This gives a more consistent aggregate measure by standardizing country coverage for each period shown. Group aggregates also include countries with less than 1 million population, even though country-specific data for these countries do not appear in the tables. Where missing information accounts for a third or more of the overall estimate, however, the group measure is reported as not available. The weightings used for computing the summary measures are stated in each technical note.

Germany and the Republic of Yemen, both recently unified, do not yet have fully merged statistical systems. Throughout the tables, all data for Germany refer only to the former Federal Republic, but data for the Republic of Yemen, where they are shown, refer to the whole country. As in previous editions, the data for China do not include Taiwan, China, but footnotes to Tables 14, 15, 16, and 18 provide estimates of the international transactions for Taiwan, China.

The table format of this edition follows that used in previous years. In each group, economies are listed in ascending order of GNP per capita, except those for which no such figure can be calculated. These are italicized and in alphabetical order at the end of the group deemed to be appropriate. This

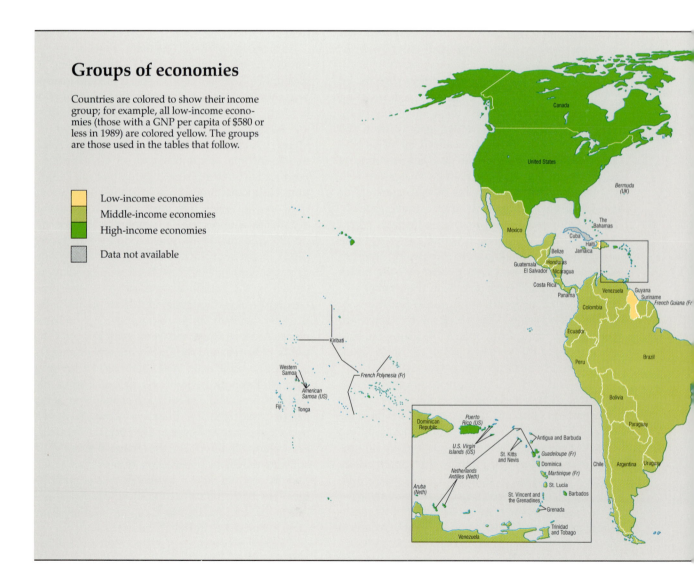

Groups of economies

Countries are colored to show their income group; for example, all low-income economies (those with a GNP per capita of $580 or less in 1989) are colored yellow. The groups are those used in the tables that follow.

Low-income economies
Middle-income economies
High-income economies

Data not available

order is used in all tables except Table 19, which covers only high-income OPEC and OECD countries. The alphabetical list in the key shows the reference number for each economy; here, too, italics indicate economies with no estimates of GNP per capita. Economies in the high-income group marked by the symbol † are those classified by the United Nations or otherwise regarded by their authorities as developing.

The technical notes and the footnotes to tables should be referred to in any use of the data. These notes outline the methods, concepts, definitions, and data sources used in compiling the tables. A separate list at the end of the notes gives bibliographic details of the data sources, which contain comprehensive definitions and descriptions of concepts used. It should also be noted that country notes to the *World Tables* provide additional explanations of sources used, breaks in comparability, and other exceptions to standard statistical practices that have been identified by Bank staff on national accounts and international transactions.

Comments and questions relating to the World Development Indicators should be addressed to:

Socio-Economic Data Division
International Economics Department
The World Bank
1818 H Street, N.W.
Washington, D.C. 20433.

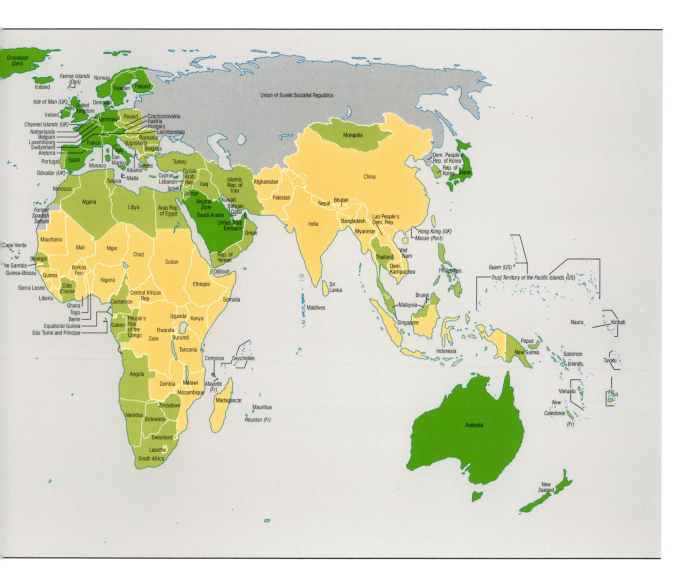

Population

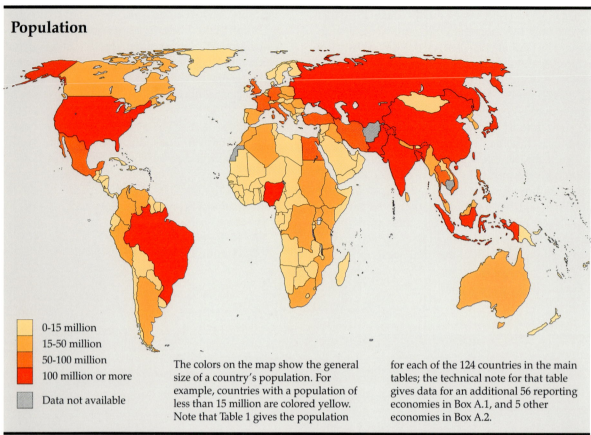

- 0-15 million
- 15-50 million
- 50-100 million
- 100 million or more
- Data not available

The colors on the map show the general size of a country's population. For example, countries with a population of less than 15 million are colored yellow. Note that Table 1 gives the population for each of the 124 countries in the main tables; the technical note for that table gives data for an additional 56 reporting economies in Box A.1, and 5 other economies in Box A.2.

Fertility and mortality

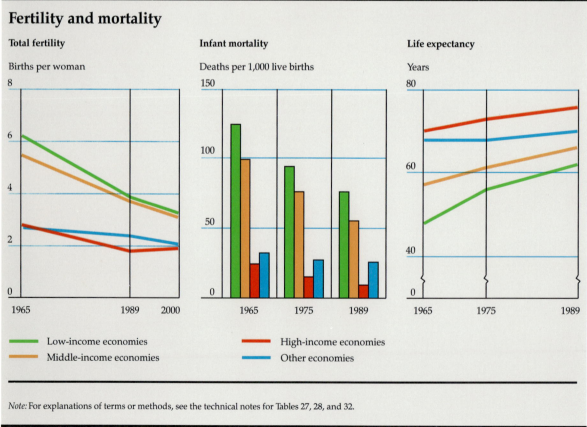

Total fertility

Births per woman

Infant mortality

Deaths per 1,000 live births

Life expectancy

Years

- Low-income economies
- Middle-income economies
- High-income economies
- Other economies

Note: For explanations of terms or methods, see the technical notes for Tables 27, 28, and 32.

Share of agriculture in GDP

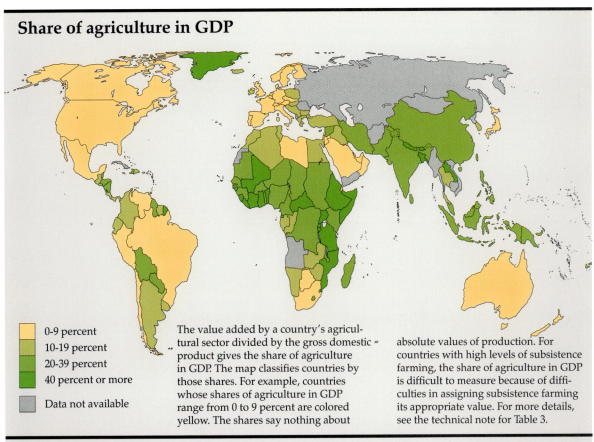

0-9 percent
10-19 percent
20-39 percent
40 percent or more

Data not available

The value added by a country's agricultural sector divided by the gross domestic product gives the share of agriculture in GDP. The map classifies countries by those shares. For example, countries whose shares of agriculture in GDP range from 0 to 9 percent are colored yellow. The shares say nothing about absolute values of production. For countries with high levels of subsistence farming, the share of agriculture in GDP is difficult to measure because of difficulties in assigning subsistence farming its appropriate value. For more details, see the technical note for Table 3.

External balances of low- and middle-income economies

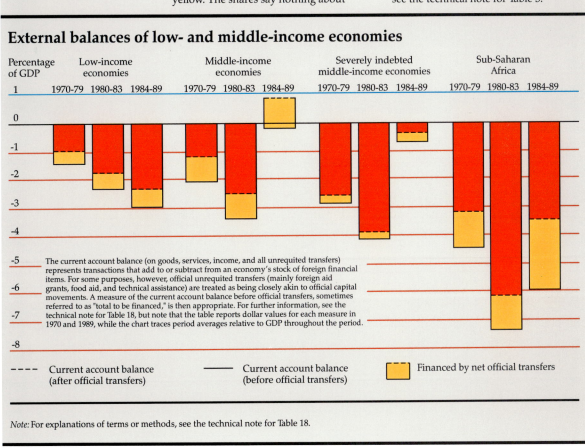

The current account balance (on goods, services, income, and all unrequited transfers) represents transactions that add to or subtract from an economy's stock of foreign financial items. For some purposes, however, official unrequited transfers (mainly foreign aid grants, food aid, and technical assistance) are treated as being closely akin to official capital movements. A measure of the current account balance before official transfers, sometimes referred to as "total to be financed," is then appropriate. For further information, see the technical note for Table 18, but note that the table reports dollar values for each measure in 1970 and 1989, while the chart traces period averages relative to GDP throughout the period.

---- Current account balance (after official transfers)

—— Current account balance (before official transfers)

Financed by net official transfers

Note: For explanations of terms or methods, see the technical note for Table 18.

Table 1. Basic Indicators

		Population (millions) mid-1989	Area (thousands of square kilometers)	GNP per capita[a] Dollars 1989	Average annual growth rate (percent) 1965–89	Average annual rate of inflation[a] (percent) 1965–80	1980–89	Life expectancy birth (years) 1989	Adult illiteracy (percent) Female 1985	Total 1985
	Low-income economies	**2,948.4** *t*	**36,664** *t*	**330** *w*	**2.9** *w*	**8.0** *w*	**9.1** *w*	**62** *w*	**58** *w*	**44** *w*
	China and India	**1,946.4** *t*	**12,849** *t*	**350** *w*	**3.6** *w*	**3.2** *w*	**6.6** *w*	**65** *w*	**56** *w*	**42** *w*
	Other low-income	**1,002.0** *t*	**23,816** *t*	**300** *w*	**1.4** *w*	**19.2** *w*	**14.9** *w*	**55** *w*	**62** *w*	**51** *w*
1	Mozambique	15.3	802	80	. .	. .	34.9	49	78	62
2	Ethiopia	49.5	1,222	120	–0.1	3.4	2.0	48	. .	*38*
3	Tanzania[b]	23.8	945	130	–0.1	9.6	26.1	49	. .	. .
4	Somalia	6.1	638	170	0.3	10.2	42.8	48	94	88
5	Bangladesh	110.7	144	180	0.4	14.8	10.6	51	78	67
6	Lao PDR	4.1	237	180	. .	. .	. .	49	24	56
7	Malawi	8.2	118	180	1.0	7.4	14.6	48	69	59
8	Nepal	18.4	141	180	0.6	7.8	9.1	52	88	74
9	Chad	5.5	1,284	190	–1.2	6.2	1.5	47	89	75
10	Burundi	5.3	28	220	3.6	5.0	3.7	49	74	66
11	Sierra Leone	4.0	72	220	0.2	7.9	54.1	42	79	71
12	Madagascar	11.3	587	230	–1.9	7.7	17.8	51	38	33
13	Nigeria	113.8	924	250	0.2	14.7	14.2	51	69	58
14	Uganda	16.8	236	250	–2.8	21.4	108.1	49	55	43
15	Zaire	34.5	2,345	260	–2.0	24.7	59.4	53	55	39
16	Mali	8.2	1,240	270	1.7	9.0	3.6	48	89	83
17	Niger	7.4	1,267	290	–2.4	7.5	3.4	45	91	86
18	Burkina Faso	8.8	274	320	1.4	6.4	4.6	48	94	87
19	Rwanda	6.9	26	320	1.2	12.5	4.0	49	67	53
20	India	832.5	3,288	340	1.8	7.5	7.7	59	71	57
21	China	1,113.9	9,561	350	5.7	–0.4	5.8	70	45	31
22	Haiti	6.4	28	360	0.3	7.3	6.8	55	65	62
23	Kenya	23.5	580	360	2.0	7.2	9.0	59	51	41
24	Pakistan	109.9	796	370	2.5	10.3	6.7	55	81	70
25	Benin	4.6	113	380	–0.1	7.4	7.5	51	84	74
26	Central African Rep.	3.0	623	390	–0.5	8.2	6.5	51	71	60
27	Ghana	14.4	239	390	–1.5	22.9	43.6	55	57	40
28	Togo	3.5	57	390	0.0	7.1	5.1	54	72	59
29	Zambia	7.8	753	390	–2.0	6.3	38.3	54	33	24
30	Guinea	5.6	246	430	. .	. .	. .	43	83	72
31	Sri Lanka	16.8	66	430	3.0	9.4	10.9	71	17	13
32	Lesotho	1.7	30	470	5.0	6.7	12.8	56	16	26
33	Indonesia	178.2	1,905	500	4.4	35.5	8.3	61	35	26
34	Mauritania	1.9	1,026	500	–0.5	7.6	9.4	46	. .	. .
35	*Afghanistan*	. .	652	. .	. .	4.9	. .	. .	. .	. .
36	*Bhutan*	1.4	47	. .	. .	. .	. .	48	. .	. .
37	*Kampuchea, Dem.*	. .	181	. .	. .	. .	. .	. .	. .	. .
38	*Liberia*	2.5	111	. .	. .	6.3	. .	54	77	65
39	*Myanmar*	40.8	677	. .	. .	. .	. .	61	. .	. .
40	*Sudan*	24.5	2,506	. .	. .	11.5	. .	50	. .	. .
41	*Viet Nam*	64.8	330	. .	. .	. .	. .	66	. .	. .
	Middle-income economies	**1,104.5** *t*	**40,406** *t*	**2,040** *w*	**2.3** *w*	**20.9** *w*	**73.0** *w*	**66** *w*	**31** *w*	**25** *w*
	Lower-middle-income	**681.8** *t*	**23,921** *t*	**1,360** *w*	**2.0** *w*	**22.2** *w*	**65.7** *w*	**65** *w*	**32** *w*	**26** *w*
42	Angola	9.7	1,247	610	. .	. .	. .	46	. .	59
43	Bolivia	7.1	1,099	620	–0.8	15.9	391.9	54	35	26
44	Egypt, Arab Rep.	51.0	1,001	640	4.2	6.4	11.0	60	70	56
45	Senegal	7.2	197	650	–0.7	6.5	7.3	48	81	72
46	Yemen, Rep.	11.2	528	650	. .	. .	. .	48	. .	. .
47	Zimbabwe	9.5	391	650	1.2	5.8	11.0	64	33	26
48	Philippines	60.0	300	710	1.6	11.7	14.8	64	15	14
49	Cote d'Ivoire	11.7	322	790	0.8	9.4	3.1	53	69	57
50	Dominican Rep.	7.0	49	790	2.5	6.7	19.1	67	23	23
51	Morocco	24.5	447	880	2.3	5.9	7.4	61	78	67
52	Papua New Guinea	3.8	463	890	0.2	8.1	5.6	54	65	55
53	Honduras	5.0	112	900	0.6	5.7	4.7	65	42	41
54	Guatemala	8.9	109	910	0.9	7.1	13.4	63	53	45
55	Congo, People's Rep.	2.2	342	940	3.3	6.8	0.3	54	45	37
56	Syrian Arab Rep.	12.1	185	980	3.1	7.9	15.0	66	57	40
57	Cameroon	11.6	475	1,000	3.2	9.0	6.6	57	55	44
58	Peru	21.2	1,285	1,010	–0.2	20.6	160.3	62	22	15
59	Ecuador	10.3	284	1,020	3.0	10.9	34.4	66	20	18
60	Namibia	1.7	824	1,030	. .	. .	13.4	57	. .	. .
61	Paraguay	4.2	407	1,030	3.0	9.3	23.2	67	15	12
62	El Salvador	5.1	21	1,070	–0.4	7.0	16.8	63	31	28
63	Colombia	32.3	1,139	1,200	2.3	17.5	24.3	69	13	12
64	Thailand	55.4	513	1,220	4.2	6.2	3.2	66	12	9
65	Jamaica	2.4	11	1,260	–1.3	12.8	18.5	73	. .	. .
66	Tunisia	8.0	164	1,260	3.3	6.7	7.5	66	59	46

Note: Economies with populations of less than 1 million are included only as part of the country groups in the main tables, but are shown in greater detail in Box A.1. Other economies not listed in the main tables nor in Box A.1, but also included in the aggregates, are shown in greater detail in Box A.2. For data comparability and coverage throughout the tables, see the technical notes. Figures in italics are for years other than those specified.

		Population (millions) mid-1989	Area (thousands of square kilometers)	GNP per capita[a] Dollars 1989	GNP per capita[a] Average annual growth rate (percent) 1965-89	Average annual rate of inflation[a] (percent) 1965-80	Average annual rate of inflation[a] (percent) 1980-89	Life expectancy birth (years) 1989	Adult illiteracy (percent) Female 1985	Adult illiteracy (percent) Total 1985
67	Turkey	55.0	779	1,370	2.6	20.8	41.4	66	38	26
68	Botswana	1.2	582	1,600	8.5	8.4	12.0	67	31	29
69	Jordan[c]	3.9	89	1,640	. .	. .	. .	67	37	25
70	Panama	2.4	77	1,760	1.6	5.4	2.5	73	12	12
71	Chile	13.0	757	1,770	0.3	129.9	20.5	72	. .	6
72	Costa Rica	2.7	51	1,780	1.4	11.2	24.8	75	7	6
73	Poland	37.9	313	1,790	. .	. .	38.1	71	. .	. .
74	Mauritius	1.1	2	1,990	3.0	11.8	8.5	70	23	17
75	Mexico	84.6	1,958	2,010	3.0	13.0	72.7	69	12	10
76	Argentina	31.9	2,767	2,160	-0.1	78.3	334.8	71	5	5
77	Malaysia	17.4	330	2,160	4.0	4.9	1.5	70	34	27
78	Algeria	24.4	2,382	2,230	2.5	10.5	5.2	65	63	50
79	Bulgaria	9.0	111	2,320	. .	. .	1.4	72	. .	. .
80	*Lebanon*	. .	10	. .	. .	9.3	. .	. .	. .	. .
81	*Mongolia*	2.1	1,565	. .	. .	. .	. .	62	. .	. .
82	*Nicaragua*	3.7	130	. .	. .	8.9	. .	64	. .	. .
	Upper-middle-income	**422.7 t**	**16,485 t**	**3,150 w**	**2.6 w**	**19.8 w**	**78.7 w**	**67 w**	**28 w**	**24 w**
83	Venezuela	19.2	912	2,450	-1.0	10.4	16.0	70	15	13
84	South Africa	35.0	1,221	2,470	0.8	9.8	14.1	62	. .	. .
85	Brazil	147.3	8,512	2,540	3.5	31.3	227.8	66	24	22
86	Hungary	10.6	93	2,590	. .	2.6	7.5	71	d	d
87	Uruguay	3.1	177	2,620	1.2	57.8	59.2	73	4	5
88	Yugoslavia	23.7	256	2,920	3.2	15.2	96.9	72	14	9
89	Gabon	1.1	268	2,960	0.9	12.8	-1.0	53	47	38
90	Iran, Islamic Rep.	53.3	1,648	3,200	0.5	15.5	13.5	63	61	49
91	Trinidad and Tobago	1.3	5	3,230	0.4	14.1	5.8	71	5	4
92	Czechoslovakia	15.6	128	3,450	. .	. .	1.6	72	. .	. .
93	Portugal	10.3	92	4,250	3.0	11.7	19.1	75	20	16
94	Korea, Rep.	42.4	99	4,400	7.0	18.4	5.0	70	. .	. .
95	Oman	1.5	212	5,220	6.4	19.9	-6.6	65	. .	. .
96	Libya	4.4	1,760	5,310	-3.0	15.4	0.2	62	50	33
97	Greece	10.0	132	5,350	2.9	10.3	18.2	77	12	8
98	*Iraq*	18.3	438	. .	. .	. .	. .	63	13	11
99	*Romania*	23.2	238	. .	. .	. .	. .	71	d	d
	Low- and middle-income	**4,052.8 t**	**77,071 t**	**800 w**	**2.5 w**	**16.7 w**	**53.7 w**	**63 w**	**51 w**	**40 w**
	SubSaharan Africa	**480.4 t**	**23,066 t**	**340 w**	**0.3 w**	**11.4 w**	**19.0 w**	**51 w**	**65 w**	**52 w**
	East Asia	**1,552.2 t**	**15,582 t**	**540 w**	**5.2 w**	**9.3 w**	**6.0 w**	**68 w**	**41 w**	**29 w**
	South Asia	**1,130.8 t**	**5,158 t**	**320 w**	**1.8 w**	**8.2 w**	**7.9 w**	**58 w**	**72 w**	**59 w**
	Europe, M.East, & N.Africa	**433.2 t**	**11,658 t**	**2,180 w**	**. .**	**13.1 w**	**21.8 w**	**65 w**	**51 w**	**40 w**
	Latin America & Caribbean	**421.2 t**	**20,385 t**	**1,950 w**	**1.9 w**	**31.5 w**	**160.7 w**	**67 w**	**19 w**	**17 w**
	Severely indebted	**554.3 t**	**21,059 t**	**1,730 w**	**2.1 w**	**29.1 w**	**140.5 w**	**66 w**	**28 w**	**24 w**
	High-income economies	**830.4 t**	**33,875 t**	**18,330 w**	**2.4 w**	**7.6 w**	**4.6 w**	**76 w**	**. .**	**. .**
	OECD members	**772.6 t**	**31,165 t**	**19,090 w**	**2.5 w**	**7.5 w**	**4.3 w**	**76 w**	**. .**	**. .**
	†Other	**57.8 t**	**2,710 t**	**8,250 w**	**3.8 w**	**13.0 w**	**14.0 w**	**72 w**	**. .**	**. .**
100	†Saudi Arabia	14.4	2,150	6,020	2.6	17.9	-4.4	64	. .	. .
101	Ireland	3.5	70	8,710	2.1	11.6	7.8	74	. .	. .
102	Spain	38.8	505	9,330	2.4	12.3	9.4	77	8	6
103	†Israel	4.5	21	9,790	2.7	25.2	117.1	76	7	5
104	†Hong Kong	5.7	1	10,350[e]	6.3	8.1	7.1	78	19	12
105	†Singapore	2.7	1	10,450	7.0	5.1	1.5	74	21	14
106	New Zealand	3.3	269	12,070	0.8	10.2	11.4	75	d	d
107	Australia	16.8	7,687	14,360	1.7	9.3	7.8	77	d	d
108	United Kingdom	57.2	245	14,610	2.0	10.7	6.1	76	d	d
109	Italy	57.5	301	15,120	3.0	11.4	10.3	76	d	d
110	Netherlands	14.8	37	15,920	1.8	7.4	1.9	77	d	d
111	†Kuwait	2.0	18	16,150	-4.0	15.9	-2.7	74	37	30
112	Belgium	10.0	31	16,220	. .	. .	4.5	76	d	d
113	Austria	7.6	84	17,300	2.9	6.0	3.8	76	d	d
114	France	56.2	552	17,820	2.3	8.6	6.5	77	d	d
115	†United Arab Emirates	1.5	84	18,430	. .	. .	1.1	71	. .	. .
116	Canada	26.2	9,976	19,030	4.0	5.5	4.6	77	d	d
117	Germany[f]	62.0	249	20,440	2.4	5.2	2.7	75	d	d
118	Denmark	5.1	43	20,450	1.8	9.3	6.0	75	d	d
119	United States	248.8	9,373	20,910	1.6	6.5	4.0	76	d	d
120	Sweden	8.5	450	21,570	1.8	8.0	7.4	77	d	d
121	Finland	5.0	338	22,120	3.2	10.5	7.0	75	d	d
122	Norway	4.2	324	22,290	3.4	7.7	5.6	77	d	d
123	Japan	123.1	378	23,810	4.3	7.6	1.3	79	d	d
124	Switzerland	6.6	41	29,880	4.6	1.6	3.6	78	d	d
	Other economies	**322.8 t**	**22,663 t**	**. .**	**. .**	**. .**	**. .**	**70 w**	**. .**	**. .**
	World	**5,206.1 t**	**133,609 t**	**3,980 w**	**1.6 w**	**9.1 w**	**13.2 w**	**65 w**	**57 w**	**. .**
	Oil exporters (excl. USSR)	**265.2 t**	**12,120 t**	**1,840 w**	**1.2 w**	**14.5 w**	**7.3 w**	**58 w**	**. .**	**47 w**

† Economies classified by United Nations or otherwise regarded by their authorities as developing.   a. See the technical notes.   b. In all tables GDP and GNP data cover mainland Tanzania only.   c. In all tables GDP and GNP data for Jordan cover the East Bank only.   d. According to Unesco, illiteracy is less than 5 percent.   e. In all tables GNP data for Hong Kong refer to GDP.   f. In all tables data refer to the former Federal Republic of Germany only; for former German Democratic Republic data, see Box A.2.

Table 2. Growth of production

		GDP		Agriculture		Industry		Manufacturing[a]		Services, etc.[b]	
		Average annual growth rate (percent)									
		1965–80	1980–89	1965–80	1980–89	1965–80	1980–89	1965–80	1980–89	1965–80	1980–89
	Low-income economies	**4.8** w	**6.2** w	**2.6** w	**4.0** w	**7.6** w	**8.6** w	**7.2** w	**11.5** w	**5.5** w	**6.2** w
	China and India	**5.0** w	**7.6** w	**2.7** w	**4.8** w	**7.2** w	**10.6** w	**7.3** w	**12.4** w	**5.7** w	**7.5** w
	Other low-income	**4.6** w	**3.4** w	**2.5** w	**2.5** w	**8.5** w	**3.1** w	**6.9** w	**7.4** w	**5.2** w	**4.4** w
1	Mozambique	..	−1.4	..	0.7	..	−4.9	..	..	..	−4.4
2	Ethiopia	2.7	1.9	1.2	−0.4	3.5	3.3	5.1	3.6	5.2	4.1
3	Tanzania	3.9	2.6	1.6	4.2	4.2	−1.0	5.6	−1.6	6.7	1.5
4	Somalia	3.5	3.0	..	3.8	..	2.5	..	0.2	..	1.2
5	Bangladesh[c]	2.5	3.5	1.5	2.1	3.8	5.0	6.8	2.7	3.4	4.9
6	Lao PDR[c]	..	..	..	..	..	..	..	..	..	..
7	Malawi	5.5	2.7	*4.1*	2.2	*6.4*	2.4	..	3.1	*6.7*	3.3
8	Nepal	1.9	4.6	1.1	4.5	..	..	..	..	..	..
9	Chad[c]	0.1	6.5	−0.3	2.5	−0.6	10.5	..	..	0.2	9.3
10	Burundi	7.1	*4.3*	6.7	*3.1*	17.4	5.8	6.0	*6.1*	1.4	*6.3*
11	Sierra Leone	2.7	0.6	3.9	2.4	−0.8	−3.4	0.7	−3.4	4.3	0.3
12	Madagascar[c]	1.6	0.8	..	2.4	..	0.5	..	..	..	0.0
13	Nigeria	6.1	−0.4	1.7	1.3	13.1	−2.1	14.6	0.8	7.6	−0.4
14	Uganda	0.6	2.5	1.2	2.2	−4.3	4.6	−3.7	4.2	1.1	2.9
15	Zaire[c]	1.8	1.9	..	2.6	..	1.4	..	2.0	..	1.9
16	Mali[c]	4.2	3.8	2.8	1.5	1.8	7.9	..	..	7.6	5.9
17	Niger[c]	0.3	−1.6	−3.4	*1.8*	11.4	*−3.3*	..	..	3.4	−6.5
18	Burkina Faso	..	5.0	..	5.8	..	3.9	..	2.4	..	4.8
19	Rwanda[c]	4.9	1.5	..	−1.4	..	1.6	..	1.3	..	4.7
20	India	3.6	5.3	2.5	2.9	4.2	6.9	4.5	7.3	4.4	6.5
21	China[c]	6.9	9.7	2.8	6.3	10.0	12.6	9.5[d]	14.5[d]	10.3	9.3
22	Haiti[c]	2.9	−0.5	1.0	−0.4	7.1	−1.6	6.2	−2.1	2.7	0.1
23	Kenya	6.8	4.1	5.0	3.2	9.7	3.7	10.5	4.8	6.6	4.9
24	Pakistan	5.2	6.4	3.3	4.4	6.4	7.3	5.7	7.9	5.9	7.1
25	Benin	2.2	*1.8*	..	4.2	..	5.8	..	7.4	..	*−1.0*
26	Central African Rep.	2.8	1.4	2.1	2.9	5.3	2.5	..	1.9	2.0	−0.5
27	Ghana[c]	1.3	2.8	1.6	0.9	1.4	3.2	2.5	4.3	1.1	5.3
28	Togo[c]	4.3	1.4	1.9	5.7	6.8	0.1	..	−0.2	4.8	−0.5
29	Zambia[c]	2.0	0.8	2.2	*4.1*	2.1	0.3	5.3	2.5	1.5	*0.1*
30	Guinea[c]	..	..	..	..	..	..	..	..	..	..
31	Sri Lanka	4.0	4.0	2.7	2.2	4.7	4.4	3.2	6.2	4.6	4.9
32	Lesotho	6.8	3.7	..	−0.8	..	4.8	..	13.4	..	4.8
33	Indonesia[c]	7.0	5.3	4.3	3.2	11.9	5.3	12.0	12.7	7.3	6.6
34	Mauritania	2.1	1.4	−2.0	1.5	2.2	5.2	..	..	6.5	0.1
35	*Afghanistan*	2.9	..	..	..	..	..	..	..	..	..
36	*Bhutan*	..	*8.1*	..	5.8	..	15.4	..	*11.9*	..	7.4
37	*Kampuchea, Dem.*	..	..	..	..	..	..	..	..	..	..
38	*Liberia*	3.3	..	5.5	..	2.2	..	10.0	..	2.4	..
39	*Myanmar*	..	..	..	..	..	..	..	..	..	..
40	*Sudan*	3.8	..	2.9	..	3.1	..	..	..	4.9	..
41	*Viet Nam*	..	..	..	..	..	..	..	..	..	..
	Middle-income economies	**6.2** w	**2.9** w	**3.4** w	**2.6** w	**6.5** w	**3.0** w	..	**3.3** w	**7.5** w	**2.8** w
	Lower-middle-income	**5.5** w	**2.5** w	**3.4** w	**2.1** w	**6.2** w	**2.6** w	**6.1** w	**2.5** w	**6.1** w	**2.3** w
42	Angola	..	..	..	..	..	..	..	..	..	..
43	Bolivia[c]	4.4	−0.9	3.8	1.9	3.7	−3.8	5.4	−3.3	5.6	−0.5
44	Egypt, Arab Rep.	7.3	5.4	2.7	2.6	6.9	4.8	..	..	10.4	7.1
45	Senegal[c]	2.1	3.1	1.4	2.9	4.6	3.9	3.0	3.3	1.4	2.9
46	Yemen, Rep.[c]	..	..	..	..	..	..	..	..	..	..
47	Zimbabwe	5.0	2.7	..	2.9	..	2.2	..	2.6	..	2.9
48	Philippines[c]	5.9	0.7	4.6	2.0	8.0	−0.8	7.5	0.5	5.2	1.2
49	Côte d'Ivoire	6.8	1.2	3.3	2.3	10.4	−1.7	*9.1*	8.2	8.6	0.4
50	Dominican Rep.[c]	8.0	2.4	6.3	1.8	10.8	2.9	8.9	1.1	7.3	2.3
51	Morocco[c]	5.7	4.1	2.4	6.7	6.1	2.8	..	4.1	6.8	4.2
52	Papua New Guinea[c]	4.1	2.1	3.1	1.7	..	3.1	..	1.6	..	1.7
53	Honduras	5.0	2.3	2.0	1.8	6.8	2.7	7.5	3.7	6.2	2.3
54	Guatemala[c]	5.9	0.4	5.1	0.8	7.3	−0.6	6.5	*−1.2*	5.7	0.6
55	Congo, People's Rep.[c]	6.2	3.9	3.1	3.2	9.9	4.7	..	6.8	4.7	3.2
56	Syrian Arab Rep.[c]	9.1	1.6	5.9	−0.9	12.0	5.2	..	..	9.4	1.2
57	Cameroon[c]	5.1	3.2	4.2	1.9	7.8	2.3	7.0	8.1	4.8	4.6
58	Peru[c]	3.9	0.4	1.0	3.6	4.4	−0.5	3.8	0.4	4.3	0.4
59	Ecuador[c]	8.8	1.9	3.4	4.3	13.7	1.8	11.5	0.2	7.6	1.3
60	Namibia	..	0.4	..	−1.0	..	−2.0	..	1.4	..	3.0
61	Paraguay[c]	7.0	2.2	4.9	3.4	9.1	−0.1	7.0	1.8	7.5	2.7
62	El Salvador[c]	4.3	0.6	3.6	−1.2	5.3	−0.6	4.6	*−0.3*	4.3	1.5
63	Colombia	5.7	3.5	4.5	2.6	5.7	5.0	6.4	3.1	6.4	2.8
64	Thailand[c]	7.3	7.0	4.6	4.1	9.5	8.1	11.2	8.1	7.6	7.4
65	Jamaica[c]	1.4	1.2	0.5	0.6	−0.1	1.4	0.4	2.1	2.7	1.0
66	Tunisia	6.5	3.4	5.5	1.6	7.4	2.4	9.9	5.9	6.5	4.5

Note: For data comparability and coverage, see the technical notes.   Figures in italics are for years other than those specified.

		GDP		Agriculture		Industry		Manufacturing[a]		Services, etc.[b]	
	Average annual growth rate (percent)	1965–80	1980–89	1965–80	1980–89	1965–80	1980–89	1965–80	1980–89	1965–80	1980–89
67	Turkey	6.2	5.1	3.2	3.0	7.2	6.3	7.5	7.4	7.6	5.0
68	Botswana[c]	13.9	11.3	9.7	–4.0	24.0	13.0	13.5	5.3	11.5	11.9
69	Jordan	..	..	..	..	..	..	..	..	..	..
70	Panama[c]	5.5	0.5	2.4	1.9	5.9	–3.5	4.7	–1.4	6.0	1.3
71	Chile[c]	1.9	2.7	1.6	4.1	0.8	3.1	0.7	2.9	2.7	2.3
72	Costa Rica[c]	6.3	2.8	4.2	2.8	8.7	2.7	..	..	6.0	2.8
73	Poland[c]	..	2.5	..	..	..	..	..	..	..	..
74	Mauritius	5.2	5.9	..	3.0	..	9.1	..	10.9	..	4.9
75	Mexico[c]	6.5	0.7	3.2	0.8	7.6	0.4	7.4	0.7	6.6	0.9
76	Argentina[c]	3.4	–0.3	1.4	0.3	3.3	–1.1	2.7	–0.6	4.0	0.2
77	Malaysia[c]	7.4	4.9	..	3.9	..	6.5	..	8.0	..	3.9
78	Algeria[c]	..	3.5	..	5.3	..	3.8	..	7.5	..	2.5
79	Bulgaria	..	3.3	..	–2.7	..	5.5	..	..	..	1.9
80	*Lebanon[c]*	..	..	..	..	..	..	..	..	..	..
81	*Mongolia*	..	..	..	..	..	..	..	..	..	..
82	*Nicaragua[c]*	2.5	–1.6	3.8	–2.7	4.2	–2.4	5.1	–3.3	1.1	–0.5
	Upper-middle-income	**6.8 w**	**3.2 w**	..	**3.0 w**	..	**3.2 w**	..	..	..	**3.1 w**
83	Venezuela[c]	3.7	1.0	3.9	3.4	1.5	1.4	5.8	4.9	6.3	0.4
84	South Africa	4.1	1.5	..	2.7	..	0.4	..	0.5	..	2.5
85	Brazil	9.0	3.0	3.8	3.0	10.1	2.7	9.8	2.2	9.5	3.2
86	Hungary[c]	5.6	1.6	2.7	2.0	6.4	0.6	..	..	6.2	2.2
87	Uruguay	2.4	0.1	1.0	0.5	3.1	–1.2	..	–0.2	2.3	0.7
88	Yugoslavia	6.1	1.3	3.1	1.0	7.8	1.4	..	..	5.5	1.2
89	Gabon[c]	9.5	1.2	..	..	..	..	..	..	..	..
90	Iran, Islamic Rep.	6.1	3.4	4.5	5.7	2.2	2.9	10.0	–1.1	13.5	2.1
91	Trinidad and Tobago	*5.0*	–5.5	*0.0*	–6.2	*5.0*	–6.4	2.6	–8.4	5.8	–3.9
92	Czechoslovakia[c]	..	1.7	..	*0.4*	..	2.0	..	..	..	*1.4*
93	Portugal[c]	5.3	2.5	..	..	..	..	..	..	..	..
94	Korea, Rep.[c]	9.9	9.7	3.0	3.3	16.4	12.4	18.7	13.1	9.6	9.1
95	Oman[c]	13.0	*12.8*	..	*5.1*	..	*13.7*	..	*27.0*	..	*10.5*
96	Libya	4.2	..	10.7	..	1.2	..	13.7	..	15.5	..
97	Greece	5.8	1.6	2.3	0.3	7.1	0.9	8.4	*0.2*	6.2	2.5
98	*Iraq*	..	..	..	..	..	..	..	..	..	..
99	*Romania*	..	..	..	..	..	..	..	..	..	..
	Low- and middle-income	**5.8 w**	**3.8 w**	**3.0 w**	**3.3 w**	**6.7 w**	**4.5 w**	**7.8 w**	**6.0 w**	**7.1 w**	**3.5 w**
	Sub-Saharan Africa	**4.2 w**	**2.1 w**	**1.9 w**	**2.0 w**	**7.5 w**	**0.7 w**	..	**3.4 w**	**4.5 w**	**2.3 w**
	East Asia	**7.3 w**	**7.9 w**	**3.2 w**	**5.2 w**	**10.9 w**	**10.4 w**	**10.7 w**	**12.6 w**	**8.3 w**	**7.7 w**
	South Asia	**3.7 w**	**5.1 w**	**2.5 w**	**2.9 w**	**4.4 w**	**6.7 w**	**4.6 w**	**7.1 w**	**4.5 w**	**6.3 w**
	Europe, M.East, & N.Africa	..	**2.9 w**	..	**2.9 w**	..	**3.1 w**	..	..	..	**2.7 w**
	Latin America & Caribbean	**6.1 w**	**1.6 w**	**3.1 w**	**1.9 w**	**6.7 w**	**1.6 w**	**7.2 w**	**1.5 w**	**6.8 w**	**1.6 w**
	Severely indebted	**6.1 w**	**1.9 w**	**3.0 w**	**2.1 w**	**6.9 w**	**1.5 w**	**7.3 w**	**1.5 w**	**6.8 w**	**1.9 w**
	High-income economies	**3.8 w**	**3.0 w**	..	**1.5 w**	..	**2.1 w**	..	**3.4 w**	**4.6 w**	**3.1 w**
	OECD members	**3.8 w**	**3.0 w**	..	**1.3 w**	..	**2.2 w**	..	**3.3 w**	**4.5 w**	**3.1 w**
	†Other	**8.2 w**	**2.4 w**	..	**6.4 w**	..	**–0.7 w**	..	**7.7 w**	..	**5.3 w**
100	†Saudi Arabia[c]	10.6	–1.8	4.1	14.6	11.6	–4.4	8.1	8.8	10.5	2.4
101	Ireland	5.3	*1.8*	2.2[e]	–8.4	10.1[e]	–4.3	..	..	5.2[e]	*3.4*
102	Spain[c]	4.6	3.1	..	..	..	..	..	..	..	..
103	†Israel[c]	6.8	3.2	..	..	..	..	..	..	..	..
104	†Hong Kong	8.6	*7.1*	..	..	..	..	..	..	..	..
105	†Singapore[c]	10.0	6.1	2.8	–5.7	11.9	5.0	13.2	5.9	9.4	7.0
106	New Zealand[c]	2.4	2.2	..	..	..	..	..	..	..	..
107	Australia[c]	4.0	3.5	..	*3.0*	..	*3.0*	..	*1.7*	..	*3.6*
108	United Kingdom	2.9	2.6	–2.8[e]	–7.2	0.8[e]	–0.6	–0.5[e]	2.9	3.8[e]	4.8
109	Italy[c]	4.3	2.4	0.9[e]	*0.9*	3.9[e]	*1.6*	5.8[e]	*2.3*	4.0[e]	*2.8*
110	Netherlands[c]	3.9	1.7	4.3[e]	*3.6*	2.3[e]	*1.1*	..	..	3.8[e]	*1.6*
111	†Kuwait[c]	1.6	0.7	..	18.8	..	1.0	..	–0.2	..	0.6
112	Belgium[c]	..	1.8	*0.4*	*2.5*	5.1	*1.1*	5.9	2.0	4.3	*1.6*
113	Austria[c]	4.1	1.9	2.1	*1.3*	4.3	*1.3*	4.5	*1.8*	4.2	*2.0*
114	France[c]	3.8	2.1	..	*2.4*	..	*0.3*	..	*–0.1*	..	*2.7*
115	†United Arab Emirates	..	–4.5	..	*9.3*	..	*–8.7*	..	*2.7*	..	*3.7*
116	Canada	..	..	..	..	..	..	..	..	..	..
117	Germany[c]	3.3	*1.9*	1.4	*1.6*	2.8	*0.0*	3.3	*0.8*	3.7	*3.0*
118	Denmark	2.6	2.2	0.8	*2.5*	1.8	*3.6*	3.1	*2.1*	3.2	*1.7*
119	United States[c]	2.7	*3.3*	1.0	*3.2*	1.7	*2.9*	2.5	*3.8*	3.4	*3.3*
120	Sweden	..	1.8	..	*0.9*	..	*3.1*	..	*3.0*	..	*1.0*
121	Finland	4.1	3.0	*0.0*	*–1.4*	4.3	*2.9*	4.9	*3.3*	4.8	*3.3*
122	Norway	4.4	3.6	–0.4	*0.4*	5.7	*4.8*	2.6	*1.5*	4.1	*3.0*
123	Japan[c]	6.6	*4.0*	–0.6	*0.4*	7.4	*5.2*	8.2	*6.7*	6.7	*3.2*
124	Switzerland[c]	5.7	2.1	..	..	..	..	..	..	..	..
	Other economies	..	..	..	..	..	..	..	..	..	..
	World	**4.1 w**	**3.1 w**	..	**2.6 w**	..	**2.4 w**	..	**3.7 w**	..	**3.2 w**
	Oil exporters (excl. USSR)	**6.6 w**	**1.2 w**	**3.9 w**	**5.4 w**	**6.1 w**	**–1.1 w**	**8.4 w**	**3.2 w**	**10.0 w**	**1.9 w**

a. Because manufacturing is generally the most dynamic part of the industrial sector, its growth rate is shown separately. b. Services, etc. include unallocated items. c. GDP and its components are at purchaser values. d. World Bank estimate. e. Data refer to the period 1970–80.

Table 3. Structure of production

		GDP (millions of dollars)		Distribution of gross domestic product (percent)							
				Agriculture		Industry		Manufacturing[a]		Services, etc.[b]	
		1965	1989	1965	1989	1965	1989	1965	1989	1965	1989
	Low-income economies	**163,040** *t*	**956,340** *t*	**44** *w*	**32** *w*	**28** *w*	**37** *w*	**20** *w*	**27** *w*	**28** *w*	**31** *w*
	China and India	**117,730** *t*	**653,040** *t*	**44** *w*	**31** *w*	**32** *w*	**41** *w*	**24** *w*	**32** *w*	**24** *w*	**28** *w*
	Other low-income	**44,490** *t*	**301,160** *t*	**44** *w*	**33** *w*	**17** *w*	**28** *w*	**8** *w*	**14** *w*	**37** *w*	**39** *w*
1	Mozambique	. .	1,100	. .	64	. .	22	. .	. .	. .	14
2	Ethiopia	1,180	5,420	58	42	14	16	7	11	28	42
3	Tanzania	790	2,540	46	66	14	7	8	4	40	27
4	Somalia	220	1,090	71	65	6	10	3	5	24	26
5	Bangladesh[c]	4,380	20,240	53	44	11	14	5	7	36	41
6	Lao PDR[c]	. .	630	. .	. .	. .	. .	. .	. .	. .	. .
7	Malawi	220	1,410	50	35	13	19	. .	11	37	45
8	Nepal	730	2,810	65	58	11	14	3	6	23	28
9	Chad[c]	290	1,020	42	36	15	20	12	16	43	44
10	Burundi	150	*960*	. .	56	. .	15	. .	*10*	. .	29
11	Sierra Leone	320	890	34	46	28	11	6	6	38	42
12	Madagascar[c]	750	2,280	25	31	*14*	14	. .	12	*61*	54
13	Nigeria	5,850	28,920	54	31	13	44	6	10	33	25
14	Uganda	1,100	4,460	52	67	13	7	8	5	35	26
15	Zaire[c]	4,150	9,610	22	30	32	32	. .	10	46	38
16	Mali[c]	*260*	2,080	*65*	50	9	12	5	6	25	38
17	Niger[c]	670	2,040	68	36	3	13	2	8	29	51
18	Burkina Faso	350	2,460	37	35	24	26	11	15	39	39
19	Rwanda[c]	150	2,170	75	37	7	23	2	15	18	41
20	India	50,530	235,220	44	30	22	29	16	18	34	41
21	China[c]	67,200	417,830	44	32	39	48	31[d]	34[d]	17	20
22	Haiti[c]	350	2,370	. .	*31*	. .	38	. .	15	. .	*31*
23	Kenya	920	7,130	35	31	18	20	11	12	47	49
24	Pakistan	5,450	35,820	40	27	20	24	14	16	40	49
25	Benin	220	1,600	59	46	8	12	. .	5	33	42
26	Central African Rep.	140	1,050	46	42	16	15	4	8	38	43
27	Ghana[c]	2,050	5,260	44	49	19	17	10	10	38	34
28	Togo[c]	190	1,340	45	33	21	23	10	8	34	44
29	Zambia[c]	1,060	4,700	14	13	54	47	6	24	32	40
30	Guinea[c]	. .	2,750	. .	30	. .	33	. .	3	. .	38
31	Sri Lanka	1,770	6,340	28	26	21	27	17	16	51	47
32	Lesotho	50	*340*	65	*24*	5	*30*	1	*14*	30	*46*
33	Indonesia[c]	3,840	93,970	56	23	13	37	8	17	31	39
34	Mauritania	160	910	32	37	36	24	4	. .	32	38
35	*Afghanistan*	600	. .	. .	. .	. .	. .	. .	. .	. .	. .
36	*Bhutan*	. .	280	. .	45	. .	25	. .	6	. .	30
37	*Kampuchea, Dem.*	. .	. .	. .	. .	. .	. .	. .	. .	. .	. .
38	*Liberia*	270	. .	27	. .	40	. .	3	. .	34	. .
39	*Myanmar*	. .	. .	. .	. .	. .	. .	. .	. .	. .	. .
40	*Sudan*	1,330	. .	54	. .	9	. .	4	. .	37	. .
41	*Viet Nam*	. .	. .	. .	. .	. .	. .	. .	. .	. .	. .
	Middle-income economies	**206,000** *t*	**2,118,080** *t*	**19** *w*	**12** *w*	**34** *w*	**36** *w*	**20** *w*	. .	**45** *w*	**50** *w*
	Lower-middle-income	**117,580** *t*	**911,200** *t*	**21** *w*	**14** *w*	**30** *w*	**35** *w*	**20** *w*	**23** *w*	**48** *w*	**51** *w*
42	Angola	. .	7,720	. .	. .	. .	. .	. .	. .	. .	. .
43	Bolivia[c]	710	4,520	23	32	31	30	15	*13*	46	38
44	Egypt, Arab Rep.	4,550	31,580	29	19	27	30	. .	*14*	45	52
45	Senegal[c]	810	4,660	25	22	18	31	14	20	56	47
46	Yemen, Rep.[c]	. .	. .	. .	. .	. .	. .	. .	. .	. .	. .
47	Zimbabwe	960	5,250	18	13	35	39	20	25	47	49
48	Philippines[c]	6,010	44,350	26	24	28	33	20	22	46	43
49	Côte d'Ivoire	760	7,170	47	46	19	24	11	*17*	33	30
50	Dominican Rep.[c]	890	6,650	23	15	22	26	16	11	55	59
51	Morocco[c]	2,950	22,390	23	16	28	34	16	17	49	50
52	Papua New Guinea[c]	340	3,520	42	28	18	30	. .	10	41	42
53	Honduras	460	4,320	40	21	19	25	12	14	41	54
54	Guatemala[c]	1,330	8,150	. .	18	. .	26	. .	. .	. .	56
55	Congo, People's Rep.[c]	200	2,270	19	14	19	35	. .	9	62	51
56	Syrian Arab Rep.[c]	1,470	11,460	29	22	22	23	. .	. .	49	55
57	Cameroon[c]	810	11,080	33	27	20	27	10	15	47	46
58	Peru[c]	5,020	28,610	18	8	30	30	17	21	53	62
59	Ecuador[c]	1,150	10,380	27	15	22	39	18	21·	50	47
60	Namibia	. .	1,650	. .	11	. .	38	. .	5	. .	50
61	Paraguay[c]	440	4,130	37	29	19	22	16	16	45	48
62	El Salvador[c]	800	5,860	29	12	22	21	18	16	49	67
63	Colombia	5,910	39,410	27	17	27	36	19	21	47	47
64	Thailand[c]	4,390	69,680	32	15	23	38	14	21	45	47
65	Jamaica[c]	970	3,880	10	5	37	45	17	18	53	50
66	Tunisia	880	8,920	22	14	24	33	9	16	54	53

Note: For data comparability and coverage, see the technical notes.   Figures in italics are for years other than those specified.

		GDP (millions of dollars)		Agriculture		Industry		Manufacturing[a]		Services, etc.[b]	
		1965	1989	1965	1989	1965	1989	1965	1989	1965	1989
67	Turkey	7,660	71,600	34	17	25	35	16	23	41	48
68	Botswana[c]	50	2,500	34	3	19	57	12	4	47	40
69	Jordan	. .	3,910	. .	6	. .	29	. .	16	. .	65
70	Panama[c]	660	4,550	18	11	19	15	12	7	63	75
71	Chile[c]	5,940	25,250	9	. .	40	. .	24	. .	52	. .
72	Costa Rica[c]	590	5,220	24	17	23	27	. .	. .	53	56
73	Poland[c]	. .	68,290	. .	. .	. .	. .	. .	. .	. .	. .
74	Mauritius	190	1,740	16	13	23	32	14	24	61	56
75	Mexico[c]	21,640	200,730	14	9	27	32	20	23	59	59
76	Argentina[c]	16,500	53,070	17	14	42	33	33	35	42	53
77	Malaysia[c]	3,130	37,480	28	. .	25	. .	9	. .	47	. .
78	Algeria[c]	. .	39,780	. .	16	. .	44	. .	14	. .	40
79	Bulgaria	. .	15,570	. .	11	. .	59	. .	. .	. .	29
80	*Lebanon*[c]	1,150	. .	12	. .	21	. .	. .	. .	67	. .
81	*Mongolia*	. .	. .	. .	. .	. .	. .	. .	. .	. .	. .
82	*Nicaragua*[c]	570	*3,430*	25	29	24	*23*	18	*19*	51	*48*
	Upper-middle-income	88,730 *t*	. .	18 *w*	. .	38 *w*	. .	. .	. .	42 *w*	. .
83	Venezuela[c]	9,820	43,830	6	6	40	46	. .	28	55	48
84	South Africa	10,540	80,370	10	6	42	44	23	24	48	50
85	Brazil	19,450	*319,150*	19	9	33	*43*	26	*31*	48	*48*
86	Hungary[c]	. .	29,060	. .	14	. .	36	. .	. .	. .	50
87	Uruguay	930	7,170	15	11	32	28	. .	22	53	61
88	Yugoslavia	11,190	71,760	23	10	42	42	. .	. .	35	48
89	Gabon[c]	230	3,440	26	10	34	47	7	10	40	43
90	Iran, Islamic Rep.	6,170	150,250	26	23	36	15	12	7	38	62
91	Trinidad and Tobago	690	4,200	8	3	48	41	. .	8	44	56
92	Czechoslovakia[c]	. .	50,470	. .	6	. .	57	. .	. .	. .	36
93	Portugal[c]	3,740	44,880	. .	9	. .	37	. .	26	. .	54
94	Korea, Rep.[c]	3,000	211,880	38	10	25	44	18	26	37	46
95	Oman[c]	60	*7,700*	61	*3*	23	*80*	0	*4*	16	*18*
96	Libya	1,500	*22,990*	5	*5*	63	*50*	3	*7*	33	*45*
97	Greece	5,270	*39,910*	24	*16*	26	*29*	16	*18*	49	*55*
98	*Iraq*	2,430	. .	18	. .	46	. .	8	. .	36	. .
99	*Romania*			. .	. .	. .	. .	. .	. .	. .	. .
	Low- and middle-income	374,030 *t*	3,078,460 *t*	30 *w*	19 *w*	31 *w*	38 *w*	21 *w*	. .	37 *w*	44 *w*
	Sub-Saharan Africa	29,120 *t*	161,820 *t*	41 *w*	32 *w*	20 *w*	27 *w*	8 *w*	11 *w*	39 *w*	38 *w*
	East Asia	90,700 *t*	895,230 *t*	42 *w*	24 *w*	35 *w*	44 *w*	27 *w*	33 *w*	23 *w*	34 *w*
	South Asia	64,510 *t*	317,170 *t*	44 *w*	32 *w*	21 *w*	26 *w*	15 *w*	17 *w*	35 *w*	41 *w*
	Europe, M.East, & N.Africa		787,990 *t*	. .	. .	. .	. .	. .	. .	. .	. .
	Latin America & Caribbean	95,470 *t*	809,230 *t*	16 *w*	. .	33 *w*	. .	23 *w*	. .	51 *w*	. .
	Severely indebted	109,860 *t*	934,670 *t*	17 *w*	. .	33 *w*	. .	22 *w*	. .	50 *w*	. .
	High-income economies	1,413,280 *t*	14,764,510 *t*	5 *w*	. .	42 *w*	. .	32 *w*	. .	54 *w*	. .
	OECD members	1,389,560 *t*	14,292,220 *t*	5 *w*	. .	43 *w*	. .	32 *w*	. .	54 *w*	. .
	†Other	17,580 *t*	477,340 *t*	8 *w*	4 *w*	45 *w*	41 *w*	14 *w*	. .	46 *w*	54 *w*
100	†Saudi Arabia[c]	2,300	80,890	8	8	60	45	9	8	31	48
101	Ireland	2,340	29,570	. .	*11*	. .	*10*	. .	*3*	. .	*79*
102	Spain[c]	23,750	379,360	. .	*5*	. .	*9*	. .	*18*	. .	*86*
103	†Israel[c]	3,590	46,030	. .	. .	. .	. .	24	*21*	. .	. .
104	†Hong Kong	2,150	*52,540*	2	*0*	40	*28*	24	21	58	*72*
105	†Singapore[c]	970	28,360	3	*0*	24	*37*	15	*26*	74	*63*
106	New Zealand[c]	5,470	41,360	. .	*8*	. .	*28*	. .	*17*	. .	*64*
107	Australia[c]	23,700	281,940	9	*4*	39	*32*	26	*15*	51	*64*
108	United Kingdom	89,750	717,870	3	*2*	46	*37*	34	*20*	51	*62*
109	Italy[c]	66,700	865,720	. .	*4*	. .	*34*	. .	*22*	. .	*63*
110	Netherlands[c]	19,910	221,680	. .	*4*	. .	*31*	. .	*20*	. .	*65*
111	†Kuwait[c]	2,100	23,530	0	*1*	70	*56*	3	*9*	29	*43*
112	Belgium[c]	16,840	156,830	5	*2*	41	*31*	30	*22*	53	*67*
113	Austria[c]	9,480	126,480	9	*3*	46	*37*	33	*27*	45	*60*
114	France[c]	99,300	955,790	. .	*3*	. .	*29*	. .	*21*	. .	*67*
115	†United Arab Emirates	. .	28,270	. .	*2*	. .	*55*	. .	*8*	. .	*43*
116	Canada	46,570	488,590	6	. .	40	. .	26	*13*	54	. .
117	Germany[c]	114,820	1,189,100	4	*2*	53	*37*	40	*32*	43	*62*
118	Denmark	8,880	89,140	9	*4*	36	*29*	23	*20*	55	*67*
119	United States[c]	698,990	5,156,440	3	*2*	38	*29*	28	*17*	59	*69*
120	Sweden	19,610	166,520	. .	*3*	. .	*34*	. .	*23*	. .	*63*
121	Finland	7,540	100,860	16	*6*	37	*36*	23	*22*	47	*58*
122	Norway	7,080	95,000	8	*3*	33	*34*	21	*15*	59	*63*
123	Japan[c]	91,290	2,818,520	10	*3*	44	*41*	34	*30*	46	*56*
124	Switzerland[c]	13,920	174,960	. .	. .	. .	. .	. .	. .	. .	. .
	Other economies	. .	. .	. .	. .	. .	. .	. .	. .	. .	. .
	World	2,003,700 *t*	19,981,540 *t*	10 *w*	. .	40 *w*	. .	30 *w*	. .	51 *w*	. .
	Oil exporters (excl. USSR)	34,470 *t*	453,320 *t*	20 *w*	14 *w*	37 *w*	35 *w*	10 *w*	9 *w*	42 *w*	49 *w*

a. Because manufacturing is generally the most dynamic part of the industrial sector, its share of GDP is shown separately. b. Services, etc. include unallocated items. c. GDP and its components are shown at purchaser values. d. World Bank estimate.

209

Table 4. Agriculture and food

		Value added in agriculture (millions of current dollars)		Cereal imports (thousands of metric tons)		Food aid in cereals (thousands of metric tons)		Fertilizer consumption (hundreds of grams of plant nutrient per hectare of arable land)		Average index of food production per capita (1979–81=100)
		1970	1989	1974	1989	1974/75	1988/89	1970/71	1987/88	1987–89
	Low-income economies	**89,314 t**	**305,959 t**	**22,608 t**	**28,763 t**	**6,002 t**	**5,235 t**	**171 t**	**802 t**	**116 w**
	China and India	**60,621 t**	**205,278 t**	**11,294 t**	**15,014 t**	**1,582 t**	**531 t**	**241 t**	**1,185 t**	**122 w**
	Other low-income	**28,269 t**	**99,716 t**	**11,314 t**	**13,749 t**	**4,420 t**	**4,704 t**	**72 t**	**310 t**	**103 w**
1	Mozambique	..	704	62	400	34	424	22	21	83
2	Ethiopia	931	2,254	118	690	54	573	4	39	89
3	Tanzania	473	1,795	431	83	148	76	31	92	90
4	Somalia	167	705	42	186	111	73	29	40	97
5	Bangladesh[a]	3,636	8,962	1,866	2,204	2,076	1,161	157	770	93
6	Lao PDR[a]	..	..	53	64	8	20	2	6	116
7	Malawi	119	498	17	86	0	217	52	203	85
8	Nepal	579	1,633	18	26	0	9	27	232	107
9	Chad[a]	142	364	37	37	20	15	7	17	101
10	Burundi	159	535	7	6	6	6	5	20	98
11	Sierra Leone	108	409	72	145	10	38	17	3	89
12	Madagascar[a]	243	717	114	103	7	76	61	21	93
13	Nigeria	5,080	8,874	389	240	7	0	2	94	96
14	Uganda	929	2,986	36	16	..	17	14	2	87
15	Zaire[a]	805	2,846	343	323	1	55	8	9	94
16	Mali[a]	207	1,048	281	89	107	62	31	59	97
17	Niger[a]	420	744	155	105	73	83	1	8	86
18	Burkina Faso	121	871	99	120	28	49	3	57	115
19	Rwanda[a]	135	799	3	10	19	2	3	20	77
20	India	23,916	71,345	5,261	1,014	1,582	308	137	517	113
21	China[a]	36,705	133,934	6,033	14,000	0	223	410	2,361	128
22	Haiti[a]	..	692	83	251	25	49	4	25	93
23	Kenya	484	2,208	15	119	2	112	238	421	101
24	Pakistan	3,352	9,681	1,274	2,171	584	416	146	829	103
25	Benin	121	729	7	104	9	16	36	49	114
26	Central African Rep.	60	442	7	28	1	0	12	4	90
27	Ghana[a]	1,030	2,570	177	244	33	46	13	38	109
28	Togo[a]	85	446	6	111	11	11	3	76	89
29	Zambia[a]	191	617	93	123	5	66	73	183	97
30	Guinea[a]	..	812	63	183	49	42	19	6	90
31	Sri Lanka	545	1,648	951	1,177	271	272	555	1,094	87
32	Lesotho	23	83	48	140	14	34	10	125	80
33	Indonesia[a]	4,340	22,032	1,919	2,356	301	69	133	1,068	124
34	Mauritania	58	339	115	207	48	70	11	55	88
35	Afghanistan	..	..	5	260	10	208	24	97	..
36	Bhutan	..	125	3	20	0	2	..	10	121
37	Kampuchea, Dem.	..	..	223	50	226	11	11	2	..
38	Liberia	91	..	42	158	3	28	63	94	95
39	Myanmar	..	..	26	..	9	0	21	125	120
40	Sudan	757	..	125	556	46	198	28	40	87
41	Viet Nam	..	..	1,854	258	64	100	513	651	111
	Middle-income economies	**50,052 t**	**258,932 t**	**42,817 t**	**80,767 t**	**1,926 t**	**4,548 t**	**370 t**	**703 t**	**101 w**
	Lower-middle-income	**31,154 t**	**129,238 t**	**24,693 t**	**49,426 t**	**1,654 t**	**4,510 t**	**309 t**	**592 t**	**99 w**
42	Angola	..	..	149	248	0	79	33	29	84
43	Bolivia[a]	202	1,440	209	172	22	95	7	19	102
44	Egypt, Arab Rep.	1,942	5,858	3,877	8,543	610	1,427	1,312	3,505	109
45	Senegal[a]	208	1,028	341	515	27	53	17	40	106
46	Yemen, Rep.[a]	..	..	306	1,378	33	85	..	63	..
47	Zimbabwe	214	664	56	52	0	10	446	505	90
48	Philippines[a]	1,996	10,429	817	1,626	89	135	287	612	86
49	Côte d'Ivoire	462	3,295	172	693	4	19	74	90	96
50	Dominican Rep.[a]	345	1,012	252	601	16	228	334	556	94
51	Morocco[a]	789	3,679	891	1,329	75	238	117	376	120
52	Papua New Guinea[a]	240	1,000	71	243	..	0	58	381	97
53	Honduras	212	890	52	172	31	67	156	190	88
54	Guatemala[a]	..	1,472	138	214	9	277	298	656	103
55	Congo, People's Rep.[a]	49	311	34	82	2	2	114	25	98
56	Syrian Arab Rep.[a]	435	2,475	339	1,578	47	31	68	404	86
57	Cameroon[a]	364	2,978	81	345	4	6	34	71	96
58	Peru[a]	1,351	2,177	637	1,065	37	146	300	622	101
59	Ecuador[a]	401	1,526	152	536	13	89	133	232	106
60	Namibia	..	187	..	0	..	..	..	..	95
61	Paraguay[a]	191	1,217	71	5	10	1	98	69	115
62	El Salvador[a]	292	685	75	186	4	197	1,043	1,262	90
63	Colombia	1,806	6,622	502	716	28	12	287	945	102
64	Thailand[a]	1,837	10,561	97	346	0	83	59	328	104
65	Jamaica[a]	93	210	340	296	1	365	873	914	92
66	Tunisia	245	1,235	307	1,655	59	284	76	222	96

Note: For data comparability and coverage, see the technical notes.   Figures in italics are for years other than those specified.

		Value added in agriculture (millions of current dollars)		Cereal imports (thousands of metric tons)		Food aid in cereals (thousands of metric tons)		Fertilizer consumption (hundreds of grams of plant nutrient per hectare of arable land)		Average index of food production per capita (1979–81 = 100)
		1970	1989	1974	1989	1974/75	1988/89	1970/71	1987/88	1987–89
67	Turkey	3,383	11,857	1,276	3,061	16	3	157	637	97
68	Botswana[a]	28	75	21	77	5	33	15	7	68
69	Jordan	. .	241	171	671	79	25	74	362	117
70	Panama[a]	149	493	63	109	3	. .	387	657	92
71	Chile[a]	558	. .	1,737	178	323	14	313	544	107
72	Costa Rica[a]	222	897	110	357	1	84	1,001	1,806	89
73	Poland[a]	. .	. .	4,185	2,893	. .	. .	1,678	2,223	106
74	Mauritius	30	222	160	209	22	21	2,095	3,075	100
75	Mexico[a]	4,462	18,050	2,881	7,050	. .	291	232	753	98
76	Argentina[a]	2,250	7,339	0	4	. .	. .	26	45	91
77	Malaysia[a]	1,198	. .	1,023	2,299	1	10	489	1,596	142
78	Algeria[a]	492	6,187	1,816	7,461	54	39	163	320	97
79	Bulgaria	. .	1,758	649	1,384	. .	. .	1,411	1,804	100
80	*Lebanon*[a]	136	. .	354	558	26	32	1,354	671	. .
81	*Mongolia*	. .	. .	28	59	. .	. .	22	184	91
82	*Nicaragua*[a]	199	. .	44	140	3	32	215	433	63
	Upper-middle-income	19,594 *t*	. .	18,124 *t*	31,341 *t*	271 *t*	38 *t*	465 *t*	865 *t*	103 *w*
83	Venezuela[a]	826	2,654	1,270	1,804	. .	. .	170	1,580	88
84	South Africa	1,362	4,635	127	296	. .	. .	422	541	90
85	Brazil	4,392	*27,810*	2,485	2,015	31	15	186	485	115
86	Hungary[a]	1,010	4,048	408	249	. .	. .	1,497	2,595	113
87	Uruguay	268	773	70	81	6	. .	485	420	106
88	Yugoslavia	2,212	7,229	992	192	. .	. .	770	1,328	98
89	Gabon[a]	60	353	24	50	. .	. .	. .	46	81
90	Iran, Islamic Rep.	2,120	34,563	2,076	6,500	. .	23	60	658	87
91	Trinidad and Tobago	40	118	208	284	. .	. .	880	450	86
92	Czechoslovakia[a]	. .	*3,266*	1,296	216	. .	. .	2,404	3,031	121
93	Portugal[a]	. .	. .	1,861	1,226	. .	. .	428	1,026	100
94	Korea, Rep.[a]	2,311	21,663	2,679	10,267	234	. .	2,450	3,920	96
95	Oman[a]	40	202	52	200	. .	. .	. .	417	. .
96	Libya	93	. .	612	1,515	. .	. .	62	416	109
97	Greece	1,569	. .	1,341	465	. .	. .	861	1,542	100
98	*Iraq*	579	. .	870	4,891	. .	. .	34	397	98
99	*Romania*	. .	. .	1,381	556	. .	. .	565	1,301	109
	Low- and middle-income	141,602 *t*	571,792 *t*	65,426 *t*	109,529 *t*	7,928 *t*	9,783 *t*	256 *t*	758 *t*	112 *w*
	Sub-Saharan Africa	15,597 *t*	52,090 *t*	4,208 *t*	7,411 *t*	910 *t*	2,610 *t*	34 *t*	76 *t*	95 *w*
	East Asia	49,792 *t*	211,600 *t*	14,938 *t*	31,795 *t*	923 *t*	651 *t*	365 *t*	1,712 *t*	123 *w*
	South Asia	32,884 *t*	103,077 *t*	9,404 *t*	6,634 *t*	4,522 *t*	2,169 *t*	135 *t*	541 *t*	112 *w*
	Europe, M.East, & N.Africa	20,496 *t*	116,812 *t*	25,193 *t*	46,909 *t*	1,010 *t*	2,394 *t*	575 *t*	1,058 *t*	99 *w*
	Latin America & Caribbean	18,661 *t*	. .	11,556 *t*	16,484 *t*	563 *t*	1,960 *t*	177 *t*	464 *t*	105 *w*
	Severely indebted	23,513 *t*	. .	20,373 *t*	29,501 *t*	1,274 *t*	2,705 *t*	351 *t*	647 *t*	105 *w*
	High-income economies	82,405 *t*	. .	78,976 *t*	75,503 *t*			1,032 *t*	1,238 *t*	99 *w*
	OECD members	80,527 *t*	. .	72,941 *t*	64,224 *t*			1,029 *t*	1,221 *t*	98 *w*
	†Other	1,880 *t*	18,155 *t*	6,035 *t*	11,279 *t*			1,423 *t*	3,445 *t*	123 *w*
100	†Saudi Arabia[a]	219	6,150	482	5,560			54	3,678	. .
101	Ireland	559	*3,307*	640	379			3,067	6,815	105
102	Spain[a]	. .	*18,160*	4,675	2,224			593	989	111
103	†Israel[b]	295	. .	1,176	1,890	53	4	1,401	2,237	106
104	†Hong Kong	62	*184*	657	826			. .	. .	61
105	†Singapore[a]	44	97	682	925			2,500	18,333	86
106	New Zealand[a]	897	. .	92	190			7,745	7,086	107
107	Australia[a]	2,157	*10,402*	2	26			232	286	96
108	United Kingdom	2,993	. .	7,540	2,908			2,631	3,555	105
109	Italy[a]	8,365	*30,579*	8,101	7,649			896	1,901	100
110	Netherlands[a]	1,827	*9,155*	7,199	5,932			7,493	6,877	110
111	†Kuwait[a]	8	238	101	597			. .	750	. .
112	Belgium[a]	920	*3,165*	4,585[c]	4,004[c]			5,648[c]	5,098[c]	116[c]
113	Austria[a]	992	*4,042*	164	81			2,426	2,214	109
114	France[a]	1,221	*31,843*	654	917			2,435	2,990	105
115	†United Arab Emirates	. .	481	132	596			. .	1,632	. .
116	Canada	3,265	. .	1,513	1,067			191	484	103
117	Germany[a]	5,951	*18,307*	7,164	4,524			4,263	4,208	112
118	Denmark	882	*3,942*	462	171			2,234	2,330	120
119	United States[a]	27,812	. .	460	2,147			816	937	92
120	Sweden	. .	*4,879*	300	120			1,646	1,357	94
121	Finland	1,205	*5,808*	222	214			1,930	2,164	102
122	Norway	624	*2,757*	713	545			2,443	2,704	109
123	Japan[b]	12,467	*72,773*	19,557	27,370			3,547	4,327	97
124	Switzerland	. .	. .	1,458	651			3,831	4,306	102
	Other economies	. .	. .	10,533 *t*	41,874 *t*	. .	1 *t*	464 *t*	1,209 *t*	110 *w*
	World	249,704 *t*	. .	154,934 *t*	226,907 *t*	7,981 *t*	9,787 *t*	497 *t*	954 *t*	110 *w*
	Oil exporters (excl. USSR)	9,822 *t*	65,457 *t*	8,166 *t*	29,579 *t*	63 *t*	143 *t*	49 *t*	408 *t*	101 *w*

a. Value added in agriculture data are at purchaser values. b. Value added in agriculture data refer to net domestic product at factor cost. c. Includes Luxembourg.

211

Table 5. Commercial energy

		Average annual energy growth rate (percent)				Energy consumption per capita (kilograms of oil equivalent)		Energy imports as a percentage of merchandise exports	
		Energy production		Energy consumption					
		1965–80	1980–89	1965–80	1980–89	1965	1989	1965	1989
Low-income economies		**10.0** w	**4.6** w	**8.3** w	**5.2** w	**125** w	**330** w	**7** w	**4** w
China and India		**9.1** w	**5.5** w	**8.8** w	**5.3** w	**146** w	**437** w	**8** w	**3** w
Other low-income		**12.4** w	**0.9** w	**5.6** w	**4.0** w	**72** w	**124** w	**6** w	**6** w
1	Mozambique	19.8	–34.7	2.2	1.8	81	84	13	*2*
2	Ethiopia	7.5	6.0	4.1	2.3	10	20	8	*25*
3	Tanzania	7.3	3.4	3.7	2.3	37	37	. .	*4*
4	Somalia	. .	0.0	16.7	1.8	14	78	9	*8*
5	Bangladesh	. .	12.8	. .	7.6	. .	51	. .	*4*
6	Lao PDR	. .	0.4	4.2	2.6	24	38	. .	. .
7	Malawi	18.2	4.1	8.0	0.3	25	41	7	*17*
8	Nepal	18.4	11.3	6.2	8.9	6	24	. .	*2*
9	Chad	. .	0.0	. .	0.2	. .	17	23	*6*
10	Burundi	. .	10.2	6.0	7.8	5	21	11	*1*
11	Sierra Leone	. .	0.0	0.8	–0.6	109	76	11	*4*
12	Madagascar	3.9	8.9	3.5	1.6	34	40	8	*2*
13	Nigeria	17.3	0.3	12.9	5.5	34	135	7	*4*
14	Uganda	–0.5	3.2	–0.5	3.7	36	25	1	*0*
15	Zaire	9.4	2.2	3.6	1.6	74	73	6	*4*
16	Mali	38.6	8.2	7.0	2.6	14	24	16	*2*
17	Niger	. .	14.0	12.5	3.1	8	40	9	*2*
18	Burkina Faso	. .	0.0	10.5	0.0	7	17	11	*2*
19	Rwanda	8.8	5.4	15.2	4.0	8	40	10	*2*
20	India	5.6	7.5	5.8	6.1	100	226	8	*24*
21	China	10.0	5.5	9.8	5.5	178	591	. .	*3*
22	Haiti	. .	5.0	8.4	1.9	24	51	. .	*2*
23	Kenya	13.1	7.8	4.5	0.5	110	98	20	*4*
24	Pakistan	6.5	5.8	3.5	6.2	135	213	7	*21*
25	Benin	. .	7.8	9.9	4.5	21	45	14	*6*
26	Central African Rep.	6.7	0.7	2.2	6.5	22	36	7	*2*
27	Ghana	17.7	–5.1	7.8	–2.6	76	129	6	*4*
28	Togo	2.9	10.1	10.7	–1.3	27	51	6	*12*
29	Zambia	25.7	1.5	4.0	0.8	464	372	. .	. .
30	Guinea	16.5	0.2	2.3	1.2	56	71	. .	*4*
31	Sri Lanka	10.4	8.1	2.2	4.2	106	173	6	*5*
32	Lesotho	. .	0.0	. .	0.0	. .	0	a	a
33	Indonesia	9.9	0.7	8.4	3.9	91	263	3	*6*
34	Mauritania	. .	0.0	9.5	0.4	48	114	2	*18*
35	*Afghanistan*	15.7	2.2	5.6	7.6	30	. .	8	*1*
36	*Bhutan*	. .	0.0	. .	0.6	. .	13	. .	. .
37	*Kampuchea, Dem.*	. .	5.6	7.6	2.3	19	. .	. .	. .
38	*Liberia*	14.6	–0.8	7.9	–7.5	182	165	6	*2*
39	*Myanmar*	8.4	3.9	4.9	4.2	39	70	4	*4*
40	*Sudan*	17.8	1.7	2.0	1.0	67	57	5	*3*
41	*Viet Nam*	5.3	1.5	–2.6	2.2	. .	97	. .	*30*
Middle-income economies		**3.7** w	**3.5** w	**6.2** w	**3.1** w	**663** w	**1,242** w	**9** w	**14** w
Lower-middle-income		**6.4** w	**4.1** w	**6.0** w	**3.2** w	**516** w	**888** w	**9** w	**13** w
42	Angola	. .	5.3	. .	2.3	. .	203	2	*1*
43	Bolivia	9.5	–0.1	7.7	–0.3	156	246	1	*2*
44	Egypt, Arab Rep.	10.7	5.7	6.2	6.3	313	636	11	*10*
45	Senegal	. .	0.0	7.4	–1.1	79	153	8	*10*
46	Yemen, Rep.	. .	1.8	. .	23.8	. .	234	. .	*13*
47	Zimbabwe	–0.7	0.7	5.2	1.2	441	525	. .	*0*
48	Philippines	9.0	8.9	5.8	–1.9	160	217	12	*17*
49	Côte d'Ivoire	11.1	–0.1	8.6	2.4	101	168	5	*2*
50	Dominican Rep.	10.9	5.9	11.5	2.4	127	336	7	*13*
51	Morocco	2.5	0.0	7.9	2.6	124	244	5	*25*
52	Papua New Guinea	13.7	6.3	13.0	2.3	56	231	7	. .
53	Honduras	14.0	4.5	7.6	2.7	111	193	5	*3*
54	Guatemala	12.5	4.9	6.8	–0.0	150	170	9	*6*
55	Congo, People's Rep.	41.1	6.2	7.8	4.0	90	211	8	*0*
56	Syrian Arab Rep.	56.3	3.4	12.4	4.2	212	896	13	*3*
57	Cameroon	13.0	12.5	6.3	5.5	67	141	6	*2*
58	Peru	6.6	–2.2	5.0	1.5	395	520	3	*9*
59	Ecuador	35.0	4.7	11.9	2.0	162	648	11	*3*
60	Namibia	. .	. .	. .	. .	. .	. .	a	a
61	Paraguay	. .	11.4	9.7	4.6	84	226	14	*26*
62	El Salvador	9.0	3.7	7.0	2.0	140	226	6	*13*
63	Colombia	1.0	9.4	6.0	2.7	413	754	1	*4*
64	Thailand	9.0	30.5	10.1	6.1	82	331	11	*10*
65	Jamaica	–0.9	5.0	6.1	–2.2	703	902	12	*24*
66	Tunisia	20.4	–0.9	8.5	6.3	170	546	12	14

Note: For data comparability and coverage, see the technical notes.   Figures in italics are for years other than those specified.

		Average annual energy growth rate (percent)				Energy consumption per capita (kilograms of oil equivalent)		Energy imports as a percentage of merchandise exports	
		Energy production		Energy consumption					
		1965-80	1980-89	1965-80	1980-89	1965	1989	1965	1989
67	Turkey	4.3	9.2	8.5	7.3	258	837	12	28
68	Botswana	8.8	2.4	9.5	2.2	191	423	a	a
69	Jordan	. .	16.4	9.3	6.8	226	773	42	49
70	Panama	6.9	9.2	5.8	4.2	576	1,636	61	54
71	Chile	1.8	2.9	3.0	1.7	652	836	5	9
72	Costa Rica	8.2	6.6	8.8	3.1	267	614	8	5
73	Poland	4.0	0.8	4.8	0.6	2,027	3,333	. .	. .
74	Mauritius	2.1	5.9	7.2	2.5	160	369	6	1
75	Mexico	9.7	1.9	7.9	0.7	605	1,288	4	4
76	Argentina	4.5	3.3	4.3	3.2	975	1,718	8	5
77	Malaysia	36.9	15.2	6.7	7.5	313	920	11	4
78	Algeria	5.3	4.1	11.9	12.5	226	1,906	0	2
79	Bulgaria	1.3	3.6	6.1	4.7	1,788	4,719	. .	. .
80	Lebanon	2.0	-2.9	2.0	3.6	713	. .	50	7
81	Mongolia	. .	3.5	. .	3.4	. .	1,245	. .	. .
82	Nicaragua	2.6	1.4	6.5	2.1	172	259	6	6
	Upper-middle-income	**2.5 w**	**2.6 w**	**6.3 w**	**2.8 w**	**881 w**	**1,890 w**	**8 w**	**14 w**
83	Venezuela	-3.1	-0.4	4.6	3.3	2,319	2,595	0	2
84	South Africa	5.1	4.6	4.3	3.3	1,744	2,432	10ᵃ	10ᵃ
85	Brazil	8.6	8.1	9.9	4.5	286	897	14	14
86	Hungary	0.8	0.9	3.8	1.0	1,825	3,106	12	11
87	Uruguay	4.7	9.7	1.3	-0.9	765	779	13	12
88	Yugoslavia	3.5	3.0	6.0	3.3	898	2,241	7	21
89	Gabon	13.7	3.4	14.7	3.0	153	1,155	3	0
90	Iran, Islamic Rep.	3.6	8.0	8.9	4.2	537	1,019	0	3
91	Trinidad and Tobago	3.8	-4.4	6.6	0.9	2,776	5,349	59	5
92	Czechoslovakia	1.0	0.0	3.2	0.6	3,374	4,945	. .	. .
93	Portugal	3.6	5.5	6.5	3.5	506	1,470	13	16
94	Korea, Rep.	4.1	9.5	12.1	7.2	238	1,832	18	12
95	Oman	23.0	8.8	30.5	10.7	14	2,556	. .	1
96	Libya	0.6	-3.7	18.2	6.0	222	3,049	2	2
97	Greece	10.5	7.3	8.5	2.5	615	2,046	29	14
98	Iraq	6.2	5.4	7.4	5.2	399	752	0	0
99	Romania	4.3	0.6	6.6	1.0	1,536	3,514	. .	. .
	Low- and middle-income	**5.4 w**	**3.9 w**	**6.9 w**	**4.0 w**	**275 w**	**575 w**	**8 w**	**10 w**
	Sub-Saharan Africa	**15.5 w**	**1.8 w**	**5.7 w**	**2.5 w**	**72 w**	**73 w**	**7 w**	**28 w**
	East Asia	**10.0 w**	**5.1 w**	**9.4 w**	**5.1 w**	**164 w**	**487 w**	**10 w**	**8 w**
	South Asia	**5.8 w**	**6.2 w**	**5.7 w**	**6.1 w**	**99 w**	**197 w**	**7 w**	**. .**
	Europe, M.East, & N.Africa	**4.1 w**	**3.1 w**	**5.7 w**	**3.1 w**	**909 w**	**1,658 w**	**9 w**	**19 w**
	Latin America & Caribbean	**1.9 w**	**2.5 w**	**6.9 w**	**2.6 w**	**514 w**	**1,010 w**	**8 w**	**5 w**
	Severely indebted	**2.7 w**	**2.0 w**	**6.1 w**	**1.9 w**	**642 w**	**1,017 w**	**7 w**	**7 w**
	High-income economies	**3.1 w**	**0.4 w**	**3.1 w**	**1.2 w**	**3,641 w**	**4,867 w**	**11 w**	**10 w**
	OECD members	**2.1 w**	**1.6 w**	**3.0 w**	**1.0 w**	**3,748 w**	**5,182 w**	**11 w**	**10 w**
	†Other	**7.6 w**	**-5.1 w**	**6.5 w**	**6.5 w**	**1,397 w**	**2,131 w**	**6 w**	**10 w**
100	†Saudi Arabia	11.5	-8.7	7.2	9.8	1,759	4,307	0	0
101	Ireland	0.1	4.7	3.9	1.4	1,504	2,499	14	5
102	Spain	3.6	6.5	6.5	2.9	901	2,204	31	19
103	†Israel	-15.2	-12.3	4.4	1.6	1,574	2,019	13	10
104	†Hong Kong	. .	0.0	8.4	4.1	413	1,629	6	6
105	†Singapore	. .	0.0	10.8	3.3	670	6,165	17	15
106	New Zealand	4.7	6.8	3.6	5.4	2,622	5,282	7	6
107	Australia	10.5	6.1	5.0	1.8	3,287	5,291	10	6
108	United Kingdom	3.6	0.2	0.9	0.4	3,481	3,624	13	7
109	Italy	1.3	0.5	3.7	0.5	1,568	2,721	16	13
110	Netherlands	15.4	-3.6	5.0	0.6	3,134	4,948	12	10
111	†Kuwait	-1.6	2.6	2.1	4.3	. .	4,944	0	0
112	Belgium	-3.9	7.5	2.9	0.1	3,402	4,804	. .	. .
113	Austria	0.8	-0.4	4.0	0.8	2,060	3,479	10	7
114	France	-0.9	7.2	3.7	0.7	2,468	3,778	16	10
115	†United Arab Emirates	14.7	0.3	36.6	10.1	105	10,554	. .	1
116	Canada	5.7	3.7	4.5	1.8	6,007	9,959	7	5
117	Germany	-0.1	0.0	3.0	-0.1	3,197	4,383	8	6
118	Denmark	2.6	44.0	2.4	-0.2	2,911	3,598	13	7
119	United States	1.1	0.5	2.3	1.0	6,535	7,794	8	16
120	Sweden	4.9	5.0	2.5	1.6	4,162	6,228	12	7
121	Finland	3.8	6.4	5.1	2.5	2,233	5,547	11	10
122	Norway	12.4	7.7	4.1	2.1	4,650	8,940	11	3
123	Japan	-0.4	4.1	6.1	2.3	1,474	3,484	19	16
124	Switzerland	3.7	0.5	3.1	1.1	2,501	3,913	8	4
	Other economies	**5.0 w**	**. .**	**4.6 w**	**. .**	**2,455 w**	**. .**	**. .**	**. .**
	World	**4.1**	**1.8 w**	**4.1 w**	**2.1 w**	**1,146 w**	**1,222 w**	**10 w**	**10 w**
	Oil exporters (excl. USSR)	**5.9 w**	**-0.3 w**	**8.1 w**	**4.1 w**	**438 w**	**974 w**	**3 w**	**5 w**

a. Figures for the Southern African Customs Union comprising South Africa, Namibia, Lesotho, Botswana and Swaziland are included in South African data; trade among the component territories is excluded.

Table 6. Structure of manufacturing

		Value added in manufacturing (millions of current dollars)		Distribution of manufacturing value added (percent; current prices)									
				Food, beverages, and tobacco		Textiles and clothing		Machinery and transport equipment		Chemicals		Other[a]	
		1970	1988	1970	1988	1970	1988	1970	1988	1970	1988	1970	1988
	Low-income economies	**46,114** *t*	**227,368** *t*										
	China and India	**38,393** *t*	**185,094** *t*										
	Other low-income	**7,078** *t*	**39,091** *t*										
1	Mozambique	..	..	51	..	13	..	5	..	3	..	28	..
2	Ethiopia	149	579	46	48	31	19	0	2	2	4	21	27
3	Tanzania	116	111	36	..	28	..	5	..	4	..	26	..
4	Somalia	26	53	88	59	6	13	0	2	1	13	6	13
5	Bangladesh[b]	387	1,390	30	22	47	35	3	5	11	22	10	17
6	Lao PDR[b]	..	..	..	..	..	..	..	..	..	..	..	..
7	Malawi	..	154	51	..	17	..	3	..	10	..	20	..
8	Nepal	32	165	..	41	..	24	..	3	..	6	..	26
9	Chad[b]	51	163	..	..	..	..	..	..	..	..	..	..
10	Burundi	16	92	53	..	25	..	0	..	6	..	16	..
11	Sierra Leone	22	53	..	65	..	1	..	..	..	4	..	30
12	Madagascar[b]	..	275	36	..	28	..	6	..	7	..	23	..
13	Nigeria	543	2,989	36	..	26	..	1	..	6	..	31	..
14	Uganda	158	213	40	..	20	..	2	..	4	..	34	..
15	Zaire[b]	..	982	38	..	16	..	7	..	10	..	29	..
16	Mali[b]	25	135	36	..	40	..	4	..	5	..	14	..
17	Niger[b]	30	167	..	..	..	..	..	..	..	..	..	..
18	Burkina Faso	65	376	69	..	9	..	2	..	1	..	19	..
19	Rwanda[b]	8	328	86	65	0	3	3	0	2	5	8	28
20	India	7,928	43,511	13	10	21	13	20	27	14	17	32	33
21	China[b]	30,465[c]	141,583[c]	..	12	..	14	..	25	..	11	..	38
22	Haiti[b]	..	362	..	..	..	..	..	..	..	..	..	..
23	Kenya	174	849	33	40	9	10	16	12	9	9	33	28
24	Pakistan	1,462	5,749	24	34	38	15	6	11	9	10	23	29
25	Benin	19	80	..	..	..	..	..	..	..	..	..	..
26	Central African Rep.	12	87	..	..	..	..	..	..	..	..	..	..
27	Ghana[b]	252	528	34	40	16	6	4	1	4	7	41	47
28	Togo[b]	25	106	..	..	..	..	..	..	..	..	..	..
29	Zambia[b]	181	1,149	49	..	9	..	5	..	10	..	27	..
30	Guinea[b]	..	85	..	..	..	..	..	..	..	..	..	..
31	Sri Lanka	321	984	26	54	19	18	10	1	11	4	33	23
32	Lesotho	3	49	..	..	..	..	..	..	..	..	..	..
33	Indonesia[b]	994	15,574	..	26	..	13	..	3	..	9	..	49
34	Mauritania	10	..	..	..	..	..	..	..	..	..	..	..
35	*Afghanistan*	..	..	..	..	..	..	..	..	..	..	..	..
36	*Bhutan*	..	16	..	..	..	..	..	..	..	..	..	..
37	*Kampuchea, Dem.*	..	..	..	..	..	..	..	..	..	..	..	..
38	*Liberia*	15	..	..	..	..	..	..	..	..	..	..	..
39	*Myanmar*	..	..	..	..	..	..	..	..	..	..	..	..
40	*Sudan*	140	..	39	..	34	..	3	..	5	..	19	..
41	*Viet Nam*	..	..	..	..	..	..	..	..	..	..	..	..
	Middle-income economies	**68,813** *t*	**500,413** *t*										
	Lower-middle-income	**35,612** *t*	**202,745** *t*										
42	Angola	..	..	..	..	..	..	..	..	..	..	..	..
43	Bolivia[b]	135	568	33	32	34	8	1	1	6	5	26	54
44	Egypt, Arab Rep.	..	..	17	29	35	20	9	9	12	17	27	25
45	Senegal[b]	141	939	51	48	19	15	2	6	6	7	22	24
46	Yemen, Rep.[b]	..	..	..	..	..	..	..	..	..	..	..	..
47	Zimbabwe	293	1,327	24	35	16	15	9	9	11	10	40	32
48	Philippines[b]	1,622	9,834	39	41	8	7	8	9	13	10	32	32
49	Côte d'Ivoire	149	..	27	..	16	..	10	..	5	..	42	..
50	Dominican Rep.[b]	275	743	74	..	5	..	1	..	6	..	14	..
51	Morocco[b]	641	3,894	..	..	..	..	..	..	..	..	..	..
52	Papua New Guinea[b]	35	340	23	..	1	..	35	..	4	..	37	..
53	Honduras	91	615	58	51	10	7	1	2	4	5	28	35
54	Guatemala[b]	..	..	42	38	14	11	4	4	12	18	27	29
55	Congo, People's Rep.[b]	..	198	65	..	4	..	1	..	8	..	22	..
56	Syrian Arab Rep.[b]	..	..	37	33	40	19	3	5	2	5	20	38
57	Cameroon[b]	119	1,708	50	..	15	..	4	..	3	..	27	..
58	Peru[b]	1,430	6,101	25	28	14	14	7	11	7	9	47	38
59	Ecuador[b]	305	2,156	43	31	14	13	3	7	8	8	32	41
60	Namibia	..	79	..	..	..	..	..	..	..	..	..	..
61	Paraguay[b]	99	662	56	..	16	..	1	..	5	..	21	..
62	El Salvador[b]	194	962	40	36	30	15	3	6	8	17	18	26
63	Colombia	1,487	8,149	31	30	20	15	8	10	11	13	29	31
64	Thailand[b]	1,130	14,760	43	29	13	18	9	13	6	7	29	33
65	Jamaica[b]	221	685	46	..	7	..	..	..	10	..	36	..
66	Tunisia	121	1,411	29	20	18	20	4	4	13	9	36	47

Note: For data comparability and coverage, see the technical notes.   Figures in italics are for years other than those specified.

		Value added in manufacturing (millions of current dollars)		Distribution of manufacturing value added (percent; current prices)									
				Food, beverages, and tobacco		Textiles and clothing		Machinery and transport equipment		Chemicals		Other[a]	
		1970	1988	1970	1988	1970	1988	1970	1988	1970	1988	1970	1988
67	Turkey	1,930	16,793	26	18	15	16	8	14	7	11	45	41
68	Botswana[b]	5	99	..	54	..	10	..	0	..	6	..	30
69	Jordan	..	619	21	25	14	4	7	1	6	8	52	62
70	Panama[b]	127	329	41	53	9	6	1	2	5	8	44	30
71	Chile[b]	2,092	..	17	23	12	7	11	4	5	8	55	57
72	Costa Rica[b]	..	..	48	47	12	8	6	6	7	8	28	31
73	Poland[b]	..	..	20	9	19	16	24	32	8	7	28	36
74	Mauritius	26	419	75	23	6	51	5	3	3	5	12	18
75	Mexico[b]	8,449	46,932	28	22	15	11	13	13	11	14	34	40
76	Argentina[b]	5,750	18,646	20	22	18	11	17	14	7	12	38	41
77	Malaysia[b]	500	..	26	18	3	6	8	23	9	13	54	39
78	Algeria[b]	682	5,446	32	20	20	17	9	13	4	3	35	47
79	Bulgaria	..	..	..	..	..	..	..	..	..	..	..	..
80	Lebanon[b]	..	..	27	..	19	..	1	..	3	..	49	..
81	Mongolia	..	..	..	..	..	..	..	..	..	..	..	..
82	Nicaragua[b]	159	642	53	..	14	..	2	..	8	..	23	..
	Upper-middle-income	**32,492** t	..										
83	Venezuela[b]	2,140	12,373	30	22	13	9	9	11	8	12	39	46
84	South Africa	3,914	19,046	15	14	13	8	17	20	10	11	45	48
85	Brazil	10,429	98,880	16	14	13	10	22	21	10	13	39	42
86	Hungary[b]	..	..	12	8	13	10	28	30	8	14	39	38
87	Uruguay	..	1,576	34	31	21	18	7	10	6	10	32	31
88	Yugoslavia	..	..	10	14	15	16	23	25	7	9	45	37
89	Gabon[b]	22	331	37	..	7	..	6	..	6	..	44	..
90	Iran, Islamic Rep.	1,501	10,695	30	..	20	..	18	..	6	..	26	..
91	Trinidad and Tobago	198	357	18	46	3	5	7	8	2	3	70	38
92	Czechoslovakia[b]	..	..	9	8	12	10	34	36	6	7	39	39
93	Portugal[b]	..	..	18	16	19	23	13	13	10	10	39	38
94	Korea, Rep.[b]	1,880	54,212	26	11	17	15	11	32	11	9	36	33
95	Oman[b]	..	319	..	..	..	..	..	..	..	..	..	..
96	Libya	81	1,500	64	..	5	..	0	..	12	..	20	..
97	Greece	1,642	7,170	20	21	20	25	13	11	7	8	40	36
98	Iraq	325	..	26	14	14	9	7	10	3	16	50	50
99	Romania	..	..	..	..	..	..	..	..	..	..	..	..
	Low- and middle-income	**116,441** t	**728,404** t										
	Sub-Saharan Africa	**3,595** t	**18,133** t										
	East Asia	**37,466** t	**250,728** t										
	South Asia	**10,357** t	**52,644** t										
	Europe, M.East, & N.Africa	..	..										
	Latin America & Caribbean	**34,769** t	**211,640** t										
	Severely indebted	**38,653** t	**242,284** t										
	High-income economies	**644,505** t	..										
	OECD members	**637,343** t	..										
	†Other	**5,631** t	**103,254** t										
100	†Saudi Arabia[b]	372	6,606	..	..	..	..	..	..	..	..	..	..
101	Ireland	785	1,019	31	25	19	4	13	33	7	16	30	22
102	Spain[b]	..	..	13	19	15	8	16	24	11	10	45	39
103	†Israel[b]	..	..	15	15	14	9	23	29	7	8	41	39
104	†Hong Kong	1,013	10,781	4	6	41	38	16	22	2	2	36	33
105	†Singapore[b]	379	7,406	12	5	5	4	28	52	4	12	51	27
106	New Zealand[b]	1,777	7,123	24	25	13	10	15	16	4	5	43	45
107	Australia[b]	9,047	41,697	16	18	9	8	24	19	7	8	43	46
108	United Kingdom	35,739	140,879	13	13	9	6	31	32	10	12	37	38
109	Italy[b]	29,016	192,884	10	8	13	13	24	32	13	10	40	36
110	Netherlands[b]	8,545	45,236	17	19	8	3	27	25	13	14	36	38
111	†Kuwait[b]	120	2,089	5	7	4	5	1	3	4	4	86	81
112	Belgium[b]	8,226	33,809	17	20	12	8	22	23	9	14	40	36
113	Austria[b]	4,873	33,723	17	16	12	7	19	26	6	7	45	44
114	France[b]	68,201	202,734	12	13	10	7	26	30	8	9	44	42
115	†United Arab Emirates	..	2,126	..	..	..	..	..	..	..	..	..	..
116	Canada	16,924	..	16	14	8	6	23	26	7	9	46	46
117	Germany[b]	70,888	377,173	13	9	8	4	32	41	9	13	38	32
118	Denmark	2,929	18,088	20	22	8	5	24	23	8	10	40	40
119	United States[b]	253,711	865,605	12	12	8	5	31	35	10	10	39	38
120	Sweden	..	38,742	10	10	6	2	30	34	5	9	49	46
121	Finland	2,588	22,370	13	13	10	5	20	23	6	7	51	53
122	Norway	2,416	13,941	15	19	7	2	23	23	7	8	49	48
123	Japan[b]	73,339	831,779	8	9	8	5	34	38	11	10	40	38
124	Switzerland[b]	..	..	10	..	7	..	31	..	9	..	42	..
	Other economies	..	..										
	World	**860,368** t	..										
	Oil exporters (excl. USSR)	**6,157** t	**46,844** t										

a. Includes unallocable data; see the technical notes.   b. Value added in manufacturing data are at purchaser values.   c. World Bank estimate.

Table 7. Manufacturing earnings and output

		Earnings per employee					Total earnings as a percentage of value added				Gross output per employee (1980=100)			
		Growth rate		Index (1980=100)										
		1970–80	1980–88	1986	1987	1988	1970	1986	1987	1988	1970	1986	1987	1988
Low-income economies														
China and India														
Other low-income														
1	Mozambique	..	..	..	..	..	29	..	..	..	..	..	..	..
2	Ethiopia	−4.6	0.2	97	106	100	24	19	20	20	61	114	115	118
3	Tanzania	..	−12.7	..	..	..	42	..	..	..	122	..	..	..
4	Somalia	−5.1	..	..	..	..	28	27	..	..	..	..	..	..
5	Bangladesh	−3.0	0.0	99	94	95	26	30	29	28	116	115	122	131
6	Lao PDR	..	..	..	..	..	..	..	..	..	..	..	..	..
7	Malawi	..	1.4	..	..	..	37	..	..	..	126	..	..	..
8	Nepal	..	..	..	..	..	..	22	25	..	..	..	..	..
9	Chad	..	..	..	..	..	..	..	..	..	..	..	..	..
10	Burundi	−7.5	..	..	..	..	..	..	..	..	..	..	..	..
11	Sierra Leone	..	..	..	..	..	..	..	..	..	..	..	..	..
12	Madagascar	−0.9	−10.3	..	..	..	36	..	..	..	106	..	..	..
13	Nigeria	−0.8	..	..	..	..	18	..	..	..	105	..	..	..
14	Uganda	..	..	..	..	..	..	..	..	..	..	..	..	..
15	Zaire	..	..	..	..	..	..	..	..	..	..	..	..	..
16	Mali	..	..	..	..	..	46	..	..	..	..	..	..	..
17	Niger	..	0.4	61	68	..	..	7	7	6	..	..	..	..
18	Burkina Faso	..	..	..	..	..	..	..	..	..	..	..	..	..
19	Rwanda	..	..	..	..	..	22	10	..	..	..	..	..	..
20	India	0.4	3.4	123	130	..	47	49	49	..	83	155	167	..
21	China	..	4.2	124	..	..	..	15	..	..	..	131	..	..
22	Haiti	−3.3	4.6	116	153	157	..	..	..	..	..	..	..	..
23	Kenya	−3.4	−0.1	97	102	106	50	44	44	44	42	165	186	182
24	Pakistan	3.4	5.0	127	..	..	21	19	..	..	51	146	..	..
25	Benin	..	..	..	..	..	..	..	..	..	..	..	..	..
26	Central African Rep.	..	..	..	..	..	..	..	..	..	..	85	..	..
27	Ghana	..	7.8	170	..	..	23	14	..	..	193	133	..	..
28	Togo	..	..	..	..	..	..	..	..	..	..	..	..	..
29	Zambia	−3.2	..	..	..	..	34	..	..	..	109	..	..	..
30	Guinea	..	..	..	..	..	..	..	..	..	..	..	..	..
31	Sri Lanka	..	1.7	102	105	..	..	..	17	..	70	132	130	..
32	Lesotho	..	..	..	..	..	..	..	..	..	..	..	..	..
33	Indonesia	5.0	6.0	144	..	..	26	19	..	..	42	162	..	..
34	Mauritania	..	..	..	..	..	..	..	..	..	..	..	..	..
35	*Afghanistan*	..	..	..	..	..	..	..	..	..	..	..	..	..
36	*Bhutan*	..	..	..	..	..	..	..	..	..	..	..	..	..
37	*Kampuchea, Dem.*	..	..	..	..	..	..	..	..	..	..	..	..	..
38	*Liberia*	..	1.7	99	..	..	..	..	..	..	..	..	..	..
39	*Myanmar*	..	..	..	..	..	..	..	..	..	..	..	..	..
40	*Sudan*	..	..	..	..	..	31	..	..	..	..	..	..	..
41	*Viet Nam*	..	..	..	..	..	..	..	..	..	..	..	..	..
Middle-income economies														
Lower-middle-income														
42	Angola	..	..	..	..	..	..	..	..	..	..	..	..	..
43	Bolivia	0.0	−10.3	41	50	46	43	24	28	26	65	32	35	34
44	Egypt, Arab Rep.	4.1	0.5	103	..	..	54	56	..	..	89	191	..	..
45	Senegal	−4.9	..	..	..	..	..	44	..	..	..	..	..	..
46	Yemen, Rep.	..	..	..	..	..	..	..	..	..	..	..	..	..
47	Zimbabwe	1.6	−0.9	100	98	100	43	36	35	34	98	116	115	116
48	Philippines	−3.7	4.0	120	145	..	21	21	26	25	102	112	121	..
49	Côte d'Ivoire	−0.9	..	..	..	..	27	..	..	..	52	..	..	..
50	Dominican Rep.	−1.1	−4.4	..	..	..	35	..	..	..	63	..	..	..
51	Morocco	..	−3.6	76	80	..	..	..	..	..	..	95	95	..
52	Papua New Guinea	2.9	−1.9	..	..	..	40	..	..	..	..	..	..	..
53	Honduras	..	..	..	..	..	..	41	41	40	..	..	..	..
54	Guatemala	−3.2	−2.7	85	89	89	..	22	19	19	..	..	..	..
55	Congo, People's Rep.	..	..	..	..	..	34	..	..	..	..	..	..	..
56	Syrian Arab Rep.	2.6	−5.5	87	70	64	33	35	32	..	70	158	207	..
57	Cameroon	3.2	..	..	..	..	30	..	..	..	80	..	..	..
58	Peru	..	−3.0	86	95	..	..	18	18	..	82	63	70	..
59	Ecuador	3.3	−1.3	103	98	95	27	38	36	35	83	109	114	101
60	Namibia	..	..	..	..	..	..	..	..	..	..	..	..	..
61	Paraguay	..	..	..	..	..	..	..	..	..	..	..	..	..
62	El Salvador	2.4	−9.4	..	..	..	28	..	..	..	71	87	..	..
63	Colombia	−0.2	3.2	116	114	115	25	16	17	15	86	127	150	148
64	Thailand	1.0	6.3	142	..	..	25	23	24	24	68	135	..	..
65	Jamaica	−0.2	..	..	..	..	43	..	..	..	..	..	..	..
66	Tunisia	4.2	..	..	..	..	44	..	..	..	95	..	..	..

Note: For data comparability and coverage, see the technical notes. Figures in italics are for years other than those specified.

216

		Earnings per employee					Total earnings as a percentage of value added				Gross output per employee (1980=100)			
		Growth rate		Index (1980=100)										
		1970-80	1980-88	1986	1987	1988	1970	1986	1987	1988	1970	1986	1987	1988
67	Turkey	6.1	−3.3	81	86	82	26	16	17	16	108	154	169	172
68	Botswana	2.6	−5.7	71	. .	. .	. .	36	. .	. .	. .	56	. .	. .
69	Jordan	. .	−1.1	99	99	. .	37	28	25	. .	. .	. .	. .	. .
70	Panama	0.2	3.2	125	124	123	32	33	32	37	67	84	90	. .
71	Chile	8.1	−1.7	98	99	105	19	17	17	17	60	. .	. .	. .
72	Costa Rica	. .	. .	. .	. .	. .	41	30	33	31	. .	. .	. .	. .
73	Poland	. .	. .	. .	. .	. .	24	23	22	23	. .	. .	. .	. .
74	Mauritius	1.8	−1.0	86	93	98	34	44	43	44	139	72	69	68
75	Mexico	1.2	−5.2	70	71	72	44	20	20	20	77	112	106	111
76	Argentina	−1.5	1.4	111	103	97	30	21	19	18	71	103	136	125
77	Malaysia	2.0	4.4	133	130	140	29	30	29	30	96	. .	. .	. .
78	Algeria	−1.0	. .	. .	. .	. .	45	. .	. .	. .	120	. .	. .	. .
79	Bulgaria	. .	. .	. .	. .	. .	. .	. .	. .	. .	. .	. .	. .	. .
80	*Lebanon*	. .	. .	. .	. .	. .	. .	. .	. .	. .	. .	. .	. .	. .
81	*Mongolia*	. .	. .	. .	. .	. .	. .	. .	. .	. .	. .	. .	. .	. .
82	*Nicaragua*	. .	−10.0	. .	. .	. .	16	. .	. .	. .	210	. .	. .	. .

Upper-middle-income

		1970-80	1980-88	1986	1987	1988	1970	1986	1987	1988	1970	1986	1987	1988
83	Venezuela	3.8	0.1	106	102	98	31	27	25	28	118	121	138	182
84	South Africa	2.7	0.0	101	100	104	46	49	49	48	. .	. .	. .	. .
85	Brazil	4.0	0.0	113	110	109	22	17	15	15	71	114	124	116
86	Hungary	*3.6*	2.2	111	112	125	28	34	33	39	41	111	112	111
87	Uruguay	. .	1.0	108	116	118	. .	25	26	26	. .	113	120	130
88	Yugoslavia	1.3	−1.5	97	93	88	39	33	30	26	59	98	89	97
89	Gabon	. .	. .	. .	. .	. .	. .	. .	. .	. .	. .	. .	. .	. .
90	Iran, Islamic Rep.	. .	. .	. .	. .	. .	25	. .	. .	. .	84	. .	. .	. .
91	Trinidad and Tobago	. .	−0.7	. .	. .	. .	. .	72	70	. .	. .	. .	. .	. .
92	Czechoslovakia	. .	. .	. .	. .	. .	49	41	40	39	. .	. .	. .	. .
93	Portugal	2.5	0.2	95	100	107	34	39	36	37	. .	. .	. .	. .
94	Korea, Rep.	10.0	5.9	128	144	153	25	26	27	27	40	146	166	191
95	Oman	. .	. .	. .	. .	. .	. .	. .	. .	. .	. .	. .	. .	. .
96	Libya	. .	. .	. .	. .	. .	37	. .	. .	. .	45	. .	. .	. .
97	Greece	4.9	*1.1*	111	103	. .	32	43	43	. .	56	114	112	. .
98	*Iraq*	. .	. .	. .	. .	. .	36	25	. .	. .	. .	. .	. .	. .
99	*Romania*	. .	. .	. .	. .	. .	. .	. .	. .	. .	. .	. .	. .	. .

Low- and middle-income
  Sub-Saharan Africa
  East Asia
  South Asia
  Europe, M.East, & N.Africa
  Latin America & Caribbean

Severely indebted

High-income economies
  OECD members
  †Other

		1970-80	1980-88	1986	1987	1988	1970	1986	1987	1988	1970	1986	1987	1988
100	†Saudi Arabia	. .	. .	. .	. .	. .	. .	. .	. .	. .	. .	. .	. .	. .
101	Ireland	4.1	2.3	105	111	119	49	33	32	31	. .	. .	. .	. .
102	Spain	4.4	0.8	101	104	107	52	38	37	37	. .	112	. .	. .
103	†Israel	8.8	−4.5	65	93	72	36	40	63	43	. .	. .	. .	. .
104	†Hong Kong	*6.4*	4.5	124	135	137	. .	60	57	56	. .	. .	. .	. .
105	†Singapore	3.0	5.2	148	146	148	36	32	29	28	73	111	121	122
106	New Zealand	1.1	−1.0	97	. .	. .	62	58	. .	. .	. .	124	. .	. .
107	Australia	2.9	0.2	104	103	103	53	48	47	47	. .	117	119	121
108	United Kingdom	1.7	2.8	115	119	124	52	43	41	41	. .	. .	. .	. .
109	Italy	4.3	0.8	102	105	110	41	42	41	41	51	126	129	139
110	Netherlands	2.5	*0.3*	100	104	. .	52	46	47	. .	68	107	110	. .
111	†Kuwait	. .	3.8	123	. .	. .	12	28	. .	. .	. .	74	. .	. .
112	Belgium	4.6	−0.1	100	102	. .	46	46	46	. .	51	118	126	. .
113	Austria	3.4	1.9	110	113	119	47	56	56	57	65	113	113	118
114	France	. .	*1.2*	. .	. .	. .	. .	. .	. .	. .	72	106	108	116
115	†United Arab Emirates	. .	. .	. .	. .	. .	. .	. .	. .	. .	. .	. .	. .	. .
116	Canada	1.8	0.4	101	100	104	53	45	44	44	. .	. .	. .	. .
117	Germany	3.5	1.7	107	110	113	46	43	43	42	60	106	103	108
118	Denmark	2.5	0.5	100	103	104	56	53	53	53	. .	. .	. .	. .
119	United States	0.1	1.8	108	107	107	47	39	37	36	63	116	124	. .
120	Sweden	0.4	0.6	100	102	103	52	37	35	34	. .	. .	. .	. .
121	Finland	2.6	2.6	115	118	122	47	49	46	44	. .	. .	. .	. .
122	Norway	2.6	1.7	107	109	110	50	60	59	56	74	117	117	123
123	Japan	3.1	1.9	112	113	117	32	37	35	34	45	116	122	132
124	Switzerland	. .	. .	. .	. .	. .	. .	. .	. .	. .	. .	. .	. .	. .

Other economies

World
  Oil exporters (excl. USSR)

Table 8. Growth of consumption and investment

		General government consumption		Private consumption, etc.		Gross domestic investment	
		Average annual growth rate (percent)					
		1965–80	*1980–89*	*1965–80*	*1980–89*	*1965–80*	*1980–89*
	Low-income economies	**5.7 w**	**6.8 w**	**4.1 w**	**5.1 w**	**7.5 w**	**7.6 w**
	China and India	**5.0 w**	**8.6 w**	**4.0 w**	**6.5 w**	**7.2 w**	**9.8 w**
	Other low-income	**6.7 w**	**3.8 w**	**4.3 w**	**2.2 w**	**8.3 w**	**1.5 w**
1	Mozambique	. .	–2.7	. .	0.9	. .	0.4
2	Ethiopia	6.4	. .	3.0	. .	–0.1	. .
3	Tanzania	a	8.1	3.5	2.4	6.2	2.1
4	Somalia	12.7	7.0	4.5	0.9	12.1	–2.7
5	Bangladesh	a	a	2.8	3.9	0.0	–0.1
6	Lao PDR	. .	. .	. .	. .	. .	. .
7	Malawi	5.7	3.9	3.6	2.2	9.1	–4.5
8	Nepal	. .	. .	. .	. .	. .	. .
9	Chad	. .	. .	. .	. .	. .	. .
10	Burundi	7.3	*5.4*	7.5	2.4	9.0	9.3
11	Sierra Leone	a	0.5	3.0	–2.3	–1.0	–3.3
12	Madagascar	2.0	0.6	1.2	–0.6	1.5	0.1
13	Nigeria	13.9	–2.6	6.9	–4.8	14.7	–12.9
14	Uganda	a	. .	1.4	. .	–5.7	. .
15	Zaire	0.7	4.0	1.8	1.9	6.6	3.3
16	Mali	1.9	3.0	5.2	2.7	1.8	10.8
17	Niger	2.9	1.8	–1.4	–0.9	6.3	–7.7
18	Burkina Faso	8.7	7.3	2.5	3.3	8.5	6.9
19	Rwanda	6.2	4.6	4.5	0.3	9.0	8.8
20	India	4.7	8.2	2.6	5.6	4.5	4.5
21	China	5.6	9.3	6.2	7.5	10.7	13.7
22	Haiti	1.9	–1.4	2.4	0.3	14.8	–3.8
23	Kenya	10.6	1.7	5.2	5.1	7.2	0.4
24	Pakistan	4.7	10.9	4.5	4.5	2.4	5.7
25	Benin	0.7	–0.1	1.9	2.7	10.4	–9.3
26	Central African Rep.	–1.1	–2.5	4.9	2.1	–5.4	5.7
27	Ghana	3.8	–2.3	1.2	2.2	–1.3	6.9
28	Togo	9.5	1.7	1.2	5.1	9.0	–2.9
29	Zambia	5.1	–5.4	–0.7	*4.1*	–3.6	–4.5
30	Guinea	. .	. .	. .	. .	. .	. .
31	Sri Lanka	1.1	8.3	4.1	3.9	11.5	–0.7
32	Lesotho	12.4	–0.4	9.9	0.6	17.8	4.4
33	Indonesia	11.4	4.4	5.2	4.3	16.1	6.8
34	Mauritania	10.0	–3.5	1.3	3.5	19.2	–5.4
35	*Afghanistan*	. .	. .	. .	. .	. .	. .
36	*Bhutan*	. .	. .	. .	. .	. .	. .
37	*Kampuchea, Dem.*	. .	. .	. .	. .	. .	. .
38	*Liberia*	3.4	. .	3.2	. .	6.4	. .
39	*Myanmar*	. .	. .	. .	. .	. .	. .
40	*Sudan*	0.2	. .	4.4	. .	6.4	. .
41	*Viet Nam*	. .	. .	. .	. .	. .	. .
	Middle-income economies	**7.2 w**	**2.3 w**	**5.9 w**	**2.8 w**	**8.5 w**	**–0.3 w**
	Lower-middle-income	**6.7 w**	**1.9 w**	**4.9 w**	**2.4 w**	**7.5 w**	**–1.4 w**
42	Angola	. .	. .	. .	. .	. .	. .
43	Bolivia	8.2	–1.9	3.1	1.7	4.4	–11.6
44	Egypt, Arab Rep.	a	3.8	6.7	3.6	11.3	0.6
45	Senegal	2.9	1.6	1.7	2.9	3.9	3.9
46	Yemen, Rep.	. .	. .	. .	. .	. .	. .
47	Zimbabwe	10.6	9.4	5.1	–2.2	0.9	2.7
48	Philippines	7.7	1.4	4.9	3.1	8.5	–7.8
49	Côte d'Ivoire	13.2	–6.3	6.9	7.3	10.7	–12.1
50	Dominican Rep.	0.2	1.8	7.8	0.8	13.5	5.4
51	Morocco	10.9	4.7	5.4	2.8	11.4	4.5
52	Papua New Guinea	0.1	–0.3	5.3	1.3	1.4	–1.7
53	Honduras	6.9	4.8	4.8	2.2	6.8	–0.5
54	Guatemala	6.2	2.4	5.1	0.5	7.4	–2.4
55	Congo, People's Rep.	5.5	4.0	1.9	3.7	4.5	–10.7
56	Syrian Arab Rep.	. .	–3.0	. .	2.6	. .	–5.1
57	Cameroon	5.0	6.4	4.1	3.0	9.9	1.7
58	Peru	6.3	–1.5	4.9	1.6	0.3	–4.5
59	Ecuador	12.2	–2.2	7.2	1.9	9.5	–3.2
60	Namibia	. .	4.3	. .	1.1	. .	–7.0
61	Paraguay	5.1	4.8	6.6	1.9	13.5	–1.9
62	El Salvador	7.0	3.1	4.2	0.3	6.6	2.7
63	Colombia	6.7	3.6	5.8	2.9	5.8	0.3
64	Thailand	9.5	5.6	6.4	7.2	8.0	5.7
65	Jamaica	9.7	0.1	2.9	2.1	–3.1	3.7
66	Tunisia	7.2	3.6	8.8	3.5	4.6	–4.4

Note: For data comparability and coverage, see the technical notes.   Figures in italics are for years other than those specified.

		Average annual growth rate (percent)					
		General government consumption		Private consumption, etc.		Gross domestic investment	
		1965–80	1980–89	1965–80	1980–89	1965–80	1980–89
67	Turkey	6.1	2.7	5.4	5.6	8.8	3.7
68	Botswana	12.0	12.5	10.2	6.8	21.0	0.4
69	Jordan	. .	. .	. .	. .	. .	. .
70	Panama	7.4	1.0	4.6	1.4	5.9	−15.6
71	Chile	4.0	−0.2	0.9	1.1	0.5	2.7
72	Costa Rica	6.8	0.9	5.1	3.0	9.4	4.9
73	Poland	a	1.9	5.7	2.1	. .	2.1
74	Mauritius	7.1	2.8	6.4	4.7	8.3	15.0
75	Mexico	8.5	2.1	5.9	0.7	8.5	−5.0
76	Argentina	3.2	−1.3	2.8	0.3	4.6	−7.8
77	Malaysia	8.5	2.5	6.2	3.3	10.4	1.3
78	Algeria	8.6	4.0	5.0	3.1	15.9	−1.1
79	Bulgaria	. .	6.5	. .	2.6	. .	4.2
80	*Lebanon*	. .	. .	. .	. .	. .	. .
81	*Mongolia*	. .	. .	. .	. .	. .	. .
82	*Nicaragua*	6.1	9.5	2.2	−5.6	. .	0.7
	Upper-middle-income	**7.5** *w*	**2.6** *w*	**6.8** *w*	**3.2** *w*	**9.4** *w*	**0.6** *w*
83	Venezuela	. .	1.8	. .	0.7	. .	−3.8
84	South Africa	5.3	3.7	3.8	2.2	4.1	−4.5
85	Brazil	6.8	7.1	8.7	2.4	11.3	0.7
86	Hungary	a	2.0	5.7	1.5	7.0	−1.2
87	Uruguay	3.2	1.2	2.3	0.0	8.0	−7.9
88	Yugoslavia	3.6	0.8	10.1	−1.8	6.5	−0.4
89	Gabon	10.7	*3.3*	7.5	−0.2	14.1	−4.9
90	Iran, Islamic Rep.	14.6	−3.5	4.0	6.8	11.5	0.3
91	Trinidad and Tobago	8.9	1.4	3.4	−7.3	12.1	−7.7
92	Czechoslovakia	. .	3.7	. .	2.0	. .	−1.0
93	Portugal	8.1	2.5	6.6	5.0	4.6	−2.7
94	Korea, Rep.	7.7	5.7	8.0	7.8	15.9	11.6
95	Oman	. .	a	. .	13.6	. .	*18.4*
96	Libya	19.7	. .	19.1	. .	7.3	. .
97	Greece	6.6	2.8	5.1	2.9	5.3	−1.7
98	*Iraq*	. .	. .	. .	. .	. .	. .
99	*Romania*	. .	. .	. .	. .	. .	. .
	Low- and middle-income	**6.9** *w*	**3.3** *w*	**5.3** *w*	**3.5** *w*	**8.2** *w*	**2.0** *w*
	Sub-Saharan Africa	**7.0** *w*	**1.1** *w*	**4.0** *w*	**0.7** *w*	**8.6** *w*	**−3.9** *w*
	East Asia	**7.4** *w*	**5.8** *w*	**6.3** *w*	**6.4** *w*	**11.1** *w*	**9.9** *w*
	South Asia	**4.6** *w*	**8.7** *w*	**2.9** *w*	**5.4** *w*	**4.3** *w*	**4.1** *w*
	Europe, M.East, & N.Africa	. .	**1.2** *w*	. .	**3.6** *w*	. .	**−0.1** *w*
	Latin America & Caribbean	**6.2** *w*	**3.1** *w*	**6.1** *w*	**1.4** *w*	**8.1** *w*	**−2.3** *w*
	Severely indebted	**6.4** *w*	**2.9** *w*	**6.1** *w*	**1.8** *w*	**8.3** *w*	**−2.0** *w*
	High-income economies	**2.6** *w*	**2.6** *w*	**4.0** *w*	**3.1** *w*	**3.7** *w*	**4.2** *w*
	OECD members	**2.5** *w*	**2.6** *w*	**4.0** *w*	**3.0** *w*	**3.6** *w*	**4.3** *w*
	†Other	. .	. .	. .	. .	. .	. .
100	†Saudi Arabia	a	. .	20.0	. .	27.5	. .
101	Ireland	6.1	−0.4	4.6	1.1	6.3	−2.3
102	Spain	5.1	4.9	4.7	2.6	3.7	5.3
103	†Israel	8.8	0.5	5.9	5.1	5.9	0.9
104	†Hong Kong	7.7	5.3	9.0	7.1	8.6	3.0
105	†Singapore	10.2	7.1	7.8	5.6	13.3	2.8
106	New Zealand	3.4	0.9	2.2	1.6	1.5	4.8
107	Australia	5.0	3.5	4.1	3.4	2.7	3.7
108	United Kingdom	2.3	1.0	2.8	3.4	1.3	6.9
109	Italy	3.5	2.9	4.6	2.6	3.4	2.1
110	Netherlands	3.0	1.1	4.6	1.5	1.6	2.1
111	†Kuwait	a	0.5	5.9	0.7	11.9	−5.1
112	Belgium	. .	0.5	. .	1.6	. .	2.1
113	Austria	3.6	1.3	4.0	2.1	4.6	2.4
114	France	3.6	2.3	3.6	2.4	3.8	1.8
115	†United Arab Emirates	. .	−3.9	. .	−5.0	. .	−8.7
116	Canada	6.9	2.1	7.2	3.6	5.3	5.6
117	Germany	3.5	1.5	3.8	1.5	1.7	1.9
118	Denmark	4.8	1.0	2.3	2.0	1.2	4.2
119	United States	0.8	3.3	3.3	3.7	2.8	4.7
120	Sweden	4.1	1.6	2.3	1.9	1.2	4.2
121	Finland	5.3	3.6	3.8	4.6	2.9	2.9
122	Norway	5.5	3.2	4.0	3.0	4.4	2.0
123	Japan	5.2	2.6	6.3	3.2	6.9	5.7
124	Switzerland	7.3	2.6	6.2	1.4	3.7	4.7
	Other economies	. .	. .	. .	. .	. .	. .
	World	**2.9** *w*	**2.7** *w*	**4.2** *w*	**3.1** *w*	**4.4** *w*	**3.7** *w*
	Oil exporters (excl. USSR)	. .	. .	. .	. .	. .	. .

a. General government consumption figures are not available separately; they are included in private consumption, etc.

Table 9. Structure of demand

						Distribution of gross domestic product (percent)						
	General government consumption		Private consumption, etc.		Gross domestic investment		Gross domestic savings		Exports of goods and nonfactor services		Resource balance	
	1965	1989	1965	1989	1965	1989	1965	1989	1965	1989	1965	1989
Low-income economies	**11** w	**9** w	**70** w	**64** w	**19** w	**28** w	**18** w	**26** w	**7** w	**14** w	**-1** w	**-2** w
China and India	**12** w	**8** w	**68** w	**62** w	**21** w	**31** w	**20** w	**30** w	**4** w	**11** w	**0** w	**-2** w
Other low-income	**9** w	**12** w	**77** w	**70** w	**14** w	**21** w	**12** w	**18** w	**16** w	**19** w	**-2** w	**-4** w
1 Mozambique	..	25	..	95	..	33	..	-19	..	16	..	-53
2 Ethiopia	11	26	77	69	13	13	12	5	12	12	-1	-8
3 Tanzania	10	12	74	93	15	21	16	-5	26	16	1	-26
4 Somalia	8	23	84	91	11	21	8	-14	17	8	-3	-35
5 Bangladesh	9	8	83	91	11	12	8	1	10	8	-4	-11
6 Lao PDR	..	15	..	87	..	11	..	-2	..	14	..	-13
7 Malawi	16	15	84	81	14	19	0	4	19	19	-14	-15
8 Nepal	a	11	100	82	6	19	0	7	8	13	-6	-12
9 Chad	20	21	74	92	12	9	6	-13	19	22	-6	-22
10 Burundi	7	17	89	78	6	18	4	5	10	12	-2	-13
11 Sierra Leone	8	10	83	85	12	11	8	5	30	13	-3	-6
12 Madagascar	16	8	84	84	7	13	0	8	13	17	-7	-5
13 Nigeria	5	9	83	70	14	13	12	21	13	34	-2	8
14 Uganda	10	7	78	91	11	13	12	2	26	6	1	-11
15 Zaire	10	10	64	75	11	13	26	16	31	27	15	3
16 Mali	10	10	84	79	18	27	5	11	12	16	-13	-15
17 Niger	6	12	90	85	8	10	3	3	9	17	-5	-6
18 Burkina Faso	5	13	90	85	10	19	4	2	6	9	-6	-17
19 Rwanda	14	14	81	80	10	15	5	6	12	9	-5	-9
20 India	9	12	76	67	17	24	15	21	4	8	-2	-3
21 China	14	6	61	59	24	36	25	36	4	14	1	-1
22 Haiti	8	10	90	85	7	12	2	5	13	12	-5	-8
23 Kenya	15	19	70	61	14	25	15	20	31	23	1	-6
24 Pakistan	11	17	76	72	21	18	13	11	8	14	-8	-6
25 Benin	11	8	87	87	11	9	3	5	13	20	-8	-4
26 Central African Rep.	22	15	67	87	21	9	11	-1	27	19	-11	-11
27 Ghana	14	9	77	84	18	12	8	6	17	19	-10	-6
28 Togo	11	17	65	69	22	21	23	13	32	45	1	-7
29 Zambia	15	10	45	85	25	9	40	5	49	28	15	-4
30 Guinea	..	10	..	71	..	18	..	19	..	27	..	1
31 Sri Lanka	13	10	74	78	12	21	13	12	38	27	1	-9
32 Lesotho	18	19	109	136	11	66	-26	-55	16	15	-38	-121
33 Indonesia	5	9	87	53	8	35	8	37	5	26	0	2
34 Mauritania	19	13	54	79	14	15	27	8	42	50	13	-7
35 *Afghanistan*	a	..	99	..	11	..	1	..	11	..	-10	..
36 *Bhutan*	..	14	..	67	..	39	..	19	..	30	..	-20
37 *Kampuchea, Dem.*	..	..	..	..	..	..	..	..	..	..	..	..
38 *Liberia*	12	..	61	..	17	..	27	..	50	..	10	..
39 *Myanmar*	..	..	..	..	..	..	..	..	..	..	..	..
40 *Sudan*	12	..	79	..	10	..	9	..	15	..	-1	..
41 *Viet Nam*	..	..	..	..	..	..	..	..	..	..	..	..
Middle-income economies	**11** w	**12** w	**67** w	**62** w	**22** w	**25** w	**21** w	**27** w	**17** w	**25** w	**0** w	**2** w
Lower-middle-income	**10** w	**12** w	**71** w	**66** w	**19** w	**22** w	**19** w	**23** w	**15** w	**25** w	**-1** w	**0** w
42 Angola	..	..	..	..	..	..	..	..	..	..	..	..
43 Bolivia	9	11	74	80	22	13	17	9	21	19	-5	-4
44 Egypt, Arab Rep.	19	13	67	80	18	24	14	7	18	22	-4	-17
45 Senegal	17	16	75	73	12	15	8	11	24	27	-4	-5
46 Yemen, Rep.	..	..	..	..	..	..	..	..	..	..	..	..
47 Zimbabwe	12	24	65	55	15	21	23	21	..	30	8	1
48 Philippines	9	9	70	73	21	19	21	18	17	25	0	-1
49 Côte d'Ivoire	11	18	61	69	22	10	29	13	37	35	7	3
50 Dominican Rep.	19	6	75	76	10	26	6	18	16	32	-4	-8
51 Morocco	12	16	76	65	10	24	12	19	18	23	1	-6
52 Papua New Guinea	34	25	64	64	22	23	2	11	18	41	-20	-12
53 Honduras	10	16	75	73	15	13	15	11	27	22	0	-2
54 Guatemala	7	8	82	84	13	14	10	8	17	17	-3	-5
55 Congo, People's Rep.	14	21	80	60	22	13	5	19	36	51	-17	6
56 Syrian Arab Rep.	14	15	76	61	10	13	10	24	17	33	0	11
57 Cameroon	13	12	75	69	13	18	12	19	24	19	-1	1
58 Peru	10	10	59	68	34	20	31	22	16	13	-3	2
59 Ecuador	9	9	80	71	14	22	11	20	16	27	-3	-2
60 Namibia	..	28	..	56	..	17	..	15	..	55	..	-1
61 Paraguay	7	6	79	79	15	21	14	15	15	34	-1	-6
62 El Salvador	9	12	79	82	15	16	12	6	27	13	-2	-10
63 Colombia	8	10	75	66	16	20	17	24	11	18	1	4
64 Thailand	10	10	72	61	20	31	19	29	16	36	-1	-2
65 Jamaica	8	14	69	60	27	29	23	26	33	47	-4	-4
66 Tunisia	15	17	71	64	28	23	14	19	19	45	-13	-4

Note: For data comparability and coverage, see the technical notes. Figures in italics are for years other than those specified.

		General government consumption		Private consumption, etc.		Gross domestic investment		Gross domestic savings		Exports of goods and nonfactor services		Resource balance	
		Distribution of gross domestic product (percent)											
		1965	1989	1965	1989	1965	1989	1965	1989	1965	1989	1965	1989
67	Turkey	12	11	74	68	15	22	13	21	6	22	−1	−1
68	Botswana	24	20	89	43	6	24	−13	37	32	64	−19	13
69	Jordan	. .	24	. .	78	. .	18	. .	−2	. .	53	. .	−20
70	Panama	11	22	73	67	18	3	16	11	36	34	−2	9
71	Chile	11	10	73	66	15	20	16	24	14	38	1	3
72	Costa Rica	13	16	78	63	20	24	9	21	23	35	−10	−4
73	Poland	. .	a	. .	67	. .	33	. .	33	. .	18	. .	0
74	Mauritius	13	12	74	66	17	29	13	21	36	67	−4	−8
75	Mexico	6	11	75	71	20	17	19	18	8	16	−2	1
76	Argentina	8	10	69	71	19	12	22	19	8	16	3	7
77	Malaysia	15	14	61	52	20	30	24	34	42	74	4	4
78	Algeria	15	16	66	53	22	31	19	31	22	21	−3	0
79	Bulgaria	. .	7	. .	63	. .	32	. .	30	. .	31	. .	−2
80	*Lebanon*	10	. .	81	. .	22	. .	9	. .	36	. .	−13	. .
81	*Mongolia*	. .	. .	. .	. .	. .	. .	. .	. .	. .	. .	. .	. .
82	*Nicaragua*	8	. .	74	. .	21	. .	18	. .	29	. .	−3	. .
	Upper-middle-income	12 w	12 w	61 w	59 w	24 w	27 w	25 w	30 w	20 w	24 w	1 w	4 w
83	Venezuela	10	9	56	64	25	13	34	27	26	34	9	14
84	South Africa	11	20	62	54	28	21	27	26	26	28	0	6
85	Brazil	11	9	67	65	20	22	22	26	8	7	2	3
86	Hungary	a	11	75	59	26	26	25	30	. .	36	−1	3
87	Uruguay	15	13	68	72	11	9	18	15	19	24	7	6
88	Yugoslavia	18	6	52	40	30	48	30	53	22	34	0	5
89	Gabon	11	20	52	47	31	26	37	33	43	48	6	7
90	Iran, Islamic Rep.	13	11	63	61	17	30	24	28	20	3	6	−1
91	Trinidad and Tobago	12	18	67	56	26	19	21	26	65	43	−5	7
92	Czechoslovakia	. .	22	. .	48	. .	28	. .	30	. .	35	. .	2
93	Portugal	12	13	68	66	25	30	20	21	27	36	−5	−10
94	Korea, Rep.	9	10	83	52	15	35	8	37	9	34	−7	3
95	Oman	. .	. .	. .	. .	. .	. .	. .	. .	. .	. .	. .	. .
96	Libya	14	. .	36	. .	29	. .	50	. .	53	. .	21	. .
97	Greece	12	22	73	69	26	18	15	9	9	24	−11	−9
98	*Iraq*	20	. .	50	. .	16	. .	31	. .	38	. .	15	. .
99	*Romania*	. .	. .	. .	. .	. .	. .	. .	. .	. .	. .	. .	. .
	Low- and middle-income	11 w	11 w	68 w	62 w	20 w	26 w	20 w	27 w	13 w	21 w	−1 w	1 w
	Sub-Saharan Africa	10 w	14 w	73 w	73 w	14 w	15 w	14 w	13 w	23 w	25 w	1 w	−3 w
	East Asia	13 w	8 w	64 w	57 w	22 w	34 w	23 w	35 w	7 w	25 w	0 w	0 w
	South Asia	8 w	12 w	77 w	69 w	17 w	22 w	14 w	18 w	6 w	9 w	−3 w	−4 w
	Europe, M.East, & N.Africa	13 w	14 w	65 w	59 w	22 w	29 w	21 w	28 w	19 w	. .	−2 w	−2 w
	Latin America & Caribbean	9 w	9 w	69 w	67 w	20 w	20 w	21 w	24 w	13 w	14 w	1 w	3 w
	Severely indebted	10 w	9 w	68 w	67 w	21 w	21 w	22 w	23 w	14 w	15 w	1 w	2 w
	High-income economies	22 w	17 w	61 w	61 w	17 w	22 w	17 w	22 w	13 w	23 w	1 w	1 w
	OECD members	22 w	17 w	61 w	61 w	17 w	22 w	17 w	22 w	13 w	21 w	1 w	0 w
	†Other	14 w	19 w	57 w	54 w	25 w	23 w	27 w	28 w	48 w	69 w	2 w	4 w
100	†Saudi Arabia	18	32	34	47	14	21	48	21	60	37	34	−1
101	Ireland	17	14	72	57	22	21	10	29	35	67	−9	10
102	Spain	13	15	68	63	23	25	19	22	10	19	−3	−3
103	†Israel	20	29	65	59	29	16	15	12	19	34	−13	−4
104	†Hong Kong	7	7	64	58	36	27	29	35	71	135	−7	8
105	†Singapore	10	11	80	46	22	35	10	43	123	191	−12	8
106	New Zealand	14	14	64	58	23	32	22	28	22	27	−1	−3
107	Australia	16	18	60	59	26	26	23	23	15	16	−3	−3
108	United Kingdom	23	18	65	64	13	21	12	18	18	24	−1	−4
109	Italy	18	15	61	62	20	24	21	23	13	19	1	−1
110	Netherlands	21	17	59	60	20	19	19	23	43	58	−1	4
111	†Kuwait	13	23	26	46	16	19	60	31	68	56	45	12
112	Belgium	16	15	64	63	19	20	20	22	36	73	0	3
113	Austria	20	17	59	55	22	27	21	28	25	40	−1	1
114	France	19	18	58	60	21	21	22	22	13	23	1	0
115	†United Arab Emirates	. .	19	. .	41	. .	25	. .	40	. .	55	. .	15
116	Canada	21	19	60	59	20	23	20	23	19	25	0	0
117	Germany	21	19	56	54	23	22	23	27	19	35	0	6
118	Denmark	19	25	59	53	24	19	22	23	29	35	−2	3
119	United States	25	20	63	67	12	15	12	13	6	12	1	−1
120	Sweden	21	26	56	52	24	22	23	22	22	33	−1	1
121	Finland	18	18	62	54	22	30	21	28	20	24	−2	−2
122	Norway	16	20	56	48	29	27	28	32	41	41	−1	5
123	Japan	12	9	59	57	28	33	30	34	11	15	1	2
124	Switzerland	11	13	60	58	30	30	29	29	29	38	−1	0
	Other economies	. .	. .	. .	. .	. .	. .	. .	. .	. .	. .	. .	. .
	World	19 w	16 w	63 w	62 w	18 w	23 w	18 w	23 w	12 w	21 w	0 w	1 w
	Oil exporters(excl. USSR)	11 w	18 w	60 w	54 w	20 w	24 w	28 w	28 w	29 w	26 w	9 w	4 w

a. General government consumption figures are not available separately; they are included in private consumption, etc.

Table 10. Structure of consumption

		Percentage share of total household consumption[a]										
		Food		Clothing and footwear	Gross rents; fuel and power		Medical care	Education	Transport and communication		Other consumption	
		Total	Cereals and tubers		Total	Fuel and power			Total	Automobiles	Total	Other consumer durables
Low-income economies												
China and India												
Other low-income												
1	Mozambique	..	..	..	..	..	..	..	..	..	..	..
2	Ethiopia	50	24	6	14	7	3	2	8	1	17	2
3	Tanzania	64	32	10	8	3	3	3	2	0	10	3
4	Somalia	..	..	..	..	..	..	..	..	..	..	..
5	Bangladesh	59	36	8	17	7	2	1	3	0	10	3
6	Lao PDR	..	..	..	..	..	..	..	..	..	..	..
7	Malawi	55	28	5	12	2	3	4	7	2	15	3
8	Nepal	57	38	12	14	6	3	1	1	0	13	2
9	Chad	..	..	..	..	..	..	..	..	..	..	..
10	Burundi	..	..	..	..	..	..	..	..	..	..	..
11	Sierra Leone	56	22	4	15	6	2	3	12	..	9	1
12	Madagascar	59	26	6	12	6	2	4	4	1	14	1
13	Nigeria	52	18	7	10	2	3	4	4	1	20	6
14	Uganda	..	..	..	..	..	..	..	..	..	..	..
15	Zaire	55	15	10	11	3	3	1	6	0	14	3
16	Mali	57	22	6	8	6	2	4	10	1	13	1
17	Niger	..	..	..	..	..	..	..	..	..	..	..
18	Burkina Faso	..	..	..	..	..	..	..	..	..	..	..
19	Rwanda	30	11	11	16	6	3	4	9	..	28	9
20	India	52	18	11	10	3	3	4	7	0	13	3
21	China	61[b]	..	13	8	3	1	1	1	..	15	..
22	Haiti	..	..	..	..	..	..	..	..	..	..	..
23	Kenya	39	16	7	12	2	3	9	8	1	22	6
24	Pakistan	54	17	9	15	6	3	3	1	0	15	5
25	Benin	37	12	14	12	2	5	4	14	2	15	5
26	Central African Rep.	..	..	..	..	..	..	..	..	..	..	..
27	Ghana	50	..	13	11	..	3	5[c]	3	..	15	..
28	Togo	..	..	..	..	..	..	..	..	..	..	..
29	Zambia	37	8	10	11	5	7	13	5	1	16	1
30	Guinea	..	..	..	..	..	..	..	..	..	..	..
31	Sri Lanka	43	18	7	6	3	2	3	15	1	25	5
32	Lesotho	..	..	..	..	..	..	..	..	..	..	..
33	Indonesia	48	21	7	13	7	2	4	4	0	22	5
34	Mauritania	..	..	..	..	..	..	..	..	..	..	..
35	*Afghanistan*	..	..	..	..	..	..	..	..	..	..	..
36	*Bhutan*	..	..	..	..	..	..	..	..	..	..	..
37	*Kampuchea, Dem.*	..	..	..	..	..	..	..	..	..	..	..
38	*Liberia*	..	..	..	..	..	..	..	..	..	..	..
39	*Myanmar*	..	..	..	..	..	..	..	..	..	..	..
40	*Sudan*	60	..	5	15	4	5	3	2	..	11	..
41	*Viet Nam*	..	..	..	..	..	..	..	..	..	..	..
Middle-income economies												
Lower-middle-income												
42	Angola	..	..	..	..	..	..	..	..	..	..	..
43	Bolivia	33	..	9	12	1	5	7	12	..	22	..
44	Egypt, Arab Rep.	50	10	11	9	3	3	6	4	1	18	3
45	Senegal	50	15	11	12	4	2	5	6	0	14	2
46	Yemen, Rep.	..	..	..	..	..	..	..	..	..	..	..
47	Zimbabwe	40	9	11	13	5	4	7	6	1	20	3
48	Philippines	51	20	4	19	5	2	4	4	2	16	2
49	Côte d'Ivoire	40	14	10	5	1	9	4	10	..	23	3
50	Dominican Rep.	46	13	3	15	5	8	3	4	0	21	8
51	Morocco	40	12	11	9	2	4	6	8	1	22	5
52	Papua New Guinea	..	..	..	..	..	..	..	..	..	..	..
53	Honduras	39	..	9	21	..	8	5[c]	3	..	15	..
54	Guatemala	36	10	10	14	5	13	4	3	0	20	5
55	Congo, People's Rep.	42	19	6	11	4	3	1	17	1	20	4
56	Syrian Arab Rep.	..	..	..	..	..	..	..	..	..	..	..
57	Cameroon	24	8	7	17	3	11	9	12	1	21	3
58	Peru	35	8	7	15	3	4	6	10	0	24	7
59	Ecuador	30	..	10	7[d]	1[d]	5	6[c]	12[e]	..	30	..
60	Namibia	..	..	..	..	..	..	..	..	..	..	..
61	Paraguay	30	6	12	21	4	2	3	10	1	22	3
62	El Salvador	33	12	9	7	2	8	5	10	1	28	7
63	Colombia	29	..	6	12	2	7	6	13	..	27	..
64	Thailand	30	7	16	7	3	5	5	13	0	24	5
65	Jamaica	39	..	4	15	7	3[f]	..	17	..	22	..
66	Tunisia	37	7	10	13	4	6	9	7	1	18	5

Note: For data comparability and coverage, see the technical notes.   Figures in italics are for years other than those specified.

Percentage share of total household consumption[a]

		Food		Clothing and footwear	Gross rents; fuel and power		Medical care	Education	Transport and communication		Other consumption	
		Total	Cereals and tubers		Total	Fuel and power			Total	Automobiles	Total	Other consumer durables
67	Turkey	40	8	15	13	7	4	1	5	2	22	7
68	Botswana	35	13	8	6	..	5	8	6	..	35	..
69	Jordan	35	..	5	6	..	5	8	6	..	24	6
70	Panama	38	7	3	11	3	8	9	7	0	29	5
71	Chile	29	7	8	13	2	5	6	11	0	28	..
72	Costa Rica	33	8	8	9	1	7	8	8	0	28	9
73	Poland	29	..	9	7	2	6	7	8	2	34	9
74	Mauritius	24	7	5	19	3	5	7	11	1	29	4
75	Mexico	35[b]	..	10	8	..	5	5	12	..	25	..
76	Argentina	35	4	6	9	2	4	6	13	0	26	6
77	Malaysia	23	..	4	9	..	5	7	19	..	33	..
78	Algeria	..	..	..	..	..	..	..	..	..	..	..
79	Bulgaria	..	..	..	..	..	..	..	..	..	..	..
80	Lebanon	..	..	..	..	..	..	..	..	..	..	..
81	Mongolia	..	..	..	..	..	..	..	..	..	..	..
82	Nicaragua	..	..	..	..	..	..	..	..	..	..	..
	Upper-middle-income											
83	Venezuela	23	..	7	10	..	8	5[c]	11	..	36	..
84	South Africa	26	..	7	12	..	4[f]	..	17	..	34	..
85	Brazil	35	9	10	11	2	6	5	8	1	27	8
86	Hungary	25	..	9	10	5	5	7	9	2	35	8
87	Uruguay	31	7	7	12	2	6	4	13	0	27	5
88	Yugoslavia	27	..	10	9	4	6	5	11	2	32	9
89	Gabon	..	..	..	..	..	..	..	..	..	..	..
90	Iran, Islamic Rep.	37	10	9	23	2	6	5	6	1	14	5
91	Trinidad and Tobago	..	..	..	..	..	..	..	..	..	..	..
92	Czechoslovakia	..	..	..	..	..	..	..	..	..	..	..
93	Portugal	34	..	10	8	3	6	5	13	3	24	7
94	Korea, Rep.	35	14	6	11	5	5	9	9	..	25	5
95	Oman	..	..	..	..	..	..	..	..	..	..	..
96	Libya	..	..	..	..	..	..	..	..	..	..	..
97	Greece	30	..	8	12	3	6	5	13	2	26	5
98	Iraq	..	..	..	..	..	..	..	..	..	..	..
99	Romania	..	..	..	..	..	..	..	..	..	..	..
	Low- and middle-income											
	Sub-Saharan Africa											
	East Asia											
	South Asia											
	Europe, M.East, & N.Africa											
	Latin America & Caribbean											
	Severely indebted											
	High-income economies											
	OECD members											
	†Other											
100	†Saudi Arabia	..	..	..	..	..	..	..	..	..	..	..
101	Ireland	22	4	5	11	5	10	7	11	3	33	5
102	Spain	24	3	7	16	3	7	5	13	3	28	6
103	†Israel	21	..	5	20	2	9	12	10	..	23	..
104	†Hong Kong	12	1	9	15	2	6	5	9	1	44	15
105	†Singapore	19	..	8	11	..	7	12	13	..	30	..
106	New Zealand	12	2	6	14	2	9	6	19	6	34	9
107	Australia	13	2	5	21	2	10	8	13	4	31	7
108	United Kingdom	12	2	6	17	4	8	6	14	4	36	7
109	Italy	19	2	8	14	4	10	7	11	3	31	7
110	Netherlands	13	2	6	18	6	11	8	10	3	33	8
111	†Kuwait	..	..	..	..	..	..	..	..	..	..	..
112	Belgium	15	2	6	17	7	10	9	11	3	31	7
113	Austria	16	2	9	17	5	10	8	15	3	26	7
114	France	16	2	6	17	5	13	7	13	3	29	7
115	†United Arab Emirates	..	..	..	..	..	..	..	..	..	..	..
116	Canada	11	2	6	21	4	5	12	14	5	32	8
117	Germany	12	2	7	18	5	13	6	13	4	31	9
118	Denmark	13	2	5	19	5	8	9	13	5	33	7
119	United States	13	2	6	18	4	14	8	14	5	27	7
120	Sweden	13	2	5	19	4	11	8	11	2	32	7
121	Finland	16	3	4	15	4	9	8	14	4	34	6
122	Norway	15	2	6	14	5	10	8	14	6	32	7
123	Japan	16	4	6	17	3	10	8	9	1	34	6
124	Switzerland	17	..	4	17	6	15	..	9	..	38	..
	Other economies											
	World											
	Oil exporters (excl. USSR)											

a. Data refer to either 1980 or 1985.   b. Includes beverages and tobacco.   c. Refers to government expenditure.   d. Excludes fuel.   e. Includes fuel.   f. Excludes government expenditure.

Table 11. Central government expenditure

		Percentage of total expenditure															
		Defense		Education		Health		Housing, amenities; social security and welfare[a]		Economic services		Other[a]		Total expenditure as a percentage of GNP		Overall surplus/deficit as a percentage of GNP	
		1972	1989	1972	1989	1972	1989	1972	1989	1972	1989	1972	1989	1972	1989	1972	1989
Low-income economies																	
China and India																	
Other low-income																	
1	Mozambique	..	..	..	..	..	..	..	..	..	..	..	..	..	..	..	..
2	Ethiopia	..	..	14.4	10.6	5.7	3.6	4.4	9.3	22.9	30.1	52.6	46.5	13.7	35.2	-1.4	-6.8
3	Tanzania	11.9	..	17.3	..	7.2	..	2.1	..	39.0	..	22.6	..	19.7	..	-5.0	..
4	Somalia[b]	23.3	..	5.5	..	7.2	..	1.9	..	21.6	..	40.5	..	13.5	..	0.6	..
5	Bangladesh[b]	5.1	..	14.8	..	5.0	..	9.8	..	39.3	..	25.9	..	9.4	..	-1.9	..
6	Lao PDR	..	..	..	..	..	..	..	..	..	..	..	..	..	..	..	..
7	Malawi[b]	3.1	5.3	15.8	12.3	5.5	7.3	5.8	0.4	33.1	36.9	36.7	37.9	22.1	29.5	-6.2	-6.0
8	Nepal	7.2	5.2	7.2	10.0	4.7	5.0	0.7	5.0	57.2	49.0	23.0	25.8	8.5	22.0	-1.2	-10.1
9	Chad	24.6	..	14.8	..	4.4	..	1.7	..	21.8	..	32.7	..	14.9	..	-2.7	..
10	Burundi	10.3	..	23.4	..	6.0	..	2.7	..	33.9	..	23.8	..	19.9	..	0.0	..
11	Sierra Leone[b]	3.6	..	15.5	..	5.3	..	2.7	..	24.6	..	48.3	..	23.9	..	-4.4	..
12	Madagascar	3.6	..	9.1	..	4.2	..	9.9	..	40.5	..	32.7	..	16.7	..	-2.0	..
13	Nigeria[b]	40.2	2.8	4.5	2.8	3.6	0.8	0.8	1.5	19.6	35.9	31.4	56.2	8.3	28.1	-0.7	-10.5
14	Uganda	23.1	..	15.3	..	5.3	..	7.3	..	12.4	..	36.6	..	21.8	..	-8.1	..
15	Zaire	11.1	14.0	15.1	6.1	2.4	4.3	2.1	4.6	13.2	25.9	56.2	45.1	13.7	18.4	-2.6	-6.8
16	Mali	..	8.0	..	9.0	..	2.1	..	3.1	..	5.3	..	72.4	..	28.9	..	-4.6
17	Niger	..	..	..	..	..	..	..	..	..	..	..	..	..	..	..	..
18	Burkina Faso	11.5	17.9	20.6	14.0	8.2	5.2	6.6	0.2	15.5	7.0	37.6	55.7	8.4	11.2	0.3	0.3
19	Rwanda	25.6	..	22.2	..	5.7	..	2.6	..	22.0	..	21.9	..	12.5	..	-2.7	..
20	India	26.2	17.2	2.3	2.7	1.5	1.7	3.2	5.0	19.9	22.1	46.9	51.3	10.5	17.7	-3.2	-6.7
21	China	..	..	..	..	..	..	..	..	..	..	..	..	..	..	..	..
22	Haiti	..	..	..	..	..	..	..	..	..	..	..	..	14.5	..	..	..
23	Kenya[b]	6.0	12.2	21.9	22.1	7.9	5.9	3.9	2.6	30.1	17.9	30.2	39.2	21.0	28.0	-3.9	-4.4
24	Pakistan	39.9	..	1.2	..	1.1	..	3.2	..	21.4	..	33.2	..	16.9	21.5	-6.9	-7.0
25	Benin	..	..	..	..	..	..	..	..	..	..	..	..	..	..	..	..
26	Central African Rep.	..	..	..	..	..	..	..	..	..	..	..	..	..	25.7	..	..
27	Ghana[b]	7.9	3.2	20.1	25.7	6.3	9.0	4.1	11.9	15.1	19.2	46.6	31.1	19.5	14.0	-5.8	0.4
28	Togo	..	11.1	..	19.9	..	5.2	..	8.5	..	31.2	..	24.1	..	32.5	..	-2.6
29	Zambia[b]	0.0	0.0	19.0	8.6	7.4	7.4	1.3	2.0	26.7	24.8	45.7	57.2	34.0	20.0	-13.8	-4.6
30	Guinea	..	..	..	..	..	..	..	..	..	..	..	..	..	..	..	..
31	Sri Lanka	3.1	5.4	13.0	10.7	6.4	6.2	19.5	15.1	20.2	20.6	37.7	42.0	25.2	29.8	-5.1	-7.5
32	Lesotho	0.0	..	22.4	..	7.4	..	6.0	..	21.6	..	42.7	..	14.5	..	3.5	..
33	Indonesia	18.6	8.3	7.4	10.0	1.4	1.8	0.9	1.7	30.5	..	41.3	78.2	15.1	20.6	-2.5	-2.1
34	Mauritania	..	..	..	..	..	..	..	..	..	..	..	..	..	33.5	..	-4.2
35	Afghanistan	..	..	..	..	..	..	..	..	..	..	..	..	..	..	..	..
36	Bhutan	..	0.0	..	13.0	..	5.7	..	4.4	..	51.4	..	25.5	..	45.1	..	0.9
37	Kampuchea, Dem.	..	..	..	..	..	..	..	..	..	..	..	..	..	..	..	..
38	Liberia	5.3	..	15.2	..	9.8	..	3.5	..	25.8	..	40.5	..	16.7	..	1.1	..
39	Myanmar	31.6	18.7	15.0	13.7	6.1	5.0	7.5	14.8	20.1	31.7	19.7	16.2	..	..	..	..
40	Sudan[b]	24.1	..	9.3	..	5.4	..	1.4	..	15.8	..	44.1	..	19.2	..	-0.8	..
41	Viet Nam	..	..	..	..	..	..	..	..	..	..	..	..	..	..	..	..
Middle-income economies																	
Lower-middle-income																	
42	Angola	..	..	..	..	..	..	..	..	..	..	..	..	..	..	..	..
43	Bolivia	..	11.6	..	20.3	..	6.6	..	14.6	..	24.7	..	22.2	..	16.8	0.0	-1.6
44	Egypt, Arab Rep.	..	14.4	..	11.9	..	2.5	..	17.6	..	9.8	..	43.8	..	40.2	..	-6.9
45	Senegal	..	..	..	..	..	..	..	..	..	..	..	..	18.8	..	-2.8	..
46	Yemen, Rep.	..	..	..	..	..	..	..	..	..	..	..	..	..	..	..	..
47	Zimbabwe	..	16.5	..	23.4	..	7.6	..	3.9	..	22.4	..	26.2	..	40.8	..	-9.1
48	Philippines[b]	10.9	13.0	16.3	17.1	3.2	4.3	4.3	2.0	17.6	25.9	47.7	37.7	13.4	15.7	-2.0	-2.8
49	Côte d'Ivoire	..	..	..	..	..	..	..	..	..	..	..	..	..	..	..	..
50	Dominican Rep.	8.5	..	14.2	..	11.7	..	11.8	..	35.4	..	18.3	..	17.7	20.4	-0.2	..
51	Morocco	12.3	15.1	19.2	17.0	4.8	3.0	8.4	7.3	25.6	21.4	29.7	36.0	22.8	29.1	-3.9	-4.6
52	Papua New Guinea[b]	..	4.7	..	15.3	..	9.4	..	3.1	..	20.8	..	46.6	..	29.0	..	-0.9
53	Honduras	12.4	..	22.3	..	10.2	..	8.7	..	28.3	..	18.1	..	16.1	..	-2.9	..
54	Guatemala	..	..	..	..	..	..	..	..	..	..	..	..	9.9	12.0	-2.2	-1.8
55	Congo, People's Rep.	..	..	..	..	..	..	..	..	..	..	..	..	..	..	..	..
56	Syrian Arab Rep.	37.2	40.4	11.3	10.4	1.4	1.5	3.6	4.5	39.9	25.0	6.7	18.2	29.0	26.7	-3.5	-2.5
57	Cameroon	..	6.7	..	12.0	..	3.4	..	8.7	..	48.1	..	21.2	..	20.9	..	-3.3
58	Peru[b]	14.5	20.2	23.6	15.6	5.5	5.5	1.8	..	30.9	18.3	23.6	40.4	16.1	11.6	-0.9	-4.8
59	Ecuador[b]	15.7	14.9	27.5	23.4	4.5	9.8	0.8	2.0	28.9	17.6	22.6	32.3	13.4	14.2	0.2	0.0
60	Namibia	..	..	..	..	..	..	..	..	..	..	..	..	..	..	..	..
61	Paraguay	13.8	10.4	12.1	11.4	3.5	3.0	18.3	26.7	19.6	9.5	32.7	39.1	13.1	8.9	-1.7	0.8
62	El Salvador[b]	6.6	27.9	21.4	17.6	10.9	7.4	7.6	5.2	14.4	15.0	39.0	26.9	12.8	10.5	-1.0	-1.9
63	Colombia	..	..	..	..	..	..	..	..	..	..	..	..	13.1	14.6	-2.5	-0.7
64	Thailand	20.2	17.8	19.9	19.3	3.7	6.3	7.0	5.3	25.6	20.4	23.5	30.9	16.7	15.1	-4.2	3.1
65	Jamaica	..	..	..	..	..	..	..	..	..	..	..	..	..	..	..	..
66	Tunisia	4.9	5.7	30.5	14.6	7.4	5.9	8.8	22.0	23.3	24.4	25.1	27.3	23.1	37.5	-0.9	-4.5

Note: For data comparability and coverage, see the technical notes.   Figures in italics are for years other than those specified.

		Defense		Education		Health		Housing, amenities; social security and welfare[a]		Economic services		Other[a]		Total expenditure as a percentage of GNP		Overall surplus/deficit as a percentage of GNP	
		1972	1989	1972	1989	1972	1989	1972	1989	1972	1989	1972	1989	1972	1989	1972	1989
67	Turkey	15.5	11.6	18.1	15.7	3.2	2.9	3.1	3.1	42.0	19.8	18.1	46.9	22.7	23.7	-2.2	-4.6
68	Botswana[b]	0.0	12.4	10.0	20.1	6.0	5.5	21.7	11.5	28.0	20.2	34.5	30.4	33.7	50.1	-23.8	27.1
69	Jordan	33.5	25.9	9.4	15.3	3.8	4.1	10.5	12.4	26.6	14.6	16.2	27.7	..	38.4	..	-9.9
70	Panama	0.0	7.9	20.7	19.1	15.1	19.8	10.8	23.5	24.2	6.1	29.1	23.6	27.6	31.7	-6.5	-5.8
71	Chile	6.1	8.4	14.5	10.1	10.3	5.9	39.8	33.9	15.3	8.8	16.3	33.0	43.2	32.5	-13.0	-0.2
72	Costa Rica	2.6	1.7	28.5	17.0	4.0	27.2	26.5	16.7	21.2	11.4	17.2	25.9	19.0	27.8	-4.5	-2.3
73	Poland	..	..	..	..	..	..	..	..	..	..	..	..	..	40.4	..	-2.4
74	Mauritius	0.8	1.0	13.5	15.3	10.3	9.2	18.0	18.5	13.9	17.2	43.4	38.8	16.3	24.2	-1.2	-1.5
75	Mexico	4.5	2.2	16.4	12.3	4.5	1.7	25.4	10.3	35.8	12.4	13.4	61.1	11.4	21.2	-2.9	-4.8
76	Argentina	10.0	8.6	20.0	9.3	..	2.0	20.0	40.9	30.0	20.5	20.0	18.7	19.6	15.5	0.0	-4.9
77	Malaysia	..	..	..	..	..	..	..	..	..	..	..	..	26.5	30.1	-9.4	-2.6
78	Algeria	..	..	..	..	..	..	..	..	..	..	..	..	..	..	..	..
79	Bulgaria	..	..	..	..	..	..	..	..	..	..	..	..	..	..	..	..
80	Lebanon	..	..	..	..	..	..	..	..	..	..	..	..	..	..	..	..
81	Mongolia	..	..	..	..	..	..	..	..	..	..	..	..	..	..	..	..
82	Nicaragua	12.3	..	16.6	..	4.0	..	16.4	..	27.2	..	23.4	..	15.8	..	-4.0	..
Upper-middle-income																	
83	Venezuela	10.3	..	18.6	..	11.7	..	9.2	..	25.4	..	24.8	..	18.1	..	-0.2	..
84	South Africa	..	..	..	..	..	..	..	..	..	..	..	..	21.8	33.0	-4.2	-7.5
85	Brazil	8.3	4.3	8.3	4.2	6.7	6.1	35.0	21.0	23.3	7.6	18.3	56.7	29.1	30.6	-0.3	-14.9
86	Hungary	..	3.7	..	2.6	..	2.1	..	29.9	..	25.1	..	36.7	..	58.6	..	-2.0
87	Uruguay	5.6	8.2	9.5	7.9	1.6	4.5	52.3	50.9	9.8	9.5	21.2	19.1	25.0	25.8	-2.5	-1.7
88	Yugoslavia	16.7	53.4	..	..	16.7	..	33.3	6.0	16.7	19.6	16.7	21.0	21.1	5.3	-0.4	0.3
89	Gabon[b]	..	..	..	..	..	..	..	..	..	..	..	..	37.0	..	-11.9	..
90	Iran, Islamic Rep.	24.1	11.7	10.4	19.3	3.6	7.1	6.1	17.2	30.6	13.8	25.2	30.9	30.8	17.5	-4.6	-8.0
91	Trinidad and Tobago	..	..	..	..	..	..	..	..	..	..	..	..	..	36.9	..	-4.5
92	Czechoslovakia	..	..	..	..	..	..	..	..	..	..	..	..	..	..	..	..
93	Portugal	..	5.7	..	10.0	..	8.2	..	27.0	..	9.8	..	39.3	..	43.3	..	-5.0
94	Korea, Rep.	25.8	24.9	15.8	18.5	1.2	2.0	5.9	9.9	25.6	19.7	25.7	24.9	18.0	16.9	-3.9	0.2
95	Oman	39.3	41.9	3.7	10.3	5.9	5.1	3.0	9.9	24.4	11.8	23.6	21.0	62.1	48.6	-15.3	-9.9
96	Libya	..	..	..	..	..	..	..	..	..	..	..	..	..	..	..	..
97	Greece	14.9	..	9.1	..	7.4	..	30.6	..	26.4	..	11.7	..	27.5	..	-1.7	..
98	Iraq	..	..	..	..	..	..	..	..	..	..	..	..	..	..	..	..
99	Romania	5.4	9.1	2.9	5.0	0.5	5.1	16.2	31.4	61.8	47.8	13.1	1.6	..	..	..	..

Low- and middle-income
Sub-Saharan Africa
East Asia
South Asia
Europe, M.East, & N.Africa
Latin America & Caribbean
Severely indebted

High-income economies
OECD members
†Other

		Defense		Education		Health		Housing		Economic		Other		Total		Overall	
100	†Saudi Arabia	..	2.8	..	11.8	..	12.4	..	30.3	..	15.4	..	27.3	32.7	57.9	-5.5	-10.7
101	Ireland	..	..	..	..	..	..	..	..	..	..	..	..	..	..	..	..
102	Spain	6.5	6.5	8.3	5.1	0.9	12.5	49.8	37.0	17.5	10.4	17.0	28.5	19.6	34.3	-0.5	-4.0
103	†Israel	42.9	26.1	7.1	10.1	0.0	3.9	7.1	22.3	7.1	10.4	35.7	27.2	43.9	49.1	-15.7	-3.9
104	†Hong Kong	..	..	..	..	..	..	..	..	..	..	..	..	..	..	..	..
105	†Singapore	35.3	21.2	15.7	19.0	7.8	5.2	3.9	13.8	9.9	16.0	27.3	24.8	16.7	23.3	1.3	6.9
106	New Zealand[b]	5.8	4.8	16.9	12.5	14.8	12.7	25.6	33.8	16.5	9.0	20.4	27.1	31.1	45.9	-4.2	2.2
107	Australia	14.2	8.9	4.2	7.3	7.0	9.9	20.3	29.3	14.4	6.9	39.9	37.8	20.2	27.0	0.3	0.5
108	United Kingdom	16.7	12.5	2.6	2.9	12.2	14.3	26.5	34.8	11.1	6.7	30.8	28.8	31.8	34.6	-2.7	1.3
109	Italy	6.3	3.6	16.1	8.3	13.5	11.3	44.8	38.6	18.4	11.5	0.9	26.6	29.5	47.9	-8.7	-10.6
110	Netherlands	6.8	5.0	15.2	11.0	12.1	11.6	38.1	40.6	9.1	8.2	18.7	23.7	41.0	54.5	0.0	-4.5
111	†Kuwait	8.4	19.9	15.0	14.0	5.5	7.4	14.2	20.5	16.6	14.5	40.1	23.7	34.4	31.0	17.4	..
112	Belgium	6.7	4.7	15.5	12.1	1.5	1.7	41.0	43.9	18.9	9.8	16.4	27.9	39.3	50.7	-4.3	-7.5
113	Austria	3.3	2.7	10.2	9.2	10.1	12.8	53.8	48.3	11.2	10.1	11.4	16.8	29.6	39.3	-0.2	-4.1
114	France	..	6.1	..	6.9	..	21.0	..	40.7	..	6.5	..	18.8	32.3	42.6	0.7	-1.9
115	†United Arab Emirates[b]	24.4	43.9	16.5	15.0	4.3	6.9	6.1	3.6	18.3	4.3	30.5	26.3	3.8	13.0	0.3	-0.6
116	Canada	7.6	7.3	3.5	2.9	7.6	5.5	35.3	37.0	19.5	10.8	26.5	36.5	20.1	23.1	-1.3	-2.9
117	Germany	12.4	8.7	1.5	0.7	17.5	18.3	46.9	49.4	11.3	7.5	10.4	15.5	24.2	29.0	0.7	-0.1
118	Denmark	7.3	5.4	16.0	9.2	10.0	1.2	41.6	37.8	11.3	6.9	13.7	39.6	32.6	41.8	2.7	4.2
119	United States	32.2	24.6	3.2	1.8	8.6	12.9	35.3	29.3	10.6	8.0	10.1	23.3	19.1	23.0	-1.5	-2.8
120	Sweden	12.5	6.5	14.8	8.7	3.6	1.0	44.3	55.9	10.6	8.0	14.3	19.8	27.9	40.6	-1.2	4.1
121	Finland	6.1	5.1	15.3	14.1	10.6	10.6	28.4	36.5	27.9	20.6	11.6	13.1	24.3	29.3	1.2	2.1
122	Norway	9.7	7.8	9.9	9.1	12.3	10.6	39.9	39.6	20.2	17.5	8.0	15.4	35.0	42.7	-1.5	-1.0
123	Japan[b]	..	..	..	..	..	..	..	..	..	..	..	..	12.7	16.5	-1.9	-2.6
124	Switzerland	15.1	..	4.2	..	10.0	..	39.5	..	18.4	..	12.8	..	13.3	..	0.9	..

Other economies

World
Oil exporters (excl. USSR)

a. See the technical notes.　　b. Data are for budgetary accounts only.

Table 12. Central government current revenue

		Percentage of total current revenue													
		Tax revenue												Total current revenue as a percentage of GNP	
		Taxes on income, profit, and capital gains		Social security contributions		Domestic taxes on goods and services		Taxes on international trade and transactions		Other taxes[a]		Nontax revenue			
		1972	1989	1972	1989	1972	1989	1972	1989	1972	1989	1972	1989	1972	1989
Low-income economies															
China and India															
Other low-income															
1	Mozambique	..	..	..	..	..	..	..	..	..	..	..	..	..	..
2	Ethiopia	23.0	26.6	0.0	0.0	29.8	21.0	30.4	19.6	5.6	2.2	11.1	30.7	10.5	25.2
3	Tanzania	29.9	..	0.0	..	29.1	..	21.7	..	0.5	..	18.8	..	15.8	..
4	Somalia[b]	10.7	..	0.0	..	24.7	..	45.3	..	5.2	..	14.0	..	13.7	..
5	Bangladesh[b]	3.7	11.7	0.0	0.0	22.4	33.2	18.0	31.5	3.8	7.1	52.2	16.5	8.6	8.8
6	Lao PDR	..	..	..	..	..	..	..	..	..	..	..	..	..	..
7	Malawi[b]	31.4	38.9	0.0	0.0	24.2	35.4	20.0	15.8	0.5	0.5	23.8	9.5	16.0	21.2
8	Nepal	4.1	11.7	0.0	0.0	26.5	36.1	36.7	30.5	19.0	5.6	13.7	16.2	5.2	9.5
9	Chad	16.7	20.8	0.0	0.0	12.3	8.6	45.2	46.2	20.5	12.7	5.3	11.6	10.8	6.2
10	Burundi	18.1	..	1.2	..	18.3	..	40.3	..	15.6	..	6.5	..	11.5	..
11	Sierra Leone[b]	32.7	26.3	0.0	0.0	14.6	25.7	42.4	44.6	0.3	0.3	9.9	3.1	19.5	9.0
12	Madagascar	13.1	..	7.2	..	29.9	..	33.6	..	5.5	..	10.8	..	14.7	..
13	Nigeria[b]	43.0	44.2	0.0	0.0	26.3	6.4	17.5	16.4	0.2	-14.4	13.0	47.4	9.4	15.7
14	Uganda	22.1	5.5	0.0	0.0	32.8	19.1	36.3	75.3	0.3	0.0	8.5	0.0	13.7	5.3
15	Zaire	22.5	35.9	2.3	0.8	12.1	11.9	57.8	45.5	1.6	2.3	3.6	3.6	9.9	9.4
16	Mali	..	10.8	..	4.4	..	28.6	..	12.0	..	30.8	..	13.5	..	18.9
17	Niger	..	..	..	..	..	..	..	..	..	..	..	..	..	..
18	Burkina Faso	16.8	15.0	0.0	8.2	18.0	13.4	51.8	38.9	3.2	6.5	10.2	18.1	8.6	11.4
19	Rwanda	17.9	..	4.4	..	14.1	..	41.7	..	13.8	..	8.1	..	9.8	..
20	India	21.3	13.5	0.0	0.0	44.5	35.5	20.1	26.7	0.9	0.4	13.2	23.9	10.2	15.4
21	China	..	..	..	..	..	..	..	..	..	..	..	..	..	..
22	Haiti	..	..	..	..	..	..	..	..	..	..	..	..	..	..
23	Kenya[b]	35.6	28.4	0.0	0.0	19.9	43.6	24.3	18.2	1.4	1.1	18.8	8.7	18.0	22.3
24	Pakistan	13.6	10.8	0.0	0.0	35.9	33.4	34.2	32.9	0.5	0.2	15.8	22.7	12.5	17.8
25	Benin	..	..	..	..	..	..	..	..	..	..	..	..	..	..
26	Central African Rep.	..	23.9	..	0.0	..	13.1	..	45.2	..	11.4	..	6.4	..	13.1
27	Ghana[b]	18.4	28.7	0.0	0.0	29.4	28.3	40.6	35.2	0.2	0.1	11.5	7.8	15.1	13.8
28	Togo	..	30.5	..	6.3	..	7.7	..	32.3	..	1.1	..	22.2	..	30.2
29	Zambia[b]	49.7	38.1	0.0	0.0	20.2	37.0	14.3	15.8	0.1	4.9	15.6	4.2	23.2	11.0
30	Guinea	..	..	..	..	..	..	..	..	..	..	..	..	..	..
31	Sri Lanka	19.1	11.0	0.0	0.0	34.7	48.1	35.4	28.5	2.1	4.1	8.7	8.3	20.0	21.6
32	Lesotho	14.3	10.7	0.0	0.0	2.0	22.3	62.9	55.7	9.5	0.1	11.3	11.2	11.7	21.6
33	Indonesia	45.5	55.9	0.0	0.0	22.8	24.5	17.6	5.6	3.5	5.7	10.6	8.3	13.4	18.4
34	Mauritania	..	32.3	..	0.0	..	19.4	..	36.8	..	1.4	..	10.1	..	21.8
35	Afghanistan	..	..	..	..	..	..	..	..	..	..	..	..	..	..
36	Bhutan	..	9.2	..	0.0	..	18.0	..	0.9	..	0.7	..	71.2	..	..
37	Kampuchea, Dem.	..	..	..	..	..	..	..	..	..	..	..	..	..	..
38	Liberia	40.4	33.9	0.0	0.0	20.3	25.1	31.6	34.6	3.1	2.3	4.6	4.2	17.0	17.8
39	Myanmar	28.7	9.5	0.0	0.0	34.2	27.7	13.4	15.9	0.0	0.0	23.8	46.8	..	..
40	Sudan[b]	11.8	..	0.0	..	30.4	..	40.5	..	1.5	..	15.7	..	18.0	..
41	Viet Nam	..	..	..	..	..	..	..	..	..	..	..	..	..	..
Middle-income economies															
Lower-middle-income															
42	Angola	..	..	..	..	..	..	..	..	..	..	..	..	..	..
43	Bolivia	..	4.9	..	8.3	..	34.5	..	8.7	..	6.7	..	37.0	..	14.1
44	Egypt, Arab Rep.	..	14.9	..	14.2	..	11.3	..	13.2	..	10.6	..	35.8	..	35.9
45	Senegal	17.5	..	0.0	..	24.5	..	30.9	..	23.9	..	3.2	..	16.9	..
46	Yemen, Rep.	..	..	..	..	..	..	..	..	..	..	..	..	..	..
47	Zimbabwe	..	45.3	..	0.0	..	25.7	..	17.1	..	1.2	..	10.7	..	35.0
48	Philippines[b]	13.8	26.1	0.0	0.0	24.3	33.2	23.0	22.7	29.7	4.0	9.3	14.0	12.4	12.8
49	Côte d'Ivoire	..	..	..	..	..	..	..	..	..	..	..	..	..	..
50	Dominican Rep.	17.9	17.8	3.9	3.8	19.0	21.3	40.4	41.7	1.7	2.1	17.0	13.4	17.2	17.6
51	Morocco	16.4	18.9	5.9	5.2	45.7	46.2	13.2	14.3	6.1	7.2	12.6	8.2	18.5	22.1
52	Papua New Guinea[b]	..	44.6	..	0.0	..	10.5	..	24.9	..	1.8	..	18.1	..	23.2
53	Honduras	19.2	..	3.0	..	33.8	..	28.2	..	2.3	..	13.5	..	13.2	..
54	Guatemala	12.7	18.1	0.0	0.0	36.1	23.2	26.2	33.8	15.6	7.2	9.4	17.7	8.9	9.7
55	Congo, People's Rep.	19.4	..	0.0	..	40.3	..	26.5	..	6.3	..	7.5	..	18.4	..
56	Syrian Arab Rep.	6.8	24.7	0.0	0.0	10.4	8.9	17.3	7.2	12.1	12.2	53.4	47.0	25.3	24.4
57	Cameroon	..	45.2	..	6.4	..	20.2	..	14.0	..	9.1	..	5.1	..	17.8
58	Peru[b]	16.0	16.8	0.0	0.0	34.0	54.5	14.0	18.3	26.0	6.0	10.0	4.5	14.6	6.9
59	Ecuador[b]	19.6	48.9	0.0	0.0	19.1	24.8	52.4	18.4	5.1	4.7	3.8	3.1	13.6	14.1
60	Namibia	..	..	..	..	..	..	..	..	..	..	..	..	..	..
61	Paraguay	8.8	12.9	10.4	13.2	26.1	25.4	24.8	11.7	17.0	24.3	12.9	12.4	11.5	10.0
62	El Salvador[b]	15.2	22.4	0.0	0.0	25.6	45.5	36.1	16.8	17.2	11.3	6.0	3.9	11.6	8.5
63	Colombia	37.1	25.8	13.7	9.6	15.2	27.7	19.8	17.9	7.1	8.2	7.1	10.7	10.6	12.6
64	Thailand	12.1	20.6	0.0	0.0	46.3	45.4	28.7	22.2	1.8	3.2	11.2	8.6	12.5	17.9
65	Jamaica	..	..	..	..	..	..	..	..	..	..	..	..	..	..
66	Tunisia	15.9	12.9	7.1	11.1	31.6	20.1	21.8	27.9	7.8	5.1	15.7	22.8	23.6	32.1

Note: For data comparability and coverage, see the technical notes.   Figures in italics are for years other than those specified.

		Percentage of total current revenue													
		Tax revenue												Total current revenue as a percentage of GNP	
		Taxes on income, profit, and capital gains		Social security contributions		Domestic taxes on goods and services		Taxes on international trade and transactions		Other taxes[a]		Nontax revenue			
		1972	1989	1972	1989	1972	1989	1972	1989	1972	1989	1972	1989	1972	1989
67	Turkey	30.8	43.3	0.0	0.0	31.0	29.5	14.6	6.3	6.1	3.1	17.5	17.7	20.6	19.0
68	Botswana[b]	19.9	41.0	0.0	0.0	2.4	0.9	47.2	12.1	0.4	0.1	30.0	46.0	30.7	82.9
69	Jordan	9.4	9.1	0.0	0.0	15.6	16.2	36.2	35.1	3.1	7.5	35.6	32.1	..	22.5
70	Panama	23.3	17.2	22.4	30.1	13.2	14.9	16.0	6.2	7.7	3.0	17.3	28.6	21.8	27.8
71	Chile	14.3	23.3	28.6	6.0	28.6	37.1	14.3	9.8	0.0	-0.2	14.3	24.1	30.2	30.8
72	Costa Rica	18.0	9.2	13.9	29.6	37.7	17.0	18.9	32.4	1.6	-2.6	9.8	14.3	15.3	26.1
73	Poland	..	30.4	..	21.4	..	30.4	..	6.2	..	6.5	..	5.1	..	38.7
74	Mauritius	22.7	12.9	0.0	4.4	23.3	20.9	40.2	48.5	5.5	5.2	8.2	8.2	15.6	24.6
75	Mexico	37.3	35.8	18.6	10.5	32.2	56.7	13.6	8.0	-8.5	-19.3	6.8	8.2	10.1	15.8
76	Argentina	..	4.3	..	43.4	..	22.4	..	11.4	..	10.3	..	8.2	..	13.2
77	Malaysia	25.2	28.6	0.1	0.8	24.2	20.3	27.9	18.0	1.4	2.5	21.2	29.8	20.3	26.3
78	Algeria	..	..	..	..	..	..	..	..	..	..	..	..	..	..
79	Bulgaria	..	..	..	..	..	..	..	..	..	..	..	..	..	..
80	Lebanon	..	..	..	..	..	..	..	..	..	..	..	..	..	..
81	Mongolia	..	..	..	..	..	..	..	..	..	..	..	..	..	..
82	Nicaragua	9.5	14.4	14.0	10.5	37.3	48.5	24.4	7.1	9.0	10.6	5.8	8.9	12.8	40.7
	Upper-middle-income														
83	Venezuela	54.2	43.0	6.0	4.2	6.7	8.8	6.1	23.4	1.1	2.3	25.9	18.2	18.5	22.8
84	South Africa	54.8	52.0	1.2	1.5	21.5	30.7	4.6	3.8	5.0	2.9	12.8	9.2	21.2	27.4
85	Brazil	20.0	9.8	27.7	11.3	35.4	9.5	7.7	1.6	3.1	2.0	6.2	65.8	18.9	42.0
86	Hungary	..	18.2	..	29.4	..	32.4	..	5.3	..	0.2	..	14.5	..	56.5
87	Uruguay	4.7	8.5	30.0	26.7	24.5	43.2	6.1	10.4	22.0	4.9	12.6	6.2	22.7	24.3
88	Yugoslavia	..	..	60.0	..	20.0	66.4	20.0	31.3	..	..	..	2.3	20.7	5.6
89	Gabon[b]	18.2	..	6.0	..	9.5	..	44.9	..	4.2	..	17.2	..	26.1	..
90	Iran, Islamic Rep.	7.9	19.3	2.7	14.7	6.4	7.8	14.6	6.7	4.9	7.6	63.6	43.9	26.2	9.5
91	Trinidad and Tobago	..	53.7	..	0.0	..	20.2	..	7.8	..	1.4	..	16.9	..	30.9
92	Czechoslovakia	..	..	..	..	..	..	..	..	..	..	..	..	..	..
93	Portugal	..	20.0	..	27.1	..	39.0	..	3.7	..	2.6	..	7.6	..	37.1
94	Korea, Rep.	29.0	34.8	0.7	4.4	41.7	32.4	10.7	10.9	5.3	5.5	12.6	12.2	13.1	18.1
95	Oman	71.1	23.7	0.0	0.0	0.0	0.7	3.0	2.6	2.3	0.8	23.6	72.1	47.4	38.2
96	Libya	..	..	..	..	..	..	..	..	..	..	..	..	..	..
97	Greece	12.2	..	24.5	..	35.5	..	6.7	..	12.0	..	9.2	..	25.4	..
98	Iraq	..	..	..	..	..	..	..	..	..	..	..	..	..	..
99	Romania	6.0	0.0	8.2	14.0	0.0	0.0	0.0	0.0	0.0	10.6	85.8	75.4	..	..

Low- and middle-income
Sub-Saharan Africa
East Asia
South Asia
Europe, M.East, & N.Africa
Latin America & Caribbean

Severely indebted

High-income economies
OECD members
†Other

		1972	1989	1972	1989	1972	1989	1972	1989	1972	1989	1972	1989	1972	1989
100	†Saudi Arabia	..	..	..	..	..	..	..	..	..	..	..	..	..	..
101	Ireland	28.3	34.0	9.0	13.3	32.1	31.6	16.7	7.6	3.2	3.0	10.6	10.5	30.1	46.8
102	Spain	15.9	22.7	38.9	38.4	23.4	27.8	10.0	2.8	0.7	1.3	11.1	7.1	19.7	29.4
103	†Israel	40.0	38.0	0.0	8.1	20.0	31.2	20.0	2.3	10.0	5.4	10.0	15.0	31.3	40.2
104	†Hong Kong	..	..	..	..	..	..	..	..	..	..	..	..	..	..
105	†Singapore	24.4	20.9	0.0	0.0	17.6	19.5	11.1	2.7	15.5	11.1	31.4	45.7	21.5	27.5
106	New Zealand[b]	61.4	53.6	0.0	0.0	19.9	26.2	4.1	2.0	4.5	3.2	10.0	15.0	29.8	43.5
107	Australia	58.3	62.7	0.0	0.0	21.9	22.0	5.2	4.6	2.1	0.6	12.5	10.0	22.2	27.1
108	United Kingdom	39.4	38.8	15.6	18.2	27.1	31.1	1.7	0.1	5.4	2.3	10.8	9.6	32.6	35.6
109	Italy	16.6	36.3	39.2	29.3	31.7	29.3	0.4	0.0	4.3	2.3	7.7	2.9	24.9	38.2
110	Netherlands	32.5	27.4	36.7	39.1	22.3	21.9	0.5	0.0	3.4	2.8	4.7	8.7	43.4	49.0
111	†Kuwait	68.8	0.6	0.0	0.0	19.7	0.4	1.5	1.3	0.2	0.0	9.9	97.7	55.2	66.1
112	Belgium	31.3	36.4	32.4	34.7	28.9	23.3	1.0	0.0	3.3	2.8	3.1	2.8	35.1	43.7
113	Austria	20.7	17.9	30.0	37.0	28.3	26.2	5.4	1.6	10.2	8.5	5.5	8.7	29.7	34.9
114	France	16.8	17.4	37.0	43.5	37.9	28.8	0.3	0.0	3.0	3.4	4.9	6.9	33.4	40.9
115	†United Arab Emirates[b]	0.0	0.0	0.0	3.1	0.0	39.7	0.0	0.0	0.0	0.0	100.0	57.2	0.2	1.3
116	Canada	54.0	53.7	8.8	14.2	15.9	19.6	11.0	3.5	-0.6	0.0	10.9	9.0	21.1	20.2
117	Germany	19.7	18.1	46.6	53.0	28.1	23.0	0.8	0.0	0.8	0.2	4.0	5.8	25.3	29.0
118	Denmark	40.0	39.4	5.1	2.8	42.1	40.3	3.1	0.1	2.8	3.3	6.8	14.2	35.5	42.3
119	United States	59.4	52.5	23.6	33.9	7.1	3.2	1.6	1.6	2.5	0.8	5.7	8.0	17.6	20.1
120	Sweden	27.0	19.6	21.6	30.1	34.0	27.6	1.5	0.5	4.7	8.9	11.3	13.4	32.4	44.4
121	Finland	30.0	33.0	7.8	9.4	47.7	45.5	3.1	1.1	5.8	4.4	5.5	6.6	26.5	31.1
122	Norway	22.6	14.6	20.6	26.0	48.0	36.6	1.6	0.5	1.0	1.5	6.2	20.9	36.8	43.3
123	Japan[b]	64.8	67.2	0.0	0.0	22.6	15.0	3.5	1.4	6.8	11.2	2.4	5.3	11.2	14.1
124	Switzerland	13.9	..	37.3	..	21.5	..	16.7	..	2.6	..	8.0	..	14.5	..

Other economies

World
Oil exporters (excl. USSR)

a. See the technical notes.   b. Data are for budgetary accounts only.

227

Table 13. Money and interest rates

		Monetary holdings, broadly defined					Average annual inflation (GDP deflator)	Nominal interest rates of banks (average annual percentage)			
		Average annual nominal growth rate (percent)		Average outstanding as a percentage of GDP				Deposit rate		Lending rate	
		1965–80	1980–89	1965	1980	1989	1980–89	1980	1989	1980	1989
	Low-income economies										
	China and India										
	Other low-income										
1	Mozambique	..	..	..	..	..	35.0	..	..	..	..
2	Ethiopia	12.7	11.9	12.5	25.3	45.4	2.0	..	6.70	..	6.00
3	Tanzania	19.7	21.5	..	37.2	..	25.9	4.00	17.00	11.50	31.00
4	Somalia	20.4	50.0	12.7	17.8	17.6	42.8	4.50	25.00	7.50	33.67
5	Bangladesh	..	22.0	..	16.9	27.3	10.6	8.25	12.00	11.33	16.00
6	Lao PDR	..	..	..	..	8.7	..	7.20	14.00	4.80	15.00
7	Malawi	15.4	17.7	17.6	20.5	..	14.6	7.92	12.75	16.67	23.00
8	Nepal	17.9	19.6	8.4	21.9	33.4	9.1	4.00	8.50	14.00	15.00
9	Chad	12.5	12.2	9.3	20.0	21.6	1.5	5.50	4.25	11.00	11.50
10	Burundi	15.7	9.8	10.1	13.3	17.5	3.6	2.50	4.00	12.00	12.00
11	Sierra Leone	15.9	53.2	11.7	20.6	18.6	54.2	9.17	20.00	11.00	29.67
12	Madagascar	12.2	17.5	15.8	22.3	21.4	17.8	5.63	11.50	9.50	..
13	Nigeria	28.5	12.7	9.9	21.5	18.6	14.6	5.27	13.09	8.43	35.00
14	Uganda	23.2	77.8	..	12.7	7.8	108.1	6.80	36.17	10.80	40.00
15	Zaire	28.2	62.7	8.4	6.2	6.4	59.4	..	..	..	..
16	Mali	14.4	10.9	..	17.9	21.3	3.6	13.71	9.53	9.38	8.75
17	Niger	18.3	6.1	3.8	13.3	18.1	3.8	6.19	5.25	9.38	8.00
18	Burkina Faso	17.1	12.5	6.9	13.8	18.5	4.7	13.55	9.49	9.38	8.75
19	Rwanda	19.0	9.7	15.8	13.6	17.8	4.0	6.25	6.31	13.50	12.00
20	India	15.3	17.0	23.7	36.2	45.6	7.7	..	..	16.50	16.50
21	China	..	25.5	..	33.5	66.7	5.7	5.40	..	..	..
22	Haiti	20.3	7.8	9.9	26.1	33.2	6.8	10.00	..	..	..
23	Kenya	18.6	14.6	..	36.8	37.8	9.1	5.75	12.00	10.58	17.25
24	Pakistan	14.7	13.7	40.7	38.7	37.5	6.7	..	..	..	..
25	Benin	17.3	4.2	10.6	21.1	18.8	7.5	13.71	9.53	9.38	7.13
26	Central African Rep.	12.7	5.9	13.5	18.9	17.8	6.7	5.50	7.50	10.50	12.50
27	Ghana	25.9	45.9	20.3	16.2	13.9	43.9	11.50	16.50	19.00	25.58
28	Togo	20.3	7.3	10.9	29.0	34.0	5.2	12.71	9.53	9.38	8.75
29	Zambia	12.7	28.9	..	32.6	..	38.3	7.00	11.44	9.50	18.39
30	Guinea	..	..	..	..	..	..	..	..	..	..
31	Sri Lanka	15.4	15.5	32.3	35.3	36.6	10.8	14.50	16.43	19.00	13.17
32	Lesotho	..	18.5	..	..	43.9	13.2	9.60	12.82	11.00	18.75
33	Indonesia	54.4	24.6	..	13.2	30.2	8.3	6.00	18.60	..	21.70
34	Mauritania	20.7	11.3	5.7	20.5	21.9	9.2	..	6.00	..	12.00
35	Afghanistan	14.0	22.0	14.4	26.8	..	..	9.00	9.00	13.00	13.00
36	Bhutan	..	20.0	..	..	..	..	..	6.50	..	15.00
37	Kampuchea, Dem.	..	..	..	..	..	..	..	..	..	..
38	Liberia	..	..	..	..	..	..	10.30	6.77	18.40	13.82
39	Myanmar	11.5	11.1	..	..	..	..	1.50	1.50	8.00	8.00
40	Sudan	21.6	37.0	14.1	32.5	17.0	..	6.00	..	..	..
41	Viet Nam	..	..	..	..	..	..	..	..	..	..
	Middle-income economies										
	Lower-middle-income										
42	Angola	..	..	..	..	..	..	..	..	..	..
43	Bolivia	24.3	306.0	10.9	16.2	21.7	392.2	18.00	..	28.00	..
44	Egypt, Arab Rep.	17.7	21.8	35.3	52.2	91.7	11.1	8.33	11.67	13.33	18.33
45	Senegal	15.6	7.2	15.3	26.6	23.6	7.3	6.19	5.25	9.38	6.96
46	Yemen, Rep.	..	..	..	..	..	..	..	..	..	..
47	Zimbabwe	..	18.1	..	54.6	50.7	10.9	3.52	8.85	17.54	13.00
48	Philippines	17.7	16.1	19.9	19.0	21.1	14.8	12.25	14.13	14.00	19.27
49	Côte d'Ivoire	20.4	5.7	21.8	25.8	30.5	3.7	13.55	9.53	9.38	8.75
50	Dominican Rep.	18.5	25.8	18.0	21.8	23.9	19.1	..	..	..	..
51	Morocco	15.7	14.5	29.4	..	50.5	7.4	4.88	8.50	7.00	9.00
52	Papua New Guinea	..	8.4	..	32.9	33.6	5.6	6.90	8.23	11.15	14.62
53	Honduras	14.8	12.0	15.4	22.8	33.8	4.8	7.00	8.63	18.50	15.38
54	Guatemala	16.3	15.0	15.2	20.5	22.8	13.4	9.00	13.00	11.00	16.00
55	Congo, People's Rep.	14.2	10.0	16.5	14.7	19.3	0.6	6.50	8.00	11.00	12.50
56	Syrian Arab Rep.	21.9	19.8	24.6	40.9	..	15.1	5.00	..	..	..
57	Cameroon	19.0	9.2	11.7	18.3	20.8	6.6	7.50	7.50	13.00	14.00
58	Peru	25.9	193.0	18.8	16.5	9.2	160.2	..	..	..	..
59	Ecuador	22.6	31.8	15.6	20.2	16.1	34.5	..	40.24	9.00	30.08
60	Namibia	..	..	..	..	..	13.2	..	..	..	..
61	Paraguay	21.3	20.0	12.1	19.8	..	23.2	..	..	..	..
62	El Salvador	14.3	16.5	21.6	28.1	26.9	16.7	..	..	..	..
63	Colombia	26.5	..	19.8	23.7	..	24.3	..	27.70	19.00	28.21
64	Thailand	17.9	18.0	23.6	37.6	65.0	3.2	12.00	9.50	18.00	15.00
65	Jamaica	17.2	25.1	24.3	35.4	56.8	18.5	10.29	19.04	13.00	25.56
66	Tunisia	17.4	15.5	30.2	42.1	..	7.5	2.50	7.37	7.25	9.87

Note: For data comparability and coverage, see the technical notes.   Figures in italics are for years other than those specified.

| | | Monetary holdings, broadly defined | | | | | Average annual inflation (GDP deflator) | Nominal interest rates of banks (average annual percentage) | | | |
| | | Average annual nominal growth rate (percent) | | Average outstanding as a percentage of GDP | | | | Deposit rate | | Lending rate | |
		1965–80	1980–89	1965	1980	1989	1980–89	1980	1989	1980	1989
67	Turkey	27.5	55.0	23.0	17.2	22.6	41.4	10.95	53.45	25.67	50.00
68	Botswana	..	27.1	..	30.7	30.3	12.1	5.00	5.58	8.48	7.67
69	Jordan	19.1	13.0	..	88.8	119.1	2.2	..	..	..	..
70	Panama	..	..	..	..	..	2.6	..	..	..	..
71	Chile	116.0	..	16.3	22.6	..	20.5	37.46	26.60	47.14	38.28
72	Costa Rica	24.6	25.9	19.3	38.8	38.2	24.8	..	15.62	..	29.17
73	Poland	..	53.0	..	58.4	42.0	38.1	3.00	21.00	8.00	16.67
74	Mauritius	21.8	21.7	27.3	41.1	60.6	8.5	9.25	11.06	12.90	16.13
75	Mexico	21.9	62.0	25.1	27.5	15.3	72.8	20.63	36.25	28.10	54.00
76	Argentina	86.0	342.0	..	22.2	12.4	334.5	79.40	432.75	..	430.38
77	Malaysia	21.5	12.6	26.3	69.8	117.4	1.5	6.23	3.00	7.75	7.00
78	Algeria	22.3	14.9	32.1	58.5	96.9	5.2	..	..	..	..
79	Bulgaria	..	..	..	..	..	1.5	..	..	..	..
80	Lebanon	16.2	64.0	83.4	176.1	..	..	..	17.54	..	39.86
81	Mongolia	..	..	..	..	..	..	..	..	..	..
82	Nicaragua	15.0	..	15.4	22.1	..	..	7.50	..	..	..
	Upper-middle-income										
83	Venezuela	22.9	15.1	17.4	43.0	32.0	16.0	..	29.23	..	22.57
84	South Africa	14.0	16.5	56.6	49.5	54.0	14.0	5.54	18.13	9.50	19.83
85	Brazil	43.4	..	20.6	18.4	..	227.9	115.00	5,922.36	..	..
86	Hungary	..	7.6	..	46.5	43.0	7.5	3.00	9.00	9.00	13.00
87	Uruguay	65.8	61.4	28.0	31.2	40.7	59.2	50.30	84.70	66.62	127.58
88	Yugoslavia	25.7	133.0	43.6	59.1	50.5	96.8	5.88	5,644.83	11.50	4353.75
89	Gabon	25.2	5.8	16.2	15.2	24.0	–1.0	7.50	8.75	12.50	12.50
90	Iran, Islamic Rep.	28.4	..	21.6	54.5	..	14.0	..	..	..	..
91	Trinidad and Tobago	23.1	9.0	21.3	32.0	..	5.4	6.57	6.28	10.00	13.31
92	Czechoslovakia	..	..	..	..	..	1.5	2.67	2.48	..	..
93	Portugal	19.5	21.4	77.7	96.3	98.7	19.2	19.00	13.00	18.75	19.59
94	Korea, Rep.	35.5	20.4	11.1	31.7	50.3	5.1	19.50	10.00	18.00	11.25
95	Oman	..	12.4	..	13.8	28.6	–6.6	..	8.66	..	10.01
96	Libya	29.2	2.3	14.2	34.7	75.8	0.2	5.13	5.50	7.00	7.00
97	Greece	21.4	25.1	35.0	61.6	..	18.2	14.50	17.14	21.25	23.26
98	Iraq	..	..	19.7	..	..	..	..	..	..	..
99	Romania	..	7.5	..	..	..	..	..	..	..	..

Low- and middle-income
  Sub-Saharan Africa
  East Asia
  South Asia
  Europe, M.East, & N.Africa
  Latin America & Caribbean

Severely indebted

High-income economies
  OECD members
  †Other

100	†Saudi Arabia	32.1	9.4	16.4	18.6	63.7	–5.2	..	..	..	..
101	Ireland	16.1	6.1	..	58.1	42.7	8.1	12.00	4.54	15.96	9.42
102	Spain	19.7	10.0	59.2	75.2	64.7	9.4	13.05	9.55	16.85	15.84
103	†Israel	60.0	106.0	15.3	56.4	64.4	117.1	..	14.10	176.93	31.63
104	†Hong Kong	..	..	..	..	69.3	7.1	..	..	..	..
105	†Singapore	17.6	12.8	58.4	74.4	117.5	1.5	9.37	3.21	11.72	6.21
106	New Zealand	12.8	16.4	56.5	53.4	11.5	11.4	11.00	16.32	12.63	20.84
107	Australia	15.9	12.9	50.0	61.8	70.2	7.8	8.58	15.29	10.58	21.69
108	United Kingdom	13.8	23.0	47.8	45.9	..	6.1	14.13	6.07	16.17	13.92
109	Italy	17.9	12.2	69.0	81.8	75.7	10.3	12.70	6.92	19.03	14.21
110	Netherlands	14.7	5.8	54.4	79.0	87.7	1.9	5.96	3.49	13.50	10.75
111	†Kuwait	17.8	5.1	28.1	33.1	74.8	–2.9	4.50	4.50	6.80	6.80
112	Belgium	10.4	6.8	59.2	57.0	58.0	4.8	7.69	5.13	..	11.08
113	Austria	13.3	7.3	48.9	72.5	84.9	3.8	5.00	2.98	..	..
114	France	15.0	9.9	53.7	69.7	76.2	6.5	6.25	5.92	18.73	16.01
115	†United Arab Emirates	..	11.1	..	19.0	59.9	1.1	9.47	..	12.13	..
116	Canada	15.3	8.3	40.2	64.3	66.7	4.6	12.87	12.09	14.25	13.33
117	Germany	10.1	5.6	46.1	60.4	64.3	2.7	7.95	5.50	12.04	9.94
118	Denmark	11.5	15.6	46.0	42.6	..	6.0	10.80	8.27	17.20	13.44
119	United States	9.2	8.9	64.1	58.9	66.2	3.9	13.07	9.09	15.27	10.92
120	Sweden	10.7	10.4	46.8	46.5	49.6	7.4	11.25	9.21	15.12	14.05
121	Finland	14.7	14.2	39.1	39.5	52.1	7.0	..	5.75	9.77	10.31
122	Norway	12.8	11.4	51.9	52.9	59.9	5.6	5.00	9.63	12.63	14.39
123	Japan	15.0	8.8	106.7	134.0	..	1.3	5.50	2.32	8.35	5.29
124	Switzerland	7.1	7.8	101.1	107.4	123.8	3.6	7.75	8.08	5.56	5.85

Other economies

World
  Oil exporters (excl. USSR)

Table 14. Growth of merchandise trade

	Merchandise trade (millions of dollars)		Average annual growth rate (percent)[a]				Terms of trade (1987 = 100)	
	Exports 1989	Imports 1989	Exports 1965–80	Exports 1980–89	Imports 1965–80	Imports 1980–89	1985	1989
Low-income economies	**120,136** *t*	**131,918** *t*	**5.6** *w*	**5.2** *w*	**4.3** *w*	**3.0** *w*	**107** *m*	**102** *m*
China and India	**68,061** *t*	**78,355** *t*	. .	**10.0** *w*	. .	**9.1** *w*	**103** *m*	**103** *m*
Other low-income	**52,075** *t*	**53,563** *t*	**6.2** *w*	**0.8** *w*	**5.3** *w*	**−3.2** *w*	**107** *m*	**102** *m*
1 Mozambique	92	680	. .	−12.6	. .	0.4	94	91
2 Ethiopia	420	1,100	−0.5	0.4	−0.9	6.4	117	107
3 Tanzania	260	840	−4.2	−8.2	*1.7*	−2.9	101	108
4 Somalia	82	133	4.4	−4.6	4.4	−9.0	107	111
5 Bangladesh	1,305	3,524	. .	7.6	. .	7.8	109	94
6 Lao PDR	. .	. .	. .	. .	. .	. .	. .	. .
7 Malawi	267	505	5.1	2.9	3.3	−0.8	104	101
8 Nepal	156	580	. .	*11.2*	. .	*11.6*	98	*100*
9 Chad	137	435	. .	. .	. .	. .	. .	. .
10 Burundi	78	187	. .	2.6	. .	6.9	133	86
11 Sierra Leone	137	189	−2.4	−2.5	. .	−4.2	106	78
12 Madagascar	312	340	0.6	−2.2	−0.4	−2.9	98	108
13 Nigeria	9,000	3,600	11.1	−2.3	14.6	−19.5	167	86
14 Uganda	273	652	−2.9	4.3	. .	1.7	143	88
15 Zaire	2,302	1,993	. .	0.6	. .	1.6	111	98
16 Mali	271	500	9.5	5.6	. .	4.6	95	102
17 Niger	250	370	12.8	−3.8	6.6	−8.2	126	79
18 Burkina Faso	75	410	3.6	0.8	5.7	−1.5	108	98
19 Rwanda	88	333	7.9	−0.8	. .	10.9	116	121
20 India	15,523	19,215	3.0	5.8	1.2	3.5	96	101
21 China*	52,538	59,140	. .	11.5	. .	11.7	109	104
22 Haiti	240	330	*5.5*	−6.9	*7.0*	−5.1	89	97
23 Kenya	1,110	2,100	3.9	1.6	2.2	1.0	114	107
24 Pakistan	4,642	7,119	−1.8	8.5	0.4	4.2	90	99
25 Benin	*111*	*431*	. .	. .	. .	. .	. .	. .
26 Central African Rep.	92	88	−1.3	−3.7	−4.8	3.2	107	113
27 Ghana	1,020	940	−2.6	5.6	−1.4	−1.5	106	82
28 Togo	245	472	. .	3.1	8.5	−1.0	118	107
29 Zambia	1,347	873	−0.7	−3.2	−7.6	−4.5	71	90
30 Guinea	430	465	. .	. .	. .	. .	. .	. .
31 Sri Lanka	1,554	2,229	0.2	6.7	−1.2	2.3	103	100
32 Lesotho[b]	. .	. .	. .	. .	. .	. .	. .	. .
33 Indonesia	21,773	16,360	9.6	2.4	. .	−0.4	134	97
34 Mauritania	360	370	4.0	3.4	. .	1.6	113	114
35 *Afghanistan*	*466*	*765*	. .	. .	. .	. .	. .	. .
36 *Bhutan*	. .	. .	. .	. .	. .	. .	. .	. .
37 *Kampuchea, Dem.*	. .	. .	. .	. .	. .	. .	. .	. .
38 *Liberia*	370	217	4.4	0.3	1.5	2.2	97	115
39 *Myanmar*	215	191	−2.0	−11.7	. .	−15.9	106	124
40 *Sudan*	520	1,390	−0.3	0.0	2.3	−3.7	106	106
41 *Viet Nam*	1,320	1,670	. .	. .	. .	. .	. .	. .
Middle-income economies	**396,324** *t*	**400,367** *t*	**2.6** *w*	**5.5** *w*	**5.1** *w*	**0.9** *w*	**110** *m*	**103** *m*
Lower-middle-income	**172,262** *t*	**183,853** *t*	**4.3** *w*	**5.2** *w*	**4.4** *w*	**0.2** *w*	**111** *m*	**103** *m*
42 Angola	*2,187*	*1,073*	. .	. .	. .	. .	. .	. .
43 Bolivia	817	615	2.7	−0.8	5.0	−2.4	167	117
44 Egypt, Arab Rep.	2,565	7,434	−0.1	9.2	3.6	6.5	131	82
45 Senegal	600	1,150	2.6	2.5	. .	0.7	106	103
46 Yemen Arab Rep.	. .	. .	. .	. .	. .	. .	. .	. .
47 Zimbabwe	1,300	1,090	. .	*3.1*	. .	−7.4	100	95
48 Philippines	7,747	10,732	4.6	1.3	2.9	0.4	93	107
49 Côte d'Ivoire	2,970	2,380	5.5	3.1	7.6	−1.1	110	91
50 Dominican Rep.	911	2,241	0.3	1.2	5.0	4.4	109	117
51 Morocco	3,337	5,492	3.7	5.7	6.5	2.2	88	80
52 Papua New Guinea	1,281	1,535	*14.1*	6.4	. .	2.7	111	81
53 Honduras	1,100	1,000	3.1	2.1	2.5	0.1	111	120
54 Guatemala	323	404	4.8	−11.7	4.6	−15.6	108	107
55 Congo, People's Rep.	830	590	10.3	6.2	0.6	−1.5	145	90
56 Syrian Arab Rep.	3,006	2,097	11.4	5.7	8.5	−8.4	125	84
57 Cameroon	900	1,320	4.9	−3.3	5.6	−1.8	139	101
58 Peru	3,714	1,839	1.6	0.4	−1.4	−6.7	111	88
59 Ecuador	2,354	1,860	15.1	5.0	*6.3*	−3.2	153	102
60 Namibia[b]	. .	. .	. .	. .	. .	. .	. .	. .
61 Paraguay	670	600	6.5	7.0	3.7	−1.4	108	120
62 El Salvador	610	1,140	1.0	−1.6	2.7	0.0	126	114
63 Colombia	5,739	5,010	1.4	9.8	5.3	−3.3	140	84
64 Thailand	20,059	25,768	8.6	12.8	4.1	8.4	91	99
65 Jamaica	982	1,806	−0.4	−2.1	−1.9	1.1	95	106
66 Tunisia	2,932	4,366	10.8	4.1	10.4	−0.1	105	99
* Data for Taiwan, China, are:	66,475	50,523	*15.6*	13.4	*12.2*	9.6	105	112

Note: For data comparability and coverage, see the technical notes.   Figures in italics are for years other than those specified.

		Merchandise trade (millions of dollars)		Average annual growth rate (percent)[a]				Terms of trade (1987 = 100)	
				Exports		Imports			
		Exports 1989	Imports 1989	1965–80	1980–89	1965–80	1980–89	1985	1989
67	Turkey	11,626	15,788	5.5	11.4	7.7	7.4	82	96
68	Botswana[b]	..	..	..	..	..	..	..	..
69	Jordan	926	2,119	11.2	9.1	9.7	–1.0	95	112
70	Panama	297	964	–5.7	0.1	–1.9	–4.8	130	152
71	Chile	8,190	6,496	8.0	4.9	1.4	–1.5	102	126
72	Costa Rica	1,362	1,743	7.0	3.1	6.0	4.7	111	109
73	Poland	13,155	10,085	..	2.4	..	1.4	94	120
74	Mauritius	987	1,326	3.1	10.5	5.2	10.7	83	108
75	Mexico	22,975	22,084	7.7	3.7	5.7	–4.7	133	98
76	Argentina	9,567	4,200	4.7	0.6	1.8	–8.2	110	110
77	Malaysia	25,053	22,496	4.6	9.8	2.2	3.7	117	97
78	Algeria	8,600	8,380	1.8	2.9	13.0	–5.8	174	88
79	Bulgaria	..	..	..	..	..	..	..	..
80	Lebanon	700	2,281	..	..	..	..	..	..
81	Mongolia	..	..	..	..	..	..	..	..
82	Nicaragua	250	1,000	2.8	–7.8	1.3	–4.2	111	110
	Upper-middle-income	**224,062** *t*	**216,515** *t*	**8.5** *w*	**5.7** *w*	**5.8** *w*	**1.6** *w*	**104** *m*	**103** *m*
83	Venezuela	12,953	7,837	–9.5	11.3	8.1	–4.3	174	118
84	South Africa[b]	13,500	16,952	7.8	–8.0	–0.1	–6.6	105	94
85	Brazil	34,392	18,281	9.3	5.6	8.2	–1.6	92	124
86	Hungary	9,605	8,818	..	5.7	..	1.6	104	87
87	Uruguay	1,599	1,203	4.6	2.8	1.2	–2.6	89	110
88	Yugoslavia	13,343	14,799	5.6	0.4	6.6	–0.7	95	121
89	Gabon	1,160	950	8.6	–0.2	..	–1.7	140	96
90	Iran, Islamic Rep.	13,000	9,550	..	21.6	..	6.5	160	68
91	Trinidad and Tobago	1,578	1,222	–5.5	–5.1	–5.8	–14.2	156	92
92	Czechoslovakia	14,455	14,277	..	..	..	..	..	..
93	Portugal	12,798	19,043	3.4	11.7	3.7	8.2	85	105
94	Korea, Rep.	62,283	61,347	27.2	13.8	15.2	10.4	103	108
95	Oman	3,933	2,255	..	..	..	..	..	..
96	Libya	6,760	5,100	3.3	–1.3	11.7	–9.0	196	91
97	Greece	7,353	16,103	11.9	4.1	5.2	3.5	94	97
98	Iraq	11,400	11,000	..	..	..	..	..	..
99	Romania	..	..	..	..	..	..	..	..
	Low- and middle-income	**516,460** *t*	**532,285** *t*	**3.3** *w*	**5.4** *w*	**5.0** *w*	**1.4** *w*	**108** *m*	**103** *m*
	Sub-Saharan Africa	**30,884** *t*	**31,805** *t*	**6.1** *w*	**–0.6** *w*	**5.7** *w*	**–5.9** *w*	**109** *m*	**104** *m*
	East Asia	**195,268** *t*	**202,642** *t*	**10.0** *w*	**10.0** *w*	**7.2** *w*	**7.6** *w*	**106** *m*	**102** *m*
	South Asia	**23,395** *t*	**32,858** *t*	**2.2** *w*	**6.2** *w*	**1.3** *w*	**3.8** *w*	**101** *m*	**100** *m*
	Europe, M.East, & N.Africa	**141,379** *t*	**163,596** *t*	**3.7** *w*	**5.8** *w*	**6.7** *w*	**1.7** *w*	**104** *m*	**96** *m*
	Latin America & Caribbean	**112,034** *t*	**84,433** *t*	**–1.0** *w*	**3.6** *w*	**4.1** *w*	**–3.7** *w*	**111** *m*	**110** *m*
	Severely indebted	**140,081** *t*	**114,839** *t*	**–0.2** *w*	**3.9** *w*	**5.1** *w*	**–1.2** *w*	**110** *m*	**108** *m*
	High-income economies	**2,385,816** *t*	**2,513,829** *t*	**7.4** *w*	**3.9** *w*	**4.6** *w*	**4.9** *w*	**98** *m*	**100** *m*
	OECD members	**2,173,621** *t*	**2,280,495** *t*	**7.3** *w*	**4.1** *w*	**4.2** *w*	**5.1** *w*	**94** *m*	**100** *m*
	†Other	**212,195** *t*	**233,334** *t*	**8.8** *w*	**2.4** *w*	**11.7** *w*	**3.3** *w*	**117** *m*	**100** *m*
100	†Saudi Arabia	26,200	21,500	8.8	–11.3	25.9	–9.9	176	92
101	Ireland	20,693	17,419	10.0	7.4	4.8	3.3	97	100
102	Spain	44,450	71,298	12.4	7.4	4.4	8.4	91	107
103	†Israel	10,735	13,101	8.9	7.7	6.2	4.8	105	102
104	†Hong Kong	28,731	72,154	9.1	6.2	8.3	11.0	97	100
105	†Singapore	44,600	49,605	4.7	8.1	7.0	5.8	99	98
106	New Zealand	8,586	8,757	3.8	3.5	1.1	3.4	88	100
107	Australia	33,205	39,869	5.4	4.1	1.0	5.0	111	122
108	United Kingdom	152,403	197,714	5.1	2.7	1.4	5.0	103	103
109	Italy	140,691	149,503	7.7	3.7	3.5	4.3	84	95
110	Netherlands	107,799	104,220	8.0	4.5	4.4	3.3	101	100
111	†Kuwait	11,476	6,295	18.5	1.2	11.8	–6.3	175	77
112	Belgium[c]	100,737	99,336	7.8	4.7	5.2	3.0	94	97
113	Austria	32,444	38,854	8.2	5.1	6.1	4.5	87	90
114	France	172,561	190,186	8.5	3.3	4.3	2.9	96	102
115	†United Arab Emirates	15,000	9,600	..	0.8	..	–3.6	171	96
116	Canada	114,066	113,230	5.4	6.0	2.5	8.8	110	110
117	Germany	340,628	268,601	7.2	4.4	5.3	3.4	82	96
118	Denmark	27,997	26,592	5.4	5.3	1.7	4.5	93	102
119	United States	346,948	491,512	6.4	2.3	5.5	8.2	100	102
120	Sweden	51,497	48,920	4.9	4.9	1.8	3.5	94	101
121	Finland	23,265	24,611	5.9	3.2	3.1	4.9	85	104
122	Norway	27,030	23,632	8.2	6.8	3.0	2.9	130	89
123	Japan	275,040	207,356	11.4	4.6	4.9	5.4	71	96
124	Switzerland	51,444	58,150	6.2	3.8	4.5	4.1	86	99
	Other economies	..	..	..	..	..	..	..	..
	World	**2,902,276** *t*	**3,046,114** *t*	**6.7** *w*	**4.1** *w*	**4.7** *w*	**4.3** *w*	**106** *m*	**101** *m*
	Oil exporters (excl. USSR)	**119,130** *t*	**86,874** *t*	**2.0** *w*	**–2.4** *w*	**11.4** *w*	**–7.4** *w*	**171** *m*	**91** *m*

a. See the technical notes.   b. Figures are for the Southern African Customs Union comprising South Africa, Namibia, Lesotho, Botswana, and Swaziland; trade between the component territories is excluded.   c. Includes Luxembourg.

Table 15. Structure of merchandise imports

<table>
<tr><th></th><th colspan="10">Percentage share of merchandise imports</th></tr>
<tr><th></th><th colspan="2">Food</th><th colspan="2">Fuels</th><th colspan="2">Other
primary
commodities</th><th colspan="2">Machinery
and transport
equipment</th><th colspan="2">Other
manufactures</th></tr>
<tr><th></th><th>1965</th><th>1989</th><th>1965</th><th>1989</th><th>1965</th><th>1989</th><th>1965</th><th>1989</th><th>1965</th><th>1989</th></tr>

<tr><td>Low-income economies</td><td>19 w</td><td>10 w</td><td>5 w</td><td>6 w</td><td>6 w</td><td>9 w</td><td>34 w</td><td>33 w</td><td>34 w</td><td>42 w</td></tr>
<tr><td>China and India</td><td>. .</td><td>8 w</td><td>. .</td><td>5 w</td><td>. .</td><td>10 w</td><td>. .</td><td>32 w</td><td>. .</td><td>45 w</td></tr>
<tr><td>Other low-income</td><td>17 w</td><td>14 w</td><td>5 w</td><td>7 w</td><td>3 w</td><td>6 w</td><td>33 w</td><td>36 w</td><td>42 w</td><td>37 w</td></tr>

<tr><td>1 Mozambique</td><td>17</td><td>35</td><td>8</td><td>1</td><td>7</td><td>3</td><td>24</td><td>34</td><td>45</td><td>26</td></tr>
<tr><td>2 Ethiopia</td><td>7</td><td>17</td><td>6</td><td>10</td><td>5</td><td>3</td><td>37</td><td>44</td><td>44</td><td>26</td></tr>
<tr><td>3 Tanzania</td><td>12</td><td>8</td><td>9</td><td>1</td><td>1</td><td>4</td><td>34</td><td>45</td><td>44</td><td>43</td></tr>
<tr><td>4 Somalia</td><td>33</td><td>29</td><td>5</td><td>3</td><td>5</td><td>2</td><td>24</td><td>38</td><td>33</td><td>29</td></tr>
<tr><td>5 Bangladesh</td><td>. .</td><td>31</td><td>. .</td><td>2</td><td>. .</td><td>4</td><td>. .</td><td>27</td><td>. .</td><td>36</td></tr>

<tr><td>6 Lao PDR</td><td>. .</td><td>. .</td><td>. .</td><td>. .</td><td>. .</td><td>. .</td><td>. .</td><td>. .</td><td>. .</td><td>. .</td></tr>
<tr><td>7 Malawi</td><td>16</td><td>10</td><td>5</td><td>12</td><td>2</td><td>1</td><td>21</td><td>43</td><td>57</td><td>35</td></tr>
<tr><td>8 Nepal</td><td>. .</td><td>9</td><td>. .</td><td>1</td><td>. .</td><td>5</td><td>. .</td><td>44</td><td>. .</td><td>41</td></tr>
<tr><td>9 Chad</td><td>13</td><td>16</td><td>20</td><td>2</td><td>3</td><td>3</td><td>21</td><td>46</td><td>42</td><td>33</td></tr>
<tr><td>10 Burundi</td><td>18</td><td>7</td><td>6</td><td>5</td><td>7</td><td>3</td><td>15</td><td>42</td><td>55</td><td>44</td></tr>

<tr><td>11 Sierra Leone</td><td>19</td><td>25</td><td>9</td><td>3</td><td>1</td><td>3</td><td>29</td><td>39</td><td>41</td><td>31</td></tr>
<tr><td>12 Madagascar</td><td>20</td><td>16</td><td>5</td><td>2</td><td>2</td><td>4</td><td>25</td><td>40</td><td>48</td><td>38</td></tr>
<tr><td>13 Nigeria</td><td>9</td><td>10</td><td>6</td><td>7</td><td>3</td><td>3</td><td>34</td><td>38</td><td>48</td><td>43</td></tr>
<tr><td>14 Uganda</td><td>8</td><td>9</td><td>1</td><td>0</td><td>3</td><td>1</td><td>37</td><td>50</td><td>51</td><td>40</td></tr>
<tr><td>15 Zaire</td><td>19</td><td>15</td><td>7</td><td>6</td><td>4</td><td>3</td><td>33</td><td>46</td><td>37</td><td>30</td></tr>

<tr><td>16 Mali</td><td>21</td><td>20</td><td>6</td><td>1</td><td>3</td><td>2</td><td>23</td><td>36</td><td>47</td><td>42</td></tr>
<tr><td>17 Niger</td><td>13</td><td>16</td><td>6</td><td>2</td><td>4</td><td>3</td><td>21</td><td>39</td><td>55</td><td>41</td></tr>
<tr><td>18 Burkina Faso</td><td>25</td><td>16</td><td>4</td><td>0</td><td>12</td><td>2</td><td>19</td><td>46</td><td>40</td><td>36</td></tr>
<tr><td>19 Rwanda</td><td>12</td><td>8</td><td>7</td><td>0</td><td>4</td><td>2</td><td>28</td><td>53</td><td>50</td><td>36</td></tr>
<tr><td>20 India</td><td>22</td><td>8</td><td>5</td><td>17</td><td>14</td><td>12</td><td>37</td><td>18</td><td>22</td><td>45</td></tr>

<tr><td>21 China*</td><td>. .</td><td>9</td><td>. .</td><td>3</td><td>. .</td><td>10</td><td>. .</td><td>31</td><td>. .</td><td>47</td></tr>
<tr><td>22 Haiti</td><td>31</td><td>23</td><td>6</td><td>1</td><td>5</td><td>2</td><td>14</td><td>26</td><td>44</td><td>47</td></tr>
<tr><td>23 Kenya</td><td>13</td><td>9</td><td>11</td><td>2</td><td>2</td><td>4</td><td>32</td><td>44</td><td>42</td><td>40</td></tr>
<tr><td>24 Pakistan</td><td>20</td><td>16</td><td>3</td><td>14</td><td>5</td><td>8</td><td>38</td><td>32</td><td>34</td><td>30</td></tr>
<tr><td>25 Benin</td><td>23</td><td>29</td><td>6</td><td>2</td><td>2</td><td>6</td><td>17</td><td>17</td><td>53</td><td>47</td></tr>

<tr><td>26 Central African Rep.</td><td>13</td><td>15</td><td>7</td><td>1</td><td>2</td><td>4</td><td>29</td><td>39</td><td>49</td><td>40</td></tr>
<tr><td>27 Ghana</td><td>13</td><td>11</td><td>4</td><td>5</td><td>2</td><td>7</td><td>33</td><td>40</td><td>48</td><td>37</td></tr>
<tr><td>28 Togo</td><td>18</td><td>26</td><td>4</td><td>6</td><td>2</td><td>2</td><td>32</td><td>25</td><td>45</td><td>41</td></tr>
<tr><td>29 Zambia</td><td>. .</td><td>. .</td><td>. .</td><td>. .</td><td>. .</td><td>. .</td><td>. .</td><td>. .</td><td>. .</td><td>. .</td></tr>
<tr><td>30 Guinea</td><td>. .</td><td>22</td><td>. .</td><td>5</td><td>. .</td><td>2</td><td>. .</td><td>36</td><td>. .</td><td>35</td></tr>

<tr><td>31 Sri Lanka</td><td>41</td><td>19</td><td>8</td><td>4</td><td>4</td><td>4</td><td>12</td><td>27</td><td>34</td><td>46</td></tr>
<tr><td>32 Lesotho[a]</td><td>. .</td><td>. .</td><td>. .</td><td>. .</td><td>. .</td><td>. .</td><td>. .</td><td>. .</td><td>. .</td><td>. .</td></tr>
<tr><td>33 Indonesia</td><td>6</td><td>8</td><td>3</td><td>8</td><td>2</td><td>10</td><td>39</td><td>38</td><td>50</td><td>37</td></tr>
<tr><td>34 Mauritania</td><td>9</td><td>23</td><td>4</td><td>18</td><td>1</td><td>1</td><td>56</td><td>29</td><td>30</td><td>29</td></tr>
<tr><td>35 Afghanistan</td><td>17</td><td>9</td><td>4</td><td>1</td><td>1</td><td>1</td><td>8</td><td>26</td><td>69</td><td>63</td></tr>

<tr><td>36 Bhutan</td><td>. .</td><td>. .</td><td>. .</td><td>. .</td><td>. .</td><td>. .</td><td>. .</td><td>. .</td><td>. .</td><td>. .</td></tr>
<tr><td>37 Kampuchea, Dem.</td><td>. .</td><td>. .</td><td>. .</td><td>. .</td><td>. .</td><td>. .</td><td>. .</td><td>. .</td><td>. .</td><td>. .</td></tr>
<tr><td>38 Liberia</td><td>18</td><td>3</td><td>8</td><td>1</td><td>1</td><td>1</td><td>33</td><td>81</td><td>39</td><td>15</td></tr>
<tr><td>39 Myanmar</td><td>15</td><td>4</td><td>4</td><td>2</td><td>5</td><td>1</td><td>18</td><td>52</td><td>58</td><td>41</td></tr>
<tr><td>40 Sudan</td><td>24</td><td>20</td><td>5</td><td>2</td><td>3</td><td>3</td><td>21</td><td>33</td><td>47</td><td>43</td></tr>
<tr><td>41 Viet Nam</td><td>. .</td><td>8</td><td>. .</td><td>23</td><td>. .</td><td>2</td><td>. .</td><td>37</td><td>. .</td><td>30</td></tr>

<tr><td>Middle-income economies</td><td>16 w</td><td>11 w</td><td>9 w</td><td>10 w</td><td>11 w</td><td>9 w</td><td>30 w</td><td>35 w</td><td>34 w</td><td>35 w</td></tr>
<tr><td>Lower-middle-income</td><td>17 w</td><td>13 w</td><td>8 w</td><td>8 w</td><td>9 w</td><td>8 w</td><td>30 w</td><td>31 w</td><td>37 w</td><td>40 w</td></tr>

<tr><td>42 Angola</td><td>18</td><td>29</td><td>2</td><td>3</td><td>2</td><td>1</td><td>24</td><td>39</td><td>54</td><td>28</td></tr>
<tr><td>43 Bolivia</td><td>20</td><td>18</td><td>1</td><td>2</td><td>2</td><td>3</td><td>34</td><td>38</td><td>42</td><td>40</td></tr>
<tr><td>44 Egypt, Arab Rep.</td><td>28</td><td>27</td><td>7</td><td>3</td><td>10</td><td>8</td><td>23</td><td>26</td><td>31</td><td>36</td></tr>
<tr><td>45 Senegal</td><td>37</td><td>21</td><td>6</td><td>5</td><td>4</td><td>3</td><td>15</td><td>34</td><td>38</td><td>37</td></tr>
<tr><td>46 Yemen, Rep.</td><td>. .</td><td>. .</td><td>. .</td><td>. .</td><td>. .</td><td>. .</td><td>. .</td><td>. .</td><td>. .</td><td>. .</td></tr>

<tr><td>47 Zimbabwe</td><td>. .</td><td>3</td><td>. .</td><td>1</td><td>. .</td><td>5</td><td>. .</td><td>55</td><td>. .</td><td>36</td></tr>
<tr><td>48 Philippines</td><td>20</td><td>11</td><td>10</td><td>13</td><td>7</td><td>7</td><td>33</td><td>20</td><td>30</td><td>50</td></tr>
<tr><td>49 Côte d'Ivoire</td><td>18</td><td>20</td><td>6</td><td>4</td><td>2</td><td>2</td><td>28</td><td>30</td><td>46</td><td>44</td></tr>
<tr><td>50 Dominican Rep.</td><td>25</td><td>14</td><td>10</td><td>6</td><td>2</td><td>3</td><td>23</td><td>30</td><td>40</td><td>47</td></tr>
<tr><td>51 Morocco</td><td>36</td><td>13</td><td>5</td><td>15</td><td>9</td><td>11</td><td>18</td><td>28</td><td>31</td><td>33</td></tr>

<tr><td>52 Papua New Guinea</td><td>25</td><td>16</td><td>4</td><td>11</td><td>1</td><td>1</td><td>25</td><td>37</td><td>45</td><td>36</td></tr>
<tr><td>53 Honduras</td><td>12</td><td>12</td><td>6</td><td>4</td><td>1</td><td>2</td><td>26</td><td>29</td><td>56</td><td>53</td></tr>
<tr><td>54 Guatemala</td><td>11</td><td>8</td><td>7</td><td>9</td><td>2</td><td>3</td><td>29</td><td>34</td><td>50</td><td>45</td></tr>
<tr><td>55 Congo, People's Rep.</td><td>15</td><td>17</td><td>6</td><td>0</td><td>1</td><td>2</td><td>34</td><td>40</td><td>44</td><td>41</td></tr>
<tr><td>56 Syrian Arab Rep.</td><td>22</td><td>21</td><td>10</td><td>2</td><td>8</td><td>3</td><td>16</td><td>32</td><td>43</td><td>42</td></tr>

<tr><td>57 Cameroon</td><td>12</td><td>16</td><td>5</td><td>1</td><td>3</td><td>2</td><td>28</td><td>36</td><td>51</td><td>44</td></tr>
<tr><td>58 Peru</td><td>17</td><td>22</td><td>3</td><td>10</td><td>5</td><td>5</td><td>41</td><td>26</td><td>34</td><td>36</td></tr>
<tr><td>59 Ecuador</td><td>10</td><td>9</td><td>9</td><td>4</td><td>4</td><td>7</td><td>33</td><td>34</td><td>44</td><td>46</td></tr>
<tr><td>60 Namibia[a]</td><td>. .</td><td>. .</td><td>. .</td><td>. .</td><td>. .</td><td>. .</td><td>. .</td><td>. .</td><td>. .</td><td>. .</td></tr>
<tr><td>61 Paraguay</td><td>14</td><td>12</td><td>14</td><td>23</td><td>2</td><td>2</td><td>37</td><td>30</td><td>33</td><td>33</td></tr>

<tr><td>62 El Salvador</td><td>16</td><td>16</td><td>5</td><td>7</td><td>3</td><td>5</td><td>28</td><td>32</td><td>48</td><td>40</td></tr>
<tr><td>63 Colombia</td><td>8</td><td>9</td><td>1</td><td>4</td><td>10</td><td>7</td><td>45</td><td>37</td><td>35</td><td>43</td></tr>
<tr><td>64 Thailand</td><td>7</td><td>6</td><td>9</td><td>8</td><td>5</td><td>9</td><td>31</td><td>39</td><td>49</td><td>38</td></tr>
<tr><td>65 Jamaica</td><td>22</td><td>19</td><td>9</td><td>14</td><td>4</td><td>4</td><td>23</td><td>21</td><td>42</td><td>42</td></tr>
<tr><td>66 Tunisia</td><td>16</td><td>15</td><td>6</td><td>9</td><td>6</td><td>10</td><td>31</td><td>24</td><td>41</td><td>41</td></tr>

<tr><td>* Data for Taiwan, China, are:</td><td>14</td><td>7</td><td>5</td><td>9</td><td>17</td><td>13</td><td>36</td><td>37</td><td>28</td><td>34</td></tr>
</table>

Note: For data comparability and coverage, see the technical notes.   Figures in italics are for years other than those specified.

		Percentage share of merchandise imports									
		Food		Fuels		Other primary commodities		Machinery and transport equipment		Other manufactures	
		1965	1989	1965	1989	1965	1989	1965	1989	1965	1989
67	Turkey	6	8	10	21	10	13	37	26	37	33
68	Botswana[a]	..	..	..	..	..	..	..	..	..	..
69	Jordan	30	19	6	16	5	4	18	23	42	38
70	Panama	12	15	21	17	1	2	21	18	45	48
71	Chile	20	5	6	12	9	5	35	41	30	37
72	Costa Rica	9	8	5	4	2	4	29	28	54	57
73	Poland	..	11	..	17	..	10	..	32	..	29
74	Mauritius	35	9	5	1	2	3	15	40	42	48
75	Mexico	5	16	2	4	10	8	50	34	33	37
76	Argentina	7	4	10	9	21	9	25	35	38	43
77	Malaysia	27	11	12	5	7	6	22	45	32	33
78	Algeria	27	28	0	2	5	8	15	28	52	35
79	Bulgaria	..	..	..	..	..	..	..	..	..	..
80	Lebanon	29	26	9	2	9	3	17	19	36	50
81	Mongolia	..	..	..	..	..	..	..	..	..	..
82	Nicaragua	13	14	5	3	1	1	30	39	51	42
	Upper-middle-income	**14 w**	**10 w**	**10 w**	**12 w**	**14 w**	**10 w**	**31 w**	**34 w**	**32 w**	**35 w**
83	Venezuela	12	12	1	1	5	9	44	47	39	31
84	South Africa[a]	5	6	5	1	10	4	42	52	37	38
85	Brazil	20	5	21	30	9	8	22	29	28	28
86	Hungary	12	7	11	12	21	9	27	33	28	38
87	Uruguay	10	7	17	14	14	7	24	33	36	39
88	Yugoslavia	16	8	6	19	19	11	28	26	32	36
89	Gabon	16	17	5	1	1	2	37	43	40	38
90	Iran, Islamic Rep.	16	22	0	4	6	4	36	34	42	37
91	Trinidad and Tobago	12	21	49	6	2	6	16	27	21	40
92	Czechoslovakia	..	6	..	28	..	10	..	36	..	20
93	Portugal	16	12	8	11	18	7	27	37	30	34
94	Korea, Rep.	15	6	7	13	26	17	13	34	38	30
95	Oman	..	20	..	2	..	2	..	34	..	43
96	Libya	14	14	4	4	3	1	36	34	43	47
97	Greece	16	16	8	6	11	7	35	31	30	40
98	Iraq	24	27	0	0	7	5	25	29	44	39
99	Romania	..	..	..	..	..	..	..	..	..	..
	Low- and middle-income	**17 w**	**11 w**	**8 w**	**10 w**	**10 w**	**8 w**	**31 w**	**34 w**	**35 w**	**37 w**
	Sub-Saharan Africa	**17 w**	**16 w**	**6 w**	**4 w**	**2 w**	**3 w**	**29 w**	**40 w**	**45 w**	**37 w**
	East Asia	**16 w**	**7 w**	**9 w**	**9 w**	**7 w**	**10 w**	**28 w**	**36 w**	**38 w**	**38 w**
	South Asia	**25 w**	**10 w**	**4 w**	**17 w**	**11 w**	**11 w**	**35 w**	**18 w**	**26 w**	**44 w**
	Europe, M.East, & N.Africa	**19 w**	**15 w**	**9 w**	**11 w**	**15 w**	**9 w**	**26 w**	**33 w**	**31 w**	**33 w**
	Latin America & Caribbean	**13 w**	**9 w**	**9 w**	**11 w**	**8 w**	**7 w**	**34 w**	**35 w**	**36 w**	**38 w**
	Severely indebted	**16 w**	**12 w**	**8 w**	**10 w**	**12 w**	**8 w**	**32 w**	**33 w**	**33 w**	**37 w**
	High-income economies	**20 w**	**10 w**	**11 w**	**9 w**	**19 w**	**8 w**	**20 w**	**34 w**	**31 w**	**39 w**
	OECD members	**20 w**	**10 w**	**11 w**	**9 w**	**19 w**	**8 w**	**20 w**	**34 w**	**31 w**	**39 w**
	†Other	**23 w**	**9 w**	**6 w**	**6 w**	**12 w**	**7 w**	**20 w**	**35 w**	**38 w**	**45 w**
100	†Saudi Arabia	31	15	1	0	4	2	27	37	37	45
101	Ireland	19	11	8	6	9	4	25	38	39	42
102	Spain	20	11	10	12	14	8	27	38	28	31
103	†Israel	16	9	6	8	11	5	28	24	38	54
104	†Hong Kong	26	8	3	2	11	5	13	26	46	59
105	†Singapore	24	7	13	14	18	5	14	42	30	33
106	New Zealand	8	7	7	6	9	4	33	40	43	42
107	Australia	6	5	8	5	9	4	37	45	41	42
108	United Kingdom	32	10	11	5	24	9	11	37	23	37
109	Italy	24	13	16	12	24	12	15	29	21	34
110	Netherlands	16	13	10	10	12	6	25	29	37	41
111	†Kuwait	26	16	1	0	2	2	32	43	39	40
112	Belgium[b]	14	10	9	8	21	10	24	24	32	48
113	Austria	15	5	7	6	12	8	31	37	35	44
114	France	20	10	15	9	18	8	20	33	27	40
115	†United Arab Emirates	..	13	..	1	..	2	..	38	..	46
116	Canada	10	6	7	5	9	5	40	53	34	32
117	Germany	24	11	8	8	20	9	13	31	35	42
118	Denmark	15	12	11	7	10	6	25	30	39	44
119	United States	20	6	10	11	20	5	14	41	36	36
120	Sweden	12	6	11	8	11	7	30	40	36	40
121	Finland	10	5	10	10	11	8	35	40	34	37
122	Norway	11	6	7	4	12	8	38	43	32	39
123	Japan	23	16	20	21	38	18	9	14	11	31
124	Switzerland	17	6	6	4	9	6	24	31	43	53
	Other economies	..	..	..	..	..	..	..	..	..	..
	World	**19 w**	**10 w**	**10 w**	**9 w**	**17 w**	**8 w**	**22 w**	**34 w**	**32 w**	**39 w**
	Oil exporters (excl. USSR)	**17 w**	**15 w**	**6 w**	**3 w**	**4 w**	**4 w**	**31 w**	**35 w**	**42 w**	**43 w**

a. Figures are for the Southern African Customs Union comprising South Africa, Namibia, Lesotho, Botswana, and Swaziland; trade between the component territories is excluded.   b. Includes Luxembourg.

Table 16. Structure of merchandise exports

		Fuels minerals, and metals		Other primary commodities		Machinery and transport equipment		Other manufactures		Textiles and clothing[a]	
		1965	1989	1965	1989	1965	1989	1965	1989	1965	1989
	Low-income economies	**16 w**	**25 w**	**60 w**	**23 w**	**1 w**	**6 w**	**23 w**	**46 w**	**12 w**	**22 w**
	China and India	..	**11 w**	..	**18 w**	..	**10 w**	..	**62 w**	..	**28 w**
	Other low-income	**22 w**	**43 w**	**65 w**	**30 w**	**1 w**	**1 w**	**11 w**	**26 w**	**4 w**	**12 w**
1	Mozambique	14	9	84	43	0	1	2	47	1	0
2	Ethiopia	0	3	100	94	0	0	0	3	0	1
3	Tanzania	1	4	86	84	0	1	13	11	0	6
4	Somalia	0	0	86	96	4	1	10	3	..	0
5	Bangladesh	..	1	..	28	..	0	..	71	..	58
6	Lao PDR	..	..	..	..	..	..	..	..	..	..
7	Malawi	0	0	99	94	0	0	1	5	0	5
8	Nepal	..	0	..	13	..	3	..	84	..	73
9	Chad	5	4	92	90	0	1	3	4	0	3
10	Burundi	0	0	94	93	0	0	6	6	1	1
11	Sierra Leone	25	41	14	21	0	0	60	38	0	0
12	Madagascar	4	6	90	85	1	0	4	9	1	6
13	Nigeria	32	94	65	5	..	0	2	1	0	0
14	Uganda	13	0	86	99	0	0	1	0	0	0
15	Zaire	72	85	20	6	0	0	8	9	0	0
16	Mali	1	0	96	90	1	2	2	8	1	1
17	Niger	0	..	95	..	1	..	4	..	1	..
18	Burkina Faso	1	0	94	88	1	1	4	10	2	1
19	Rwanda	40	1	60	98	0	0	1	1	..	0
20	India	10	8	41	19	1	7	47	66	36	23
21	China*	..	11	..	19	..	7	..	63	..	25
22	Haiti	14	0	62	14	3	16	20	70	3	43
23	Kenya	13	2	77	85	0	1	10	12	0	1
24	Pakistan	2	1	62	33	1	0	35	66	29	54
25	Benin	1	26	94	71	2	0	3	3	0	0
26	Central African Rep.	1	0	45	47	0	0	54	52	0	0
27	Ghana	13	29	86	63	0	0	1	8	0	0
28	Togo	33	53	62	38	1	1	4	7	0	0
29	Zambia	..	92	..	3	..	1	..	5	..	0
30	Guinea	..	83	..	6	..	0	..	11	..	0
31	Sri Lanka	0	3	99	43	0	4	1	50	0	38
32	Lesotho[b]	..	..	..	..	..	..	..	..	..	..
33	Indonesia	43	47	53	21	3	1	1	31	0	9
34	Mauritania	94	45	5	54	1	0	0	0	0	0
35	*Afghanistan*	0	43	87	40	..	1	13	17	12	13
36	*Bhutan*	..	..	..	..	..	..	..	..	..	..
37	*Kampuchea, Dem.*	..	..	..	..	..	..	..	..	..	..
38	*Liberia*	72	35	25	24	1	21	3	19	0	0
39	*Myanmar*	5	11	94	73	0	1	0	15	0	4
40	*Sudan*	1	1	99	95	..	2	0	2	0	1
41	*Viet Nam*	..	12	..	75	..	2	..	10	..	5
	Middle-income economies	**27 w**	**26 w**	**46 w**	**21 w**	**14 w**	**20 w**	**13 w**	**33 w**	**3 w**	**11 w**
	Lower-middle-income	**22 w**	**29 w**	**62 w**	**32 w**	**8 w**	**12 w**	**8 w**	**28 w**	**2 w**	**9 w**
42	Angola	6	95	76	2	1	0	17	3	0	0
43	Bolivia	93	80	3	15	0	1	4	4	0	1
44	Egypt, Arab Rep.	8	46	71	18	0	0	20	35	15	27
45	Senegal	9	19	88	72	1	1	2	8	1	1
46	Yemen, Rep.	..	..	..	..	..	..	..	..	..	..
47	Zimbabwe	..	17	..	40	..	1	..	43	..	3
48	Philippines	11	12	84	26	0	10	6	52	1	7
49	Côte d'Ivoire	2	1	93	91	1	0	4	7	1	2
50	Dominican Rep.	10	2	88	28	0	5	2	65	0	35
51	Morocco	40	23	55	30	0	4	5	42	1	20
52	Papua New Guinea	0	54	90	37	..	1	10	8	..	0
53	Honduras	6	1	90	87	0	1	4	11	1	7
54	Guatemala	0	2	86	81	1	0	13	16	4	11
55	Congo, People's Rep.	4	76	45	15	2	1	49	7	0	0
56	Syrian Arab Rep.	1	77	89	16	1	1	9	6	7	3
57	Cameroon	17	48	77	49	3	0	2	3	0	1
58	Peru	45	55	54	26	0	1	1	17	0	9
59	Ecuador	2	49	96	48	0	0	2	2	1	0
60	Namibia[b]	..	..	..	..	..	..	..	..	..	..
61	Paraguay	0	0	92	92	0	0	8	8	0	1
62	El Salvador	2	1	82	79	1	5	16	15	6	11
63	Colombia	18	26	75	49	0	1	6	24	2	6
64	Thailand	11	3	86	43	0	15	3	39	0	17
65	Jamaica	28	16	41	26	0	1	31	58	4	13
66	Tunisia	31	23	51	11	0	6	19	60	2	29
*	Data for Taiwan, China, are:	2	2	28	6	15	36	54	57	25	15

Note: For data comparability and coverage, see the technical notes.   Figures in italics are for years other than those specified.

		Fuels minerals, and metals		Other primary commodities		Machinery and transport equipment		Other manufactures		Textiles and clothing [a]	
		1965	1989	1965	1989	1965	1989	1965	1989	1965	1989
67	Turkey	9	8	89	26	0	5	2	61	1	35
68	Botswana[b]	..	..	..	..	..	..	..	..	..	..
69	Jordan	33	45	60	10	2	1	5	44	1	5
70	Panama	35	2	63	78	0	0	2	19	1	7
71	Chile	89	57	7	33	1	1	4	9	0	1
72	Costa Rica	0	1	84	69	1	4	15	27	2	18
73	Poland	..	19	..	14	..	32	..	34		6
74	Mauritius	0	0	100	38	0	1	0	61	0	51
75	Mexico	22	41	62	14	1	24	15	21	3	2
76	Argentina	1	4	93	64	1	6	5	26	0	3
77	Malaysia	34	19	60	37	2	27	4	17	0	5
78	Algeria	57	96	39	0	2	2	2	2	0	0
79	Bulgaria	..	..	..	..	..	..	..	..	..	..
80	Lebanon	14	6	52	24	14	8	19	63	2	8
81	Mongolia	..	..	..	..	..	..	..	..	..	..
82	Nicaragua	4	1	90	96	0	1	6	2	0	0
	Upper-middle-income	**32 w**	**25 w**	**28 w**	**13 w**	**22 w**	**25 w**	**18 w**	**37 w**	**5 w**	**12 w**
83	Venezuela	97	91	1	1	0	1	2	7	0	0
84	South Africa[b]	24	46	44	20	3	3	29	31	1	2
85	Brazil	9	15	83	33	2	20	7	32	1	3
86	Hungary	5	8	25	24	32	30	37	38	9	6
87	Uruguay	0	0	95	61	0	3	5	35	2	14
88	Yugoslavia	10	8	33	12	24	28	33	52	8	8
89	Gabon	52	69	37	21	1	1	10	9	0	0
90	Iran, Islamic Rep.	88	89	8	5	0	1	4	6	4	5
91	Trinidad and Tobago	84	62	9	7	0	1	7	30	0	0
92	Czechoslovakia	..	4	..	5	..	55	..	36	..	6
93	Portugal	4	6	34	15	3	19	58	59	24	29
94	Korea, Rep.	15	2	25	5	3	38	56	55	27	23
95	Oman	..	87	..	3	..	7	..	3	..	0
96	Libya	99	97	1	0	..	0	0	3	0	0
97	Greece	8	13	78	35	2	3	11	48	3	27
98	Iraq	95	98	4	0	0	1	1	1	0	0
99	Romania	..	..	..	..	..	..	..	..	..	..
	Low- and middle-income	**25 w**	**26 w**	**49 w**	**21 w**	**11 w**	**17 w**	**15 w**	**36 w**	**6 w**	**13 w**
	Sub-Saharan Africa	**24 w**	**53 w**	**68 w**	**36 w**	**0 w**	**1 w**	**7 w**	**10 w**	**0 w**	**2 w**
	East Asia	**22 w**	**12 w**	**67 w**	**19 w**	**1 w**	**22 w**	**10 w**	**47 w**	**2 w**	**33 w**
	South Asia	**6 w**	**6 w**	**57 w**	**24 w**	**1 w**	**5 w**	**35 w**	**65 w**	**28 w**	**33 w**
	Europe, M.East, & N.Africa	**21 w**	**34 w**	**35 w**	**12 w**	**21 w**	**20 w**	**23 w**	**33 w**	**8 w**	**12 w**
	Latin America & Caribbean	**43 w**	**33 w**	**50 w**	**33 w**	**1 w**	**12 w**	**6 w**	**24 w**	**1 w**	**3 w**
	Severely indebted	**33 w**	**29 w**	**45 w**	**29 w**	**11 w**	**15 w**	**11 w**	**28 w**	**3 w**	**5 w**
	High-income economies	**12 w**	**9 w**	**20 w**	**12 w**	**30 w**	**40 w**	**38 w**	**40 w**	**7 w**	**5 w**
	OECD members	**9 w**	**7 w**	**21 w**	**12 w**	**31 w**	**41 w**	**39 w**	**40 w**	**7 w**	**4 w**
	†Other	**59 w**	**27 w**	**17 w**	**6 w**	**3 w**	**26 w**	**23 w**	**40 w**	**10 w**	**12 w**
100	†Saudi Arabia	98	91	1	1	1	2	1	7	0	0
101	Ireland	3	2	63	26	5	32	29	40	7	4
102	Spain	9	8	51	18	10	36	29	37	6	4
103	†Israel	6	2	28	10	2	27	63	60	9	6
104	†Hong Kong	1	1	5	2	7	23	87	73	52	39
105	†Singapore	21	18	44	9	10	47	24	26	6	5
106	New Zealand	1	9	94	67	0	5	5	19	0	2
107	Australia	13	32	73	35	5	5	10	27	1	1
108	United Kingdom	7	10	9	8	42	40	42	40	7	3
109	Italy	8	3	14	7	30	37	47	52	15	12
110	Netherlands	12	12	32	25	21	21	35	42	9	4
111	†Kuwait	98	96	1	0	1	1	0	3	0	0
112	Belgium[c]	13	9	11	11	20	25	55	55	12	7
113	Austria	8	5	17	8	20	34	55	52	12	8
114	France	8	5	21	18	26	35	45	41	10	5
115	†United Arab Emirates	..	91	..	2	..	2	..	5	..	1
116	Canada	28	19	35	19	15	39	22	24	1	1
117	Germany	7	4	5	6	46	49	42	41	5	5
118	Denmark	2	4	55	32	22	25	21	39	4	4
119	United States	8	6	27	16	37	43	28	34	3	2
120	Sweden	9	6	23	10	35	43	33	41	2	2
121	Finland	3	5	40	14	12	29	45	52	2	3
122	Norway	21	56	28	10	17	13	34	21	2	1
123	Japan	2	1	7	1	31	65	60	32	17	2
124	Switzerland	3	3	7	4	30	32	60	61	10	5
	Other economies	..	..	..	..	..	..	..	..	..	..
	World	**15 w**	**12 w**	**26 w**	**14 w**	**25 w**	**35 w**	**34 w**	**39 w**	**7 w**	**6 w**
	Oil exporters (excl. USSR)	**80 w**	**92 w**	**16 w**	**2 w**	**0 w**	**1 w**	**3 w**	**5 w**	..	**1 w**

Percentage share of merchandise exports

a. Textiles and clothing is a subgroup of other manufactures.   b. Figures are for the Southern African Customs Union comprising South Africa, Namibia, Lesotho, Botswana, and Swaziland; trade between the component territories is excluded.   c. Includes Luxembourg.

Table 17. OECD imports of manufactured goods: origin and composition

		Value of imports of manufactures, by origin (millions of dollars)[a]		Composition of 1989 imports of manufactures (percent)[a]				
		1969	1989[a]	Textiles and clothing	Chemicals	Electrical machinery and electronics	Transport equipment	Others
	Low-income economies	**1,484** t	**47,562** t	**40** w	**6** w	**6** w	**3** w	**45** w
	China and India	**865** t	**34,903** t	**40** w	**6** w	**8** w	**1** w	**45** w
	Other low-income	**619** t	**12,659** t	**42** w	**4** w	**1** w	**9** w	**43** w
1	Mozambique	7	7	23	2	20	3	52
2	Ethiopia	4	62	13	8	3	3	74
3	Tanzania	30	52	40	3	2	8	48
4	Somalia	0	2	2	2	7	10	78
5	Bangladesh	0	882	84	0	0	0	16
6	Lao PDR	0	3	79	4	0	1	16
7	Malawi	0	13	70	0	2	1	28
8	Nepal	2	177	93	0	1	0	5
9	Chad	0	1	27	3	6	1	62
10	Burundi	2	2	9	1	3	2	86
11	Sierra Leone	89	82	0	0	0	0	99
12	Madagascar	8	40	64	12	1	0	23
13	Nigeria	17	160	3	28	2	4	64
14	Uganda	1	5	1	0	3	63	33
15	Zaire	51	312	0	1	0	0	98
16	Mali	0	17	2	1	3	1	94
17	Niger	0	283	0	98	0	1	1
18	Burkina Faso	0	6	10	1	3	1	85
19	Rwanda	0	1	0	4	5	4	88
20	India	608	8,125	40	5	1	1	54
21	China	257	26,778	39	7	10	1	43
22	Haiti	13	389	54	2	15	0	29
23	Kenya	17	124	5	3	5	16	71
24	Pakistan	193	2,357	81	1	0	1	18
25	Benin	0	4	1	0	1	1	97
26	Central African Rep.	11	67	0	0	0	0	99
27	Ghana	17	68	0	2	1	0	96
28	Togo	1	17	1	0	0	2	96
29	Zambia	6	36	17	1	1	11	70
30	Guinea	31	124	0	35	0	0	64
31	Sri Lanka	8	913	70	1	0	0	28
32	Lesotho[b]	. .	. .	. .	. .	. .	. .	. .
33	Indonesia	22	4,612	33	3	1	0	62
34	Mauritania	3	3	6	1	2	55	36
35	*Afghanistan*	9	46	91	0	0	1	8
36	*Bhutan*	0	2	0	0	3	2	95
37	*Kampuchea, Dem.*	0	1	24	4	4	3	70
38	*Liberia*	46	1,670	0	0	0	63	37
39	*Myanmar*	4	27	32	1	1	1	65
40	*Sudan*	0	8	7	2	4	6	82
41	*Viet Nam*	1		. .	. .	. .	. .	. .
	Middle-income economies	**4,307** t	**155,938** t	**25** w	**7** w	**17** w	**7** w	**44** w
	Lower-middle-income	**1,291** t	**64,526** t	**24** w	**6** w	**23** w	**7** w	**40** w
42	Angola	2	250	0	0	0	1	99
43	Bolivia	1	32	19	6	0	0	75
44	Egypt, Arab Rep.	31	570	61	5	2	7	25
45	Senegal	10	68	9	7	2	1	81
46	Yemen, Rep.	0	5	4	3	18	12	63
47	Zimbabwe	0	331	13	0	1	0	86
48	Philippines	111	4,291	34	3	28	1	34
49	Côte d'Ivoire	7	231	18	3	1	0	78
50	Dominican Rep.	5	1,474	48	1	6	0	46
51	Morocco	22	1,672	64	17	7	1	11
52	Papua New Guinea	13	31	5	3	2	5	85
53	Honduras	3	136	68	2	0	0	29
54	Guatemala	5	206	77	7	0	1	16
55	Congo, People's Rep.	4	126	0	2	0	0	97
56	Syrian Arab Rep.	3	28	52	4	2	4	38
57	Cameroon	3	60	28	1	1	7	63
58	Peru	13	452	49	9	3	1	38
59	Ecuador	3	73	13	3	1	8	75
60	Namibia	. .	. .	. .	. .	. .	. .	. .
61	Paraguay	4	77	27	14	0	0	59
62	El Salvador	1	116	57	1	25	0	17
63	Colombia	41	903	23	7	0	0	70
64	Thailand	30	8,197	24	2	14	1	59
65	Jamaica	62	765	33	63	0	0	4
66	Tunisia	15	1,494	62	16	7	1	14

Note: For data comparability and coverage, see the technical notes.   Figures in italics are for years other than those specified.

		Value of imports of manufactures, by origin (millions of dollars)[a]		Composition of 1989 imports of manufactures (percent)[a]				
		1969	1989[a]	Textiles and clothing	Chemicals	Electrical machinery and electronics	Transport equipment	Others
67	Turkey	35	5,313	70	5	3	2	21
68	Botswana[b]	. .	. .	. .	. .	. .	. .	. .
69	Jordan	1	83	5	37	5	23	30
70	Panama[c]	19	1,276	4	1	0	73	21
71	Chile	14	497	11	36	1	1	51
72	Costa Rica	4	561	64	1	11	1	23
73	Poland	230	2,880	20	16	7	9	48
74	Mauritius	1	663	81	0	0	0	18
75	Mexico	393	21,306	4	4	35	13	43
76	Argentina	89	1,658	12	18	1	3	66
77	Malaysia	34	7,761	15	4	55	1	25
78	Algeria	19	226	0	27	1	3	69
79	Bulgaria	44	374	21	24	6	1	49
80	Lebanon	15	147	15	4	3	3	76
81	Mongolia	0	5	73	4	2	0	21
82	Nicaragua	3	4	8	11	14	5	63
	Upper-middle-income	**3,016 t**	**91,412 t**	**26 w**	**7 w**	**12 w**	**7 w**	**48 w**
83	Venezuela	19	653	3	15	4	6	71
84	South Africa[b]	565	3,505	3	14	1	3	78
85	Brazil	136	11,674	7	9	5	14	65
86	Hungary	163	2,504	23	20	10	4	44
87	Uruguay	18	324	53	3	0	1	43
88	Yugoslavia	380	7,195	28	10	9	10	44
89	Gabon	8	89	0	67	1	1	31
90	Iran, Islamic Rep.	127	511	90	0	1	0	9
91	Trinidad and Tobago	37	313	1	73	0	0	26
92	Czechoslovakia	390	2,642	16	18	4	5	57
93	Portugal	390	9,803	39	6	8	9	38
94	Korea, Rep.	365	42,601	26	2	19	6	46
95	Oman	1	152	5	0	21	15	59
96	Libya	5	307	0	93	1	1	6
97	Greece	138	3,893	55	5	3	7	31
98	Iraq	5	142	1	19	2	9	69
99	Romania	124	2,102	28	7	3	3	59
	Low- and middle-income	**5,792 t**	**203,500 t**	**28 w**	**6 w**	**14 w**	**6 w**	**45 w**
	Sub-Saharan Africa	**385 t**	**5,043 t**	**15 w**	**9 w**	**1 w**	**22 w**	**53 w**
	East Asia	**911 t**	**96,190 t**	**30 w**	**4 w**	**18 w**	**3 w**	**45 w**
	South Asia	**815 t**	**12,497 t**	**54 w**	**3 w**	**1 w**	**1 w**	**42 w**
	Europe, M.East, & N.Africa	**2,167 t**	**42,841 t**	**40 w**	**10 w**	**7 w**	**6 w**	**37 w**
	Latin America & Caribbean	**949 t**	**43,424 t**	**11 w**	**9 w**	**19 w**	**13 w**	**49 w**
	Severely indebted	**1,273 t**	**49,712 t**	**14 w**	**8 w**	**20 w**	**10 w**	**48 w**
	High-income economies	**103,679 t**	**1,364,833 t**	**6 w**	**13 w**	**11 w**	**19 w**	**51 w**
	OECD members	**100,844 t**	**1,262,684 t**	**5 w**	**13 w**	**11 w**	**20 w**	**51 w**
	†Other	**2,835 t**	**102,149 t**	**17 w**	**5 w**	**18 w**	**4 w**	**56 w**
100	†Saudi Arabia	5	1,697	0	59	1	19	21
101	Ireland	426	12,883	7	25	11	2	56
102	Spain	601	23,799	5	10	7	30	48
103	†Israel	295	7,247	8	14	10	3	65
104	†Hong Kong	1,605	23,814	41	1	14	1	44
105	†Singapore	63	16,815	6	6	31	4	54
106	New Zealand	94	1,727	9	22	7	4	58
107	Australia	437	5,901	3	37	4	8	48
108	United Kingdom	9,381	88,190	5	18	10	12	55
109	Italy	6,749	95,052	16	8	8	10	58
110	Netherlands	4,857	59,605	7	30	9	9	46
111	†Kuwait	6	225	1	40	6	27	26
112	Belgium[d]	6,557	65,999	9	20	6	19	47
113	Austria	1,379	22,605	10	9	12	5	63
114	France	7,448	108,863	6	17	8	23	46
115	†United Arab Emirates	. .	607	27	25	3	6	39
116	Canada	7,499	70,015	1	8	6	40	45
117	Germany	19,517	236,407	5	14	10	21	49
118	Denmark	1,219	14,952	7	15	11	4	62
119	United States	19,238	184,431	2	12	13	20	53
120	Sweden	3,314	36,500	2	9	10	19	61
121	Finland	972	14,432	4	8	8	5	75
122	Norway	886	7,845	2	21	7	12	58
123	Japan	7,064	174,094	1	3	19	30	46
124	Switzerland	3,201	39,230	6	22	10	2	61
	Other economies	**722 t**	**12,725 t**	**4 w**	**15 w**	**12 w**	**11 w**	**58 w**
	World	**110,193 t**	**1,581,058 t**	**9 w**	**12 w**	**12 w**	**17 w**	**51 w**
	Oil exporters (excl. USSR)	**243 t**	**5,576 t**	**12 w**	**36 w**	**2 w**	**9 w**	**40 w**

Note: Data cover high-income OECD countries only. a. Trade data are based on the UN Comtrade database, Revision 1 SITC for the year 1969 and Revision 2 SITC for 1989. b. Figures for Lesotho and Botswana are included with South Africa. c. Excludes the Canal Zone. d. Includes Luxembourg.

Table 18. Balance of payments and reserves

		Current account balance (millions of dollars)				Net workers' remittances (millions of dollars)		Gross international reserves		
		After official transfers		Before official transfers				Millions of dollars		In months of import coverage
		1970	1989	1970	1989	1970	1989	1970	1989	1989
	Low-income economies							**3,613** t	**50,839** t	**3.5** w
	China and India							**1,023** t	**34,663** t	**4.4** w
	Other low-income							**2,590** t	**16,176** t	**2.5** w
1	Mozambique	..	−405[a]	..	−793[a]	..	..	..	..	..
2	Ethiopia	−32	−169[a]	−43	−378[a]	..	..	72	123	1.1
3	Tanzania	−36	−158	−37	−628	..	0	65	54	0.5
4	Somalia	−6	−151[a]	−18	−482[a]	..	..	21	23	0.5
5	Bangladesh	−114[a]	−729	−234[a]	−1,402	0[a]	771	..	929	2.8
6	Lao PDR	..	−67[a]	..	−107[a]	..	0[a]	6	*16*	*1.3*
7	Malawi	−35	−118[a]	−46	−173[a]	−4	..	29	105	2.1
8	Nepal	−1[a]	−254	−25[a]	−308	..	0	94	276	4.3
9	Chad	2	−5[a]	−33	−242[a]	−6	−21[a]	2	133	3.4
10	Burundi	2[a]	−29	−2[a]	−161	..	..	15	107	4.5
11	Sierra Leone	−16	*−3*	−20	*−11*	..	0	39	4	*0.5*
12	Madagascar	10	−128	−42	−283	−26	−11	37	245	3.7
13	Nigeria	−368	−143	−412	−254	..	−19	223	2,041	2.8
14	Uganda	20	−240[a]	19	−418[a]	−5	..	57	14	0.2
15	Zaire	−64	−460[a]	−141	−736[a]	−98	..	189	282	1.1
16	Mali	−2	−81	−22	−317	−1	39	1	123	2.1
17	Niger	0	−111	−32	−243	−3	−40	19	217	4.6
18	Burkina Faso	9	−91[a]	−21	−327[a]	16	147[a]	36	270	4.4
19	Rwanda	7	−105[a]	−12	−233[a]	−4	−17	8	70	2.1
20	India	−380[a]	−7,538[a]	−590[a]	−8,038[a]	80	2,650	1,023	8,048	3.0
21	China*	−81[a]	−4,530	−81[a]	−4,701	0[a]	138	..	23,053	4.4
22	Haiti	11	−63	4	−169	13	59	4	20	1.1
23	Kenya	−49	−587	−86	−868	..	−3	220	317	1.3
24	Pakistan	−667	−1,351	−705	−1,943	86	1,902	195	1,302	1.6
25	Benin	−3	−3[a]	−23	−58[a]	0	57[a]	16	8	0.2
26	Central African Rep.	−12	−8[a]	−24	−159[a]	−4	−29	1	118	4.1
27	Ghana	−68	−98	−76	−311	−9	3	43	436	3.7
28	Togo	3	−46	−14	−118	−3	4	35	290	5.7
29	Zambia	108	5	107	−67	−48	−21	515	*139*	*1.1*
30	Guinea	..	−126	..	−223	..	0	..	..	..
31	Sri Lanka	−59	−372[a]	−71	−546[a]	3	338[a]	43	269	1.2
32	Lesotho	18[a]	−37	−1[a]	−174	29[a]	..	..	49	0.9
33	Indonesia	−310	−1,368	−376	−1,540	..	125	160	6,444	2.9
34	Mauritania	−5	111[a]	−13	−158[a]	−6	4[a]	3	87	1.6
35	Afghanistan	..	−217	..	−305	..	..	49	631	10.4
36	*Bhutan*	..	−3[a]	..	−66[a]	..	0[a]	..	66	..
37	*Kampuchea, Dem.*	..	..	..	..	..	..	..	..	..
38	*Liberia*	−16[a]	*−118*	−27[a]	*−163*	−18[a]	*51*	..	8	..
39	*Myanmar*	−63	−204[a]	−81	−204	..	0	98	364	4.7
40	*Sudan*	−42	−945[a]	−43	−1,216[a]	..	297[a]	22	176	0.9
41	*Viet Nam*	..	..	..	..	..	..	243	..	..
	Middle-income economies							**15,855** t	**153,347** t	**3.1** w
	Lower-middle-income							**7,076** t	**71,910** t	**2.8** w
42	Angola	..	−20[a]	..	−20[a]	..	..	..	..	..
43	Bolivia	4	−264	2	−399	..	−1	46	563	5.2
44	Egypt, Arab Rep.	−148	−1,691[a]	−452	−2,828[a]	29	4,254[a]	165	2,495	1.7
45	Senegal	−16	−180[a]	−66	−397[a]	−16	30	22	31	0.2
46	Yemen, Rep.	−34[a]	−423	−52[a]	−531	39[a]	190	..	280	1.7
47	Zimbabwe	−14[a]	−107[a]	−26[a]	−185[a]	..	..	59	274	1.7
48	Philippines	−48	−1,465	−138	−1,822	..	360	255	2,398	2.0
49	Côte d'Ivoire	−38	−983[a]	−73	−1,044	−56	0[a]	119	33	0.1
50	Dominican Rep.	−102	−205[a]	−103	−289[a]	25	306[a]	32	171	0.8
51	Morocco	−124	−790	−161	−1,055	27	1,325	142	771	1.2
52	Papua New Guinea	−89[a]	−445	−239[a]	−662	..	46	..	410	2.4
53	Honduras	−64	−275	−68	−331	..	..	20	28	0.2
54	Guatemala	−8	−313	−8	−418	..	40	79	524	3.0
55	Congo, People's Rep.	−45[a]	−65	−53[a]	−127	−3[a]	−55	9	21	0.2
56	Syrian Arab Rep.	−69	784[a]	−72	−578[a]	7	225	57	*533*	2.2
57	Cameroon	−30	−295[a]	−47	−295[a]	−11	3[a]	81	92	0.5
58	Peru	202	508	146	353	..	..	339	1,597	4.5
59	Ecuador	−113	−532[a]	−122	−629[a]	..	..	76	707	2.4
60	Namibia	..	..	..	..	..	..	..	..	..
61	Paraguay	−16	−86[a]	−19	−86[a]	..	..	18	447	3.7
62	El Salvador	9	−186	7	−463	..	242	64	454	3.6
63	Colombia	−293	42	−333	42	6	459	207	3,862	5.4
64	Thailand	−250	−2,455	−296	−2,652	..	..	911	10,508	4.3
65	Jamaica	−153	−213	−149	−369	29	71	139	108	0.5
66	Tunisia	−53	−159	−88	−374	20	482	60	1,037	2.3
*	Data for Taiwan, China, are:	1	11,384	2	11,392	..	..	627	78,652	14.2

Note: For data comparability and coverage, see the technical notes. Figures in italics are for years other than those specified.

		Current account balance (millions of dollars)				Net workers' remittances (millions of dollars)		Gross international reserves			
		After official transfers		Before official transfers				Millions of dollars		In months of import coverage	
		1970	1989	1970	1989	1970	1989	1970	1989	1989	
67	Turkey	−44	966	−57	543	273	3,040	440	6,298	3.5	
68	Botswana	−30[a]	366[a]	−35[a]	173[a]	−9[a]	..	..	2,841	19.5	
69	Jordan	−20	−82[a]	−130	−704[a]	..	561[a]	258	771	2.5	
70	Panama	−64	39[a]	−79	−69[a]	..	..	16	119	0.6	
71	Chile	−91	−905	−95	−1,087	..	..	392	3,500	3.9	
72	Costa Rica	−74	−382	−77	−503	..	..	16	746	3.7	
73	Poland	..	−985	..	−1,872	..	..	..	2,504	1.5	
74	Mauritius	8	−71	5	−80	..	..	46	542	4.1	
75	Mexico	−1,068	−5,447	−1,098	−5,603	..	321	756	6,740	1.9	
76	Argentina	−163	−1,292	−160	−1,292	..	0	682	3,217	2.9	
77	Malaysia	8	−145	2	−239	..	..	667	8,733	3.6	
78	Algeria	−125	−1,254	−163	−1,254	178	355	352	3,086	3.1	
79	Bulgaria	..	..	..	..	..	..	..	..	..	
80	*Lebanon*	..	..	..	..	..	..	405	4,636	..	
81	*Mongolia*	..	..	..	..	..	..	..	..	..	
82	*Nicaragua*	−40	−448	−43	−617	..	..	49	..	..	
	Upper-middle-income							8,779 *t*	81,437 *t*	3.5 *w*	
83	Venezuela	−104	2,496	−98	2,512	−87	−368	1,047	8,702	8.0	
84	South Africa	−1,215	1,579	−1,253	1,507	..	..	1,057	2,195	1.1	
85	Brazil	−837	1,040[a]	−861	1,040[a]	..	..	1,190	10,505	3.5	
86	Hungary	−25	−572[a]	−25	−572[a]	..	0	..	1,846	1.6	
87	Uruguay	−45	153[a]	−55	145[a]	..	..	186	1,548	9.1	
88	Yugoslavia	−372	2,427	−378	2,430	441	6,290	143	4,899	2.5	
89	Gabon	−3	−175[a]	−15	−194[a]	−8	*−151*	15	40	0.2	
90	Iran, Islamic Rep.	−507	−2,476	−511	−2,476	..	..	217	..	..	
91	Trinidad and Tobago	−109	−141[a]	−104	−141[a]	3	0[a]	43	268	1.6	
92	Czechoslovakia	146	1,038	156	1,060	..	..	113	3,609	2.5	
93	Portugal	−158[a]	−575	−158[a]	−1,404	504[a]	3,379	1,565	16,389	9.4	
94	Korea, Rep.	−623	5,056	−706	5,008	..	0	610	15,342	2.7	
95	Oman	..	852	..	844	..	..	13	1,470	..	
96	Libya	645	−1,823	758	−1,786	−134	−496	1,596	5,776	*8.9*	
97	Greece	−422	−2,573	−424	−5,175	333	1,350	318	4,585	3.1	
98	*Iraq*	105	..	104	..	..	..	472	..	..	
99	*Romania*	−23	..	−23	..	..	..	..	2,731	..	
	Low- and middle-income							19,468 *t*	204,186 *t*	3.2 *w*	
	Sub-Saharan Africa							2,028 *t*	9,707 *t*	2.4 *w*	
	East Asia							2,885 *t*	67,513 *t*	3.4 *w*	
	South Asia							1,453 *t*	14,874 *t*	3.5 *w*	
	Europe, M.East, & N.Africa							6,581 *t*	65,836 *t*	3.3 *w*	
	Latin America & Caribbean							5,464 *t*	44,062 *t*	3.3 *w*	
	Severely indebted							5,510 *t*	47,950 *t*	2.7 *w*	
	High-income economies							75,667 *t*	858,580 *t*	3.1 *w*	
	OECD members							72,921 *t*	801,066 *t*	3.1 *w*	
	†Other							2,746 *t*	57,515 *t*	4.0 *w*	
100	†Saudi Arabia	71	−6,774	152	−4,275	−183	*−6,158*	670	18,590	7.6	
101	Ireland	−198	517	−228	−1,153	..	..	698	4,201	2.0	
102	Spain	79	−10,934	79	−12,378	469	1,425	1,851	47,770	6.5	
103	†Israel	−562	1,148	−766	−2,162	..	..	452	5,684	3.3	
104	†Hong Kong	225	..	225	..	..	..	..	..	..	
105	†Singapore	−572	2,338	−585	2,407	..	..	1,012	20,345	4.3	
106	New Zealand	−232	−2,039	−222	−1,999	16	300	258	3,027	2.5	
107	Australia	−777	−16,181	−682	−16,005	..	..	1,709	16,961	3.0	
108	United Kingdom	1,985	−31,159	2,393	−24,227	..	..	2,918	42,381	1.5	
109	Italy	800	−10,632	1,096	−7,094	446	*1,227*	5,547	73,455	5.1	
110	Netherlands	−588	6,962	−617	8,105	−49	−72	3,362	34,129	3.0	
111	†Kuwait	853[a]	9,323	853[a]	9,534	..	−1,287	209	4,120	4.6	
112	Belgium[b]	717	3,197	904	4,962	38	−213	2,963	23,059	1.8	
113	Austria	−75	−94	−73	−22	−7	293	1,806	16,882	3.6	
114	France	−204	−4,299	18	1,420	−641	−1,782	5,199	57,434	2.6	
115	†United Arab Emirates	90[a]	*2,700*	100[a]	*2,800*	..	..	..	4,776	..	
116	Canada	1,008	−14,091	960	−13,722	..	..	4,733	22,512	1.7	
117	Germany	852	55,477	1,899	67,721	−1,366	−3,992	13,879	98,877	3.4	
118	Denmark	−544	−1,414	−510	−1,192	..	..	488	7,054	1.9	
119	United States	2,330	−110,060	4,680	−96,630	−650	−1,050	15,237	168,584	2.9	
120	Sweden	−265	−5,179	−160	−3,922	..	28	775	11,993	2.1	
121	Finland	−240	−5,128	−233	−4,663	..	..	455	5,914	2.1	
122	Norway	−242	226	−200	1,007	..	−23	813	14,260	4.3	
123	Japan	1,990	56,990	2,170	60,280	..	..	4,876	93,673	5.8	
124	Switzerland	161	8,495	203	8,511	−313	*−1,549*	5,317	58,510	8.9	
	Other economies										
	World							95,135 *t*	1,062,766 *t*	3.1 *w*	
	Oil exporters (excl. USSR)							4,750 *t*	46,736 *t*	4.5 *w*	

a. World Bank estimate.   b. Includes Luxembourg.

Table 19. Official development assistance from OECD and OPEC members

OECD: Total net flows[a]	1965	1970	1975	1980	1985	1986	1987	1988	1989
					Millions of US dollars				
101 Ireland	0	0	8	30	39	62	51	57	49
106 New Zealand	..	14	66	72	54	75	87	104	87
107 Australia	119	212	552	667	749	752	627	1,101	1,020
108 United Kingdom	472	500	904	1,854	1,530	1,737	1,871	2,645	2,587
109 Italy	60	147	182	683	1,098	2,404	2,615	3,193	3,613
110 Netherlands	70	196	608	1,630	1,136	1,740	2,094	2,231	2,094
112 Belgium	102	120	378	595	440	547	687	601	703
113 Austria	10	11	79	178	248	198	201	301	283
114 France	752	971	2,093	4,162	3,995	5,105	6,525	6,865	7,450
116 Canada	96	337	880	1,075	1,631	1,695	1,885	2,347	2,320
117 Germany	456	599	1,689	3,567	2,942	3,832	4,391	4,731	4,949
118 Denmark	13	59	205	481	440	695	859	922	937
119 United States	4,023	3,153	4,161	7,138	9,403	9,564	9,115	10,141	7,676
120 Sweden	38	117	566	962	840	1,090	1,375	1,534	1,799
121 Finland	2	7	48	110	211	313	433	608	706
122 Norway	11	37	184	486	574	798	890	985	917
123 Japan	244	458	1,148	3,353	3,797	5,634	7,342	9,134	8,949
124 Switzerland	12	30	104	253	302	422	547	617	558
Total	6,480	6,968	13,855	27,296	29,429	36,663	41,595	48,114	46,697
					As a percentage of donor GNP				
101 Ireland	0.00	0.00	0.09	0.16	0.24	0.28	0.19	0.20	0.17
106 New Zealand	..	0.23	0.52	0.33	0.25	0.30	0.26	0.27	0.22
107 Australia	0.53	0.59	0.65	0.48	0.48	0.47	0.34	0.46	0.38
108 United Kingdom	0.47	0.41	0.39	0.35	0.33	0.31	0.28	0.32	0.31
109 Italy	0.10	0.16	0.11	0.15	0.26	0.40	0.35	0.39	0.42
110 Netherlands	0.36	0.61	0.75	0.97	0.91	1.01	0.98	0.98	0.94
112 Belgium	0.60	0.46	0.59	0.50	0.55	0.48	0.48	0.39	0.46
113 Austria	0.11	0.07	0.21	0.23	0.38	0.21	0.17	0.24	0.23
114 France	0.76	0.66	0.62	0.63	0.78	0.70	0.74	0.72	0.78
116 Canada	0.19	0.41	0.54	0.43	0.49	0.48	0.47	0.50	0.44
117 Germany	0.40	0.32	0.40	0.44	0.47	0.43	0.39	0.39	0.41
118 Denmark	0.13	0.38	0.58	0.74	0.80	0.89	0.88	0.89	0.94
119 United States	0.58	0.32	0.27	0.27	0.24	0.23	0.20	0.21	0.15
120 Sweden	0.19	0.38	0.82	0.78	0.86	0.85	0.88	0.86	0.97
121 Finland	0.02	0.06	0.18	0.22	0.40	0.45	0.49	0.59	0.63
122 Norway	0.16	0.32	0.66	0.87	1.01	1.17	1.09	1.13	1.04
123 Japan	0.27	0.23	0.23	0.32	0.29	0.29	0.31	0.32	0.32
124 Switzerland	0.09	0.15	0.19	0.24	0.31	0.30	0.31	0.32	0.30
					National currencies				
101 Ireland (millions of pounds)	0	0	4	15	37	46	34	37	35
106 New Zealand (millions of dollars)	..	13	55	74	109	143	146	158	145
107 Australia (millions of dollars)	106	189	402	591	966	1,121	895	1,404	1,287
108 United Kingdom (millions of pounds)	169	208	409	798	1,180	1,194	1,142	1,485	1,578
109 Italy (billions of lire)	38	92	119	585	2,097	3,578	3,389	4,156	4,954
110 Netherlands (millions of guilders)	253	710	1,538	3,241	3,773	4,263	4,242	4,400	4,436
112 Belgium (millions of francs)	5,100	6,000	13,902	17,399	26,145	24,525	25,648	21,949	27,677
113 Austria (millions of schillings)	260	286	1,376	2,303	5,132	3,023	2,541	3,717	3,743
114 France (millions of francs)	3,713	5,393	8,971	17,589	35,894	35,357	39,218	40,814	47,482
116 Canada (millions of dollars)	104	353	895	1,257	2,227	2,354	2,500	2,888	2,747
117 Germany (millions of deutsche marks)	1,824	2,192	4,155	6,484	8,661	8,323	8,004	8,292	9,292
118 Denmark (millions of kroner)	90	443	1,178	2,711	4,657	5,623	5,848	6,196	6,844
119 United States (millions of dollars)	4,023	3,153	4,161	7,138	9,403	9,564	9,115	10,141	7,659
120 Sweden (millions of kronor)	197	605	2,350	4,069	7,226	7,765	8,718	9,742	11,599
121 Finland (millions of markkaa)	6	29	177	414	1,308	1,587	1,902	2,550	3,026
122 Norway (millions of kroner)	79	264	962	2,400	4,946	5,901	5,998	6,412	6,329
123 Japan (billions of yen)	88	165	341	760	749	950	1,062	1,169	1,232
124 Switzerland (millions of francs)	52	131	268	424	743	759	815	900	912

Summary

	1965	1970	1975	1980	1985	1986	1987	1988	1989
					Billions of US dollars				
ODA (current prices)	6.5	7.0	13.9	27.3	29.4	36.7	41.6	48.1	46.7
ODA (1987 prices)	27.4	24.7	29.1	36.6	39.3	41.2	41.6	44.8	43.6
GNP (current prices)	1,350.3	2,040.0	3,959.3	7,393.5	8,490.0	10,387.0	12,050.0	13,480.0	13,950.0
					Percent				
ODA as a share of GNP	0.48	0.34	0.35	0.37	0.35	0.35	0.35	0.36	0.33
					Index (1987 = 100)				
GDP deflator[c]	23.66	28.24	47.65	74.62	74.92	89.06	100.00	107.36	106.99

OECD: Total bilateral flows to low-income economies[a]

		1965	1970	1975	1980	1984	1985	1986	1987	1988	1989
		As a percentage of donor GNP									
101	Ireland	..	..	..	..	0.03	0.05	0.06	0.07	−0.07	0.06
106	New Zealand	..	..	0.14	0.01	0.00	0.00	0.00	0.06	0.03	..
107	Australia	0.08	0.10	0.04	0.06	0.05	0.04	0.05	0.11	0.08	..
108	United Kingdom	0.23	0.09	0.11	0.11	0.09	0.09	0.09	0.09	0.10	0.10
109	Italy	0.04	0.06	0.01	0.01	0.09	0.12	0.16	0.16	0.16	0.15
110	Netherlands	0.08	0.24	0.24	0.30	0.29	0.27	0.32	0.31	0.31	0.28
112	Belgium	0.56	0.30	0.31	0.24	0.20	0.23	0.20	0.14	0.10	0.14
113	Austria	0.06	0.05	0.02	0.03	0.01	0.02	0.01	0.04	−0.04	0.05
114	France	0.12	0.09	0.10	0.08	0.14	0.14	0.13	0.14	0.14	0.15
116	Canada	0.10	0.22	0.24	0.11	0.15	0.15	0.12	0.14	0.14	0.08
117	Germany	0.14	0.10	0.12	0.08	0.11	0.14	0.12	0.11	0.11	0.11
118	Denmark	0.02	0.10	0.20	0.28	0.28	0.32	0.32	0.32	0.36	0.40
119	United States	0.26	0.14	0.08	0.03	0.03	0.04	0.03	0.03	0.04	0.02
120	Sweden	0.07	0.12	0.41	0.36	0.30	0.31	0.38	0.29	0.31	0.29
121	Finland	..	..	0.06	0.08	0.13	0.17	0.18	0.18	0.23	0.22
122	Norway	0.04	0.12	0.25	0.31	0.34	0.40	0.47	0.38	0.42	0.40
123	Japan	0.13	0.11	0.08	0.08	0.07	0.09	0.10	0.07	0.07	0.06
124	Switzerland	0.02	0.05	0.10	0.08	0.12	0.12	0.12	0.10	0.10	0.11
	Total	0.20	0.13	0.11	0.07	0.07	0.09	0.09	0.09	0.09	0.08

OPEC: Total net flows[d]

		1976	1980	1982	1983	1984	1985	1986	1987	1988	1989
		Millions of US dollars									
13	Nigeria	80	35	58	35	51	45	52	30	14	..
	Qatar	180	277	139	20	10	8	18	0	4	1
78	Algeria	11	81	129	37	52	54	114	39	13	41
83	Venezuela	109	135	125	142	90	32	85	24	49	..
90	Iran, Islamic Rep.	751	−72	−193	10	52	−72	69	−10	39	..
96	Libya	98	376	44	144	24	57	68	63	129	82
98	Iraq	123	864	52	−10	−22	−32	−21	−37	−28	37
100	Saudi Arabia	2,791	5,682	3,854	3,259	3,194	2,630	3,517	2,888	2,098	1,171
111	Kuwait	706	1,140	1,161	997	1,020	771	715	316	108	169
115	United Arab Emirates	1,028	1,118	406	351	88	122	87	15	−17	25
	Total OPEC	5,877	9,636	5,775	4,985	4,559	3,615	4,704	3,328	2,409	..
	Total OAPEC[e]	4,937	9,538	5,785	4,798	4,366	3,610	4,498	3,284	2,307	..
		As a percentage of donor GNP									
13	Nigeria	0.19	0.04	0.08	0.04	0.06	0.06	0.11	0.13	0.03	..
	Qatar	7.35	4.16	2.13	0.40	0.18	0.15	0.47	0.00	0.08	..
78	Algeria	0.07	0.20	0.31	0.08	0.10	0.10	0.19	0.06	0.02	..
83	Venezuela	0.35	0.23	0.19	0.22	0.16	0.00	0.08	0.02	0.04	..
90	Iran, Islamic Rep.	1.16	−0.08	−0.15	0.01	0.03	−0.04	0.04	−0.01	0.02	..
96	Libya	0.66	1.16	0.15	0.51	0.10	0.24	0.34	0.25	0.52	..
98	Iraq	0.76	2.36	0.13	−0.02	−0.05	−0.07	−0.05	−0.08	−0.05	1.46
100	Saudi Arabia	5.95	4.87	2.50	2.69	3.20	2.98	4.67	3.88	2.70	0.54
111	Kuwait	4.82	3.52	4.34	3.83	3.95	3.17	2.91	1.23	0.41	0.10
115	United Arab Emirates	8.95	4.06	2.22	1.26	0.32	0.45	0.41	0.07	−0.07	
	Total OPEC	2.32	1.85	0.96	0.82	0.76	0.61	0.95	0.63	0.45	..
	Total OAPEC[e]	4.23	3.22	1.81	1.70	1.60	1.39	1.80	1.10	0.86	..

a. Organisation of Economic Co-operation and Development.   b. Preliminary estimates.   c. See the technical notes.   d. Organization of Petroleum Exporting Countries.   e. Organization of Arab Petroleum Exporting Countries.

Table 20. Official development assistance: receipts

Net disbursement of ODA from all sources

		Millions of dollars							Per capita (dollars) 1989	As a percentage of GNP 1989
		1983	1984	1985	1986	1987	1988	1989		
Low-income economies		**12,338** *t*	**12,397** *t*	**13,833** *t*	**16,781** *t*	**18,517** *t*	**21,865** *t*	**21,467** *t*	**7.3** *w*	**2.2** *w*
China and India		**2,509** *t*	**2,471** *t*	**2,532** *t*	**3,254** *t*	**3,300** *t*	**4,086** *t*	**4,101** *t*	**2.1** *w*	**0.6** *w*
Other low-income		**9,829** *t*	**9,926** *t*	**11,301** *t*	**13,528** *t*	**15,216** *t*	**17,779** *t*	**17,366** *t*	**17.4** *w*	**5.6** *w*
1	Mozambique	211	259	300	422	651	893	759	49.4	59.2
2	Ethiopia	339	364	715	636	634	970	702	14.2	11.6
3	Tanzania	594	558	487	681	882	982	918	38.5	32.0
4	Somalia	343	350	353	511	580	433	440	72.2	38.9
5	Bangladesh	1,049	1,200	1,152	1,455	1,635	1,592	1,791	16.2	8.9
6	Lao PDR	30	34	37	48	58	77	141	34.8	22.5
7	Malawi	117	158	113	198	280	366	394	47.9	24.9
8	Nepal	201	198	236	301	347	399	488	26.5	16.0
9	Chad	95	115	182	165	198	264	239	43.2	23.5
10	Burundi	140	141	142	187	202	188	198	37.3	18.6
11	Sierra Leone	66	61	66	87	68	102	99	24.5	10.5
12	Madagascar	183	153	188	316	321	304	320	28.4	12.6
13	Nigeria	48	33	32	59	69	120	339	3.0	1.1
14	Uganda	137	163	182	198	279	363	397	23.7	8.4
15	Zaire	315	312	325	448	627	576	637	18.5	6.6
16	Mali	215	321	380	372	366	427	470	57.2	22.6
17	Niger	175	161	304	307	353	371	296	39.8	14.5
18	Burkina Faso	184	189	198	284	281	298	284	32.4	11.1
19	Rwanda	150	165	181	211	245	252	238	34.5	11.0
20	India	1,840	1,673	1,592	2,120	1,839	2,097	1,874	2.3	0.7
21	China	669	798	940	1,134	1,462	1,989	2,227	2.0	0.5
22	Haiti	134	135	153	175	218	147	198	31.1	8.4
23	Kenya	400	411	438	455	572	809	967	41.1	11.7
24	Pakistan	735	749	801	970	879	1,408	1,119	10.2	2.8
25	Benin	86	77	95	138	138	162	247	53.8	14.7
26	Central African Rep.	93	114	104	139	176	196	189	64.0	17.1
27	Ghana	110	216	203	371	373	474	543	37.6	10.3
28	Togo	112	110	114	174	126	199	182	51.9	13.6
29	Zambia	217	239	328	464	430	478	388	49.6	8.3
30	Guinea	68	123	119	175	213	262	346	62.2	12.6
31	Sri Lanka	473	466	484	570	502	598	558	33.2	7.9
32	Lesotho	108	101	94	88	107	108	118	68.5	26.0
33	Indonesia	744	673	603	711	1,246	1,632	1,830	10.3	1.9
34	Mauritania	176	175	209	225	182	184	195	101.8	19.4
35	*Afghanistan*	14	7	17	2	45	72	95	. .	. .
36	*Bhutan*	13	18	24	40	42	41	40	28.5	. .
37	*Kampuchea, Dem.*	37	17	13	13	14	19	25	. .	. .
38	*Liberia*	118	133	90	97	78	65	58	23.3	. .
39	*Myanmar*	302	275	356	416	367	451	220	5.4	. .
40	*Sudan*	962	622	1,128	945	898	937	760	31.0	. .
41	*Viet Nam*	106	109	114	147	111	148	138	2.1	. .
Middle-income economies		**11,180** *t*	**11,432** *t*	**11,760** *t*	**13,317** *t*	**14,547** *t*	**13,722** *t*	**11,628** *t*	**12.0** *w*	**0.6** *w*
Lower-middle-income		**9,620** *t*	**9,982** *t*	**10,156** *t*	**11,142** *t*	**12,115** *t*	**11,337** *t*	**10,973** *t*	**17.4** *w*	**1.3** *w*
42	Angola	75	95	92	131	135	159	140	14.4	1.8
43	Bolivia	174	172	202	322	318	394	432	60.8	9.6
44	Egypt, Arab Rep.	1,463	1,794	1,791	1,716	1,773	1,537	1,578	30.9	4.7
45	Senegal	323	368	295	567	641	568	652	90.5	14.0
46	Yemen, Rep.	. .	. .	. .	. .	. .	. .	. .	. .	. .
47	Zimbabwe	208	298	237	225	294	273	266	27.9	4.5
48	Philippines	429	397	486	956	770	854	831	13.8	1.9
49	Côte d'Ivoire	156	128	125	186	254	439	409	34.9	4.4
50	Dominican Rep.	100	188	207	93	130	118	141	20.2	2.1
51	Morocco	398	352	785	403	447	481	443	18.1	2.0
52	Papua New Guinea	333	322	259	263	322	380	334	87.5	9.5
53	Honduras	190	286	272	283	258	321	256	51.5	5.2
54	Guatemala	76	65	83	135	241	235	256	28.7	3.1
55	Congo, People's Rep.	108	98	71	110	152	89	91	41.3	4.0
56	Syrian Arab Rep.	813	641	610	728	684	191	139	11.5	1.2
57	Cameroon	129	186	159	224	213	284	470	40.7	4.2
58	Peru	297	310	316	272	292	272	300	14.2	1.0
59	Ecuador	64	136	136	147	203	136	162	15.7	1.6
60	Namibia	0	0	6	15	17	23	44	25.5	2.3
61	Paraguay	51	50	50	66	81	75	91	21.7	2.2
62	El Salvador	290	261	345	341	426	420	446	86.8	7.6
63	Colombia	86	88	62	63	78	62	62	1.9	0.2
64	Thailand	431	475	481	496	504	563	697	12.6	1.0
65	Jamaica	181	170	169	178	168	193	258	108.3	6.6
66	Tunisia	205	178	163	222	274	316	247	30.9	2.5

Note: For data comparability and coverage, see the technical notes.   Figures in italics are for years other than those specified.

		Net disbursement of ODA from all sources								
		Millions of dollars							Per capita (dollars)	As a percentage of GNP
		1983	1984	1985	1986	1987	1988	1989	1989	1989
67	Turkey	356	242	179	339	376	269	122	2.2	0.2
68	Botswana	104	102	96	102	156	151	162	133.1	6.5
69	Jordan	787	687	538	564	579	415	280	71.8	6.3
70	Panama	47	72	69	52	40	22	17	7.2	0.4
71	Chile	0	2	40	−5	21	44	61	4.7	0.2
72	Costa Rica	252	218	280	196	228	187	224	81.9	4.3
73	Poland	. .	. .	. .	. .	. .	. .	. .	. .	. .
74	Mauritius	41	36	28	56	65	59	57	53.8	2.7
75	Mexico	132	83	144	252	155	173	97	1.1	0.0
76	Argentina	48	49	39	88	99	152	215	6.7	0.4
77	Malaysia	177	327	229	192	363	104	139	8.0	0.4
78	Algeria	95	122	173	165	214	171	153	6.3	0.3
79	Bulgaria	. .	. .	. .	. .	. .	. .	. .	. .	. .
80	*Lebanon*	127	77	83	62	101	141	132	. .	. .
81	*Mongolia*	. .	. .	. .	. .	. .	3	4	1.9	. .
82	*Nicaragua*	120	114	102	150	141	213	227	60.8	. .
	Upper-middle-income	**1,560** *t*	**1,451** *t*	**1,604** *t*	**2,175** *t*	**2,432** *t*	**2,386** *t*	**655** *t*	**2.0** *w*	**0.1** *w*
83	Venezuela	10	14	11	16	19	18	21	1.1	0.0
84	South Africa	. .	. .	. .	. .	. .	. .	. .	. .	. .
85	Brazil	101	161	123	178	289	210	189	1.3	0.0
86	Hungary	. .	. .	. .	. .	. .	. .	. .	. .	. .
87	Uruguay	3	4	5	27	18	41	38	12.3	0.5
88	Yugoslavia	3	3	11	19	35	44	43	1.8	0.1
89	Gabon	64	76	61	79	82	106	134	121.3	3.9
90	Iran, Islamic Rep.	48	13	16	27	71	82	89	1.7	0.1
91	Trinidad and Tobago	5	5	7	19	34	9	6	4.8	0.1
92	Czechoslovakia	. .	. .	. .	. .	. .	. .	. .	. .	. .
93	Portugal	43	97	101	139	64	106	79	7.6	0.2
94	Korea, Rep.	8	−37	−9	−18	11	10	−9	−0.2	0.0
95	Oman	71	67	78	84	16	1	16	10.8	. .
96	Libya	6	5	5	11	6	6	11	2.5	0.1
97	Greece	13	13	11	19	35	37	33	3.3	0.1
98	*Iraq*	13	4	26	33	91	10	5	0.3	. .
99	*Romania*	. .	. .	. .	. .	. .	. .	. .	. .	. .
	Low- and middle-income	**23,518** *t*	**23,829** *t*	**25,593** *t*	**30,098** *t*	**33,063** *t*	**35,587** *t*	**33,095** *t*	**8.5** *w*	**1.1** *w*
	Sub-Saharan Africa	**7,716** *t*	**7,941** *t*	**9,006** *t*	**11,093** *t*	**12,492** *t*	**14,079** *t*	**13,148** *t*	**27.7** *w*	**7.9** *w*
	East Asia	**3,428** *t*	**3,553** *t*	**3,577** *t*	**4,529** *t*	**5,548** *t*	**6,411** *t*	**6,357** *t*	**4.1** *w*	**0.7** *w*
	South Asia	**4,623** *t*	**4,585** *t*	**4,655** *t*	**5,888** *t*	**5,630** *t*	**6,613** *t*	**6,090** *t*	**5.4** *w*	**1.7** *w*
	Europe, M.East, & N.Africa	**4,934** *t*	**4,749** *t*	**5,028** *t*	**4,888** *t*	**5,247** *t*	**4,268** *t*	**3,803** *t*	**11.4** *w*	**0.6** *w*
	Latin America & Caribbean	**2,818** *t*	**3,001** *t*	**3,328** *t*	**3,700** *t*	**4,146** *t*	**4,216** *t*	**3,697** *t*	**8.8** *w*	**0.4** *w*
	Severely indebted	**4,266** *t*	**4,684** *t*	**5,222** *t*	**5,861** *t*	**6,079** *t*	**6,129** *t*	**6,226** *t*	**12.3** *w*	**0.6** *w*
	High-income economies	. .	. .	. .	. .	. .	. .	. .	. .	. .
	OECD members	. .	. .	. .	. .	. .	. .	. .	. .	. .
	†Other	**1,929** *t*	**1,831** *t*	**2,405** *t*	**2,498** *t*	**1,840** *t*	**1,675** *t*	**1,324** *t*	**42.8** *w*	**0.5** *w*
100	†Saudi Arabia	44	36	29	31	22	19	16	1.1	0.0
101	Ireland									
102	Spain									
103	†Israel	1,345	1,256	1,978	1,937	1,251	1,241	1,192	264.4	2.6
104	†Hong Kong	9	14	20	18	19	22	23	4.0	0.0
105	†Singapore	15	41	24	29	23	22	95	35.4	0.3
106	New Zealand									
107	Australia									
108	United Kingdom									
109	Italy									
110	Netherlands									
111	†Kuwait	5	4	4	5	3	6	4	2.0	0.0
112	Belgium									
113	Austria									
114	France									
115	†United Arab Emirates	4	3	4	34	115	−12	−6	−3.9	0.0
116	Canada									
117	Germany									
118	Denmark									
119	United States									
120	Sweden									
121	Finland									
122	Norway									
123	Japan									
124	Switzerland									
	Other economies	**13** *t*	**12** *t*	**18** *t*	**18** *t*	**30** *t*	**20** *t*	. .	. .	. .
	World	**25,459** *t*	**25,673** *t*	**28,016** *t*	**32,614** *t*	**34,932** *t*	**37,282** *t*	**34,419** *t*	**8.7** *w*	**1.1** *w*
	Oil exporters (excl. USSR)	**750** *t*	**706** *t*	**648** *t*	**847** *t*	**966** *t*	**692** *t*	**881** *t*	**3.3** *w*	**0.2** *w*

Table 21. Total external debt

		Long-term debt (millions of dollars)				Use of IMF credit (millions of dollars)		Short-term debt (millions of dollars)		Total external debt (millions of dollars)	
		Public and publicly guaranteed		Private nonguaranteed							
		1970	1989	1970	1989	1970	1989	1970	1989	1970	1989
Low-income economies											
China and India											
Other low-income											
1	Mozambique	..	3,885	..	245	0	56	..	551	..	4,737
2	Ethiopia	169	2,876	0	0	0	30	..	107	..	3,013
3	Tanzania	250	4,505	15	13	0	129	..	272	..	4,918
4	Somalia	77	1,814	0	0	0	150	..	173	..	2,137
5	Bangladesh	15	9,926	0	0	0	719	..	68	..	10,712
6	Lao PDR	8	939	0	0	0	8	..	2	..	949
7	Malawi	122	1,242	0	4	0	101	..	48	..	1,394
8	Nepal	3	1,290	0	0	0	52	..	18	..	1,359
9	Chad	33	317	0	0	3	24	..	28	..	368
10	Burundi	7	810	0	0	8	40	..	17	..	867
11	Sierra Leone	59	512	0	0	0	105	..	440	..	1,057
12	Madagascar	89	3,345	0	0	0	165	..	97	..	3,607
13	Nigeria	452	31,668	115	406	0	0	..	759	..	32,832
14	Uganda	138	1,489	0	0	0	225	..	95	..	1,809
15	Zaire	311	7,571	0	0	0	628	..	643	..	8,843
16	Mali	238	2,055	0	0	9	55	..	46	..	2,157
17	Niger	32	1,127	0	259	0	85	..	108	..	1,578
18	Burkina Faso	21	685	0	0	0	1	..	71	..	756
19	Rwanda	2	606	0	0	3	1	..	45	..	652
20	India	7,838	54,776	100	1,478	0	1,566	..	4,689	..	62,509
21	China	..	37,043	0	0	0	908	..	6,907	..	44,857
22	Haiti	40	684	0	0	3	41	..	77	..	802
23	Kenya	319	4,001	88	632	0	415	..	641	..	5,690
24	Pakistan	3,064	14,669	5	138	45	933	..	2,770	..	18,509
25	Benin	41	1,046	0	0	0	10	..	121	..	1,177
26	Central African Rep.	24	642	0	0	0	35	..	38	..	716
27	Ghana	488	2,279	10	33	46	737	..	29	..	3,078
28	Togo	40	946	0	0	0	75	..	164	..	1,186
29	Zambia	624	4,095	30	0	0	900	..	1,879	..	6,874
30	Guinea	312	1,967	0	0	3	61	..	148	..	2,176
31	Sri Lanka	317	4,238	0	103	79	366	..	394	..	5,101
32	Lesotho	8	312	0	0	0	10	..	2	..	324
33	Indonesia	2,497	40,851	461	4,626	139	608	..	7,026	..	53,111
34	Mauritania	27	1,777	0	0	0	69	..	165	..	2,010
35	*Afghanistan*	..	..	..	..	..	..	..	..	..	..
36	*Bhutan*	..	77	0	0	0	0	..	2	..	79
37	*Kampuchea, Dem.*	..	..	..	..	..	..	..	..	..	..
38	*Liberia*	158	1,091	0	0	4	299	..	371	..	1,761
39	*Myanmar*	106	4,045	0	0	17	2	..	124	..	4,171
40	*Sudan*	298	8,261	0	496	31	884	..	3,324	..	12,965
41	*Viet Nam*	..	..	..	..	..	..	..	..	..	..
Middle-income economies											
Lower-middle-income											
42	Angola	..	..	..	..	..	..	..	..	..	..
43	Bolivia	480	3,605	11	200	6	252	..	302	..	4,359
44	Egypt, Arab Rep.	1,781	39,751	0	1,081	49	161	..	7,806	..	48,799
45	Senegal	102	3,508	31	33	0	316	..	282	..	4,139
46	Yemen, Rep.	..	4,775	0	0	0	1	..	909	..	5,685
47	Zimbabwe	229	2,568	0	68	0	29	..	423	..	3,088
48	Philippines	625	22,992	919	783	69	1,177	..	3,951	..	28,902
49	Côte d'Ivoire	256	8,156	11	4,071	0	370	..	2,816	..	15,412
50	Dominican Rep.	212	3,281	141	105	7	123	..	558	..	4,066
51	Morocco	712	19,507	15	200	28	850	..	294	..	20,851
52	Papua New Guinea	36	1,370	173	958	0	3	..	165	..	2,496
53	Honduras	90	2,823	19	84	0	35	..	407	..	3,350
54	Guatemala	106	2,089	14	110	0	73	..	330	..	2,601
55	Congo, People's Rep.	119	3,535	0	0	0	12	..	770	..	4,316
56	Syrian Arab Rep.	233	3,934	0	0	10	0	..	1,268	..	5,202
57	Cameroon	131	3,708	9	378	0	113	..	545	..	4,743
58	Peru	856	12,669	1,799	1,589	10	758	..	4,859	..	19,875
59	Ecuador	193	9,421	49	158	14	325	..	1,407	..	11,311
60	Namibia	..	..	..	..	..	..	..	..	..	..
61	Paraguay	112	2,098	0	27	0	0	..	365	..	2,490
62	El Salvador	88	1,657	88	39	7	5	..	149	..	1,851
63	Colombia	1,297	14,001	283	1,272	55	0	..	1,614	..	16,887
64	Thailand	324	12,424	402	4,658	0	273	..	6,112	..	23,466
65	Jamaica	160	3,594	822	42	0	383	..	303	..	4,322
66	Tunisia	541	6,085	0	225	13	270	..	319	..	6,899

Note: For data comparability and coverage, see the technical notes. Figures in italics are for years other than those specified.

| | | Long-term debt (millions of dollars) | | | | Use of IMF credit (millions of dollars) | | Short-term debt (millions of dollars) | | Total external debt (millions of dollars) | |
| | | Public and publicly guaranteed | | Private nonguaranteed | | | | | | | |
		1970	1989	1970	1989	1970	1989	1970	1989	1970	1989
67	Turkey	1,846	34,781	42	795	74	48	..	5,977	..	41,600
68	Botswana	17	509	0	0	0	0	..	4	..	513
69	Jordan	120	6,404	0	0	0	97	..	918	..	7,418
70	Panama	194	3,575	0	0	0	320	..	1,906	..	5,800
71	Chile	2,067	10,850	501	3,148	2	1,270	..	2,973	..	18,241
72	Costa Rica	134	3,480	112	304	0	35	..	650	..	4,468
73	Poland	24	34,747	0	0	0	0	..	8,577	..	43,324
74	Mauritius	32	631	0	106	0	63	..	32	..	832
75	Mexico	3,196	76,257	2,770	3,999	0	5,091	..	10,295	..	95,642
76	Argentina	1,880	51,429	3,291	1,800	0	3,100	..	8,416	..	64,745
77	Malaysia	390	14,461	50	1,377	0	0	..	2,738	..	18,576
78	Algeria	945	23,609	0	0	0	619	..	1,840	..	26,067
79	Bulgaria	..	..	..	..	..	..	..	..	..	..
80	*Lebanon*	64	234	0	0	0	0	..	286	..	520
81	*Mongolia*	..	..	..	..	..	..	..	..	..	..
82	*Nicaragua*	147	7,546	0	0	8	0	..	1,659	..	9,205

Upper-middle-income

		1970	1989	1970	1989	1970	1989	1970	1989	1970	1989
83	Venezuela	718	25,339	236	4,523	0	998	..	2,284	..	33,144
84	South Africa	..	..	..	..	..	..	..	..	..	111,290
85	Brazil	3,421	84,284	1,706	6,008	0	2,423	..	18,576	..	20,605
86	Hungary	0	16,843	0	0	0	456	..	3,307	..	3,751
87	Uruguay	269	2,967	29	105	18	202	..	477	..	
88	Yugoslavia	1,199	14,303	854	3,481	0	686	..	1,181	..	19,651
89	Gabon	91	2,478	0	0	0	135	..	562	..	3,175
90	Iran, Islamic Rep.	..	..	..	..	..	..	..	..	..	
91	Trinidad and Tobago	101	1,680	0	0	0	205	..	127	..	2,012
92	Czechoslovakia	..	..	..	..	..	..	..	..	..	..
93	Portugal	485	14,644	268	696	0	0	..	2,950	..	18,289
94	Korea, Rep.	1,816	17,351	175	5,961	0	0	..	9,800	..	33,111
95	Oman	..	2,626	0	0	0	0	..	348	..	2,974
96	Libya	..	..	..	..	..	..	..	..	..	..
97	Greece	..	..	..	..	..	..	..	..	..	..
98	*Iraq*	..	..	..	..	..	..	..	..	..	..
99	*Romania*	..	0	0	0	0	0	..	500	..	500

Low- and middle-income
 Sub-Saharan Africa
 East Asia
 South Asia
 Europe, M.East, & N.Africa
 Latin America & Caribbean

Severely indebted

High-income economies
 OECD members
 †Other

100	†Saudi Arabia
101	Ireland
102	Spain
103	†Israel
104	†Hong Kong
105	†Singapore
106	New Zealand
107	Australia
108	United Kingdom
109	Italy
110	Netherlands
111	†Kuwait
112	Belgium
113	Austria
114	France
115	†United Arab Emirates
116	Canada
117	Germany
118	Denmark
119	United States
120	Sweden
121	Finland
122	Norway
123	Japan
124	Switzerland

Other economies

World
 Oil exporters (excl. USSR)

Table 22. Flow of public and private external capital

		Disbursements (millions of dollars)				Repayment of principal (millions of dollars)				Interest payments (millions of dollars)			
		Long-term public and publicly guaranteed		Private nonguaranteed		Long-term public and publicly guaranteed		Private nonguaranteed		Long-term public and publicly guaranteed		Private nonguaranteed	
		1970	1989	1970	1989	1970	1989	1970	1989	1970	1989	1970	1989
Low-income economies **China and India** **Other low-income**													
1	Mozambique	..	177	..	14	..	13	..	4	..	31	..	3
2	Ethiopia	28	297	0	0	15	174	0	0	6	72	0	0
3	Tanzania	51	158	8	0	10	37	3	0	7	28	1	0
4	Somalia	4	75	0	0	1	7	0	0	0	10	0	0
5	Bangladesh	0	1,015	0	0	0	174	0	0	0	139	0	0
6	Lao PDR	6	134	0	0	1	9	0	0	0	2	0	0
7	Malawi	40	114	0	1	3	27	0	1	4	29	0	0
8	Nepal	1	241	0	0	2	29	0	0	0	25	0	0
9	Chad	6	80	0	0	3	3	0	0	0	2	0	0
10	Burundi	1	88	0	0	0	19	0	0	0	14	0	0
11	Sierra Leone	8	7	0	0	11	1	0	0	3	1	0	0
12	Madagascar	11	160	0	0	5	59	0	0	2	113	0	0
13	Nigeria	56	1,426	25	99	38	471	30	14	20	1,270	8	10
14	Uganda	27	138	0	0	4	88	0	0	5	28	0	0
15	Zaire	32	283	0	0	28	69	0	0	9	27	0	0
16	Mali	23	183	0	0	0	22	0	0	0	14	0	0
17	Niger	12	127	0	40	2	18	0	37	1	14	0	21
18	Burkina Faso	2	100	0	0	2	16	0	0	0	16	0	0
19	Rwanda	0	68	0	0	0	14	0	0	0	8	0	0
20	India	883	5,919	25	223	289	1,613	25	309	187	2,820	6	135
21	China	..	6,902	0	0	..	2,401	0	0	..	2,508	0	0
22	Haiti	4	29	0	0	3	15	0	0	0	9	0	0
23	Kenya	35	471	41	20	17	207	12	34	13	158	4	33
24	Pakistan	489	1,754	3	77	114	779	1	33	77	446	0	10
25	Benin	2	151	0	0	1	7	0	0	0	12	0	0
26	Central African Rep.	2	66	0	0	2	6	0	0	1	7	0	0
27	Ghana	42	434	0	9	14	136	0	8	12	61	0	2
28	Togo	5	65	0	0	2	24	0	0	1	33	0	0
29	Zambia	351	138	11	0	35	91	6	0	29	63	2	0
30	Guinea	90	257	0	0	11	67	0	0	4	32	0	0
31	Sri Lanka	66	404	0	0	30	183	0	2	12	107	0	1
32	Lesotho	0	52	0	0	0	14	0	0	0	7	0	0
33	Indonesia	441	5,963	195	1,329	59	4,234	61	868	25	2,527	21	454
34	Mauritania	5	96	0	0	3	55	0	0	0	25	0	0
35	*Afghanistan*	..	..	..	..	..	..	..	..	..	..	..	..
36	*Bhutan*	..	12	0	0	..	2	0	0	..	2	0	0
37	*Kampuchea, Dem.*	..	..	..	..	..	..	..	..	..	..	..	..
38	*Liberia*	7	1	0	0	11	1	0	0	6	1	0	0
39	*Myanmar*	22	215	0	0	20	121	0	0	3	69	0	0
40	*Sudan*	53	237	0	0	22	46	0	0	12	12	0	0
41	*Viet Nam*	..	..	..	..	..	..	..	..	..	..	..	..
Middle-income economies **Lower-middle-income**													
42	Angola	..	..	..	..	..	..	..	..	..	..	..	..
43	Bolivia	55	327	3	0	17	140	2	0	7	95	1	0
44	Egypt, Arab Rep.	397	2,004	0	142	310	1,270	0	192	56	1,085	0	107
45	Senegal	19	301	1	8	5	122	3	8	2	146	0	1
46	Yemen, Rep.	..	532	..	0	..	146	..	0	..	56	..	0
47	Zimbabwe	0	619	0	31	5	241	0	13	5	136	0	7
48	Philippines	141	1,584	276	119	74	950	186	35	26	1,620	19	77
49	Côte d'Ivoire	78	231	4	900	29	150	2	529	12	192	0	234
50	Dominican Rep.	38	199	22	0	7	102	20	15	4	76	8	9
51	Morocco	168	1,053	8	8	37	609	3	8	24	1,061	1	5
52	Papua New Guinea	43	292	111	285	0	171	20	183	1	74	8	86
53	Honduras	29	133	10	20	3	68	3	8	3	43	1	3
54	Guatemala	37	182	6	0	20	157	2	3	6	90	1	6
55	Congo, People's Rep.	18	134	0	0	6	175	0	0	3	94	0	0
56	Syrian Arab Rep.	60	249	0	0	31	272	0	0	6	113	0	0
57	Cameroon	29	633	11	82	5	62	2	131	4	73	1	39
58	Peru	148	367	240	181	100	107	233	15	43	91	119	5
59	Ecuador	41	859	7	63	16	437	11	25	7	399	3	12
60	Namibia	..	..	..	..	..	..	..	..	..	..	..	..
61	Paraguay	14	202	0	0	7	76	0	1	4	65	0	0
62	El Salvador	8	186	24	0	6	86	16	16	4	53	6	4
63	Colombia	253	2,079	0	177	78	1,708	59	443	44	1,197	15	187
64	Thailand	51	1,275	169	2,525	23	1,397	107	883	16	872	17	233
65	Jamaica	15	301	165	0	6	159	164	9	9	211	54	3
66	Tunisia	89	910	0	30	47	667	0	40	18	376	0	11

Note: For data comparability and coverage, see the technical notes. Figures in italics are for years other than those specified.

		Disbursements (millions of dollars)				Repayment of principal (millions of dollars)				Interest payments (millions of dollars)			
		Long-term public and publicly guaranteed		Private nonguaranteed		Long-term public and publicly guaranteed		Private nonguaranteed		Long-term public and publicly guaranteed		Private nonguaranteed	
		1970	1989	1970	1989	1970	1989	1970	1989	1970	1989	1970	1989
67	Turkey	331	4,276	1	432	128	3,441	3	268	42	2,607	2	60
68	Botswana	6	64	0	0	0	36	0	0	0	33	0	0
69	Jordan	15	1,030	0	0	3	200	0	0	2	254	0	0
70	Panama	67	1	0	0	24	2	0	0	7	1	0	0
71	Chile	408	669	247	846	166	568	41	270	78	1,080	26	207
72	Costa Rica	30	128	30	0	21	131	20	0	7	162	7	0
73	Poland	30	273	0	0	6	674	0	0	0	767	0	0
74	Mauritius	2	52	0	48	1	47	0	5	2	39	0	3
75	Mexico	772	2,880	603	1,086	475	2,440	542	1,800	216	7,104	67	793
76	Argentina	482	1,009	424	70	344	1,443	428	69	121	1,319	217	200
77	Malaysia	45	1,456	12	675	47	2,221	9	592	22	1,133	3	88
78	Algeria	313	5,024	0	0	35	5,221	0	0	10	1,851	0	0
79	Bulgaria	..	..	..	..	..	..	..	..	..	..	..	..
80	*Lebanon*	12	25	0	0	2	20	0	0	1	14	0	0
81	*Mongolia*	..	..	..	..	..	..	..	..	..	..	..	..
82	*Nicaragua*	44	282	0	0	16	18	0	0	7	10	0	0
Upper-middle-income													
83	Venezuela	216	1,239	67	0	42	578	25	160	40	1,987	13	564
84	South Africa	..	..	..	..	..	..	..	..	..	..	..	..
85	Brazil	892	2,185	900	850	256	3,260	200	1,757	135	3,619	89	747
86	Hungary	0	2,245	0	0	0	1,651	0	0	0	1,185	0	0
87	Uruguay	37	295	13	0	47	157	4	55	16	273	2	1
88	Yugoslavia	179	171	465	837	170	797	204	858	73	1,135	32	239
89	Gabon	26	128	0	0	9	63	0	0	3	107	0	0
90	Iran, Islamic Rep.	..	..	..	..	..	..	..	..	..	..	..	..
91	Trinidad and Tobago	8	56	0	0	10	65	0	0	6	138	0	0
92	Czechoslovakia	..	..	..	..	..	..	..	..	..	..	..	..
93	Portugal	18	3,335	20	180	63	2,157	22	99	29	1,012	5	45
94	Korea, Rep.	444	2,100	32	1,798	198	3,856	7	1,749	71	1,381	5	562
95	Oman	..	559	0	0	..	375	0	0	..	226	0	0
96	Libya	..	..	..	..	..	..	..	..	..	..	..	..
97	Greece	..	..	..	..	..	..	..	..	..	..	..	..
98	*Iraq*	..	..	..	..	..	..	..	..	..	..	..	..
99	*Romania*	..	26	0	0	..	1,646	0	0	..	105	0	0

Low- and middle-income
  Sub-Saharan Africa
  East Asia
  South Asia
  Europe, M.East, & N.Africa
  Latin America & Caribbean

Severely indebted

High-income economies
  OECD members
  †Other

100	†Saudi Arabia
101	Ireland
102	Spain
103	†Israel
104	†Hong Kong

105	†Singapore
106	New Zealand
107	Australia
108	United Kingdom
109	Italy

110	Netherlands
111	†Kuwait
112	Belgium
113	Austria
114	France

115	†United Arab Emirates
116	Canada
117	Germany
118	Denmark
119	United States

120	Sweden
121	Finland
122	Norway
123	Japan
124	Switzerland

Other economies

World
  Oil exporters (excl. USSR)

Table 23. Aggregate net resource flows and net transfers

| | | Net flows on long-term debt (millions of dollars) | | | | | | | | | | | |
| | | Public and publicly guaranteed | | Private nonguaranteed | | Official grants | | Net foreign direct investment | | Aggregate net resource flows | | Aggregate net transfers | |
		1970	1989	1970	1989	1970	1989	1970	1989	1970	1989	1970	1989
Low-income economies													
China and India													
Other low-income													
1	Mozambique	..	164	0	10	0	553	..	0	..	727	..	693
2	Ethiopia	13	123	0	0	6	422	4	..	23	545	10	473
3	Tanzania	40	120	5	0	6	544	..	0	52	664	44	636
4	Somalia	4	68	0	0	9	278	5	..	17	347	16	336
5	Bangladesh	0	841	0	0	..	767	..	0	0	1,607	0	1,469
6	Lao PDR	4	125	0	0	28	48	..	..	33	173	32	171
7	Malawi	37	87	0	1	7	187	9	..	52	275	41	246
8	Nepal	-2	213	0	0	16	163	..	0	14	375	14	351
9	Chad	3	77	0	0	11	132	1	-12	15	197	13	195
10	Burundi	1	68	0	0	7	60	0	1	8	129	8	112
11	Sierra Leone	-3	5	0	0	1	51	8	..	7	57	-1	56
12	Madagascar	5	101	0	0	20	136	10	6	36	243	29	130
13	Nigeria	18	955	-5	85	40	79	205	2,082	259	3,201	-207	900
14	Uganda	23	50	0	0	2	165	4	0	29	215	11	188
15	Zaire	3	214	0	0	37	134	42	12	83	360	44	272
16	Mali	23	161	0	0	12	203	..	-3	34	361	32	344
17	Niger	11	109	0	3	15	155	0	18	26	285	23	249
18	Burkina Faso	0	84	0	0	13	130	0	2	13	215	11	195
19	Rwanda	0	54	0	0	10	95	0	16	10	164	10	146
20	India	594	4,307	0	-86	157	756	0	425	751	5,402	559	2,447
21	China	..	4,500	0	0	..	311	..	1,400	..	6,211	..	3,696
22	Haiti	1	14	0	0	2	78	3	9	6	102	2	85
23	Kenya	17	264	30	-14	4	384	14	69	64	703	-2	405
24	Pakistan	375	975	2	44	79	408	23	170	479	1,597	395	1,099
25	Benin	1	144	0	0	9	95	7	1	17	241	13	228
26	Central African Rep.	-1	60	0	0	6	76	1	..	7	137	5	129
27	Ghana	28	297	0	1	9	193	68	15	104	507	79	437
28	Togo	3	41	0	0	7	65	0	..	11	106	4	58
29	Zambia	316	48	5	0	2	215	-297	..	26	263	-65	200
30	Guinea	80	191	0	0	1	109	..	10	80	310	76	278
31	Sri Lanka	36	222	0	-2	14	200	0	27	50	447	30	317
32	Lesotho	0	38	0	0	8	42	..	13	8	93	7	86
33	Indonesia	383	1,730	134	461	84	212	83	735	683	3,137	510	-1,647
34	Mauritania	1	41	0	0	3	126	1	3	5	171	-8	146
35	*Afghanistan*	..	..	..	..	..	..	..	..	..	..	..	..
36	*Bhutan*	..	10	0	0	0	17	..	..	..	26	..	24
37	*Kampuchea, Dem.*	..	..	..	..	..	..	..	..	..	..	..	..
38	*Liberia*	-4	0	0	0	1	24	28	..	25	24	19	23
39	*Myanmar*	2	94	0	0	16	76	..	154	17	323	14	254
40	*Sudan*	30	190	0	0	2	458	..	0	32	648	16	636
41	*Viet Nam*	..	..	..	..	..	..	..	..	..	..	..	..
Middle-income economies													
Lower-middle-income													
42	Angola	..	..	..	..	..	..	..	200	..	200	..	200
43	Bolivia	38	187	1	0	..	171	-76	-25	-37	333	-61	223
44	Egypt, Arab Rep.	87	734	0	-50	150	504	..	1,586	238	2,773	182	1,548
45	Senegal	14	178	-2	0	16	244	5	-20	33	402	16	254
46	Yemen, Rep.	..	386	0	0	10	106	0	0	..	492	..	386
47	Zimbabwe	-5	378	0	18	..	135	..	-9	-5	522	-9	379
48	Philippines	67	634	90	84	16	304	-29	482	144	1,505	76	-487
49	Côte d'Ivoire	49	80	2	371	12	220	31	..	94	672	33	218
50	Dominican Rep.	31	97	2	-15	10	42	72	110	115	234	102	149
51	Morocco	131	444	5	0	23	99	20	167	179	710	134	-412
52	Papua New Guinea	43	121	91	102	144	275	..	186	278	684	268	314
53	Honduras	26	65	7	12	0	115	8	37	41	230	17	109
54	Guatemala	17	25	4	-3	4	130	29	80	55	232	18	136
55	Congo, People's Rep.	13	-41	0	0	5	22	30	0	48	-20	45	-213
56	Syrian Arab Rep.	29	-23	0	0	11	24	..	..	41	1	35	-112
57	Cameroon	24	571	9	-49	21	117	16	31	70	670	61	559
58	Peru	48	259	7	166	20	114	-70	59	4	598	-231	480
59	Ecuador	26	421	-4	39	2	34	89	80	112	574	83	44
60	Namibia	..	..	..	..	..	..	..	..	..	..	..	..
61	Paraguay	7	126	0	-1	2	13	4	21	13	159	5	79
62	El Salvador	2	99	8	-16	2	235	4	0	15	318	-1	261
63	Colombia	174	371	-59	-266	21	34	39	546	175	685	22	-1,503
64	Thailand	28	-122	62	1,642	6	123	43	1,650	139	3,293	87	1,946
65	Jamaica	9	143	1	-9	3	113	161	28	174	274	5	-48
66	Tunisia	42	243	0	-10	42	110	16	74	99	416	61	-75

Note: For data comparability and coverage, see the technical notes.   Figures in italics are for years other than those specified.

| | | Net flows on long-term debt (millions of dollars) | | | | Official grants | | Net foreign direct investment | | Aggregate net resource flows | | Aggregate net transfers | |
| | | Public and publicly guaranteed | | Private nonguaranteed | | | | | | | | | |
		1970	1989	1970	1989	1970	1989	1970	1989	1970	1989	1970	1989
67	Turkey	203	835	−2	163	21	68	58	663	280	1,729	202	−1,041
68	Botswana	6	29	0	0	9	68	6	129	21	226	20	−122
69	Jordan	12	830	0	0	41	102	..	0	53	932	51	679
70	Panama	44	−1	0	0	..	5	33	12	77	16	51	−20
71	Chile	242	101	206	576	11	30	−79	259	380	966	172	−706
72	Costa Rica	9	−3	10	0	4	134	26	115	49	245	31	38
73	Poland	24	−402	0	0	..	..	..	−7	24	−409	24	−1,176
74	Mauritius	1	5	0	42	3	19	2	26	5	92	3	33
75	Mexico	297	440	61	−714	11	59	323	2,241	692	2,026	50	−7,123
76	Argentina	139	−435	−4	1	1	27	11	1,028	147	621	−264	−1,572
77	Malaysia	−2	−765	3	83	4	18	94	1,846	99	1,182	−92	−1,481
78	Algeria	279	−197	0	0	56	55	45	−59	379	−201	219	−2,052
79	Bulgaria	..	..	..	..	..	..	..	..	..	..	..	..
80	*Lebanon*	10	5	0	0	2	73	..	..	12	78	11	64
81	*Mongolia*	..	..	..	..	..	..	..	..	..	..	..	..
82	*Nicaragua*	28	264	0	0	2	163	15	..	45	428	15	418
	Upper-middle-income												
83	Venezuela	174	662	41	−160	..	4	−23	77	192	583	−429	−2,193
84	South Africa	..	..	..	..	..	..	318	7	..	..	..	..
85	Brazil	636	−1,076	700	−908	26	41	407	782	1,770	−1,160	1159	−7,725
86	Hungary	0	594	0	0	..	..	..	125	0	719	0	−466
87	Uruguay	−10	138	9	−55	2	13	..	1	1	98	−18	−177
88	Yugoslavia	9	−626	261	−21	−8	4	..	..	262	−643	158	−2,017
89	Gabon	17	66	0	0	10	27	−1	80	26	172	15	116
90	Iran, Islamic Rep.	..	..	..	..	..	..	25	..	..	..	..	..
91	Trinidad and Tobago	−3	−10	0	0	1	6	83	36	81	32	16	−106
92	Czechoslovakia	..	..	..	..	..	..	..	..	..	..	..	..
93	Portugal	−45	1,178	−1	81	..	65	15	1,546	−31	2,870	−65	1,744
94	Korea, Rep.	246	−1,756	25	49	119	1	66	453	456	−1,253	374	−3,417
95	Oman	..	184	0	0	0	0	..	..	..	184	..	−42
96	Libya	..	..	..	..	..	..	139	..	..	..	..	..
97	Greece	..	..	..	..	..	..	50	752	..	..	..	..
98	*Iraq*	..	..	..	..	..	..	24	..	..	..	..	..
99	*Romania*	..	−1,620	0	0	..	..	..	..	..	−1,620	..	−1,725

Low- and middle-income
Sub-Saharan Africa
East Asia
South Asia
Europe, M.East, & N.Africa
Latin America & Caribbean

Severely indebted

High-income economies
  OECD members
  †Other

100	†Saudi Arabia
101	Ireland
102	Spain
103	†Israel
104	†Hong Kong

105	†Singapore
106	New Zealand
107	Australia
108	United Kingdom
109	Italy

110	Netherlands
111	†Kuwait
112	Belgium
113	Austria
114	France

115	†United Arab Emirates
116	Canada
117	Germany
118	Denmark
119	United States

120	Sweden
121	Finland
122	Norway
123	Japan
124	Switzerland

Other economies

World
  Oil exporters (excl. USSR)

Table 24. Total external debt ratios

		Total external debt as a percentage of				Total debt service as a percentage of exports of goods and services		Interest payments as a percentage of exports of goods and services	
		Exports of goods and services		GNP					
		1980	1989	1980	1989	1980	1989	1980	1989
	Low-income economies	**95.3** w	**214.1** w	**13.7** w	**32.3** w	**9.8** w	**20.2** w	**4.7** w	**9.8** w
	China and India	**70.5** w	**130.8** w	**5.3** w	**15.9** w	**6.5** w	**14.7** w	**2.6** w	**8.1** w
	Other low-income	**106.9** w	**322.2** w	**27.0** w	**71.0** w	**11.4** w	**27.4** w	**5.7** w	**12.0** w
1	Mozambique	. .	1,744.7	. .	426.8	. .	23.1	. .	17.1
2	Ethiopia	136.2	416.8	19.6	50.6	7.6	38.7	4.7	11.6
3	Tanzania	334.1	931.4	50.2	186.1	21.1	16.5	9.7	7.7
4	Somalia	252.0	2,253.4	109.5	202.8	4.9	34.1	0.9	14.7
5	Bangladesh	345.6	437.6	31.7	53.3	23.2	19.9	6.4	7.8
6	Lao PDR	. .	1,116.4	. .	152.6	. .	15.6	. .	3.2
7	Malawi	260.8	411.3	72.1	91.4	27.7	28.0	16.7	11.8
8	Nepal	85.5	330.5	10.3	43.5	3.2	16.0	2.1	6.9
9	Chad	305.9	163.3	30.2	36.7	8.3	5.2	0.7	1.7
10	Burundi	180.1	754.3	18.1	81.9	9.5	32.9	4.8	13.8
11	Sierra Leone	155.6	. .	40.2	119.5	22.9	. .	5.7	. .
12	Madagascar	242.3	779.8	31.5	154.1	17.2	52.0	10.9	27.8
13	Nigeria	32.2	389.6	9.0	119.3	4.2	21.3	3.3	15.6
14	Uganda	221.7	664.9	42.7	39.0	13.2	77.0	3.3	17.0
15	Zaire	202.2	371.0	33.5	96.6	22.5	21.5	11.0	4.2
16	Mali	227.5	488.7	45.5	105.2	5.1	15.0	2.3	4.8
17	Niger	132.8	416.7	34.5	79.4	21.7	32.1	12.9	12.6
18	Burkina Faso	88.8	182.2	19.6	29.6	5.9	9.4	3.1	5.1
19	Rwanda	103.4	415.2	16.3	30.2	4.2	18.5	2.8	7.9
20	India	135.7	259.5	11.9	24.0	9.1	26.4	4.1	14.3
21	China	22.1	77.3	1.5	10.8	4.6	9.8	1.6	5.5
22	Haiti	72.9	203.0	20.9	34.2	6.2	13.1	1.8	4.3
23	Kenya	171.3	294.1	50.2	71.7	22.3	33.3	11.7	14.1
24	Pakistan	208.9	242.4	42.5	46.9	18.0	23.2	7.6	9.7
25	Benin	100.8	303.5	36.5	71.9	4.9	6.7	3.5	4.4
26	Central African Rep.	94.8	336.0	24.4	65.8	4.9	14.2	1.6	5.2
27	Ghana	108.3	343.8	29.7	59.9	12.5	48.9	4.3	12.3
28	Togo	180.1	239.2	93.4	91.2	9.0	18.2	5.8	8.6
29	Zambia	201.0	453.6	90.9	158.8	25.3	11.3	8.8	4.2
30	Guinea	201.9	292.8	. .	85.3	19.8	15.2	6.0	5.0
31	Sri Lanka	123.4	223.0	46.1	73.5	12.0	17.8	5.7	6.7
32	Lesotho	19.5	65.0	11.2	39.0	1.5	4.5	0.6	1.5
33	Indonesia	94.2	210.7	28.0	59.4	13.9	35.2	6.5	14.9
34	Mauritania	306.7	394.8	125.7	213.2	17.3	20.1	7.9	7.2
35	*Afghanistan*	. .	. .	. .	. .	. .	. .	. .	. .
36	*Bhutan*	. .	. .	. .	. .	. .	. .	. .	. .
37	*Kampuchea, Dem.*	. .	. .	. .	. .	. .	. .	. .	. .
38	*Liberia*	111.8	. .	62.8	. .	8.8	. .	5.8	. .
39	*Myanmar*	269.9	643.7	. .	. .	25.4	30.4	9.4	10.9
40	*Sudan*	499.4	1,234.4	65.7	. .	25.5	9.2	12.8	4.8
41	*Viet Nam*	. .	. .	. .	. .	. .	. .	. .	. .
	Middle-income economies	**148.6** w	**184.4** w	**36.1** w	**46.1** w	**26.1** w	**23.1** w	**13.3** w	**11.1** w
	Lower-middle-income	**155.4** w	**227.4** w	**37.7** w	**67.7** w	**25.4** w	**26.6** w	**12.8** w	**12.9** w
42	Angola	. .	. .	. .	. .	. .	. .	. .	. .
43	Bolivia	258.2	488.9	93.3	102.2	35.0	31.3	21.1	14.3
44	Egypt, Arab Rep.	208.4	333.6	95.0	159.0	20.8	20.5	9.0	10.3
45	Senegal	162.2	320.7	50.3	93.2	28.6	29.4	10.4	14.6
46	Yemen, Rep.	78.5	253.6	38.6	70.6	3.4	11.6	2.0	4.7
47	Zimbabwe	45.4	169.7	14.9	53.9	3.8	26.0	1.5	9.9
48	Philippines	212.5	226.4	49.5	65.3	26.5	26.3	18.2	17.1
49	Côte d'Ivoire	160.7	463.9	58.8	182.2	28.3	40.9	13.0	15.6
50	Dominican Rep.	133.8	165.5	31.5	63.3	25.3	13.0	12.0	4.6
51	Morocco	223.8	328.4	53.1	98.4	32.7	32.2	17.0	18.4
52	Papua New Guinea	66.1	161.5	29.2	73.7	13.8	34.3	6.6	11.2
53	Honduras	152.0	303.0	61.5	72.5	21.4	13.1	12.4	6.2
54	Guatemala	63.6	171.1	14.9	32.6	7.9	19.0	3.7	7.7
55	Congo, People's Rep.	145.2	363.9	97.0	215.0	10.5	27.0	6.6	11.9
56	Syrian Arab Rep.	82.3	. .	21.0	47.1	11.4	. .	4.7	. .
57	Cameroon	136.7	224.3	36.8	44.2	15.2	17.3	8.1	7.9
58	Peru	207.7	432.2	51.0	73.5	46.5	6.8	19.9	3.6
59	Ecuador	201.6	392.3	53.8	117.0	33.9	36.2	15.9	17.1
60	Namibia	. .	. .	. .	. .	. .	. .	. .	. .
61	Paraguay	121.8	183.1	20.7	61.1	18.6	11.9	8.5	6.2
62	El Salvador	71.1	177.3	25.9	32.1	7.5	16.6	4.7	6.3
63	Colombia	117.1	208.3	20.9	45.8	16.0	45.9	11.6	19.3
64	Thailand	96.3	87.1	25.9	34.1	18.7	15.9	9.4	6.1
65	Jamaica	129.3	188.0	76.5	133.8	19.0	26.4	10.8	11.8
66	Tunisia	96.0	136.7	41.6	71.9	14.8	22.6	6.9	8.5

Note: For data comparability and coverage, see the technical notes.   Figures in italics are for years other than those specified.

		Total external debt as a percentage of				Total debt service as a percentage of exports of goods and services		Interest payments as a percentage of exports of goods and services	
		Exports of goods and services		GNP					
		1980	1989	1980	1989	1980	1989	1980	1989
67	Turkey	332.9	190.0	34.3	53.8	28.0	32.1	14.9	14.1
68	Botswana	17.8	26.5	16.2	23.2	1.9	3.5	1.1	1.7
69	Jordan	79.2	246.0	. .	181.2	8.4	19.6	4.3	11.7
70	Panama	70.3	257.8	92.3	142.5	11.5	0.1	6.0	0.0
71	Chile	192.5	187.7	45.2	78.3	43.1	27.5	19.0	16.8
72	Costa Rica	224.5	236.2	59.5	91.2	29.0	19.2	14.6	10.5
73	Poland	54.9	262.9	16.4	66.3	17.9	9.4	5.2	5.3
74	Mauritius	80.6	57.2	41.5	41.0	9.1	9.8	5.9	3.7
75	Mexico	259.2	264.0	30.3	51.2	49.5	39.6	27.4	25.7
76	Argentina	242.4	537.0	48.4	119.7	37.3	36.1	20.8	17.7
77	Malaysia	44.6	64.5	28.0	51.6	6.3	14.6	4.0	4.8
78	Algeria	130.0	248.8	47.1	56.8	27.1	68.9	10.4	19.1
79	Bulgaria	. .	. .	. .	. .	. .	. .	. .	. .
80	*Lebanon*	. .	. .	. .	. .	. .	. .	. .	. .
81	*Mongolia*	. .	. .	. .	. .	. .	. .	. .	. .
82	*Nicaragua*	422.3	2,652.9	104.9	. .	21.5	8.6	12.7	3.4
	Upper-middle-income	**139.4** w	**127.7** w	**34.0** w	**26.5** w	**27.1** w	**18.5** w	**14.0** w	**8.7** w
83	Venezuela	131.9	211.5	42.1	79.9	27.2	25.0	13.8	20.3
84	South Africa	. .	. .	. .	. .	. .	. .	. .	. .
85	Brazil	304.8	301.6	31.2	24.1	63.1	31.3	33.8	15.5
86	Hungary	95.9	161.0	44.8	74.5	18.5	26.3	10.5	11.7
87	Uruguay	104.4	170.5	16.5	46.5	18.8	29.4	10.6	15.3
88	Yugoslavia	103.1	76.5	25.6	26.2	20.8	14.5	7.2	5.8
89	Gabon	62.2	169.1	39.2	101.8	17.7	11.9	6.3	8.6
90	Iran, Islamic Rep.	. .	. .	. .	. .	. .	. .	. .	. .
91	Trinidad and Tobago	24.6	107.0	14.0	53.9	6.8	12.3	1.6	8.9
92	Czechoslovakia	. .	. .	. .	. .	. .	. .	. .	. .
93	Portugal	99.2	94.3	40.4	41.4	18.3	18.2	10.5	6.6
94	Korea, Rep.	130.6	44.7	48.7	15.8	19.7	11.4	12.7	3.8
95	Oman	15.4	. .	11.2	39.0	6.4	. .	1.8	. .
96	Libya	. .	. .	. .	. .	. .	. .	. .	. .
97	Greece	. .	. .	. .	. .	. .	. .	. .	. .
98	*Iraq*	. .	. .	. .	. .	. .	. .	. .	. .
99	Romania	80.3	. .	. .	. .	12.6	. .	4.9	. .
	Low- and middle-income	**134.4** w	**191.7** w	**27.6** w	**41.2** w	**21.8** w	**22.4** w	**11.0** w	**10.7** w
	Sub-Saharan Africa	**96.8** w	**362.0** w	**26.8** w	**96.9** w	**10.9** w	**22.1** w	**5.7** w	**10.2** w
	East Asia	**89.5** w	**90.2** w	**16.7** w	**23.7** w	**13.6** w	**15.5** w	**7.7** w	**6.7** w
	South Asia	**162.7** w	**272.8** w	**17.3** w	**29.6** w	**12.1** w	**24.8** w	**5.1** w	**12.3** w
	Europe, M.East, & N.Africa	**115.3** w	**185.9** w	**35.7** w	**55.5** w	**19.0** w	**24.1** w	**8.1** w	**9.9** w
	Latin America & Caribbean	**202.8** w	**288.5** w	**35.1** w	**45.8** w	**38.5** w	**31.0** w	**20.3** w	**17.6** w
	Severely indebted	**195.8** w	**292.7** w	**37.9** w	**54.0** w	**36.0** w	**28.5** w	**18.6** w	**16.3** w

High-income economies
  OECD members
  †Other

100	†Saudi Arabia
101	Ireland
102	Spain
103	†Israel
104	†Hong Kong
105	†Singapore
106	New Zealand
107	Australia
108	United Kingdom
109	Italy
110	Netherlands
111	†Kuwait
112	Belgium
113	Austria
114	France
115	†United Arab Emirates
116	Canada
117	Germany
118	Denmark
119	United States
120	Sweden
121	Finland
122	Norway
123	Japan
124	Switzerland

Other economies

World
  Oil exporters (excl. USSR)

Table 25. Terms of external public borrowing

		Commitments (millions of dollars)		Average interest rate (percent)		Average maturity (years)		Average grace period (years)		Public loans with variable interest rates, as a percentage of public debt	
		1970	1989	1970	1989	1970	1989	1970	1989	1970	1989
	Low-income economies	..	32,958 *t*	..	5.6 *w*	..	22 *w*	..	7 *w*	..	20.5 *w*
	China and India	..	14,587 *t*	..	7.0 *w*	..	17 *w*	..	5 *w*	..	25.5 *w*
	Other low-income	3,331 *t*	18,371 *t*	3.2 *w*	4.4 *w*	29 *w*	26 *w*	9 *w*	8 *w*	0.2 *w*	17.9 *w*
1	Mozambique	..	294	..	1.0	..	40	..	10	..	4.9
2	Ethiopia	21	601	4.4	2.8	32	29	7	8	0.1	5.2
3	Tanzania	284	106	1.2	0.8	39	43	11	10	1.6	2.4
4	Somalia	22	128	0.0	0.8	20	40	16	10	0.0	1.1
5	Bangladesh	0	1,023	0.0	1.2	0	37	0	10	0.0	0.0
6	Lao PDR	12	163	3.0	0.6	28	41	4	21	0.0	0.0
7	Malawi	14	113	3.8	0.7	29	39	6	10	0.0	3.7
8	Nepal	17	341	2.8	1.3	27	38	6	10	0.0	0.6
9	Chad	10	182	5.7	1.2	8	40	1	10	0.0	0.0
10	Burundi	1	81	2.9	1.2	5	37	2	10	0.0	0.2
11	Sierra Leone	25	111	2.9	1.5	27	22	6	12	10.6	1.2
12	Madagascar	23	86	2.3	0.7	39	29	9	10	0.0	7.3
13	Nigeria	65	1,613	6.0	7.1	14	19	4	5	2.7	38.3
14	Uganda	12	261	3.8	2.4	28	24	6	7	0.0	0.4
15	Zaire	258	292	6.5	1.1	12	41	4	10	0.0	5.3
16	Mali	34	272	1.1	1.0	25	33	9	9	0.0	0.4
17	Niger	19	143	1.2	3.8	40	27	8	9	0.0	9.5
18	Burkina Faso	9	246	2.3	2.1	36	31	8	8	0.0	0.3
19	Rwanda	9	136	0.8	1.5	50	35	10	9	0.0	0.0
20	India	954	7,771	2.5	6.4	34	20	8	6	0.0	17.1
21	China	..	6,817	..	7.8	..	15	..	4	..	37.8
22	Haiti	5	60	4.8	1.4	10	35	1	9	0.0	0.8
23	Kenya	50	716	2.6	2.7	37	31	8	8	0.1	4.3
24	Pakistan	951	2,125	2.8	5.6	31	21	12	6	0.0	10.7
25	Benin	7	189	1.8	1.6	32	32	7	9	0.0	0.8
26	Central African Rep.	7	104	2.0	1.2	36	38	8	10	0.0	0.0
27	Ghana	51	567	2.0	2.8	37	33	10	9	0.0	1.5
28	Togo	3	86	4.5	1.4	17	36	4	9	0.0	3.9
29	Zambia	557	56	4.2	9.1	27	7	9	2	0.0	14.3
30	Guinea	68	249	2.9	1.8	13	32	5	9	0.0	8.2
31	Sri Lanka	81	258	3.0	3.7	27	29	5	7	0.0	3.5
32	Lesotho	0	21	5.5	3.2	20	28	2	8	0.0	0.0
33	Indonesia	530	7,068	2.6	6.1	34	21	9	7	0.0	31.0
34	Mauritania	7	183	6.0	2.5	11	27	3	7	0.0	5.7
35	*Afghanistan*	..	..	..	..	..	..	..	..	..	..
36	*Bhutan*	..	2	..	1.0	..	39	..	10	..	0.0
37	*Kampuchea, Dem.*	..	..	..	..	..	..	..	..	..	..
38	*Liberia*	12	0	6.7	0.0	19	0	5	0	0.0	11.3
39	*Myanmar*	48	13	4.1	0.0	16	20	5	8	0.0	0.0
40	*Sudan*	98	216	1.8	1.1	17	38	9	10	0.0	15.0
41	*Viet Nam*	..	..	..	..	..	..	..	..	..	..
	Middle-income economies	8,092 *t*	47,810 *t*	6.2 *w*	7.6 *w*	16 *w*	15 *w*	5 *w*	5 *w*	2.7 *w*	52.6 *w*
	Lower-middle-income	5,402 *t*	34,279 *t*	5.9 *w*	7.4 *w*	17 *w*	15 *w*	5 *w*	5 *w*	1.4 *w*	48.2 *w*
42	Angola	..	..	..	..	..	..	..	..	..	..
43	Bolivia	24	323	1.9	4.0	48	28	4	8	0.0	25.5
44	Egypt, Arab Rep.	771	1,464	5.3	6.5	21	15	9	5	0.0	9.1
45	Senegal	7	297	3.9	1.7	23	32	7	9	0.0	1.6
46	Yemen, Rep.	..	202	..	2.4	..	27	..	7	..	2
47	Zimbabwe	0	435	0.0	7.6	0	13	0	3	0.0	26.0
48	Philippines	171	2,572	7.3	5.0	11	20	2	6	0.8	43.0
49	Côte d'Ivoire	71	512	5.8	7.3	19	19	5	6	9.0	53.1
50	Dominican Rep.	20	137	2.4	5.2	28	14	5	6	0.0	29.2
51	Morocco	187	1,410	4.6	7.1	20	17	3	4	0.0	40.1
52	Papua New Guinea	91	312	6.4	5.8	22	19	8	5	0.0	28.0
53	Honduras	23	75	4.1	6.3	30	19	7	3	0.0	19.5
54	Guatemala	50	153	3.7	7.5	26	14	6	3	10.3	10.9
55	Congo, People's Rep.	31	93	2.8	5.9	18	16	6	6	0.0	31.7
56	Syrian Arab Rep.	14	260	4.4	6.8	9	20	2	5	0.0	1.7
57	Cameroon	42	685	4.7	7.4	29	17	8	5	0.0	10.7
58	Peru	125	608	7.4	5.7	14	15	4	5	0.0	32.3
59	Ecuador	78	590	6.2	7.5	20	13	4	3	0.0	64.3
60	Namibia	..	..	..	..	..	..	..	..	..	..
61	Paraguay	14	60	5.7	5.2	25	17	6	2	0.0	34.0
62	El Salvador	12	33	4.7	5.4	23	21	6	6	0.0	3.8
63	Colombia	363	2,893	6.0	9.0	21	14	5	5	0.0	46.0
64	Thailand	106	1,344	6.8	7.5	19	14	4	5	0.0	34.3
65	Jamaica	24	222	6.0	7.9	16	15	3	4	0.0	24.1
66	Tunisia	144	1,388	3.5	7.2	28	16	6	4	0.0	20.2

Note: For data comparability and coverage, see the technical notes.   Figures in italics are for years other than those specified.

		Commitments (millions of dollars)		Average interest rate (percent)		Average maturity (years)		Average grace period (years)		Public loans with variable interest rates, as a percentage of public debt	
		1970	1989	1970	1989	1970	1989	1970	1989	1970	1989
67	Turkey	489	4,674	3.6	7.9	19	13	5	6	0.9	30.5
68	Botswana	38	77	0.6	5.0	39	24	10	6	0.0	13.8
69	Jordan	36	436	3.7	5.2	16	18	5	5	0.0	27.3
70	Panama	111	0	6.9	0.0	15	0	4	0	0.0	60.2
71	Chile	361	736	6.8	8.2	12	16	3	5	0.0	69.5
72	Costa Rica	58	244	5.6	8.1	28	19	6	1	7.5	47.5
73	Poland	0	247	0.0	9.3	0	6	0	3	0.0	64.0
74	Mauritius	14	76	0.0	5.4	24	18	2	8	6.0	19.8
75	Mexico	858	2,994	7.9	8.3	12	15	3	5	5.7	79.3
76	Argentina	494	234	7.3	8.5	12	8	3	2	0.0	83.2
77	Malaysia	84	1,451	6.1	7.9	19	12	5	7	0.0	48.1
78	Algeria	378	6,500	5.7	8.2	12	13	3	3	2.8	32.3
79	Bulgaria	. .	. .	. .	. .	. .	. .	. .	. .	. .	. .
80	*Lebanon*	7	15	2.9	7.3	21	29	1	5	0.0	15.3
81	*Mongolia*	. .	. .	. .	. .	. .	. .	. .	. .	. .	. .
82	Nicaragua	23	265	7.1	4.9	18	17	4	3	0.0	18.4
	Upper-middle-income	**2,691** *t*	**13,531** *t*	**6.7** *w*	**8.0** *w*	**15** *w*	**14** *w*	**4** *w*	**4** *w*	**6.0** *w*	**63.8** *w*
83	Venezuela	188	1,582	7.6	8.9	8	12	2	4	2.6	87.1
84	South Africa	. .	. .	. .	. .	. .	. .	. .	. .	. .	. .
85	Brazil	1,439	3,063	7.0	8.5	14	13	3	3	11.8	71.0
86	Hungary[a]	0	2,323	0.0	8.5	0	9	0	5	0.0	64.4
87	Uruguay	71	453	7.9	8.8	12	12	3	4	0.7	72.9
88	Yugoslavia	199	34	7.1	8.7	17	10	6	4	3.3	69.4
89	Gabon	33	135	5.1	7.1	11	16	1	5	0.0	10.5
90	Iran, Islamic Rep.	. .	. .	. .	. .	. .	. .	. .	. .	. .	. .
91	Trinidad and Tobago	3	40	7.4	6.1	10	24	1	6	0.0	47.2
92	Czechoslovakia	. .	. .	. .	. .	. .	. .	. .	. .	. .	. .
93	Portugal	59	3,705	4.3	6.7	17	18	4	5	0.0	31.2
94	Korea, Rep.	691	1,409	5.8	8.3	19	20	6	2	1.2	27.1
95	Oman	. .	731	. .	7.7	. .	12	. .	5	. .	54.1
96	Libya	. .	. .	. .	. .	. .	. .	. .	. .	. .	. .
97	Greece	. .	. .	. .	. .	. .	. .	. .	. .	. .	. .
98	*Iraq*	. .	. .	. .	. .	. .	. .	. .	. .	. .	. .
99	*Romania*	. .	0	. .	0.0	. .	0	. .	0	. .	0.0
	Low- and middle-income	**12,377** *t*	**80,768** *t*	**5.1** *w*	**6.7** *w*	**21** *w*	**18** *w*	**6** *w*	**5** *w*	**1.7** *w*	**43.3** *w*
	Sub-Saharan Africa	**1,903** *t*	**9,663** *t*	**3.6** *w*	**3.9** *w*	**26** *w*	**27** *w*	**8** *w*	**7** *w*	**0.9** *w*	**19.5** *w*
	East Asia	**1,689** *t*	**21,213** *t*	**5.0** *w*	**6.8** *w*	**23** *w*	**18** *w*	**6** *w*	**6** *w*	**0.5** *w*	**35.7** *w*
	South Asia	**2,052** *t*	**11,556** *t*	**2.7** *w*	**5.6** *w*	**32** *w*	**22** *w*	**10** *w*	**7** *w*	**0.0** *w*	**12.5** *w*
	Europe, M.East, & N.Africa	**2,363** *t*	**23,501** *t*	**4.8** *w*	**7.5** *w*	**19** *w*	**14** *w*	**6** *w*	**4** *w*	**1.0** *w*	**36.8** *w*
	Latin America & Caribbean	**4,370** *t*	**14,835** *t*	**7.0** *w*	**8.2** *w*	**14** *w*	**14** *w*	**4** *w*	**4** *w*	**4.0** *w*	**68.3** *w*
	Severely indebted	**4,979** *t*	**20,083** *t*	**6.8** *w*	**7.4** *w*	**15** *w*	**15** *w*	**4** *w*	**5** *w*	**3.8** *w*	**61.3** *w*

High-income economies
  OECD members
  †Other

100	†Saudi Arabia
101	Ireland
102	Spain
103	†Israel
104	†Hong Kong
105	†Singapore
106	New Zealand
107	Australia
108	United Kingdom
109	Italy
110	Netherlands
111	†Kuwait
112	Belgium
113	Austria
114	France
115	†United Arab Emirates
116	Canada
117	Germany
118	Denmark
119	United States
120	Sweden
121	Finland
122	Norway
123	Japan
124	Switzerland

Other economies

World
  Oil exporters (excl. USSR)

a. Includes debt in convertible currencies only.

Table 26. Population growth and projections

		Average annual growth of population (percent)			Population (millions)			Hypothetical size of stationary population (millions)	Age structure of population (percent)			
									0–14 years		15–64 years	
		1965–80	1980–89	1989–2000[a]	1989	2000[a]	2025[a]		1989	2025[a]	1989	2025[a]
	Low-income economies	**2.3 w**	**2.0 w**	**1.9 w**	**2,948 t**	**3,633 t**	**5,201 t**		**35.5 w**	**26.9 w**	**60.0 w**	**65.3 w**
	China and India	**2.2 w**	**1.7 w**	**1.5 w**	**1,946 t**	**2,300 t**	**2,950 t**		**31.4 w**	**22.3 w**	**63.3 w**	**67.3 w**
	Other low-income	**2.5 w**	**2.7 w**	**2.6 w**	**1,002 t**	**1,333 t**	**2,251 t**		**43.3 w**	**32.8 w**	**53.6 w**	**62.6 w**
1	Mozambique	2.5	2.7	3.1	15	21	41	87	44.0	37.7	52.9	59.0
2	Ethiopia	2.7	3.0	3.4	49	72	159	435	46.6	43.2	50.6	54.3
3	Tanzania	2.9	3.1	3.3	24	34	66	140	46.7	37.7	50.3	59.2
4	Somalia	2.6	3.0	3.1	6	9	17	39	45.9	39.7	51.2	57.2
5	Bangladesh	2.7	2.6	2.1	111	139	196	295	44.6	26.3	52.7	69.1
6	Lao PDR	1.9	2.7	3.1	4	6	10	21	44.0	37.0	53.1	59.5
7	Malawi	2.9	3.4	3.6	8	12	27	72	46.5	43.0	50.8	54.4
8	Nepal	2.4	2.6	2.5	18	24	37	60	43.0	29.0	54.9	65.9
9	Chad	2.0	2.4	2.7	6	7	14	29	41.8	37.2	54.7	58.9
10	Burundi	1.9	2.9	3.5	5	8	16	39	46.3	41.4	50.8	56.2
11	Sierra Leone	2.0	2.4	2.6	4	5	10	24	43.2	40.5	53.7	56.3
12	Madagascar	2.5	2.9	3.1	11	16	29	54	46.2	35.1	50.3	61.7
13	Nigeria	2.5	3.4	3.2	114	160	298	580	47.6	35.2	50.2	61.3
14	Uganda	2.9	3.2	3.5	17	25	51	119	48.6	40.6	49.1	57.0
15	Zaire	2.8	3.1	3.0	34	48	86	164	46.1	34.4	51.3	62.0
16	Mali	2.1	2.5	3.0	8	11	24	60	46.6	41.3	50.4	56.1
17	Niger	2.6	3.4	3.3	7	11	24	76	47.1	44.7	50.4	52.9
18	Burkina Faso	2.1	2.6	2.9	9	12	23	51	45.3	38.5	51.7	58.7
19	Rwanda	3.3	3.2	4.1	7	11	24	74	48.3	44.3	49.4	53.4
20	India	2.3	2.1	1.7	833	1,007	1,350	1,876	37.1	24.1	58.6	68.4
21	China	2.2	1.4	1.4	1,114	1,294	1,597	1,890	27.2	20.7	66.9	66.4
22	Haiti	1.7	1.9	2.1	6	8	12	21	40.1	31.0	55.8	64.0
23	Kenya	3.6	3.9	3.4	24	34	62	114	50.3	31.9	46.7	64.6
24	Pakistan	3.1	3.2	3.2	110	155	279	518	45.3	33.9	52.2	62.4
25	Benin	2.7	3.2	3.0	5	6	11	21	47.4	33.4	49.8	63.2
26	Central African Rep.	1.9	2.7	2.7	3	4	7	13	42.3	33.7	54.8	62.6
27	Ghana	2.2	3.4	3.1	14	20	35	63	46.7	32.8	50.2	63.5
28	Togo	3.0	3.5	3.3	4	5	9	18	47.9	35.4	49.1	61.4
29	Zambia	3.0	3.7	3.6	8	12	24	52	49.2	38.5	48.6	58.8
30	Guinea	1.5	2.5	2.8	6	8	15	34	46.2	40.4	51.3	56.8
31	Sri Lanka	1.8	1.5	1.1	17	19	24	28	32.5	21.0	62.3	66.0
32	Lesotho	2.3	2.7	2.7	2	2	4	6	43.2	29.2	53.2	66.0
33	Indonesia	2.4	2.1	1.6	178	213	282	371	36.8	23.3	59.3	68.2
34	Mauritania	2.4	2.4	2.8	2	3	5	14	44.4	42.4	52.4	55.0
35	*Afghanistan*	2.4	..	..	..	..	..	..	..	..	..	..
36	*Bhutan*	1.6	2.1	2.4	1	2	3	5	40.1	32.8	56.7	62.9
37	*Kampuchea, Dem.*	0.3	..	..	..	..	..	..	..	..	..	..
38	*Liberia*	3.0	3.2	3.0	2	3	6	11	44.8	32.6	51.9	63.2
39	*Myanmar*	2.3	2.1	2.1	41	51	70	96	37.5	24.0	58.4	68.5
40	*Sudan*	3.0	2.8	2.8	24	33	57	106	44.8	33.7	52.1	62.5
41	*Viet Nam*	..	2.1	2.2	65	83	119	167	40.1	24.2	55.7	68.8
	Middle-income economies	**2.3 w**	**2.1 w**	**1.9 w**	**1,104 t**	**1,354 t**	**1,954 t**		**36.2 w**	**26.4 w**	**58.7 w**	**65.0 w**
	Lower-middle-income	**2.5 w**	**2.3 w**	**2.0 w**	**682 t**	**842 t**	**1,224 t**		**37.9 w**	**26.3 w**	**57.5 w**	**65.8 w**
42	Angola	2.8	2.6	3.0	10	14	27	65	44.8	40.1	52.3	56.8
43	Bolivia	2.5	2.7	2.8	7	10	16	27	43.9	31.1	52.9	64.6
44	Egypt, Arab Rep.	2.1	2.5	1.8	51	62	86	120	39.2	24.4	56.5	67.6
45	Senegal	2.9	3.0	3.2	7	10	20	46	46.9	39.6	50.6	57.9
46	Yemen, Rep.	2.3	3.4	3.7	11	17	38	113	48.2	44.1	48.8	54.1
47	Zimbabwe	3.1	3.5	2.7	10	13	20	29	45.8	25.4	51.5	68.7
48	Philippines	2.8	2.5	1.8	60	73	101	137	40.1	23.9	56.4	68.4
49	Côte d'Ivoire	4.1	4.1	3.8	12	18	37	85	48.9	39.5	48.8	57.6
50	Dominican Rep.	2.7	2.3	1.8	7	9	11	15	38.1	23.2	58.4	68.0
51	Morocco	2.5	2.6	2.3	25	32	48	72	41.0	25.9	55.2	67.9
52	Papua New Guinea	2.4	2.5	2.4	4	5	7	11	41.2	27.6	56.3	67.8
53	Honduras	3.2	3.5	2.9	5	7	11	18	45.0	28.1	51.7	66.9
54	Guatemala	2.8	2.9	2.8	9	12	20	33	45.7	28.9	51.5	66.4
55	Congo, People's Rep.	2.8	3.4	3.4	2	3	7	16	45.0	39.2	51.0	57.8
56	Syrian Arab Rep.	3.4	3.6	3.7	12	18	36	69	48.3	34.9	49.0	61.3
57	Cameroon	2.7	3.2	3.2	12	16	33	69	46.9	37.0	49.3	59.5
58	Peru	2.8	2.3	2.1	21	27	37	50	38.4	23.8	58.1	68.4
59	Ecuador	3.1	2.7	2.2	10	13	19	26	40.1	24.0	56.3	68.4
60	Namibia	2.4	3.1	3.0	2	2	4	7	45.6	31.2	51.2	64.4
61	Paraguay	2.8	3.2	2.8	4	6	10	16	41.1	30.2	55.4	63.7
62	El Salvador	2.8	1.4	2.1	5	6	10	16	44.7	27.7	52.1	67.4
63	Colombia	2.5	2.0	1.6	32	38	51	64	35.9	22.2	60.0	67.9
64	Thailand	2.9	1.9	1.3	55	64	83	103	33.4	21.6	61.9	68.2
65	Jamaica	1.3	1.3	0.5	2	3	3	4	33.8	20.9	59.2	67.9
66	Tunisia	2.1	2.5	2.1	8	10	14	19	38.4	23.7	57.5	68.3

Note: For data comparability and coverage, see the technical notes.   Figures in italics are for years other than those specified.

		Average annual growth of population (percent)			Population (millions)			Hypothetical size of stationary population (millions)	Age structure of population (percent)			
									0–14 years		15–64 years	
		1965–80	1980–89	1989–2000ª	1989	2000ª	2025ª		1989	2025ª	1989	2025ª
67	Turkey	2.4	2.4	2.0	55	68	92	121	35.1	23.1	60.7	67.6
68	Botswana	3.5	3.4	2.6	1	2	2	4	47.3	25.3	48.9	68.9
69	Jordan	2.6	3.3	2.8	4	5	9	16	35.6	32.7	40.4	63.1
70	Panama	2.6	2.2	1.6	2	3	4	5	35.4	21.9	59.9	67.2
71	Chile	1.7	1.7	1.3	13	15	19	23	30.7	21.3	63.4	65.7
72	Costa Rica	2.7	2.4	1.9	3	3	5	6	36.2	22.1	59.6	66.3
73	Poland	0.8	0.7	0.4	38	39	44	49	25.1	19.7	65.1	62.3
74	Mauritius	1.6	1.0	0.9	1	1	1	2	29.8	18.9	65.1	66.8
75	Mexico	3.1	2.1	1.8	85	103	142	185	38.1	22.9	58.3	68.3
76	Argentina	1.6	1.4	1.1	32	36	44	54	29.9	21.5	61.1	65.0
77	Malaysia	2.5	2.6	2.2	17	22	31	43	37.8	23.6	58.2	67.4
78	Algeria	3.1	3.0	2.8	24	33	52	78	44.0	25.7	52.1	68.5
79	Bulgaria	0.5	0.2	–0.4	9	8	8	9	19.4	17.9	64.5	61.1
80	*Lebanon*	1.7	. .	. .	. .	. .	. .	. .	. .	. .	. .	. .
81	*Mongolia*	2.6	2.7	2.6	2	3	4	6	40.9	25.9	55.6	67.9
82	*Nicaragua*	3.1	3.4	3.1	4	5	9	14	46.1	28.4	51.3	66.4
	Upper-middle-income	**2.0** *w*	**1.9** *w*	**1.8** *w*	**423** *t*	**512** *t*	**730** *t*		**33.4** *w*	**26.6** *w*	**60.7** *w*	**63.6** *w*
83	Venezuela	3.5	2.8	2.2	19	24	34	45	38.5	23.3	57.9	67.5
84	South Africa	2.4	2.4	2.3	35	45	65	96	38.2	25.3	57.9	67.1
85	Brazil	2.4	2.2	1.7	147	178	236	304	35.5	22.8	60.1	66.9
86	Hungary	0.4	–0.2	–0.1	11	10	10	11	19.7	17.7	66.9	61.6
87	Uruguay	0.4	0.6	0.6	3	3	4	4	25.9	20.0	62.7	63.9
88	Yugoslavia	0.9	0.7	0.6	24	25	28	30	23.1	18.6	67.7	62.1
89	Gabon	3.6	3.7	2.8	1	1	3	6	38.7	38.2	56.5	57.5
90	Iran, Islamic Rep.	3.1	3.5	3.3	53	77	158	420	44.0	38.8	53.0	56.9
91	Trinidad and Tobago	1.2	1.7	1.3	1	1	2	2	33.6	22.2	60.7	65.8
92	Czechoslovakia	0.5	0.3	0.3	16	16	18	19	23.4	19.1	64.9	62.9
93	Portugal	0.4	0.6	0.4	10	11	11	11	21.3	16.5	65.9	63.4
94	Korea, Rep.	2.0	1.2	0.9	42	47	53	56	26.4	18.0	68.7	66.0
95	Oman	3.6	4.7	3.9	1	2	5	10	45.9	36.8	51.7	58.5
96	Libya	4.3	4.2	3.6	4	6	14	36	46.0	39.5	51.4	56.7
97	Greece	0.7	0.4	0.2	10	10	10	9	19.5	15.4	66.6	60.6
98	*Iraq*	3.4	3.6	3.4	18	26	48	85	46.6	32.0	50.7	63.6
99	*Romania*	1.1	0.4	0.5	23	24	27	31	23.5	20.0	66.2	63.6
	Low- and middle-income	**2.3** *w*	**2.1** *w*	**1.9** *w*	**4,053** *t*	**4,987** *t*	**7,155** *t*		**35.7** *w*	**26.7** *w*	**59.7** *w*	**65.2** *w*
	Sub-Saharan Africa	**2.7** *w*	**3.2** *w*	**3.2** *w*	**480** *t*	**679** *t*	**1,311** *t*		**46.8** *w*	**37.4** *w*	**50.6** *w*	**59.4** *w*
	East Asia	**2.2** *w*	**1.6** *w*	**1.5** *w*	**1,552** *t*	**1,822** *t*	**2,307** *t*		**29.8** *w*	**21.5** *w*	**64.8** *w*	**66.9** *w*
	South Asia	**2.4** *w*	**2.3** *w*	**1.9** *w*	**1,131** *t*	**1,396** *t*	**1,959** *t*		**38.7** *w*	**25.8** *w*	**57.4** *w*	**67.5** *w*
	Europe, M.East, & N.Africa	**1.9** *w*	**2.0** *w*	**2.0** *w*	**433** *t*	**533** *t*	**813** *t*		**35.4** *w*	**29.5** *w*	**58.3** *w*	**62.5** *w*
	Latin America & Caribbean	**2.5** *w*	**2.1** *w*	**1.8** *w*	**421** *t*	**513** *t*	**700** *t*		**36.6** *w*	**23.6** *w*	**58.9** *w*	**67.1** *w*
	Severely indebted	**2.4** *w*	**2.1** *w*	**1.8** *w*	**554** *t*	**673** *t*	**926** *t*		**36.6** *w*	**24.4** *w*	**58.6** *w*	**66.4** *w*
	High-income economies	**0.9** *w*	**0.7** *w*	**0.6** *w*	**830** *t*	**884** *t*	**965** *t*		**20.5** *w*	**17.8** *w*	**66.8** *w*	**60.7** *w*
	OECD members	**0.8** *w*	**0.6** *w*	**0.5** *w*	**773** *t*	**813** *t*	**862** *t*		**19.7** *w*	**16.8** *w*	**67.1** *w*	**60.6** *w*
	†Other	**2.8** *w*	**2.4** *w*	**1.8** *w*	**58** *t*	**71** *t*	**103** *t*		**32.1** *w*	**26.4** *w*	**61.9** *w*	**61.9** *w*
100	†Saudi Arabia	4.6	5.0	3.7	14	21	43	89	45.1	36.3	51.8	59.1
101	Ireland	1.2	0.4	0.3	4	4	4	5	27.2	19.7	61.6	64.9
102	Spain	1.0	0.4	0.4	39	41	43	41	20.9	16.2	66.8	63.0
103	†Israel	2.8	1.7	1.8	5	6	7	9	31.8	21.2	60.2	65.1
104	†Hong Kong	2.0	1.5	0.9	6	6	7	6	21.6	15.9	69.6	61.3
105	†Singapore	1.6	1.2	1.0	3	3	3	4	23.7	18.0	70.8	61.5
106	New Zealand	1.3	0.7	0.8	3	4	4	4	23.4	18.7	67.4	62.7
107	Australia	1.8	1.4	1.4	17	19	23	24	22.4	18.1	66.9	63.0
108	United Kingdom	0.2	0.2	0.3	57	59	61	62	19.0	17.5	65.5	61.2
109	Italy	0.5	0.2	0.0	58	58	55	46	17.0	14.3	68.7	61.0
110	Netherlands	0.9	0.5	0.4	15	16	16	14	17.8	15.4	69.2	59.7
111	†Kuwait	7.1	4.4	3.1	2	3	4	5	36.1	21.3	62.5	64.9
112	Belgium	0.3	0.1	0.2	10	10	10	9	18.2	15.9	67.1	59.8
113	Austria	0.3	0.1	0.1	8	8	8	7	17.8	15.3	67.3	60.5
114	France	0.7	0.4	0.4	56	59	63	63	20.3	17.3	66.1	60.6
115	†United Arab Emirates	16.5	4.6	2.3	2	2	3	3	30.9	22.2	67.4	60.7
116	Canada	1.3	0.9	0.8	26	29	32	31	21.1	16.9	67.9	60.7
117	Germany	0.3	0.0	–0.1	62	62	57	61	15.1	14.3	69.5	58.8
118	Denmark	0.5	0.0	0.0	5	5	5	4	17.2	15.3	67.5	60.2
119	United States	1.0	1.0	0.8	249	272	309	319	21.6	18.0	66.1	61.1
120	Sweden	0.5	0.2	0.4	8	9	9	9	17.5	17.6	64.6	59.3
121	Finland	0.3	0.4	0.2	5	5	5	5	19.4	16.3	67.6	58.8
122	Norway	0.6	0.4	0.4	4	4	5	5	19.2	17.1	64.4	61.0
123	Japan	1.2	0.6	0.4	123	129	131	121	19.0	15.7	69.3	58.8
124	Switzerland	0.5	0.5	0.4	7	7	7	6	16.9	15.8	68.2	58.3
	Other economies	**1.0** *w*	**1.0** *w*	**0.7** *w*	**323** *t*	**349** *t*	**404** *t*		**25.8** *w*	**20.2** *w*	**64.8** *w*	**63.5** *w*
	World	**2.0** *w*	**1.8** *w*	**1.6** *w*	**5,206** *t*	**6,220** *t*	**8,524** *t*		**32.6** *w*	**25.4** *w*	**61.1** *w*	**64.6** *w*
	Oil exporters (excl. USSR)	**3.0** *w*	**3.4** *w*	**3.1** *w*	**265** *t*	**373** *t*	**692** *t*		**44.9** *w*	**34.8** *w*	**51.9** *w*	**60.9** *w*

a. For the assumptions used in the projections, see the technical notes.

Table 27. Demography and fertility

		Crude birth rate (per 1,000 population)		Crude death rate (per 1,000 population)		Women of childbearing age as a percentage of all women		Total fertility rate			Assumed year of reaching net reproduction rate of 1	Married women of childbearing age using contraception (percent)[b]
		1965	1989	1965	1989	1965	1989	1965	1989	2000[a]		1987
	Low-income economies	**42** w	**31** w	**16** w	**10** w	**46** w	**51** w	**6.3** w	**3.9** w	**3.3** w		
	China and India	**41** w	**26** w	**14** w	**8** w	**46** w	**53** w	**6.3** w	**3.2** w	**2.5** w		
	Other low-income	**46** w	**40** w	**21** w	**13** w	**46** w	**46** w	**6.3** w	**5.5** w	**4.7** w		
1	Mozambique	49	46	27	17	47	45	6.8	6.4	6.2	2040	..
2	Ethiopia	43	52	20	18	46	43	5.8	7.5	7.3	2050	..
3	Tanzania	49	47	23	17	45	45	6.6	6.5	6.1	2040	..
4	Somalia	50	48	26	18	45	44	6.7	6.8	6.6	2045	..
5	Bangladesh	47	37	21	14	44	46	6.8	4.9	3.6	2015	32
6	Lao PDR	45	47	23	17	47	45	6.1	6.7	6.0	2040	..
7	Malawi	56	54	26	19	46	45	7.8	7.6	7.4	2050	..
8	Nepal	46	41	24	15	50	47	6.0	5.7	4.6	2025	15
9	Chad	45	44	28	19	47	46	6.0	5.9	6.6	2040	..
10	Burundi	47	48	24	15	44	45	6.4	6.8	6.6	2045	9
11	Sierra Leone	48	47	31	23	47	46	6.4	6.5	6.5	2045	..
12	Madagascar	47	46	22	16	47	44	6.6	6.5	5.8	2030	..
13	Nigeria	51	47	23	15	45	44	6.9	6.6	5.6	2035	..
14	Uganda	49	51	19	16	44	43	7.0	7.3	6.6	2045	5
15	Zaire	47	45	21	14	47	45	6.0	6.1	5.4	2035	..
16	Mali	50	50	27	19	46	45	6.5	7.0	7.0	2050	5
17	Niger	48	51	29	20	45	44	7.1	7.1	7.3	2055	..
18	Burkina Faso	48	47	26	18	47	45	6.4	6.5	6.3	2045	..
19	Rwanda	52	52	17	17	45	43	7.5	8.3	7.6	2055	..
20	India	45	31	20	11	48	49	6.2	4.1	3.0	2015	40
21	China	38	22	10	7	45	56	6.4	2.5	2.1	2000	74
22	Haiti	41	36	21	13	45	48	6.1	4.9	4.2	2035	11
23	Kenya	52	46	20	10	41	41	8.0	6.7	5.2	2035	27
24	Pakistan	48	46	21	12	43	45	7.0	6.6	5.4	2035	..
25	Benin	49	46	24	15	44	44	6.8	6.4	5.2	2035	..
26	Central African Rep.	34	42	24	15	47	46	4.5	5.8	5.3	2035	..
27	Ghana	47	45	18	13	45	44	6.8	6.3	5.1	2030	13
28	Togo	50	49	22	14	46	44	6.5	6.7	5.5	2035	..
29	Zambia	49	49	20	13	46	44	6.6	6.7	6.1	2040	..
30	Guinea	46	48	29	21	45	45	5.9	6.5	6.5	2045	..
31	Sri Lanka	33	21	8	6	47	53	4.9	2.5	2.1	1995	62
32	Lesotho	42	41	18	12	47	45	5.8	5.7	4.5	2025	..
33	Indonesia	43	27	20	9	47	51	5.5	3.3	2.4	2005	45
34	Mauritania	47	48	26	19	47	45	6.5	6.8	6.8	2050	..
35	*Afghanistan*	53	..	29	..	49	..	7.1	..	..	..	..
36	*Bhutan*	42	39	23	17	48	48	5.9	5.5	5.4	2035	..
37	*Kampuchea, Dem.*	44	..	20	..	47	..	6.2	..	..	..	..
38	*Liberia*	46	44	20	14	47	44	6.4	6.4	5.2	2035	6
39	*Myanmar*	40	30	18	9	46	50	5.8	3.9	2.9	2010	..
40	*Sudan*	47	44	24	15	46	45	6.7	6.4	5.4	2035	..
41	*Viet Nam*	..	32	..	7	..	48	..	4.0	2.9	2015	58
	Middle-income economies	**37** w	**29** w	**13** w	**8** w	**45** w	**49** w	**5.5** w	**3.7** w	**3.1** w		
	Lower-middle-income	**40** w	**30** w	**14** w	**8** w	**45** w	**49** w	**5.9** w	**3.9** w	**3.2** w		
42	Angola	49	47	29	19	47	45	6.4	6.5	6.6	2045	..
43	Bolivia	46	42	21	13	46	46	6.6	5.9	4.8	2030	30
44	Egypt, Arab Rep.	43	32	19	10	43	48	6.8	4.2	3.1	2015	38
45	Senegal	47	45	23	16	45	44	6.4	6.5	6.3	2045	12
46	Yemen, Rep.	49	53	27	18	47	43	7.0	7.7	7.5	2055	..
47	Zimbabwe	55	37	17	7	42	46	8.0	5.1	3.4	2015	43
48	Philippines	42	30	12	7	44	50	6.8	3.9	2.7	2010	44
49	Côte d'Ivoire	52	50	22	14	44	42	7.4	7.3	6.4	2045	..
50	Dominican Rep.	47	30	13	6	43	51	6.9	3.6	2.7	2010	50
51	Morocco	49	36	18	9	45	48	7.1	4.7	3.6	2020	36
52	Papua New Guinea	43	36	20	11	47	48	6.2	5.1	4.0	2020	..
53	Honduras	51	39	17	8	44	46	7.4	5.3	4.1	2025	41
54	Guatemala	46	39	17	8	44	45	6.7	5.5	4.3	2025	23
55	Congo, People's Rep.	42	48	18	15	45	43	5.7	6.5	6.3	2045	..
56	Syrian Arab Rep.	48	45	16	7	..	43	7.7	6.6	5.5	2035	..
57	Cameroon	40	44	20	12	47	42	5.2	6.5	5.9	2040	..
58	Peru	45	31	16	9	44	50	6.7	3.9	2.8	2010	46
59	Ecuador	45	32	13	7	43	49	6.8	4.1	3.0	2015	44
60	Namibia	46	43	22	12	46	44	6.1	6.0	4.8	2030	..
61	Paraguay	41	36	8	6	41	48	6.6	4.7	4.0	2030	45
62	El Salvador	46	35	13	8	44	46	6.7	4.7	3.8	2025	47
63	Colombia	43	25	11	6	43	53	6.5	2.9	2.2	2000	63
64	Thailand	41	22	10	7	44	54	6.3	2.5	2.1	1995	66
65	Jamaica	38	22	9	7	42	51	5.7	2.5	2.1	1995	55
66	Tunisia	44	30	16	7	43	49	7.0	4.0	2.8	2010	50

Note: For data comparability and coverage, see the technical notes.   Figures in italics are for years other than those specified.

		Crude birth rate (per 1,000 population)		Crude death rate (per 1,000 population)		Women of childbearing age as a percentage of all women		Total fertility rate			Assumed year of reaching net reproduction rate of 1	Married women of childbearing age using contraception (percent)[b]
		1965	1989	1965	1989	1965	1989	1965	1989	2000[a]		1987
67	Turkey	41	29	15	8	45	50	5.7	3.6	2.7	2010	77
68	Botswana	53	36	19	6	45	44	6.9	4.9	3.1	2015	33
69	Jordan	53	43	21	6	45	45	8.0	6.3	5.2	2035	..
70	Panama	40	25	9	5	44	52	5.7	2.9	2.2	2000	..
71	Chile	34	23	11	6	45	53	4.8	2.6	2.1	2000	..
72	Costa Rica	45	26	8	4	42	52	6.3	3.1	2.3	2005	68
73	Poland	17	15	7	10	47	48	2.5	2.1	2.1	2030	..
74	Mauritius	36	18	8	6	45	55	4.8	1.9	1.8	2030	78
75	Mexico	45	28	11	6	43	51	6.7	3.4	2.4	2005	53
76	Argentina	23	20	9	9	50	47	3.1	2.8	2.3	2005	..
77	Malaysia	40	30	12	5	44	51	6.3	3.7	3.0	2015	..
78	Algeria	50	36	18	8	44	45	7.4	5.2	3.7	2020	..
79	Bulgaria	15	12	8	12	51	46	2.1	1.9	1.9	2030	..
80	Lebanon	40	..	12	..	42	..	6.2	..	..		..
81	Mongolia	43	35	16	9	46	48	5.9	4.8	3.7	2020	..
82	Nicaragua	49	40	16	7	43	46	7.2	5.4	4.2	2025	..
	Upper-middle-income	**33** w	**27** w	**12** w	**8** w	**46** w	**50** w	**4.8** w	**3.4** w	**3.0** w		
83	Venezuela	42	29	8	5	44	50	6.1	3.6	2.7	2010	..
84	South Africa	40	34	16	10	46	49	6.1	4.3	3.4	2020	..
85	Brazil	39	27	11	8	45	51	5.6	3.3	2.4	2005	65
86	Hungary	13	12	11	13	48	47	1.8	1.8	1.8	2030	73
87	Uruguay	21	17	10	10	49	47	2.8	2.3	2.1	1995	..
88	Yugoslavia	21	15	9	9	50	49	2.7	2.0	2.0	2030	..
89	Gabon	31	42	22	15	48	47	4.1	5.7	6.1	2045	..
90	Iran, Islamic Rep.	46	44	18	9	42	47	7.1	6.1	5.4	2055	..
91	Trinidad and Tobago	33	25	8	6	46	52	4.3	2.8	2.3	2005	53
92	Czechoslovakia	16	14	10	11	46	48	2.4	2.0	2.0	2030	..
93	Portugal	23	12	10	9	48	49	3.1	1.6	1.7	2030	..
94	Korea, Rep.	35	16	11	6	46	57	4.9	1.8	1.8	2030	70
95	Oman	50	44	24	6	47	43	7.2	7.1	5.9	2040	..
96	Libya	49	44	17	9	45	44	7.4	6.7	5.8	2050	..
97	Greece	18	11	8	9	51	47	2.3	1.5	1.6	2030	..
98	Iraq	49	42	18	8	45	44	7.2	6.2	5.1	2030	..
99	Romania	15	16	9	10	50	48	1.9	2.1	2.1	1985	..
	Low- and middle-income	**41** w	**30** w	**15** w	**10** w	**46** w	**50** w	**6.1** w	**3.9** w	**3.3** w		
	Sub-Saharan Africa	**48** w	**47** w	**23** w	**15** w	**45** w	**44** w	**6.6** w	**6.6** w	**6.0** w		
	East Asia	**39** w	**23** w	**11** w	**7** w	**45** w	**54** w	**6.2** w	**2.7** w	**2.3** w		
	South Asia	**45** w	**33** w	**20** w	**11** w	**47** w	**48** w	**6.3** w	**4.4** w	**3.4** w		
	Europe, M.East, & N.Africa	**33** w	**30** w	**14** w	**10** w	**46** w	**47** w	**4.8** w	**4.1** w	**3.7** w		
	Latin America & Caribbean	**40** w	**28** w	**12** w	**7** w	**45** w	**50** w	**5.8** w	**3.5** w	**2.6** w		
	Severely indebted	**37** w	**28** w	**12** w	**8** w	**45** w	**49** w	**5.6** w	**3.6** w	**2.8** w		
	High-income economies	**20** w	**14** w	**10** w	**9** w	**47** w	**50** w	**2.8** w	**1.8** w	**1.9** w		
	OECD members	**19** w	**13** w	**10** w	**9** w	**47** w	**50** w	**2.7** w	**1.7** w	**1.8** w		
	†Other	**34** w	**24** w	**8** w	**6** w	**45** w	**51** w	**5.0** w	**3.5** w	**3.2** w		
100	†Saudi Arabia	48	42	20	8	45	42	7.3	7.1	5.9	2040	..
101	Ireland	22	16	12	9	42	49	4.0	2.2	2.1	1990	..
102	Spain	21	12	8	8	49	49	2.9	1.4	1.6	2030	59
103	†Israel	26	22	6	7	46	49	3.8	2.9	2.3	2005	..
104	†Hong Kong	27	14	6	5	45	56	4.5	1.6	1.6	2030	72
105	†Singapore	31	18	6	5	45	59	4.7	1.9	1.9	2030	..
106	New Zealand	23	16	9	8	45	52	3.6	2.0	2.0	2030	..
107	Australia	20	15	9	7	47	53	3.0	1.9	1.9	2030	..
108	United Kingdom	18	14	12	11	45	48	2.9	1.8	1.9	2030	..
109	Italy	19	10	10	10	48	49	2.7	1.3	1.4	2030	..
110	Netherlands	20	12	8	9	47	53	3.0	1.5	1.6	2030	76
111	†Kuwait	48	27	7	3	45	52	7.4	3.7	2.7	2010	..
112	Belgium	17	12	12	11	44	48	2.6	1.6	1.6	2030	..
113	Austria	18	11	13	11	43	48	2.7	1.5	1.5	2030	..
114	France	18	14	11	10	43	48	2.8	1.8	1.8	2030	..
115	†United Arab Emirates	41	23	14	4	47	47	6.8	4.6	3.7	2020	..
116	Canada	21	14	8	7	47	53	3.1	1.7	1.7	2030	..
117	Germany	18	10	12	11	45	48	2.5	1.4	1.4	2030	78
118	Denmark	18	11	10	12	47	50	2.6	1.5	1.6	2030	..
119	United States	19	15	9	9	46	52	2.9	1.9	1.9	2030	..
120	Sweden	16	13	10	12	47	47	2.4	2.0	2.0	2030	..
121	Finland	17	12	10	10	48	49	2.4	1.7	1.7	2030	..
122	Norway	18	13	10	10	45	48	2.9	1.8	1.8	2030	..
123	Japan	19	11	7	7	56	50	2.0	1.7	1.7	2030	..
124	Switzerland	19	12	10	10	48	50	2.6	1.6	1.7	2030	..
	Other economies	**20** w	**18** w	**8** w	**10** w	**47** w	**47** w	**2.7** w	**2.4** w	**2.1** w		
	World	**35** w	**27** w	**14** w	**9** w	**46** w	**50** w	**5.2** w	**3.5** w	**3.0** w		
	Oil exporters (excl. USSR)	**49** w	**43** w	**20** w	**11** w	**44** w	**45** w	**6.9** w	**6.1** w	**5.2** w		

a. For assumptions used in the projections, see the technical notes for Table 26.   b. Figures include women whose husbands practice contraception; see the technical notes.

Table 28. Health and nutrition

		Population per				Births attended by health staff (percent)	Babies with low birth weight (percent)	Infant mortality rate (per 1,000 live births)		Daily calorie supply (per capita)	
		Physician		Nursing person							
		1965	1984	1965	1984	1985	1985	1965	1989	1965	1988
	Low-income economies	**9,750** w	**5,890** w	**6,050** w	**2,180** w			**124** w	**70** w	**1,988** w	**2,331** w
	China and India	**2,930** w	**1,650** w	**4,420** w	**1,650** w			**114** w	**58** w	**2,001** w	**2,407** w
	Other low-income	**28,130** w	**14,890** w	**10,300** w	**3,670** w			**146** w	**94** w	**1,960** w	**2,182** w
1	Mozambique	18,000	. .	5,370	. .	28	15	179	137	1,704	1,632
2	Ethiopia	70,190	78,770	5,970	5,390	58	. .	165	133	1,802	1,658
3	Tanzania	21,700	24,980	2,100	5,490	74	14	138	112	1,800	2,151
4	Somalia	36,840	16,080	3,950	1,530	2	. .	165	128	1,410	1,736
5	Bangladesh	8,100	6,730	. .	8,980	. .	31	144	106	1,984	1,925
6	Lao PDR	24,320	1,360	4,880	530	. .	39	148	105	2,133	2,637
7	Malawi	47,320	11,340	40,980	. .	59	10	200	147	2,196	2,009
8	Nepal	46,180	30,220	87,650	4,680	10	. .	171	124	1,887	2,078
9	Chad	72,480	38,360	13,610	3,390	. .	11	183	127	2,374	1,852
10	Burundi	55,910	21,030	7,320	4,380	12	14	142	70	2,383	2,253
11	Sierra Leone	16,840	13,620	4,470	1,090	25	14	208	149	1,976	1,806
12	Madagascar	10,620	9,780	3,650	. .	62	10	201	117	2,375	2,101
13	Nigeria	29,530	6,440	6,160	900	. .	25	166	100	2,166	2,039
14	Uganda	11,110	. .	3,130	. .	. .	10	121	99	2,343	2,013
15	Zaire	34,740	12,940	. .	1,800	. .	. .	141	94	2,135	2,034
16	Mali	51,510	25,390	3,360	1,350	27	17	207	167	1,843	2,181
17	Niger	65,540	39,670	6,210	460	47	20	180	130	1,930	2,340
18	Burkina Faso	73,960	265,250	4,150	1,680	. .	18	190	135	1,841	2,061
19	Rwanda	72,480	35,090	7,450	3,690	. .	17	141	118	1,660	1,786
20	India	4,880	2,520	6,500	1,700	39	30	150	95	2,103	2,104
21	China	1,600	1,010	3,000	1,610	. .	6	90	30	1,931	2,632
22	Haiti	14,350	7,130	13,210	2,280	20	17	158	94	2,045	1,911
23	Kenya	13,280	10,050	1,930	. .	. .	13	112	68	2,169	1,973
24	Pakistan	. .	2,910	9,910	4,900	24	25	149	106	1,797	2,200
25	Benin	32,390	15,940	2,540	1,750	34	10	166	112	1,976	2,145
26	Central African Rep.	34,020	. .	3,000	. .	. .	15	157	100	2,016	1,980
27	Ghana	13,740	20,460	3,730	1,670	73	17	120	86	1,912	2,209
28	Togo	23,240	8,700	4,990	1,240	. .	20	156	90	2,345	2,133
29	Zambia	11,380	7,150	5,820	740	. .	14	121	76	2,042	2,026
30	Guinea	47,050	. .	4,110	. .	. .	18	191	140	2,006	2,042
31	Sri Lanka	5,820	5,520	3,220	1,290	87	28	63	20	2,164	2,319
32	Lesotho	20,060	18,610	4,700	. .	28	10	142	96	2,024	2,307
33	Indonesia	31,700	9,460	9,490	1,260	43	14	128	64	1,796	2,670
34	Mauritania	36,530	11,900	. .	1,180	23	10	178	123	1,796	2,528
35	*Afghanistan*	15,770	. .	24,430	. .	. .	. .	206	. .	2,304	. .
36	*Bhutan*	. .	9,730	. .	. .	3	. .	171	125	. .	. .
37	*Kampuchea, Dem.*	22,410	. .	3,670	. .	. .	. .	134	. .	2,271	. .
38	*Liberia*	12,560	9,350	2,330	1,380	89	. .	176	137	2,110	2,270
39	*Myanmar*	11,860	3,740	11,370	900	97	16	122	66	1,917	2,572
40	*Sudan*	23,500	10,190	3,360	1,260	20	15	160	104	1,853	1,996
41	*Viet Nam*	. .	950	. .	590	. .	18	. .	43	. .	2,233
	Middle-income economies	**3,800** w	**2,180** w	**2,110** w	**980** w			**97** w	**51** w	**2,482** w	**2,834** w
	Lower-middle-income	**5,010** w	**2,910** w	**2,150** w	**1,020** w			**104** w	**51** w	**2,407** w	**2,738** w
42	Angola	13,150	17,790	3,820	1,020	15	17	192	132	1,843	1,725
43	Bolivia	3,300	1,540	3,990	2,480	36	15	160	106	1,854	2,086
44	Egypt, Arab Rep.	2,300	770	2,030	. .	24	7	145	68	2,336	3,213
45	Senegal	19,490	. .	2,440	2,030	. .	10	160	82	2,452	1,989
46	Yemen, Rep.	31,580	. .	. .	1,970	. .	. .	197	125	1,994	2,322
47	Zimbabwe	8,010	6,700	990	1,000	69	15	103	46	2,044	2,232
48	Philippines	. .	6,570	1,140	2,680	. .	18	72	42	1,896	2,255
49	Côte d'Ivoire	20,640	. .	2,000	. .	20	14	149	92	2,334	2,365
50	Dominican Rep.	1,700	1,760	1,640	1,210	57	16	110	61	1,834	2,357
51	Morocco	12,120	4,760	2,290	1,050	. .	9	145	69	2,066	2,820
52	Papua New Guinea	12,640	6,070	620	880	34	25	143	59	1,903	2,236
53	Honduras	5,370	1,510	1,530	670	50	20	128	66	1,972	2,164
54	Guatemala	3,690	2,180	8,250	850	19	10	112	55	2,046	2,352
55	Congo, People's Rep.	14,210	. .	950	. .	. .	12	129	115	2,236	2,512
56	Syrian Arab Rep.	5,400	1,260	. .	890	37	9	114	44	2,195	3,168
57	Cameroon	26,720	. .	5,830	. .	. .	13	143	90	1,990	2,161
58	Peru	1,650	1,040	900	. .	55	9	130	79	2,325	2,269
59	Ecuador	3,000	820	2,320	610	27	10	112	61	2,123	2,338
60	Namibia	. .	. .	. .	. .	. .	. .	145	101	1,882	1,889
61	Paraguay	1,850	1,460	1,550	1,000	22	6	73	32	2,586	2,816
62	El Salvador	. .	2,830	1,300	930	35	15	120	55	1,859	2,415
63	Colombia	2,500	1,240	890	660	51	15	86	38	2,175	2,561
64	Thailand	7,160	6,290	4,970	710	33	12	88	28	2,134	2,287
65	Jamaica	1,990	2,050	340	490	89	8	49	16	2,232	2,572
66	Tunisia	8,000	2,150	. .	370	60	7	145	46	2,150	2,964

Note: For data comparability and coverage, see the technical notes.   Figures in italics are for years other than those specified.

		Population per				Births attended by health staff (percent)	Babies with low birth weight (percent)	Infant mortality rate (per 1,000 live births)		Daily calorie supply (per capita)	
		Physician		Nursing person							
		1965	1984	1965	1984	1985	1985	1965	1989	1965	1988
67	Turkey	2,900	1,390	. .	1,030	78	7	172	61	2,670	3,080
68	Botswana	27,450	6,900	17,710	700	52	8	112	39	1,982	2,269
69	Jordan	4,690	1,120	1,800	1,270	75	7	114	53	2,277	2,907
70	Panama	2,130	1,000	1,600	390	83	8	56	22	2,254	2,468
71	Chile	2,120	1,230	600	370	97	7	101	19	2,588	2,584
72	Costa Rica	2,010	960	630	450	93	9	72	17	2,367	2,782
73	Poland	800	490	410	190	. .	8	42	16	3,292	3,451
74	Mauritius	3,930	1,900	2,030	. .	90	9	65	21	2,212	2,679
75	Mexico	2,080	1,242	980	880	. .	15	82	40	2,570	3,135
76	Argentina	600	370	610	980	. .	6	58	30	3,207	3,118
77	Malaysia	6,200	1,930	1,320	1,010	82	9	55	22	2,307	2,686
78	Algeria	8,590	2,340	11,770	300	. .	9	154	69	1,683	2,726
79	Bulgaria	600	280	410	160	100	. .	31	13	3,440	3,614
80	Lebanon	1,010	. .	2,030	. .	. .	. .	56	. .	2,494	
81	Mongolia	730	. .	320	. .	99	10	113	64	2,333	2,458
82	Nicaragua	2,560	1,500	1,390	530	. .	15	121	57	2,398	2,361
	Upper-middle-income	**2,190** w	**1,160** w	**2,070** w	**930** w			**87** w	**50** w	**2,593** w	**2,990** w
83	Venezuela	1,210	700	560	. .	82	9	65	35	2,319	2,547
84	South Africa	2,050	. .	. .	490	. .	12	124	68	2,615	3,035
85	Brazil	2,500	1,080	3,100	1,210	73	8	104	59	2,415	2,709
86	Hungary	630	310	240	170	99	10	39	17	3,170	3,601
87	Uruguay	880	510	590	. .	. .	8	47	22	2,812	2,770
88	Yugoslavia	1,200	550	850	260	. .	7	72	24	3,244	3,505
89	Gabon	. .	2,790	760	270	92	16	153	98	1,805	2,396
90	Iran, Islamic Rep.	3,890	2,840	4,270	1,110	. .	9	152	90	2,219	3,100
91	Trinidad and Tobago	3,810	950	560	260	90	. .	42	15	2,497	2,960
92	Czechoslovakia	540	280	200	140	100	6	26	12	3,396	3,564
93	Portugal	1,240	410	1,160	. .	. .	8	65	13	2,567	3,382
94	Korea, Rep.	2,680	1,160	2,970	580	65	9	62	23	2,254	2,878
95	Oman	23,790	1,700	6,420	390	60	14	191	36	. .	. .
96	Libya	3,860	690	850	. .	76	5	138	77	1,803	3,384
97	Greece	710	350	600	450	. .	6	34	11	3,045	3,699
98	Iraq	5,000	1,740	2,910	1,660	50	9	119	67	2,150	2,962
99	Romania	760	570	400	. .	99	6	44	27	2,988	3,357
	Low- and middle-income	**8,150** w	**4,990** w	**5,010** w	**1,880** w			**117** w	**65** w	**2,122** w	**2,468** w
	Sub-Saharan Africa	**33,200** w	**26,640** w	**5,410** w	**2,170** w			**157** w	**107** w	**2,034** w	**2,011** w
	East Asia	**5,600** w	**2,400** w	**4,130** w	**1,530** w			**95** w	**35** w	**1,943** w	**2,596** w
	South Asia	**6,220** w	**3,510** w	**8,380** w	**2,720** w			**147** w	**95** w	**2,058** w	**2,116** w
	Europe, M.East, & N.Africa	**4,100** w	**1,640** w	**3,130** w	**1,200** w			**106** w	**58** w	**2,668** w	**3,131** w
	Latin America & Caribbean	**2,380** w	**1,230** w	**2,100** w	**1,020** w			**94** w	**50** w	**2,451** w	**2,724** w
	Severely indebted	**2,940** w	**1,830** w	**1,660** w	**1,180** w			**93** w	**51** w	**2,513** w	**2,805** w
	High-income economies	**940** w	**470** w	**470** w	**140** w			**25** w	**9** w	**3,082** w	**3,398** w
	OECD members	**870** w	**450** w	**420** w	**130** w			**24** w	**8** w	**3,100** w	**3,417** w
	†Other	**4,430** w	**810** w	**2,440** w	**280** w			**65** w	**27** w	**2,323** w	**2,945** w
100	†Saudi Arabia	9,400	740	6,060	340	78	6	148	67	1,842	2,832
101	Ireland	950	680	170	140	. .	4	25	8	3,569	3,699
102	Spain	800	320	1,220	260	96	. .	38	8	2,768	3,543
103	†Israel	400	350	300	110	99	7	27	10	2,791	3,138
104	†Hong Kong	2,520	1,070	1,250	240	. .	4	27	7	2,537	2,899
105	†Singapore	1,900	1,310	600	. .	100	7	26	8	2,286	2,892
106	New Zealand	820	580	570	80	99	5	20	10	3,266	3,459
107	Australia	720	440	150	110	99	6	19	8	3,015	3,322
108	United Kingdom	870	. .	200	. .	98	7	20	9	3,350	3,252
109	Italy	1,850	230	790	. .	. .	7	36	9	3,104	3,566
110	Netherlands	860	450	270	. .	. .	4	14	7	3,090	3,354
111	†Kuwait	790	640	270	200	99	7	64	15	2,796	3,132
112	Belgium	700	330	590	. .	100	5	24	9	. .	. .
113	Austria	720	390	350	180	. .	6	28	8	3,239	3,478
114	France	830	320	380	. .	. .	5	22	7	3,218	3,310
115	†United Arab Emirates	. .	1,020	. .	390	96	. .	103	24	2,709	3,552
116	Canada	770	510	190	. .	99	6	24	7	3,128	3,447
117	Germany	640	380	500	230	. .	5	24	8	3,103	3,514
118	Denmark	740	400	190	60	. .	6	19	8	3,393	3,577
119	United States	670	470	310	70	100	7	25	10	3,236	3,666
120	Sweden	910	390	310	. .	100	4	13	6	2,880	3,007
121	Finland	1,300	440	180	60	. .	4	17	6	3,125	3,170
122	Norway	790	450	340	60	100	4	17	8	3,036	3,253
123	Japan	970	660	410	180	100	5	18	4	2,679	2,848
124	Switzerland	710	700	270	. .	. .	5	18	7	3,504	3,547
	Other economies	**510** w	**530** w	**300** w	**290** w			**30** w	**24** w	**3,129** w	**3,358** w
	World	**6,060** w	**4,200** w	**3,720** w	**1,630** w			**92** w	**54** w	**2,390** w	**2,669** w
	Oil exporters (excl. USSR)	**16,870** w	**4,490** w	**5,450** w	**900** w			**149** w	**86** w	**2,114** w	**2,491** w

Table 29. Education

		Percentage of age group enrolled in education									Primary net enrollment (percent)		Primary pupil-teacher ratio	
		Primary				Secondary				Tertiary (total)					
		Total		Female		Total		Female							
		1965	1988	1965	1988	1965	1988	1965	1988	1965	1988	1975	1988	1965	1988
	Low-income economies	**73** *w*	**105** *w*	..	**95** *w*	**20** *w*	**37** *w*	..	**29** *w*	**2** *w*	..	..	..	..	..
	China and India	**83** *w*	**119** *w*	..	**108** *w*	**25** *w*	**43** *w*	..	**34** *w*	**2** *w*	..	..	..	..	..
	Other low-income	**49** *w*	**75** *w*	**37** *w*	**68** *w*	**9** *w*	**25** *w*	**5** *w*	**20** *w*	**1** *w*	**3** *w*	..	**67** *w*	**42** *w*	**40** *w*
1	Mozambique	37	68	26	59	3	5	2	4	0	0	..	45	..	61
2	Ethiopia	11	36	6	28	2	15	1	12	0	1	..	26	41	43
3	Tanzania	32	66	25	66	2	4	1	3	0	0	..	50	52	33
4	Somalia	10	..	4	13	2	..	1	..	0	3	16	..	26	..
5	Bangladesh	49	59	31	49	13	18	3	11	1	5	..	62	45	58
6	Lao PDR	40	*110*	30	98	2	27	1	22	0	2	..	70	37	27
7	Malawi	44	72	32	65	2	4	1	3	0	*1*	..	55	..	63
8	Nepal	20	86	4	57	5	30	2	17	1	5	..	64	..	..
9	Chad	34	*51*	13	29	1	6	0	2	..	*1*	..	38	83	..
10	Burundi	26	70	15	50	1	4	1	3	0	*1*	..	46	40	62
11	Sierra Leone	29	53	21	40	5	18	3	..	0	*1*	..	..	32	..
12	Madagascar	65	97	59	95	8	19	5	19	1	4	..	66	71	40
13	Nigeria	32	62	24	48	5	16	3	7	0	..	..	..	33	39
14	Uganda	67	77	50	50	4	8	2	8	0	*1*	..	53	..	30
15	Zaire	70	76	45	65	5	22	2	14	0	..	..	..	37	37
16	Mali	24	*23*	16	*17*	4	6	2	4	0	*1*	..	18	46	38
17	Niger	11	30	7	21	1	7	0	4	..	1	..	..	42	41
18	Burkina Faso	12	*32*	8	*24*	1	6	1	4	0	*1*	..	27	47	65
19	Rwanda	53	64	43	66	2	6	1	5	0	0	..	64	67	57
20	India	74	99	57	83	27	41	13	29	5	..	..	..	42	..
21	China	89	134	..	126	*24*	44	..	37	0	2	..	100	..	23
22	Haiti	50	*83*	44	*80*	5	19	3	17	0	..	..	*44*	..	..
23	Kenya	54	93	40	91	4	23	2	19	0	2	88	..	34	33
24	Pakistan	40	*40*	20	*28*	12	19	5	11	2	5	..	..	42	*41*
25	Benin	34	63	21	43	3	16	2	9	0	3	..	50	41	35
26	Central African Rep.	56	67	28	51	2	11	1	6	..	1	..	49	54	70
27	Ghana	69	73	57	66	13	39	7	30	1	2	..	..	32	24
28	Togo	55	*101*	32	78	5	24	2	12	0	3	..	73	50	52
29	Zambia	53	97	46	92	7	..	3	..	..	2	..	..	51	47
30	Guinea	31	30	19	19	5	9	2	4	0	1	..	23	..	40
31	Sri Lanka	93	*107*	86	*105*	35	71	35	74	2	4	..	100	..	14
32	Lesotho	94	*112*	114	*123*	4	25	4	30	0	4	..	..	57	56
33	Indonesia	72	119	65	117	12	48	7	43	1	..	72	100	..	28
34	Mauritania	13	52	6	*43*	1	16	0	10	..	3	..	..	20	50
35	*Afghanistan*	16	..	5	..	2	..	1	..	0	..	..	..	53	..
36	*Bhutan*	7	26	1	20	0	5	..	2	..	..	..	..	..	37
37	*Kampuchea, Dem.*	77	..	56	..	9	..	4	..	1	..	..	..	48	..
38	*Liberia*	41	*35*	23	..	5	..	3	..	1	*3*	..	..	..	..
39	*Myanmar*	71	*103*	65	*100*	15	..	11	23	1	..	..	..	48	..
40	*Sudan*	29	49	21	..	4	20	2	..	1	2	..	..	..	..
41	*Viet Nam*	..	..	..	..	..	..	..	..	..	..	..	..	..	..
	Middle-income economies	**92** *w*	**104** *w*	**86** *w*	**102** *w*	**26** *w*	**55** *w*	**23** *w*	**56** *w*	**7** *w*	**17** *w*	..	**89** *w*	**36** *w*	**28** *w*
	Lower-middle-income	**89** *w*	**103** *w*	**81** *w*	**101** *w*	**25** *w*	**54** *w*	**22** *w*	**54** *w*	**7** *w*	**17** *w*	..	**89** *w*	**38** *w*	**29** *w*
42	Angola	39	..	26	..	5	..	4	..	0	..	..	..	..	..
43	Bolivia	73	*91*	60	85	18	*37*	15	35	5	18	73	83	28	27
44	Egypt, Arab Rep.	75	90	60	79	26	69	15	58	7	20	..	..	39	30
45	Senegal	40	59	29	49	7	16	3	10	1	3	..	50	43	54
46	Yemen, Rep.	13	..	3	..	3	..	1	..	..	..	..	..	42	..
47	Zimbabwe	110	128	92	126	6	51	5	42	0	4	..	*100*	..	39
48	Philippines	113	110	111	111	41	71	40	71	19	28	95	98	31	33
49	Côte d'Ivoire	60	..	41	..	6	19	2	12	0	..	..	..	47	..
50	Dominican Rep.	87	*101*	87	*103*	12	74	12	..	2	..	..	73	53	*33*
51	Morocco	57	67	35	53	11	36	5	30	1	*10*	47	55	39	26
52	Papua New Guinea	44	71	35	65	4	13	2	9	..	2	..	..	19	32
53	Honduras	80	*106*	79	*108*	10	*32*	9	..	1	9	..	91	..	39
54	Guatemala	50	77	45	70	8	21	7	..	2	9	53	..	33	35
55	Congo, People's Rep.	114	..	94	..	10	..	5	..	1	8	..	..	60	66
56	Syrian Arab Rep.	78	110	52	104	28	57	13	47	8	*18*	87	99	36	26
57	Cameroon	94	*111*	75	*102*	5	27	2	21	0	*3*	69	80	47	*51*
58	Peru	99	..	90	..	25	..	21	..	8	26	..	..	36	..
59	Ecuador	91	*117*	88	*116*	17	56	16	57	3	26	78	..	37	*31*
60	Namibia	..	..	..	..	..	..	..	..	..	..	..	..	..	..
61	Paraguay	102	104	96	102	13	29	13	29	4	9	83	90	30	25
62	El Salvador	82	80	79	81	17	29	17	31	2	17	..	72	34	45
63	Colombia	84	*114*	86	*115*	17	*56*	16	56	3	*14*	..	73	36	29
64	Thailand	78	87	74	..	14	28	11	..	2	*16*	..	..	35	19
65	Jamaica	109	103	106	105	51	63	50	68	3	4	90	97	..	*34*
66	Tunisia	91	*116*	65	105	16	44	9	38	2	7	..	85	56	30

Note: For data comparability and coverage, see the technical notes.   Figures in italics are for years other than those specified.

		Percentage of age group enrolled in education										Primary net enrollment (percent)		Primary pupil-teacher ratio	
		Primary				Secondary				Tertiary (total)					
		Total		Female		Total		Female							
		1965	1988	1965	1988	1965	1988	1965	1988	1965	1988	1975	1988	1965	1988
67	Turkey	101	117	83	113	16	46	9	34	4	11	. .	84	46	31
68	Botswana	65	116	71	119	3	33	3	33	. .	3	58	97	40	32
69	Jordan	95	. .	83	. .	38	. .	23	. .	2	. .	. .	. .	38	18
70	Panama	102	106	99	104	34	59	36	63	7	28	87	90	30	22
71	Chile	124	102	122	101	34	74	36	76	6	18	94	90	52	. .
72	Costa Rica	106	100	105	99	24	41	25	42	6	24	92	85	27	32
73	Poland	104	100	102	99	69	81	69	83	18	20	96	99	28	16
74	Mauritius	101	105	97	105	26	53	18	53	3	2	82	95	34	23
75	Mexico	92	117	90	115	17	53	13	53	4	15	. .	99	47	31
76	Argentina	101	111	102	114	28	74	31	78	14	41	96	. .	20	. .
77	Malaysia	90	102	84	102	28	57	22	57	2	7	. .	. .	. .	21
78	Algeria	68	96	53	87	7	62	5	53	1	9	77	89	43	28
79	Bulgaria	103	104	102	103	54	75	55	76	17	25	96	91	23	17
80	*Lebanon*	106	. .	93	. .	26	. .	20	. .	14	. .	. .	. .	. .	. .
81	*Mongolia*	98	102	97	103	66	92	66	96	8	22	. .	95	32	31
82	*Nicaragua*	69	99	69	104	14	43	13	58	2	8	65	76	34	32
	Upper-middle-income	98 w	104 w	94 w	103 w	28 w	58 w	24 w	58 w	6 w	16 w	80 w	90 w	32 w	26 w
83	Venezuela	94	106	94	107	27	54	28	59	7	27	81	89	34	26
84	South Africa	90	. .	88	. .	15	. .	14	. .	4	. .	. .	. .	. .	. .
85	Brazil	108	104	108	. .	16	38	16	45	2	11	71	84	28	24
86	Hungary	101	96	100	97	. .	71	. .	72	13	15	. .	93	23	14
87	Uruguay	106	109	106	108	44	77	46	. .	8	48	. .	77	. .	23
88	Yugoslavia	106	94	103	94	65	80	59	79	13	18	. .	. .	31	. .
89	Gabon	134	. .	122	. .	11	. .	5	. .	. .	5	. .	. .	39	46
90	Iran, Islamic Rep.	63	116	40	109	18	53	11	44	2	7	. .	96	32	29
91	Trinidad and Tobago	93	100	90	100	36	82	34	85	2	5	87	88	34	24
92	Czechoslovakia	99	94	97	94	29	85	35	88	14	18	. .	. .	23	21
93	Portugal	84	126	83	127	42	59	34	63	5	18	91	100	32	. .
94	Korea, Rep.	101	104	99	104	35	87	25	84	6	37	99	100	62	36
95	Oman	. .	100	. .	95	. .	42	. .	34	. .	4	32	82	. .	27
96	Libya	78	. .	44	. .	14	. .	4	. .	1	. .	. .	. .	31	. .
97	Greece	110	102	109	102	49	95	41	93	10	28	97	97	36	23
98	*Iraq*	74	96	45	87	28	47	14	37	4	14	79	84	22	23
99	*Romania*	101	97	100	. .	39	79	32	80	10	10	. .	. .	23	. .
	Low- and middle-income	78 w	105 w	63 w	97 w	22 w	42 w	14 w	36 w	3 w	8 w	. .	89 w	39 w	29 w
	Sub-Saharan Africa	41 w	67 w	31 w	60 w	4 w	18 w	2 w	14 w	0 w	2 w	. .	47 w	42 w	42 w
	East Asia	88 w	128 w	. .	123 w	23 w	46 w	. .	41 w	1 w	5 w	. .	100 w	. .	24 w
	South Asia	68 w	90 w	52 w	76 w	24 w	37 w	12 w	26 w	4 w	. .	. .	42 w	. .	. .
	Europe, M.East, & N.Africa	85 w	98 w	73 w	92 w	32 w	60 w	27 w	55 w	8 w	14 w	. .	84 w	35 w	27 w
	Latin America & Caribbean	98 w	107 w	96 w	108 w	19 w	48 w	19 w	52 w	4 w	17 w	. .	86 w	34 w	28 w
	Severely indebted	97 w	103 w	93 w	100 w	27 w	54 w	25 w	55 w	8 w	19 w	81 w	89 w	34 w	27 w
	High-income economies	104 w	103 w	105 w	102 w	61 w	93 w	59 w	94 w	21 w	40 w	88 w	96 w	25 w	19 w
	OECD members	104 w	103 w	106 w	103 w	63 w	95 w	61 w	96 w	21 w	41 w	88 w	96 w	25 w	19 w
	†Other	88 w	89 w	75 w	86 w	37 w	62 w	32 w	59 w	7 w	17 w	72 w	65 w	28 w	20 w
100	†Saudi Arabia	24	71	11	65	4	44	1	35	1	13	42	56	22	16
101	Ireland	108	101	108	101	51	98	50	102	12	25	91	89	. .	27
102	Spain	115	111	114	110	38	105	29	111	6	32	100	100	34	25
103	†Israel	95	95	95	97	48	83	51	87	20	34	. .	. .	. .	19
104	†Hong Kong	103	106	99	105	29	74	25	76	5	. .	92	. .	29	27
105	†Singapore	105	111	100	110	45	69	41	70	10	. .	100	. .	29	26
106	New Zealand	106	106	104	105	75	87	74	88	15	36	100	100	22	19
107	Australia	99	106	99	106	62	99	61	101	16	29	98	98	28	17
108	United Kingdom	92	107	92	107	66	83	66	84	12	23	97	100	. .	20
109	Italy	112	95	110	95	47	76	41	76	11	26	97	. .	22	13
110	Netherlands	104	117	104	117	61	104	57	102	17	32	92	100	31	17
111	†Kuwait	116	93	103	92	52	81	43	79	. .	17	68	79	23	18
112	Belgium	109	100	108	100	75	99	72	100	15	33	. .	83	21	15
113	Austria	106	102	105	101	52	80	52	82	9	31	89	91	20	11
114	France	134	114	133	113	56	94	59	98	18	35	98	100	30	21
115	†United Arab Emirates	. .	104	. .	104	. .	62	. .	68	0	9	. .	93	. .	18
116	Canada	105	105	104	104	56	105	55	106	26	62	. .	97	26	17
117	Germany	. .	105	. .	105	. .	94	. .	92	11	32	. .	90	24	17
118	Denmark	98	97	99	99	83	107	67	108	14	31	. .	. .	11	11
119	United States	100	100	. .	100	. .	98	. .	99	40	60	72	95	25	21
120	Sweden	95	101	96	101	62	90	60	92	13	31	100	100	20	16
121	Finland	92	100	89	100	76	108	80	116	11	40	. .	. .	23	. .
122	Norway	97	97	98	97	64	94	62	96	11	35	100	96	21	16
123	Japan	100	102	100	101	82	95	81	96	13	30	99	100	29	22
124	Switzerland	87	. .	87	. .	37	. .	35	. .	8	25	. .	. .	. .	. .
	Other economies	103 w	105 w	103 w	100 w	70 w	98 w	77 w	90 w	29 w	23 w	. .	96 w	12 w	10 w
	World	85 w	104 w	74 w	98 w	31 w	54 w	29 w	46 w	9 w	16 w	84 w	91 w	33 w	26 w
	Oil exporters (excl. USSR)	50 w	87 w	37 w	81 w	11 w	40 w	7 w	34 w	1 w	12 w	73 w	88 w	33 w	27 w

Table 30. Income distribution and ICP estimates of GDP

		ICP estimates of GDP per capita[a]			Percentage share of household income, by percentile group of households[b]						
		United States = 100		Current international dollars		Lowest	Second	Third	Fourth	Highest	Highest
		1985	1989	1989	Year	20 percent	quintile	quintile	quintile	20 percent	10 percent

Low-income economies											
China and India											
Other low-income											
1	Mozambique	..	..	..		..	..	..	..	..	..
2	Ethiopia	1.6	1.6	330		..	..	..	..	..	..
3	Tanzania	2.6	2.3	490		..	..	..	..	..	..
4	Somalia	..	..	..		..	..	..	..	..	..
5	Bangladesh	5.0	4.7	960	1985–86[c]	10.0	13.7	17.2	21.9	37.2	23.2
6	Lao PDR	..	..	..		..	..	..	..	..	..
7	Malawi	3.6	3.2	660		..	..	..	..	..	..
8	Nepal	..	..	..		..	..	..	..	..	..
9	Chad	..	..	..		..	..	..	..	..	..
10	Burundi	..	..	..		..	..	..	..	..	..
11	Sierra Leone	3.0	2.6	540		..	..	..	..	..	..
12	Madagascar	3.9	3.4	700		..	..	..	..	..	..
13	Nigeria	7.2	6.2	1,290		..	..	..	..	..	..
14	Uganda	..	..	..		..	..	..	..	..	..
15	Zaire	..	..	..		..	..	..	..	..	..
16	Mali	2.4	2.5	520		..	..	..	..	..	..
17	Niger	..	..	..		..	..	..	..	..	..
18	Burkina Faso	..	..	..		..	..	..	..	..	..
19	Rwanda	3.8	3.0	620		..	..	..	..	..	..
20	India	4.5	4.7	980	1983[c]	8.1	12.3	16.3	22.0	41.4	26.7
21	China	..	..	..		..	..	..	..	..	..
22	Haiti	..	..	..		..	..	..	..	..	..
23	Kenya	5.3	5.2	1,070		..	..	..	..	..	..
24	Pakistan	8.1	8.2	1,700	1984–85[d]	7.8	11.2	15.0	20.6	45.6	31.3
25	Benin	6.5	5.0	1,040		..	..	..	..	..	..
26	Central African Rep.	..	..	..		..	..	..	..	..	..
27	Ghana	..	..	..	1987–88[c]	6.5	10.9	15.7	22.3	44.6	29.1
28	Togo	..	..	..		..	..	..	..	..	..
29	Zambia	4.7	4.3	900		..	..	..	..	..	..
30	Guinea	..	..	..		..	..	..	..	..	..
31	Sri Lanka	11.2	10.5	2,160	1985–86[e]	4.8	8.5	12.1	18.4	56.1	43.0
32	Lesotho	..	..	..		..	..	..	..	..	..
33	Indonesia	..	..	..	1987[c]	8.8	12.4	16.0	21.5	41.3	26.5
34	Mauritania	..	..	..		..	..	..	..	..	..
35	*Afghanistan*	..	..	..		..	..	..	..	..	..
36	*Bhutan*	..	..	..		..	..	..	..	..	..
37	*Kampuchea, Dem.*	..	..	..		..	..	..	..	..	..
38	*Liberia*	..	..	..		..	..	..	..	..	..
39	*Myanmar*	..	..	..		..	..	..	..	..	..
40	*Sudan*	..	..	..		..	..	..	..	..	..
41	*Viet Nam*	..	..	..		..	..	..	..	..	..
Middle-income economies											
Lower-middle-income											
42	Angola	..	..	..		..	..	..	..	..	..
43	Bolivia	..	..	..		..	..	..	..	..	..
44	Egypt, Arab Rep.	15.8	15.3	3,160		..	..	..	..	..	..
45	Senegal	7.0	6.5	1,340		..	..	..	..	..	..
46	Yemen, Rep.	..	..	..		..	..	..	..	..	..
47	Zimbabwe	9.9	8.8	1,830		..	..	..	..	..	..
48	Philippines	10.8	11.0	2,280	1985[d]	5.5	9.7	14.8	22.0	48.0	32.1
49	Côte d'Ivoire	10.2	8.2	1,700	1986–87[c]	5.0	8.0	13.1	21.3	52.7	36.3
50	Dominican Rep.	..	..	..		..	..	..	..	..	..
51	Morocco	13.1	12.5	2,590	1984–85[d]	9.8	13.0	16.4	21.4	39.4	25.4
52	Papua New Guinea	..	..	..		..	..	..	..	..	..
53	Honduras	..	..	..		..	..	..	..	..	..
54	Guatemala	..	..	..	1979–81	5.5	8.6	12.2	18.7	55.0	40.8
55	Congo, People's Rep.	16.4	12.8	2,650		..	..	..	..	..	..
56	Syrian Arab Rep.	..	..	..		..	..	..	..	..	..
57	Cameroon	14.0	10.0	2,070		..	..	..	..	..	..
58	Peru	..	..	..	1985–86[c]	4.4	8.5	13.7	21.5	51.9	35.8
59	Ecuador	..	..	..		..	..	..	..	..	..
60	Namibia	..	..	..		..	..	..	..	..	..
61	Paraguay	..	..	..		..	..	..	..	..	..
62	El Salvador	..	..	..		..	..	..	..	..	..
63	Colombia				1988[e]	4.0	8.7	13.5	20.8	53.0	37.1
64	Thailand	16.0	20.2	4,190		..	..	..	..	..	..
65	Jamaica	..	..	..	1988[c]	5.4	9.9	14.4	21.2	49.2	33.4
66	Tunisia	19.8	18.0	3,720		..	..	..	..	..	..

Note: For data comparability and coverage, see the technical notes.   Figures in italics are for years other than those specified.

		ICP estimates of GDP per capita[a]		Current international dollars	Percentage share of household income, by percentile group of households[b]						
		United States = 100				Lowest	Second	Third	Fourth	Highest	Highest
		1985	1989	1989	Year	20 percent	quintile	quintile	quintile	20 percent	10 percent
67	Turkey	21.8	22.3	4,610		. .	. .	. .	. .	. .	. .
68	Botswana	16.1	19.3	3,990	1985–86	2.5	6.5	11.8	20.2	59.0	42.8
69	Jordan	. .	. .	. .		. .	. .	. .	. .	. .	. .
70	Panama	. .	. .	. .		. .	. .	. .	. .	. .	. .
71	Chile	. .	. .	. .		. .	. .	. .	. .	. .	. .
72	Costa Rica	. .	. .	. .	1986[e]	3.3	8.3	13.2	20.7	54.5	38.8
73	Poland	24.5	24.0	4,980	1987[e]	9.7	14.2	18.0	22.9	35.2	21.0
74	Mauritius	24.8	29.1	6,030		. .	. .	. .	. .	. .	. .
75	Mexico	. .	. .	. .		. .	. .	. .	. .	. .	. .
76	Argentina	. .	. .	. .		. .	. .	. .	. .	. .	. .
77	Malaysia	. .	. .	. .	1987[e]	4.6	9.3	13.9	21.2	51.2	34.8
78	Algeria	. .	. .	. .		. .	. .	. .	. .	. .	. .
79	Bulgaria	. .	. .	. .		. .	. .	. .	. .	. .	. .
80	*Lebanon*	. .	. .	. .		. .	. .	. .	. .	. .	. .
81	*Mongolia*	. .	. .	. .		. .	. .	. .	. .	. .	. .
82	*Nicaragua*	. .	. .	. .		. .	. .	. .	. .	. .	. .
Upper-middle-income											
83	Venezuela	. .	. .	. .	1987[e]	4.7	9.2	14.0	21.5	50.6	34.2
84	South Africa	. .	. .	. .							
85	Brazil	. .	. .	. .	1983	2.4	5.7	10.7	18.6	62.6	46.2
86	Hungary	31.2	30.0	6,200	1983[e]	10.9	15.3	18.7	22.8	32.4	18.7
87	Uruguay	. .	. .	. .		. .	. .	. .	. .	. .	. .
88	Yugoslavia	29.2	25.7	5,320	1987[e]	6.1	11.0	16.5	23.7	42.8	26.6
89	Gabon	. .	. .	. .		. .	. .	. .	. .	. .	. .
90	Iran, Islamic Rep.	27.9	21.4	4,430		. .	. .	. .	. .	. .	. .
91	Trinidad and Tobago	. .	. .	. .		. .	. .	. .	. .	. .	. .
92	Czechoslovakia	. .	. .	. .		. .	. .	. .	. .	. .	. .
93	Portugal	33.8	37.2	7,700		. .	. .	. .	. .	. .	. .
94	Korea, Rep.	24.1	32.5	6,720		. .	. .	. .	. .	. .	. .
95	Oman	. .	. .	. .		. .	. .	. .	. .	. .	. .
96	Libya	. .	. .	. .		. .	. .	. .	. .	. .	. .
97	Greece	35.5	34.2	7,090		. .	. .	. .	. .	. .	. .
98	*Iraq*	. .	. .	. .		. .	. .	. .	. .	. .	. .
99	*Romania*	. .	. .	. .		. .	. .	. .	. .	. .	. .
Low- and middle-income											
Sub-Saharan Africa											
East Asia											
South Asia											
Europe, M.East, & N.Africa											
Latin America & Caribbean											
Severely indebted											
High-income economies											
OECD members											
†Other											
100	†Saudi Arabia	. .	. .	. .		. .	. .	. .	. .	. .	. .
101	Ireland	40.9	41.3	8,540							
102	Spain	46.0	51.2	10,600	1980–81	6.9	12.5	17.3	23.2	40.0	24.5
103	†Israel	. .	. .	. .	1979	6.0	12.1	17.8	24.5	39.6	23.5
104	†Hong Kong	61.7	75.7	15,660	1980	5.4	10.8	15.2	21.6	47.0	31.3
105	†Singapore	. .	. .	. .	1982–83	5.1	9.9	14.6	21.4	48.9	33.5
106	New Zealand	60.9	56.9	11,780	1981–82	5.1	10.8	16.2	23.2	44.7	28.7
107	Australia	71.1	69.0	14,290	1985	4.4	11.1	17.5	24.8	42.2	25.8
108	United Kingdom	66.1	68.0	14,070	1979	5.8	11.5	18.2	25.0	39.5	23.3
109	Italy	65.6	67.3	13,920	1986	6.8	12.0	16.7	23.5	41.0	25.3
110	Netherlands	68.2	65.9	13,630	1983	6.9	13.2	17.9	23.7	38.3	23.0
111	†Kuwait	. .	. .	. .		. .	. .	. .	. .	. .	. .
112	Belgium	64.7	66.1	13,680	1978–79	7.9	13.7	18.6	23.8	36.0	21.5
113	Austria	66.1	66.3	13,710		. .	. .	. .	. .	. .	. .
114	France	69.3	70.0	14,480	1979	6.3	12.1	17.2	23.5	40.8	25.5
115	†United Arab Emirates	. .	. .	. .		. .	. .	. .	. .	. .	. .
116	Canada	92.5	92.9	19,230	1987	5.7	11.8	17.7	24.6	40.2	24.1
117	Germany	73.8	73.5	15,220	1984	6.8	12.7	17.8	24.1	38.7	23.4
118	Denmark	74.2	69.3	14,340	1981	5.4	12.0	18.4	25.6	38.6	22.3
119	United States	100.0	100.0	20,690	1985	4.7	11.0	17.4	25.0	41.9	25.0
120	Sweden	76.9	75.7	15,670	1981	8.0	13.2	17.4	24.5	36.9	20.8
121	Finland	69.5	73.6	15,230	1981	6.3	12.1	18.4	25.5	37.6	21.7
122	Norway	84.4	83.5	17,280	1979	6.2	12.8	18.9	25.3	36.7	21.2
123	Japan	71.5	75.9	15,710	1979	8.7	13.2	17.5	23.1	37.5	22.4
124	Switzerland	. .	. .	. .	1982	5.2	11.7	16.4	22.1	44.6	29.8
Other economies											
World											
Oil exporters (excl. USSR)											

a. ICP refers to the United Nations' International Comparison Program. Data for 1985 are preliminary Phase V results; those for 1989 are estimated from the 1985 values.   b. These estimates should be treated with caution; see technical notes for details of different distribution measures.   c. Data refer to per capita expenditure.   d. Data refer to household expenditure.   e. Data refer to per capita income.

263

Table 31. Urbanization

		Urban population				Population in capital city as a percentage of		Population in cities of 1 million or more in 1990, as a percentage of			
		As a percentage of total population		Average annual growth rate (percent)				Urban		Total	
		1965	1989	1965-80	1980-89	Urban 1990	Total 1990	1965	1990	1965	1990
	Low-income economies	**17** *w*	**36** *w*	**3.5** *w*	**..**	**10** *w*	**3** *w*	**41** *w*	**31** *w*	**7** *w*	**9** *w*
	China and India	**18** *w*	**42** *w*	**2.9** *w*	**..**	**3** *w*	**1** *w*	**42** *w*	**29** *w*	**8** *w*	**9** *w*
	Other low-income	**14** *w*	**25** *w*	**4.9** *w*	**..**	**25** *w*	**6** *w*	**37** *w*	**34** *w*	**5** *w*	**9** *w*
1	Mozambique	5	26	10.2	10.7	38	10	68	38	3	10
2	Ethiopia	8	13	4.9	5.3	29	4	27	30	2	4
3	Tanzania	5	31	11.3	10.8	21	7	38	18	2	6
4	Somalia	20	36	5.2	5.5	31	11	..	..	..	..
5	Bangladesh	6	16	6.9	6.6	36	6	50	47	3	8
6	Lao PDR	8	18	5.3	6.1	52	10	..	..	..	..
7	Malawi	5	12	7.4	6.3	31	4	..	..	..	..
8	Nepal	4	9	6.4	7.4	20	2	..	..	..	..
9	Chad	9	29	8.0	6.5	43	13	..	..	..	..
10	Burundi	2	5	6.9	5.6	82	4	..	..	..	..
11	Sierra Leone	15	32	5.2	5.4	52	17	..	..	..	..
12	Madagascar	12	24	5.2	6.3	23	6	..	..	..	..
13	Nigeria	17	35	5.7	6.2	19	7	23	24	4	8
14	Uganda	7	10	4.7	5.1	38	4	..	..	..	..
15	Zaire	26	39	4.6	4.6	25	10	17	25	5	10
16	Mali	13	19	4.4	3.6	41	8	..	..	..	..
17	Niger	7	19	7.2	7.7	39	8	..	..	..	..
18	Burkina Faso	5	9	4.1	5.4	51	5	..	..	..	..
19	Rwanda	3	7	7.5	8.1	54	4	..	..	..	..
20	India	19	27	3.7	3.8	4	1	32	32	6	9
21	China	18	53	2.3	..	2	1	49	27	9	9
22	Haiti	18	28	3.7	3.7	56	16	47	56	8	16
23	Kenya	9	23	8.1	8.2	26	6	41	27	4	6
24	Pakistan	24	32	4.3	4.6	1	0	44	42	10	13
25	Benin	13	37	8.9	5.2	12	4	..	..	..	..
26	Central African Rep.	27	46	4.3	4.9	51	24	..	..	..	..
27	Ghana	26	33	3.2	4.2	22	7	27	22	7	7
28	Togo	11	25	6.6	6.9	55	14	..	..	..	..
29	Zambia	23	49	6.6	6.2	24	12	..	..	..	..
30	Guinea	12	25	4.9	5.7	89	23	47	88	5	23
31	Sri Lanka	20	21	2.3	1.3	17	4	..	..	..	..
32	Lesotho	6	20	7.5	7.1	17	4	..	..	..	..
33	Indonesia	16	30	4.8	5.4	17	5	42	33	7	10
34	Mauritania	9	45	10.6	7.7	83	39	..	..	..	..
35	*Afghanistan*	9	..	6.0	..	..	..	41	..	4	..
36	*Bhutan*	3	5	3.9	5.2	22	1	..	..	..	..
37	*Kampuchea, Dem.*	11	..	-0.5	..	..	..	..	..	..	..
38	*Liberia*	22	45	6.2	6.1	57	26	..	..	..	..
39	*Myanmar*	21	25	3.2	2.4	32	8	23	32	5	8
40	*Sudan*	13	22	5.9	3.9	35	8	30	35	4	8
41	*Viet Nam*	..	22	..	3.4	22	5	..	30	..	7
	Middle-income economies	**42** *w*	**58** *w*	**3.8** *w*	**3.4** *w*	**26** *w*	**14** *w*	**42** *w*	**41** *w*	**18** *w*	**25** *w*
	Lower-middle-income	**40** *w*	**53** *w*	**3.7** *w*	**3.5** *w*	**31** *w*	**16** *w*	**41** *w*	**41** *w*	**17** *w*	**23** *w*
42	Angola	13	28	6.4	5.8	61	17	49	61	6	17
43	Bolivia	40	51	3.1	4.3	33	17	28	33	11	17
44	Egypt, Arab Rep.	41	46	2.7	3.1	37	17	53	52	22	24
45	Senegal	33	38	3.3	4.0	52	20	40	53	13	20
46	Yemen, Rep.	11	28	6.6	7.3	11	3	..	..	..	..
47	Zimbabwe	14	27	6.0	6.0	31	9	..	..	..	..
48	Philippines	32	42	4.0	3.8	32	14	28	32	9	14
49	Côte d'Ivoire	23	40	7.6	4.7	44	18	30	45	7	18
50	Dominican Rep.	35	59	5.2	4.2	51	31	46	51	16	31
51	Morocco	32	47	4.3	4.3	9	4	39	36	12	17
52	Papua New Guinea	5	16	8.2	4.5	32	5	..	..	..	..
53	Honduras	26	43	5.5	5.5	35	15	..	..	..	..
54	Guatemala	34	39	3.5	3.4	23	9	..	..	..	..
55	Congo, People's Rep.	32	40	3.5	4.8	68	28	..	..	..	..
56	Syrian Arab Rep.	40	50	4.5	4.4	32	16	58	60	23	30
57	Cameroon	16	40	7.6	6.1	16	6	..	..	..	..
58	Peru	52	70	4.3	3.1	41	29	37	41	19	29
59	Ecuador	37	55	4.7	4.5	21	12	50	49	19	28
60	Namibia	17	27	4.6	5.3	30	8	..	..	..	..
61	Paraguay	36	47	3.8	4.6	47	22	..	..	..	..
62	El Salvador	39	44	3.2	2.0	25	11	..	..	..	..
63	Colombia	54	69	3.7	3.0	21	15	38	39	20	27
64	Thailand	13	22	5.1	4.7	57	13	66	57	8	13
65	Jamaica	38	52	2.8	2.4	51	27	..	..	..	..
66	Tunisia	40	54	4.0	2.9	37	20	35	37	14	20

Note: For data comparability and coverage, see the technical notes.   Figures in italics are for years other than those specified.

| | | Urban population | | | | Population in capital city as a percentage of | | Population in cities of 1 million or more in 1990 as a percentage of | | | |
| | | As a percentage of total population | | Average annual growth rate (percent) | | | | Urban | | Total | |
		1965	1989	1965–80	1980–89	Urban 1990	Total 1990	1965	1990	1965	1990
67	Turkey	34	60	4.1	6.0	8	5	41	35	14	22
68	Botswana	4	26	12.5	10.1	38	10	. .	. .	. .	. .
69	Jordan	46	67	4.4	4.6	53	32	33	38	15	26
70	Panama	44	53	3.4	2.9	37	20	. .	. .	. .	. .
71	Chile	72	85	2.6	2.3	42	36	39	42	28	36
72	Costa Rica	38	47	3.5	3.3	77	36	62	72	24	34
73	Poland	50	61	1.9	1.4	10	6	32	28	16	18
74	Mauritius	37	41	2.5	0.4	36	15	. .	. .	. .	. .
75	Mexico	55	72	4.4	3.0	32	23	41	45	22	32
76	Argentina	76	86	2.2	1.8	41	36	53	49	40	42
77	Malaysia	26	42	4.6	4.9	22	10	16	22	4	10
78	Algeria	38	51	3.9	4.9	23	12	24	23	9	12
79	Bulgaria	46	67	2.5	1.2	20	14	21	19	10	13
80	*Lebanon*	50	. .	4.5	. .	. .	. .	. .	. .	. .	. .
81	*Mongolia*	42	52	4.0	2.9	42	22	. .	. .	. .	. .
82	*Nicaragua*	43	59	4.6	4.6	44	26	36	44	15	26
	Upper-middle-income	**44** *w*	**66** *w*	**4.1** *w*	**3.3** *w*	**17** *w*	**11** *w*	**43** *w*	**40** *w*	**19** *w*	**28** *w*
83	Venezuela	70	84	4.8	2.7	25	21	34	29	24	27
84	South Africa	47	59	3.2	3.7	11	6	40	30	19	18
85	Brazil	50	74	4.3	3.5	2	2	48	47	24	35
86	Hungary	43	61	1.9	1.2	33	20	43	33	19	20
87	Uruguay	81	85	0.7	0.8	45	39	53	45	43	39
88	Yugoslavia	31	55	3.5	2.9	12	7	11	12	3	7
89	Gabon	21	45	7.3	6.4	57	26	. .	. .	. .	. .
90	Iran, Islamic Rep.	37	56	5.2	4.9	22	12	43	41	16	23
91	Trinidad and Tobago	30	68	5.6	3.8	12	8	. .	. .	. .	. .
92	Czechoslovakia	51	77	2.4	1.7	11	8	15	11	8	8
93	Portugal	24	33	1.8	2.0	46	15	44	46	11	16
94	Korea, Rep.	32	71	5.8	3.6	36	26	74	69	24	50
95	Oman	4	10	7.5	8.7	41	4	. .	. .	. .	. .
96	Libya	26	69	9.8	6.5	. .	. .	55	65	14	45
97	Greece	48	62	2.0	1.2	55	34	59	55	28	34
98	*Iraq*	51	71	5.3	4.4	30	21	40	29	20	21
99	*Romania*	38	52	2.9	1.2	18	9	21	18	8	9
	Low- and middle-income	**24** *w*	**42** *w*	**3.7** *w*	**6.8** *w*	**15** *w*	**6** *w*	**41** *w*	**33** *w*	**10** *w*	**13** *w*
	Sub-Saharan Africa	**14** *w*	**28** *w*	**5.8** *w*	**6.0** *w*	**31** *w*	**9** *w*	**30** *w*	**29** *w*	**4** *w*	**9** *w*
	East Asia	**19** *w*	**47** *w*	**3.0** *w*	**. .**	**9** *w*	**3** *w*	**48** *w*	**30** *w*	**9** *w*	**11** *w*
	South Asia	**18** *w*	**26** *w*	**3.9** *w*	**3.9** *w*	**8** *w*	**2** *w*	**35** *w*	**34** *w*	**6** *w*	**9** *w*
	Europe, M.East, & N.Africa	**38** *w*	**54** *w*	**3.4** *w*	**3.4** *w*	**22** *w*	**11** *w*	**36** *w*	**36** *w*	**14** *w*	**19** *w*
	Latin America & Caribbean	**53** *w*	**71** *w*	**3.9** *w*	**3.1** *w*	**23** *w*	**16** *w*	**44** *w*	**45** *w*	**24** *w*	**33** *w*
	Severely indebted	**49** *w*	**64** *w*	**3.7** *w*	**3.0** *w*	**24** *w*	**15** *w*	**42** *w*	**43** *w*	**21** *w*	**28** *w*
	High-income economies	**71** *w*	**77** *w*	**1.4** *w*	**0.9** *w*	**11** *w*	**9** *w*	**37** *w*	**37** *w*	**27** *w*	**28** *w*
	OECD members	**72** *w*	**77** *w*	**1.2** *w*	**0.8** *w*	**10** *w*	**8** *w*	**37** *w*	**36** *w*	**26** *w*	**28** *w*
	†Other	**63** *w*	**77** *w*	**3.8** *w*	**3.0** *w*	**45** *w*	**39** *w*	**54** *w*	**53** *w*	**42** *w*	**47** *w*
100	†Saudi Arabia	39	76	8.5	6.6	17	13	23	29	9	23
101	Ireland	49	57	2.1	0.7	46	26	. .	. .	. .	. .
102	Spain	61	78	2.2	1.2	17	13	26	28	16	22
103	†Israel	81	91	3.5	2.0	12	11	43	45	34	41
104	†Hong Kong	89	94	2.1	1.7	100	94	90	100	81	94
105	†Singapore	100	100	1.6	1.2	100	100	100	100	100	100
106	New Zealand	79	84	1.6	0.8	12	10	. .	. .	. .	. .
107	Australia	83	86	2.0	1.4	2	1	60	59	50	51
108	United Kingdom	87	89	0.3	0.2	14	13	33	26	28	23
109	Italy	62	69	1.0	0.6	8	5	42	37	26	25
110	Netherlands	86	89	1.2	0.5	8	7	18	16	16	14
111	†Kuwait	78	95	8.2	5.0	53	50	100	55	78	53
112	Belgium	93	97	0.4	0.2	10	10	. .	. .	. .	. .
113	Austria	51	58	0.8	0.7	47	27	51	47	26	28
114	France	67	74	1.3	0.6	20	15	30	26	20	19
115	†United Arab Emirates	41	78	23.7	4.1	. .	. .	. .	. .	. .	. .
116	Canada	73	77	1.5	1.1	4	3	37	39	27	30
117	Germany	79	86	0.7	0.2	1	1	19	15	15	13
118	Denmark	77	87	1.1	0.4	31	27	38	31	29	27
119	United States	72	75	1.2	1.2	2	1	49	48	35	36
120	Sweden	77	84	0.9	0.3	23	19	17	23	13	20
121	Finland	44	60	2.6	0.4	34	20	27	34	12	20
122	Norway	58	75	1.9	1.0	21	16	. .	. .	. .	. .
123	Japan	67	77	2.1	0.7	19	15	37	36	25	27
124	Switzerland	53	60	1.0	1.0	7	4	. .	. .	. .	. .
	Other economies	**52** *w*	**65** *w*	**2.3** *w*	**1.5** *w*	**6** *w*	**4** *w*	**25** *w*	**23** *w*	**13** *w*	**15** *w*
	World	**36** *w*	**49** *w*	**2.6** *w*	**4.5** *w*	**14** *w*	**6** *w*	**39** *w*	**33** *w*	**14** *w*	**16** *w*
	Oil exporters (excl. USSR)	**30** *w*	**50** *w*	**5.5** *w*	**5.1** *w*	**23** *w*	**11** *w*	**30** *w*	**30** *w*	**10** *w*	**16** *w*

Table 32. Women in Development

		Health and welfare							Education							
		Under 5 mortality rate (per 1,000 live births)		Life expectancy at birth (years)				Maternal mortality (per 100,000 live births)	Percentage of cohort persisting to grade 4				Females per 100 males			
				Female		Male			Female		Male		Primary		Secondary[a]	
		Female 1989	Male 1989	1965	1989	1965	1989	1980	1970	1984	1970	1984	1965	1988	1965	1988
	Low-income economies	**92** w	**98** w	**50** w	**63** w	**48** w	**61** w		..	..	..	..	..	..	**40** w	**61** w
	China and India	**71** w	**74** w	**52** w	**66** w	**50** w	**64** w		..	..	..	..	..	..	**42** w	**61** w
	Other low-income	**134** w	**145** w	**45** w	**56** w	**43** w	**54** w		**63** w	**75** w	**72** w	**73** w	**49** w	**76** w	**34** w	**60** w
1	Mozambique	193	214	39	50	36	47	479[b]	..	..	..	..	..	78	85	54
2	Ethiopia	188	208	43	49	42	46	2,000[b]	57	45	56	50	38	64	28	67
3	Tanzania	176	197	45	51	41	47	370[b]	82	88	88	89	60	99	33	54
4	Somalia	204	227	40	49	37	46	1,100	46	59	51	65	27	..	11	..
5	Bangladesh	162	146	44	51	45	52	600	..	..	..	30	44	77	14	46
6	Lao PDR	163	183	42	51	39	48	..	..	..	..	..	59	78	59	73
7	Malawi	237	251	40	48	38	47	250	55	64	60	65	..	80	40	60
8	Nepal	187	178	40	51	41	52	..	..	..	..	..	..	..	17	..
9	Chad	203	225	38	48	35	45	700	..	..	..	..	23	40	6	18
10	Burundi	102	118	45	51	42	48	..	47	84	45	84	42	75	10	52
11	Sierra Leone	239	264	34	44	31	40	450	..	..	..	..	55	..	37	..
12	Madagascar	162	180	45	52	42	50	300	65	..	63	..	83	95	64	94
13	Nigeria	155	174	43	54	40	49	1,500	64	..	66	..	63	..	43	..
14	Uganda	151	171	47	50	44	47	300	..	..	..	..	..	82	30	54
15	Zaire	143	161	45	54	42	51	800[b]	56	..	65	..	48	78	15	..
16	Mali	210	239	39	49	37	46	..	52	68	89	75	49	59	30	42
17	Niger	208	231	38	47	35	43	420[b]	75	76	74	88	46	56	19	42
18	Burkina Faso	190	210	40	49	37	46	600	71	84	68	82	48	59	27	46
19	Rwanda	188	209	45	51	42	47	210	63	82	65	81	69	97	37	35
20	India	134	118	44	59	46	58	500	42	..	45	..	57	..	35	51
21	China	31	41	59	71	56	69	44	..	76	..	77	..	84	47	69
22	Haiti	125	142	47	57	44	54	340	..	..	..	..	..	..	44	..
23	Kenya	98	114	50	61	46	57	510[b]	84	75	84	73	57	94	38	70
24	Pakistan	139	133	45	55	47	55	600	56	..	60	..	31	49	27	39
25	Benin	154	173	43	53	41	49	1,680[b]	59	64	67	63	44	51	44	39
26	Central African Rep.	154	173	41	52	40	49	600	67	67	67	74	34	62	19	40
27	Ghana	130	148	49	56	46	53	1,070[b]	77	..	82	..	71	80	34	66
28	Togo	136	154	44	55	40	52	476[b]	85	77	88	70	42	63	26	32
29	Zambia	112	128	46	56	43	52	110	93	97	99	..	78	90	39	..
30	Guinea	224	249	36	44	34	43	..	..	62	..	67	..	45	19	31
31	Sri Lanka	22	28	64	73	63	69	90	94	97	73	99	86	93	102	106
32	Lesotho	128	146	50	58	47	54	..	87	86	70	75	157	125	100	153
33	Indonesia	80	95	45	63	43	60	800	67	78	89	99	..	93	..	79
34	Mauritania	196	218	39	48	36	45	119	..	91	..	96	31	70	11	44
35	*Afghanistan*	..	..	35	..	35	..	..	64	..	71	..	17	..	23	..
36	*Bhutan*	187	180	40	48	41	49	..	..	26	..	29	..	59	..	41
37	*Kampuchea, Dem.*	..	..	46	..	43	..	..	..	..	..	..	56	..	26	..
38	*Liberia*	170	195	46	55	43	53	173	..	..	..	..	..	..	33	..
39	*Myanmar*	82	98	49	63	46	59	140	39	..	58	..	..	..	57	..
40	*Sudan*	161	181	41	52	39	49	607[b]	..	81	..	80	55	..	30	..
41	*Viet Nam*	48	61	..	69	..	64	110	..	..	..	..	..	..	..	..
	Middle-income economies	**60** w	**72** w	**59** w	**68** w	**56** w	**63** w		**78** w	**85** w	**78** w	**90** w	**83** w	**89** w	**81** w	**104** w
	Lower-middle-income	**63** w	**74** w	**58** w	**68** w	**54** w	**63** w		**79** w	**82** w	**79** w	**87** w	**80** w	**89** w	**71** w	**100** w
42	Angola	211	234	37	47	34	44	..	..	..	..	..	..	..	89	..
43	Bolivia	144	162	47	56	42	52	480	..	..	..	..	68	87	57	..
44	Egypt, Arab Rep.	99	114	50	61	48	59	500	85	..	93	..	64	75	41	68
45	Senegal	123	140	42	50	40	47	530[b]	..	88	..	92	57	69	35	51
46	Yemen, Rep.	175	194	41	49	39	48	..	..	..	..	..	14	29	..	..
47	Zimbabwe	60	72	50	66	46	62	150[b]	74	87	80	87	..	95	..	88
48	Philippines	47	60	57	66	54	62	80	..	82	..	76	94	97	96	..
49	Côte d'Ivoire	141	159	44	55	40	51	..	77	82	83	83	51	..	19	44
50	Dominican Rep.	75	83	57	69	54	65	56	..	52	..	70	..	162	104	..
51	Morocco	87	103	51	63	48	60	327[b]	78	77	83	79	42	63	31	66
52	Papua New Guinea	72	87	44	55	44	54	1,000	76	..	84	..	61	79	27	60
53	Honduras	73	87	51	67	48	63	82	38	63	35	59	..	100	69	..
54	Guatemala	66	80	50	65	48	60	110	33	62	73	73	80	82	67	..
55	Congo, People's Rep.	170	183	47	57	41	51	..	86	82	89	89	71	95	29	76
56	Syrian Arab Rep.	58	70	54	68	51	64	280	92	96	95	97	47	87	28	70
57	Cameroon	119	136	47	59	44	55	303	59	85	58	86	66	85	28	64
58	Peru	91	107	52	64	49	60	310	..	..	..	..	82	..	69	..
59	Ecuador	75	82	57	68	55	64	220	69	..	70	..	91	96	46	91
60	Namibia	121	141	47	59	44	56	..	..	..	..	..	..	..	..	..
61	Paraguay	34	45	67	69	63	65	469	70	75	71	76	88	93	89	99
62	El Salvador	66	80	56	67	53	59	74	56	..	56	..	86	102	75	92
63	Colombia	40	50	61	72	57	66	130	57	75	51	67	102	100	57	99
64	Thailand	29	39	58	68	54	64	270	71	..	69	..	89	..	68	..
65	Jamaica	16	23	67	75	64	71	100	..	..	..	..	..	97	121	..
66	Tunisia	53	66	52	67	51	66	1,000[c]	..	90	..	94	52	82	37	74

Note: For data comparability and coverage, see the technical notes.   Figures in italics are for years other than those specified.

		Health and welfare							Education							
		Under 5 mortality rate (per 1,000 live births)		Life expectancy at birth (years)				Maternal mortality (per 100,000 live births)	Percentage of cohort persisting to grade 4				Females per 100 males			
				Female		Male			Female		Male		Primary		Secondary[a]	
		Female 1989	Male 1989	1965	1989	1965	1989	1980	1970	1984	1970	1984	1965	1988	1965	1988
67	Turkey	76	83	55	69	52	64	207	76	97	81	98	66	89	37	60
68	Botswana	42	55	49	69	46	65	300	97	95	90	95	129	107	77	103
69	Jordan	64	71	52	69	49	65	. .	90	99	92	. .	72	94	40	96
70	Panama	22	30	65	75	62	70	90	97	90	97	89	93	92	100	105
71	Chile	20	26	63	75	57	68	55	86	96	83	97	96	96	106	106
72	Costa Rica	19	23	66	77	63	73	26	93	92	91	90	94	94	110	103
73	Poland	17	22	72	75	66	67	12	99	. .	97	. .	93	95	217	262
74	Mauritius	21	30	63	72	59	67	99	97	99	97	99	90	88	53	97
75	Mexico	43	53	61	73	58	66	92	. .	72	. .	95	91	94	53	89
76	Argentina	31	42	69	74	63	68	85	92	. .	69	. .	96	. .	60	172
77	Malaysia	22	31	60	72	56	68	59	. .	100	. .	99	. .	95	. .	101
78	Algeria	87	95	51	66	49	64	129	90	. .	95	. .	62	80	45	76
79	Bulgaria	14	19	73	75	66	70	22	91	95	100	98	93	94	. .	180
80	*Lebanon*	. .	. .	64	. .	60	. .	. .	. .	. .	. .	. .	. .	. .	. .	. .
81	*Mongolia*	79	94	51	63	49	61	140	. .	. .	. .	. .	. .	100	. .	107
82	*Nicaragua*	69	84	52	66	49	63	65	48	64	45	58	99	107	69	168
	Upper-middle-income	**57** w	**68** w	**61** w	**72** w	**58** w	**65** w		**77** w	**90** w	**76** w	**97** w	**88** w	**89** w	**95** w	**111** w
83	Venezuela	36	46	65	73	61	67	65	84	82	61	89	98	96	109	*119*
84	South Africa	85	100	54	65	49	58	550[c]	. .	. .	. .	. .	. .	. .	87	. .
85	Brazil	64	78	59	69	55	63	150	56	. .	54	. .	98	. .	93	. .
86	Hungary	17	23	72	74	67	67	28	90	97	99	97	94	96	197	194
87	Uruguay	23	29	72	76	65	69	56	. .	99	. .	99	. .	95	110	. .
88	Yugoslavia	27	32	68	75	64	69	27	91	. .	99	. .	91	. .	86	*94*
89	Gabon	151	171	44	55	41	51	124[b]	73	80	78	78	84	98	39	*81*
90	Iran, Islamic Rep.	105	124	52	63	52	63	. .	75	79	74	99	46	*80*	44	68
91	Trinidad and Tobago	16	21	67	74	63	69	81	78	99	74	96	97	98	107	*100*
92	Czechoslovakia	12	17	73	75	67	68	8	96	97	98	97	93	97	195	*159*
93	Portugal	15	19	68	78	62	72	15	92	. .	92	. .	95	. .	92	*114*
94	Korea, Rep.	23	32	58	73	55	67	34	96	100	96	99	91	94	59	87
95	Oman	38	50	45	67	43	63	. .	82	96	82	99	. .	87	. .	71
96	Libya	88	104	51	64	48	60	. .	92	. .	95	. .	39	. .	13	. .
97	Greece	13	16	72	80	69	74	12	97	98	96	99	90	94	86	*101*
98	*Iraq*	83	91	53	65	51	61	. .	84	90	90	92	42	79	29	63
99	*Romania*	25	34	70	73	66	68	180	90	. .	89	. .	94	. .	147	*233*
	Low- and middle-income	**84** w	**91** w	**52** w	**65** w	**50** w	**62** w		**61** w	**78** w	**65** w	**79** w	**66** w	**83** w	**52** w	**70** w
	Sub-Saharan Africa	**159** w	**178** w	**43** w	**53** w	**41** w	**49** w		**66** w	**73** w	**69** w	**74** w	**56** w	**78** w	**36** w	**59** w
	East Asia	**39** w	**50** w	**55** w	**70** w	**52** w	**67** w		. .	**78** w	. .	**81** w	. .	**86** w	**50** w	**72** w
	South Asia	**127** w	**121** w	**45** w	**58** w	**46** w	**58** w		**45** w	. .	**48** w	. .	**54** w	. .	**34** w	**50** w
	Europe, M.East, & N.Africa	**74** w	**85** w	**60** w	**68** w	**56** w	**64** w		**86** w	**90** w	**89** w	**95** w	**70** w	**80** w	**88** w	**104** w
	Latin America & Caribbean	**56** w	**67** w	**60** w	**70** w	**56** w	**64** w		**64** w	**75** w	**59** w	**86** w	**95** w	**98** w	**77** w	**110** w
	Severely indebted	**60** w	**72** w	**60** w	**68** w	**56** w	**63** w		**75** w	**79** w	**72** w	**87** w	**88** w	**90** w	**90** w	**119** w
	High-income economies	**10** w	**13** w	**74** w	**79** w	**67** w	**73** w		**95** w	**97** w	**94** w	**96** w	**95** w	**94** w	**93** w	**99** w
	OECD members	**9** w	**11** w	**74** w	**80** w	**68** w	**73** w		**96** w	**97** w	**94** w	**96** w	**96** w	**95** w	**94** w	**100** w
	†Other	**30** w	**37** w	**67** w	**74** w	**62** w	**70** w		**94** w	**94** w	**94** w	**94** w	**59** w	**89** w	**66** w	**87** w
100	†Saudi Arabia	75	89	50	66	47	62	52	93	*93*	91	*93*	29	80	8	66
101	Ireland	9	12	73	77	69	71	7	. .	. .	. .	. .	. .	95	113	*101*
102	Spain	9	11	74	80	69	74	10	76	97	76	96	93	93	70	*101*
103	†Israel	11	15	74	78	71	74	5	*96*	98	*96*	98	. .	98	127	*121*
104	†Hong Kong	8	10	71	80	64	75	4	94	. .	92	. .	85	92	72	*104*
105	†Singapore	8	10	68	77	64	71	11	99	. .	99	. .	85	. .	91	. .
106	New Zealand	11	15	74	78	68	72	. .	. .	98	. .	98	94	95	. .	*98*
107	Australia	8	11	74	80	68	73	11	. .	97	. .	94	95	95	92	99
108	United Kingdom	9	12	74	79	68	73	7	. .	. .	. .	. .	. .	. .	94	96
109	Italy	10	13	73	80	68	73	13	. .	. .	. .	. .	93	. .	80	. .
110	Netherlands	8	10	76	81	71	74	5	99	. .	96	. .	95	. .	93	*111*
111	†Kuwait	15	21	65	76	61	71	18	*96*	92	*98*	93	66	. .	63	67
112	Belgium	10	12	74	80	68	73	10	. .	87	. .	85	94	96	85	*103*
113	Austria	9	13	73	79	66	72	11	95	99	92	100	95	94	95	94
114	France	8	11	75	81	68	73	13	97	96	90	99	95	*94*	108	*108*
115	†United Arab Emirates	24	33	59	73	56	69	. .	97	95	93	92	. .	94	. .	101
116	Canada	8	10	75	81	69	74	2	95	97	92	93	94	*93*	94	95
117	Germany	8	11	73	79	67	72	11	97	97	96	96	. .	*96*	82	97
118	Denmark	9	11	75	78	70	72	4	98	100	96	100	96	*96*	104	*105*
119	United States	11	13	74	79	67	72	9	. .	96	. .	94	. .	*94*	. .	. .
120	Sweden	7	8	76	80	72	75	4	98	. .	96	. .	96	95	104	107
121	Finland	7	9	73	79	66	72	5	. .	99	. .	98	90	95	115	*112*
122	Norway	9	11	76	81	71	74	. .	99	99	98	99	96	95	95	103
123	Japan	6	7	73	82	68	76	15	100	100	100	100	96	95	101	99
124	Switzerland	7	9	75	81	69	74	5	*94*	99	*93*	99	. .	96	. .	99
	Other economies	**24** w	**33** w	**72** w	**74** w	**65** w	**66** w		. .	**100** w	. .	**99** w	**95** w	**93** w	**109** w	**102** w
	World	**68** w	**75** w	**58** w	**67** w	**55** w	**64** w		**67** w	**83** w	**70** w	**83** w	**85** w	**86** w	**58** w	**74** w
	Oil exporters (excl. USSR)	**119** w	**135** w	**48** w	**59** w	**46** w	**56** w		**74** w	**84** w	**74** w	**95** w	**59** w	**83** w	**47** w	**77** w

a. See technical notes.   b. Data refer to maternal mortality in hospitals and other medical institutions only.   c. Community data from rural areas only.

Table 33. Forests, protected areas, and water

| | | Forest area (thousands of square kilometers) | | | | Protected land areas | | | Internal renewable water resources: annual withdrawal (1970–87) | | | | |
| | | Total area 1980 | | Annual deforestation 1981–85 | | Area (thousands of square kilometers) | Number | As a percentage of total land area | Total (cubic kilometers) | As a percentage of total water resources | Per capita (cubic meters) | | |
		Total	Closed	Total	Closed						Total	Domestic	Industrial and agricultural
	Low-income economies												
	China and India												
	Other low-income												
1	Mozambique	154	9	1.20	0.10	0.00	0	0.0	0.76	1	53	13	40
2	Ethiopia	272	44	0.88	0.08	68.73	25	6.2	2.21	2	48	5	43
3	Tanzania	420	14	1.30	0.10	119.13	20	13.4	0.48	1	36	7	28
4	Somalia	91	15	0.14	0.04	0.00	0	0.0	0.81	7	167	5	162
5	Bangladesh	9	9	0.08	0.08	0.97	8	0.7	22.50	1	211	6	205
6	Lao PDR	136	84	1.30	1.00	0.00	0	0.0	0.99	0	228	18	210
7	Malawi	43	2	1.50	. .	10.67	9	11.3	0.16	2	22	7	15
8	Nepal	21	19	0.84	0.84	9.59	11	7.0	2.68	2	155	6	149
9	Chad	135	5	0.80	. .	1.14	1	0.1	0.18	0	35	6	29
10	Burundi	0	0	0.01	0.01	0.00	0	0.0	0.10	3	20	7	13
11	Sierra Leone	21	7	0.06	0.06	1.01	3	1.4	0.37	0	99	7	92
12	Madagascar	132	103	1.56	1.50	10.31	31	1.8	16.30	41	1,675	17	1,658
13	Nigeria	148	60	4.00	3.00	9.60	4	1.1	3.63	1	44	14	30
14	Uganda	60	8	0.50	0.10	13.32	18	6.7	0.20	0	20	7	14
15	Zaire	1,776	1,058	3.70	1.82	88.27	9	3.9	0.70	0	22	13	9
16	Mali	73	5	0.36	. .	8.76	6	0.7	1.36	2	159	3	156
17	Niger	26	1	0.67	0.03	16.54	4	1.3	0.29	1	44	9	35
18	Burkina Faso	47	3	0.80	0.03	7.39	7	2.7	0.15	1	20	6	14
19	Rwanda	2	1	0.05	0.03	2.62	2	10.5	0.15	2	23	6	17
20	India	640	378	0.48[a]	. .	131.70	288	4.4	380.00	18	612	18	594
21	China	1,150	978	0.00	. .	79.04	179	0.8	460.00	16	462	28	434
22	Haiti	0	0	0.02	0.02	0.08	2	0.3	0.04	0	46	11	35
23	Kenya	24	11	0.39	0.19	30.95	30	5.4	1.09	7	48	13	35
24	Pakistan	25	22	0.09	0.07	75.83	57	9.8	153.40	33	2,053	21	2,032
25	Benin	39	0	0.67	0.01	8.44	2	7.6	0.11	0	26	7	19
26	Central African Rep.	359	36	0.55	0.05	39.04	7	6.3	0.07	0	27	6	21
27	Ghana	87	17	0.72	0.22	11.75	8	5.1	0.30	1	35	12	23
28	Togo	17	3	0.12	0.02	4.63	6	8.5	0.09	1	40	25	15
29	Zambia	295	30	0.70	0.40	63.59	19	8.6	0.36	0	86	54	32
30	Guinea	107	21	0.86	0.36	0.13	1	0.1	0.74	0	115	12	104
31	Sri Lanka	17	17	0.58	0.58	7.40	38	11.4	6.30	15	503	10	493
32	Lesotho	0	0	. .	. .	0.07	1	0.2	0.05	1	34	7	27
33	Indonesia	1,169	1,139	9.20[a]	9.00[a]	140.67	141	7.8	16.59	1	96	12	84
34	Mauritania	6	0	0.13	0.01	14.83	2	1.4	0.73	10	473	57	417
35	*Afghanistan*	12	8	. .	. .	1.42	4	0.2	26.11	52	1,436	14	1,422
36	*Bhutan*	21	21	0.01	0.01	8.76	5	18.6	0.02	0	15	5	10
37	*Kampuchea, Dem.*	126	75	0.30	0.25	0.00	0	0.0	0.52	0	69	3	66
38	*Liberia*	20	20	0.46	0.46	1.31	1	1.4	0.13	0	54	15	39
39	*Myanmar*	319	319	6.77[a]	6.77[a]	1.73	2	0.3	3.96	0	103	7	96
40	*Sudan*	477	7	5.04	0.04	81.16	13	3.4	18.60	14	1,089	11	1,079
41	*Viet Nam*	101	88	1.73[a]	1.73[a]	8.58	56	2.6	5.07	1	81	11	70
	Middle-income economies												
	Lower-middle-income												
42	Angola	536	29	0.94	0.44	8.90	3	0.7	0.48	0	43	6	37
43	Bolivia	668	440	1.17	0.87	48.37	12	4.5	1.24	0	184	18	166
44	Egypt, Arab Rep.	0	0	. .	. .	6.85	9	0.7	56.40	97	1,202	84	1,118
45	Senegal	110	2	0.50	. .	21.77	9	11.3	1.36	4	201	10	191
46	Yemen, Rep.	0	0	0.00	. .	0.00	0	0.0	. .	. .	. .	. .	. .
47	Zimbabwe	198	2	0.80	0.00	27.60	19	7.1	1.22	5	129	18	111
48	Philippines	95	95	1.43[a]	1.43[a]	5.21	32	1.7	29.50	9	693	125	568
49	Côte d'Ivoire	98	45	5.10	2.90	19.58	10	6.2	0.71	1	68	15	53
50	Dominican Rep.	6	6	0.04	0.04	5.50	13	11.4	2.97	15	453	23	430
51	Morocco	32	15	0.13	. .	2.98	10	0.7	11.00	37	501	30	471
52	Papua New Guinea	382	342	0.23	0.22	0.07	3	0.0	0.10	0	25	7	18
53	Honduras	40	38	0.90	0.90	5.80	15	5.2	1.34	1	508	20	487
54	Guatemala	45	44	0.90	0.90	0.99	13	0.9	0.73	1	139	13	127
55	Congo, People's Rep.	213	213	0.22	0.22	13.53	10	4.0	0.04	0	20	12	8
56	Syrian Arab Rep.	2	1	0.00	. .	0.00	0	0.0	3.34	9	449	31	418
57	Cameroon	233	165	1.90[a]	1.00[a]	17.02	12	3.6	0.40	0	30	14	16
58	Peru	706	697	2.70	2.70	54.83	22	4.3	6.10	15	294	56	238
59	Ecuador	147	143	3.40	3.40	106.19	13	38.4	5.56	2	561	39	522
60	Namibia	184	. .	0.30	. .	. .	. .	. .	0.14	2	77	5	72
61	Paraguay	197	41	2.12	1.90	11.21	9	2.8	0.43	0	111	17	94
62	El Salvador	1	1	0.05	0.05	0.22	7	1.1	1.00	5	241	17	224
63	Colombia	517	464	8.90	8.20	56.14	35	5.4	5.34	0	179	73	105
64	Thailand	157	92	2.40[a]	1.58[a]	46.77	75	9.1	31.90	18	599	24	575
65	Jamaica	1	1	0.02	0.02	0.00	0	0.0	0.32	4	157	11	146
66	Tunisia	3	2	0.05	. .	0.45	6	0.3	2.30	53	325	42	283

Note: For data comparability and coverage, see the technical notes.   Figures in italics are for years other than those specified.

		Forest area (thousands of square kilometers)				Protected land areas			Internal renewable water resources: annual withdrawal (1970–87)				
		Total area 1980		Annual deforestation 1981–85		Area (thousands of square kilometers)	Number	As a percentage of total land area	Total (cubic kilometers)	As a percentage of total water resources	Per capita (cubic meters)		Industrial and agricultural
		Total	Closed	Total	Closed						Total	Domestic	
67	Turkey	202	89	. .	. .	2.46	15	0.3	15.60	8	317	76	241
68	Botswana	326	0	0.20	. .	100.25	9	17.7	0.09	1	98	5	93
69	Jordan	1	0	. .	. .	0.93	7	1.0	0.45	41	173	50	123
70	Panama	42	42	0.36	0.36	13.11	14	17.3	1.30	1	744	89	654
71	Chile	76	76	0.50	. .	119.83	69	16.0	16.80	4	1,625	98	1,528
72	Costa Rica	18	16	0.42[a]	0.42[a]	6.10	25	12.0	1.35	1	779	31	748
73	Poland	87	86	. .	. .	21.93	75	7.2	16.80	30	472	76	397
74	Mauritius	0	0	0.00	0.00	0.04	1	2.0	0.36	16	415	66	348
75	Mexico	484	463	6.15	5.95	55.83	47	2.9	54.20	15	901	54	847
76	Argentina	445	445	. .	. .	109.75	69	4.0	27.60	3	1,059	95	964
77	Malaysia	210	210	2.55	2.55	11.01	39	3.4	9.42	2	765	176	589
78	Algeria	18	15	0.40	. .	4.97	17	0.2	3.00	16	161	35	125
79	Bulgaria	37	33	. .	. .	1.29	39	1.2	14.18	7	1,600	112	1,488
80	Lebanon	0	0	0.00	. .	0.04	1	0.3	0.75	16	271	30	241
81	Mongolia	95	95	. .	. .	3.18	13	0.2	0.55	2	272	30	242
82	Nicaragua	45	45	1.21	1.21	0.43	6	0.4	0.89	1	370	92	277
Upper-middle-income													
83	Venezuela	339	319	2.45	1.25	86.19	43	9.8	4.10	0	387	166	221
84	South Africa	3	3	. .	. .	58.02	152	4.8	9.20	18	404	65	340
85	Brazil	5,145	3,575	b	b	200.96	160	2.4	35.04	1	212	91	121
86	Hungary	16	16	. .	. .	5.11	46	5.5	5.38	5	502	45	457
87	Uruguay	5	5	. .	. .	0.30	7	0.2	0.65	1	241	14	227
88	Yugoslavia	105	91	. .	. .	10.36	76	4.1	8.77	3	393	63	330
89	Gabon	206	205	0.15	0.15	17.53	6	6.8	0.06	0	51	37	14
90	Iran, Islamic Rep.	38	28	0.20	. .	36.26	30	2.2	45.40	39	1,362	54	1,307
91	Trinidad and Tobago	2	2	0.01	0.01	0.16	6	3.1	0.15	3	149	40	109
92	Czechoslovakia	46	44	. .	. .	19.86	66	15.8	5.80	6	379	87	292
93	Portugal	30	26	. .	. .	6.20	27	6.8	10.50	16	1,062	159	903
94	Korea, Rep.	49	49	. .	. .	5.58	17	5.7	10.70	17	298	33	265
95	Oman	0	0	. .	. .	0.54	2	0.3	0.43	22	561	17	545
96	Libya	2	1	. .	. .	1.55	3	0.1	2.62	374	262	39	222
97	Greece	58	25	. .	. .	5.34	61	4.1	6.95	12	721	58	663
98	Iraq	12	1	. .	. .	0.00	0	0.0	42.80	43	4,575	137	4,437
99	Romania	67	63	. .	. .	1.52	18	0.7	25.40	12	1,144	92	1,053
Low- and middle-income													
Sub-Saharan Africa													
East Asia													
South Asia													
Europe, M.East, & N.Africa													
Latin America & Caribbean													
Severely indebted													
High-income economies													
OECD members													
†Other													
100	†Saudi Arabia	2	0	. .	. .	8.08	5	0.4	2.33	106	321	145	177
101	Ireland	4	3	. .	. .	0.24	5	0.4	0.79	2	267	43	224
102	Spain	108	69	. .	. .	25.61	110	5.1	45.25	41	1,174	141	1,033
103	†Israel	1	1	. .	. .	2.36	19	11.6	1.90	88	447	71	375
104	†Hong Kong	. .	. .	. .	. .	0.00	. .	. .	. .	. .	. .	. .	. .
105	†Singapore	0	0	. .	. .	0.03	1	4.8	0.19	32	84	38	46
106	New Zealand	95	72	. .	. .	28.28	122	10.5	1.20	0	379	174	204
107	Australia	1,067	417	. .	. .	364.81	625	4.8	17.80	5	1,306	849	457
108	United Kingdom	22	20	. .	. .	25.69	84	10.6	28.35	24	507	101	405
109	Italy	81	64	. .	. .	12.66	100	4.3	56.20	30	983	138	845
110	Netherlands	4	3	. .	. .	1.51	47	4.4	14.47	16	1,023	51	972
111	†Kuwait	0	0	. .	. .	0.00	0	0.0	0.01	. .	10	6	4
112	Belgium	8	7	. .	. .	0.84	5	2.6	9.03	72	917	101	816
113	Austria	38	38	. .	. .	15.94	129	19.3	3.13	3	417	79	338
114	France	151	139	. .	. .	45.01	73	8.2	40.00	22	728	116	612
115	†United Arab Emirates	0	0	. .	. .	0.00	0	0.0	0.42	140	429	47	381
116	Canada	4,364	2,641	. .	. .	338.85	311	3.7	42.20	1	1,752	196	1,556
117	Germany	72	70	. .	. .	27.57	86	11.3	41.22	26	668	67	601
118	Denmark	5	5	. .	. .	2.82	58	6.7	1.46	11	289	87	202
119	United States	2,960	2,096	1.59	. .	790.40	396	8.6	467.00	19	2,162	259	1,903
120	Sweden	278	244	. .	. .	17.07	68	4.1	3.98	2	479	172	307
121	Finland	232	199	. .	. .	8.06	34	2.6	3.70	3	774	93	681
122	Norway	87	76	. .	. .	47.62	65	15.5	2.00	0	489	98	392
123	Japan	253	239	. .	. .	24.01	61	6.4	107.80	20	923	157	766
124	Switzerland	11	9	. .	. .	1.21	19	3.0	3.20	6	502	115	387
Other economies													
World													
Oil exporters (excl. USSR)													

a. Data are for the periods as follows: India 1983–87, Indonesia 1979–84, Myanmar 1975–81, Viet Nam 1976–81, Philippines 1981–88, Cameroon 1976–86, Thailand 1985–88, Costa Rica 1973–89.   b. See the technical notes for alternative estimates.

Technical notes

This fourteenth edition of the World Development Indicators provides economic, social, and natural resource indicators for selected periods or years for 184 economies and various analytical and geographical groups of economies.

The main criterion of country classification is gross national product (GNP) per capita. With the inclusion of four new World Bank members, Bulgaria, Czechoslovakia, Mongolia, and Namibia, the main tables now include country data on 124 economies. As only sparse data are available for four additional economies, these are not included in the main tables except in summary form under the heading *other economies*, where available; selected data are presented for them, and for the former German Democratic Republic, in Box A.2. Box A.1, showing basic indicators for economies with populations of less than 1 million, covers another fifty-six economies. Other changes are outlined in the introduction.

Considerable effort has been made to standardize the data; nevertheless, statistical methods, coverage, practices, and definitions differ widely among countries. In addition, the statistical systems in many developing economies are still weak, and this affects the availability and reliability of the data. Moreover, cross-country and cross-time comparisons always involve complex technical problems, which cannot be fully and unequivocally resolved. The data are drawn from the sources thought to be most authoritative, but many of them are subject to considerable margins of error.

Most social and demographic data from national sources are drawn from regular administrative files, although some come from special surveys or periodic census inquiries. In the case of survey and census data, figures for intermediate years have to be interpolated or otherwise estimated from the base reference statistics. Similarly, because not all data are up-

dated, some figures—especially those relating to current periods—may be extrapolated. Several estimates (for example, life expectancy) are derived from models based on assumptions about behavior and prevailing conditions. Issues related to the reliability of demographic indicators are reviewed in the UN's *World Population Trends and Policies*. Readers are urged to take these limitations into account in interpreting the indicators, particularly when making comparisons across economies.

A major methodological change introduced in this edition is the use of 1987 constant price series for calculating growth rates instead of the 1980 constant price series previously used.

To provide long-term trend analysis, facilitate international comparisons and include the effects of changes in intersectoral relative prices, constant price data for most economies are partially rebased to three base years and linked together. The year 1970 is the base year for data from 1960 to 1975, 1980 for 1976 to 1982, and 1987 for 1983 and beyond. These three periods are "chain-linked" to obtain 1987 prices throughout all three periods.

Chain-linking is accomplished for each of the three subperiods by rescaling; this moves the year in which current and constant price versions of the same time series have the same value, without altering the trend of either. Components of GDP are individually rescaled and summed to provide GDP and its subaggregates. In this process, a rescaling deviation may occur between the constant price GDP by industrial origin and the constant price GDP by expenditure. Such rescaling deviations are absorbed under the heading *private consumption, etc.* on the assumption that GDP by industrial origin is a more reliable estimate than GDP by expenditure.

Because private consumption is calculated as a residual, the national accounting identities are main-

Box A.1 Basic indicators for economies with populations of less than 1 million

		Population (thousands) mid-1989	Area (thousands of square kilometers)	GNP per capita[a] Dollars 1989	GNP per capita[a] Average annual growth rate (percent) 1965–89	Average annual rate of inflation[a] (percent) 1965–80	Average annual rate of inflation[a] (percent) 1980–89	Life expectancy at birth (years) 1989	Adult illiteracy (percent) Female 1985	Adult illiteracy (percent) Total 1985
1	Guinea-Bissau	960	36	180	. .	. .	53.2	40	83	69
2	The Gambia	849	11	240	0.7	8.1	14.1	44	85	75
3	Equatorial Guinea	407	28	330	. .	. .	. .	46	. .	63
4	Guyana	796	215	340	−1.6	7.9	20.0	64	5	4
5	São Tomé and Principe	120	1	340	. .	. .	18.3	66	. .	. .
6	Maldives	210	b	420	2.5	. .	6.4	61	. .	. .
7	Comoros	458	2	460	0.5	. .	5.3	55	. .	. .
8	Solomon Islands	313	29	580	. .	7.7	10.5	64	. .	. .
9	Kiribati	69	1	700	. .	. .	5.5	55	. .	. .
10	Western Samoa	163	3	700	. .	. .	9.7	66	. .	. .
11	Cape Verde	361	4	780	. .	. .	9.7	66	61	. .
12	Vanuatu	152	12	860	. .	. .	4.3	64	. .	. .
13	Swaziland	761	17	900	2.1	9.0	11.9	56	34	32
14	Tonga	98	1	910	. .	. .	7.5	67	. .	. .
15	Fiji	740	18	1,650	1.8	10.3	5.6	67	19	15
16	Belize	184	23	1,720	2.5	7.1	2.4	68	. .	. .
17	St. Lucia	148	1	1,810	. .	. .	3.6	71	. .	. .
18	Grenada	94	b	1,900	. .	. .	. .	69	. .	. .
19	Suriname	437	163	3,010	1.2	. .	6.2	67	10	10
20	Seychelles	67	b	4,230	3.2	12.2	3.4	70	. .	. .
21	Malta	350	b	5,830	7.2	3.5	2.0	73	18	16
22	Barbados	256	b	6,350	2.4	11.0	5.5	75	. .	. .
23	Cyprus	695	9	7,040	. .	. .	6.0	76	. .	. .
24	The Bahamas	249	14	11,320	1.1	6.4	6.1	68	. .	. .
25	Qatar	422	11	15,500	. .	. .	. .	70	. .	. .
26	Iceland	254	103	21,070	3.4	26.8	34.8	78	. .	. .
27	Luxembourg	377	3	24,980	6.1	4.3	4.4	75	. .	. .
28	American Samoa	38	b	c	. .	. .	. .	72	. .	. .
29	Andorra	50	. .	c	. .	. .	. .	. .	. .	. .
30	Antigua and Barbuda	78	b	d	. .	. .	6.7	74	. .	. .
31	Aruba	60	b	c	. .	. .	. .	. .	. .	. .
32	Bahrain	489	1	c	. .	. .	−1.3	69	36	27
33	Bermuda	60	b	c	. .	8.1	9.1	. .	. .	. .
34	Brunei	249	6	c	. .	. .	−5.1	75	. .	. .
35	Channel Islands	142	. .	c	. .	. .	. .	77	. .	. .
36	Djibouti	411	23	e	. .	. .	. .	48	. .	. .
37	Dominica	82	1	e	0.5	12.6	6.1	75	. .	. .
38	Faeroe Islands	47	1	c	. .	. .	. .	. .	. .	. .
39	French Guiana	90	90	d	. .	. .	. .	. .	. .	. .
40	French Polynesia	193	4	c	. .	. .	. .	72	. .	. .
41	Gibraltar	31	b	d	. .	. .	. .	. .	. .	. .
42	Greenland	56	342	c	. .	. .	. .	. .	. .	. .
43	Guadeloupe	341	2	c	. .	. .	. .	74	. .	. .
44	Guam	134	1	c	. .	. .	. .	73	. .	. .
45	Isle of Man	67	. .	c	. .	. .	. .	. .	. .	. .
46	Macao	448	b	d	. .	. .	. .	72	. .	. .
47	Martinique	338	1	d	. .	. .	. .	76	. .	. .
48	Mayotte	69	. .	c	. .	. .	. .	. .	. .	. .
49	Netherlands Antilles	189	1	c	. .	. .	. .	77	. .	. .
50	New Caledonia	162	19	d	. .	. .	. .	69	. .	. .
51	Pacific Islands, Trust Territories	169	2	d	. .	. .	. .	. .	. .	. .
52	Puerto Rico[f]	3,301	9	c	. .	. .	. .	75	. .	. .
53	Réunion	584	3	d	. .	. .	. .	72	. .	. .
54	St. Kitts and Nevis	41	b	d	. .	. .	6.4	69	. .	. .
55	St. Vincent and the Grenadines	113	b	e	1.9	10.9	5.8	70	. .	. .
56	Virgin Islands (U.S.)	109	b	c	. .	. .	. .	74	. .	. .

Note: Economies in italics are those for which 1989 GNP per capita cannot be calculated; figures in italics are for years other than those specified. a. See the technical note for Table 1. b. Less than 500 square kilometers. c. GNP per capita estimated to be in the high-income range. d. GNP per capita estimated to be in the upper-middle-income range. e. GNP per capita estimated to be in the lower-middle-income range. f. Population is more than 1 million.

Box A.2 Selected indicators for other economies

	Albania 1965	Albania 1989	Cuba 1965	Cuba 1989	Former German Democratic Republic[a] 1965	Former German Democratic Republic[a] 1989	People's Democratic Republic of Korea 1965	People's Democratic Republic of Korea 1989	USSR 1965	USSR 1989
Population (millions)	2	3	8	11	17	17	12	21	232	288
Urban population (percentage of total)	32	35	58	74	73	77	45	60	52	66
Life expectancy at birth (years)	66	72	67	76	70	74	57	70	69	70
Crude birth rate (per 1,000 population)	35	24	34	18	17	12	44	22	18	18
Crude death rate (per 1,000 population)	9	6	8	7	14	13	12	5	7	10
Population per physician	2,100	..	1,150	530	870	440	..	420	480	270
Total fertility rate	5.4	3.0	4.4	1.9	2.5	1.8	6.5	2.4	2.5	2.4
Infant mortality (per 1,000 live births)	87	26	38	12	25	8	63	27	28	24
Low birth weight (percent)	..	..	..	8	..	6	..	..	..	..
Under 5 mortality (per 1,000 live births, female)	..	28	..	14	..	9	..	27	..	25
Under 5 mortality (per 1,000 live births, male)	..	34	..	17	..	12	..	36	..	33
Daily calorie supply (per capita)	2,376	2,741	2,373	3,103	3,203	3,890	2,298	3,193	3,205	3,386
Food production per capita index (1979–81 = 100)	84	96	82	108	72	113	73	108	86	113
Primary education (female)	87	98	119	101	111	105	..	100	103	..
Primary education (total)	92	99	121	104	109	105	..	100	103	105
Area (thousands of square kilometers)	..	29	..	111	..	108	..	121	..	22,402
Population projected to year 2000 (millions)	..	4	..	12	..	15	..	25	..	307

Note: For data comparability and coverage and definitions, see the technical notes for the appropriate main table. Figures in italics are for years other than those specified.   a. Not included in the ''other economies'' country group in the main tables.

tained. Rebasing does involve incorporating in private consumption whatever statistical discrepancies arise for expenditure. The value added in the services sector also includes a statistical discrepancy, as reported by the original source.

With some exceptions, use of 1987 rather than 1980 values as country weights does not greatly alter the group indexes and growth rates reported here. Most exceptions relate to oil exporters and reflect declining shares of group GNP, trade, and so on from 1980 to 1987. This is most notable for Sub-Saharan Africa, with the dramatic decline in Nigeria's weight. In contrast, changing the base year for country series themselves, as described above, is likely to alter trends significantly. Differences of half a percentage point a year in growth rates could be quite common; larger changes may occur for economies that have undergone significant structural change, such as oil exporters.

The summary measures are calculated by simple addition when a variable is expressed in reasonably comparable units of account. Economic indicators that do not seem naturally additive are usually combined by a price-weighting scheme. The summary measures for social indicators are weighted by population.

The World Development Indicators, unlike the *World Tables*, provide data for (usually) two reference points rather than annual time series. For summary measures that cover many years, the calculation is based on the same country composition over time and across topics. The World Development Indicators permit group measures to be compiled only if the country data available for a given year account for at least two-thirds of the full group, as defined by the 1987 benchmarks. So long as that criterion is met, uncurrent reporters (and those not providing ample history) are, for years with missing data, assumed to behave like the sample of the group that does provide estimates. Readers should keep in mind that the purpose is to maintain an appropriate relationship across topics, despite myriad problems with country data, and that nothing meaningful can be deduced about behavior at the country level by working back from group indicators. In addition, the weighting process may result in discrepancies between summed subgroup figures and overall totals. This is explained more fully in the introduction to the *World Tables*.

All growth rates shown are calculated from constant price series and, unless otherwise noted, have been computed using the least-squares method. The least-squares growth rate, r, is estimated by fitting a least-squares linear regression trend line to the logarithmic annual values of the variable in the relevant period. More specifically, the regression equation takes the form $\log X_t = a + bt + e_t$, where this is equivalent to the logarithmic transformation of the compound growth rate equation, $X_t = X_o (1 + r)^t$. In these equations, X is the variable, t is time, and $a = \log X_o$ and $b = \log (1 + r)$ are the parameters to be estimated; e is the error term. If b^* is the least-squares estimate of b, then the average annual percentage growth rate, r, is obtained as $[\text{antilog} (b^*)] - 1$ and multiplied by 100 to express it as a percentage.

Table 1. Basic indicators

For basic indicators for economies with populations of less than 1 million, see Box A.1. For selected indicators for other economies and for the former German Democratic Republic, see Box A.2.

Population numbers for mid-1989 are World Bank estimates. These are normally projections from the most recent population censuses or surveys; most are from the 1980s, and for a few countries, the 1960s or 1970s. Note that refugees not permanently settled in the country of asylum are generally considered to be part of the population of their country of origin.

The data on *area* are from the Food and Agriculture Organization. Area is the total surface area, measured in square kilometers, comprising land area and inland waters.

GNP per capita figures in US dollars are calculated according to the *World Bank Atlas* method, which is described below.

GNP per capita does not, by itself, constitute or measure welfare or success in development. It does not distinguish between the aims and ultimate uses of a given product, nor does it say whether it merely offsets some natural or other obstacle, or harms or contributes to welfare. For example, GNP is higher in colder countries, where people spend money on heating and warm clothes, than in balmy climates, where people are comfortable wearing light clothes in the open air.

More generally, GNP abstracts from environmental issues, particularly natural resource use. The Bank has joined with others to see how national accounts might provide insights into these issues. The possibility of developing "satellite" accounts is being considered; such accounts could delve into practical and conceptual difficulties, such as assigning a meaningful economic value to resources that markets do not yet perceive as "scarce" and allocating costs that are essentially global within a framework that is inherently national.

GNP measures the total domestic and foreign value added claimed by residents. It comprises GDP (defined in the note for Table 2) plus net factor income from abroad, which is the income residents receive from abroad for factor services (labor and capital) less similar payments made to nonresidents who contributed to the domestic economy.

In estimating GNP per capita, the Bank recognizes that perfect cross-country comparability of GNP per capita estimates cannot be achieved. Beyond the classic, strictly intractable index number problem, two obstacles stand in the way of adequate comparability. One concerns the GNP and population estimates themselves. There are differences in national accounting and demographic reporting systems and in the coverage and reliability of underlying statistical information among various countries. The other relates to the use of official exchange rates for converting GNP data, expressed in different national currencies, to a common denomination—conventionally the US dollar—to compare them across countries.

Recognizing that these shortcomings affect the comparability of the GNP per capita estimates, the World Bank has introduced several improvements in the estimation procedures. Through its regular review of member countries' national accounts, the Bank systematically evaluates the GNP estimates, focusing on the coverage and concepts employed and, where appropriate, making adjustments to improve comparability. As part of the review, Bank staff estimates of GNP (and sometimes of population) may be developed for the most recent period.

The World Bank also systematically assesses the appropriateness of official exchange rates as conversion factors. An alternative conversion factor is used (and reported in the *World Tables*) when the official exchange rate is judged to diverge by an exceptionally large margin from the rate effectively applied to foreign transactions. This applies to only a small number of countries. For all other countries the Bank calculates GNP per capita using the *Atlas* method.

The *Atlas* conversion factor for any year is the average of the exchange rate for that year and the exchange rates for the two preceding years, after adjusting them for differences in relative inflation between the country and the United States. This three-year average smooths fluctuations in prices and exchange rates for each country. The resulting GNP in US dollars is divided by the midyear population for the latest of the three years to derive GNP per capita.

Some sixty low- and middle-income economies have suffered declining real GNP per capita in constant prices during the 1980s. In addition, significant currency and terms of trade fluctuations have affected relative income levels. For this reason the levels and ranking of GNP per capita estimates, calculated by the *Atlas* method, have sometimes changed in ways not necessarily related to the relative domestic growth performance of the economies.

The following formulas describe the procedures for computing the conversion factor for year *t*:

$$(e^*_{t-2,t}) = \frac{1}{3} \left[e_{t-2} \left(\frac{P_t}{P_{t-2}} \middle| \frac{P^\$_t}{P^\$_{t-2}} \right) + e_{t-1} \left(\frac{P_t}{P_{t-1}} \middle| \frac{P^\$_t}{P^\$_{t-1}} \right) + e_t \right]$$

and for calculating GNP per capita in US dollars for year *t*:

$$(Y^\$_t) = (Y_t / N_t \div e^*_{t-2,t})$$

where

Y_t = current GNP (local currency) for year *t*

P_t = GNP deflator for year *t*

e_t = annual average exchange rate (local currency/US dollar) for year *t*

N_t = midyear population for year *t*

$P^\$_t$ = US GNP deflator for year *t*.

Because of problems associated with the availability of comparable data and the determination of conversion factors, information on GNP per capita is not shown for some economies.

The use of official exchange rates to convert national currency figures to US dollars does not reflect the relative domestic purchasing powers of currencies. The United Nations International Comparison Program (ICP) has developed measures of real GDP on an internationally comparable scale, using purchasing power parities (PPPs) instead of exchange rates as conversion factors. Table 30 shows the most recent ICP estimates. Information on the ICP has been published in four studies and in a number of other reports. The most recent study is Phase V, parts of which have already been published by the European Communities (EC)—covering Europe and Africa—and the Organisation for Economic Co-operation and Development (OECD).

The ICP figures reported in Table 30 are preliminary and may be revised. The United Nations and its regional economic commissions, as well as other international agencies, such as the EC, the OECD, and the World Bank, are working to improve the methodology and to extend annual purchasing power comparisons to all countries. However, exchange rates remain the only generally available means of converting GNP from national currencies to US dollars.

The *average annual rate of inflation* is measured by the growth rate of the GDP implicit deflator for each of the periods shown. The GDP deflator is first calculated by dividing, for each year of the period, the value of GDP at current values by the value of GDP at constant values, both in national currency. The least-squares method is then used to calculate the growth rate of the GDP deflator for the period. This measure of inflation, like any other, has limitations. For some purposes, however, it is used as an indicator of inflation because it is the most broadly based measure, showing annual price movements for all goods and services produced in an economy.

Life expectancy at birth indicates the number of years a newborn infant would live if prevailing patterns of mortality at the time of its birth were to stay the same throughout its life. Data are from the UN Population Division, supplemented by World Bank estimates, and do not yet reflect the potentially significant impact of the human immunodeficiency virus (HIV) epidemic.

Adult illiteracy is defined here as the proportion of the population over the age of fifteen who cannot, with understanding, read and write a short, simple statement on their everyday life. This is only one of three widely accepted definitions, and its application is subject to qualifiers in a number of countries.

The summary measures for GNP per capita, life expectancy, and adult illiteracy in this table are weighted by population. Those for average annual rates of inflation are weighted by the 1987 share of country GDP valued in current US dollars.

Tables 2 and 3. Growth and structure of production

Most of the definitions used are those of the UN *System of National Accounts* (SNA), Series F, No. 2, Revision 3. Estimates are obtained from national sources, sometimes reaching the World Bank through other international agencies but more often collected during World Bank staff missions.

World Bank staff review the quality of national accounts data and in some instances, through mission work or technical assistance, help adjust national series. Because of the sometimes limited capabilities of statistical offices and basic data problems, strict international comparability cannot be achieved, especially in economic activities that are difficult to measure such as parallel market transactions, the informal sector, or subsistence agriculture.

GDP measures the total output of goods and services for final use produced by residents and nonresidents, regardless of the allocation to domestic and foreign claims. It is calculated without making deductions for depreciation of "manmade" assets or depletion and degradation of natural resources. Although SNA envisages estimates of GDP by industrial origin to be at producer prices, many countries still report such details at factor cost. International comparability of the estimates is affected by the use of differing country practices in valuation systems for reporting value added by production sectors. As a partial solution, GDP estimates are shown at purchaser values if the components are on this basis, and such instances are footnoted. However, for a few countries in Tables 2 and 3, GDP at purchaser values has been replaced by GDP at factor cost.

The figures for GDP are dollar values converted from domestic currencies using single-year official exchange rates. For a few countries where the official exchange rate does not reflect the rate effectively applied to actual foreign exchange transactions, an alternative conversion factor is used (and reported in the *World Tables*). Note that this table does not use the three-year averaging technique applied to GNP per capita in Table 1.

Agriculture covers forestry, hunting, and fishing as well as agriculture. In developing countries with high levels of subsistence farming, much of agricultural production is either not exchanged or not exchanged for money. This increases the difficulty of measuring the contribution of agriculture to GDP and reduces the reliability and comparability of such numbers. *Industry* comprises value added in mining; manufacturing (also reported as a separate subgroup); construction; and electricity, water, and gas. Value added in all other branches of economic activity, including imputed bank service charges, import duties, and any statistical discrepancies noted by national compilers, are categorized as *services, etc.*

Partially rebased, chain-linked 1987 series in domestic currencies, as explained at the beginning of the technical notes, are used to compute the growth rates in Table 2. The sectoral shares of GDP in Table 3 are based on current price series.

In calculating the summary measures for each indicator in Table 2, partially rebased constant 1987 US dollar values for each economy are calculated for each year of the periods covered; the values are aggregated across countries for each year; and the least-squares procedure is used to compute the growth rates. The average sectoral percentage shares in Table 3 are computed from group aggregates of sectoral GDP in current US dollars.

Table 4. Agriculture and food

The basic data for *value added in agriculture* are from the World Bank's national accounts series at current prices in national currencies. Value added in current prices in national currencies is converted to US dollars by applying the single-year conversion pro-

cedure, as described in the technical note for Tables 2 and 3.

The figures for the remainder of this table are from the Food and Agriculture Organization (FAO). *Cereal imports* are measured in grain equivalents and defined as comprising all cereals in the *Standard International Trade Classification* (SITC), Revision 2, Groups 041–046. *Food aid in cereals* covers wheat and flour, bulgur, rice, coarse grains, and the cereal component of blended foods. The figures are not directly comparable because of reporting and timing differences. Cereal imports are based on calendar-year data reported by recipient countries, and food aid in cereals is based on data for crop years reported by donors and international organizations, including the International Wheat Council and the World Food Programme. Furthermore, food aid information from donors may not correspond to actual receipts by beneficiaries during a given period because of delays in transportation and recording, or because aid is sometimes not reported to the FAO or other relevant international organizations. Food aid imports may also not show up in customs records. The earliest available food aid data are for 1974. The time reference for food aid is the crop year, July to June.

Fertilizer consumption measures the plant nutrients used in relation to arable land. Fertilizer products cover nitrogenous, potash, and phosphate fertilizers (which include ground rock phosphate). Arable land is defined as land under temporary crops (double-cropped areas are counted once), temporary meadows for mowing or pastures, land under market or kitchen gardens, and land temporarily fallow or lying idle, as well as land under permanent crops. The time reference for fertilizer consumption is the crop year, July to June.

The *average index of food production per capita* shows the average annual quantity of food produced per capita in 1987–89 in relation to the average produced annually in 1979–81. The estimates are derived by dividing the quantity of food production by the total population. For this index food is defined as comprising nuts, pulses, fruits, cereals, vegetables, sugar cane, sugar beet, starchy roots, edible oils, livestock, and livestock products. Quantities of food production are measured net of animal feed, seeds for use in agriculture, and food lost in processing and distribution.

The summary measures for fertilizer consumption are weighted by total arable land area; the summary measures for food production are weighted by population.

Table 5. Commercial energy

The data on energy are primarily from UN sources. They refer to commercial forms of primary energy—

petroleum and natural gas liquids, natural gas, solid fuels (coal, lignite, and so on), and primary electricity (nuclear, geothermal, and hydroelectric power)—all converted into oil equivalents. Figures on liquid fuel consumption include petroleum derivatives that have been consumed in nonenergy uses. For converting primary electricity into oil equivalents, a notional thermal efficiency of 34 percent has been assumed. The use of firewood, dried animal excrement, and other traditional fuels, although substantial in some developing countries, is not taken into account because reliable and comprehensive data are not available.

Energy imports refer to the dollar value of energy imports—Section 3 in the *Standard International Trade Classification*, Revision 1—and are expressed as a percentage of earnings from merchandise exports. Because data on energy imports do not permit a distinction between petroleum imports for fuel and those for use in the petrochemicals industry, these percentages may overestimate the dependence on imported energy.

The summary measures of energy production and consumption are computed by aggregating the respective volumes for each of the years covered by the periods and then applying the least-squares growth rate procedure. For energy consumption per capita, population weights are used to compute summary measures for the specified years.

The summary measures of energy imports as a percentage of merchandise exports are computed from group aggregates for energy imports and merchandise exports in current dollars.

Table 6. Structure of manufacturing

The basic data for *value added in manufacturing* are from the World Bank's national accounts series at current prices in national currencies. Value added in current prices in national currencies is converted to US dollars by applying the single-year conversion procedure, as described in the technical note for Tables 2 and 3.

The data for *distribution of manufacturing value added* among industries are provided by the United Nations Industrial Development Organization, and distribution calculations are from national currencies in current prices.

The classification of manufacturing industries is in accordance with the UN *International Standard Industrial Classification of All Economic Activities* (ISIC), Revision 2. *Food, beverages, and tobacco* comprise ISIC Division 31; *textiles and clothing,* Division 32; *machinery and transport equipment,* Major Groups 382–84; and *chemicals,* Major Groups 351 and 352. *Other* comprises wood and related products (Division 33), paper and related products (Division 34), petroleum and related

products (Major Groups 353–56), basic metals and mineral products (Divisions 36 and 37), fabricated metal products and professional goods (Major Groups 381 and 385), and other industries (Major Group 390). When data for textiles, machinery, or chemicals are shown as not available, they are also included in *other.*

Summary measures given for value added in manufacturing are totals calculated by the aggregation method noted at the beginning of the technical notes.

Table 7. Manufacturing earnings and output

Four indicators are shown—two relate to real earnings per employee, one to labor's share in total value added generated, and one to labor productivity in the manufacturing sector. The indicators are based on data from the United Nations Industrial Development Organization (UNIDO), although the deflators are from other sources, as explained below.

Earnings per employee are in constant prices and are derived by deflating nominal earnings per employee by the country's consumer price index (CPI). The CPI is from the International Monetary Fund's *International Financial Statistics. Total earnings as a percentage of value added* are derived by dividing total earnings of employees by value added in current prices, to show labor's share in income generated in the manufacturing sector. *Gross output per employee* is in constant prices and is presented as an index of overall labor productivity in manufacturing with 1980 as the base year. To derive this indicator, UNIDO data on gross output per employee in current prices are adjusted using the implicit deflators for value added in manufacturing or in industry, taken from the World Bank's national accounts data files.

To improve cross-country comparability, UNIDO has, where possible, standardized the coverage of establishments to those with five or more employees.

The concepts and definitions are in accordance with the *International Recommendations for Industrial Statistics,* published by the United Nations. Earnings (wages and salaries) cover all remuneration to employees paid by the employer during the year. The payments include (a) all regular and overtime cash payments and bonuses and cost of living allowances; (b) wages and salaries paid during vacation and sick leave; (c) taxes and social insurance contributions and the like, payable by the employees and deducted by the employer; and (d) payments in kind.

The value of gross output is estimated on the basis of either production or shipments. On the production basis it consists of (a) the value of all products of the establishment, (b) the value of industrial services rendered to others, (c) the value of goods shipped in the same condition as received, (d) the value of electricity sold, and (e) the net change in the value of work-in-progress between the beginning and the end of the reference period. In the case of estimates compiled on a shipment basis, the net change between the beginning and the end of the reference period in the value of stocks of finished goods is also included. "Value added" is defined as the current value of gross output less the current cost of (a) materials, fuels, and other supplies consumed, (b) contract and commission work done by others, (c) repair and maintenance work done by others, and (d) goods shipped in the same condition as received.

The term "employees" in this table combines two categories defined by the UN, regular employees and persons engaged. Together these groups comprise regular employees, working proprietors, active business partners, and unpaid family workers; they exclude homeworkers. The data refer to the average number of employees working during the year.

Tables 8 and 9. Growth of consumption and investment; structure of demand

GDP is defined in the note for Tables 2 and 3, but for these two tables it is in purchaser values.

General government consumption includes all current expenditure for purchases of goods and services by all levels of government. Capital expenditure on national defense and security is regarded as consumption expenditure.

Private consumption, etc., is the market value of all goods and services, including durable products (such as cars, washing machines, and home computers) purchased or received as income in kind by households and nonprofit institutions. It excludes purchases of dwellings but includes imputed rent for owner-occupied dwellings (see the note for Table 10 for details). In practice, it includes any statistical discrepancy in the use of resources. At constant prices, it also includes the rescaling deviation from partial rebasing, which is explained at the beginning of the technical notes.

Gross domestic investment consists of outlays on additions to the fixed assets of the economy plus net changes in the level of inventories.

Gross domestic savings are calculated by deducting total consumption from GDP.

Exports of goods and nonfactor services represent the value of all goods and nonfactor services provided to the rest of the world; they include merchandise, freight, insurance, travel, and other nonfactor services. The value of factor services, such as investment income, interest, and labor income, is excluded. Current transfers are also excluded.

The *resource balance* is the difference between exports of goods and nonfactor services and imports of goods and nonfactor services.

Partially rebased 1987 series in constant domestic

currency units are used to compute the indicators in Table 8. Distribution of GDP in Table 9 is calculated from national accounts series in current domestic currency units.

The summary measures are calculated by the method explained in the note for Tables 2 and 3.

Table 10. Structure of consumption

Percentage shares of selected items in total household consumption expenditure are computed from details of GDP (expenditure at national market prices) defined in the UN *System of National Accounts* (SNA), mostly as collected from International Comparison Program (ICP) Phases IV (1980) and V (1985). For countries not covered by the ICP, less detailed national accounts estimates are included, where available, in order to present a general idea of the broad structure of consumption. The data cover eighty-four countries (including Bank staff estimates for China) and refer to the most recent estimates, generally for 1980 and 1985. Where they refer to other years the figures are shown in italics. *Consumption* here refers to private (nongovernment) consumption as defined in the SNA and in the notes for Tables 2 and 3, 4, and 9, except that education and medical care comprise government as well as private outlays. This ICP concept of "enhanced consumption" reflects who uses rather than who pays for consumption goods, and it improves international comparability because it is less sensitive to differing national practices regarding the financing of health and education services.

Cereals and tubers, a major subitem of *food,* comprise the main staple products: rice, flour, bread, all other cereals and cereal preparations, potatoes, yams, and other tubers. For high-income OECD members, however, this subitem does not include tubers. *Gross rents; fuel and power* consist of actual and imputed rents and repair and maintenance charges, as well as the subitem *fuel and power* (for heating, lighting, cooking, air conditioning, and so forth). Note that this item excludes energy used for transport (rarely reported to be more than 1 percent of total consumption in low- and middle-income economies). As mentioned, *medical care* and *education* include government as well as private consumption expenditure. *Transport and communication* also includes the purchase of *automobiles,* which are reported as a subitem. *Other consumption,* the residual group, includes beverages and tobacco, nondurable household goods and household services, recreational services, and services (including meals) supplied by hotels and restaurants; carry-out food is recorded here. It also includes the separately reported subitem *other consumer durables,* comprising household appliances, furniture, floor coverings, recreational equipment, and watches and jewelry.

Estimating the structure of consumption is one of the weakest aspects of national accounting in low- and middle-income economies. The structure is estimated through household expenditure surveys and similar survey techniques. It therefore shares any bias inherent in the sample frame. Since, conceptually, expenditure is not identical to consumption, other apparent discrepancies occur and data for some countries should be treated with caution. For example, some countries limit surveys to urban areas or, even more narrowly, to capital cities. This tends to produce lower than average shares for food and high shares for transport and communication, gross rents, fuel and power, and other consumption. Controlled food prices and incomplete national accounting for subsistence activities also contribute to low food shares.

Table 11. Central government expenditure

The data on central government finance in Tables 11 and 12 are from the IMF *Government Finance Statistics Yearbook* (1990) and IMF data files. The accounts of each country are reported using the system of common definitions and classifications found in the IMF *Manual on Government Finance Statistics* (1986).

For complete and authoritative explanations of concepts, definitions, and data sources, see these IMF sources. The commentary that follows is intended mainly to place these data in the context of the broad range of indicators reported in this edition.

The shares of *total expenditure* and *current revenue* by category are calculated from series in national currencies. Because of differences in coverage of available data, the individual components of central government expenditure and current revenue shown in these tables may not be strictly comparable across all economies.

Moreover, inadequate statistical coverage of state, provincial, and local governments dictates the use of central government data; this may seriously understate or distort the statistical portrayal of the allocation of resources for various purposes, especially in countries where lower levels of government have considerable autonomy and are responsible for many economic and social services. In addition, "central government" can mean either of two accounting concepts: consolidated or budgetary. For most countries, central government finance data have been consolidated into one overall account, but for others only the budgetary central government accounts are available. Since all central government units are not always included in the budgetary accounts, the overall picture of central government activities is usually incomplete. Countries reporting budgetary data are footnoted.

It must be emphasized that for these and other reasons the data presented, especially those for education and health, are not comparable across countries. In many economies private health and education services are substantial; in others public services represent the major component of total expenditure but may be financed by lower levels of government. Caution should therefore be exercised in using the data for cross-country comparisons. Central government expenditure comprises the expenditure by all government offices, departments, establishments, and other bodies that are agencies or instruments of the central authority of a country. It includes both current and capital (development) expenditure.

Defense comprises all expenditure, whether by defense or other departments, on the maintenance of military forces, including the purchase of military supplies and equipment, construction, recruiting, and training. Also in this category are closely related items such as military aid programs. Defense does not include expenditure on public order and safety, which are classified separately.

Education comprises expenditure on the provision, management, inspection, and support of preprimary, primary, and secondary schools; of universities and colleges; and of vocational, technical, and other training institutions. Also included is expenditure on the general administration and regulation of the education system; on research into its objectives, organization, administration, and methods; and on such subsidiary services as transport, school meals, and school medical and dental services. Note that Table 10 provides an alternative measure of expenditure on education, private as well as public, relative to household consumption.

Health covers public expenditure on hospitals, maternity and dental centers, and clinics with a major medical component; on national health and medical insurance schemes; and on family planning and preventive care. Note that Table 10 provides a more comprehensive measure of expenditure on medical care, private as well as public, relative to household consumption.

Housing, amenities; social security and welfare cover expenditure on housing (excluding interest subsidies, which are usually classified with "other"), such as income-related schemes; on provision and support of housing and slum clearance activities; on community development; and on sanitary services. These categories also cover compensation for loss of income to the sick and temporarily disabled; payments to the elderly, the permanently disabled, and the unemployed; family, maternity, and child allowances; and the cost of welfare services, such as care of the aged, the disabled, and children. Many expenditures relevant to environmental defense, such as pollution abatement, water supply, sanitary affairs, and refuse collection, are included indistinguishably in this category.

Economic services comprise expenditure associated with the regulation, support, and more efficient operation of business; economic development; redress of regional imbalances; and creation of employment opportunities. Research, trade promotion, geological surveys, and inspection and regulation of particular industry groups are among the activities included.

Other covers interest payments and items not included elsewhere; for a few economies it also includes amounts that could not be allocated to other components (or adjustments from accrual to cash accounts).

Total expenditure is more narrowly defined than the measure of general government consumption given in Table 9 because it excludes consumption expenditure by state and local governments. At the same time, central government expenditure is more broadly defined because it includes government's gross domestic investment and transfer payments.

Overall surplus/deficit is defined as current and capital revenue and official grants received, less total expenditure and lending minus repayments.

Table 12. Central government current revenue

Information on data sources and comparability is given in the note for Table 11. Current revenue by source is expressed as a percentage of *total current revenue*, which is the sum of tax revenue and nontax revenue and is calculated from national currencies.

Tax revenue comprises compulsory, unrequited, nonrepayable receipts for public purposes. It includes interest collected on tax arrears and penalties collected on nonpayment or late payment of taxes and is shown net of refunds and other corrective transactions. *Taxes on income, profit, and capital gains* are taxes levied on the actual or presumptive net income of individuals, on the profits of enterprises, and on capital gains, whether realized on land sales, securities, or other assets. Intragovernmental payments are eliminated in consolidation. *Social security contributions* include employers' and employees' social security contributions as well as those of self-employed and unemployed persons. *Domestic taxes on goods and services* include general sales and turnover or value added taxes, selective excises on goods, selective taxes on services, taxes on the use of goods or property, and profits of fiscal monopolies. *Taxes on international trade and transactions* include import duties, export duties, profits of export or import monopolies, exchange profits, and exchange taxes. *Other taxes* include employers' payroll or labor taxes, taxes on property, and taxes not allocable to other categories. They may include negative values that are adjust-

ments, for instance, for taxes collected on behalf of state and local governments and not allocable to individual tax categories.

Nontax revenue comprises receipts that are not a compulsory nonrepayable payment for public purposes, such as fines, administrative fees, or entrepreneurial income from government ownership of property. Proceeds of grants and borrowing, funds arising from the repayment of previous lending by governments, incurrence of liabilities, and proceeds from the sale of capital assets are not included.

Table 13. Money and interest rates

The data on monetary holdings are based on the IMF's *International Financial Statistics* (IFS). *Monetary holdings, broadly defined*, comprise the monetary and quasi-monetary liabilities of a country's financial institutions to residents other than the central government. For most countries, monetary holdings are the sum of money (IFS line 34) and quasi-money (IFS line 35). Money comprises the economy's means of payment: currency outside banks and demand deposits. Quasi-money comprises time and savings deposits and similar bank accounts that the issuer will readily exchange for money. Where nonmonetary financial institutions are important issuers of quasi-monetary liabilities, these are also included in the measure of monetary holdings.

The growth rates for monetary holdings are calculated from year-end figures, while the average of the year-end figures for the specified year and the previous year is used for the ratio of monetary holdings to GDP.

The *nominal interest rates of banks*, also from IFS, represent the rates paid by commercial or similar banks to holders of their quasi-monetary liabilities (deposit rate) and charged by the banks on loans to prime customers (lending rate). The data are, however, of limited international comparability partly because coverage and definitions vary, and partly because countries differ in the scope available to banks for adjusting interest rates to reflect market conditions.

Since interest rates (and growth rates for monetary holdings) are expressed in nominal terms, much of the variation among countries stems from differences in inflation. For easy reference, the Table 1 indicator of recent inflation is repeated in this table.

Table 14. Growth of merchandise trade

The main data source for current trade values is the UN Commodity Trade (Comtrade) data file supplemented by data from United Nations Conference on Trade and Development (UNCTAD) and World Bank estimates. The statistics on merchandise trade are based on countries' customs returns.

Merchandise *exports* and *imports*, with some exceptions, cover international movements of goods across customs borders; trade in services is not included. Exports are valued f.o.b. (free on board) and imports c.i.f. (cost, insurance, and freight), unless otherwise specified in the foregoing sources. These values are in current dollars.

The growth rates of merchandise exports and imports are based on constant price data, which are obtained from export or import value data as deflated by the corresponding price index. The World Bank uses its own price indexes, which are based on international prices for primary commodities and unit value indexes for manufactures. These price indexes are country-specific and disaggregated by broad commodity groups. This ensures consistency between data for a group of countries and those for individual countries. Such consistency will increase as the World Bank continues to improve its trade price indexes for an increasing number of countries. These growth rates can differ from those derived from national practices because national price indexes may use different base years and weighting procedures from those used by the World Bank.

The *terms of trade*, or the net barter terms of trade, measure the relative movement of export prices against that of import prices. Calculated as the ratio of a country's index of average export prices to its average import price index, this indicator shows changes over a base year in the level of export prices as a percentage of import prices. The terms of trade index numbers are shown for 1985 and 1989, where 1987 = 100. The price indexes are from the source cited above for the growth rates of exports and imports.

The summary measures for the growth rates are calculated by aggregating the 1987 constant US dollar price series for each year and then applying the least-squares growth rate procedure for the periods shown.

Tables 15 and 16. Structure of merchandise imports and exports

The shares in these tables are derived from trade values in current dollars reported in the UN trade data system and the UN *Yearbook of International Trade Statistics*, supplemented by other secondary sources and World Bank estimates, as explained in the technical note for Table 14.

Merchandise *exports* and *imports* are also defined in that note.

The categorization of exports and imports follows the *Standard International Trade Classification* (SITC),

Series M, No. 34, Revision 1. Estimates from secondary sources also usually follow this definition. For some countries, data for certain commodity categories are unavailable and the full breakdown cannot be shown.

In Table 15, *food* commodities are those in SITC Sections 0, 1, and 4 and Division 22 (food and live animals, beverages, oils and fats, and oilseeds and nuts). Unlike previous years, Division 12, tobacco, is included in *food*, rather than *other primary commodities*; thus the data are not strictly comparable with those of previous years, particulartly if tobacco is a major import item. *Fuels* are the commodities in SITC Section 3 (mineral fuels, and lubricants and related materials). *Other primary commodities* comprise SITC Section 2 (crude materials, excluding fuels), less Division 22 (oilseeds and nuts), plus Division 68 (nonferrous metals). *Machinery and transport equipment* are the commodities in SITC Section 7. *Other manufactures*, calculated residually from the total value of manufactured imports, represent SITC Sections 5 through 9, less Section 7 and Division 68.

In Table 16, *fuels, minerals, and metals* are the commodities in SITC Section 3 (mineral fuels, and lubricants and related materials), Divisions 27 and 28 (minerals and crude fertilizers, and metalliferous ores), and Division 68 (nonferrous metals). *Other primary commodities* comprise SITC Sections 0, 1, 2, and 4 (food and live animals, beverages and tobacco, inedible crude materials, oils, fats, and waxes), less Divisions 27 and 28. *Machinery and transport equipment* are the commodities in SITC Section 7. *Other manufactures* represent SITC Sections 5 through 9, less Section 7 and Division 68. *Textiles and clothing*, representing SITC Divisions 65 and 84 (textiles, yarns, fabrics, and clothing), are a subgroup of *other manufactures*.

The summary measures in Table 15 are weighted by total merchandise imports of individual countries in current dollars; those in Table 16 by total merchandise exports of individual countries in current dollars. (See the technical note for Table 14.)

Table 17. OECD imports of manufactured goods: origin and composition

The data are from the United Nations, reported by high-income OECD economies, which are the OECD members excluding Greece, Portugal, and Turkey.

The table reports the value of *imports of manufactures* of high-income OECD countries by the economy of origin, and the composition of such imports by major manufactured product groups.

The table replaces one in past editions on the origin and destination of manufactured exports, which was based on exports reported by individual economies. Since there was a lag of several years in reporting by many developing economies, estimates based on various sources were used to fill the gaps. Until these estimates can be improved, this table, based on up-to-date and consistent but less comprehensive data, is included instead. Manufactured imports of the predominant markets from individual economies are the best available proxy of the magnitude and composition of the manufactured exports of these economies to all destinations taken together.

Manufactured goods are the commodities in the *Standard International Trade Classification* (SITC), Revision 1, Sections 5 through 9 (chemical and related products, basic manufactures, manufactured articles, machinery and transport equipment, and other manufactured articles and goods not elsewhere classified), excluding Division 68 (nonferrous metals). This definition is somewhat broader than the one used to define exporters of manufactures.

The major manufactured product groups reported are defined as follows: *textiles and clothing* (SITC Sections 65 and 84), *chemicals* (SITC Section 5), *electrical machinery and electronics* (SITC Section 72), *transport equipment* (SITC Section 73), and *others*, defined as the residual. SITC Revision 1 data are used for the year 1969, whereas the equivalent data in Revision 2 are used for the year 1989.

Table 18. Balance of payments and reserves

The statistics for this table are mostly as reported by the IMF but do include recent estimates by World Bank staff and, in rare instances, the Bank's own coverage or classification adjustments to enhance international comparability. Values in this table are in US dollars converted at current exchange rates.

The *current account balance after official transfers* is the difference between (a) exports of goods and services (factor and nonfactor) as well as inflows of unrequited transfers (private and official) and (b) imports of goods and services as well as all unrequited transfers to the rest of the world.

The *current account balance (before official transfers)* is the current account balance that treats net official unrequited transfers as akin to official capital movements. The difference between the two balance of payments measures is essentially foreign aid in the form of grants, technical assistance, and food aid, which, for most developing countries, tends to make current account deficits smaller than the financing requirement.

Net workers' remittances cover payments and receipts of income by migrants who are employed or expect to be employed for more than a year in their new economy, where they are considered residents. These remittances are classified as private unrequited transfers and are included in the balance of payments

current account balance, whereas those derived from shorter-term stays are included in services as labor income. The distinction accords with internationally agreed guidelines, but many developing countries classify workers' remittances as a factor income receipt (and hence a component of GNP). The World Bank adheres to international guidelines in defining GNP and, therefore, may differ from national practices.

Gross international reserves comprise holdings of monetary gold, special drawing rights (SDRs), the reserve position of members in the IMF, and holdings of foreign exchange under the control of monetary authorities. The data on holdings of international reserves are from IMF data files. The gold component of these reserves is valued throughout at year-end (December 31) London prices: that is, $37.37 an ounce in 1970 and $401.00 an ounce in 1989. The reserve levels for 1970 and 1989 refer to the end of the year indicated and are in current dollars at prevailing exchange rates. Because of differences in the definition of international reserves, in the valuation of gold, and in reserve management practices, the levels of reserve holdings published in national sources do not have strictly comparable significance. Reserve holdings at the end of 1989 are also expressed in terms of the number of months of imports of goods and services they could pay for.

The summary measures are computed from group aggregates for gross international reserves and total imports of goods and services in current dollars.

Table 19. Official development assistance from OECD and OPEC members

Official development assistance (ODA) consists of net disbursements of loans and grants made on concessional financial terms by official agencies of the members of the Development Assistance Committee (DAC) of the Organisation for Economic Co-operation and Development (OECD) and members of the Organization of Petroleum Exporting Countries (OPEC) to promote economic development and welfare. Although this definition is meant to exclude purely military assistance, the borderline is sometimes blurred; the definition used by the country of origin usually prevails. ODA also includes the value of technical cooperation and assistance. All data shown are supplied by the OECD, and all US dollar values are converted at official exchange rates.

Total net flows are net disbursements to developing countries and multilateral institutions. The disbursements to multilateral institutions are now reported for all DAC members on the basis of the date of issue of notes; some DAC members previously reported on the basis of the date of encashment. *Total bilateral flows to low-income economies* exclude unallocated bilateral flows and all disbursements to multilateral institutions.

The nominal values shown in the summary for ODA from high-income OECD countries were converted at 1987 prices using the dollar GDP deflator. This deflator is based on price increases in OECD countries (excluding Greece, Portugal, and Turkey) measured in dollars. It takes into account the parity changes between the dollar and national currencies. For example, when the dollar depreciates, price changes measured in national currencies have to be adjusted upward by the amount of the depreciation to obtain price changes in dollars.

The table, in addition to showing totals for OPEC, shows totals for the Organization of Arab Petroleum Exporting Countries (OAPEC). The donor members of OAPEC are Algeria, Iraq, Kuwait, Libya, Qatar, Saudi Arabia, and United Arab Emirates. ODA data for OPEC and OAPEC are also obtained from the OECD.

Table 20. Official development assistance: receipts

Net disbursements of ODA from all sources consist of loans and grants made on concessional financial terms by all bilateral official agencies and multilateral sources to promote economic development and welfare. They include the value of technical cooperation and assistance. The disbursements shown in this table are not strictly comparable with those shown in Table 19 since the receipts are from all sources; disbursements in Table 19 refer only to those made by high-income members of the OECD and members of OPEC. Net disbursements equal gross disbursements less payments to the originators of aid for amortization of past aid receipts. Net disbursements of ODA are shown per capita and as a percentage of GNP.

The summary measures of per capita ODA are computed from group aggregates for population and for ODA. Summary measures for ODA as a percentage of GNP are computed from group totals for ODA and for GNP in current US dollars.

Table 21. Total external debt

The data on debt in this and successive tables are from the World Bank Debtor Reporting System, supplemented by World Bank estimates. That system is concerned solely with developing economies and does not collect data on external debt for other groups of borrowers or from economies that are not members of the World Bank. The dollar figures on debt shown in Tables 21 through 25 are in US dollars converted at official exchange rates.

The data on debt include private nonguaranteed

debt reported by twenty-seven developing countries and complete or partial estimates for an additional twenty others that do not report, but for which this type of debt is known to be significant.

Public loans are external obligations of public debtors, including the national government, its agencies, and autonomous public bodies. *Publicly guaranteed loans* are external obligations of private debtors that are guaranteed for repayment by a public entity. These two categories are aggregated in the tables. *Private nonguaranteed loans* are external obligations of private debtors that are not guaranteed for repayment by a public entity.

Use of IMF credit denotes repurchase obligations to the IMF for all uses of IMF resources, excluding those resulting from drawings in the reserve tranche. It is shown for the end of the year specified. It comprises purchases outstanding under the credit tranches, including enlarged access resources, and all of the special facilities (the buffer stock, compensatory financing, extended fund, and oil facilities), Trust Fund loans, and operations under the enhanced structural adjustment facilities. Use of IMF credit outstanding at year-end (a stock) is converted to US dollars at the dollar-SDR exchange rate in effect at year-end.

Short-term debt is debt with an original maturity of one year or less. Available data permit no distinctions between public and private nonguaranteed short-term debt.

Total external debt is defined for the purpose of this Report as the sum of public, publicly guaranteed, and private nonguaranteed long-term debt, use of IMF credit, and short-term debt.

Table 22. Flow of public and private external capital

Data on disbursements, repayment of principal (amortization), and payment of interest are for public, publicly guaranteed, and private nonguaranteed long-term loans.

Disbursements are drawings on long-term loan commitments during the year specified.

Repayment of principal is the actual amount of principal (amortization) paid in foreign currency, goods, or services in the year specified.

Interest payments are actual amounts of interest paid in foreign currency, goods, or services in the year specified.

Table 23. Aggregate net resource flows and net transfers

Net flows on long-term debt are disbursements less the repayment of principal on public, publicly guaranteed, and private nonguaranteed long-term debt. *Of-*

ficial grants are transfers made by an official agency in cash or in kind in respect of which no legal debt is incurred by the recipient. Data on official grants exclude grants for technical assistance.

Net foreign direct investment is defined as investment that is made to acquire a lasting interest (usually 10 percent of the voting stock) in an enterprise operating in a country other than that of the investor (defined according to residency), the investor's purpose being an effective voice in the management of the enterprise. *Aggregate net resource flows* are the sum of net flows on long-term debt (excluding IMF), plus official grants (excluding technical assistance), and net foreign direct investment. *Aggregate net transfers* are equal to aggregate net resource flows minus interest payments on long-term loans and foreign direct investment profits.

Table 24. Total external debt ratios

Total external debt as a percentage of exports of goods and services represents public, publicly guaranteed, private nonguaranteed long-term debt, use of IMF credit, and short-term debt drawn at year-end, net of repayments of principal and write-offs, and, throughout this table, goods and services include workers' remittances. For estimating *total external debt as a percentage of GNP*, the debt figures are converted into US dollars from currencies of repayment at end-of-year official exchange rates. GNP is converted from national currencies to US dollars by applying the conversion procedure described in the technical note for Tables 2 and 3.

Total debt service as a percentage of goods and services is the sum of principal repayments and interest payments on total external debt (as defined in the note for Table 21). It is one of several conventional measures used to assess a country's ability to service debt.

Interest payments as a percentage of exports of goods and services are actual payments made on total external debt.

The summary measures are weighted by exports of goods and services in current dollars and by GNP in current dollars, respectively.

Table 25. Terms of external public borrowing

Commitments refer to the public and publicly guaranteed loans for which contracts were signed in the year specified. They are reported in currencies of repayment and converted into US dollars at average annual official exchange rates.

Figures for *interest rates*, *maturities*, and *grace periods* are averages weighted by the amounts of the loans. Interest is the major charge levied on a loan and is usually computed on the amount of principal drawn and outstanding. The maturity of a loan is the interval between the agreement date, when a loan agreement is signed or bonds are issued, and the date of final repayment of principal. The grace period is the interval between the agreement date and the date of the first repayment of principal.

Public loans with variable interest rates, as a percentage of public debt, refer to interest rates that float with movements in a key market rate; for example, the London interbank offered rate (LIBOR) or the US prime rate. This column shows the borrower's exposure to changes in international interest rates.

The summary measures in this table are weighted by the amounts of the loans.

Table 26. Population growth and projections

Population growth rates are period averages calculated from midyear populations.

Population estimates for mid-1989 and estimates of fertility and mortality are made by the World Bank from data provided by the UN Population Division, the UN Statistical Office, and country statistical offices. Estimates take into account the results of the latest population censuses, which, in some cases, are neither recent nor accurate. Note that refugees not permanently settled in the country of asylum are generally considered to be part of the population of their country of origin.

The projections of population for 2000, 2025, and the year in which the population will eventually become stationary (see definition below) are made for each economy separately. Information on total population by age and sex, fertility, mortality, and international migration is projected on the basis of generalized assumptions until the population becomes stationary.

A stationary population is one in which age- and sex-specific mortality rates have not changed over a long period, and during which fertility rates have remained at replacement level; that is, when the net reproduction rate (defined in the note for Table 27) equals 1. In such a population, the birth rate is constant and equal to the death rate, the age structure is constant, and the growth rate is zero.

Population projections are made age cohort by age cohort. Mortality, fertility, and migration are projected separately and the results are applied iteratively to the 1985 base-year age structure. For the projection period 1985 to 2005, the changes in mortality are country specific: increments in life expectancy and decrements in infant mortality are based on previous trends for each country. When female secondary school enrollment is high, mortality is assumed to decline more quickly. Infant mortality is projected separately from adult mortality. Note that the data do not yet reflect the potentially significant impact of the human immunodeficiency virus (HIV) epidemic.

Projected fertility rates are also based on previous trends. For countries in which fertility has started to decline (termed "fertility transition"), this trend is assumed to continue. It has been observed that no country with a life expectancy of less than 50 years has experienced a fertility decline; for these countries fertility transition is delayed, and then the average decline of the group of countries in fertility transition is applied. Countries with below-replacement fertility are assumed to have constant total fertility rates until 1995–2000 and then to regain replacement level by 2030.

International migration rates are based on past and present trends in migration flows and migration policy. Among the sources consulted are estimates and projections made by national statistical offices, international agencies, and research institutions. Because of the uncertainty of future migration trends, it is assumed in the projections that net migration rates will reach zero by 2025.

The estimates of the size of the stationary population are speculative. *They should not be regarded as predictions.* They are included to show the implications of recent fertility and mortality trends on the basis of generalized assumptions. A fuller description of the methods and assumptions used to calculate the estimates is contained in *World Population Projections, 1989–90 Edition.*

Table 27. Demography and fertility

The *crude birth rate* and *crude death rate* indicate respectively the number of live births and deaths occurring per thousand population in a year. They come from the sources mentioned in the note to Table 26.

Women of childbearing age are those from age 15 to 49.

The *total fertility rate* represents the number of children that would be born to a woman if she were to live to the end of her childbearing years and bear children at each age in accordance with prevailing age-specific fertility rates. The rates given are from the sources mentioned in the note for Table 26.

The *net reproduction rate* (NRR), which measures the number of daughters a newborn girl will bear during her lifetime, assuming fixed age-specific fertility and mortality rates, reflects the extent to which a cohort of newborn girls will reproduce themselves. An NRR of 1 indicates that fertility is at replacement level: at this rate women will bear, on average, only enough daughters to replace themselves in the population. As with the size of the stationary population, the assumed year of reaching replacement-level fertility

is speculative and should not be regarded as a prediction.

Married women of childbearing age using contraception are women who are practicing, or whose husbands are practicing, any form of contraception. Contraceptive usage is generally measured for women age 15 to 49. A few countries use measures relating to other age groups, especially 15 to 44.

Data are mainly derived from demographic and health surveys, contraceptive prevalence surveys, World Bank country data, and Mauldin and Segal's article "Prevalence of Contraceptive Use: Trends and Issues" in volume 19 of *Studies in Family Planning* (1988). For a few countries for which no survey data are available, and for several African countries, program statistics are used. Program statistics may understate contraceptive prevalence because they do not measure use of methods such as rhythm, withdrawal, or abstinence, nor use of contraceptives not obtained through the official family planning program. The data refer to rates prevailing in a variety of years, generally not more than two years before the year specified in the table.

All summary measures are country data weighted by each country's share in the aggregate population.

Table 28. Health and nutrition

The estimates of *population per physician* and *per nursing person* are derived from World Health Organization (WHO) data and are supplemented by data obtained directly by the World Bank from national sources. The data refer to a variety of years, generally no more than two years before the year specified. The figure for physicians, in addition to the total number of registered practitioners in the country, includes medical assistants whose medical training is less than that of qualified physicians but who nevertheless dispense similar medical services, including simple operations. Nursing persons include graduate, practical, assistant, and auxiliary nurses, as well as paraprofessional personnel such as health workers, first aid workers, traditional birth attendants, and so on. The inclusion of auxiliary and paraprofessional personnel provides more realistic estimates of available nursing care. Because definitions of doctors and nursing personnel vary—and because the data shown are for a variety of years—the data for these two indicators are not strictly comparable across countries.

Data on *births attended by health staff* show the percentage of births recorded where a recognized health service worker was in attendance. The data are from WHO, supplemented by UNICEF data. They are based on national sources, derived mostly from official community reports and hospital records; some reflect only births in hospitals and other medical institutions. Sometimes smaller private and rural hospitals are excluded, and sometimes even relatively primitive local facilities are included. The coverage is therefore not always comprehensive, and the figures should be treated with extreme caution.

Babies with low birth weight are children born weighing less than 2,500 grams. Low birth weight is frequently associated with maternal malnutrition and tends to raise the risk of infant mortality and lead to poor growth in infancy and childhood, thus increasing the incidence of other forms of retarded development. The figures are derived from both WHO and UNICEF sources and are based on national data. The data are not strictly comparable across countries since they are compiled from a combination of surveys and administrative records that may not have representative national coverage.

The *infant mortality rate* is the number of infants who die before reaching one year of age, per thousand live births in a given year. The data are from the UN publication *Mortality of Children under Age 5: Projections, 1950–2025* as well as from the World Bank.

The *daily calorie supply (per capita)* is calculated by dividing the calorie equivalent of the food supplies in an economy by the population. Food supplies comprise domestic production, imports less exports, and changes in stocks; they exclude animal feed, seeds for use in agriculture, and food lost in processing and distribution. These estimates are from the Food and Agriculture Organization.

The summary measures in this table are country figures weighted by each country's share in the aggregate population.

Table 29. Education

The data in this table refer to a variety of years, generally not more than two years distant from those specified; however, figures for females sometimes refer to a year earlier than that for overall totals. The data are mostly from Unesco.

Primary school enrollment data are estimates of children of all ages enrolled in primary school. Figures are expressed as the ratio of pupils to the population of school-age children. Although many countries consider primary school age to be 6 to 11 years, others do not. For some countries with universal primary education, the gross enrollment ratios may exceed 100 percent because some pupils are younger or older than the country's standard primary school age.

The data on *secondary* school enrollment are calculated in the same manner, but again the definition of secondary school age differs among countries. It is most commonly considered to be 12 to 17 years. Late entry of more mature students as well as repetition

and the phenomenon of "bunching" in final grades can influence these ratios.

The *tertiary* enrollment ratio is calculated by dividing the number of pupils enrolled in all post-secondary schools and universities by the population in the 20–24 age group. Pupils attending vocational schools, adult education programs, two-year community colleges, and distance education centers (primarily correspondence courses) are included. The distribution of pupils across these different types of institutions varies among countries. The youth population—that is, 20 to 24 years—has been adopted by Unesco as the denominator since it represents an average tertiary level cohort even though people above and below this age group may be registered in tertiary institutions.

Primary net enrollment is the percentage of school-age children who are enrolled in school. Unlike gross enrollment, the net ratios correspond to the country's primary school–age group. This indicator gives a much clearer idea of how many children in the age group are actually enrolled in school, without the number being inflated by over- (or under-) age children.

The *primary pupil-teacher ratio* is the number of pupils enrolled in school in a country, divided by the number of teachers in the education system.

The summary measures in this table are country enrollment rates weighted by each country's share in the aggregate population.

Table 30. Income distribution and ICP estimates of GDP

The data in this table refer to the ICP estimates of GDP and the distribution of income or expenditure accruing to percentile groups of households ranked by total household income, per capita income, or expenditure.

The first column presents preliminary results of the UN International Comparison Program (ICP), Phase V, for 1985. ICP recasts traditional national accounts through special price collections and disaggregation of GDP by expenditure components. More comprehensive ICP results are expected to be available by the end of 1991. The figures given here are subject to change and should be regarded as indicative only. ICP Phase V details are prepared by national statistical offices. The results are coordinated by the UN Statistical Office (UNSO) with support from other international agencies, particularly the Statistical Office of the European Communities (Eurostat) and the Organisation for Economic Co-operation and Development (OECD). The World Bank, the Economic Commission for Europe, and the Economic and Social Commission for Asia and the Pacific also contribute to this exercise.

A total of sixty-four countries participated in ICP Phase V, and preliminary results are now available for fifty-seven. For one country (Nepal), total GDP data were not available, and comparisons were made for consumption only; two countries with populations of less than 1 million—Luxembourg, with 81.3 as its estimated index of GDP per capita, and Swaziland, with 13.6—have been omitted from this table. Data for the remaining seven countries, all Caribbean, are expected soon.

Although the GDP per capita figures are presented as indexes to the US value, the underlying data are expressed in US dollars. However, these dollar values, which are different from those shown in Tables 1 and 3 (see the technical notes for these tables), are obtained by special conversion factors designed to equalize purchasing powers of currencies in the respective countries. This conversion factor, commonly known as the purchasing power parity (PPP), is defined as the number of units of a country's currency required to buy the same amounts of goods and services in the domestic market as one dollar would buy in the United States. The computation of PPPs involves obtaining implicit quantities from national accounts expenditure data and specially collected price data and revaluing the implicit quantities in each country at a single set of average prices. The PPP rate thus equalizes dollar prices in every country, and cross-country comparisons of GDP based on them reflect differences in quantities of goods and services free of any price-level differentials. This procedure is designed to bring cross-country comparisons in line with cross-time real value comparisons that are based on constant price series.

The figures presented here are the results of a two-step exercise. Countries within a region or group such as the OECD are first compared using their own group average prices. Next, since group average prices may differ from each other, making the countries belonging to different groups not comparable, the group prices are adjusted to make them comparable at the world level. The adjustments, done by UNSO, are based on price differentials observed in a network of "link" countries representing each group. However, the linking is done in a manner that retains in the world comparison the relative levels of GDP observed in the group comparisons.

The two-step process was adopted because the relative GDP levels and rankings of two countries may change when more countries are brought into the comparison. It was felt that this should not be allowed to happen within geographic regions; that is, that the relationship of, say, Ghana and Senegal should not be affected by the prices prevailing in the United States. Thus overall GDP per capita levels are calculated at "regional" prices and then linked together. The linking is done by revaluing GDPs of all the countries at average "world" prices and reallocating the new regional totals on the basis of each country's share in the original comparison.

Such a method does not permit the comparison of more detailed quantities (such as food consumption). Hence these subaggregates and more detailed expenditure categories are calculated using world prices. These quantities are indeed comparable internationally, but they do not add up to the indicated GDPs because they are calculated at a different set of prices.

Some countries belong to several regional groups. Some groups have priority; others are equal. Thus fixity is always maintained between members of the European Communities, even within the OECD and world comparison. For Finland and Austria, however, the bilateral relationship that prevails within the OECD comparison is also the one used within the global comparison. However, a significantly different relationship (based on Central European prices) prevails in the comparison within that group, and this is the relationship presented in the separate publication of the European comparison.

The estimates in the second column are calculated from the actual ICP results reported in the first, by applying average annual growth rates of GNP computed from World Bank files. The numbers do not reflect changes in terms of trade. The estimates in the third column are calculated from those in the second by expressing the values in 1985 "international dollars" and multiplying them by the US inflation rate measured by the implicit GNP deflator. The ICP estimates are expressed in "international dollars," which have the same purchasing power over total US GDP as the US dollar in a given year, but with a purchasing power over subaggregates determined by average international prices rather than by US relative prices.

For further details on the ICP procedures, readers may consult the ICP Phase IV report, *World Comparisons of Purchasing Power and Real Product for 1980* (New York: United Nations, 1986).

The income distribution data cover rural and urban areas for all countries. The data refer to different years between 1979 and 1989 and are drawn from a variety of sources. These include the Economic Commission for Latin America and the Caribbean, the Luxembourg Income Study, the OECD, the UN's *National Accounts Statistics: Compendium of Income Distribution Statistics, 1985*, the World Bank, and national sources. Data for many countries have been updated, and some of the income distribution data previously published have been deleted because they refer to years long past.

In many countries the collection of income distribution data is not systematically organized or integrated with the official statistical system. The data are derived from surveys designed for other purposes, most often consumer expenditure surveys, that also collect information on income. These surveys use a variety of income concepts and sample designs, and in many cases their geographic coverage is too limited to provide reliable nationwide estimates of income distribution. Although the data presented here represent the best available estimates, they do not avoid all these problems and should be interpreted with caution.

Similarly, the scope of the indicator is limited for certain countries, and data for other countries are not fully comparable. Because households vary in size, a distribution in which households are ranked according to per capita household income, rather than according to total household income, is superior for many purposes. The distinction is important because households with low per capita incomes frequently are large households, whose total income may be high, whereas many households with low household incomes may be small households with high per capita income. Information on the distribution of per capita household income exists for only a few countries and is infrequently updated. Where possible, distributions are ranked according to per capita income; more often they are ranked by household income, with others ranked by per capita expenditure or household expenditure. Since the size of household is likely to be small for low-income households (for instance, single-person households and couples without children), the distribution of household income may overstate the income inequality. Also, since household savings tend to increase faster as income levels increase, the distribution of expenditure is inclined to understate the income inequality. The World Bank's Living Standards Measurement Study and the Social Dimensions of Adjustment project (the latter covering Sub-Saharan African countries) are assisting a few countries in improving their collection and analysis of data on income distribution.

Table 31. Urbanization

Data on urban population and agglomeration in large cities are from the UN's *Prospects of World Urbanization*, supplemented by data from the World Bank. The growth rates of urban population are calculated from the World Bank's population estimates; the estimates of urban population shares are calculated from both sources just cited.

Because the estimates in this table are based on different national definitions of what is urban, cross-country comparisons should be made with caution.

The summary measures for urban population as a percentage of total population are calculated from country percentages weighted by each country's share in the aggregate population; the other summary measures in this table are weighted in the same fashion, using urban population.

Table 32. Women in development

This table provides some basic indicators disaggregated to show differences between the sexes that illustrate the condition of women in society. The measures reflect the demographic status of women and their access to health and education services. Statistical anomalies become even more apparent when social indicators are analyzed by gender, because reporting systems are often weak in areas related specifically to women. Indicators drawn from censuses and surveys, such as those on population, tend to be about as reliable for women as for men; but indicators based largely on administrative records, such as maternal and infant mortality, are less reliable. More resources are now being devoted to develop better information on these topics, but the reliability of data, even in the series shown, still varies significantly.

The *under 5 mortality rate* shows the probability of a newborn baby dying before reaching age 5. The rates are derived from life tables based on estimated current life expectancy at birth and on infant mortality rates. In general throughout the world more males are born than females. Under good nutritional and health conditions and in times of peace, male children under 5 have a higher death rate than females. These columns show that female-male differences in the risk of dying by age 5 vary substantially. In industrial market economies, female babies have a 23 percent lower risk of dying by age 5 than male babies; the risk of dying by age 5 is actually higher for females than for males in some lower-income economies. This suggests differential treatment of males and females with respect to food and medical care.

Such discrimination particularly affects very young girls, who may get a smaller share of scarce food or receive less prompt costly medical attention. This pattern of discrimination is not uniformly associated with development. There are low- and middle-income countries (and regions within countries) where the risk of dying by age 5 for females relative to males approximates the pattern found in industrial countries. In many other countries, however, the numbers starkly demonstrate the need to associate women more closely with development. The health and welfare indicators in both Table 28 and in this table's maternal mortality column draw attention, in particular, to the conditions associated with childbearing. This activity still carries the highest risk of death for women of reproductive age in developing countries. The indicators reflect, but do not measure, both the availability of health services for women and the general welfare and nutritional status of mothers.

Life expectancy at birth is defined in the note to Table 1.

Maternal mortality refers to the number of female deaths that occur during childbirth per 100,000 live births. Because deaths during childbirth are defined more widely in some countries to include complications of pregnancy or the period after childbirth, or of abortion, and because many pregnant women die because of lack of suitable health care, maternal mortality is difficult to measure consistently and reliably across countries. The data in these two series are drawn from diverse national sources and collected by the World Health Organization (WHO), although many national administrative systems are weak and do not record vital events in a systematic way. The data are derived mostly from official community reports and hospital records, and some reflect only deaths in hospitals and other medical institutions. Sometimes smaller private and rural hospitals are excluded, and sometimes even relatively primitive local facilities are included. The coverage is therefore not always comprehensive, and the figures should be treated with extreme caution.

Clearly, many maternal deaths go unrecorded, particularly in countries with remote rural populations; this accounts for some of the very low numbers shown in the table, especially for several African countries. Moreover, it is not clear whether an increase in the number of mothers in hospital reflects more extensive medical care for women or more complications in pregnancy and childbirth because of poor nutrition, for instance. (Table 28 shows data on low birth weight.)

These time series attempt to bring together readily available information not always presented in international publications. WHO warns that there are inevitably gaps in the series, and it has invited countries to provide more comprehensive figures. They are reproduced here, from the 1986 WHO publication *Maternal Mortality Rates,* supplemented by the UNICEF publication *The State of the World's Children 1989,* as part of the international effort to highlight data in this field. The data refer to any year from 1977 to 1984.

The *education* indicators, based on Unesco sources, show the extent to which females have equal access to schooling.

Percentage of cohort persisting to grade 4 is the percentage of children starting primary school in 1970 and 1984, respectively, who continued to the fourth grade by 1973 and 1987. Figures in italics represent earlier or later cohorts. The data are based on enroll-

ment records. The slightly higher persistence ratios for females in some African countries may indicate male participation in activities such as animal herding.

All things being equal, and opportunities being the same, the ratios for *females per 100 males* should be close to 100. However, inequalities may cause the ratios to move in different directions. For example, the number of females per 100 males will rise at secondary school level if male attendance declines more rapidly in the final grades because of males' greater job opportunities, conscription into the army, or migration in search of work. In addition, since the numbers in these columns refer mainly to general secondary education, they do not capture those (mostly males) enrolled in technical and vocational schools or in full-time apprenticeships, as in Eastern Europe.

All summary measures are country data weighted by each country's share in the aggregate population.

Table 33. Forests, protected areas, and water

This new table on natural resources is a first step toward including environmental data in the assessment of development and the planning of economic strategies. It provides a partial picture of the status of forests, the extent of areas protected for conservation or other environmentally related purposes, and the availability and use of freshwater. The data reported here are drawn from the most authoritative sources available, cited in World Resources Institute's *World Resources 1990–91.* Perhaps even more than other data in this Report, however, these data should be used with caution. While they accurately characterize major differences in resources and uses between countries, true comparability is limited because of variation in data collection, statistical methods, definitions, and government resources.

No conceptual framework has yet been agreed upon that integrates natural resource and traditional economic data. Nor are the measures shown in this table intended to be final indicators of natural resource wealth, environmental health, or resource depletion. They have been chosen because they are available for most countries, are testable, and reflect some general conditions of the environment.

The *total area* of forest refers to the total natural stands of woody vegetation in which trees predominate. These estimates are derived from country statistics assembled by the Food and Agriculture Organization of the United Nations (FAO) in 1980. Some of them are based on more recent inventories or satellite-based assessments performed during the 1980s. In 1992 the FAO will complete and publish an assessment of world forest extent and health that should modify some of these estimates substantially. The total area of *closed* forest refers to those forest areas where trees cover a high proportion of the ground and there is no continuous ground cover.) Closed forest, for members of the Economic Commission for Europe (ECE), however, is defined as those forest areas where tree crowns cover more than 20 percent of the area. These natural stands do not include tree plantations.

Total annual deforestation refers to both closed and open forest. (Open forest is defined as at least a 10 percent tree cover with a continuous ground cover.) In the ECE countries open forest has 5–20 percent crown cover or a mixture of bush and stunted trees. Deforestation is defined as the permanent conversion of forest land to other uses including pasture, shifting cultivation, mechanized agriculture, or infrastructure development. Assessments of annual deforestation, both in open and closed forest, are difficult to make and are usually undertaken as special studies. The estimates shown here for 1981–85 were calculated in 1980, projecting the rate of deforestation during the first five years of the decade. Figures in italics are estimates from other periods and are based on more recent or better assessments than those used in the 1980 projections.

Special note should be taken of Brazil—the country with the world's largest tropical closed forest—which now undertakes annual deforestation assessments. Deforested areas do not include areas logged but intended for regeneration, nor areas degraded by fuelwood gathering, acid precipitation, or forest fires. In temperate industrialized countries the permanent conversion of remaining forest to other uses is relatively rare. Brazil is unique in having several assessments of forest extent and deforestation that use a common methodology based on images from Landsat satellites. Closed forest deforestation in the Legal Amazon of Brazil during 1990 is estimated at 13,800 square kilometers, down from the 17,900 square kilometers estimated in 1989. Between 1978 and 1988, deforestation in this region averaged about 21,000 square kilometers, having peaked in 1987 and declined greatly thereafter. By 1990, cumulative deforestation (both recent and historical) within the Legal Amazon totaled 415,000 square kilometers. Deforestation outside the Legal Amazon also occurs, but there is much less information on its extent. A 1980 estimate, that open forest deforestation in Brazil totaled about 1.05 million hectares, is the most recent available.

Protected land areas are nationally protected areas of at least 1,000 hectares that fall into one of five management categories: scientific reserves and strict nature reserves, national parks of national or international significance (not materially affected by human activity), natural monuments and natural landscapes

with some unique aspects, managed nature reserves and wildlife sanctuaries, and protected landscapes and seascapes (which may include cultural landscapes). This table does not include sites protected only under local or provincial law or areas where consumptive uses of wildlife are allowed. These data are subject to variations in definition and in reporting to the organizations, such as the World Conservation Monitoring Centre, that compile and disseminate these data.

Internal renewable water resources data are subject to variation in collection and estimation methods but accurately show the magnitude of water use in both total and per capita terms. These data, however, also hide what can be significant variation in total renewable water resources from one year to another. They also fail to distinguish the variation in water availability within a country both seasonally and geographically. Because freshwater resources are based on long-term averages, their estimation explicitly excludes decade-long cycles of wet and dry. These data are compiled from national, international, and professional publications from a variety of years. In the absence of other measures, estimates of sectoral withdrawals are modeled when necessary (based on information on industry, irrigation practices, livestock populations, crop mix, and precipitation). Data from small countries and arid regions are thought less reliable than those from large countries and more humid zones. These data do not include freshwater created by desalination plants.

Annual withdrawal refers to the average annual flows of rivers and underground waters that are derived from precipitation falling within the country. The *total* withdrawn and the *percentage* withdrawn of the total renewable resource are both reported in this table. The total water withdrawn for use can exceed the total renewable resource of a country for two reasons. Water might be withdrawn from a lake or river shared with another country, or it might be withdrawn from an aquifer that is not part of the renewable cycle. *Domestic* use includes drinking water, municipal use or supply, and uses for public services, commercial establishments, and homes. Direct withdrawals for *industrial* use, including withdrawals for cooling thermoelectric plants, are combined in the final column of this table with withdrawals for *agriculture* (irrigation and livestock production). Estimates of per capita use are based on 1987 population estimates, the base year of most of the resource and withdrawal estimates.

Data sources

Production and domestic absorption	UN Department of International Economic and Social Affairs. Various years. *Statistical Yearbook*. New York. ———. Various years. *Energy Statistics Yearbook*. Statistical Papers, series J. New York. UN International Comparison Program Phases IV (1980) and V (1985) reports, and data from ECE, ESCAP, Eurostat, OECD, and UN. FAO, IMF, UNIDO, and World Bank data; national sources.
Fiscal and monetary accounts	International Monetary Fund. *Government Finance Statistics Yearbook*. Vol. 11. Washington, D.C. ———. Various years. *International Financial Statistics*. Washington, D.C. UN Department of International Economic and Social Affairs. Various years. *World Energy Supplies*. Statistical Papers, series J. New York. IMF data.
Core international transactions	International Monetary Fund. Various years. *International Financial Statistics*. Washington, D.C. UN Conference on Trade and Development. Various years. *Handbook of International Trade and Development Statistics*. Geneva. UN Department of International Economic and Social Affairs. Various years. *Monthly Bulletin of Statistics*. New York. ———. Various years. *Yearbook of International Trade Statistics*. New York. FAO, IMF, UN, and World Bank data.
External finance	Organisation for Economic Co-operation and Development. Various years. *Development Co-operation*. Paris. ———. 1988. *Geographical Distribution of Financial Flows to Developing Countries*. Paris. IMF, OECD, and World Bank data; World Bank Debtor Reporting System.
Human and natural resources	Bulatao, Rodolfo A., Eduard Bos, Patience W. Stephens, and My T. Vu. 1990. *World Population Projections, 1989–90 Edition*. Baltimore, Md.: Johns Hopkins University Press. Institute for Resource Development/Westinghouse. 1987. *Child Survival: Risks and the Road to Health*. Columbia, Md. Mauldin, W. Parker, and Holden J. Segal. 1988. ''Prevalence of Contraceptive Use: Trends and Issues.'' *Studies in Family Planning* 19, 6: 335–53. Sivard, Ruth. 1985. *Women—A World Survey*. Washington, D.C.: World Priorities. UN Department of International Economic and Social Affairs. Various years. *Demographic Yearbook*. New York. ———. Various years. *Population and Vital Statistics Report*. New York. ———. Various years. *Statistical Yearbook*. New York. ———. 1989. *Levels and Trends of Contraceptive Use as Assessed in 1988*. New York. ———. 1988. *Mortality of Children under Age 5: Projections 1950–2025*. New York. ———. 1989. *Prospects of World Urbanization*. New York. ———. 1989. *World Population Prospects: 1988*. New York. UN Educational Scientific and Cultural Organization. Various years. *Statistical Yearbook*. Paris. ———. 1988. *Compendium of Statistics on Illiteracy*. Paris. UNICEF. 1989. *The State of the World's Children 1989*. Oxford: Oxford University Press. World Health Organization. Various years. *World Health Statistics Annual*. Geneva. ———. 1986. *Maternal Mortality Rates: A Tabulation of Available Information*, 2nd edition. Geneva. ———. Various years. *World Health Statistics Report*. Geneva. World Resources Institute. 1990. *World Resources 1990–91*. New York. FAO and World Bank data.